STUDIES IN THE
NATIONAL INCOME AND EXPENDITURE OF
THE UNITED KINGDOM

a series published under the joint auspices of the

NATIONAL INSTITUTE OF ECONOMIC AND SOCIAL RESEARCH, LONDON

and

DEPARTMENT OF APPLIED ECONOMICS
UNIVERSITY OF CAMBRIDGE

GENERAL EDITOR
RICHARD STONE
P. D. LEAKE PROFESSOR OF FINANCE AND ACCOUNTING
AND FELLOW OF KING'S COLLEGE, CAMBRIDGE

4

DOMESTIC CAPITAL FORMATION IN THE UNITED KINGDOM

1920-1938

STUDIES IN THE
NATIONAL INCOME AND EXPENDITURE
OF THE UNITED KINGDOM

The scope of the series is the measurement and analysis of the size, trend and interrelationships of the components of the British national income, output, expenditure, saving and asset formation. The investigations published in these *Studies* are confined to those undertaken at the National Institute of Economic and Social Research or at the Cambridge University Department of Applied Economics by members of their respective staffs and others working in direct collaboration with them. The production of a jointly sponsored series under a single editorship is being carried out in order that the intellectual unity underlying the many segments of research should be emphasized and made plain.

The National Institute of Economic and Social Research and the Department of Applied Economics assume no responsibility for the views expressed in these *Studies*.

The titles in this series are:

1 *The Measurement of Consumers' Expenditure and Behaviour in the United Kingdom, 1920–1938*, vol. I, by RICHARD STONE, assisted by D. A. ROWE and by W. J. CORLETT, RENEE HURSTFIELD, MURIEL POTTER

2 *The Measurement of Consumers' Expenditure and Behaviour in the United Kingdom, 1920–1938*, vol. II, by RICHARD STONE and D. A. ROWE

3 *Consumers' Expenditure in the United Kingdom, 1900–1919*, by A. R. PREST, assisted by A. A. ADAMS

4 *Domestic Capital Formation in the United Kingdom, 1920–1938*, by C. H. FEINSTEIN

5 *Wages and Salaries in the United Kingdom, 1920–1938*, by AGATHA L. CHAPMAN, assisted by ROSE KNIGHT

6 *National Income, Expenditure and Output of the United Kingdom, 1860–1960*, by C. H. FEINSTEIN

DOMESTIC CAPITAL FORMATION
IN THE UNITED KINGDOM
1920-1938

BY

C. H. FEINSTEIN

DEPARTMENT OF APPLIED ECONOMICS
UNIVERSITY OF CAMBRIDGE

CAMBRIDGE
AT THE UNIVERSITY PRESS
1965

PUBLISHED BY
THE SYNDICS OF THE CAMBRIDGE UNIVERSITY PRESS

Bentley House, 200 Euston Road, London, N.W.1
American Branch: 32 East 57th Street, New York, N.Y. 10022.
West African Office: P.O. Box 33, Ibadan, Nigeria

©

CAMBRIDGE UNIVERSITY PRESS

1965

Printed in Great Britain
by Spottiswoode, Ballantyne & Co. Ltd.
London and Colchester

Library of Congress Catalogue card No. 64-21572

CONTENTS

LIST OF TABLES

Tables are numbered according to the chapter in which they appear. Thus 7.00 refers to the estimates for Electricity, gas and water as a whole (Chapter 7), 7.10 to the estimates for Electricity (7.1).

Unless otherwise stated the tables in chapters 5 to 12 refer to the standard set of estimates for 1920–38 of capital formation, depreciation and capital stock on three price bases for each of the main types of asset. In the tables marked by an asterisk the estimates for fixed assets are shown in total only.

na

LIST OF FIGURES

FOREWORD

Ten years have passed since a volume was last published in this series and many readers may have thought that the whole enterprise had lost its impetus and that the remaining volumes would never appear. It is therefore a particular pleasure for me to be writing this foreword and at the same time to be able to announce progress in other directions as well: the second volume on consumers' expenditure has reached an advanced stage in printing; and a final volume on national income and expenditure 1860 to 1960, which will complete and pull together the work in earlier volumes in a form consistent with the post-war estimates of the Central Statistical Office, is in active preparation by Dr. C. H. Feinstein.

The present study has had a long and, alas, chequered career. It was started in 1950 when Dr. K. Maywald came to work on capital formation at this Department. In the years that followed Dr. Maywald set about systematically collecting and organizing all the information he could find which could in any way contribute to this work. His energy and thoroughness are apparent in the detail in which the many branches of activity are treated in this volume. As the work proceeded, a number of articles written by Dr. Maywald appeared in the Department's series of reprints and a summary of preliminary results was published in 1960 in *The London and Cambridge Economic Bulletin*. In the course of this work Dr. Maywald had at various times the assistance of the late Mr. Arthur Adams and also of Mr. J. J. C. McGibbon until the latter left the Department to join the staff of the O.E.E.C. in Paris.

The study was written up in sections and by 1959 the complete work was assembled. It then seemed to me and also to Mr. W. B. Reddaway, who had succeeded me as the Director of the Department, that certain changes of substance and presentation were needed before the study could be sent for printing. In the discussions that followed we were unable to get Dr. Maywald to see eye to eye with us and decided eventually to ask Dr. Feinstein to undertake the task of preparing a final version for publication. This involved a considerable amount of reworking of the basic material, as well as a careful discussion of many problems in the text, and we are extremely grateful to Dr. Feinstein for the skill and patience with which he has discharged a task which proved more arduous than any of us had expected. The result is the present volume. Though Dr. Maywald agreed to cooperate in the early stages of this work, he was unwilling in the end to associate his name with the final product. All of us concerned regretted this decision very much but there seemed to be no alternative but to let the work go forward under the name of Dr. Feinstein.

I should like to conclude this short account of the origins of this volume by expressing my warm personal thanks to Mr. Reddaway who played the major part in editing it and bore the brunt of the discussions that led to its final form.

DEPARTMENT OF APPLIED ECONOMICS RICHARD STONE
May 1964 *General Editor*

PREFACE

The statistical work presented in this book was originally planned and undertaken by Dr. K. Maywald, and I should like here to express my high regard for the exceptional care and enterprise which Dr. Maywald brought to his task of discovering relevant data and of shaping what must often have seemed to be quite intractable material into the required series.

My own association with this study did not begin until 1959, when a first set of estimates had already been completed by Dr. Maywald.[1] Many of these series have been retained without alteration, but a number of what were considered to be major improvements were made in the hope that these would reduce the repairs required during such future life as the estimates may enjoy. It must be said quite clearly that there is still scope for further improvements, but the period of gestation has already been unduly long and it did not seem that readers' interests would be best served by still further delays in publication. The alterations made consisted, firstly, of straightforward statistical adjustments where it was possible to use what were, in my judgement, more reliable estimating procedures and the resulting differences were large enough to warrant the revision: this affected mainly the estimates for dwellings, farm buildings and shops and certain other buildings in the sector Distribution and other services. Secondly, significant changes were made in the conceptual approach to certain problems, in particular those raised by the estimates for such civil engineering works as roads, harbours and the permanent way and works of the railway, and this too led to substantial differences in the final estimates.

Apart from these alterations my main work was the writing of the introductory chapters, the detailed description of the methods of estimation (for which I was able to draw on the drafts by Dr. Maywald), the evaluation of the results and the comparison with other estimates. The present text was very largely written after Dr. Maywald's association with the study had ended. He is not necessarily committed to any of the views expressed in it, and is not in any way responsible for the use made of his original estimates or for any errors in the revised series.

An historical investigation of this magnitude could not have been undertaken without the assistance of a large number of individuals and organizations and I should like to acknowledge their willing co-operation.

The Editor of this volume, Mr. W. B. Reddaway, has contributed immeasurably to every aspect of the work, and it is impossible to express adequately my gratitude for the time which he has devoted to this study and for the quite exceptional knowledge and insight which he has so generously imparted. Our many discussions on points of theory and method were always a stimulating and rewarding experience for me. Professor Stone and Miss Phyllis Deane were kind enough to read various drafts and to assist in many ways, and the main part of chapter 1 owes a great deal to Professor Stone. I have also profited greatly from discussions with Mr. G. Dean of the Central Statistical Office.

Information and assistance was freely supplied by numerous firms, institutions and government departments. We are especially indebted to the Share and Loan Department of the Stock Exchange and to the officials of Moodies Services, Ltd. for permission to use their extensive collections of company accounts; to the many firms which gave us additional information about their accounts; to the official departments which answered our endless stream of enquiries about published and unpublished material; and to the Statistics and Intelligence Division of the Board of Inland Revenue which made available much indispensable information and by their extensive co-operation made possible the construction of the estimates for individual trade groups in manufacturing, distribution and other sectors.

The co-operation of all these individuals has helped to strengthen the estimates and to remove many defects but they are not, of course, responsible for those errors which remain.

I would also like to record my thanks to Mr. R. Grasby for drawing the graphs; and to Mrs. L. Silk, Miss M. Clarke and other members of the staff of the Department of Applied Economics for their ever-willing assistance in the long task of computation and typing.

It might be of assistance to readers to indicate briefly the plan of this study. Chapter 1 is a general discussion of the concepts underlying the estimates of

---

[1] A summary of these preliminary results was published by Dr. Maywald under the title 'Domestic Capital Formation in the United Kingdom', *The London and Cambridge Economic Bulletin*, No. 34, *The Times Review of Industry*, June 1960.

gross and net capital formation and of the capital stock and chapter 2 outlines the main methods used to derive the estimates. Chapter 3 summarizes the main findings and also contains a short discussion of certain aspects of capital formation in the inter-war years. In chapter 4 a 'supply-side' estimate of aggregate gross fixed capital formation is constructed on the basis of information in the Censuses of Production; this is designed mainly as a check on estimates obtained in later chapters from other information, but some use is also made of it in the derivation of certain estimates. The coverage, sources and methods of estimation of the 'ownership-side' series derived for the eight individual sectors and their component sub-sectors are then described in full in chapters 5 to 12. There is an overall evaluation of the results in chapter 13; and in chapter 14 a detailed comparison is made with previous estimates by other authors and by the Central Statistical Office. Chapters 2, 3, 13 and 14 are likely to be the most useful for the reader whose main interest is in the final results rather than the detailed working, but no series should be used without careful reference to the appropriate chapter to ascertain the reliability of the estimates. Many are very approximate.

C. H. FEINSTEIN

CAMBRIDGE
1963

CHAPTER 1

CONCEPTS AND DEFINITIONS OF CAPITAL FORMATION

1.1 INTRODUCTION

The primary purpose of the present investigations was to provide the section on capital formation in the collective series *Studies in the National Income and Expenditure of the United Kingdom* for the period 1920 to 1938. This means that its principal concern is with three basic flow concepts: gross investment, depreciation and net investment, classified by industry and by type of asset.

In addition to the measurement of these flows, the study also includes estimates of the accumulated stocks of the different types of fixed asset available in different industries. These estimates of capital stock were necessary in order to complete the full set of estimates of the flows, and have their own intrinsic interest.

No attempt will be made here to discuss in detail the conceptual problems which arise in the definition of these flows and stocks of assets, either as to what would be logically desirable or what should be adopted as a practical objective. These matters have been the subject of much discussion in recent years among economists and statisticians actually engaged in making estimates, and the results of their growing experience can be found in recommendations by international organizations, and in particular in two reports by the United Nations.[1]

In general the objectives described in these reports are accepted here, and no more than a brief treatment will be given to explain the essential nature of the estimates and to emphasize points of special importance or difficulty.

1.2 THE SCOPE OF THE ESTIMATES

The estimates of capital formation given in this volume relate primarily to the assets used for productive purposes by business enterprises, whether they are conducted privately by individuals or corporate bodies, or by public authorities. Other categories of assets, such as private dwelling houses, schools, public buildings and roads are also included by a conventional extension of the term 'productive purposes'. These assets are included even though, for example, private owners of dwelling houses do not normally keep accounts or make any allowance for the depreciation of their property.

Two important categories of asset, consumers' durable goods and armaments, are by general convention excluded from the estimates of capital formation. They are, however, covered by other volumes in this series.[2]

The following are the flows and stocks covered by the estimates made in the present study:

A. *Flows during the year*:
   1. Purchases of fixed assets
   2. Sales of fixed assets
   3. Gross fixed capital formation
   4. Depreciation
   5. Net fixed capital formation
   6. Scrapping of fixed assets
   7. Change in stock-in-trade plus work in progress

B. *Stocks of assets at the end of the year*:
   8. Stock of fixed assets at (a) depreciated value
       (b) first cost value
   9. Stock-in-trade and work in progress

The definition and interrelation of these concepts is briefly explored in the following sections.

1.3 STOCKS AND FLOWS

If one attempts to account for the revenues and expenses of any productive activity so as to find how much is being gained in that activity, two types of

---

[1] [**77**] United Nations, *Studies in Methods*: Series F, No. 3. *Concepts and Definitions of Capital Formation* (New York, 1953); [**78**] Series F. No. 8. *Methods of National Income Estimation* (New York, 1955).

Other important sources are: [**57**] Central Statistical Office, *National Income Statistics, Sources and Methods*, H.M.S.O. (London, 1956); [**109**] R. W. Goldsmith, 'A Perpetual Inventory of National Wealth', *Conference on Research in Income and Wealth*, vol. fourteen, National Bureau of Economic Research (New York, 1951); and [**131**] *Problems of Capital Formation, Studies in Income and Wealth*, vol. nineteen, National Bureau of Economic Research (Princeton, 1957).

[2] [**139**] R. Stone. *Measurement of Consumers' Expenditure and Behaviour in the United Kingdom, 1920–1938*, vol. I (Cambridge, 1954); vol. II, in preparation. J. E. G. Utting. *Income and Expenditure of Public Authorities in the United Kingdom, 1920–1938* (Unpublished estimates).

problem arise. The first is concerned with making sure that incomings and outgoings match one another in time; the second is concerned with making sure that items of cost are properly valued. In many cases no difficulty will arise; items such as fuel and raw materials which are bought and used up in the production of goods sold within the period are clearly chargeable against the revenue from sales in the period. But apart from these current expenses of production, most activities involve the use of durable capital equipment which, though only bought from time to time, is used up more or less continuously in the process of production. It would be quite inappropriate to charge the cost of this durable equipment against revenue in the period in which it was incurred, and so it is charged in the first instance to capital account, and only the amount estimated to correspond to the use of the period is entered in the production account. In this way the cost of using up durable equipment is charged as far as possible against the periods in which the using-up takes place.

This generally accepted procedure enables goods bought for productive purposes to be divided into two classes: those which are charged directly against the proceeds of production; and those which are charged in the first place against capital or, in accounting terminology, entered on the balance sheet and subsequently written off, by means of charges for depreciation, against the proceeds of production. It is usual to treat only durable equipment in this way and to recognize that the use of this equipment involves expenses for repair and maintenance which are normally treated as direct current costs and not as capital expenditure.

Let us assume for the moment that prices are always constant. Then for all forms of fixed assets (durable equipment) the clearest connexion between the total stock and the annual flows can be seen from the following identity:

(1) *Depreciated value of stock at end of year*
    equals *Depreciated value of stock at beginning of year*
    plus *Gross investment during the year*
    less *Depreciation during the year*.[1]

It will be noted that the stock of fixed assets in this identity is taken at its depreciated or written-down value, i.e. after deducting all depreciation due on assets which have not been scrapped and are still included in the total stock. It is, therefore, subject to all the errors and arbitrariness inherent in the concept of depreciation (see 1.4), quite apart from imperfections in the statistical data.

This problem of depreciation can, in principle, be avoided by preparing estimates of the stock of fixed assets which record the gross or first cost value[2] of every asset. As long as they are not scrapped, assets remain in the stock at this first cost value, irrespective of their age or condition. The relation of this estimate of the stock of fixed assets to the annual flows is seen from the following identity:

(2) *First cost value of stock at end of year*
    equals *First cost value of stock at beginning of year*
    plus *Assets purchased during the year*
    less *First cost value of assets scrapped or sold during the year*.

The measurement of fixed capital thus has two distinct sets of estimates: one for the depreciated value of the assets and a second for the first cost value. Both sets of estimates are made in this study, and the meaning of the flows and stocks in identities (1) and (2) will be further discussed in 1.4 and 1.6.

A third identity arises from a problem which was ignored in the above classification of goods into those charged directly to current production and those charged in the first instance to capital account. Having charged materials and fuel to current production it is not possible to leave the matter there since the quantities bought in the year may be greater or less than the amount used in production during the year. If the amount bought is greater (less) than the amount used, then the stock-in-trade at the end of the year will be higher (lower) than the stock-in-trade at the beginning of the year. In constructing the balance sheet at the end of the year, this discrepancy is adjusted by adding the net increase in stock-in-trade during the year to the stock-in-trade at the beginning of the year and adding the same amount in the production account to the revenue from the sale of output. Any change in stocks of finished products and work in progress (the excess or deficit of output over sales) is treated in a similar way.

Thus for all forms of stock-in-trade (and work in progress) the connexion between the total stock and the annual flows can be seen from the identity:

(3) *Stock-in-trade at end of year*
    equals *Stock-in-trade at beginning of year*
    plus *Net increase in component items during the year*.

The meaning of these terms will be further discussed in 1.5.

The changes over the year contained in the stock-flow identities (1) and (3) above constitute net investment (or net capital formation) in fixed capital and stock-in-trade respectively.

---

[1] Strictly there should also be a deduction for capital losses and an addition for capital gain. This point is discussed on p. 4 below.

[2] As is explained below (p. 6) this is not necessarily the historic price of the asset but may also be valued at current or constant prices.

1.4 NET INVESTMENT IN FIXED CAPITAL

Reference to the two stock-flow identities for fixed capital formation (1) and (2) above, shows that there are three flows to be discussed here: gross investment, depreciation and scrapping. These words stand for somewhat complicated concepts which will now be discussed.

(I) GROSS INVESTMENT

At this stage let us again put aside all complications due to fluctuating prices. Gross investment is then equal to the additions to the stock of fixed assets of each type of asset, whether purchased new or second-hand, less any reductions to the stock through sales. Several points should be noted in connexion with this statement.

First, there is the crucial problem of the value at which these various transactions are entered in the national accounts. This problem is quite independent of fluctuating prices and arises even though we are assuming that prices remain constant. Assets purchased, whether new or second-hand, are valued at their cost to the enterprise, including costs of installation, legal fees, etc. From this a deduction should be made equal to the proceeds of assets sold during the year (whether for further use or for scrap). This gives the identity:

(4) *Gross investment in fixed capital during the year* equals *Cost of purchases of new or second-hand assets* less *Proceeds of assets sold or scrapped.*

Second, there is an inevitable arbitrariness in deciding where to draw the line between fixed assets which are subject to depreciation and other goods which are bought for the purposes of production. Generally speaking the length of life will be the main criterion, but this will usually be modified in the light of business practices whereby certain expenditures, for example on hand tools and replacement parts, are charged to current expenses. As already stated the important item of repair and maintenance is also normally regarded as a current expense which, by definition, does not add to the original life of the asset or alter the service which the asset yields, and no attempt is made to add it to the stock of fixed assets and then write it off through depreciation.

This is in contrast to the treatment of major alterations and improvements to assets, where the usual procedure is to include them as part of gross investment in fixed capital, and this practice is followed in the present study. It will be appreciated, however, that the distinction between this item and the expenditure on ordinary repairs not so included, is in practice not always easy to make.[1]

Third, when considering gross investment in a single industry or other sector of the economy the sale of existing assets (for example, to other industries) should, in principle, be deducted, and purchases should be included. For the economy as a whole these transactions largely cancel out, except that gross investment should have a net positive item for the margins earned by dealers in second-hand assets, including their reward for any reconditioning work; and a negative item in respect of sales of assets abroad, notably second-hand ships, or to final consumers, as when a used car is sold by a business to a private individual.

(II) DEPRECIATION

Depreciation is the amount which it *seems* right to charge against the production of the year to allow for the fact that equipment originally charged to capital account has become older, more worn and perhaps also more obsolete during the year. There are various ways in which this might be measured, but all methods are inherently arbitrary.[2] In principle it might, for example, be possible to measure the actual physical using-up during the year and take this, plus an allowance for obsolescence, etc. as the basis of the charge for depreciation. In practice, however, both in business and national income accounting, the calculation is almost always made either from initial estimates of the expected life of each type of asset, or from initial estimates of the proportion of the remaining value at the beginning of each year that should be deemed to be used up during the year.

Leaving aside for the moment the complications due to technical change and fluctuations in price, these two customary methods operate as follows. On the first, or straight line method, $1/n$th of the value of an asset is charged against production in each of its estimated n years of life. On the second, or reducing balance method, it is assumed at the outset that an asset will never be entirely written off while it remains 'on the books', but that $1/m$th, say, of what is left at the beginning of each year will be used during the year. Thus in the first year depreciation will be $1/m$; the amount left at the end of the first year will be $(m-1)/m$ and so the depreciation in the second year will be $(m-1)/m^2$, and so on until the asset is sold or scrapped.

---

[1] The appendix to this chapter contains a further discussion of the treatment of maintenance and improvements in certain more complex cases.

[2] Cf. [**106**] E. F. Denison 'Theoretical Aspects of Quality Change, Capital Consumption and Net Capital Formation' in *Problems of Capital Formation, Studies in Income and Wealth*, vol. nineteen.

A third method which was at one time widely used by public utilities such as railways and gas companies, was the renewals method. On this method nothing was charged for depreciation in any year until a new asset was bought to replace one which was worn out or obsolete, and the entire cost of the renewal (often including an element of improvement) was then charged as depreciation in that one year. There are a number of serious objections to this method and it is today rarely used.

Several points should be noted in connexion with the concept of depreciation. First, however the estimates are made, they can at best represent the result of applying a reasonable rate at a particular time. There is always the likelihood that unforeseeable developments will affect the actual life of the asset. Technical innovations, for example, may make the asset obsolescent before the original estimated allowances for depreciation have actually written it off. If it is scrapped in these circumstances, or sold for less than its book value, a capital loss will be incurred and this ought to be included with depreciation in identity (1) above.[1]

Conversely, the asset may turn out to be both economically and technically usable for some years after it has been completely written off.[2] It seems likely that the accounting assumptions frequently employed in estimating depreciation tend on the whole to be conservative, so that the phenomenon of fully depreciated assets still in use, particularly as reserve capacity, may be quite usual. This would mean that the estimates of the stock of fixed assets at depreciated values understated the stock of assets actually in use. The estimates at first cost values should not be affected since, in principle, all assets remain in the stock at their first cost value until they are scrapped; but in practice this may not be achieved since the rate of scrapping has also generally to be assumed.

In this context it must be noted that in national income accounting the object is to make the best possible estimates of depreciation which are not biased one way or the other, but that in principle these estimates are appropriate to the time at which they are first made. They are not retrospectively revised if, at a later date, it becomes possible to see that the estimate made was too high or too low.

Second, the actual estimates of depreciation are considerably affected by the choice of depreciation formula. As indicated above, the straight line method writes off the same amount in every year during the life of each asset, whereas the reducing balance method writes off progressively smaller amounts each year. If the same effective life is assumed the choice of the reducing balance method with its higher depreciation

charges in the earlier years leads to a considerably lower depreciated value for the stock of fixed assets (relatively to the same first cost value) than the straight line method.[3]

Third, the word 'depreciation' is used here to describe the flow as a whole, i.e. wear and tear, obsolescence, and other operating provisions connected with durable equipment, such as the provision for accidental loss and damage.

The concept of net investment in fixed capital is thus derived from the two concepts which have been discussed in this section by the following identity:

(5) *Net investment during the year*
    equals *Gross investment during the year*
    less *Depreciation during the year*

Some further and more complex aspects of depreciation, concerning assets which are, in a sense, permanently maintained in their original condition, are considered in the appendix to this chapter.

(III) SCRAPPING

Even at the conceptual level scrapping presents almost as much difficulty as depreciation. Has a machine been scrapped if it is no longer used, but is kept in reserve in the factory for possible emergencies? If an eighteenth-century building which has repeatedly been radically altered is finally scrapped, what is the value of the scrapping at first cost?

These problems would be formidable even if full information on the treatment of old assets were available. In practice there is virtually no information on this subject. A working assumption has, therefore, been generally made in this study that assets are scrapped when the writing off of depreciation has reduced their value to 10% of the first cost in the case of most plant,

---

[1] On the other side, allowance should also be made for capital profits on assets sold for more than their book value.

In practice, however, there is virtually no information available to the statistician on the sale of old assets, and in the present study a working assumption has generally been made that the proceeds from the occasional known sales of old assets (for example, for ships, or buildings in the cotton industry) were equal to their estimated depreciated value at the time of the sale. On this assumption the need for an item showing capital gains or losses falls away.

[2] As noted above (p. 3) the reducing balance method of depreciation, if applied consistently, never *completely* writes off an asset. The book value may, however, be reduced below scrap value, or below the point where the enterprise would normally expect to scrap the asset and write off the remainder in one sum.

[3] If we assume, for example, a stationary stock of assets with a life of 5 years, built up by regular inflows and with the assets scrapped when 90% of their first cost value has been written off, the depreciated value is 46% of the first cost value when depreciation is written off by the straight line method, and 30.8% when the reducing balance method is used. This example is taken from the schematic table in chapter 2, p. 12, where the question is considered in more detail.

ships and vehicles,[1] and to zero for all other assets. Assets due to be scrapped, therefore, have 10% or zero value in the set of estimates at depreciated values, although it is the first cost value of assets due for scrapping on the above working assumption which is taken for the estimates at first cost values.

1.5 NET INVESTMENT IN STOCK-IN-TRADE AND WORK IN PROGRESS

In order to be able to produce and to meet orders, enterprises require stocks of the materials which they use in production and the products which they make. If their products take a long time to make, as is the case with ships and heavy generating equipment for example, they are likely to have at the end of any period a certain amount of unfinished products or work in progress. In general, this will be different from the amount they had at the beginning of the period. As we have noted above (p. 2) any increase (decrease) in these stocks and work in progress represents positive (negative) net investment.

In the case of stocks, the component items can, in principle, be measured in terms of quantity, and there is then no difficulty in discovering how these quantities have changed over the year. The sum of the quantity changes each multiplied by the average current price during the year of the input or output in question gives net investment in stocks. The difficulty of actual measurement arises because this amount of detailed information is never available. The calculations have, therefore, to be made by adjusting the opening and closing stocks, which are valued at different prices, to a common standard of values, namely the average current price during the year. This is difficult because even if the basis of valuation is known, for example where all stocks are valued at cost and materials are withdrawn for purposes of production in the order in which they entered the stockpile, it will not be easy to find out exactly when the materials in a stockpile were actually bought. There is the further difficulty that different firms use different bases of valuation so that the recorded totals of stocks at different dates for a whole industry often reflect a mixed system of valuations.

The corresponding need to estimate work in progress arises if an order is worked on but not completed in a year. The value of the materials and work embodied in it during the year, including overhead charges but not a mark-up for profits, is then part of net investment. Similarly if an order is completed in a year the value of the materials and work embodied in it up to the beginning of that year is a deduction from net investment. Accordingly if the value of unfinished work at the beginning of the year is subtracted from the value of unfinished work at the end of the year the result will be the net addition to work in progress over the year.

1.6 ALTERNATIVE CONCEPTS OF THE STOCK OF FIXED ASSETS

In the case of fixed assets the accumulated stock available at any point of time can be regarded in two distinct ways. If we take cars as an example and neglect differences between different makes of car, the first method is to treat each car available for use as one car, whether it is brand new or twenty years old. The second method is to take the age of the car into account and to treat an old car as equivalent to a fraction of a new car, deriving the fraction from its age and assumed length of life. Except when the age composition of the stock is constant, these two measures do not remain in constant proportion to each other.

The first may accord best with the idea of the capacity of the stock—one can still ride about in a twenty-year-old car if it has been looked after—but it must be remembered that, with technical progress, the older versions of particular pieces of equipment may be greatly inferior to the new versions. The second concept accords not so much with the current capacity of the stock as with the total expected future life, that is, to follow the car example, the total number of future car-years of use that may be expected from the present stock.

The first concept corresponds to the estimates made in this study of the stock of fixed assets at their original or first cost values. The second corresponds to the estimates at depreciated or written-down values. In this connexion two major points must be emphasized. First, the present study starts wherever possible from objective *ex post* estimates of the value of the stock of fixed assets, i.e. from actual costs as indicated by recorded transactions. This approach is conceptually quite distinct from the subjective *ex ante* estimates of the 'market value', based in principle on discounted future income streams. Second, the present estimates of the stock of fixed assets involve certain conventional and rather conservative assumptions about rates of depreciation and scrapping. The estimates may therefore differ from the measurements which might be made by an appropriately valued physical census of the fixed assets which *actually* existed (or were 'in use') in the United Kingdom at the same dates, though the estimates are not, in principle, different.

---

[1] The 10% scrap value is accepted for these assets in the standard rates of depreciation allowed for tax purposes by the Board of Inland Revenue.

It should be noted, however, that an estimate of the actual stock of assets at one date (based, for example, on Inhabited House Duty records for buildings, or the register of ships) has in fact been used as a *starting-point* for many of the stock series. With this starting point the figures for the stock of fixed assets in other years have been found by the additions and subtractions indicated in the stock-flow identities (1) and (2) above. In this way the need to estimate the flows for many years back into the nineteenth century was avoided, and the cumulative discrepancy between the actual depreciation written off and assets scrapped, and the depreciation and scrappings assumed due on the assumptions used in the present estimates, was considerably reduced, though not entirely eliminated.

Finally it must be stressed that the assets have been left at their assumed 'book values' and are not adjusted to take account of possible revised estimates of their expected future life made in the light of contemporary knowledge.[1]

1.7 ALTERNATIVE PRICE BASES

Up to this point we have considered the stocks and flows of different kinds of fixed asset on the assumption that prices are always the same. When we allow for changing prices there is clearly more than one price basis on which the stocks and flows of assets can be measured.

For the depreciated and the first cost value of the stock of fixed assets three price bases are given:

(i) *At historical prices*. Each type of asset included in the stock is valued at the prices of the year in which it was acquired, or at its cost as recorded by the enterprise. This gives the first cost value at historical prices; and a fraction of this, which increases with the age of the stock, is deducted for accumulated depreciation to give the depreciated value at historical prices.

(ii) *At constant prices*. Each type of asset included in the stock is valued at the prices of the same year, 1930 in this study, so that the effect of price changes is eliminated. For each asset the first cost value at historical prices is in principle adjusted to 1930 prices by means of a price index covering each year in which the stock was accumulated; and the same fraction as before is deducted for accumulated depreciation to obtain the depreciated value at 1930 prices.

(iii) *At current prices*. Each type of asset included in the stock is valued at the prices of the current year in question, irrespective of the prices ruling when it was acquired. The first cost value at current prices of each asset is obtained from the corresponding first cost value at constant prices by means of a price index; its depre-

ciated value at current prices is then obtained from the first cost value at current prices by deducting the same fraction for accumulated depreciation as in (i).

For gross investment in fixed capital only two of the above price bases exist, since historical prices and current prices are automatically identical for a newly-acquired asset.

For depreciation of fixed capital all three price bases apply, since depreciation is simply a fraction of the first cost (or depreciated) value of the stock of fixed assets on each of the three price bases; and hence all three apply to net investment (although the estimate at historical prices is not generally of interest). All three price bases are also applicable for the estimates of the first cost value of assets scrapped or sold.

For the change in stock-in-trade and work in progress, as for gross investment, there can only be two price bases, since the values at historical and current prices will automatically be identical.

The problem of changes in the quality or productive capacity of capital goods raises a number of important and complex theoretical issues which cannot be considered here.[2] It must, however, be emphasized that the price indices used in the present study (as in most others) to revalue each type of asset do not, in general, make allowance for such quality changes. In almost all cases the price indices reflect only the changes in the cost of the inputs of labour and material required to construct the capital goods. A major implication of this is that the estimates of depreciation at current or 1930 prices represent a deduction from gross capital formation of the cost of replacing that part of the capital stock which has become worn-out or obsolete during the year with other assets of the same *cost*, even though the quality of the new assets acquired at that cost may be appreciably higher. The corresponding estimates of net capital formation are not, therefore, a measure of the change in the *quality or productive capacity* of the assets.

---

[1] Cf. p. 4 above. This treatment is analogous to that of a company which shows the assets in its balance sheet at a book value (equal to cost less accumulated depreciation), differing considerably from an up-to-date valuation of the current written-down replacement cost which it has had made, say, for the purpose of fire insurance. The company might from time to time desire to revalue the assets on its balance sheet at the new and more appropriate value, and the difference would usually be credited or debited to a 'capital reserve' without passing through any annual profit and loss account. In principle such a practice would also be useful in the national accounts: the annual 'income' flows would be unaffected, but the stocks of capital assets in the national balance sheet would be brought into line with the assets actually in existence, instead of those 'on the books'. If these adjustments showed that the depreciation allowances were consistently much too high, they might then be reduced for future years. As already indicated, no such adjustment has been made in the present study.

[2] For further discussion see [**106**] Denison; [**56**] Central Statistical Office, *National Income and Expenditure, 1961*, p. 81; and [**80**] *A Critique of the United States Income and Product Accounts, Studies in Income and Wealth*, vol. twenty-two, National Bureau of Economic Research (Princeton, *1958*), pp. 87–9 and 256–62.

APPENDIX 1.1

THE TREATMENT OF ASSETS WHICH DO NOT HAVE A NORMAL LIFE-CYCLE

The object of this appendix is to discuss certain cases which do not fit easily into the system of concepts set out above. In the main we shall be dealing with the cases where the difficulty arises not so much from the type of accounting records which have been kept, as from the essential nature of the underlying economic realities; the records do, however, tend to make things yet more difficult. We shall start by ignoring the problems which arise out of changing prices, since although price changes aggravate the problem, there is a very real difficulty even with stable prices.

It is useful to begin by noting that in the field of capital formation and the related concepts covered in this book, as in the field of national income statistics in general, it is essential to adopt a reasonably consistent and economically meaningful pattern of accounting, even though some of the people, firms and government agencies concerned with the transactions may adopt a different system, or keep no accounts at all. It is also not sufficient to add up the things which the various people have recorded, even if they have given them names which correspond to concepts in our system, without some attempt at standardization. This procedure of forcibly making the records conform to a common pattern is bound to come up against difficulties, where the underlying nature of the economic events does not readily lend itself to the system of accounting and the conventions adopted for national income estimates; but we must attempt to make our record of the events in a way that does conform to the standard pattern, even when, as in the present study, we base our records on data derived from business and public authority accounts.

THE SIMPLEST CASE

To appreciate the difficulties which arise in such cases, it is helpful to set up a simplified picture of the events for which the system is well designed. Thus we could visualize the life history of a capital asset as follows:

(a) First there is capital expenditure on new construction to create it—which we record as gross investment.

(b) It is then used for a period, during which there may be expenditures on maintaining it, including the insertion of spare parts and the like; these expenditures are charged to current operating costs, and therefore do not appear in this study at all.

(c) The asset is then scrapped, and perhaps replaced, the reason being possibly that it has become physically less efficient than it was when it was new, or that the amount of expenditure for maintenance has risen too high, or that it has become obsolete through the introduction of new models and so on.

(d) In order to provide for the replacement, an annual charge, called depreciation, is made against the operating expenses, and in the balance sheet the accumulated value of this depreciation is subtracted from the initial value of the asset.

So long as assets broadly conform to this pattern in their life history, the various magnitudes which have been described in the chapter are relatively free from ambiguity, though owing to the uncertain life of the asset there is necessarily uncertainty about the amount which should be charged for depreciation in each year.

MINOR COMPLICATIONS

The system of accounting can also cope quite easily with some kinds of minor complications. Thus it is fairly common for some major improvement to be made to the asset in the course of its life. We can usefully distinguish two cases here:

(a) Where the improvement consists in adding something quite new to the asset (for example, stabilizers are installed on a ship which was built without them).

(b) Where the improvement consists in replacing some fairly substantial part of the asset with something better (for example, the old engine of

the ship is scrapped and replaced by a better one).

The first case presents no difficulties, since the stabilizers constitute gross investment, and records can be kept in respect of them without affecting the records for the main ship.

In the second case the expenditure on the new engine will again constitute gross investment but we also have to take heed of the fact that the original engine has been scrapped. So far as the 'first cost' set of records is concerned, this will require that an item corresponding with the initial cost of the original engine is recorded as scrapped, and subtracted from the first cost value of the original ship, whilst the cost of the new engine is added on. In the set of records which deals with depreciation and depreciated values it *may* be considered that there has been a capital loss equal to the written-down value of the original engine, but more commonly the written-down value of the ship with its new engine will be found by adding the cost of the latter to the written-down value of the original ship. Allowances for depreciation in future years will simply be found by continuing the system in respect of the original ship (including its engine) and adding an allowance in respect of the capital cost of the new engine.

So long as the asset itself broadly follows the simple life-cycle, the real awkwardness which arises with major 'improvements' done during the course of its life is to distinguish these from minor improvements and maintenance expenditure, including the installation of spare parts. In many cases there is no sharp dividing line, so that the figures for gross investment in the year in which the dubious expenditure is incurred may be substantially increased by taking a broad view of what constitutes major improvements, or reduced by taking a broad view of what constitutes maintenance. Correspondingly, the figures for depreciation in subsequent years will move in the same direction, since if the item is capitalized by classing it as 'investment', then it must be written off, and the effective life of the dubious items is likely to be short.

This problem of 'how gross' to make the figures for gross investment is a fairly familiar one in national income research, and there is a substantial literature on the subject. Less has been said, however, about its implications for a series of measurements of the stock of fixed assets, such as is attempted in this study. Particularly for the series of first cost values, a broad view of gross investment has to be accompanied by a broad view of 'partial scrapping' since otherwise the first cost value of an old building which has frequently been 'improved' will come to include the whole of its original cost, plus the whole of the expenditure on the improvements, even though some part of the original construction was effectively scrapped when the improvement was made.

REALLY AWKWARD CASES

So long as we are concerned with assets which broadly conform to the pattern indicated at the start of this appendix, it is not too serious to have to adopt somewhat arbitrary criteria to deal with the awkward cases, since these only represent a minor element in the total. The real problem with which this appendix is concerned arises with assets where the awkward cases are the rule rather than the exception. As an example, one might think of a railway track.

At the stage of initial construction there is no particular problem since there is a clear capital cost to be treated as gross investment. This applies also to any subsequent expenditure on additions to the mileage of track or other major extensions, and in what follows we shall assume such expenditure to be nil. The difficulty comes from the absence, in many cases, of anything which seems to constitute the 'scrapping' and 'replacement' which would normally bring the life history to a close. Instead, we seem to be faced with a situation in which maintenance is clearly necessary, but in which (at least if we take a broad view of 'maintenance') the asset seems to be everlasting.

Further consideration of the problem suggests that it arises from two principal features of assets of this type. First is the fact that in most cases the asset is not renewed as a whole but piece by piece in successive accounting periods (and not all pieces may require renewal). With the railway track for example, the embankment may never require renewal provided it is properly maintained, but the track itself will require not only continual running repairs to individual rails but also, from time to time, the renewal of whole sections. Only part of the track will be renewed within any one accounting period, but ultimately the permanent way as a whole will have been renewed. The second feature is that this piecemeal renewal is frequently a mixture of both maintenance and improvement. If, for example, the worn-out rails are replaced by new rails of a more durable type, the one action both does the necessary maintenance and improves on the original standard.

These features raise difficult conceptual problems for both the 'flow' and the 'stock' series which we are attempting to measure. As a first step we shall ignore the problem of gradual improvement in the course of maintenance, and we shall assume that prices remain constant. The initial problem is to determine what, if

any, part of the annual expenditure on maintenance, repairs and renewals should be classified as gross investment.

At one extreme we might say that none of this expenditure should be capitalized, but that we should take a very broad view of 'maintenance'. It would thus include, as a charge against revenue, not only repairs but also all renewals whether, say, the replacement of an individual rail or the relaying of whole sections of the track. On this view there would also be no depreciation and no scrapping to include in our records of flows, and our capital stock series would show continuously uniform figures for the depreciated and the first cost value, both equal to the original capital outlay.[1] The assumption made is thus, in effect, that current expenditure maintains the economic life of the asset and thereby gives it an essentially permanent character. This treatment is clearly rather artificial: complete renewals should almost certainly be capitalized (as they are for other assets), though naturally it is essential to adopt appropriate criteria for deciding what constitutes 'complete renewals' for assets of this type (see below); and the view that the whole asset is everlasting takes no account of obsolescence, or of the gradual deterioration to which civil engineering works are subject even with regular maintenance.[2] Furthermore, in this particular case, it is necessary to take account of the fact that the permanent way and works also includes what are certainly quite short-lived items such as signal boxes and telegraph equipment.

The other extreme would be to capitalize all expenditure on maintenance, repairs and renewals, thus taking a very broad view of 'gross investment'. If this expenditure was capitalized there would then have to be corresponding depreciation and scrapping; and one assumption which might be made is that depreciation was equal—either year-by-year or, preferably, over the average of a number of years—to the expenditure on maintenance, etc. A similar treatment might be adopted for scrapping. The broad view of 'gross investment' would thus be matched by a broad view of depreciation and scrapping. The depreciated and first cost values of the capital stock would again be equal and would be roughly constant, with perhaps some minor fluctuations according to the amount of maintenance expenditure actually done each year.

This approach is equally subject to a number of serious objections, in particular it would not be in accordance with generally accepted national accounting conventions to capitalize *all* expenditure on repairs, and the view of the whole asset as everlasting has been criticized above.

In the present study we have attempted to find a solution somewhere between these extremes. The main task is to distinguish that part of expenditure on maintenance, repairs and renewals which should be treated as gross investment rather than as maintenance. It is not possible to establish comprehensive criteria for this in general terms but a few illustrative cases may be given. Thus if it is possible, in practice, to separate out such items as the relaying with new materials of whole sections of track, the complete resurfacing of an approach road or the building of a new signal box to replace one that has deteriorated, it is these major renewals of parts of the way and works which might more properly be treated as gross investment. On the other hand, routine adjustment of minor defects on the permanent way and works (such as the replacement of loose rails, the patching of the roadway or the repainting of the signal box) would not be capitalized. Clearly, however, there is an element of arbitrariness in the decision as to where to draw the line, but an important point in favour of an approach along these lines is that it is reasonably consistent with the treatment adopted for other assets.

If an approach along these lines is accepted a corresponding treatment has to be employed for depreciation and scrapping. For depreciation it would be possible to take a rate which would give figures equal to the renewals element of gross investment[3] (averaged over a reasonable period, excluding the initial years) plus perhaps an allowance for obsolescence; or to take a long, and admittedly arbitrary, length of life and depreciate the whole asset over this period. This second approach would allow for obsolescence, for the fact that parts of the railway such as the station and other buildings do clearly deteriorate with use and age, even if regular maintenance is done, and for the fact that even for an asset like a road or tunnel the maintenance expenditure required may ultimately become so heavy that it is more economic to build a new one than to

---

[1] On the simplest view they would both be equal to the original capital outlay. It would be more appropriate, however, to recognize that little would be needed in the way of maintenance when the track was new although something of the nature of depreciation would be taking place; and unless this is subsequently made good by maintenance in excess of current depreciation it might be better to think of the depreciated value as levelling out at, say, a constant 80% of the original cost.

[2] Cf. [**132**] P. Redfern, 'Net Investment in Fixed Assets in the United Kingdom, 1938–1953', *Journal of the Royal Statistical Society*, Series A (General) vol. 118 (1955), pp. 147–8.

[3] It will be remembered that we are assuming that there is no element of improvement in the renewals. When this assumption is relaxed it is no longer possible to equate the renewal including an improvement element) with the depreciation of the original asset. Similarly if prices change it is illegitimate to equate the expenditure on renewals (measured at current prices) and the depreciation of the original asset (measured at the historic prices at which the asset was acquired) even where no improvement is involved.

keep the existing one in use.[1] By taking a long life such as 100 years for the permanent way as a whole one could implicitly assume that the possibly longer life of, say, the embankment, was offset by the undoubtedly shorter life of some of the buildings and equipment. One other advantage of this second approach is its consistency with the method adopted for estimates of depreciation in other sectors. For these reasons it was the method adopted for the present estimates of depreciation of the permanent way and similar assets.

For scrapping, measured at first cost, one would want the same series as for the renewals element of gross investment,[2] plus the original cost of any assets scrapped or abandoned without replacement.

The two series for the stock of fixed assets—at first cost and at depreciated value—would then logically follow if one had information from the start of the enterprise. They would inevitably accumulate all the conceptual problems of the flows but some of these largely cancel out—for example, if investment is taken too gross (at the expense of maintenance) so is depreciation. It is worth emphasizing, however, that the concept of the first cost value of a railway track, or a harbour or other asset of this type is a somewhat sophisticated one, built up from the original capital outlay, with a large number of deductions for elements of it which we regard as scrapped, and an even larger number of additions for replacements and improvements. There is no straightforward asset, or collection of physically separate assets, which has a clear-cut 'first cost'.

THE PROBLEM OF GRADUAL IMPROVEMENT

Even at a conceptual level, the difficulties begin to increase when we take account of the fact that a considerable amount of the 'maintenance' expenditure on the track includes an important element of improvement and modernization. The first implication of this is that the improvement element should in principle be capitalized if it adds to the economic life or performance of the asset. This further means that the original cost of assets scrapped and replaced each year should not be taken as equal to the value of the replacement expenditure, but only to that part which does not constitute an improvement. Similarly with depreciation, if the first of the two approaches mentioned on p. 9 is adopted, depreciation should be equated with the replacement element and not the improvement element of the renewal. These points will in turn be reflected in the estimates of the capital stock. Thus the first cost value should show the original capital outlay and any subsequent expenditure on extensions and major improvements plus the improvement element in the renewals.

THE PROBLEM OF CHANGING PRICES

Finally, we must introduce the problem of changing prices. These greatly enhance the practical difficulty of actually preparing estimates, but they also raise interesting conceptual points, especially for the series at historical prices.

Essentially the problem arises from the fact that the logical basis for taking depreciation (or scrapping) as broadly equal to the renewals element of gross investment depends on both being measured at the same price level: like the renewals basis of accounting, it rests on the assumption that if on the average the real capital is maintained essentially in the same condition, the renewals balance the depreciation *in real terms*. In a set of figures 'at historical prices', depreciation is necessarily measured at the prices at which the assets were acquired, whereas renewals are of course measured in the prices of the year in which the renewal is done. In a period of high prices like 1921, for example, if depreciation was equal to renewals in real terms, it would be much less than this at historical prices.

This also greatly increases the importance of the question of 'how gross to take gross investment'. If we treat almost all expenditure on the railway track as gross investment (with depreciation correspondingly large, but measured at its lower historical price level), then the series for the depreciated value of the track at historical prices will show a fairly rapid rise as more and more of the track is valued at the higher post-war price. If, on the other hand, we treat almost all expenditure (other than extensions) as maintenance, the rise in the depreciated value would be much slower because pre-1914 prices would continue to predominate.

A similar point emerges, of course, with the series at first cost. The 'very gross' view of investment implies a high rate of scrapping, so that the value of the assets rapidly moves on to a post-war price basis; the narrow view of gross investment leaves the original assets standing in the books at pre-war prices.

The first cost series also raises a problem to which the answer is perhaps clear in conceptual terms, but which is very awkward in practice. If, for example, some rails are renewed, and this is treated as gross investment, we have to treat the old ones as scrapped and remove their first-cost value from the totals using historical prices; since the first-cost value of the various rails will differ (quite apart from quality problems) we need in principle to identify the particular rails which have been scrapped.[3]

---

[1] Cf. [**132**] Redfern, p. 148.

[2] See footnote (3), p. 9.

[3] For the series at depreciated values there is little or no problem, because the replaced rails will have been written down to a very low figure.

CHAPTER 2
METHODS OF ESTIMATION

2.1 INTRODUCTION

This chapter is designed to provide a general introduction to the methods used in preparing the estimates described in subsequent chapters. A tabular synopsis of the methods used for all the main estimates is set out in Table 2.10. A detailed explanation is given in the following sections of the more important methods which are used on several occasions; methods used only for one or two sectors are merely noted here, and the reader is referred to the relevant chapters for a more complete account.

It is convenient at the outset to emphasize two points. First, no systematic information is available covering the whole field for which estimates of capital formation and of the stock of assets are required. The totals have to be built up by adding together estimates for the constituent parts derived from a wide variety of sources, with all the consequent problems of duplication or omission. Second, there are many stages at which it was necessary to make extremely broad assumptions and rough estimates or guesses in order to complete a series, but in general it was considered that even a poor approximation would be preferable to complete omission. The effect of both these points is considered more fully in chapter 13 where the complete national totals are discussed and an indication given of their coverage and probable errors.

2.2 THE STANDARD ESTIMATES

The economy was divided into eight major sectors and these in turn were sub-divided into appropriate trade groups. For each of these sectors and trade groups a complete set of *standard estimates* was made for each year from 1920 to 1938. These standard estimates have four aspects. First, a separate set of estimates is given, wherever appropriate, for each of the following groups of assets:

1 Building and civil engineering work (with a separate estimate where appropriate for the value of the stock of land).
2 Plant and machinery, vehicles, ships, furniture and fittings and other equipment.

3 All fixed assets ($= 1+2$).
4 Stock-in-trade and work in progress.

Wherever possible each type of asset in groups (1) and (2) is given separately.

Second, for each group of *fixed* assets a complete set of estimates contains the following eight series:

(a) The year's purchases of new and secondhand assets.
(b) The proceeds of assets scrapped or sold.
(c) Gross capital formation ($= a-b$).
(d) Depreciation.
(e) Net capital formation ($= c-d$).
(f) The depreciated value of the stock of assets held at the end of each year.
(g) The first cost value of assets scrapped or sold.
(h) The first cost value of the stock of assets held at the end of each year.

Where appropriate, the estimates also contain:

(i) The value of the stock of land held at the end of each year.[1]

Third, each of the series in this set is estimated on three price bases:[2]

A. At historical prices.
B. At current prices.
C. At constant (1930) prices.

Fourth, for stock-in-trade and work in progress the total stocks at the end of each year are shown at current

---

[1] Where the estimates were derived from company accounts this series for land is generally shown combined with the depreciated value of all man-made fixed assets, to correspond with the information initially derived from the balance sheets; but this is given in addition to the separate estimates of the depreciated value of man-made assets.

It should be noted that for the economy as a whole the transfer of ownership of land (or other existing assets) makes no net contribution to the total gross capital formation except for the professional fees, stamp duties and other costs incurred in connection with the transfer. For individual sectors or sub-sectors, however, the cost of land might be treated as a component of gross capital formation by the purchasing sector and as a deduction from capital formation by the sector selling the land. This practice has not been adopted in the present estimates and wherever possible the cost of land is excluded from the estimates of gross fixed capital formation. (Cf. [57] *Sources and Methods*, p. 283).

[2] For estimates of the year's purchases and of the proceeds of assets scrapped or sold (and hence of gross capital formation) the series at historical and current prices are identical.

and at 1930 prices. The increase in the value of stocks at current and 1930 prices can be derived from the annual change in these series.

The symbols used above: (1) to (4) for the types of asset, (a) to (i) for the series and A to C for the price

illustrated in the following simple numerical example. It is assumed that the assets have a life of 5 years, that depreciation is written off on the reducing balance method, and that the assets have a scrap value equal to 10% of their cost.

(1)	(2)	(3)	(4)	(5)	(6)	(7)
Year	Purchases during the year	Depreciation during the year	First cost value of assets scrapped during the year	First cost value at end of year	Accumulated Depreciation at end of year	Depreciated value at end of year
1	100	37	—	100	37	63
2	200	97	—	300	134	166
3	300	172	—	600	306	294
4	400	256	—	1,000	562	438
5	500	346	—	1,500	908	592
6	500	399	100	1,900	1,217	683
7	500	429	200	2,200	1,466	734
8	500	444	300	2,400	1,640	760
9	500	450	400	2,500	1,730	770
10	500	450	500	2,500	1,730	770

Source

(2) is the assumed inflow, constant after year 5.

(3) 90% of each year's purchase written off over 5 years by the reducing balance method. The formula is $0 \cdot 1 = (1-r)^L$. With the length of life, $L = 5$, depreciation $r = 0 \cdot 369$, and is applied to the depreciated value at the beginning of the year plus gross capital formation during the year. For example, depreciation for year 10 is $0 \cdot 369 (770 + 450) = 450$.

(4) Assets scrapped at the end of 5 years, $= (1)$ lagged by 5 years.

(The proceeds of assets scrapped, taken as equal to their depreciated value, is assumed to be 10% of their first cost value, e.g. 50 in year 10. Gross capital formation would therefore be 450 and net capital formation 0).

(5) Cumulating (2) and deducting (4).

(6) Cumulating (3) and deducting the depreciation written off assets scrapped.

(7) = (5) less (6).

bases, are followed throughout this study and all entries in the tables and in the technical notes to the tables are made with this notation. In order to save space the complete set of standard estimates is not reproduced in every table. Series (a), (b), (e) and (g) on each price basis are usually omitted.

Using the standard notation given above and the symbol Δ to indicate the change in the stock of capital during a year, the conceptual relationship between the series can be set out as follows:

(1)   (b) $= (a) - (d) - \Delta(f)$ (Note: This identity holds only when the proceeds of assets scrapped or sold equals their depreciated value).

(2)   (c) $= (a) - (b)$

(2′) $= \Delta(f) + (d)$

(3)   (e) $= (c) - (d)$

(3′) $= \Delta(f)$

(4)   (g) $= (a) - \Delta(h)$

Identities (1), (2′), (3′) and (4) involve a change in the *value* of the stock of assets between the end of one year and the end of the next, and so apply only to the series at historical and at constant prices.

The relationship between the main series is further

In addition to the standard estimates, occasional *supplementary estimates* are given where additional information of some interest is available, but the resulting series do not form part of the national totals.

2.3   ESTIMATES OF GROSS FIXED CAPITAL FORMATION OR OF THE YEAR'S PURCHASES

There are basically three types of information from which estimates of gross fixed capital formation or of the year's purchases of fixed assets can be derived: (i) from the censuses of production (the supply side); (ii) from the accounts of the owners (the ownership side); and (iii) from comprehensive statistics (kept for such purposes as taxation and licensing, or the regulation of building activity) of all assets of a particular type. We shall briefly consider the approach to estimates of capital formation based on each of these sources, and also a further approach which represents a combination of the first and third types of information.

(I) INFORMATION FROM THE CENSUSES OF PRODUCTION

The census of production is the nearest to a comprehensive source. It provides relatively accurate information

on the output during a year of almost all the types of assets relevant to capital formation. It does, however, present a number of difficulties:

(*a*) It has to be adjusted by the exclusion of capital goods exported and the addition of capital goods imported, and this requires an alignment of the classification in the production and overseas trade statistics.

(*b*) An allowance has to be made for transport and other costs not paid by the producers.

(*c*) It is often uncertain how the output of any particular good should be classified. For example, an item such as a car will be a capital good for the purpose of this study if purchased by a business, but not if purchased by an individual for his personal use.

(*d*) As it approaches the problem from the supply side it provides extensive information on the type of asset supplied, but it nevertheless allows little classification according to the purchasing industry.

(*e*) The inter-war censuses do not cover all types of capital formation; and give no information on sales or scrapping of capital goods.

(*f*) Censuses are not available for every year. The output of capital goods in the remaining years has, therefore, to be estimated by interpolation and extrapolation, using such indicators of movement as are available.

(II) INFORMATION FROM THE OWNERS' ACCOUNTS

The second main approach starts from the accounts kept by the companies, public authorities, and other purchasers of assets. The local authorities, the Post Office and a few other public utilities show explicitly their expenditure during each year on new capital assets, including those which they produce themselves, and some also show the receipts from the sale (as scrap, or for further use) of discarded assets. In most cases, however, the figures for gross capital formation have to be inferred from information in the balance sheets on the book value of the stock of assets at the beginning and end of the year. In the normal case, where a regular charge for depreciation is made, the book value at which the assets will be shown in the balance sheets can be taken as corresponding to our concept of the depreciated value at historical prices, and gross capital formation can be obtained by the identity:

Gross fixed capital formation during the year
equals *change in the depreciated value of the stock of fixed assets during the year*
plus *depreciation during the year.*

(If the actual depreciation written off by the company is not known it has to be estimated; this point is discussed below, p. 29).

Where the first cost value of the stock of assets is shown, the gross capital formation can be inferred from the change between the beginning and end of the year, plus the first cost value of assets scrapped, and this may require a special estimate of the scrapping (see below, p. 22).

In a few cases, in particular the public utilities, local authorities, and the Post Office, aggregate accounts are available for all units in the trade group. In most cases, however, including almost all capital formation in manufacturing and distribution, it is possible to obtain accounts for only a portion of the firms in each trade group.[1] This problem of incomplete coverage was overcome by taking those accounts which were available, generally including those for nearly all the largest companies in each trade group, and treating these as a sample. The method used to obtain the necessary estimates is discussed in some detail in appendix 2.1. An essential feature is the way in which the figure for the stock of all fixed assets obtained from the sample of company accounts was grossed-up to give an estimate for the industry as a whole. This was done for each industry for one year (usually 1937) on the basis of the proportion of the industry's figure for wear and tear allowances accounted for by our sample in the relevant tax year (1938–9).

The appendix also describes how the figures for years other than 1937 were produced. The basic idea was that the accounts of the sample companies were linked year by year to form a chain of figures by which the grossed-up industry total for 1937 could be extrapolated. Special precautions were taken to deal with problems such as the amalgamation of two or more companies or the revaluation of assets.

One great advantage of using the information given in accounts is that it enables estimates to be made for many separate industries and trades. Its main disadvantage (apart from the errors introduced by the use of samples) is that in the inter-war years the accounts seldom distinguished between the different types of fixed assets purchased, and where a classification was given it was seldom uniform from one company to another. To meet this difficulty various devices were adopted. In the case of the manufacturing and distribution sectors, a special estimate was made of the depreciated value of the plant, machinery and vehicles

---

[1] In the important case of dwellings this approach breaks down altogether because accounts are not normally kept by individual owner-occupiers. Gross capital formation has, therefore, to be estimated by one of the other methods.

owned at the end of each year. This was obtained in several ways: for example, by grossing-up data from a sub-sample of company accounts giving the necessary data in 1937, and extrapolating this in the same way as for all fixed assets. The value of other assets was then obtained as the residual. Further particulars of this and other methods used are given in appendix 2.1, p. 27. In other cases the pattern of asset formation found in the accounts of a few large units within the group was applied to the group as a whole. A classification of assets purchased by water supply undertakings, for example, was based on the information available in the more informative accounts of the Metropolitan Water Board.

(III) COMPREHENSIVE INFORMATION ON SPECIFIC TYPES OF ASSETS

A third approach can be adopted for estimating the purchases of four important types of assets: dwellings, ships, motor vehicles (in various categories) and railway rolling stock. For all these assets comprehensive series are available from which the *quantities* purchased each year can be derived.[1] In the case of motor vehicles, for example, the licensing regulations provide annual data on the number of new vehicles in various categories (such as cars, buses and lorries) registered for the first time. Similarly, the register kept by the Board of Trade shows the tonnage of all ships added to the register each year.

These quantity series were then multiplied by appropriate average costs per unit to obtain estimates of the value of the assets purchased or work done. The tonnage of shipping, for example, was multiplied by an estimate of the average cost per ton of a new ship. The methods used are described in more detail in the relevant sectors.

The major limitation of this approach is that it is based entirely on the technical character of the asset and takes no account of its ownership. It thus raises some awkward problems when combined with other estimates classified largely on the basis of the ownership of the assets. In the case of ships and railway rolling stock (except private wagons) it was assumed that all the assets were purchased by shipping companies and railway companies respectively. Similarly it could be assumed that all dwellings were owned by a special 'ownership of dwellings sector,' and that all buses and taxis were owned by road passenger transport undertakings. In the case of other motor vehicles such as lorries, and passenger cars used for business purposes, no such assumption was possible as these assets are owned by a large number of trade groups and their purchases are covered by the accounts for these trade

groups. The information obtained for these vehicles by this third approach is, therefore, presented only as a supplementary estimate, not directly incorporated in the national totals.

(IV) ALLOCATION OF THE OUTPUT OF BUILDING WORK DONE BY TYPE OF BUILDING

The method used to derive an estimate of purchases of shops, hotels, cinemas and theatres and farm buildings is a combination of the first and third approaches outlined above. The total output of building work was estimated for each year by interpolation and extrapolation of the census of production data. The proportion of this total in the form of shops and other specific types of building was then determined by means of a classification of new building work done. This classification was found in the Inland Revenue Statistics of buildings assessed to Income Tax, Schedule A for the first time, and in the analysis by certain local authorities of building plans approved. Further explanation is given in chapter 10.

2.4 ESTIMATES OF THE STOCK OF FIXED ASSETS

The censuses of production provide no information on the stock of fixed assets, and estimates have to be derived in one of two ways:

(*a*) One method is to reconstruct the first cost and depreciated values of the stock by cumulating the appropriate flows over the life of the asset. This requires estimates of the inflows (purchases) and outflows (depreciation, scrapping and sales) back to the first year in which assets still in the stock at the beginning of the investigated period were acquired.

The major disadvantages of this 'perpetual inventory' method are, first, that it is greatly dependent on assumptions about the actual length of life of each type of asset—a subject on which there is very little reliable information; and, second, that it requires estimates of gross capital formation, and appropriate price series for years far back into the nineteenth century, where the data are again very inadequate.

(*b*) The alternative method, and the one adopted wherever possible in this study, is to obtain a starting-point in the inter-war period for the estimate and then to use the perpetual invention method for other years. The starting-point can be obtained either from information in the accounts of the owners of the assets, or from

---

[1] The statistics of rolling stock do not include privately owned wagons and a separate estimate was made for these. See chapter 9, p. 156.

statistics on the stock of specific types of asset, kept for such purposes as taxation and licensing. These sources of information generally yield an estimate of either the depreciated value or the first cost value of the capital stock. Having obtained one of these values, therefore, the second problem is to derive the other value from it. This requires some indication of the age-structure of the stock of assets.

Before discussing these two problems—the starting-point and the derivation of the other value—there are three points which may be noted:

First, where information was obtained from accounts it was usually at historical prices. Estimates obtained by valuing data in real terms were usually made at constant prices. The methods used in each case to convert the series to the two other price bases are considered in 2.7, p. 24.

Second, in some cases, for example, ships, an estimate of either value of the capital stock could be made (on one price basis) for every year of the period. In others an estimate could only be obtained for one year, generally 1919, and estimates of purchases and depreciation (or scrapping) were then required in order to derive the depreciated (or first cost) values in other years by means of the identities given on p. 12.

Third, as in the case of the capital formation, there was not always sufficient information on each type of asset owned. A breakdown of the estimated total stock of fixed assets had then to be made and this was done in the ways indicated above, p. 13. The breakdown was always made at the earliest stage possible and all subsequent stages were separately estimated for each type of asset.

(I) THE STARTING-POINT FOR THE ESTIMATE OF THE CAPITAL STOCK

Five main methods were used to obtain estimates of the capital stock (on one price basis) for one or more years:

(a) The aggregated accounts for the public utilities show the accumulated capital expenditure on each type of fixed asset. This was generally taken as the equivalent of the first cost value at historical prices. Where a sample of accounts was used, as in Manufacturing, Distribution and Mining, the calculations described in appendix 2.1 normally yielded estimates of the depreciated value of all fixed assets (including land) at historical prices.

A standard assumption was made that land represented 7% of the first cost value of the buildings and sites.[1]

(b) Estimates of the first cost value of ships, motor vehicles, railway rolling stock, cotton spindles and other plant, and agricultural machinery and tractors were obtained by valuing the total registered or recorded quantity (number or tonnage) of these assets.

(c) The first cost value of dwellings at 1930 prices was calculated for end-1938 by cumulating the estimated gross capital formation at 1930 prices. These estimates were obtained by valuing the number of dwellings built each year at the appropriate average 1930 cost per dwelling. The series were carried back for a sufficient number of years to account for the total number of dwellings at the end of 1938. This total was derived from data for 1931 obtained from the enumeration of buildings in the 1931 *Census of Population.*

(d) Shops, and hotels, inns, etc., were assessed to Inhabited House Duty and their gross annual value is known from this source for many years up to 1913/14. The annual value in 1913/14 of each of these types of building was capitalized by using the ratio established for dwellings of first cost value (as obtained above) to gross annual value assessed for Inhabited House Duty.

(e) The fifth method was based on the local authority loans for particular services which were outstanding in 1919 and 1938. The loans outstanding were taken as equivalent to the depreciated value of all fixed assets at historical prices. In a variant of this method the first cost value at historical prices of all fixed assets owned by gas supply undertakings was taken as equivalent to the total paid-up capital and loans issued in 1937.

(II) THE RELATIONSHIP BETWEEN THE FIRST COST AND THE DEPRECIATED VALUE OF THE CAPITAL STOCK

The relationship between these two values of the capital stock (on any one price basis) depends essentially on the age-structure of the stock of assets: the spread of purchases over the years in which the stock was accumulated, and the assumed length of life of the asset.

There are a few cases where direct information on both the depreciated and the first cost value is available, for example in the Post Office *Accounts*, or the age-composition of the tonnage of ships on the official register. For dwellings, the accumulated depreciation at the end of 1938 was estimated by cumulating the gross fixed capital formation since 1839 and writing off depreciation by the straight line method at 1% of the cumulated total building at the end of each year from

---

[1] This proportion was adopted after consideration of the opinion given at the time by valuers and other authorities. See [**136**] J. C. Stamp, *British Incomes and Property* (London, 1916), p. 345; and [**123**] K. Maywald, 'Fire Insurance and the Capital Coefficient in Great Britain, 1866–1952', *Economic History Review*, vol. IX (1956), p. 101.

1839 to 1938. An allowance equal to 10% of the first cost value was added to the depreciated value for all buildings in the end-1938 stock which had survived for more than 100 years. A similar cumulation of expenditure over the assumed life of the asset was used to estimate the accumulated depreciation on roads, on the permanent way and works of the railway and on docks and harbours.

In the majority of cases, however, it was necessary to find some way of imputing an age-structure to the stock of assets and the relationship between the depreciated and first cost values could then be established.[1] This was generally done in one of two ways:

(a) *Age-structure of building derived from Inhabited House Duty Assessments*

The age-structure of most types of building was estimated by reference to records of their gross annual value each year as assessed for Inhabited House Duty. This information was used in the following sectors:

Chapter	Sector or Type of Building	Class of Building Assessed to Inhabited House Duty
8	Manufacturing	Premises not used as dwellings, i.e. Houses, etc., used solely for Trade, etc.
10	Wholesale distribution	
	Shops	Residential shops and Lock-up shops*
	Hotels, inns, etc.	Hotels, Public houses, and Coffee houses
	Cinemas, theatres, halls, etc.	
11	Schools and Libraries	Hospitals, Schools, Royal and Diplomatic residences, etc.
	Hospitals	
	Central Government buildings	

* The gross annual value of lock-up shops is only known for one year (1911/12) and in other years it was assumed to move in the same way as Premises not used as dwellings, of which it forms a part.

These records generally do not go back to the first year in which the accumulation of the stock of assets held in 1919 began. An estimate of the age-structure at the date when the records begin is therefore required, and some arbitrary assumption was usually made: for example, that the age-structure at that date was such that the depreciated value was one-half of the first cost value.

The way in which the gross annual values were used to indicate the age-structure of the buildings can be illustrated by the estimate for factories and other buildings owned by manufacturing industry. The series available in this case begins in 1874/5 and it was assumed that the depreciated value at that date was one-half of the first cost value. It was also assumed that

the buildings had a life of 60 years, that depreciation should be written off on the straight line method, and that all the buildings were demolished at the end of their assumed life.

The calculation of the ratio of the depreciated to the first cost value was then made *in terms of gross annual values*. The accumulated depreciation at end-1919 was taken as 50% of the annual value in 1874, plus $\frac{1}{60}$ of the annual value in each year from 1875 to 1913, plus $\frac{6}{60}$ of the annual value in 1913 to cover the six years 1914 to 1919 for which detailed assessments are not available. The accumulated depreciation due on all buildings assumed to have been demolished at the end of their 60 years life was then deducted from this total. The balance was then deducted from the first cost value represented by the gross annual value in 1919.

The first cost value less the accumulated depreciation due gives the depreciated value, and the ratio of the first cost to the depreciated value obtained in this way (i.e. in terms of annual values) was 1·48. This ratio was then applied to the estimate which had been made in money terms of the depreciated value at the end of 1919.[2]

The same type of calculation was also made with other indicators: for all assets of gas supply undertakings, for example, the age-structure imputed was based on the mileage of gas mains laid.

(b) *The standard estimates of the age-structure of plant*

For most types of plant, machinery, etc., standard estimates of the relationship between the depreciated and the first cost value were used. These rest on the key assumption of a stationary stock of assets accumulated by a process of regular inflows and outflows over a long period. The results obtained with this assumption, assuming various lengths of life for the assets, are illustrated on p. 17 by a schematic calculation of the ratio of the depreciated to the first cost value.

The conclusion which emerges from an analysis of this table and of similar schematic calculations in which the assumption of a stationary stock of assets was varied, is that for assets with a life of more than about 25 years the margin of error introduced by assuming a stationary population of assets is not very great.

Where no information on the actual age-structure of the plant, machinery, vehicles, etc., was available, it was assumed to be that of a stationary stock of assets with

[1] The length of life in these calculations for each type of asset is discussed in 2.5, p. 17.
[2] It may be noted that for dwellings an estimate obtained by using the relevant Inhabited House Duty assessments as an indicator of age-structure gives a depreciated value at end-1919 equal to 64% of the first cost value. The estimate obtained by actual reconstruction of the stock at the end of each year from 1839 to 1938 (see above, p. 15) gives a ratio for end-1919 of 58%.

*Standard estimates of the age-structure of a
stationary stock of assets*

Assumed length of life of all assets in the stock	Ratio of the Depreciated to the First Cost Value Method of Depreciation	
	Straight line	Reducing balance
(1)	(2)	(3)
Years	*Per cent*	*Per cent*
5	46·0	30·8
10	50·5	34·8
15	52·0	36·2
20	52·8	36·9
25	53·2	37·3
30	53·5	37·6
35	53·7	37·8
40	53·9	38·0

(i) It is assumed that all assets have a scrap value equal to 10% of their first cost value.

(ii) The underlying calculation is illustrated in the table on p. 12, where the stock of assets with an assumed life of 5 years is stationary from year 9 onwards (because purchases have been constant for 5 years) so that the depreciated value in column (7) is 30·8% of the first cost value in column (5).

depreciation (generally) measured by the reducing balance method. The ratio of the depreciated to the first cost value was thus taken from a more complete version of the above table. The length of life used was that established for the particular type of plant for the estimates of depreciation (see 2.5). This standard estimate of the age-structure of plant and other assets was used for Manufacturing, Distribution and other services, and Mining.

2.5 DEPRECIATION

It has already been stressed that all estimates of depreciation are, in varying degrees, both arbitrary and approximate. In the present study the basic method was to provide for depreciation (including obsolescence, etc.) by either the straight line or the reducing balance method. The choice between these two conventional techniques, and also the length of life over which the asset was to be written-off, was determined wherever possible by reference to the accounting practices in use in the inter-war years as indicated, for example, by the statutory rates of loan repayment for local authorities or the rates of wear and tear allowed for income tax purposes. These rates seldom represent a realistic technical estimate of the lives of the assets, and tend to be conservative. There may also be inconsistencies between the rates used for similar assets in different sectors. However, it did not seem desirable to introduce independent estimates of the asset lives where our estimates of capital formation and capital stock were derived from accounts in which these rates were

used. There is, in any case, practically no information on which satisfactory independent estimates might be based.

There are some sectors where this resort to accounting practice was not possible, either, as with owner-occupied dwellings, because no accounts were kept, or, as with the renewals system of the public utilities, because some unacceptable method had been used. For these assets it was necessary to make rather rough estimates of the length of life on the basis of such evidence as is available and of the rates for similar assets for which accounting practice is known. The choice between the two methods was also made with a view to consistency with other sectors.

In most sectors the same rate of depreciation was used for each type of asset both for the whole of the period 1920–38 and for earlier years (where estimates of depreciation were required in order to arrive at the accumulated depreciation due at end-1919) although there will almost certainly have been changes in the durability of assets. These changes might in some cases mean longer lives, in other cases shorter lives, and there is insufficient information on this point to warrant the adoption of different lives for the same type of asset in different periods. An important exception to the foregoing are the estimates for depreciation of plant, vehicles, etc. in Manufacturing, Mining and Distribution and other services where account was taken of the changes in the rates allowed by the Inland Revenue. These are described below.

As regards the price basis on which depreciation should be measured, the usual question of 'historical cost versus replacement cost' is answered by the standard procedure in the present study whereby the estimates give one series based on historical cost, a second based on replacement cost at the prices of the year in question, and a third based on replacement cost at 1930 prices.[1]

Where the reducing balance method is used depreciation for the year is estimated from the depreciated value at the beginning of the year plus gross capital formation during the year; and it was generally assumed that the assets had a scrap value equal to 10% of their first cost, so that only 90% of each asset was written off as depreciation. Where the straight line method is used, depreciation is estimated from the first cost value at the end of year.

The methods used to measure depreciation in each sector, and the assumed lengths of life are given in Table 2.10, p. 18. For Manufacturing, Distribution and

---

[1] This refers to the current (or 1930) cost of replacing the original assets, not the cost of replacement by the technically most advanced assets currently available.

TABLE 2.10 SYNOPSIS OF METHODS OF ESTIMATION FOR MAIN FIXED ASSETS*

Part 1 *Buildings and Civil Engineering Works*

Sector	Type of asset	Basic source of information	Gross fixed capital formation = (c)† — Method of estimation	Capital stock‡				Depreciation = (d)§		Scrapping = (g)‖ — Method of estimation
				Starting point Year	Value	Depreciated value = (f) — Method of estimation	First cost value = (h) — Method of estimation	Method	Length of life	
5.1 Agriculture	Farmhouses and Farm Buildings	*Census of Production* and *Inland Revenue*	Share in all new work on buildings, as for chapter 10	1919	(h)	For 1919 ratio to (h) assumed to be 1:2	Maintenance of farm buildings (from Schedule A) assumed to be same ratio to first cost value as for all buildings. See p. 73	SL	100	Nil
6.1 Coal Mining	Buildings and Works	Sample of accounts grossed-up	Δ (f) + (d)	All	(f)	All assets from accounts, less plant, etc. and land	For 1919 ratio to (f) taken as 2:1	SL	60	Based on age-structure as indicated by output of coal, see p. 81
6.2 Other Mining and quarrying								SL	50	Total 1920–38 = $\frac{19}{50}$ of (h) in 1919
7.1 Electricity	Buildings	*Electricity Supply*	Δ (h)	All	(f) and (h)	By cumulating (c)-(d) since 1900	Accumulated capital expenditure as given in *Electricity Supply*	SL	30	Nil
7.2 Gas	Buildings	*Return of all Gas Undertakings*	Share of each type of asset in the increase in issued share and loan capital (adjusted in relation to increase in mileage of mains), + replacements (= g)	1937	(h)	For 1919 ratio to (h) based on age-structure indicated by mileage of mains	Share of each type of asset in total share and loan capital issued	SL	100 and 60	Based on age-structure as indicated by mileage of gas mains. See p. 98
	Mains							SL	60	
7.3 Water	Buildings	*Local Government Financial Statistics*, and sample of company accounts grossed-up	Share of each type of asset in local authority loan expenditure and an allowance for companies	1919 and 1938	(f)	Share of each type of asset in loans outstanding plus assets in grossed-up company accounts	For 1919 ratio to (f) based on age-structure indicated by Schedule D assessments on waterworks	SL	100	Nil
	Mains							SL	75	Total 1920–38 = $\frac{19}{75}$ of (h) in 1878
8.11 Cotton	Buildings	*International Cotton Statistics*	1920–26 proportional to plant 1927–38 assumed negligible	All	(h)	For 1919 ratio to (h) based on age-structure indicated by Inhabited House Duty assessments	Proportionately to (h) for plant	SL	60	Total 1920–38 = $\frac{19}{60}$ of (h) in 1878
8.12–8.54 All other Manufacturing	Buildings and Works	Samples of accounts grossed-up	Δ (f) + (d)	All	(f)	All assets from accounts, less plant, etc. and land	For 1919 ratio to (f) based on age-structure indicated by Inhabited House Duty assessments	SL	60	

Item	Asset	Source	Gross capital formation	Year	(h)/(f)	(h) less accumulated depreciation	For 1919 accumulated capital expenditure		Life	At current prices = revenue expenditure on complete renewals
9.1 Railways	Permanent Way and Works	Railway Returns	Δ (h) + complete renewals	1919	(h)	(h) less accumulated depreciation (based on annual estimates of (c) since 1831)	For 1919 accumulated capital expenditure as in Railway Returns	SL	100	At current prices = revenue expenditure on complete renewals
9.2 Road transport	Roads and Bridges	Road Fund Reports	Expenditure on new construction and major improvements + renewals	1919	(h)	(h) less accumulated depreciation since 1820	By cumulating annual estimates of (c) from 1820 to 1919	SL	100	Estimated total 1920–38 at 1930 prices = £19m.
9.3 Sea and Inland water transport	Harbours and Docks, Canals	Railway Returns, Local Government Financial Statistics and company accounts	Δ (h)	All	(h)	(h) less accumulated depreciation. See pp. 173–4	Estimates of accumulated capital expenditure. See pp. 173–4	SL	75	Estimated total 1920–38 at 1930 prices = £38m.
9.5 Post Office	Buildings	Commercial Accounts of the P.O.	Δ (h) + replacements	All	(f) and (h)	Prime cost less accumulated depreciation as in Commercial Accounts	Prime cost as in Commercial Accounts	SL	100	Revenue expenditure on renewals plus major transfers out of accounts
10.1 Wholesale distribution	Buildings	Sample of accounts, grossed-up	Δ (f) + (d)	All	(f)	All assets from accounts, less plant, etc. and land	For 1919 ratio to (f) based on age-structure indicated by Inhabited House Duty assessments	SL	60	Total 1920–38 = $\frac{18}{99}$ of (h) in 1878
10.2 Retail distribution	Shops	Census of Production and Inland Revenue	Share in all new work on buildings. The classification of new buildings is based mainly on the series of first assessments to Schedule A	1919	(h)	For 1919 ratio to (h) based on age-structure indicated by Inhabited House Duty Assessments	By capitalizing the gross annual value as assessed for Inhabited House Duty	SL	100	Same proportion of (h) each year as for dwellings
10.3 Services by hotels, inns, etc.	Hotels, Inns, etc.						For 1919 ratio to (f) based on age-structure found for inns, hotels, etc.	SL	100	Nil
10.6 Entertainment and sport	Cinemas, Halls, etc.	Census of Production and sample of accounts grossed-up		All	(f)	All assets from accounts less plant, etc.	For 1919 ratio to (f) based on age-structure	SL	100	Special estimate, see p. 197
11.1 Schools and libraries	Buildings	Local Government Financial Statistics and (for 11.2) Hospitals Year Books	70% of loan expenditure	1919	(f)	Share of outstanding loan debt	For 1919 ratio to (f) based on imputed age-structure	SL	100	Nil
11.2 Hospitals	Buildings		83% of loan expenditure and capital expenditure by private hospitals			Share of outstanding loan debt and allowance for private hospitals		SL	100	
11.3 Local authority non-trading services	Buildings and Works		Total loan expenditure by specified services			Outstanding loan debt of specified services		SL	33	Total 1920–38 = 19/L of (h) for 1919
12.0 Residential dwellings	Dwellings	Ministry of Health, Annual Reports and Abstract of Labour Statistics	Work done in units of completed dwellings multiplied by the estimated average value per dwelling based on the cost shown by data on building plans approved	1938	(h)	For 1938 (h) less accumulated depreciation = 1% of end-year stock from 1839 to 1938 + 90% of end-1838 stock	By cumulating gross capital formation (number of dwellings built multiplied by average cost per dwelling) for sufficient period to cover 13m. dwellings in end-1938 stock	SL	100	Special estimate from Stone, Vol. I, p. 221

For Footnotes see below p. 21

TABLE 2.10 (continued) SYNOPSIS OF METHODS OF ESTIMATION FOR MAIN FIXED ASSETS*

Part 2 *Plant and Machinery, Vehicles, Ships etc.*

Sector	Type of asset	Basic source of information	Gross fixed capital formation = (c)† — Method of estimation	Capital stock‡ — Starting point — Year	Capital stock‡ — Starting point — Value	Capital stock‡ — Depreciated value = (f) — Method of estimation	Capital stock‡ — First cost value = (h) — Method of estimation	Depreciation = (d)§ — Method	Depreciation = (d)§ — Length of life	Scrapping = (g)‖ — Method of estimation
5.1 Agriculture	Machinery	*Census of Production* and *Statistical Abstracts*	Extrapolations of census year estimates of retained output + imports	1942	(h)	By cumulating (a)–(d) since 1904	Based on census of machinery in use in May 1942	RB	(14)	3-year moving average of purchases 15 years earlier
6.1 Coal mining	Plant, vehicles, etc.	*Inland Revenue*	△ f.+d.	1937	(f)	Base year wear and tear allowances divided by average rate of depreciation and extrapolated	For 1919, ratio to (f) from schematic estimate of age-structure, see p. 84	RB	(30)	Total 1920–38 = $\frac{19}{30}$ of (h) in 1919
6.2 Other mining and quarrying								RB	(28)	Total 1920–38 = $\frac{19}{28}$ of (h) in 1919
7.1 Electricity	Plant, mains, etc.	*Electricity Supply*	(a) = △ (h) + (g)	All	(f) and (h)	By cumulating (a)–(d) since 1900	Accumulated capital expenditure as given in *Electricity Supply*	RB	av. of 25	Total 1920–38 = purchases 1895–1913
7.2 Gas	Plant, vehicles, etc.	*Return of all Gas Undertakings*	Share in increase in capital plus replacements as for buildings	1937	(h)	For 1919 ratio to (h) based on age-structure indicated by mileage of mains	Share of each type of asset in total share and loan capital issued	SL	60 or 40	Based on age-structure as indicated by mileage of mains. See p. 98
7.3 Water	Plant, vehicles, etc.	*Local Government Financial Statistics* and sample of company accounts grossed-up	Share in estimated loan expenditure as for buildings	1919 and 1938	(f)	Share of each type of asset in loans outstanding plus assets in grossed-up company accounts	For 1919, ratio to (f) based on age-structure indicated by Schedule D assessments on water-works	SL	75	Total 1920–38 = $\frac{19}{75}$ of (h) in 1878
8.11 Cotton	Plant	*International Cotton Statistics* and J. Ryan, *Economic Journal*, 1930	Estimated spindles in course of erection valued at average cost per spindle of all cotton plant	All	(h)	For 1919 ratio to (h) from schematic estimate of age-structure, see p. 16	Spindles and looms in existence valued at average cost per spindle of all cotton plant	RB	(35)	(a)−△ (h)
8.12–8.54 Other Manufacturing	Plant, vehicles, ships, etc.	*Inland Revenue* and samples of accounts grossed-up	△ (f) + (d)	1937	(f)	(i) Base year value of plant in accounts, grossed-up and extrapolated; *or* (ii) Ratio of plant to all fixed assets in sample accounts; *or* (iii) base year wear and tear allowances divided by average rate of depreciation and extrapolated	For 1919, ratio to (f) from schematic estimate of age-structure, see p. 16	RB	av. of approx. 30	Total 1920–38 = $\frac{19}{L}$ of (h) in 1919
9.1 Railways	Rolling stock	*Railway Returns* and accounts of 15 companies	New units acquired valued at average cost per unit	All	(h)	(h) minus accumulated depreciation due	Units owned valued at the average cost per unit	SL	33	(a)−△ (h)

			†	‡				§		‖
9.2 Road transport‖	Cars, lorries, buses, taxis, etc.	Motor Industry of Great Britain, and Road Fund Reports	New registrations valued at average cost per vehicle	All	(h)	Average cost per vehicle of 'survivors' (based on table of life-expectancy) minus accumulated depreciation due	Number of licences current at the average cost per vehicle	RB	8	(a)−△ (h)
9.3 Sea and Inland water transport	Ships	Statement of Navigation and Shipping	Tonnage newly registered valued at the average export value per ton	All	(h)	(h) minus accumulated depreciation due	Tonnage on the register valued at the average export value per ton	SL	20	(a)−△ (h)
9.5 Post Office	Plant, etc.	Commercial Accounts of the P.O.	△ (h)+replacements = (g)	All	(f) and (h)	Prime cost less accumulated depreciation as in Commercial Accounts	Prime cost as in Commercial Accounts	SL	(22)	Revenue expenditure on renewals plus major transfers out of accounts
10.1 Wholesale distribution	Plant, vehicles, ships, equipment etc.	Inland Revenue	△ (f)+(d)	1937	(f)	Base-year wear and tear allowances divided by average rate of depreciation and extrapolated	For 1919, ratio to (f) from schematic estimate of age-structure, see p. 16	RB	(28)	Total 1920–38 = 19/L of (h) in 1919
10.2 Retail distribution								RB	(30)	
10.5 Finance and miscellaneous services								RB	(24)	
10.6 Entertainment and sport							For 1919, ratio to (f) assumed to be 3:2	RB	25	Total 1920–28 = 19/28 of (h) in 1919 Total 1929–38 = (h) in 1928
10.3 Services by hotels, inns, etc.	Furniture, etc.	Inland Revenue and sample of accounts	Additions proportional to buildings+replacements = (g)	1919	(h)	For 1919 ratio to (h) assumed to be 1:2	For 1919, taken as 27·6% of (h) for buildings. Proportion based on sample of accounts	SL	33	Total 1920–38 = 19/L of (h) in 1919
11.1 Schools and libraries	Plant, vehicles, equipment, etc.	Local Government Financial Statistics + (for 11.2) Hospitals Year Book	20% of loan expenditure	1919	(f)	Share of outstanding loan debt	For 1919 ratio to (f) assumed to be 2:1	SL	30	Total 1920–38 = 19/L of (h) in 1919
11.2 Hospitals			10% of loan expenditure and capital expenditure by private hospitals			Share of outstanding loan debt and allowance for private hospitals		SL	30	
11.3 Local authority non-trading services			Total loan expenditure by specified services, see p. 208			Outstanding loan debt of specified services	For 1919 ratio to (f) derived from imputed age-structure, see p. 208	SL	20 or 25	

* *Price basis:* For the majority of items the description relates essentially to the series at historical prices for the stock, and at current (= historical) prices for capital formation. For conversion in each case to other price bases see p. 23.

† *Gross fixed capital formation:* For agricultural machinery, electricity supply plant, cotton industry buildings, railway rolling stock, vehicles and ships the notes in this column relate to the estimate of the year's purchases. The proceeds of assets scrapped or sold have to be deducted from this to obtain gross fixed capital formation. See p. 23.

‡ *Capital Stock:* For estimates of the ratio of the depreciated to the first cost value of the capital stock, see p. 15.

§ *Depreciation:* SL = Straight line method; RB = Reducing balance method.

For the plant, vehicles, etc. mentioned in footnote † only 90% of the original cost of the assets is written-off. Figures in brackets are approximate lives (derived from *average* rates of depreciation) in the 1920s; they would be a little shorter after 1931 when the rates were increased. See p. 22.

‖ *Scrapping:* L = length of life of assets, assumed in estimating depreciation.

The purchases L years before 1920–38 are taken as due for scrapping in 1920–38, and are roughly estimated as a fraction (19/L) of the first cost value in 1919 (or, in some cases, in 1878). This total was then generally spread in equal annual amounts. See p. 22.

¶ The estimate for all vehicles is a supplementary estimate. For the estimates for those vehicles (buses and taxis, and vehicles owned by road hauliers) specifically included in the national totals see 9.2, part 3. The remaining vehicles are covered by other estimates, mainly in chapters 8 and 10.

other services, and Mining, the depreciation at historical cost of plant, machinery, vehicles etc. was based on the statutory allowances in trading years 1936, 1937 and 1938 granted to samples of assessments investigated by the Board of Inland Revenue.[1] They are, therefore, composite rates of depreciation covering various types of plant machinery, vehicles and equipment in different proportions. The average length of life indicated by these allowances was typically about 30 years. The rates for years before 1936 were based on those in 1937 with an adjustment to take account of the change in allowances introduced with effect from 1931 and 1937.

Typical depreciation rates allowed by the Inland Revenue in 1918 (in each case on the written-down value of the asset and the assumption that the scrap value would be 10% of the original cost) were 5% for engines, $7\frac{1}{2}\%$ for other plant and machinery and 20% for motor vehicles.[2] There has been a tendency for rates agreed since then to rise, especially as the speed and precision of machinery increased. An additional allowance equal to 10% of the normal allowance was granted by the Finance Act, 1932; and the Finance Act, 1938 increased the additional allowance to 20% of the normal allowance.[3]

Since 1918 buildings such as factories or mills containing machinery have been exempt from income tax (under Schedule D) to the extent of one-sixth of the Schedule A assessment on the gross annual value of the buildings, and this is regarded as equivalent to an allowance for depreciation.[4] This allowance is not, however, included in the published wear and tear allowances.

The rates allowed by the Inland Revenue for tax purposes were not always equal to those used by the companies in their accounts. It is likely, however, that the Inland Revenue rates had some standardizing influence,[5] so that although actual and estimated depreciation will undoubtedly vary from year to year for each firm they may agree quite closely for each trade group over the period as a whole.

2.6 ASSETS SCRAPPED OR SOLD

(1) THE FIRST COST VALUE OF ASSETS SCRAPPED OR SOLD[6]

Only rarely is any information available on the scrapping of assets. In a few cases, mostly for public utilities, revenue expenditure on renewals is known and was assumed to indicate that there had been an equivalent amount of scrapping. Where independent estimates could be made of both the annual purchases and the capital stock at the end of each year, as was the case for example, for ships and vehicles, scrapping

could be derived by deducting the increase in the stock from the purchases. Finally, an estimate in real terms is available for dwellings.[7]

For a variety of long-lived buildings it seemed reasonable to assume that the value of scrapping or demolition was negligible and could be ignored. This assumption was made, for example, for farm buildings, hotels, schools and hospitals.

In all remaining cases, scrapping due (at historical prices) was estimated on the basis of the assumption that assets were scrapped at the end of the life assumed for them in the measurement of depreciation. In principle this requires information on the purchases L years before the period for which scrapping is being estimated (where L is the assumed life of the asset). Such information is not usually available and approximate estimates of the relevant purchases were made. In a few cases, such as the buildings and works owned by coal mines and gas supply undertakings, specific indicators were used for this purpose. Other estimates were derived in one of two ways:

(a) Scrapping taken as $\frac{19}{60}$ of the capital stock in 1878

This method was used for buildings owned by Wholesale distribution and most of the 22 trade groups in Manufacturing. As noted above (p. 16) the life assumed for these buildings is 60 years, and on the assumption made above the total scrapping due in the 19 years 1920 to 1938 is equal to the purchases from 1860 to 1878. These purchases were taken as equal to $\frac{19}{60}$ of the capital stock at the end of 1878. This total was then generally spread evenly over the 19 years unless some special evidence was available (for example from changes in the value of fixed assets in the samples of accounts) of exceptional scrapping in certain years.

The capital stock at the end of 1878 was in turn derived by means of the Inhabited House Duty assessments on the gross annual value of Premises not used as Dwellings. It was assumed that the 1878 first cost value

---

[1] This unpublished information was kindly made available by the Board of Inland Revenue.

[2] [48] *Statement respecting allowances for Wear and Tear and Obsolescence of Plant and Machinery, etc.* Cd. 9022 (1918).

[3] Thus if the composite rate of depreciation shown by the samples for a particular sector was 8% in 1937, the rate from 1931 to 1936 was taken as 7·3% and from 1920 to 1930 as 6·67%.

[4] [50] *Report of the Royal Commission on Income Tax*, 1920, Cmd. 615, paras. 218–19.

[5] Cf. the statement by Sir Arthur Lowes Dickinson, in evidence to the Colwyn Committee on behalf of the accountants' societies: '. . . people will not as a rule write off more depreciation than they are allowed for income tax'. [62] *Minutes of Evidence* taken before the Committee on National Debt and Taxation, H.M.S.O. (1927), para. 3421.

[6] For further details of the methods used in each trade group, see Table 2.10, p. 18.

[7] See [139] Stone, vol. I, p. 221.

was the same proportion of the 1919 first cost value as the assessed annual value in 1878 was of the annual value in 1919.[1]

The same type of estimate was made for plant and mains owned by water supply undertakings but the first cost value in 1878 was estimated by means of the Schedule D assessments on the profits of waterworks.

(b) *Scrapping taken as* 19/L *of the capital stock in* 1919

An alternative method was used for plant, vehicles, etc., owned by mines and quarries, most manufacturing industries other than cotton, distribution and other services (except entertainment) and schools and hospitals; for buildings and works owned by 'other mining and quarrying'; and for all assets owned by the local authority non-trading services covered in trade group 11.3.

For these assets the total scrapping due in the 19 years 1920 to 1938 was simply taken as equal to 19/L of the first cost value at the end of 1919 where L = the length of life used in the estimates of depreciation.[2] This gives a broadly accurate estimate of the purchases L years before the period 1920–38 unless the stock was changing at a very rapid rate before 1919, and in practice, the fact that the rate probably was growing before 1914 would be partly balanced by the stagnation during the war years. The total scrapping due obtained by this method was usually spread evenly over the period 1920 to 1938.

(II) PROCEEDS OF ASSETS SCRAPPED OR SOLD

The proceeds of assets sold as scrap or for further use is significant only for ships, but a small allowance has to be made for the following assets: agricultural machinery, electricity supply plant, cotton industry buildings, railway rolling stock, motor vehicles and tramway equipment and tramcars. Very little information is available on this item and the basic assumption made was that the proceeds at current and 1930 prices were equal to the corresponding depreciated values of the assets scrapped or sold at historical and 1930 prices, respectively.[3]

The depreciated value of assets scrapped or sold at historical and 1930 prices can be derived from the identity:

Depreciated value of scrapping or sales during the year
equals *Purchases during the year*
less *Depreciation during the year*
less *Change in the depreciated value of the stock of assets during the year.*

For the above assets the proceeds of the sales or scrapping have to be deducted from the year's purchases to obtain the gross fixed capital formation. In almost all other cases the proceeds were negligible (or were assumed to be so) and were ignored, so that gross capital formation is equal to the year's purchases.[4]

2.7 PRICE ADJUSTMENTS

(I) THE YEAR'S PURCHASES AND GROSS FIXED CAPITAL FORMATION

Three main price indices were used to convert the estimates at current (or historical) costs to 1930 prices.

Index A. The cost of civil engineering work and construction.

Index B. The cost of buildings, including dwellings.

Index C. The cost of unspecified plant and machinery.

These indices are reproduced in Table 2.70 for the period 1920–38.

Indices A and B are described in detail in a published paper,[5] and the estimates are given there back to 1845. Both include indices of the costs of materials and of labour combined with equal weights. For index A the materials included are bricks, stone, cement, wood and two series for iron. Index B includes these materials and also tiles, lead, paint and glass. In each case the indices for these materials are combined with equal weights. The cost of labour is represented in both indices by an index of wage rates in the building trades.

---

[1] The usual formula was thus to obtain the total scrapping due by multiplying the first cost value at historical prices at the end of 1919 by

$$\frac{19}{60} \times \frac{\text{gross annual value in } 1878}{\text{gross annual value in } 1919}, \text{ i.e. by } 11\%.$$

[2] Where the rate of depreciation (r) is known, and the reducing balance method has been used, the length of life over which the asset has been depreciated (L) can be obtained by the formula $0.1 = (1-r)^L$, i.e. taking logs,

$$L = \frac{\log 0.1}{\log (1-r)}$$

[3] The depreciated value at historical prices of assets scrapped or sold will differ from the depreciated value at current prices; but for the proceeds of assets sold or scrapped the two price bases are identical. The assumption made above is that the proceeds at current (or historical) prices are equal to the depreciated value at *historical* prices. Except perhaps for ships the difference between the two estimates for the depreciated value is entirely negligible and the use of the historical price series has the practical advantage that it preserves the standard identities.

[4] There are a few cases where the proceeds were high in one or two years as a result of transfers or rearrangements of accounts, and estimates were made for these years. It should also be noted that where estimates were derived from accounts the estimate of gross fixed capital formation is obtained directly from the annual change in the depreciated value of the assets plus the depreciation during the year, so that no estimate of the proceeds of assets scrapped or sold is required (or available).

[5] [122] K. Maywald. 'An Index of Building Costs in the United Kingdom, 1845–1938'. *Economic History Review*, vol. VII (1954).

TABLE 2.70 THE MAIN PRICE INDICES FOR FIXED ASSETS
(1930 = 100)

	Index A Civil Engineering Work	Index B Buildings	Index C Unspecified Plant and Machinery
1920	166·6	171·8	222·9
1921	145·9	140·5	147·2
1922	113·7	113·6	108·7
1923	106·1	106·9	109·8
1924	107·6	110·9	111·3
1925	106·9	111·1	107·9
1926	105·3	107·8	106·9
1927	105·0	105·9	105·4
1928	103·2	101·7	102·9
1929	102·1	102·2	105·7
1930	100·0	100·0	100·0
1931	99·0	96·2	93·4
1932	94·2	91·8	93·6
1933	92·6	90·0	95·4
1934	92·5	90·2	95·7
1935	93·5	92·0	98·4
1936	96·6	95·6	104·3
1937	102·6	100·4	119·1
1938	108·3	102·3	115·9

Index C has not previously been published. It was calculated by combining with equal weights an index of weekly wage rates in engineering at 31 December each year;[1] and an index of the price of materials. This index is, in turn, an unweighted average of the Board of Trade wholesale price indices for iron and steel and for non-ferrous metals.[2]

More specialized indices than these three were used where considered necessary, particularly for ships, vehicles and certain specific types of plant and machinery. These indices are described in their individual chapters.

(II) THE CAPITAL STOCK

Estimates of the capital stock (at either first cost or depreciated value) at constant prices can be converted to current prices by multiplying the series by the appropriate price index—either one of the general indices A, B or C, or the special index for the particular type of asset.

Conversion from historical to 1930 prices, however, requires, in principle, estimates of the purchases in each year that the stock was accumulated and of the prices in those years. In a very few cases, mainly the younger assets such as those in the electricity supply industry, such estimates were made. In the great majority of cases, however, a short-cut method was used. This rests essentially on the long-term stability of prices in the pre-1913 period, and the assumption that the stock of assets was accumulated in a fairly regular way before 1913. This relative stability of prices is suggested by the following table which shows how very little variation there is in the moving average of prices under indices B and C over periods of 30 years.[3]

Average Historical Prices
(30-year moving averages of price indices, 1930 = 100)

Last year of moving average	Index B Cost of Building	Index C Cost of Plant and Machinery
1893	51·9	62·0
1898	51·5	62·1
1903	51·3	62·5
1908	50·5	62·9
1913	50·8	65·3

The average historical costs of buildings accumulated in a fairly regular way during the 30 years 1864–93 would thus be about 51·9% of the costs at 1930 prices, compared with 50·8% for the average historical costs of buildings accumulated in the 30 years 1884–1913.

The working rule generally adopted for the relationship between historical and 1930 prices was thus simply to assume an average price of this sort; and in view of the stability of the averages shown above, the average price for the 30 years 1884–1913 was taken as broadly representative of the long-term trend of prices before 1914. The 1919 stock of dwellings at historical prices, for example, was taken to be 50·8% of the stock at 1930 prices, both at first cost and depreciated values. Once the stock at 1930 prices is known for one year, the remaining years can be derived by means of the usual identities.

(III) DEPRECIATION

Estimates of depreciation were made in the same way[4] at historical and at 1930 prices. Depreciation at current prices was then obtained from the series at 1930 prices by means of the appropriate price index.

(IV) FIRST COST VALUE OF ASSETS SCRAPPED OR SOLD

The ratio of average historical prices to 1930 prices was generally assumed to be the same in each year for assets scrapped as it was for the stock of assets in 1919.

---

[1] [30] *Statistical Abstracts for the United Kingdom*, annual or [1] *Abstracts of Labour Statistics of the United Kingdom*.
[2] [30] *Statistical Abstracts*.
[3] For further confirmation of this assumption, see chapter 9, p. 154.
[4] See above, p. 17.

TABLE 2.80 VALUE OF PHYSICAL INCREASE IN STOCKS: INDUSTRY, TRADE AND TRANSPORT

At Current and 1930 Prices

Value of stocks in balance sheet at end of year at current prices	Index of prices underlying balance sheet values in (1)	Value of stocks at average 1930 prices (1)÷(2)	Value of physical increase in stocks at 1930 prices	Index of average price of stocks during year	Value of physical increase at current prices (4)×(5)
£m.	Average 1930 = 100	£m.	£m.	(1930 = 100)	£m.
(1)	(2)	(3)	(4)	(5)	(6)
1920 2099	217·6	965	—	265·7	—
1921 1452	138·7	1047	82	160·1	132
1922 1266	132·6	955	−92	134·5	−124
1923 1254	137·4	913	−42	135·9	−57
1924 1276	141·8	900	−13	141·8	−18
1925 1267	127·2	996	96	135·2	130
1926 1218	121·6	1002	6	123·9	7
1927 1244	118·8	1047	45	119·0	54
1928 1238	117·1	1057	10	119·4	12
1929 1210	109·8	1102	45	115·5	52
1930 1086	91·2	1191	89	100·0	89
1931 1017	85·9	1184	−7	87·5	−6
1932 967	83·0	1165	−19	84·4	−16
1933 956	87·0	1099	−66	84·8	−56
1934 993	87·5	1135	36	88·1	32
1935 1020	89·8	1136	1	88·1	1
1936 1111	98·5	1128	−8	93·5	−7
1937 1238	104·5	1185	57	106·8	61
1938 1206	95·5	1263	78	98·0	77

Source

(1) Sum of estimates for Mining, Electricity, gas and water, Manufacturing, Transport and Distribution and other services.

(2) Index of price at balance sheet date (if prices were falling) or during period when stocks were acquired (if prices were rising) estimated as described on p. 32 below.

(4) Annual change in (3).

(5) Current weighted average of prices used in chapters 6 to 10 below for approximate conversion of book values to average 1930 prices.

The total scrapping due over the period 1920–38 at 1930 prices could thus be found by applying the same proportion to the end-1919 first cost value at 1930 prices as was applied to the corresponding value at historical prices.[1] Scrapping at current prices was then obtained from the series at 1930 prices by means of the appropriate price index.

2.8 STOCK-IN-TRADE AND WORK IN PROGRESS

Estimates of the book value of total stocks (including work in progress) were generally taken directly from aggregated accounts, or were derived from samples of accounts by the methods described in appendix 2.1, pp. 28–9. Special estimates based on physical data on livestock, crops on farms and standing timber were made for agriculture and forestry, and are given in chapter 5.

Special price indices, relating mainly to wholesale prices, were used in each trade group to convert the end-year stocks from current book values to what is, *in principle*, an approximation to the value at average 1930 prices. Since it is only an approximation, however, estimates of the value of the physical increase in stocks at current or 1930 prices cannot be obtained from these series (except in agriculture and forestry) and are not given for the industrial trade groups. An estimate for industry, trade and transport as a whole has, however, been made and is shown in Table 2.80. The methods used to obtain this aggregate estimate at current and 1930 prices are described in appendix 2.2, pp. 31–3; and the appendix also contains a brief note on the approximate estimates which can be made for the individual trade groups and sectors.

[1] See above, p. 22.

2.9 OWNERSHIP OF ASSETS—DEFINITION AND CLASSIFICATION

All estimates in the present study are classified to different sectors (and sub-sectors) and the classification is based in principle on the criterion of ownership. Two issues arise in this connexion. The first is the question of definition: whose assets should be covered. The present estimates refer in principle to all assets located in the United Kingdom, i.e. they include assets in the United Kingdom owned by non-residents and exclude assets located overseas which are owned by United Kingdom residents. This approach is essentially determined by the nature of the data available.

The second issue relates to the criteria for classification by sector, and two important issues of principle arise in connexion with the basis on which the classification is to be made.

First, since buildings and other assets may be hired, we have to decide whether the classification is to be based on the character of the owner or of the user of the asset. If, for example, a railway company owns a book-stall which it lets to a tenant, is the stall to be classified under railways or under distribution? One particular aspect of this problem is that if we follow the ownership criterion we need, in principle, a special property-owning sector for assets owned by firms whose business consists simply in letting out assets for use by others; property companies provide an important illustration of this. On the other hand, if the 'use' criterion is adopted, there is no such property-owning sector; and on this basis the book-stall in the above example would be classified under distribution.

Second, whether it is the owner or the user of the asset whom we wish to classify, the principles for classifying them need elaboration. For example, is a railway company to be regarded as having only *one* industrial classification made according to its principal activity, so that its ships, hotels, engineering workshops and so on are all put under railways? Or should we divide its activities up as much as possible, and regard the company as having, for example, a 'shipping section' whose assets would be added to those of other shipping companies? This type of problem is a familiar one—it sometimes takes the form of deciding whether to make the 'establishment' the unit of classification rather than the firm (or even the whole group of parent firm, subsidiaries and sub-subsidiaries).

The solutions to these two questions are in fact closely related: by using, wherever possible, a classification by establishment rather than by the firm as a whole, the distinction between the criteria of ownership and use is virtually eliminated. Thus the bookstalls owned by the railways can in principle be treated as a separate establishment engaged in distribution and classified as such. This is not necessarily the ideal solution but it is on the whole the most satisfactory one which can be attained with the information available. We thus made the classification on the criterion of ownership, based wherever possible on establishments rather than firms.

If we take dwellings for example, the owners include individual occupiers, property companies and enterprises which provide accommodation for their employees. In this study all these dwellings are aggregated in one sector covering the ownership of all dwellings. A property company which owns, say, dwellings and cinemas is thus split into two establishments, one classified to the Dwellings sector, the other to the sector (Entertainment and sport) covering the ownership of all cinemas. Similarly pubs owned by breweries are treated as separate establishments and classified to the sector covering the ownership of all hotels, inns and restaurants and are not included with the breweries in Manufacturing. The large number of estimates made directly from the owners' accounts also lead to a classification according to ownership. There is inevitably, however, a certain amount of duplication and omission, and the extent of this is considered in chapter 13.

APPENDIX 2.1

ESTIMATES BASED ON A SAMPLE OF COMPANY ACCOUNTS

Samples of company accounts were used for estimates for all 22 trade groups in manufacturing industry except cotton, for mining, and for wholesale distribution. Part of the estimates for retail distribution and certain other services were also obtained from this source.

The derivation of estimates of capital formation and the capital stock from company accounts raises two sets of problems:

(a) Those arising from the nature of the information typically provided by company accounts in the inter-war years.

(b) Those arising from the fact that accounts are not available covering the whole of any industry; that it is hard to assess what fraction of the industry's capital formation is covered by the sample in any one year; that this fraction may not be representative; and that it changes from year to year for a variety of reasons such as amalgamations.

The following sections of this appendix consider:

1. the methods used to overcome the difficulties presented by information in a sample of company accounts; and

2. the main characteristics of the estimates which are obtained by these methods.

I OUTLINE OF THE METHOD USED FOR ESTIMATES BASED ON A SAMPLE OF COMPANY ACCOUNTS

(a) Information available in the accounts

For the majority of trade groups the accounts give a figure for the written down value of fixed assets (and for the first cost value of land) at the end of each year, as shown in the firms' books. For plant, equipment, etc., and for buildings it was assumed that the firms would make a deduction for accumulated depreciation, and the book value was taken as corresponding to our concept of the *depreciated value*. Essentially this depreciated value is at historical cost and (after grossing up the sample) was taken as such without adjustment except for the allocation by type of asset.[1]

Net fixed capital formation for the whole industry can be obtained from the difference between the depreciated value at the beginning and end of each year of each type of asset. This figure is based on the firms' own figure for depreciation and their own idea of what expenditure should be capitalized.

Gross fixed capital formation can then be deduced by adding back the depreciation written off each year. As a rule the companies did not publish their allowance for depreciation so an estimate had to be made of the 'appropriate' amount for the year, and this was added back for the year instead. (See 2 (i), (c), p. 29).

The estimates of depreciation, and of the other series required—i.e. the first cost value of the stock of fixed assets, and the first cost value of the assets scrapped or sold—were derived by the methods described above on pp. 14–23.

The estimates obtained from the accounts are at historical prices and they were converted to current and 1930 prices by the methods outlined on p. 23.

The accounts also show the value of the *stock-in-trade* held at the end of each year, and here again an estimate for the industry as a whole has to be derived from the sample.

(b) Selection of the sample

In general no scientific method of sampling was possible. The companies in an industry which were quoted on the London Stock Exchange with an issued capital greater than £500,000 in 1920, 1930 or 1938 were usually all included, plus about one-third of the quoted companies below this size for which accounts were available. The number of accounts available tended to be smaller in the 'twenties and the early estimates are correspondingly less reliable. A direct approach was made to many companies for additional information to supplement that available in the published accounts.

---

[1] For two trade groups containing mainly buildings on which no form of depreciation allowance was given (see above, p. 22) the book value was taken as corresponding to our concept of the first cost value. This applies to buildings owned by Wholesale distribution (mainly warehouses and offices) and by Entertainment and sport (mainly cinemas and halls).

(c) Timing

Information in the company accounts relates to the assets held at the end of the company's financial year. The figures were taken without adjustment for the nearest calendar year, i.e. the estimate of assets held at the end of, say, 1930 was based on all companies in the sample whose financial year ended on any date from 1 July 1930 to 30 June 1931. It is believed that the weighted average terminal date does approximate quite closely to the end of the calendar year (Cf. p. 32 below).

(d) Grossing-up the samples for one year

The basic step was to gross-up the figure for the depreciated stock of all fixed assets (excluding land) obtained from the sample of company accounts for each trade group for one year (usually 1937) so as to obtain an estimate for the group as a whole. The companies whose accounts were available were classified into the trade group as defined by the Board of Inland Revenue,[1] and a list of our sample companies in each trade group was given to the Board. They then informed us what proportion of the total wear and tear allowances granted to each trade group in the financial year 1938/39 (trading year 1937) was allowed to the companies in our sample. If, for example, the total wear and tear allowances for the chemical industry was W, and w of this had been allowed to our sample of chemical companies, then the value of fixed assets shown by the sample companies was multiplied by $\frac{W}{w}$ to obtain the depreciated capital stock for the whole chemical industry. Allowance was made for units which were not assessed in the base year because they had made losses.

(e) Depreciated value of all Fixed Assets in other years

The movement in the depreciated value of all fixed assets between the base date and the preceding (or succeeding) year was then established by taking all the companies in the sample for which accounts were available for both dates, after eliminating any for which there seemed to be an 'unreal' movement due, for example, to amalgamations or a revaluation of assets. (Where possible, however, these cases were included after the appropriate adjustment had been made. For example, the value after a merger would be compared with the sum of the previous values for the constituent companies; or the amount by which assets had been written down in a reconstruction would be added back). In this way a chain was constructed from year to year for the whole industry until the whole period 1920 to 1938 had been covered.

(f) Allocation of the total by type of asset

The total thus obtained for all fixed assets was divided between land, buildings and civil engineering work, and plant, machinery, vehicles, etc. The first step was to estimate the depreciated value at the end of each year of the plant, etc. This was done by one of three methods, chosen in the following order of preference on the basis of the information available.

(i) The depreciated value of plant, etc., was estimated for 1937 from a sub-sample of accounts giving the necessary breakdown, grossed-up in the same way as for all fixed assets, and then extrapolated by means of a chain constructed in the same way as for all fixed assets.

(ii) The ratio of plant to all fixed assets shown by a sample of accounts available each year was applied to the corresponding estimate of all fixed assets owned by the whole industry.

(iii) The wear and tear allowed for each trade group for tax purposes is known for 1937 (income tax year 1938/9) from a census of assessments.[2] The depreciated value for a base year (which was usually 1937) was obtained by dividing the allowances[3] by the average *rate* of depreciation (i.e. the ratio of wear and tear allowances to the depreciated value of plant, etc.) established from samples of assessments for 1937. This value was then extrapolated on the basis of an index of changes in the wear and tear allowances shown in the Board of Internal Revenue's annual summaries of information for a sample of assessments.[4] Adjustments were made to eliminate the effect of the additional allowances introduced in 1931 and 1937.[5]

Land and buildings were then obtained as the residual, and in turn separated by the standard assumption that the end-year value of land represented 7% of the first cost value of buildings.[6]

(g) Stock-in-trade

Two methods were used, and the most satisfactory adopted in each case.

The first, and most usual, method was to use the ratio of stocks to net fixed assets shown by the sample companies each year.

---

[1] For details of the inter-war Inland Revenue classification, see chapter 13, p. 224.

[2] A census of assessments classified by trades was taken for three inter-war income tax years: 1928/9, 1933/4 and 1938/9. These censuses have not been published by the Board of Internal Revenue but were kindly made available for the present investigation.

[3] Adjustments were made for firms not covered by the censuses because, for example, they had made a trading loss.

[4] These summaries have not been published but were made available by the Board of Internal Revenue.

[5] See above, p. 22.

[6] See above, p. 15.

The second method was to compute a figure for the base year by the ratio method, and then to make an independent chain for stocks by using at each link all the companies which gave a suitable figure for stocks at each end of the link.

2 CHARACTERISTICS OF THE ESTIMATES DERIVED FROM THE ACCOUNTS

There are several points which may be briefly made about estimates derived from accounts.

(i) First, there are five points which would arise even if all accounts in a trade-group were available:

(a) *The basis of classification by industry*. From the nature of their origin, the estimates cover the activities of firms, classified as mainly engaged in the industry, without any attempt to eliminate the other activities which they conduct, or to include activities of a kind associated with this industry conducted as side-lines of firms classified elsewhere.

These two adjustments, if made, might of course cancel out. Their size is increased, as against, say, the Census of Production's 'carry-in and carry-out', by the use of the firm rather than the establishment as a unit of classification. But the problem is not as serious for inter-war years as it would be now, because firms did not usually consolidate the activities of parents and subsidiaries, and wherever possible the unconsolidated accounts were included in the samples.

(b) *Rented Assets*. A special corollary of the above is that the figures for any industry will include assets which the firms in it own and let to others, but *exclude* assets which they use, but do not own. This may be important in relation to rented buildings, and is perhaps less likely to cancel out.

(c) *Gross Fixed Capital Formation*. Estimates of this are unfortunately exposed to the possibility of serious error, because the firms may have written off for depreciation a sum quite different from that calculated by us as 'due' and added back to the figure for net capital formation. Accounting practices in regard to depreciation were highly variable in the inter-war years, both from company to company and from year to year. This applies more particularly to certain buildings and civil engineering works, where there was no income-tax allowance to provide a standardizing influence. The main consequence is that in years when the industry was making poor profits, gross capital formation may be overestimated, because little was allocated by the companies to depreciation; and conversely for prosperous years. In industries where net capital formation is small relative to depreciation, the errors in gross capital formation caused by this factor may be proportionately very large.

(d) *Net Fixed Capital Formation*. The values shown for this are free from the distortion caused by our depreciation estimates being different from the amounts actually written off by the firms: they represent essentially the amount of expenditure which the firms themselves decided to capitalize, less the amounts which the firms decided to write off. In consequence, however, they are also liable to be 'too high' (by more objective national accounting standards) in years of low profits, because many firms may then have decided that they could 'afford' relatively little for depreciation.

(e) *The Stock of Fixed Assets*. The initial estimate of the stock of fixed assets derived from the accounts represents the *book value* of these assets, and is thus subject to all the limitations inherent in this valuation: in particular the likelihood that different companies will have used different methods of valuation (and revaluation) in arriving at the values shown in the balance sheets. The fundamental assumptions required, and they may not always be very satisfactory, are that the book values of fixed assets (other than land) can be accepted as the equivalent of the *written-down* (or for some types of building the first cost) *value at historical prices*; and furthermore, that the short-cut methods outlined above (p. 16 and p. 24) are satisfactory both for converting the written-down value to the first cost value, and for converting both values at historical prices to the corresponding value at 1930 replacement cost.

It was assumed that depreciation would have been written off the original cost of factories and mills in the manufacturing sector but not of warehouses etc. in wholesale distribution. In fact, before 1918 no depreciation was allowed for tax purposes on any type of building and so it is very likely that there were many firms in manufacturing where no depreciation was written off for buildings. In such cases the assumption that the book value should be regarded as the equivalent of the written-down value would obviously be incorrect and the present estimates for both the first cost and the depreciated value of industrial buildings would be a good deal too high. The first cost value will also be too high if depreciation was written off, but over a longer life than the 60 years assumed in the calculation described on p. 16 above.

(ii) Second, there are three additional points which arise from the need to use a sample of accounts:

(a) *Assumption Implicit in Base-Year Grossing-up*. The method of grossing-up has three important implications:

First, as the total wear-and-tear allowances for the industry cover all kinds of firms, and not merely public companies, the method automatically extends the estimate to cover sole traders, partnerships, private companies, etc.

Second, however, this extension assumes that the ratio of 'income-tax allowance for wear-and-tear of plant and machinery, etc.' to net fixed assets (and to stocks) which is found in a sample of public companies (mostly large) can be taken as representative for the whole industry. With plant there is solid support for the assumption, since the same tax rules apply based on the reducing balance principle; for stocks it is perhaps plausible. It is less satisfactory for estimating the value of buildings owned, since small firms are more likely to rent their buildings. The assumption that the ratio of plant to buildings is the same for all firms in the industry is also not very satisfactory.

Third, the industry is effectively defined as the firms classified to it by the Board of Inland Revenue.

(b) *The Chain of Fixed Assets*. The method of preparing this necessarily involves the assumption that at each link the proportionate change in the written-down stock of capital for the industry as a whole was similar to that for the sample of (mainly large) companies whose accounts were both available and considered usable (either because there appeared to be no distortions through amalgamations, revaluations, etc., or because allowance could be made for them).

(c) *Revaluations*. The base for the chain of assets is essentially the figure shown for them in the balance-sheets of the year used for grossing-up (usually 1937). This is taken as equivalent to 'historical cost' for that year, and appropriate adjustments are made so that any revaluations which may have been made in earlier years do not disturb the comparability of the successive links in the chain. In other words our 'historical cost' in, say, 1920 will be adjusted so that it reflects (in advance) revaluations subsequently made in, say, 1932.

The effect of all these factors on the estimates actually obtained is further considered in the relevant chapters, particularly chapters 8 and 9.

APPENDIX 2.2

INVESTMENT IN STOCK-IN-TRADE AND WORK IN PROGRESS

The purpose of this appendix is, first, to describe an estimate for the value of the physical increase in stocks at current (or 1930) prices which has been made for industry, trade and transport (chapters 6 to 10) as a whole. A separate estimate is made for agriculture and forestry in chapter 5 (pp. 75 and 77) and these two estimates can be combined to obtain an estimate for the economy as a whole. Second, there is a brief discussion of the estimates available for the individual trade groups and sectors in industry, trade and transport. These were not fully adjusted to yield what would, in principle, be a correct estimate of the value of the physical increase in stocks, but a rough approximation to this can be obtained and the present comments are designed to facilitate evaluation of this approximation.

(1) INDUSTRY, TRADE AND TRANSPORT

The data which we obtain from accounts for each trade group yield estimates of the balance sheet values of stock-in-trade and work in progress (stocks). From the first difference of these values we can obtain only the annual change in the value of stocks. We cannot obtain directly the value of the physical change in stocks, i.e. the physical change in stocks during the year valued at the average current replacement cost of stocks during the year; and it is this series which is required for social accounting purposes.[1]

If we had all the necessary data we could adopt the following procedure to obtain estimates of the value of the physical change in stocks for each trade group. We would first have to make the following (or appropriately varied) conventional assumptions: that the quantity of stocks held changes at a steady rate throughout the year; that a firm assesses the cost of its stocks in the way which would be appropriate if it had used its supplies in the sequence in which they were acquired (the 'first in, first out' or FIFO hypothesis); and that for balance sheet purposes stocks are valued by firms at cost or current market price, whichever is the lower.

We then take any two successive years and assume, for purposes of illustration, that prices are falling in year 1 and rising in year 2. Let:

Quantity of stocks at end of year $1 = q_1$.
Quantity of stocks at end of year $2 = q_2$.
Market price at end of year $1 = p_1$.
Market price at end of year $2 = p_2$.
Average market price when q_1 was acquired $= p_m$ (which is greater than p_1 because prices were falling).
Average market price when q_2 was acquired $= p_n$ (which is less than p_2 because prices were rising).
Average market price during year $1 = p_a$.
Average market price during year $2 = p_b$.
Average market price during $1930 = p_c$.

Given the assumptions made above about the balance sheet values, the values at the beginning and end of year 2 will then be:

	Beginning	End
At book values	$q_1 . p_1$	$q_2 . p_n$
At average prices of year 2	$q_1 . p_b$	$q_2 . p_b$

The figure we want for the value of the physical change in stocks at average current (year 2) prices is thus $(q_2 - q_1)p_b$; and this can be obtained by multiplying the end-year book value by $\frac{p_b}{p_n}$ and the beginning value by $\frac{p_b}{p_1}$. For the value of the physical change at average 1930 prices the procedure is exactly the same except that p_c is substituted for p_b.

In order to make these adjustments in practice we therefore need to know two sets of average market prices: (a) the price during each year; and (b) the price at the end of the year if prices were falling, or during the period when the end-year stocks were acquired if prices were rising. This last series in turn requires that we must know the average period for which stocks on hand at the balance sheet date had been held. These requirements are discussed below. With the data available it is clear that any adjustments we make must be very approximate, quite apart from errors in the data

---

[1] These general concepts are more fully discussed in the Central Statistical Office publication [57] *Sources and Methods*, pp. 309–13 and 324–31. The methods used in this appendix owe a great deal to the pioneer study by T. Barna [82] 'Valuation of Stocks and the National Income', *Economica*, New Series, vol. IX (1942).

on balance sheet values from which we start. This is greatly accentuated by the fact that the adjustment should ideally be made for each individual trade group and not, as in the present case, for the aggregate stocks held.

Given these limitations and accepting the assumptions that the balance sheet data refer to the lower of cost or market value in combination with the FIFO hypothesis we then have the following practical difficulties:

(i) We need a monthly price index showing the movement in the current value of stocks. We have the weighted average of the indices which are used for each trade group in chapters 6 to 10 below to convert current values to average 1930 values, but only on an annual basis. The great majority of the component indices were, however, based on the Board of Trade wholesale price indices and our weighted average moves in fairly close agreement with the 'all articles' index. We have therefore assumed that the proportionate movement from month to month was the same for our index as for the 'all articles' index. The error introduced by this procedure is of much less consequence than the fact that our (annual) component wholesale price indices are a highly unreliable guide to the actual market prices of the stock changes.[1] More appropriate data are not available but this must be recognized as a major limitation of our estimates for investment in stocks.

(ii) Given this monthly index we can reasonably assume, when prices are falling, that the balance sheet value is based on the average price during the month to which the balance sheet is made up. When prices are rising, however, we have to take the average price during the period when the stocks on hand were purchased and this requires some assumption about the average period of turnover of stocks. Reliable information on this point is not available in the inter-war years, either for individual industries or for the economy as a whole. We have taken an average period of 4 months;[2] thus if the business year ends on 31 December, p_n in the example given above would be the average of our monthly indices for September to December. This is a very rough guess, but the results would not differ very much if we took, say, 3 or 6 months.

(iii) The final problem is that the balance sheet dates from which our data are obtained are not made up to any uniform date, but to a wide range of dates throughout the year. This has two consequences: first, the weighted mean terminal date of the balance sheets is not exactly 31 December so that the change in stocks will not relate exactly to the calendar year. Second, the prices taken to be underlying the balance sheet values (on the assumptions made in (ii) above) will also

be spread throughout the year. The first difficulty is not very important since the mean terminal date is probably quite close to the actual end of the calendar year,[3] and any variation from year to year is unlikely to be significant.

The second difficulty is more important in a period when the rate of change of prices is not constant, and means that we must obtain some evidence as to the way in which the balance sheet dates are distributed between the four quarters from 1 July to 30 June—the period covered by the balance sheets which we take as made up, on average, to 31 December. Ideally we should use a weighted average of the balance sheet dates in the actual sample of accounts from which our estimates are drawn, but this information was not collated at the time the estimates were made and is not now available. As a very approximate substitute we have taken the distribution of business year-ends between the quarters to be the same as that for all public quoted companies covered in the Board of Trade compilations of company accounts for 1955-7,[4] weighting the year-ends in each sector on the basis of the balance sheet values in these accounts for stock-in-trade and work in progress. We make one further assumption: that in each quarter the balance sheets are made up to a date in the last month of the quarter (as is commonly the case) and we can then use the percentage distribution of balance sheets as weights with which to obtain the mean price assumed to be underlying the balance sheet values at the end of each year. This index is then used to derive the estimates of the value of the physical increase in stocks at current and at 1930 prices, as shown in Table 2.80, p. 25.

Estimates of the investment in stocks are almost inevitably subject to large margins of error[5] and it will

---

[1] The primary source of error is the fact that the official wholesale price indices relate largely to raw materials and unprocessed foods whereas the physical stocks include a very large element of manufactured and semi-manufactured goods.

[2] Cf. [82] Barna, p. 350, where it was estimated that for the whole economy, the average period of turnover of stocks 'was under 5 months'.

[3] [137] J. C. Stamp, *The National Capital* (London, 1937), p. 50 quotes a sample of accounts *published* in the year ended 30 September 1930 as having a mean terminal date 25 December 1929.

[4] *Economic Trends*, No. 74, 1959, and the underlying mimeographed Board of Trade material for each quarter for each sector.

[5] The crux of the statistical difficulty is that the *change* in stocks is small in relation to the likely errors in the end-year estimates of total stocks. In our estimates the average level of stocks at current prices is approximately £1,200m. An error of only 5% in one end-year estimate of the level of stocks could thus produce an error of £60m. in the estimate of the change in stocks. If a 5% error was made in the opposite direction in the following end-year estimate of the level of stocks the error in the estimated change in stocks would be £120m. If potential and by no means improbable errors of this order of magnitude are set against the actual size of the stock changes given in Table 2.80 it is clear why any estimates must be subject to a very large margin of error.

However, if one is interested in the total stockbuilding over the 19 years covered, or over (say) a five-year period, then many of the errors cancel out, and the *absolute* error for the whole period is likely to be little greater than that for a single year.

be readily apparent that these estimates for the inter-war years are particularly imperfect and uncertain. (A comparison with the corresponding estimates by Barna is made in chapter 14, p. 252).

(II) AGRICULTURE AND FORESTRY

The estimates for this sector can be far more simply obtained since the basic estimates are derived from physical data on crops, livestock and standing timber and if these end-year series are valued at average current (or 1930) prices the required value of the physical increase in stocks is directly available. The estimates of the end-year values at current and 1930 prices are made in chapter 5 and the series for investment in stocks can be derived from this.

(III) ESTIMATES FOR INDIVIDUAL SECTORS AND TRADE GROUPS

For the five sectors of industry, trade and transport covered in chapters 6 to 10, and for their constituent trade groups, the basic estimate obtained is again the end-year book value. In order to make the same type of adjustment for each trade group or sector as was made above for the five sectors as a whole it would be necessary to calculate the appropriate price indices assumed to be underlying the separate balance sheet values, and we have not undertaken this. In the light of the data on prices, balance sheet dates, turnover of stocks, etc., at present available it is doubtful whether any worthwhile results could in fact be obtained.

An index of average prices during each year was, however, constructed for each trade group and deflation of the book values by this index yields an approximation to the value of the stocks at 1930 prices. The figure so computed for (say) end-1926 will be above (or below) the true one by the same proportion as the prices used in valuing stocks for the end-1926 balance sheets were above (or below) the average prices of 1926. The same will apply to the end-1927 figures, and the figure for stockbuilding in 1927 will have an error made up of the errors in these two figures (from which it is computed by difference). If the two errors are *in the same direction*, they will tend to cancel out: in particular the estimate for stockbuilding will be virtually correct if prices were rising (or falling) at a fairly steady rate throughout 1926 and 1927. Our approximate procedure would however yield serious errors if prices were rising markedly in 1926 and falling markedly in 1927 (or vice-versa).

3

In the notation of p. 31 we have, for example, for the stock change:

$$(q_2 . p_n)\frac{p_c}{p_b} - (q_1 . p_1)\frac{p_c}{p_a} \tag{1}$$

whereas what we actually want is:

$$(q_2 . p_n)\frac{p_c}{p_n} - (q_1 . p_1)\frac{p_c}{p_1} = (q_2 - q_1)p_c \tag{2}$$

The difference between the true investment in stocks (i.e. the value of the physical increase) in year 2 at 1930 prices as given by equation (2) and the approximation given by (1) is thus equal to:

$$\left[(q_2 . p_c)\frac{p_n}{p_b} - (q_2 . p_c)\right] - \left[(q_1 . p_c)\frac{p_1}{p_a} - (q_1 . p_c)\right]$$

$$= (q_2 . p_c) . \frac{p_n - p_b}{p_b} + (q_1 . p_c) . \frac{p_a - p_1}{p_a} \tag{3}$$

In order to illustrate the orders of magnitude of the differences between the true and approximate estimates in the above case (where prices are falling in year 1 and rising in year 2) let us assume that $q_1 . p_c$ is £180 and $q_2 . p_c$ £200 and that the rate of change of prices is $\frac{1}{2}$ per cent per month in both years.[1] We then have:

$$£(200)(1.02 - 1) + (180)(1 - 0.973) = £8.9$$

If, however, prices were falling in both years (at $\frac{1}{2}$ per cent per month) the error would be only £0.5.

From a consideration of a variety of assumptions as to the direction and rate of change of prices we can say that within a realistic range of rates of change the errors are negligible when both the direction and the rate of change of prices is the same in both years; and are still reasonably small even if the rate of change of prices either increases or decreases. However when the direction of change is not the same in both years the errors become much larger. The absolute magnitude of the error depends partly on the rate at which prices are changing and, given this, on the size of the end-year stocks. In practice, therefore, the absolute size of the error introduced in the estimates at the industry or sector level as a result of this approximation to the correct procedure will generally not be unacceptably large in relation to the accuracy of the basic data.

All the above comments apply to the estimates at 1930 prices. No *further* error is introduced in principle by the conversion to current prices since the same index of average prices can be used as would be used if the true estimates at 1930 prices were available, i.e. the index used to convert the end-year book values from current to 1930 prices.

---

[1] A rate of change of $\frac{1}{2}$ per cent per month implies a change in average annual prices of over 6% per annum. The average rate of change (disregarding sign) from 1922 to 1938 in the average annual prices of stocks given in col. (5) of Table 2.80, p. 25, was 5.5%.

CHAPTER 3
CAPITAL FORMATION BETWEEN THE WARS: A SUMMARY OF FINDINGS

3.1 INTRODUCTION

In chapters 4 to 14 we present the estimates made for individual sectors and sub-sectors and describe in detail their coverage, the methods by which they were obtained and the qualifications which must be made about the scope and accuracy of the estimates. The present chapter is designed to bring together in a convenient summary the main statistical results; in addition there is a brief commentary which touches on certain aspects emerging from the summary, such as cyclical movements, trends over the period and the relationship with other variables, but there is no attempt to undertake a full or systematic examination of the behaviour of inter-war domestic investment.

The estimates obtained are, in general, sufficiently reliable to serve as a guide to the main trends and fluctuations in domestic capital formation between the wars, and we shall not as a rule refer in this summary to the probable margins of error attached to the various series. It is, however, essential to emphasize the very imperfect nature of many of these estimates, and individual series must not be pressed into service without careful reference to the appropriate chapters to ascertain whether they are of sufficient calibre for any specific campaign for which they may be recruited.

The plan of this summary is as follows: in 3.2 we look briefly at gross domestic fixed capital formation as a total and in relation to the other components of investment and to gross national product. A rough comparison is made with investment before 1914 and after 1950. Section 3.3 contains an outline analysis of gross fixed capital formation at constant prices broken down by the industrial group of the enterprise responsible for the expenditure and by type of asset, and with a division between public and private investment. Replacement, depreciation and net fixed capital formation are reviewed in 3.4; and in 3.5 changes in the stock of fixed assets, gross and net of accumulated depreciation, are considered in total and per head, and in relation to changes in output. Finally, the results of our findings about investment in stocks and work in progress are summarised in 3.6.

3.2 INVESTMENT AND NATIONAL PRODUCT

GROSS FIXED CAPITAL FORMATION AT HOME

Measured at constant (1930) prices total gross domestic fixed capital formation (Table 3.30, p. 38 and Figure 4, p. 48) almost doubled between 1920–2 and 1938. Its movement falls into three main phases. From £285 m. in 1920–2 it climbed to £434m. in 1929–30, a rise of some 50% broken only by a slight fall in 1926. In the second phase it dropped abruptly to £378m. in 1932–3. The final phase opened in 1934 with a tremendous jump in which the previous peak was easily surpassed, and continued with an unbroken upswing which brought the total to a record level of £552m. in 1937–8. This was a little less than 50% above the level in the depression years 1932 and 1933, and 27% above the peak reached at the end of the expansion during the 1920's.

Precise comparison with pre-1914 gross fixed capital formation is not possible, but as a rough approximation a figure for 1913 (at 1930 prices) would be about £270m. and for 1902, the highest pre-war year, about £380m. It was thus not until 1925, mid-way through the expansion of the 'twenties that the peak pre-war level was bettered. Similarly approximate estimates at 1930 prices for the period after the Second World War suggest that the 1938 level was regained by 1949 and that the 1961 level was little short of double this.

TOTAL INVESTMENT, 1900–59

In Table 3.20 we show gross fixed capital formation at home together with the two other components of investment: the value of the physical increase in stocks and work in progress, and net investment abroad.[1] All the series have been converted to 1930 prices though for 1900–9 and 1950–9 the adjustment is naturally very

---

[1] Equal to the balance of payments surplus (or deficit) on current account less capital grants from overseas government. It thus represents the change in the value of all overseas assets (both real and financial) of United Kingdom residents, net of changes in United Kingdom assets owned by foreigners.

crude. We are interested here in the long-term changes in the level and composition of total investment, and the data are given in the form of annual rates during ten-year periods.

By comparison with the pre-war decades the outstanding features are, first, the more than two-fold rise in the inter-war years in the volume of capital expenditure on dwellings; second, the rather small rise between 1900–9 and 1930–8 in the annual average volume of

insufficiently appreciated) feature is that the annual rate of gross fixed capital formation (excluding dwellings) in real terms has more than doubled since the war. In sharp contrast, annual capital expenditure on dwellings was not significantly higher in the 1950's than in the 1930's. Net investment abroad has been positive but relatively small in the post-war period, about equal to the average annual rate in the inter-war years but little more than a third of the 1900–9 level.

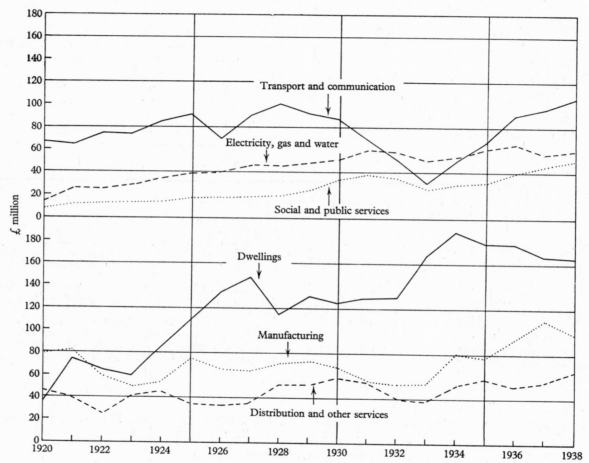

FIG. 1 Gross fixed capital formation at 1930 prices, by sector, 1920–38.

other fixed capital expenditure; and third, and perhaps most striking of all, the decline in net overseas lending from an annual average of £110m. in 1900–9[1] to £70m. in the 'twenties, and to a position in the 'thirties where there was a persistent deficit on current account, i.e. Britain was on balance a net borrower.[2] With little change in the total annual investment over these three decades there was a major shift in its composition: the share of the total invested abroad dropped from 25% in 1900–9 to −7% in 1930–8, and the proportion devoted to housebuilding expanded over the same period from 13 to 32%.

In the second comparison, between the inter-war years and the decade 1950–9, the important (and

INVESTMENT AND GROSS NATIONAL PRODUCT

The striking increase in the average level of gross-fixed capital formation (excluding dwellings) just noted is not simply a reflection of the expansion of the economy since the Second World War. In Table 3.21 the components of total investment at current prices are expressed as a percentage of the gross national product at current factor cost. The proportion of gross national

---

[1] In the exceptional period immediately before the First World War the volume of net investment abroad was very much higher, averaging some £240m. p.a. at 1930 prices in the four years 1910–13. This absorbed 46% of total investment compared with 6% for dwellings, 40% for other gross fixed capital formation and 8% for stockbuilding.

[2] This 'borrowing' includes repayment to the United Kingdom of earlier loans.

TABLE 3.20   THE COMPOSITION OF TOTAL INVESTMENT, SELECTED DECADES
1900–59

(Annual rates. At 1930 prices)

	1900–9	1920–9	1930–8	1950–9
A. £ million at 1930 prices*				
1. Gross fixed capital formation at home				
(a) Dwellings	55	95	140	155
(b) Other	265	255	310	630
2. Value of physical increase in stocks and work in progress	10	25	20	50
3. Net investment abroad†	110	70	−30	40
4. Total	440	445	440	875
B. As per cent of total investment				
5. Dwellings	13	21	32	18
6. Other	60	57	70	72
7. Stocks	2	6	5	6
8. Net investment abroad†	25	16	−7	4
9. Total	100	100	100	100

* In recognition of their very approximate nature these estimates have been rounded to the nearest £5m.
† See footnote (1), p. 34.

Source: 1900–9

1 (a) and 1 (b). Based on [108] C. H. Feinstein 'Income and Investment in the United Kingdom, 1856–1914', *Economic Journal*, Vol. LXXI (1961), pp. 369–74.

2. At current prices taken as 40% of the annual change in net national income from [108] Feinstein, p. 384, and deflated by the import average value index in [114] A. H. Imlah, *Economic Elements in the Pax Britannica* (Cambridge, Mass., 1958), p. 98 and in [154] *London and Cambridge Economic Bulletin*, No. 42, June 1962.

3. Data at current prices from [114] Imlah, pp. 74–5 deflated by the import average value index used for line 2.

Source: 1920–38

1 (a), 1 (b) and 2. From the present estimates.

3. Data at current prices from [154] *London and Cambridge Economic Bulletin* deflated by the L.C.E.B. import average value index.

Source: 1950–9

1 (a) and 1 (b). Data at 1954 prices from [56] *National Income and Expenditure, 1961* revalued by means of the indices in [132] Redfern, p.171.

2. Data at 1954 prices from [56] *National Income and Expenditure, 1961*, revalued by means of the L.C.E.B. import average value index.

3. Data at current prices from [56] *National Income and Expenditure, 1961* deflated by the L.C.E.B. import average value index.

TABLE 3.21   INVESTMENT AS A PERCENTAGE OF GROSS NATIONAL PRODUCT, SELECTED DECADES, 1900–59

(Annual rates. At current prices)

	1900–9	1920–9	1930–8	1950–9
A. £m. at current prices*				
1. Gross national product at factor cost	2,000	4,620	4,440	16,540
B. Percentage of GNP at factor cost				
2. Total investment	13·3	12·0	10·5	18·0
3. Gross fixed capital formation at home				
(a) Dwellings	1·5	2·3	3·4	3·4
(b) Other	6·9	6·7	6·9	13·0
4. Net investment abroad	4·4	2·1	−0·6	0·6
5. Stockbuilding	0·5	0·9	0·8	1·0

* Rounded to nearest £10m.

Source

1. See source for data at current prices for Table 3.22, p. 37.
2–5. See source for data at current prices for Table 3.20, above.

product devoted to fixed capital formation at home (other than for dwellings) is seen to be almost twice as high in the decade 1950–9 as in the inter-war years. If the comparison is made with the pre-1914 period the share in gross-national product of residential building was doubled between 1900–9 and the inter-war period, the share of other fixed investment was broadly unchanged and the share of net overseas investment was markedly reduced.

generating the initial recovery were exports and total capital formation, and both in absolute terms and in terms of the rate of increase between 1929 and 1937 the data suggest strongly that it was the latter which was the main driving force. Some of the factors underlying the initial expansion of fixed investment are discussed below. Once out of the trough the customary process of interaction between income and investment would come into operation. Merchandise exports in fact failed

TABLE 3.22 GROSS NATIONAL PRODUCT BY CATEGORY OF EXPENDITURE, 1929–37

(£m. At 1930 market prices)

	1929	1932	1937	Change		
				1929–32	1932–7	
	£m.	£m.	£m.	£m.	£m.	%
1. Consumers' expenditure	3,882	3,950	4,481	68	531	13
2. Public authorities' current expenditure on goods and services	441	467	637	26	170	36
3. Gross fixed capital formation at home	433	372	548	−61	176	47
4. Stockbuilding	33	−7	56	−40	63	—
5. Merchandise exports	804	495	641	−309	146	30
6. Net export of services and net income from abroad	318	219	296	−99	77	35
7. *Less* Merchandise imports	964	842	1,005	−122	163	19
8. GROSS NATIONAL PRODUCT	4,947	4,654	5,654	−293	1,000	21

Source

1. Data at current prices from [154] *London and Cambridge Economic Bulletin* No. 42, June 1962 deflated by *L.C.E.B.* consumers' expenditure average value index.

2. Data at current prices from [127] A. T. Peacock and J. Wiseman, *The Growth of Public Expenditure in the United Kingdom* (Princeton, 1961), pp. 176–8, deflated by *L.C.E.B.* consumers' expenditure average value index.

3 and 4. Present estimates.

5. Data at current prices from [154] *L.C.E.B.* deflated by *L.C.E.B.* index of the average value of exports.

6 and 7. Data at current prices from [154] *L.C.E.B.* deflated by *L.C.E.B.* index of the average value of imports. (Imports are reduced by 10% to convert them from c.i.f. to approximate f.o.b. values and a corresponding adjustment is made to net exports of services).

One further aspect which merits attention is the significance of the role played by domestic fixed capital formation in the recovery of the 1930's. The relevant data are set out in Table 3.22.

Between 1932 and 1937 the gross national product at constant prices increased by about one-fifth. The component showing the largest absolute increase in real terms was consumers' expenditure but this was more a consequence than a cause of the *initial* rise in real incomes, and the percentage increase was relatively small. Public authorities' current expenditure on goods and services rose by some 36% but as the greater part of this increase was in defence expenditure—which was not appreciably expanded until after 1935—it too made little contribution to the initial phase of recovery, although undoubtedly it did help to maintain the momentum of the upswing towards the end of the period. The two remaining categories of final expenditure which might have played a leading part in

to recover from their great fall after 1929 and although they had risen 30% by 1937 were still only 80% in volume of their previous peak level.

3.3 THE STRUCTURE OF GROSS FIXED CAPITAL FORMATION—BY SECTOR AND BY TYPE OF ASSET

Gross fixed capital formation at home at current and at 1930 prices is analysed by sector in Table 3.30 and by type of asset in Table 3.31, and the main series at 1930 prices are graphed in Figures 1 and 2. The discussion in this section will be confined entirely to the constant price series.

Gross fixed capital formation represents a process of cumulative addition to the stock of assets and it may be of interest to begin this summary by looking at the aggregate amount invested during the inter-war period in each of the main sectors and types of asset. The figures are set out in Table 3.32.

TABLE 3.30 GROSS DOMESTIC FIXED CAPITAL FORMATION BY SECTOR, 1920–38 (£M.)

	1920	1921	1922	1923	1924	1925	1926	1927	1928	1929	1930	1931	1932	1933	1934	1935	1936	1937	1938
At current prices																			
Agriculture, forestry and fishing	9	9	6	5	4	4	4	3	4	3	4	3	3	2	4	4	5	6	5
Mining and quarrying	18	11	16	18	14	14	8	9	5	12	10	8	5	8	9	6	9	10	11
Electricity, gas and water	24	35	28	30	38	41	41	48	45	49	52	56	53	47	48	56	63	60	64
Manufacturing	152	117	66	57	62	83	72	69	75	76	68	52	50	53	75	77	94	126	109
Transport and communication	117	112	150	102	95	101	76	82	100	90	87	79	51	35	46	63	86	99	111
Distribution and other services	86	55	28	45	51	39	36	39	53	54	58	51	37	37	49	55	52	58	68
Social and public services	14	15	12	13	16	19	20	20	21	25	34	37	30	24	26	30	38	47	55
Dwellings	62	104	75	64	94	119	144	156	117	133	122	122	118	151	170	165	170	168	169
Total	482	458	381	334	374	420	401	426	420	442	435	408	347	357	427	456	517	574	592
At 1930 prices																			
Agriculture, forestry and fishing	7	6	5	5	4	4	3	3	3	3	4	3	3	2	4	4	6	7	5
Mining and quarrying	10	8	14	16	13	13	7	8	5	11	10	9	6	8	9	6	10	9	10
Electricity, gas and water	14	24	23	26	35	38	39	46	44	46	52	61	58	52	54	61	65	57	60
Manufacturing	79	81	60	53	55	76	67	66	72	73	68	56	54	55	80	79	91	112	98
Transport and communication	67	64	77	75	86	93	70	89	100	94	87	78	50	33	51	66	88	96	104
Distribution and other services	46	39	25	41	45	36	35	37	52	51	58	55	40	39	52	59	52	54	62
Social and public services	8	10	12	13	14	18	18	19	20	25	34	38	33	27	29	32	40	46	52
Dwellings	36	74	66	60	85	107	134	147	115	130	122	127	128	168	188	179	178	167	165
Total	267	306	282	289	337	385	373	415	411	433	435	427	372	384	467	486	530	548	556

TABLE 3.31 GROSS DOMESTIC FIXED CAPITAL FORMATION BY TYPE OF ASSET,* 1920–38 (£M.)

	1920	1921	1922	1923	1924	1925	1926	1927	1928	1929	1930	1931	1932	1933	1934	1935	1936	1937	1938
At 1930 prices																			
Road goods vehicles	6	5	7	8	10	8	10	10	10	15	14	14	12	13	18	19	21	21	18
Buses, coaches, taxis and tramcars	9	7	10	10	10	6	11	9	10	11	10	7	5	4	5	7	8	9	10
Passenger cars owned for business use	4	4	5	6	9	11	11	13	12	13	12	10	10	13	17	21	23	25	21
Other road vehicles†	2	2	1	1	1	2	1	1	2	1	2	2	2	1	2	2	3	3	3
Railway rolling stock	8	7	3	8	11	10	9	12	9	9	7	5	4	4	6	8	10	12	9
Ships	31	22	32	19	26	30	9	21	38	30	20	10	−1	−6	5	10	24	19	22
Total ships and vehicles	60	47	58	52	67	67	51	66	81	79	65	48	32	29	53	67	89	89	83
Plant and machinery, etc.	66	96	75	81	85	97	90	104	116	108	110	135	116	95	119	122	130	130	152
Dwellings	36	74	66	60	85	107	134	147	115	130	122	127	128	168	188	179	178	167	165
Other buildings	80	61	42	49	57	60	56	54	61	72	81	56	49	53	68	77	82	105	98
Civil engineering works	25	28	41	47	43	54	42	44	38	44	57	61	47	39	39	41	51	57	58
Total	267	306	282	289	337	385	373	415	411	433	435	427	372	384	467	486	530	548	556

* This detailed classification by type of asset is subject to appreciably larger errors than the estimated division between (1) Buildings and works and (2) Plant, vehicles, ships, etc. given in Table 13.00. See chapter 13, p. 228.

† Includes tractors, agricultural vans and lorries, and horse-drawn vehicles.

TABLE 3.32   AGGREGATE GROSS DOMESTIC FIXED CAPITAL FORMATION, 1920–38
(Aggregates at 1930 prices)

	Buildings and Works		Plant, ships, vehicles, etc.		Total	
Physical Production	1920–9 £m.	1930–8 £m.	1920–9 £m.	1930–8 £m.	1920–38 £m.	%
Agriculture, forestry and fishing	4	2	39	36	81	1·0
Mining and quarrying	53	31	52	46	182	2·4
Electricity	24	26	194	342	586	7·6
Gas and water	77	95	40	57	269	3·5
Textiles	23	1	86	71	181	2·4
Metals and metal-using	77	83	141	202	503	6·5
Food, drink and tobacco	38	28	54	53	173	2·2
Chemicals, leather, clothing and paper	78	58	117	114	367	4·8
Building and building materials, etc.	29	29	39	54	151	2·0
Total Manufacturing	245	199	437	494	1,375	17·9
Services						
Railways	65	76	77	69	287	3·7
Roads and road transport*	153	143	119	101	516	6·7
Sea and inland water transport	24	17	263	106	410	5·3
Postal, telephone and telegraph communications	8	14	106	123	251	3·3
Total Transport and Communications	250	250	565	403†	1,468†	19·0
Wholesale distribution	43	45	88	83	259	3·4
Retail distribution	115	124	73	114	426	5·5
Hotels, entertainment and other services	43	45	45	60	193	2·5
Total Distribution and Other Services	201	214	206	257	878	11·4
Schools and libraries	25	65	7	17	114	1·5
Hospitals	21	59	3	7	90	1·2
Other public services	98	176	3	7	284	3·7
Total Social and Public Services	144	300	13	31	488	6·4
Total excluding dwellings	998	1,117	1,546	1,666	5,327	69·2
Dwellings	954	1,422	—	—	2,376	30·8
Total	1,952	2,539	1,546	1,666	7,703	100·0

* Excluding vehicles owned by other sectors.   † Including £4m. for civil aviation.

In the 19 years from 1920 to 1938 capital expenditure on fixed assets at 1930 prices totalled some £7,700m., made up of three roughly equal parts: 31% invested in the construction of dwellings, 32% in assets required for physical production and 37% in services of all kinds.

Within the second segment investment in manufacturing totalled £1,375m., of which one-third was for buildings and two-thirds for plant, vehicles, etc. The largest sub-group was the expanding metals and metal-using industries which were responsible for some £500m. of this, and the smallest was the contracting textiles group responsible for £180m. Electricity supply undertakings invested heavily in fixed assets, principally supply mains plant and equipment, to a total of £585m., more than double the amount required for gas and water undertakings. Investment in agriculture and mining was very low.

Of the services, transport and communications was the largest with a total of £1,470m., including £290m.

for railways, £520 m. for roads and road transport[1] and £410 m. for sea and inland water transport. Distribution and other services invested £880 m., roughly evenly divided between buildings and other assets; and capital expenditure for social and public services totalled £490 m., mainly for the construction of buildings and works.

Analysed by type of asset we again have dwellings, accounting for 31% of the total. Investment in other buildings and works totalled £2,115 m. or 27%, compared with £3,210 m. or 42% for plant and machinery, ships, vehicles and other equipment.

CYCLICAL FLUCTUATIONS

The above figures indicate the aggregate levels of capital expenditure over the period, but it is also interesting to note the differences in cyclical behaviour.

in a flat-bottomed trough during the years 1929–32. In 1933 it again led the rest of the economy[3] showing a substantial gain of £40 m. (30%) while other sectors were still falling or stationary. It rose again in 1934 to a peak of £188 m. and then dropped back slightly to end at £165 m. in 1938. The 1934 peak was thus almost 50% above the trough level of 1929–32[4] and 28% above the peak in 1927. In view of the absolute magnitude of the expenditure on dwellings, and the extent of its repercussions on a wide range of other sectors it seems likely that this lead in timing had a major impact on the rest of the economy, particularly in the initial recovery.

The pattern of expenditure at 1930 prices of the other main sectors and of the total, including dwellings, is shown below.

The most severe fall was in transport and communications, due particularly to the collapse of investment by

	Previous peak year	Trough (1933) as per cent of previous peak	Final peak (1938) as per cent of trough (1933)	Final peak (1938) as per cent of previous peak
Electricity, gas and water	1931	85	115	98
Manufacturing	1929	75	204*	153*
Transport and communications	1928	33	315	104
Distribution and other services	1930	67	159	107
Social and public services	1931	71	193	137
Total	1930	85†	149†	128†

* Peak year = 1937.   † Trough year = 1932.

Source: Table 3.30.

During the 'twenties the movements of the main sectors are very varied: expenditure on the public utilities and services rises fairly steadily while the other sectors show cyclical movements with little uniformity in timing or amplitude (Figure 1). Any explanation of the fluctuations in total capital formation must clearly take into account this diversity in the behaviour of the components and a general model is unlikely to be adequate. In the 'thirties there is more similarity in the fluctuations, reflecting the stronger force of the decline and recovery in general activity as indicated by output and employment data, but there are still significant differences in the severity of the depression and the strength of the upswing.

Our data do not represent annual turning points with great accuracy[2] but it seems clear that residential building was the first sector in which capital expenditure declined, reaching its peak (of £147 m. at 1930 prices) as early as 1927. From there it fell sharply in 1928 and then levelled off roughly 15% below this peak

the shipping sector, and there was a correspondingly strong recovery after 1933. Perhaps the most significant feature is the rapid expansion of the manufacturing sector, where strongly rising outlays from 1934 to 1937 carried gross fixed capital formation to a level more

[1] Investment in roads and road transport would be over £1,500 m. if we include (i) the goods vehicles and cars acquired by manufacturing, distribution and other sectors, and (ii) the cars acquired for private use by consumers. In Table 3.30, p. 38, (and elsewhere in this study) (i) is included as part of the respective sectors, but (ii) does not form part of the present estimates.

[2] Apart from errors of estimation the main problem is that the data taken from accounts related to a variety of financial years and not to the exact calendar years for which they are shown in our tables.

[3] '... the initial impulse of the housing boom originated ... in the late autumn of 1932 and the beginning of 1933; was translated from paper to employment on a substantial scale in the summer and autumn of 1933; and made the first outstanding impression on the official statistics of output relating to the half-year ended 31st March, 1934'. [94] Sir Harold Bellman, 'The Building Trades', *Britain in Recovery* (London, 1938), p. 405.

[4] The number of houses built continued to increase until 1936 at which point it was some 65% above the 1929–32 level. The more moderate increase in capital expenditure (at 1930 prices) essentially reflects the decline in the size of the houses built in this period (see p. 216 below).

than 50% above the 1929 peak. Capital expenditure on the social and public services rose 37% above their previous peak. One last point worth notice is the lateness of the downturn in the public utilities and the social and public services, though as we shall see this was not the result of deliberate policy.

We turn now to a slightly more detailed consideration of the main individual sectors.

Dwellings

The overall dominance of residential building (chapter 12) has already been emphasized at several points in the preceding summary. The trends in housing between the wars have been the subject of several detailed studies[1] based on the official data on the number of houses built by local authorities and private enterprise; and in view of its importance it is desirable to note briefly some of the main factors underlying the variations in residential building.

Capital expenditure on dwellings rose very swiftly after the almost complete cessation of building during the war, and in 1921 90,000 houses were completed and the value (at 1930 prices) of work done is estimated to be about £75m., of which £50m. was work done for local authorities. (See Table 3.34, p. 47). Public expenditure then dropped abruptly to £13m. in 1923 but private building was rising and the total for that year was some £60m. In order to place this initial phase in perspective it should be noted that more than 150,000 houses were completed annually at the height of the building boom which occurred at the end of the nineteenth century, but these were generally smaller houses built to lower specifications and their value at 1930 prices is estimated at approximately £70 m. p.a. After 1902 residential building declined rapidly and in 1913 only 54,000 houses were built with a value at 1930 prices of approximately £25m.

By pre-1914 standards, therefore, the construction of residential building attained a fairly high level of activity in a short space of time. In these few years, for the only time before 1945, the majority of houses were built by local authorities, in response to the intense public demand for working-class housing and the stimulus of the subsidies given under Addison's Housing Act of 1919. This phase came to an end early in 1923 after scarcities of materials and a swift increase in building costs, and in the following phase the initiative passed to the speculative builders. The new type of subsidies given under Chamberlain's 1923 Act were available to both local authorities and private enterprise but were little used by the former. However subsidized private building expanded rapidly and with unsubsidized building steady the total volume of private

expenditure on house building almost doubled: from £47m. in 1923 to £91m. in 1927. The Chamberlain subsidies were first reduced for houses completed after 30 September 1927 and then abolished two years later, but building costs were falling in the late 'twenties, and except for one year—1928—there was very little decline in the volume of total private building.

In 1924 the Labour Party enjoyed its first brief tenure of office and the Housing Act introduced in that year by Wheatley gave renewed encouragement to local authorities to build houses for letting to working-class tenants. The volume of work done rose to a maximum of £56m. in 1927, when there was a rush to complete houses before the new Conservative Government reduction in the Wheatley subsidy took effect. From this date the local authority programmes declined slowly to 1934 when expenditure was only £28m. This fall appears to have been only partly due to the uncertainty and discouragement created by changes in government policy with regard to subsidies. It has also been shown that there were important regional differences in local authority capital expenditure on housing, due partly to the diverse attitudes and circumstances of individual authorities, but also, and more significantly, associated with the varying prosperity of the regions.[2] In the most depressed areas, notably those dependent on the staple export trades, tenants' incomes were insufficient to meet economic rents, and migration seemed likely to relieve some of the shortage. Authorities in some of the more prosperous areas did maintain and expand their housing programmes but with insufficient energy to meet the demand in their own areas or to compensate for the fall in the depressed areas. From 1932 Government policy changed yet again, to one of reliance on private enterprise for the provision of new working-class housing, and the local authorities were urged to concentrate on slum clearance.

The net outcome of these differing trends in private and public building was that total capital expenditure on dwellings at 1930 prices rose according to our estimates from £60m. in 1923 to £147m. in 1927 and then dropped to an average level of £125m. in 1928–32, with both sectors contributing to the rise but with the decline almost entirely confined to the public sector.

From 1933 the private sector began to accelerate and the number of houses completed by private builders shot up from 151,000 in 1932/33 to 294,000 in 1934/35, an increase of almost 100% in the course of two years.

---

[1] See especially [**94**] Bellman, [**138**] W. F. Stolper 'British Monetary Policy and the Housing Boom', *Quarterly Journal of Economics*, vol. LVI (1941); [**92**] M. Bowley, *Housing and the State 1919–44* (London, 1945); and [**126**] E. Nevin *The Mechanism of Cheap Money* (Cardiff, 1955). In the following paragraphs we have drawn a great deal on these studies.

[2] See [**92**] Bowley, pp. 94–113.

With little support in the initial stages from the local authorities, the private sector carried the volume of expenditure on residential building to a peak of £188m. in 1934, after which it tapered off slowly. Within this total expenditure on housebuilding by the private sector increased from £97m. in 1932 to £160m. in 1934 and then declined to £113m. in 1938; public sector expenditure did not begin to rise until the end of the decade, but then moved rapidly from £31m. in 1935 to £52m. in 1938.

During the five years 1934–8 some 1,800,000 houses were built, three-quarters of them by private enterprise; the magnitude of this achievement can best be appreciated by comparison with 1953–7, the post-war quinquennium when residential building was at its highest level, and 1,500,000 houses were completed in the United Kingdom.

What are the factors which explain the dimensions and timing of this boom which in turn played such a decisive part in the general economic recovery from the depression of 1930–2? The primary explanation of the *need* for housing is not to be found in the increase in population,[1] but in the exceptionally strong and widespread desire firstly, for separate houses for families previously sharing accommodation and secondly, for modern houses appropriate in size, suburb and specification to the standards of the 1930's.

These factors account for the great need or desire for new houses, and they also explain the stability of rents in the face of several years of house-building at record levels. They cannot explain how this need was translated into an *effective demand* on the scale witnessed from 1933 onwards. For this we must turn to three forces: the steady fall in building costs after 1925, the general financial developments summarized in the phrase 'cheap money' and the gain in real incomes as a result of the fall in the cost of living associated with the favourable movement of the terms of trade. Writers on the building cycle have come forward to champion the claims of each of these factors to be considered as the single principal explanation of the boom of the 1930s, and there has perhaps been a tendency to emphasize the role played by one or other at the expense of a balanced assessment of their joint and inter-dependent contributions.

Building costs as measured by our index (p. 24 above) fell almost 20% between 1925 and 1932; and the average contract price of three-bedroom houses built for local authorities—a series which reflects changes in the efficiency of building and in the size of houses built, as well as in the basic costs of labour and material—shows a reduction of more than 30% over the same period. The cumulative effect of this substantial reduction in

costs meant a broadly corresponding downward movement in the price of new houses and must have helped greatly to bring new housing within the incomes of a wider range of potential buyers. It was, however, a process which had effectively come to an end by 1933, thereafter costs began to rise again; and since the fall had begun as early as 1926 it does not directly explain the timing of the boom.

Cheap money, in the widest sense, provides a much more powerful explanation. Late in 1931 the sequence of monetary changes occurred which initiated the new era of low interest rates, a change dramatized by the conversion of the 5% War loan to 3½% in July 1932. In a situation remarkably similar to that experienced in the genesis of the housing boom of the mid-1890's, there was a sharp swing in the preferences of investors away from gilt-edged securities and overseas lending and in favour of investment at home, especially in housing. The yield on fixed interest securities fell relative to rents and to the interest on building society shares: in 1932 the yield on the latter was 4·5%, a fifth more than that offered by 2½% Consols. Allied to this was the insecurity of foreign investment after an economic crisis in which overseas producers of primary products were deeply involved.

Both the supply of and the demand for housing were strongly and immediately affected by these financial factors. On the supply side there was a vast inflow of funds to estate agents, property companies, building societies and other media of investment in property. To the extent that the demand for houses came from investors intending to let rather than to occupy the properties there was a direct and immediate effect on the demand side. But roughly two-thirds of the demand for houses was from owner-occupiers and here the process operated principally via a change in the lending policy of building societies and other institutions from which funds could be borrowed for house purchase. In the case of the building societies, the most important single source of funds for house-purchase, three steps were taken to facilitate borrowing: (i) a reduction in the initial deposit required, (ii) a cut in the mortgage rate, and (iii) an increase in the period over which loans could be repaid. The need to find a deposit of no more than £30 to £50 brought the possibility of purchase within the resources of many thousands of would-be owner-occupiers; and the second and third changes together resulted in a very considerable reduction in the weekly cost which they would have to meet. It has been shown, for example, that on an advance of £500 a change from a 6% rate of interest and repayment over

---

[1] Between 1932 and 1938 the stock of houses in England and Wales was increased by almost a fifth, while the population grew by only 2·5%.

15 years to a 5% rate and repayment over 25 years—and this is the order of magnitude of the typical changes after 1932—reduced the weekly cost from 19s. 10d. to 13s. 8d., a fall of about one-third.[1] These financial factors were almost certainly the most important influence both on the timing of the upswing, and on the scale of its subsequent development.

The third contributory factor was the rise in real incomes. This made its major impact in 1930 and 1931, but unlike cheap money it did not persist throughout the 'thirties. Between 1929 and 1932 average annual money wage and salary earnings fell by 3% while the official cost of living index dropped by 12½%, so that for those in employment there was a rise of over 10% in estimated average annual real earnings.[2] There was a further slight rise between 1932 and 1935 but from then onwards real earnings declined. Not all of this gain will have been devoted to better housing and some of it has to be offset against the high level of unemployment at this time, but there must nevertheless have been a useful additional increase in the ability of potential owner-occupiers to give effective expression to their long-standing desire for better housing.

Finally, it should be noted that in the closing years of the period the decline in private building was to some extent offset by increased building by local authorities, primarily as part of the programme of slum clearance.

Transport and Communications

The second largest sector was Transport and communications (chapter 9) in which rail, road and sea transport are combined with the Post Office.[3]

Gross fixed capital formation by the railways, once the dominant form of investment, was of relatively small importance in the inter-war years, averaging about £15m. per year. The contrast with road transport is most marked, particularly if we include with the latter the goods vehicles and private cars owned by other sectors and by consumers. Defined thus widely capital expenditure on roads and road transport averaged some £80m. per annum, rising from £35m. in 1920–1 to £88m. in 1929–30 and £125m. in 1937–8.

Construction and improvement of roads was primarily the responsibility of local authorities, but they were very dependent on grants from the central government and capital expenditure fluctuated widely in response to changes in government policy. During the early 'twenties there was a strong upward trend, gross capital formation at 1930 prices rising, according to our estimates, from £5m. in 1920 to £17m. in 1925. In these years central grants from the Road Fund were supplemented by grants in aid of unemployment relief. There was then a turn in government policy, grants

were reduced, and capital formation slipped back to £15m. in 1928. From June 1929, with the Labour Government in office, renewed encouragement was given to road-building as a means of creating employment and capital expenditure rose in 1931 to £23m., the highest figure reached in the inter-war period. After 1931 the National Government's economy campaign took effect and annual expenditure on construction of roads was cut by more than half to £10m. in 1933 and 1934. From 1935 expansion was once again encouraged from the centre and the upswing had reached £18m. when it was cut short by the outbreak of war.

Investment in road motor vehicles (see Figure 2 and Table 3.31) had a strong upward trend throughout the period. At 1930 prices it rose from £19m. in 1920–1 to £40m. in 1929, and after a fall to £29m. in 1932 it increased again to a maximum of £58m. in 1937.[4] The expansion of public service vehicles was restrained by the Road Traffic Act of 1930, but the number of goods vehicles and private cars in use increased very rapidly after the depression.

This dynamic record of rapid long-run expansion and relatively mild cyclical contraction is completely reversed when we turn to sea and inland water transport. This includes the small expenditure on docks and canals but the dominant component is shipping. Investment in merchant ships (at 1930 prices) plunged from £38m. in 1928 to −£6m. in 1933 (Figure 2 and Table 3.31) when the estimated proceeds from ships broken up or sold abroad exceeded outlays on new ships. This spectacular drop accounted for £44m. of the £67m. reduction in the sector as a whole. For the shipping industry this crisis was the culmination of a decade of difficulty in which the much depressed volume of world trade and the increased foreign competition in trade and shipping combined to curtail the demand for new ships. In 1911–13 the tonnage launched for British shippers averaged over 1,400,000 gross tons; in 1929, the best year since the unwise excitement of 1920, it was 1,260,000 tons and in 1933 it collapsed to less than one-tenth of this. After 1933 there was a moderate

---

[1] [**120**] R. M. MacIntosh 'A Note on Cheap Money and the British Housing Boom, 1932–37': *Economic Journal*, vol. LXI (1951), p. 168.

[2] [**99**] A. L. Chapman, *Wages and Salaries in the United Kingdom, 1920–1938* (Cambridge, 1952), p. 30. The figures represent average earnings per man-year worked, not average annual earnings per person employed.

[3] For a detailed discussion of capital (and maintenance) expenditure for roads, railways and the Post Office the reader is referred to [**95**] R. F. Bretherton, F. A. Burchardt and R. S. G. Rutherford, *Public Investment and the Trade Cycle* (Oxford, 1941).

[4] These figures exclude consumers' expenditure on cars, also rising strongly throughout the period to a peak in 1937 of £58m. (at 1930 prices). The division of car purchases between consumers and business users is very approximate.

recovery to £24 m. in 1936, at which level gross capital formation was maintained until the end of the period.

The remaining component of this sector is the Post Office. Capital formation at 1930 prices rose from £5 m. in 1920 to £13 m. in 1924 and was steady at that level until 1931. There was a slight dip to £10 m. in 1933 and then a strong upswing to £24 m. in 1938. The major object of expenditure was the extension of the telephone system. Although the Post Office was the

rather different from those in other sectors. There is little overall growth during the 'twenties, and measured at constant prices the peak in 1929 falls short of that in 1925 which in turn is slightly below that of the immediate post-war boom. The sector is also unique in that the decline in the early 'twenties (from £80 m. in 1920–1 to £54 m. in 1923–4) is more severe than that of the early 'thirties (from £73 m. in 1928–9 to £55 m. in 1931–3). In the first contraction the trade groups

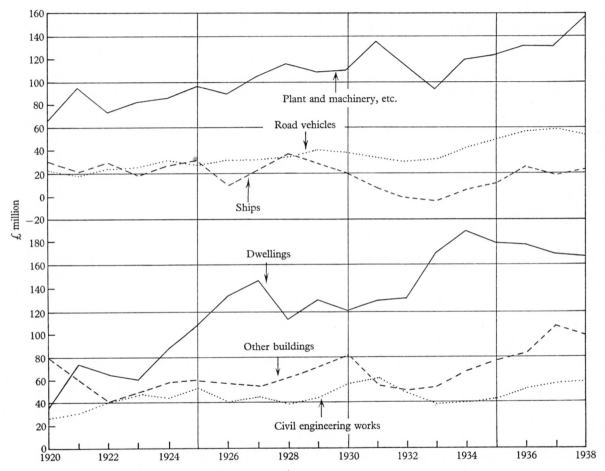

Fig. 2 Gross fixed capital formation at 1930 prices, by type of asset, 1920–38.

only sector directly controlled by the central government its fluctuations owe little to anti-cyclical policy and seem largely explicable simply as a response to the varying level of demand in the economy.

Manufacturing

The present estimates of capital formation by Manufacturing (chapter 8) break new ground in providing data for 22 separate trade groups, but the individual series are generally less reliable than the aggregate and must be used with caution.

The cyclical movements of investment in manufacturing as shown by these estimates are in some respects

which show particularly large falls include those manufacturing electrical engineering equipment, motor vehicles, food, chemicals, leather and rubber, and building materials. In the second contraction the largest declines were in cotton, rayon and silk and chemicals, the last-mentioned being especially sharp.

The pattern during the 1930's is similar to that in other sectors, but as noted on p. 40 above, the recovery was particularly strong. At its maximum of £112 m. in 1937 gross fixed capital formation by manufacturing was more than double the level in the flat-bottomed trough of 1929–33 and 53% above the peak of 1929. The upswing obtained its maximum support from

investment for the metal and metal-using trades, chemicals, paper and printing and the building and building materials industries. Its most notable feature is the extent to which the recovery took the form of increased capacity in new industries to meet the rising demand from the home market. In the critical initial phase the foundation for this direct and indirect rise in home demand was laid by the growth of real income which followed the favourable movement in the terms of trade, and by the upsurge of residential building with its wide-ranging repercussions on other sectors of the economy. In addition, protection and depreciation of the pound were contributory factors, perhaps most significantly in their psychological effect on business confidence and profit expectations, and cheap money meant that it was easier to obtain funds for expansion. Underlying all these factors were the technological innovations which were now making a real impact on

the economy after an overlong period of gestation, in many cases one going back to the two decades before the First World War. As suggested above, this initial rise in investment was itself an important factor underlying the general recovery of the economy, and this in turn increased the need for additional capacity.

The very wide variations in the extent to which industries invested in fixed assets over the period as a whole is brought out by Table 3.33 below, in which the aggregate gross fixed capital formation at 1930 prices from 1920 to 1938 is expressed as a percentage of the gross stock of capital (at 1930 prices) at the end of 1920. Gross fixed capital formation in two industries, motor vehicles and rayon and silk, amounted to more than twice the initial stock of capital; and three other industries invested at least as much as their end-1920 stock. In all five of these leading industries, however, the amounts invested were relatively small, accounting

TABLE 3.33 GROSS FIXED CAPITAL FORMATION IN MANUFACTURING, 1920–38
(£m. At 1930 prices)

	(1) First cost value of fixed assets at end-1920	(2) Gross fixed capital formation 1920–38	(3) (2) as % of (1)
Industries with an increase of more than 100%			
Motor vehicles	33	73	221
Rayon and silk	23	49	213
Tobacco	13	16	123
Leather and rubber	29	31	107
Paper and hardboard	59	61	103
	157	230	146
Industries with an increase of 50–100%			
Electrical engineering	74	67	90
Non-ferrous metals	49	36	73
Newspapers, printing and stationery	110	80	73
Clothing	79	56	71
Toys and other industries	52	32	62
Chemicals	227	138	61
Building and building materials*	206	120	58
Iron and steel	341	184	54
	1,138	713	63
Industries with an increase of less than 50%			
Food	234	113	48
Engineering and shipbuilding	311	143	46
Drink	113	44	39
Textiles (other than rayon and silk)*	665	131	20
	1,323	431	32
Total all manufacturing	2,618	1,374	52

* Covers more than one of the separate trade groups in chapter 8.
Source: Chapter 8.

together for only 17% of total fixed investment in manufacturing in the period 1920–38. In a second group of eight industries, accounting for just over half the total, capital expenditure was equal to between 50 and 100% of the end-1920 capital stock, including at the lower end three of the largest industries: chemicals, building and building materials and iron and steel. Finally there are four industries, all large, with increases of less than 50%. This group includes engineering and shipbuilding, with an increase of 46%; and textiles other than rayon and silk, where the fixed investment during the period represented only 20% of the capital stock at the end of 1920.

Electricity, gas and water

The outstanding component in this sector (chapter 7) was electricity, in which capital formation showed a more than fourfold increase over the period, a rate of growth exceeded only by the local authorities programme of school building. The two other public utilities also expanded their fixed investment but at a much more modest pace.

Capital expenditure by electricity supply undertakings increased fivefold from £9m. (at 1930 prices) in 1920 to £45m. in 1932 and then tapered off at an average level of about £40m. The initial expansion was determined by the surge forward in demand from domestic and industrial users, and was greatly stimulated by the technical economies which enabled charges to be very appreciably reduced. The need for such heavy capital outlays must also be attributed in part to the initial deficiencies in electricity supply resulting from the delays and difficulties of the pre-1914 period.

Cyclical movements were extremely mild and the decline from the peak of 1932 was essentially independent of the depression. It is largely to be explained by the fact that a programme of heavy non-recurrent expenditure (undertaken by the Central Electricity Board in connection with the construction of the Grid of high voltage transmission lines), reached its maximum of £13m. in 1932 and then fell away to less than £2m. in 1937.[1]

Distribution and other services

Gross fixed capital formation by distribution and other services (chapter 10) averaged some £46m. per annum (at 1930 prices), 80% of this on the main components, wholesale and retail distribution. For the former the initial trend was downwards until 1926–7. In the four years 1928–31 gross fixed capital formation averaged £18m. per year; it dropped to half this level in the depression years 1932–3, and expanded again to an average of £14m. in the last five years of the period.

Fixed capital formation by retail distribution rose from £13m. in 1920–1 to £22m. in 1923–4 and remained steady at between £20m. and £25m. until 1934, with very little regard to the cyclical fluctuations in other sectors. In the last five years it moved to a higher level at around £30m. Slightly more than half the expenditure was on buildings, the balance on vehicles, fittings, plant, etc.

Social and public services

The three main components of this sector (chapter 11) are local authority schools, hospitals, and local authorities' non-trading services other than roads. All three have a strong upward trend over the period, most notably the capital expenditure on educational building. This latter was mainly due to the movement of population to new suburbs and the improvement in the standards expected of school buildings. The major component of the local authority capital expenditure on non-trading services was sewerage works and the increased outlays were mainly required to keep pace with the new residential buildings. Expenditure on school buildings was sharply contracted during the depression, but the other components show little sensitivity to cyclical changes.

PUBLIC AND PRIVATE SECTORS

We can conclude this section with a comparison of gross fixed capital formation at 1930 prices by private industry and trade and by public and semi-public enterprises. In the former we include agriculture, mining, manufacturing, shipping, distribution and other services, and private expenditure on housebuilding; in the latter the capital expenditure by the local authorities, including that on housing, the post office, the public utilities and the railways. The railways and some of the electricity, gas and water supply undertakings were private companies, but they are public utilities and we have included them in the 'public and semi-public category'. The estimates at 1930 prices are set out in Table 3.34 and are graphed in Figure 3. Expenditure on dwellings by the two sectors was discussed above and the following comments relate to the totals excluding dwellings.

Until 1931 there is a striking contrast between the two sectors. The public and semi-public capital expenditure climbs steadily throughout the decade, rising from just under £60m. in 1920 to over £160m. in 1931. The private sector, on the other hand, has a fluctuating movement around a level trend, with peaks

---

[1] The study by Bretherton, Burchardt and Rutherford ([95] pp. 251–82) should be referred to for further information on this and other aspects of the capital expenditure by the industry.

TABLE 3.34   GROSS FIXED CAPITAL FORMATION IN THE PRIVATE AND THE PUBLIC AND SEMI-PUBLIC SECTORS

(£m. At 1930 prices)

| | Total | Private | | | Public and Semi-public | | |
		Dwellings	Other	Total	Dwellings	Other	Total
1920	267	17	173	190	19	58	77
1921	306	25	157	182	49	75	124
1922	282	29	138	167	37	78	115
1923	289	47	135	182	13	94	107
1924	337	67	145	212	18	107	125
1925	385	75	161	236	32	117	149
1926	373	85	123	208	49	116	165
1927	415	91	139	230	56	129	185
1928	411	74	172	246	41	124	165
1929	433	95	171	266	35	132	167
1930	435	89	162	251	33	151	184
1931	427	92	137	229	35	163	198
1932	372	97	105	202	31	139	170
1933	384	139	100	239	29	116	145
1934	467	160	155	315	28	124	152
1935	486	148	163	311	31	144	175
1936	530	140	188	328	38	164	202
1937	548	121	207	328	46	174	220
1938	556	113	202	315	52	189	241

Source. Present estimates; for definition of sectors see text. For public sector expenditure on dwellings see chapter 12, p. 217.

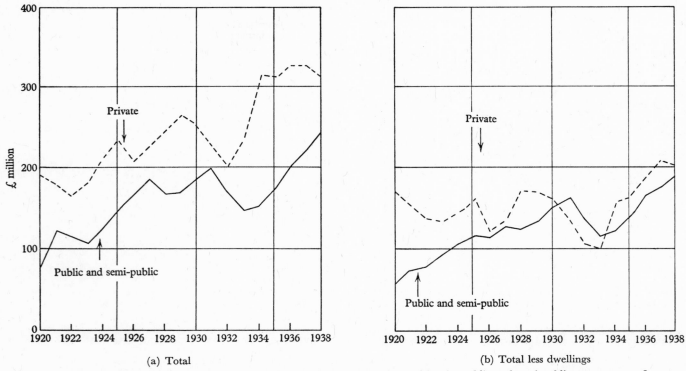

(a) Total   (b) Total less dwellings

FIG. 3 Gross fixed capital formation at 1930 prices, by the private sector and by the public and semi-public sector, 1920–38.

in 1920, 1925 and 1928–9. It then turns down two years earlier and falls further: a fall from 1929 to 1933 of just over 40%, compared with a drop of 30% from 1931 to 1933 for the public and semi-public investment. From 1933 both sectors make a strong recovery, the private sector doubling its capital expenditure and the public and semi-public enterprises showing a more modest but still substantial rise of 63%. In each case this represented an increase over the respective pre-slump peaks of almost 20%.

The overall effect of these varying movements was that the contribution of public and semi-public enterprises to fixed capital formation other than housing rose from 35% in 1920–4 to just over 50% in 1930–4, and then slipped back slightly in 1935–8. Over the period as a whole its share in the total amounted to 45%. If housing is included this proportion is diminished, the average allocation of fixed investment over the period

being 40% in the public and semi-public sector and 60% in the private sector.

3.4 REPLACEMENT, DEPRECIATION AND NET DOMESTIC FIXED CAPITAL FORMATION

The series described in the preceding sections represented the gross outlays on capital goods. But part of these outlays was required to replace assets scrapped or sold and part to make good the wear and tear and obsolescence of existing assets. We can thus consider gross fixed capital formation net of 'scrapping' (equal to that part of gross investment required for replacement) or *new* fixed capital formation, and gross fixed capital formation net of depreciation or *net* fixed capital formation. These series are shown at 1930 prices in Figure 4, and net fixed capital formation is set out by

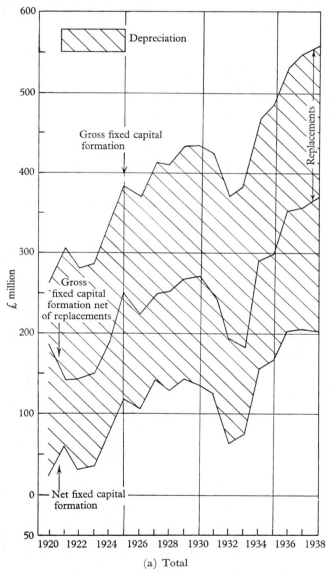

(a) Total

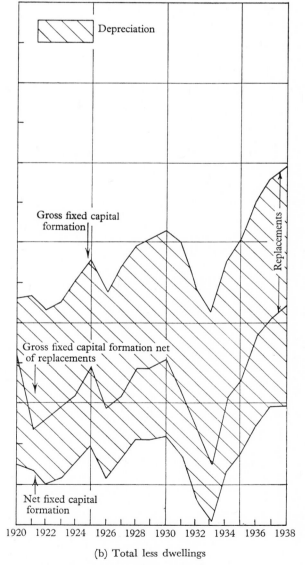

(b) Total less dwellings

Fig. 4 Gross and net fixed capital formation, replacement and depreciation at 1930 prices, 1920–38.

TABLE 3.40 NET DOMESTIC FIXED CAPITAL FORMATION BY SECTOR, 1920–38 (£M.)

	1920	1921	1922	1923	1924	1925	1926	1927	1928	1929	1930	1931	1932	1933	1934	1935	1936	1937	1938
At current prices																			
Agriculture, forestry and fishing	−7	−7	−7	−8	−8	−8	−8	−8	−7	−7	−6	−6	−6	−6	−5	−5	−5	−4	−5
Mining and quarrying	1	−2	6	8	3	3	−3	−2	−5	2	0	−2	−5	−2	−1	−4	−1	−2	−1
Electricity, gas and water	−4	11	8	9	16	18	17	22	18	19	22	26	22	15	15	20	23	15	18
Manufacturing	23	26	−4	−12	−8	14	3	0	7	6	2	−15	−16	−13	8	7	18	35	16
Transport and communication	7	12	38	13	18	25	2	12	25	12	8	1	−22	−35	−20	−8	15	22	30
Distribution and other services	26	9	−9	8	12	0	−3	1	14	14	18	10	−4	−4	8	13	7	6	15
Social and public services	−11	−6	−5	−3	−1	2	3	3	4	8	16	19	13	6	8	11	18	25	31
Dwellings	5	58	36	27	55	79	103	115	76	91	79	80	77	109	127	119	120	115	113
Total	40	101	63	42	87	133	114	143	132	145	139	113	59	70	140	153	195	212	217
At 1930 prices																			
Agriculture, forestry and fishing	−3	−4	−7	−7	−8	−8	−7	−8	−7	−7	−6	−7	−7	−7	−6	−5	−4	−4	−6
Mining and quarrying	1	−1	5	7	3	3	−3	−2	−5	1	0	−2	−5	−2	−1	−4	−1	−2	−1
Electricity, gas and water	−1	7	6	8	15	17	16	21	18	18	22	28	24	17	17	22	24	15	17
Manufacturing	16	18	−3	−9	−8	12	3	1	6	7	2	−13	−17	−15	9	6	17	32	15
Transport and communication	3	−1	11	7	16	22	−1	17	24	15	8	1	−25	−41	−20	−7	15	22	28
Distribution and other services	14	6	−8	8	11	0	−1	1	14	13	18	11	−3	−5	8	14	6	6	13
Social and public services	−6	−5	−3	−2	−1	2	2	3	4	8	16	20	14	8	9	12	19	24	30
Dwellings	3	41	32	25	50	71	96	108	75	89	79	83	83	121	140	129	126	114	110
Total	27	61	33	37	78	119	105	141	129	144	139	121	64	76	156	167	202	207	206

TABLE 3.41 NET DOMESTIC FIXED CAPITAL FORMATION BY TYPE OF ASSET,* 1920–38 (£M.)

	1920	1921	1922	1923	1924	1925	1926	1927	1928	1929	1930	1931	1932	1933	1934	1935	1936	1937	1938
At 1930 prices																			
Road vehicles	10	4	8	8	9	4	7	5	5	8	4	−2	−4	−1	8	10	13	12	4
Railway rolling stock	−1	−1	−5	0	3	2	1	4	1	0	−1	−3	−4	−4	−2	1	2	4	2
Ships	9	1	11	−2	2	7	−13	−2	13	4	−4	−13	−23	−28	−13	−10	6	1	3
Total ships and vehicles	18	4	14	6	14	13	−5	7	19	12	−1	−18	−31	−33	−7	1	21	17	9
Plant and machinery, etc.	−1	25	4	10	16	23	19	32	42	34	31	47	25	7	27	33	36	30	47
Dwellings	3	41	32	25	50	71	96	108	75	89	79	83	83	121	140	129	126	114	110
Other buildings	23	4	−16	−9	−2	1	−4	−7	−1	10	18	−7	−14	−12	3	11	15	37	30
Civil engineering works	−16	−13	−1	5	0	11	−1	1	−6	−1	12	16	1	−7	−7	−7	4	9	10
Total	27	61	33	37	78	119	105	141	129	144	139	121	64	76	156	167	202	207	206

*This detailed classification by type of asset is subject to appreciably larger errors than the estimated division between (1) Buildings and works and (2) Plant, vehicles, ships, etc. given in Table 13.00. See chapter 13, p. 228.

sector of ownership (at current and 1930 prices) in Table 3.40 and by type of asset (at 1930 prices) in Table 3.41. Whereas gross capital formation is a relatively objective concept, net capital formation is subject to all the uncertainties associated with the concept of depreciation.[1] One important warning which must be sounded is that our estimates of net capital formation do not purport to measure increases in the productive capacity of the stock of capital. It should also be noted that the estimates of scrapping are very uncertain: for

works the proportion was 32%. For plant, etc. it was as much as 87%.

The marked difference in the ratios of scrapping (replacement) to depreciation for each type of asset is due to differences in the rate of growth in the stock of assets and in the length of life over which the assets were depreciated and at the end of which they were (generally) assumed to be automatically scrapped.[2] It can in fact be shown that the ratio varies inversely with the rate of growth of gross investment and the length of

TABLE 3.42 AGGREGATE GROSS FIXED CAPITAL FORMATION, DEPRECIATION AND SCRAPPING, 1920–38

(Decade aggregates)

	Dwellings		Other buildings and works		Plant, ships, vehicles, etc.		TOTAL	
	1920–9	1930–8*	1920–9	1930–8*	1920–9	1930–8*	1920–9	1930–8*
A. £m. at 1930 prices								
1. Gross fixed capital formation	954	1,422	998	1,117	1,546	1,666	3,498	4,205
2. First cost value of assets scrapped or sold	46	89	284	369	1,110	1,196	1,440	1,654
3. Depreciation	364	437	1,020	1,007	1,240	1,423	2,624	2,867
4. G.F.C.F. less Scrapping (1–2)	908	1,333	714	748	436	470	2,058	2,551
5. G.F.C.F. less Depreciation (1–3)	590	985	−22	110	306	243	874	1,338
B. Ratios (percentage)								
6. Scrapping/Depreciation (2 as percentage of 3)	13	20	28	37	90	84	55	57
7. Scrapping/G.F.C.F. (2 as percentage of 1)	5	6	28	33	72	72	41	39
8. Depreciation/G.F.C.F. (3 as percentage of 1)	38	31	102	90	80	85	75	68

* Nine years.

most sectors they are not based on actual records of scrapping or replacement but simply reflect our assumptions as to the useful life of the assets.

The various series at 1930 prices are summarized in Table 3.42, and some very striking contrasts emerge from this, both in the relationship between the three series and in the comparison between the different types of asset. We consider first the ratio of scrapping (replacement) to depreciation. It is sometimes assumed that replacement can be taken as broadly equal to depreciation, but Table 3.42 shows that while this would be a reasonable approximation in the inter-war period for plant and other equipment, it would be very far from correct for dwellings and for other buildings and works, and so for the economy as a whole. Scrapping (demolition) of dwellings was negligible in the inter-war years, equal (at constant prices) to only 17% of the depreciation required; and for other buildings and

life of the assets.[3] For the long-lived assets such as dwellings, and to a lesser extent for other buildings and works, the ratio of scrapping to depreciation in the inter-war period was low because (a) the amount of scrapping was either negligible because the assets had not yet reached the end of their assumed lives; or, more commonly, very small because it was equal (in constant prices) to the low level of gross capital formation 60 to 100 years earlier; and (b) the amount of depreciation was relatively much higher since it was estimated as a proportion of the total stock of capital including the most recently acquired assets, so that since the rate of

---

[1] See chapter 1, p. 3 above.

[2] For dwellings our estimates of scrapping are in fact based on data on houses demolished and the first cost value at 1930 prices of the scrapping was even lower than it would have been if all houses were demolished at the end of their assumed life of 100 years.

[3] See [107] E. D. Domar, 'Depreciation, Replacement and Growth', *Economic Journal*, vol. LXIII (1953) for a full discussion of this and related issues.

growth of gross investment and thus of the stock of capital had been rising there were substantial amounts of recent gross investment on which depreciation had to be written off but for which no replacement was yet required. For plant and equipment on the other hand this difference is appreciably reduced, both because the assumed working lives of the assets are much shorter (generally about 25 to 30 years) and because the rate of growth of the capital stock over its life-span was much slower.

The result of this difference in the relative magnitude of depreciation and scrapping is reflected in lines 4 and 5 of Table 3.42 and in Figure 4, where investment net of replacement is seen to be much higher in total and for each asset than investment net of depreciation.

The second point to be considered is the ratio of depreciation to gross investment (line 8 of Table 3.42). For dwellings we find that only a third of gross fixed capital formation was required for capital consumption, leaving about two-thirds for net fixed capital formation. For other buildings and works depreciation actually exceeded gross capital formation in the 'twenties and absorbed 90% of it in the 'thirties. For plant and other equipment over 80% of gross capital formation was needed to make good capital consumption. The overall result was, therefore, that for all fixed assets net capital formation in the inter-war years amounted to £2,212 m. or only 29% of gross capital formation, and as much as £1,575 m. or over 70% of this net capital formation took the form of dwellings.

For comparison we may note that in the post-war decade 1950–9, the proportion of gross fixed capital formation required to make good depreciation was 43% for dwellings, 54% for other buildings and works and 60% for plant and other equipment, i.e. a higher proportion than in the inter-war years for dwellings but a very much lower proportion for other fixed assets. This change reflects the lower rate of growth of investment in dwellings in the post-war period and the substantially higher rate of growth of other fixed capital formation (cf. p. 35 above). The higher the rate of growth of investment the greater will be the ratio of present investment to accumulated past investment, and since depreciation is calculated as a fraction of accumulated past investment, the ratio of depreciation to gross investment is lower the higher the rate of growth of gross investment.[1]

3.5 THE STOCK OF FIXED ASSETS

The stock of fixed assets at depreciated and at first cost value is given for five years at 1930 prices, classified by sector of ownership in Table 3.50 and by type of asset in Table 3.51.

The depreciated value represents the gross stock less accumulated depreciation and the change over any period is equal to net domestic fixed capital formation during that period. We find, as would be expected in the light of the previous section, that Dwellings show by far the most substantial increase between the wars, raising their share in the total stock from 25% in 1920 to 35% in 1938. Electricity, gas and water and Social and public services gain a slightly increased share, and the remaining sectors all have a diminished share either because the total net fixed capital formation was very low or, in the case of Agriculture and Mining, because it was actually negative so that there was a contraction of the capital stock.

Analysed by type of asset the main change is that the increased share of dwellings is balanced by a fall in the proportion consisting of other buildings and works. Plant, ships, vehicles, etc., show a very slight proportionate rise and in 1938 constitute 20% of the capital stock.

The first cost value of the stock of fixed assets represents the original purchases less the first cost value of all assets scrapped or sold and in its movement and composition is broadly similar to the depreciated value.

THE PER CAPITA STOCK OF FIXED ASSETS

In this paragraph the stock of fixed assets at 1930 prices is related to the population and to the employed civilian labour force. The figures are given separately in Table 3.52 for dwellings and for other fixed assets.

For dwellings all four series show a continuous upward trend and at the end of 1938 the depreciated value of the stock of houses per head of the total population was over 70% higher than at the end of 1920. For the first cost value the increase per head was 53%.

The depreciated value of the stock of assets other than dwellings barely kept pace with the increase in total population; and per head of the employed labour force it rose between 1920 and 1925, due more to the fall in employment than to the growth in capital stock, remained steady until 1930, and thereafter declined as employment increased. The first cost value of the stock of assets other than dwellings was increased per head of the population by 13% from end-1920 to end-1938, but per head of the employed labour force it also declined slightly during the 'thirties.

THE CAPITAL : OUTPUT RATIO

This evidence of a stable (or even slightly downward) trend after 1925 in the per capita stock of fixed assets

---

[1] See [107] Domar, p. 4. The ratio varies inversely with the product of the length of life of the assets and the rate of growth of gross investment.

TABLE 3.50 STOCK OF FIXED ASSETS BY SECTOR, SELECTED YEARS, 1920–38 (£M.)

At 1930 prices

	Depreciated value*						First Cost Value*					
	1920	1925	1930	1935	1938	Change 1920–1938	1920	1925	1930	1935	1938	Change 1920–1938
Agriculture, forestry and fishing	349	315	280	248	233	−116	745	746	741	734	738	−7
Mining and quarrying	217	234	225	211	207	−10	426	457	465	470	478	52
Electricity, gas and water	505	558	653	761	817	312	879	1000	1188	1429	1582	703
Manufacturing	1346	1356	1375	1345	1409	63	2617	2691	2779	2801	2938	321
Transport and communication	1634	1689	1752	1660	1725	91	3256	3424	3604	3575	3696	440
Distribution and other services	1309	1326	1371	1396	1422	113	2068	2180	2334	2491	2595	527
Social and public services	383	374	407	470	543	160	674	722	816	947	1061	387
Dwellings	1861	2080	2527	3083	3433	1572	3268	3643	4255	5012	5473	2205
Total	7604	7932	8590	9174	9789	2185	13933	14863	16182	17459	18561	4628

* At end of year.

TABLE 3.51 STOCK OF FIXED ASSETS BY TYPE OF ASSET,† SELECTED YEARS, 1920–38 (£M.)

	Depreciated Value*						First Cost Value*					
	1920	1925	1930	1935	1938	Change 1920–1938	1920	1925	1930	1935	1938	Change 1920–1938
Road vehicles	65	98	128	139	168	103	231	326	393	435	499	268
Railway rolling stock	133	132	136	124	132	−1	372	367	356	332	332	−40
Ships	269	288	286	199	209	−60	591	612	642	547	560	−31
Plant and machinery, etc.	948	1026	1184	1323	1436	488	2249	2345	2559	2815	3059	810
Dwellings	1861	2080	2527	3083	3433	1572	3268	3643	4255	5012	5473	2205
Other buildings	2675	2653	2669	2650	2732	57	4184	4395	4653	4859	5077	893
Civil engineering works	1653	1655	1660	1656	1679	26	3038	3175	3324	3459	3561	523
Total	7604	7932	8590	9174	9789	2185	13933	14863	16182	17459	18561	4628

* At end of year.

† This detailed classification by type of asset is subject to appreciably larger errors than the estimated division between (1) Buildings and works and (2) Plant, vehicles, ships, etc. given in Table 13.00. See chapter 13, p. 228.

other than dwellings acquires added interest if considered in relation to the increase of 33% in industrial production per man-year of employment between 1924 and 1938 and of 13% in real gross national product per man-year. This indication that the ratio of capital to output declined reflects either an increase in the degree of utilization of the capital stock and/or an increase in its productive efficiency. On balance it seems likely

TABLE 3.52 THE PER CAPITA STOCK OF FIXED ASSETS, 1920–38
(£s. At 1930 prices)

	Total excluding dwellings					Dwellings				
	1920	1925	1930	1935	1938	1920	1925	1930	1935	1938
Per head of the population										
Depreciated value	131	130	132	130	134	42	46	55	66	72
First cost value	244	249	260	266	276	75	81	93	107	115
Per head of the employed labour force										
Depreciated value	338	373	373	355	344	110	133	156	179	186
First cost value	628	715	734	724	709	192	232	262	292	297

Source
  Population: [**30**] *Statistical Abstract.* Mid-year estimate of *de facto* United Kingdom population.

Employed labour force: [**99**] Chapman, p. 28. Man-years of employees in civil employment.

TABLE 3.53 CHANGES IN EMPLOYMENT, CAPITAL AND OUTPUT, 1924–38
(Per cent, per annum, compound rates)

	Employment	Capital	Output	Output per man-year
1. Agriculture and fishing	−1·5	−0·1	1·2	3·1
2. Textiles	−1·4	1·0	0·7	2·6
3. Metals and metal-using industries	2·1	1·1	3·4	1·3
4. Food, drink and tobacco	1·5	0·6	2·8	1·3
5. Other manufacturing	1·2	1·6*	2·8	1·6
6. Total manufacturing	1·0	0·7	2·8	1·8
7. Construction	2·9	*	3·9	1·0
8. Mining and quarrying	−2·1	0·4	−0·6	2·2
9. Electricity, gas and water	2·9	3·6	5·5	2·6
10. Industrial production	0·8	1·4	2·7	1·9
11. Transport and communications	0·6	0·7	1·4	·08
12. Distributive trades	3·0	1·3	1·6	−1·1
13. Total rows 1 to 12	0·8	1·1	2·3	1·5
14. Other services†	2·2	2·3	1·5	−0·5
15. Gross domestic product‡	1·1	1·2	2·0	0·9

Source: Capital
  Present estimates of first cost value of fixed assets (excluding land) at 1930 prices.

Employment
  Man-years of employees in civil work from [**99**] Chapman, pp. 18 and 98–100.

Output
  Rows 2–10 from [**119**] K. S. Lomax 'Production and Productivity Movements in the United Kingdom since 1900'. *Journal of the Royal Statistical Society*, Series A (General), vol. 122 (1959), p. 185.
  Rows 1 and 11–15 estimated by the author. (These estimates have now been published in C. H. Feinstein 'Production and Productivity in the United Kingdom, 1920–1962', *The London and Cambridge Economic Bulletin*, no. 48 (1963) p. xii.)

* Fixed assets in the construction industry are included in 'other manufacturing'.

† Insurance, banking and finance; professional services; public administration; domestic service, hotels, catering, entertainment and miscellaneous services.

‡ Excluding ownership of dwellings. Including dwellings the rate of growth of capital would be 1·7% per annum.

TABLE 3.60 STOCK-IN-TRADE AND WORK IN PROGRESS, 1920–38 (£M.)

	1920	1921	1922	1923	1924	1925	1926	1927	1928	1929	1930	1931	1932	1933	1934	1935	1936	1937	1938
At current prices																			
A. Book value of end-year stocks:																			
1. Total industry, trade and transport	2099	1452	1266	1254	1276	1267	1218	1244	1238	1210	1085	1017	967	956	993	1020	1111	1238	1206
B. Investment in stocks:																			
1. Mining and quarrying	..	3	2	1	1	–1	–4	–1	–1	–1	1	1	–1	–1	0	–1	2	2	1
2. Electricity, gas and water	..	1	2	2	3	1	1	1	1	1	1	1	–1	1	2	0	1	1	2
3. Manufacturing	..	53	18	–13	28	24	12	37	15	–8	1	15	3	–18	27	19	42	10	28
4. Transport and communications	..	4	2	–2	3	1	1	0	0	–2	4	–1	–2	–2	4	0	2	0	3
5. Distribution and other services	..	126	21	–13	–77	27	49	39	–27	23	31	50	–12	4	–33	10	–17	–42	35
6. Total industry, trade and transport	..	187	45	–25	–42	52	59	76	–12	13	38	66	–13	–16	0	28	30	–29	69
C. Value of physical increase in stocks:																			
1. Total industry, trade and transport	..	132	–124	–57	–18	130	7	54	12	52	89	–6	–16	–56	32	1	–7	61	77
2. Agriculture, forestry and fishing	44	–35	33	–8	12	3	10	–10	6	–12	2	3	17	–2	–3	4	1	–1	6
3. Total	..	97	–91	–65	–6	133	17	44	18	40	91	–3	1	–58	29	5	–6	60	83
At 1930 prices																			
D. Book value of end-year stocks:																			
1. Mining and quarrying	12	14	16	17	18	17	13	12	11	11	12	13	12	11	11	11	13	14	15
2. Electricity, gas and water	8	9	10	12	14	15	15	16	17	18	19	20	19	20	23	23	24	25	27
3. Manufacturing	376	409	423	413	434	453	463	495	508	501	502	519	522	501	531	552	596	605	633
4. Transport and communications	26	29	30	28	31	32	32	32	32	30	33	32	30	27	32	31	33	33	36
5. Distribution and other services	368	447	462	453	403	421	459	490	469	488	519	578	563	568	530	541	522	481	519
6. Total industry, trade and transport	790	908	941	923	900	938	982	1045	1037	1048	1085	1162	1146	1127	1127	1158	1188	1158	1230
E. Investment in stocks:																			
1. Total industry, trade and transport	..	118	33	–18	–23	38	44	63	–8	11	38	77	–16	–19	0	31	30	–30	72
F. Value of physical increase in stocks:																			
1. Total industry, trade and transport	..	82	–92	–42	–13	96	6	45	10	45	89	–7	–19	–66	36	1	–8	57	78
2. Agriculture, forestry and fishing	18	–29	26	–7	14	–10	11	–11	4	–12	2	8	13	–4	–2	5	1	–1	4
3. Total	..	53	–66	–49	1	86	17	34	14	33	91	–3	–6	–70	34	6	–7	56	82

.. Not available.

NOTES TO TABLE 3.60

At current prices

A. Book value of end-year stocks:

Sum of estimates in chapters 6 to 10 (For components of total see individual chapters).

B. Investment in stocks:[1]

Estimates for each sector obtained by multiplying the corresponding estimate at 1930 prices (see E below) by the implicit price index obtained from the book values in A and D.

C. Value of physical increase in stocks:

1. See Table 2.80 and pp. 31–3.

2. For agriculture, stocks of crops and livestock on farms each derived by multiplying the corresponding estimates at 1930 prices by the implied price indices obtained from total stocks on farms in Table 5.20.

For standing timber see Table 5.10.

At 1930 prices

D. Book value of end-year stocks:

Estimates in Chapters 6 to 10.

E. Investment in stocks:[1]

Annual change in book value at 1930 prices. (Only the total is given but the components can be obtained from D above).

F. Value of physical increase in stocks:

1. See Table 2.80 and pp. 31–3.

2. For agriculture, stocks of crops and livestock on farms each derived from the annual change in the estimates of total stocks in Table 5.10.

For standing timber see Table 5.20.

---

[1] See chapter 2, appendix 2.2, p. 33.

that the higher productivity of the new capital installed during the period—particularly in the new industries—was the more important factor.[1]

For all fixed assets other than dwellings the capital: output ratio fell from 2·6 in 1920–4 to 2·3 in 1935–8 if measured by the ratio of first cost value to gross national product, or from 1·4 to 1·2 if measured by the ratio of depreciated value to net national product.

A more detailed picture is given by Table 3.53. This shows, for each of the main industries and services, the compound rate of growth per annum from 1924 to 1938 in the inputs of labour (man-years of employees at work) and capital (gross stock of reproducible fixed assets at 1930 prices), in output and in productivity, defined as output per man-year.

It is an interesting feature of the table that there is very little positive association between the rate of growth of the capital stock and of productivity. Electricity, gas and water is the one sector where there is a substantial increase in both productivity and capital input. In agriculture—the sector where output per man grew most rapidly—there was no increase in fixed capital, but in this sector, as in mining and the textile industries which also do well in terms of productivity, there was a marked fall in the labour force employed, so that capital per employee did increase considerably in these sectors.

In industry as a whole output per man-year grew at almost 2% per annum but this was offset by the very poor performance of the services. In the distributive trades the number of employees is estimated to have increased at a rate of 3% per annum (from 1·6m. in 1924 to 2·4m. in 1938) and with an increase in fixed assets at a rate of only 1·3% per annum, there was a sharp fall in both capital per head and productivity. In transport and communication there was an increase in employment at 0·6% per annum and in capital (excluding the vehicles owned by manufacturing, distribution, etc.) at much the same rate, and the rate of increase in productivity was 0·8% per annum.

The remaining services are of limited significance in the present context: output can in many cases be measured only by reference to the numbers employed so that productivity is assumed to be constant, and they either employ very little fixed capital (as in finance, the professions or domestic service) or else there is very little relationship between the capital and the output of the service as a whole. In national and local government, for example, the main item of non-trading capital is in public works such as sewers and an increase in this will not be reflected in the output of the mainly administrative employees.

The sub-total in row 13 of Table 3.53 which excludes these services and also ownership of dwellings is thus a more meaningful estimate than the total in row 15. Row 13 shows that output of agriculture, industry, transport and distribution increased by 37% (2·3% per annum) from 1924 to 1938; capital per employee increased by 0·3% per annum, productivity by 1·5% per annum and the capital : output ratio thus fell by 1·2% per annum or some 15%.

3.6   STOCK-IN-TRADE AND WORK IN PROGRESS

In Table 3.60 the value of the physical increase in stock-in-trade and work in progress (stocks) is set out at current and 1930 prices for agriculture, forestry and fishing and for total industry and trade. Estimates on this basis cannot be made for the component sectors in industry and trade, but approximate estimates are available and are shown in detail at current prices and in total at 1930 prices[2] in Table 3.60. If the totals of the two estimates at 1930 prices are compared (Rows E1 and F1) the year-to-year agreement is very poor but the movement over the period from 1923 to 1938 is broadly the same in both series. On the approximate basis the total change in stocks over this period is £289m., compared with £308m. on the correctly defined (but very roughly estimated) calculation.[3]

Stockbuilding in the inter-war period represented only about 5% of total investment (Table 3.20, p. 36) and less than 1% of gross national product (Table 3.21, p. 36). The book value at 1930 prices of stocks other than farm crops, livestock and growing timber was estimated to be £941m. at end-1922 and £1,230m. at end-1938, an increase of 30%. Stocks held by manufacturing industry increased 50% from £423m. at end-1922 to £633m. at end-1938, and in distribution and other services the increase between the same dates was from £462m. to £519m., or only 12%. In other sectors of industry stocks were very low and net movements slight. Stocks on farms fell from £445m. at end-1922 to £428m. at end-1938, a small rise in the estimated value of livestock and poultry on farms being outweighed by a fairly steady fall in stocks of crops from £132m. to £90m.

---

[1] There is no reliable and comprehensive information on the degree of utilization of fixed capital but a very rough indication of the smallness of any improvement is given by the fact that the proportion of the labour force unemployed was higher in 1938 than in 1924.

[2] The detailed series at 1930 prices can be obtained from the annual change in the book value of end-year stocks at 1930 prices given in rows D.1 to D.5 of Table 3.60.

[3] See chapter 2, appendix 2.2, pp. 31–3 above for a discussion of the distinction between the two series.

CHAPTER 4

GROSS FIXED CAPITAL FORMATION ESTIMATED FROM THE SUPPLY SIDE

4.1 INTRODUCTION

In this chapter one series, gross fixed capital formation, is estimated by using data from the supply side wherever possible. This estimate was made mainly as a check on those estimates in subsequent chapters which were made independently from the ownership side.[1] It also serves as the basis for estimates of new building for shops; hotels, inns, etc.; cinemas and other places of entertainment (chapter 10, pp. 186–97); and farm buildings (chapter 5, p. 73).

The basic sources of information for these estimates are the inter-war Censuses of Production, for 1924, 1930 and 1935. These censuses classify goods primarily according to the industry by which they are produced, not the use to which they are put. It is thus necessary to decide from an examination of the detailed census returns which goods should be classified for the present purpose as *capital goods*. This decision must inevitably be rather arbitrary in some cases, since, for example, the same item may in one instance be used as a capital good, and in another may be used for current maintenance.

The estimated is described as being from the supply side but it is not possible to obtain all the information required from the censuses of production (for domestic output) and the overseas trade statistics (for imports and exports of capital goods). Adjustments have to be made for assets not covered by the censuses, for legal fees, etc., for transport and installation costs and for the proceeds of assets scrapped or sold; and it was also necessary to obtain certain information from accounts (i.e. from the ownership side) in order to complete the present estimates. This affects in particular the estimates for civil engineering work.

Details of the sources and methods of estimation used in this chapter are given first for buildings and contracting works; second for plant, machinery, vehicles, etc.; and finally for legal fees, etc., which are incurred in the process of capital formation but not included in the recorded value of the assets produced.

A detailed comparison with other estimates which have been made from the Censuses of Production will be found in chapter 14, pp. 247–9 and there is a discussion of the accuracy of the censuses themselves in chapter 13, p. 233.

4.2 BUILDING AND CONTRACTING WORK

AN OUTLINE OF THE METHOD OF ESTIMATION

The estimates in this sector were made in the following five stages:

(i) The total value of *all building and contracting work done (including all repairs and maintenance)* was estimated from the Census of Production for each of the three years in which a census was taken. This total included not only the output of the Building and contracting trade, but also work done by the contracting departments of local authorities, public utilities and certain other census trades.

(ii) Estimates of the corresponding total for the *non-census* years were then made by extrapolation based on data on numbers employed, wages and salaries paid, and indices of the cost of building materials.

(iii) The total value of the *contracting work (including repairs and maintenance)* included in the above totals was then estimated for each year. This covers the contracting work done for local authorities and the various public utilities, either by their own employees or by those of outside contractors. The estimates of the value of this work were made by combining the data given in the Censuses of Production with estimates derived from the annual summaries of the published accounts of these bodies.

(iv) The total value of the *building work (including repairs and maintenance)* done each year was obtained by deducting (iii) the value of the contracting work from (ii) the total value of all work done.

(v) The value of *new construction of buildings* each year was then obtained by deducting an estimate of work on minor repairs and maintenance of buildings each year

---

[1] See chapter 13, p. 230.

from the estimate in (iv) above. This deduction for repairs, etc., was based on estimates given in the notes on the Censuses of Production, extrapolated by means of the annual Schedule A income tax allowance for repairs to buildings.

Each of these stages is described more fully below.

work done by small building firms not covered by the censuses; and by a deduction for the duplication arising from work done by sub-contractors.

Four further points may be noted. First, the censuses only include work done by employees of gasworks and similar public utilities 'up to the meter stage'. A small

TABLE 4.20 BUILDING AND CONTRACTING WORK (£M.)
(Including Repairs and Maintenance)

	1924	1930	1935
Total value as returned for work done by employees in:[1]			
Building and contracting trades	193·5	192·2	213·1
Public utilities and local authorities	126·6	134·4	116·2
Iron and steel constructional trades	} 26·1	21·3	20·5
Other trades		12·2	17·4
	346·2	360·1	367·2
Add Allowance for:			
Small building firms not covered above[2]	15·0	55·0	88·0
Work by public utilities charged directly to consumers	1·3	1·6	2·0
	362·5	416·7	457·2
Less Work done by sub-contractors, duplicated above:[3]			
Building and contracting trades	} 8·0	9·3	19·0
Small building firms		1·1	2·0
Iron and steel constructional trades		5·6	5·4
Other trades		2·2	4·0
	354·5	398·5	426·8

Source: The details given below refer to the following Reports:

1924: [34] *Final Report* on the Third Census of Production (1924), part v.

1930: [35] *Final Report* on the Fourth Census of Production (1930), part IV.

1935: [36] *Final Report* on the Fifth Census of Production (1935), part IV, section 1.

[1] 1924: [34] *Report* p. 278 and p. 280. 1930: [35] *Report* p. 189 plus allowance for Northern Ireland p. 183 and pp. 450, *et. seq.* 1935: [36] *Report* pp. 7–8.

[2] 1924: [34] *Report* p. 273 estimates that non-reporting firms employed some 40,000 persons (8% of the total returned). Our estimate

assumes that the net output per head (£188), and the ratio of net to gross output (roughly one-half) was the same in these small non-reporting firms as in those covered by the census. (This estimate may be rather too large in the light of a comment on p. 274 of the *Report*). 1930 and 1935: [36] *Report* (1935) p. 9.

[3] 1924: [34] *Report* p. 280 states that: '... the total amount of duplication was probably not less than £8m. and not greater than £18m., but there are no means of indicating at what point within this somewhat wide range the true figure is likely to lie.' (The choice of the lower limit may again lead to some overstatement of the value of work done in 1924). 1930: Building and contracting trades: [35] *Report* p. 186 plus Northern Ireland p. 183. All Others: by analogy with the data for 1935. 1935: [36] *Report* pp. 8–9.

BUILDING AND CONTRACTING WORK DONE IN THE CENSUS YEARS

The three benchmarks derived from the census reports are given in Table 4.20. They include all building and contracting work (including repairs and maintenance) done by the building and contracting trades, by the local authorities and the public utilities, and by the iron and steel constructional trades and certain other census trades. The value of work done, as shown by the census returns, was adjusted by an allowance for

allowance was therefore made for work done beyond this stage and charged directly to consumers: for example, fitting purchasers' appliances.

Second, the censuses do not include the value of work carried out on buildings of private firms by their own employees. In the 1907 Census the value of such work was put at £5m.[1] No comparable estimate is given for the inter-war censuses, but the volume of such work is likely to have increased, and if allowance

---

[1] [34] *Report* 1924, part v, p. 278.

is made for the rise in the prices, the value of the work done by firms' own employees may represent a significant omission from the census benchmarks. A large part of such work was probably maintenance and repairs rather than new construction, and to the extent that it was maintenance the omission would not affect

ponents: work done by employees of local authorities, and work done by all employees other than those of local authorities. It was originally intended to work with a larger number of separate trade groups, but this did not prove possible. The estimates are given in Table 4.21.

TABLE 4.21   ANNUAL ESTIMATES OF TOTAL BUILDING AND CONTRACTING WORK, 1920–1938 (£M.)

	Value of work done by all employees other than those of local authorities		Value of work done by employees of local authorities		Total value of all building and contracting work done
	Wages and salaries	Materials used and other costs plus profits*	Wages and salaries	Materials used and other costs	
	(1)	(2)	(3)	(4)	(5)
1920	156·6	377·0	32·5	40·4	607
1921	138·9	290·4	29·3	32·8	491
1922	100·0	212·1	21·3	23·4	357
1923	93·9	201·2	20·2	23·2	339
1924	98·8	210·8	21·8	24·0	355
1925	109·1	229·1	24·5	25·6	388
1926	111·3	221·5	25·4	25·0	383
1927	118·8	230·3	27·7	27·4	404
1928	117·3	220·0	27·7	27·3	392
1929	117·3	221·9	28·2	27·0	394
1930	119·8	223·2	29·5	26·5	399
1931	114·7	210·9	27·2	25·2	378
1932	103·7	187·4	23·6	21·0	336
1933	109·3	199·2	23·8	21·1	353
1934	121·0	222·5	25·2	22·2	391
1935	131·6	245·1	26·3	22·6	426
1936	142·2	270·6	27·2	24·4	464
1937	152·3	302·5	27·7	27·1	510
1938	156·7	308·5	26·9	28·6	521

* Adjusted for changes in productivity 1931–8. (See p. 62).

the residual estimate of gross capital formation, as it would also be excluded from the census figure for maintenance deducted from the total work done.

Third, shaft sinking is not covered by the censuses and as the value of this work is not known, it is omitted from our estimates in Table 4.20.

Finally, no allowance was made for interest paid out of capital on works or buildings under construction.

BUILDING AND CONTRACTING WORK DONE IN THE NON-CENSUS YEARS

The interpolation and extrapolation to obtain the estimated value of building and contracting work done (including repairs and maintenance) in the non-census years was made by dividing the total into two com-

(i) *Work done by all employees other than those of Local Authorities*

The value of work done was estimated as the sum of three components: wages and salaries paid, materials used, and other costs plus profits. The value shown by the 1930 Census of Production was taken as the starting point for the estimates of the second and third components. The differences between the extrapolated series and the benchmarks for the two other census years (1924 and 1935) were then used to adjust the extrapolated series.

The first component was taken directly from Chapman's estimate of the annual wage and salary bill in the building and contracting industry.[1] The second

[1] [99] Chapman, pp. 111–14.

TABLE 4.22 GROSS FIXED CAPITAL FORMATION ESTIMATED FROM THE 'SUPPLY SIDE': BUILDING AND CONTRACTING WORK, 1920–38 (£M.)

(1) Estimate of New Building Work from the Supply Side

	1920	1921	1922	1923	1924	1925	1926	1927	1928	1929	1930	1931	1932	1933	1934	1935	1936	1937	1938
A. Total Building and Contracting work (including repairs, etc.)	(607)	491	357	339	355	388	383	404	392	394	399	378	336	353	391	426	464	510	521
B. Total Contracting Work (including repairs, etc.)																			
1. Highways, sewers and other local authority non-trading services	83·8	71·4	51·4	49·9	52·7	57·6	58·0	63·4	63·3	63·5	64·4	60·3	51·3	51·6	54·5	56·2	59·3	63·0	63·8
2. Gas mains and works	10·2	10·0	7·7	7·7	8·2	8·2	8·3	8·4	8·1	7·9	8·1	7·8	7·2	7·7	8·0	8·4	9·3	8·8	9·4
3. Electric lines and works	5·4	7·8	5·9	7·4	9·6	11·6	13·7	14·2	14·8	17·4	21·8	25·0	21·3	19·4	17·2	18·2	21·0	21·0	19·9
4. Waterworks	6·1	7·4	6·9	6·8	8·0	7·9	7·1	6·7	6·5	7·1	7·1	7·7	6·6	6·2	6·5	7·2	8·4	8·9	9·8
5. Tramway, Permanent way and lines	4·5	5·5	5·0	6·3	4·9	4·4	3·1	3·6	3·0	3·0	2·9	2·6	2·4	2·4	2·3	2·5	2·5	2·5	2·2
6. Railway way and works	34·1	38·1	32·0	29·8	29·4	30·2	25·4	28·1	25·9	26·1	26·6	29·2	27·3	20·2	21·8	22·6	23·1	26·2	31·2
7. Harbours, docks, etc.	7·7	6·4	4·8	4·8	5·4	5·6	5·0	6·4	5·0	4·2	4·5	4·4	3·7	3·4	2·9	3·0	3·3	4·3	3·7
8. Canals	2·3	1·9	1·7	1·7	1·7	1·7	1·7	1·7	1·7	1·7	1·6	1·5	1·4	1·4	1·4	1·5	1·6	1·6	1·6
9. Telegraphic and Telephonic lines and works	8·9	11·2	9·9	11·0	12·6	14·2	13·2	13·3	13·0	12·8	13·0	11·9	11·0	10·2	11·2	14·1	17·1	21·1	23·7
10. Total	163	160	125	125	132	141	135	146	141	144	150	150	132	122	125	133	145	158	165
C. Building work																			
1. Total work (A–B10)	(444)	331	232	214	223	247	248	258	251	250	249	228	204	231	266	293	319	352	356
2. Maintenance and repairs	(106)	86	70	66	68	69	72	72	74	75	77	88	90	91	92	95	99	104	108
3. New construction (C1–C2)	(338)	245	162	148	155	178	176	186	177	175	172	140	114	140	174	198	220	248	248

(2) Gross Fixed Capital Formation: Building and Contracting Work

	1920	1921	1922	1923	1924	1925	1926	1927	1928	1929	1930	1931	1932	1933	1934	1935	1936	1937	1938
D. New Contracting Work (estimated from the ownership side)																			
1. New construction (and renewals) of contracting work included in B10 above	40	54	52	56	63	70	64	67	63	67	80	91	70	56	57	62	77	89	95
2. Less New work on electrical plant included in D1	11	17	14	16	21	23	23	24	24	26	30	32	28	24	24	26	32	36	37
3. Add Mine works and buildings	13	5	9	9	6	11	4	4	0	3	7	2	2	5	3	2	4	3	3
4. Gross fixed capital formation	42	42	47	49	48	58	45	46	39	44	57	61	44	37	36	38	49	56	61
E. New Building Work																			
1. Total new construction as above (C3 (a))	(338)	245	162	148	155	178	176	186	177	175	172	140	114	140	174	198	220	248	248
2. Add legal fees, stamp duties etc.	24	13	12	12	14	14	15	16	16	15	14	10	11	15	17	19	19	19	16
3. Gross fixed capital formation	(362)	258	174	160	169	192	191	202	193	190	186	150	125	155	191	217	239	267	264

NOTES TO TABLE 4.22

(1) *Estimate of New Building Work from the Supply Side*

A. Total building and contracting work:
See p. 59.

B. Contracting work:

These estimates were made as follows: First, estimates were established from the three censuses of production of the total value of contracting work done for or by local authorities and public utilities. These estimates are set out below:

Contracting Work (including Repairs and Maintenance), 1924, 1930 and 1935 (£m.)

	1924	1930	1935
1. Local authority non-trading services:			
Highways	45·9	52·9	46·5
Sewers, sea-walls, recreation grounds, etc.[1]	6·9	11·3	10·1
	52·8	64·2	56·6
2. Gas mains and works	9·2	9·2	8·2
3. Electric lines and works	12·6	20·9	18·5
4. Waterworks (reservoirs, mains, etc.)	7·6	7·2	7·3
5. Tramways and trolley vehicles (permanent way, overhead wires, etc.)	5·0	2·9	2·3
6. Railways (permanent way, etc.)	25·6	24·5	21·8
7. Harbours, docks, etc.	5·7	4·1	3·2
8. Canals and waterways	1·7	1·3	1·7
9. Telegraphic and telephonic lines and works	13·1	13·0	13·4
	133·3	147·3	133·0

Source: The basic sources are the three [34, 35, 36] *Final Reports on the Censuses of Production:*

For 1924 and 1930: [35] *Report*, 1930, part IV, pp. 188–9 and 183.

For 1935: [36] *Report* 1935, part IV, section I, p. 7.

The figures given above include adjustments to the following items for work done for consumers, allocation of unclassified work, etc.:

For 1924 and 1930: [35] *Report* 1930, part IV: Gas, p. 471; Water, p. 512–13; Tramways, p. 543; and Railways, p. 526–8.

For 1935: [36] *Report* 1935, part IV, section IV: Gas, p. 25; Water, p. 58; Tramways, p. 79 and Railways, p. 68.

For 1935 the notes on the Census (*Final Report*, p. 9) also give an adjusted total of £141m. for the value of all contracting work done. The excess of £8m. is primarily due to the inclusion of the value of goods made and used by contractors. As this total of £141m. forms part of the estimate of £426m. for all building and contracting work done in 1935 given in the figures (p. 9) and used in Table 4.22 (see row A of Table 4.22) the benchmark for contracting work in 1935 should have been taken as £141m. and not as £133m. The effect of this error (which was discovered at a late stage after the supply side estimate of building work obtained as a residual had been completed and used in chapters 5 and 10) is thus to overstate by £8m. the supply side estimate of building work done in 1935. There is presumably a corresponding error in the other censal years and thus in the annual estimates

---

obtained by interpolation and extrapolation. The effect of this error is taken into account in the comparison with the estimates from the ownership side (see chapter 13, p. 234 below).

Second, annual estimates of total contracting work done were made for each of the nine items covered in the above table. For highways and other local authority non-trading items and for telegraphic and telephonic lines and works only a total estimate was made. For the other seven items separate estimates were made for each year of net additions and of other contracting work (including maintenance and renewals). For all these items the estimate of net additions was based on the *ownership side* estimates made in chapters 7 and 9 below for these public utilities, i.e. from their published accounts. The estimate of other contracting work was either taken directly from the same ownership side accounts, or was estimated on the basis of the *average* difference in the three census years between the census estimate of total work done and the above estimate (from the accounts) of net additions, extrapolated by reference to some appropriate indicator.[2] The estimates given in Table 4.22 are thus not the same in census years as the census estimates given above, but the differences are generally very small. The details of the methods used to obtain the annual estimates are as follows:

1. *Highways, sewers and other local-authority non-trading services:* Total contracting work done by or for local authorities assumed to be the same proportion of total building and contracting work done by local authorities (as given in Table 4.21, p. 59) as it was, on average, in the three census years.

2. *Gas mains and works: Net additions:* Capital expenditure on net additions to mains as estimated in 7.2, p. 97.

Other contracting work: Other work (maintenance and renewals) assumed to be the same proportion (34·8%) each year of total revenue expenses of gas supply undertakings, as total work done less net additions was, on average, in the three census years.

3. *Electric lines and works: Net additions:* Capital expenditure on mains transmission and on mains and services for distribution as shown annually in [27] *Electricity Supply.* (This expenditure is classified as *plant* in our estimates from the ownership side and forms part of the estimate described as plant in 7.1, p. 87).

Other contracting work: Other work (mainly renewals) estimated on the basis of the difference between the net additions and the census figures for all contracting work done, extrapolated by reference to the estimate in 7.1 of plant scrapped.

4. *Waterworks: Net additions:* Capital expenditure on net additions to mains as estimated in 7.3, p. 100.

Other contracting work: Maintenance and renewals by local authority undertakings assumed to be the same proportion each year of their total revenue expenses (20·4%) as the average maintenance expenditure on filter beds, storage and distribution by the Metropolitan Water Board was of the Board's total working expenses. This series was than raised by 26% to cover the statutory company undertakings. (Cf. 7.3, p. 100.)

5. *Tramways and trolley vehicles: Net additions:* Net change is accumulated capital expenditure on the permanent way and on electrical equipment of overhead lines as shown by the [31] Return of *Tramways and Light Railways and Trolley Undertakings* and the [67] *Report of the London Passenger Transport Board.* (In 9.2, p. 169, the expenditure on the permanent way is classified as

---

civil engineering work but the expenditure on electrical equipment of lines is included with power plant in the category of plant.)

Other contracting work: Maintenance expenditure (including renewals) on the permanent way and lines as shown by the [31] *Return* and [67] *Report* quoted above.

6. *Railway permanent way and works: Net additions:* Net change is accumulated capital expenditure on way and works as shown by the [22] *Railway Returns* and the [67] *Reports of the London Passenger Transport Board.* (See 9.1, p. 153).

Other contracting work: Maintenance expenditure (including renewals) on way and works as shown by the [22] *Railway Returns* and the [67] *Reports of the London Passenger Transport Board.*

7. *Harbours, docks, etc.: Net additions:* Net change in accumulated capital expenditure as estimated in 9.3, p. 176.

Other contracting work: Maintenance and renewals assumed to be the same proportion of revenue expenditure on local authority harbours each year as total work done less net additions was, on average, in the three census years.

8. *Canals: Net additions:* Net change in accumulated capital expenditure as estimated in 9.3, p. 176.

Other contracting work: Maintenance and renewals estimated on the basis of data for railway owned canals (in [22] *Railway Returns*) and the Manchester Ship Canal, plus an allowance for other canals. (See 9.3, p. 176).

9. *Telegraphic and telephonic lines and works:* Total contracting work (net additions plus maintenance and renewals) on lines and works assumed to be the same proportion (82·1%) each year of the total capital and maintenance expenditure on telegraph and telephone plant (as given in the [21] Post Office *Commercial Accounts*) as it was, an average in the three census years. (The total capital expenditure on telegraph and telephone plant forms part of the estimate classified as *plant* in 9.5, p. 176).

10. Total contracting work: sum of 1 to 9.

C. Building Work.
1. Total building work done: A–B 10.
2. Maintenance: See below, p. 63.
3. New construction: C1–C2.

(2) *Gross Fixed Capital Formation: Building and Contracting Work*

D. New Contracting Work
1. *New Construction (and renewals):* Total of net additions as estimated for items B1–B9 above.
2. *New work on electrical plant:* Total of net additions as estimated for items B3, B5 (part) and B9, above.
3. *Mine works and buildings:* As for Tables 6.10 and 6.20.

E. New Building Work
2. *Legal fees, stamp duties, etc.:* Share of building work in col. (6) of Table 4.40.

---

[1] Including a small amount for work on recreation and sports grounds not owned by local authorities.

[2] Adjustments were made to the extrapolated series for 1926 to allow for the abnormal effects of the general strike.

component—the value of materials used—was estimated by assuming that it varied with: (a) the number of wage-earners employed in building and contracting;[1] and (b) the fluctuations in the costs of various building materials.[2] On this assumption the value of materials used in building and contracting in 1930 (as shown by the Census of Production), per head of the numbers employed, was extrapolated by means of indices of the numbers employed and the costs of materials.

The third component was the value of other costs plus profits. This was estimated on the assumption that it moved in proportion to the total wage and salary bill in the industry. The ratio of other costs plus profits to wages and salaries in 1930 was therefore applied annually to Chapman's estimate of the wage and salary bill.

Two alternative procedures for estimating the value of work done were tried but rejected. In the first it was assumed that it was the *total value* of work done by employees, other than those of local authorities, which varied with the numbers employed and the costs of building materials. The total value per head in 1930 was then extrapolated by means of indices of these two series. In the second procedure the assumption made was that other costs plus profits moved in proportion to the cost of building materials rather than the wage and salary bill.

For 1924 the procedure adopted (taken together with the estimate below for the employees of local authorities) gives a figure of £355·4 m. for the total value of work done, and the benchmark from the census of production is £354·5 m. The two alternative procedures each overshoot the target by £8 m. For 1935 the procedure adopted gives a figure £11 m. below the census benchmark, but the two alternative procedures undershoot the target by rather more than this.

The discrepancy in 1935 was taken as an indication of an increase in productivity after 1930 and was used as the basis for an upward adjustment of the extrapolated series. The amount added was increased steadily from £2 m. in 1931 to £14 m. in 1938.

No adjustment was made to the extrapolated estimates for 1920–3 to allow for the likelihood that because of post-war disorganization, scarcities of materials, etc., productivity was lower in these years than in 1924. The figures for these years (especially 1920) are thus almost certainly overstated.

(ii) *Work done by employees of Local Authorities*

The value of work done by employees of local authorities as returned in the censuses does not include profits. It was estimated in inter-censal years as the sum of two components: (a) the total wage and salary bill of those employed on building and contracting by local authorities;[3] and (b) the other cost of work done by local authorities in 1930 per head of the number employed, extrapolated by means of indices of the numbers employed each year and of the costs of civil engineering work (index A).[4]

THE VALUE OF CONTRACTING WORK INCLUDED IN THE ESTIMATES OF THE TOTAL VALUE OF WORK DONE

The next stage was to divide the above annual estimates of all work done between building work and contracting work. For this purpose annual estimates of contracting work (including maintenance) were made by combining information from the Censuses of Production with information from the accounts of the local authorities and public utilities for or by whom this work was done. This covers all work classified in the censuses as contracting work on highways, sewers and other local authority non-trading services, gas mains and works, electric lines and works, water works, tramways (permanent way and electrical equipment of lines) and trolley vehicles, railway and works, harbours, canals and telegraphic and telephonic lines and works. The details of the methods by which these estimates were obtained are given in the Notes to Table 4.22, p. 61.

Estimates of new construction of civil engineering work as estimated from the ownership side can be found for these items in chapters 7 and 9; and as indicated in the Notes to Table 4.22 these ownership side estimates were used as the basis for certain of the items included in the estimate of total contracting work done and do not, therefore, provide an independent check on the estimates in Table 4.22.[5] It should also be observed that electrical contracting work is classified as contracting work in the censuses and therefore in Table 4.22, but, as is conventional, it is classified as plant in the estimates from the ownership side; and that renewals are included in the estimates of 'other contracting work' described in the Notes to Table 4.22 and in gross fixed capital function in the estimates on the ownership side.

NEW CONSTRUCTION OF BUILDINGS

The value of the annual new construction of buildings was then obtained by deducting the estimated annual value of repairs and maintenance of buildings from the estimated total value of building work done.

[1] [99] Chapman, pp. 111-14.
[2] [122] Maywald, p. 192.
[3] [99] Chapman, pp. 111-14.
[4] [122] Maywald, p. 193.
[5] See also chapter 13, p. 230.

The value of repair and maintenance work on buildings shown by the 1924 Census of Production was £60m., to which some £8m. must be added for non-reporting firms. The 1935 Census shows a value of £95 m.[1] For other years the Inland Revenue series of the annual maintenance allowances (Repairs, etc., to Houses and Buildings) under Schedule A of the Income Tax was used as an index to extrapolate the census figures. The very sharp and sudden fall in building costs between 1920 and 1923 is not reflected in the Schedule A allowances for these years, and an adjustment (based on the index of the costs of building materials) was therefore made in order to allow for this. The result is shown in Table 4.22.

4.3 PLANT, VEHICLES, SHIPS, ETC.

COVERAGE

The difficulties of measuring capital formation from the Censuses of Production are particularly marked in the case of fixed assets such as plant, vehicles and ships. Capital goods have to be distinguished from consumer goods and intermediate products, and replacement parts required for current maintenance have to be distinguished from complete sets of machinery. For some assets an allowance has to be made for distributive margins; and it is also necessary to combine production statistics with data on imports and exports.

Given these difficulties, and the fact that more reliable and comprehensive information for certain groups of these assets is available annually from other sources,[2] the use of Census of Production data was limited to the mechanical engineering and electrical engineering sectors. These two sectors accounted in 1930 for about 40% of the estimated total supply of plant, vehicles, ships, etc. All series are, however, included in Table 4.30 so as to provide a complete picture of the pattern of supply of new assets.

OUTLINE OF THE METHOD OF ESTIMATION FOR MECHANICAL AND ELECTRICAL ENGINEERING

Separate estimates of the value of mechanical engineering and of electrical engineering capital goods supplied to the home market each year were made in six stages. The first three refer to the six census years:

(i) In the first stage lists were made of 'potential' capital goods (i.e. those broad categories most likely to contain the items required) produced in the United Kingdom by each of these two industries in the six years for which production statistics are available. These 'census' years are the three covered by a full [34, 35, 36] Census of Production (1924, 1930 and 1935)

and the three covered by the partial [38] Import Duties Act Inquiries (1933, 1934 and 1937).

(ii) These lists were then further examined and reduced to obtain an estimate of the value of capital goods produced in the United Kingdom in these census years. This involved the elimination of replacement parts and also of all other non-capital goods on the first list such as intermediate products and consumer durables.

(iii) The value of capital goods available for the home market in these census years was then obtained by deducting the exports of capital goods and adding imports.

The next three stages refer to the estimates for the inter-censal years:

(iv) The first step was extrapolation and interpolation of the census year totals (stage (i) above) of 'potential' capital goods produced. The extrapolation was based on the total numbers employed in the two industries, the total wages and salaries paid, and indices of the cost of material used.

(v) The value of the 'potential' capital goods available for the home market in the inter-censal years, was then obtained by deducting exports less imports of the corresponding potential capital goods.

(vi) Finally, the value of capital goods available for the home market in inter-censal years was obtained by applying to the series in (v) above, ratios of the value of the capital goods available for the home market to the value of the 'potential' capital goods available for the home market, based on the data obtained for the six census years. This somewhat cumbersome procedure was necessary because it was not possible in the inter-censal years to make an accurate breakdown of the trade statistics into complete capital goods, replacement parts, intermediate products, etc.

The estimates were then completed by an allowance of 4% for costs of transport, installation, etc.

In the following sections these stages are described in more detail.

---

[1] [36] Report 1935 part IV, section 1, p. 9. The figure given in the 1930 Census cannot be used because it excluded the small firms which were responsible for a large part of total maintenance work.

[2] The assets for which more reliable information was available from other sources include ships and motor vehicles covered by statistics of new registrations, and the specialized plant, rolling stock, etc., purchased by the railways, tramways, post office and electricity supply industry, for all of which aggregate accounts are available. These sources all have the advantage of continuity and full coverage and are of a high degree of reliability. (The estimates derived from them are described in their respective chapters). A comparison with estimates for these assets made by other writers on the basis of the census data is given in chapter 14, p. 247.

It must be noted that for certain of these assets, particularly ships, the proceeds of sales abroad or scrapping have been deducted from the year's purchases to obtain the estimated gross capital formation. No information about these sales or scrapping is available from the census.

TABLE 4.30 GROSS FIXED CAPITAL FORMATION ESTIMATED FROM THE 'SUPPLY SIDE': PLANT, SHIPS, VEHICLES, etc. (£M.)

(1) Supply of Plant, Ships, Vehicles, etc.

	1920	1921	1922	1923	1924	1925	1926	1927	1928	1929	1930	1931	1932	1933	1934	1935	1936	1937	1938
A. Estimates from the Censuses:																			
1. Assets from Mechanical Engineering																			
(a) Output of 'potential' capital goods	495·8	168·2	102·9	112·8	104·4	113·0	105·4	112·6	113·4	121·5	106·4	83·2	77·0	82·2	102·3	121·7	142·9	180·2	184·5
(b) Less Exports* less retained imports	43·1	67·5	45·0	34·9	29·5	35·1	23·2	21·5	24·4	30·8	24·5	14·3	14·8	16·6	19·0	21·9	17·4	19·7	28·0
(c) 'Potential' capital goods for the home market	362·7	100·7	57·9	77·9	74·9	77·9	82·2	91·1	89·0	90·7	82·0	68·9	62·2	65·6	83·3	99·8	125·5	160·5	156·5
(d) Capital goods for the home market	265·6	73·8	42·4	57·0	54·8	57·0	60·2	66·7	65·2	66·4	60·0	48·9	43·1	44·3	58·3	71·2	89·7	95·4	112·1
2. Assets from Electrical Engineering																			
(a) Output of 'potential' capital goods	35·4	32·4	26·8	21·6	20·7	21·7	22·0	22·4	23·3	24·9	24·2	21·6	20·8	19·6	24·6	27·8	32·1	35·6	37·1
(b) Less Exports* less retained imports	2·7	6·2	4·9	4·5	6·1	6·6	7·2	7·2	6·7	5·7	5·1	3·3	3·5	3·1	3·7	5·1	5·9	7·1	10·6
(c) 'Potential' capital goods for the home market	32·7	26·2	21·9	17·1	14·6	15·1	14·8	15·2	16·6	19·2	19·1	18·3	17·3	16·5	20·9	22·7	26·2	28·5	26·5
(d) Capital goods for the home market	31·2	25·0	20·9	16·3	13·9	14·4	14·1	14·5	15·9	18·8	18·3	17·5	16·5	16·0	20·3	22·0	24·4	27·6	25·6
3. Transport and installation costs for 1 and 2	11·9	4·0	2·5	2·9	2·7	2·9	3·0	3·2	3·2	3·4	3·1	2·7	2·4	2·4	3·1	3·7	4·6	4·9	5·5
4. Total estimated from censuses (1 (d) + 2 (d) + 3)	308·7	102·8	65·8	76·2	71·4	74·3	77·3	84·4	84·3	88·6	81·4	69·1	62·0	62·7	81·7	96·9	118·7	127·9	143·2
B. Estimates from Other Sources:																			
1. Merchant ships (including fishing vessels)	64·3	59·5	101·4	39·8	35·3	36·9	19·6	19·5	40·0	34·1	30·1	14·9	5·1	4·4	7·2	17·4	28·2	28·8	26·1
2. Road goods vehicles, tractors, etc.	12·5	9·0	10·1	10·2	12·5	9·2	11·1	11·4	11·9	17·1	16·7	17·5	15·0	15·3	18·4	18·4	20·3	21·6	19·6
3. Buses and coaches, taxis, tramcars and trolley buses	14·6	11·4	13·2	12·3	11·7	7·2	12·3	11·3	11·7	11·1	12·4	11·5	7·0	4·2	5·6	8·5	9·9	11·9	13·6
4. Passenger cars for business use	9·9	7·2	9·2	11·4	14·6	17·3	17·6	17·2	15·5	14·9	13·8	10·6	9·5	11·7	14·4	17·3	18·4	20·2	17·4
5. Railway rolling stock	15·9	14·9	7·0	10·1	13·0	12·4	10·3	12·4	10·0	9·2	8·7	5·6	4·5	4·2	7·5	9·9	11·9	13·1	11·3
6. Telegraph and telephone plant	7·9	11·3	9·8	10·9	12·8	14·6	13·1	12·9	12·6	12·2	12·4	11·0	9·5	8·4	9·4	11·5	14·4	18·6	21·8
7. Electricity supply mains and services	4·6	7·0	5·0	6·5	8·7	10·8	11·7	12·8	13·1	15·8	19·6	22·2	19·6	17·3	15·6	16·5	19·3	19·7	18·6
8. Hotel furniture and fittings	3·6	3·2	2·6	2·7	2·4	2·3	2·4	2·5	2·5	2·3	2·3	2·1	1·9	2·0	2·0	2·1	2·2	2·4	2·5
9. Total	133	124	158	104	111	111	98	100	117	117	116	95	72	68	80	102	125	136	131

(2) *Gross Fixed Capital Formation: Plant, Ships, Vehicles, etc.*

C. Total 'Supply Side' Estimate

1. Total supply as above (A4+B9)	442	227	224	180	182	185	175	184	197	206	201	164	134	131	162	199	244	264	274
2. *Add* legal fees (See Table 4.40)	8	5	5	5	6	5	5	6	5	6	6	5	5	5	6	6	7	7	6
3. *Less* Proceeds of ships or vehicles scrapped or sold	9	13	11	1	9	7	12	13	20	13	10	13	10	11	11	14	12	16	7
4. Gross fixed capital formation	441	219	218	184	179	183	168	177	182	199	197	156	129	125	157	191	239	255	273

* Less 4% for transport costs, etc.

NOTES TO TABLE 4.30

(1) *Supply of Plant, Vehicles, Ships, etc.*

A. Estimates from the censuses: See pp. 66-7.

B. Estimates from other sources:

The following estimates are of the *year's purchases* of the assets at current (historical) prices and are described in detail in their respective chapters.

1. *Merchant ships:* See 5.3 and 9.3.

2. *Road goods vehicles, tractors, etc.:* For the goods vehicles see 9.2 and the supplementary estimate in Table 9.22. For the agricultural tractors, etc. see 5.1; the estimates are included in Table 5.10 but are not shown separately.

3. *Buses and taxis, tramcars, etc.:* See 9.2. The buses and taxis are given in the supplementary estimate in Table 9.22. The tramcars and trolley-buses are included in Table 9.23 but are not shown separately.

4. *Passenger cars owned for business use:* See 9.2 and the supplementary estimate in Table 9.22.

5. *Railway rolling stock:* See 9.1. The supplementary estimate for privately owned wagons is included.

6. *Telegraph and telephone plant:* See 9.5. Light, heat and power plant is excluded.

7. *Electricity supply mains and services:* This is the estimate for new construction of electric lines and works which forms part of Table 4.12, row B3. (Other electrical plant is in the estimates from the censuses in A. above).

8. *Hotel furniture and fittings:* See 10.3. This is included as a rough allowance for furniture, etc. not covered in the estimates from censuses.

(2) *Gross Fixed Capital Formation*

The proceeds of ships or vehicles sold abroad, sold to consumers or scrapped is equal to the difference between the estimates of the year's purchases given in B above and the estimates of gross fixed capital formation given in the respective sections referred to the notes on lines B1 to B8.

THE VALUE OF CAPITAL GOODS SUPPLIED IN
THE SIX 'CENSUS' YEARS

(i) *The list of 'potential' capital goods*

The first step taken was an analysis of the production statistics available for six years of the period. This resulted in a list of those categories of goods produced which warranted further examination as potential components of the present estimates of the supply of capital goods. The items contained in the mechanical engineering list of 'potential' capital goods included all goods produced or work done except marine engineering, constructional engineering, fabricated iron and steel, and repairs and jobbing. The items remaining in the electrical engineering list included all electrical machinery produced except motors for railways and tramways, but none of the electrical appliances produced except meters, commercial and medical instruments, commercial and industrial heating apparatus, electric carbons and electrodes.

This first round of elimination reduced the original scope of the census return of the value of mechanical engineering goods made and work done by approximately one-fifth, in terms of persons employed. In electrical engineering the reduction was much larger and the original census coverage was reduced by about two-thirds, in terms of persons employed. (It should be noted that a large part of the products of the electrical engineering industry enter the estimates of capital formation via the series for telegraphs and telephones, electricity supply mains and so on.)

For the three years in which data on production was taken from the Import Duties Acts Inquiries omissions in the statistics available were adjusted *pro rata* on the basis of the nearest Census of Production. Small firms (omitted from the census returns) were not responsible for any significant contribution to the output of fixed assets by these two engineering industries, and the only allowance necessary on this account was for certain complements of textile machinery.

(ii) *Division of this list into complete capital goods and other goods*

The division of the preliminary list into complete capital goods and other goods was made in two stages by detailed scrutiny of the census returns. In the first stage obviously unwanted items such as intermediate goods or any remaining consumer goods were eliminated. This covered, for example, the metal doors and frames included under 'other engineering products', and the lawn-mowers included in the censuses under agricultural machinery.

In the second stage the value of replacement parts of capital goods was eliminated. The estimates for 1924

rely partly on the later and more informative censuses, and any figures missing in the three partial censuses were derived from the nearest full census.

(iii) *Capital goods available for the home market*

The next stage was to estimate the value of the capital goods available for the home market in the six census years. This required an analysis of the items contained in the overseas trade statistics comparable to that made for the production statistics, i.e. reducing the export and import figures to correspond firstly, to the list of 'potential capital goods' and then to the list of capital goods. Where insufficient information was available, for example on replacement parts, the estimates were based on proportions derived from the nearest production statistics.

The value of goods *exported* was made comparable with the value of work done by deducting a uniform allowance of 4% for transport and other costs. This is a lower proportion than is usually used and was adopted after an examination of the actual cost of railway transport of machinery. This suggested that a deduction of 4% would be sufficient to cover not only the cost of railway transport, but also dock charges and insurance.

THE VALUE OF CAPITAL GOODS SUPPLIED IN
INTER-CENSAL YEARS

(i) *Extrapolation and interpolation of the output of 'potential' capital goods*

The 1930 census figures were taken as the basis for the extrapolation of the list of 'potential' capital goods. The estimated value of these goods in 1930 was split into two components: (a) costs of materials, and (b) wages and salaries paid, other costs and profits.

A first approximation to the value of the first component in years other than 1930 was obtained on the assumption of a constant quantity of materials per worker, i.e. by extrapolating the 1930 cost of materials by indices of the number of employed wage-earners and of the prices of materials. For materials in mechanical engineering the index of the price of unspecified plant and machinery (Index C, p. 24) was used. For electrical engineering materials, the indices used were the estimated prices of engineering stores held by the electricity supply industry and by the Post Office (pp. 91 and 179 below).

A first approximation to the value of the wages, other costs and profits was obtained (on the assumption that profits moved in proportion to wages and salaries) by extrapolating the 1930 figure by an index of Chapman's estimates of the wages and salaries paid.

In the case of mechanical engineering, the result for 1924 was £107·7m. or slightly more than the Census

benchmark of £104·4m.; for 1933 it was £81·4m. or slightly less than the benchmark of £82·2m. These discrepancies can be largely attributed to rising productivity and the series was adjusted to fit the benchmarks, assuming equally distributed changes in the correction, downwards for 1924 to 1930 and upwards for 1931 and 1932. A constant downward adjustment equal to that for 1924 was made for 1920 to 1923. For 1933 to 1935 and for 1937 the production statistics were used, and for 1936 and 1938 an upward adjustment was made based on the difference between the 1935 benchmark and the first approximation.

Similar adjustments were made in the series for electrical engineering, where the corrections required were of proportionately the same size.

(ii) *Value of 'potential' capital goods available for the home market*

In this stage the exports of 'potential' capital goods (less 4% for transport and other costs) less imports, obtained by an analysis of the overseas trade returns, were deducted from the total of the 'potential' capital goods. By adjusting for overseas trade at this level the difficulty involved in a more detailed analysis of the trade statistics into actual capital goods and replacement parts, intermediate products, etc., was avoided. This in turn meant, however, that it was not possible to make a *direct* allocation of the residual (equal to the total 'potential' capital goods available for the home market each year) into capital and other goods.

(iii) *The value of the capital goods available for the home market*

In the final stage, therefore, the value of the capital goods available for the home market in each non-census year was derived by assuming that it bore the same ratio to the potential capital goods as in the nearest census years. The actual ratio used each year was obtained by interpolation and extrapolation of the adjacent census year ratios.

Finally, an allowance of 4% was added to cover costs of transport, installation, etc.

4.4 LEGAL FEES, PROFESSIONAL SERVICES, ETC.

ASSETS INCLUDED

The contribution of legal fees, and the services of professions, etc., to capital formation may, in part, be

TABLE 4.40 LEGAL AND PROFESSIONAL FEES, STAMP DUTIES, ETC., 1920–38 (£M.)

| | Stamp duty paid on land and property | Fees charged for | | Total Fees and stamp duties = (1)+(2)+(3) | Allocated to | |
		non-industrial professional services	legal services		plant, ships, etc.	building and contracting = (4)−(5)
	(1)	(2)	(3)	(4)	(5)	(6)
1920	6·6	20·3	12·8	39·7	8·1	31·6
1921	4·2	12·9	8·0	25·1	5·3	19·8
1922	4·1	12·6	7·9	24·6	5·8	18·8
1923	4·2	12·7	8·0	24·9	5·1	19·8
1924	4·6	14·0	8·8	27·4	5·6	21·8
1925	4·7	14·3	8·9	27·9	5·3	22·6
1926	4·6	14·1	8·9	27·6	5·1	22·5
1927	4·9	15·0	9·3	29·2	5·6	23·6
1928	4·9	14·9	9·3	29·1	6·3	22·8
1929	4·8	14·7	9·1	28·6	5·9	22·7
1930	4·3	13·4	8·4	26·1	5·1	21·0
1931	3·8	11·5	7·2	22·5	4·7	17·8
1932	3·9	12·1	7·6	23·6	4·8	18·8
1933	4·7	14·6	9·1	28·4	5·1	23·3
1934	5·1	15·7	9·8	30·6	5·8	24·8
1935	5·5	17·0	10·6	33·1	6·5	26·6
1936	5·7	17·6	10·9	34·2	7·1	27·1
1937	5·2	17·3	10·6	33·1	6·8	26·3
1938	4·8	14·6	9·2	28·6	6·0	22·6

Source

(1) [**30**] *Statistical Abstract.*
(2) and (3) See p. 68.

(5) Allocation of (2) based on year's purchases of plant, vehicles, ships, etc. and of other fixed assets.

included already in the costs charged by the producers of the assets. The major part of the cost of professional services is, however, paid directly by the users. The full value of stamp duties paid on transfers of land and other property, for example, is certainly excluded from the cost at which assets are transferred between users and producers. Legal services also contribute an amount roughly proportional to the stamp duties. On the other hand, the costs of fees charged for non-industrial professional services may be paid either by the producers of assets or directly by the persons for whom the asset is being constructed.

METHODS OF ESTIMATION

Table 4.40 attempts to estimate the approximate amount of the costs excluded from the transactions between producers and users of assets. The estimate rests on the assumption that transactions in property are the predominating component and thus that fluctuation in these transactions can be accepted as the basis for the construction of the overall series.

The estimate of the costs of the non-industrial professional services (architects, surveyors, etc.) is based on information on assessments for Schedule D, Income Tax, in 1928/9, 1933/4 and 1938/9, and Chapman's estimate of wages and salaries for the 'other professional services'.[1] The total costs of these services were taken as equal to the assessed income of the self-employed, plus Chapman's estimate of wages and salaries (on the average equal to 74% of the assessed income of the self-employed), plus an allowance for all other expenses, taken as 26% of the income of self-employed. The total amount was compared with stamp duties paid in these three years and the average ratio then used to derive the annual total costs of professional services as a proportion of the annual stamp duties paid.

The corresponding estimate for legal services was derived in the same way, but using only one-quarter of the assessed income of self-employed members of the legal professions.

Total fees for non-industrial professional services were allocated between building and contracting and plant, vehicles, etc., in proportion to their respective contributions to the year's purchases. All stamp duties and legal services were allocated to building and contracting work.

The estimate required some rather arbitrary assumptions and a correspondingly wide margin of error is introduced, except for the stamp duties paid on land and real property which are taken from official records. On balance, the estimate may be somewhat too high.

---

[1] [99] Chapman, p. 203.

CHAPTER 5
AGRICULTURE, FORESTRY AND FISHING

This chapter covers the following trade groups:

5.1 Agriculture
5.2 Forestry
5.3 Fishing

The component estimates are presented in Tables 5.10, 5.20 and 5.30.

5.1 AGRICULTURE

GENERAL PROCEDURE AND SOURCE OF INFORMATION

The depreciated value of farm *land and buildings* at current prices in 1930 was obtained by multiplying the acreage under crops and permanent grass by the estimated 1930 sale value per acre of farm property.[1] This value was then split between land and buildings by deducting a separate estimate for the depreciated value of *farm buildings*. The starting point for this was an estimate of the first cost value at historical prices at the end of 1919, derived by multiplying the estimated maintenance expenditure on farm buildings by a factor relating the first cost value and maintenance expenditure for all buildings.[2]

For *tractors and agricultural machinery* the basic estimates were first made in real terms. Gross fixed capital formation was estimated mainly from information in the inter-war Censuses of Production, the Import Duties Act Enquiries, and the annual statistics of overseas trade. The first cost values were based on the first census of Agricultural tractors, machines and implements in use, taken in May 1942;[3] and on data on numbers of tractors given in the Censuses of Agricultural Production.

For *motor vehicles* used for agriculture the gross fixed capital formation was estimated in real terms from annual data on new registrations of vehicles, and the first cost value from data on licences current.[4]

Estimates of livestock, poultry and crops on farms were taken from the annual enumeration made by the Ministry of Agriculture, and valued at the market prices collected by the Ministry.[5]

ASSETS INCLUDED

The present estimates cover the main activities of the agricultural sector. Independent subsidiary activities such as fruit growing, market gardening or commercial greenhouses are not explicitly included and represent a minor omission from the sector and national totals.

For the estimates of gross capital formation in buildings the scope is determined by the classification on which the Board of Inland Revenue series of first assessments to Schedule A of 'Farmhouses and Farm Buildings' is based. In principle this should cover all such buildings, irrespective of their annual value.

For the stock of buildings the coverage depends essentially on the estimate of maintenance expenditure on farm buildings. As this is a rather approximate estimate the coverage is not very clearly defined, but it is likely that it in fact includes some farm-houses occupied by farm tenants or servants which are also included in the estimate of all dwelling-houses in chapter 12. At a very rough guess the first cost value at historical prices at end-1919 of the buildings duplicated may be between £50m. and £75m.,[6] but no correction has been made for this.

The estimate of the value of '*land*' includes all improvements other than buildings. The base year estimate was extrapolated by the changes in the acreage under crops and permanent grass, and an appropriate evaluation of improvements to, or under-maintenance of, land was not made, except in the series for the value of land at current prices where it is covered to the extent that such factors are allowed for by the changes in the estimated sale value of the land. Capital formation in the form of ditching, drainage, etc., is, therefore, an omission from the sector and national totals. No allowance was made for other agricultural land, particularly rough grazings, as no continuous series of their

---

[1] [**96**] D. K. Britton, 'The Sale Value of Farm Land between the Wars', *The Farm Economist*, vol. VI, No. 5 (1949).
[2] Based mainly on Schedule A data in the [**25**] *58th Report of the Commissioners of H.M. Inland Revenue* (1915), p. 104.
[3] [**4**] *Annual Abstract of Statistics*, No. 85 (1948), p. 159.
[4] [**30**] *Statistical Abstract*.
[5] [**2**] Ministry of Agriculture and Fisheries, *Agricultural Statistics*.
[6] See footnote (3), p. 73.

TABLE 5.10 AGRICULTURE (£M.)

	1920	1921	1922	1923	1924	1925	1926	1927	1928	1929	1930	1931	1932	1933	1934	1935	1936	1937	1938
(1) Buildings																			
A. At historical prices:																			
(c) Gross fixed capital formation	1·7	1·1	0·5	0·4	0·4	0·3	0·3	0·2	0·2	0·2	0·3	0·2	0·2	0·2	0·3	0·3	0·3	0·4	0·4
(d) Depreciation	3·2	3·2	3·2	3·2	3·2	3·2	3·2	3·2	3·2	3·2	3·2	3·2	3·2	3·3	3·3	3·3	3·3	3·3	3·3
(f) Depreciated value*	158	156	153	150	148	145	142	139	136	133	130	127	124	121	118	115	112	109	106
(h) First cost value*	320	322	322	322	323	323	324	324	324	324	324	325	325	325	325	326	326	326	327
(i) Land*	685	677	675	673	673	669	667	665	663	661	659	659	656	654	652	650	648	646	646
B. At current prices:																			
(d) Depreciation	10·8	8·8	7·2	6·7	7·0	7·0	6·8	6·7	6·4	6·5	6·3	6·1	5·8	5·7	5·7	5·8	6·1	6·4	6·5
(f) Depreciated value*	530	426	338	311	316	310	295	283	266	261	249	234	217	208	203	201	203	208	206
(h) First cost value*	1080	884	716	674	699	701	680	669	642	646	632	608	581	569	570	583	606	636	649
(i) Land*	777	626	626	659	666	668	623	593	587	455	477	503	484	525	572	520	572	571	577
C. At constant (1930) prices:																			
(c) Gross fixed capital formation	1·0	0·8	0·4	0·4	0·4	0·3	0·3	0·2	0·2	0·2	0·3	0·2	0·2	0·2	0·3	0·3	0·3	0·4	0·4
(d) Depreciation	6·3	6·3	6·3	6·3	6·3	6·3	6·3	6·3	6·3	6·3	6·3	6·3	6·3	6·3	6·3	6·3	6·3	6·3	6·3
(f) Depreciated value*	308	303	297	291	285	279	273	267	261	255	249	243	237	231	225	219	213	207	201
(h) First cost value*	629	629	630	630	631	631	631	631	632	632	632	632	632	633	633	633	634	634	634
(i) Land*	496	490	489	487	487	484	483	481	480	478	477	477	476	474	473	471	470	468	468
(2) Machinery, Vehicles, etc.																			
1. Agricultural machinery, tractors and motor vehicles																			
A. At historical prices:																			
(c) Gross fixed capital formation	5·6	6·4	4·6	3·7	2·8	2·7	2·7	2·3	2·6	2·4	2·4	2·3	2·1	1·5	2·8	3·2	3·8	4·9	4·2
(d) Depreciation	3·6	4·2	4·3	4·1	3·9	3·7	3·4	3·2	3·1	2·8	2·7	2·6	2·4	2·3	2·4	2·6	3·0	3·4	3·6
(f) Depreciated value*	16	18	18	18	17	16	15	14	14	13	13	13	12	12	12	13	13	15	15
(h) First cost value*	34	40	44	47	49	50	52	53	54	56	56	57	56	53	53	52	51	51	52
B. At current prices:																			
(d) Depreciation	4·5	5·5	4·5	3·9	3·4	3·3	3·2	3·1	2·8	2·6	2·6	2·4	2·4	2·3	2·4	2·5	2·9	3·4	3·9
(f) Depreciated value*	19	24	20	17	15	15	14	14	13	12	12	12	12	11	11	11	13	15	16
(h) First cost value*	54	66	58	54	50	51	52	56	51	51	52	49	50	48	47	44	45	48	53
C. At 1930 prices:																			
(c) Gross fixed capital formation	4·2	4·8	3·7	3·7	2·7	2·6	2·6	2·2	2·5	2·4	2·4	2·4	2·1	1·5	2·9	3·7	4·4	5·5	4·3
(d) Depreciation	3·5	3·7	3·7	3·6	3·4	3·3	3·1	2·9	2·8	2·6	2·6	2·5	2·4	2·3	2·5	2·7	3·2	3·7	3·9
(f) Depreciated value*	16	16	16	16	15	15	14	13	13	13	12	12	12	11	12	12	14	16	16
(h) First cost value*	43	46	47	49	50	51	51	52	52	52	52	52	51	48	48	48	49	51	52
2. Horse-drawn vehicles†																			
C. At 1930 prices:																			
(c) Gross fixed capital formation	0·6	0·6	0·6	0·6	0·5	0·5	0·5	0·5	0·5	0·4	0·4	0·4	0·4	0·4	0·4	0·4	0·4	0·4	0·4
(d) Depreciation	0·4	0·4	1·1	1·5	1·3	1·4	1·0	1·2	1·1	0·9	0·9	0·7	0·6	0·6	0·7	0·5	0·5	0·4	0·5
(f) Depreciated value*	20	20	20	19	18	17	16	16	15	15	14	14	14	13	13	13	14	13	13
(h) First cost value*	60	60	58	56	54	51	49	47	45	44	42	42	41	40	39	39	39	39	38

(3) All Fixed Assets (excluding Land)

A. At historical prices:

(c) Gross fixed capital formation	8·2	8·3	5·7	4·6	3·8	3·5	3·5	3·0	3·0	3·1	3·0	2·9	2·7	2·1	3·5	3·8	4·5	5·8	5·0
(d) Depreciation	7·5	8·1	8·3	8·3	8·1	7·9	7·3	7·3	6·7	6·6	6·3	6·1	6·1	6·1	6·2	6·4	6·8	7·1	7·3
(f) Depreciated value*	184	184	181	177	173	169	165	161	157	153	150	146	143	139	136	134	131	130	128
(h) First cost value*	385	392	395	397	398	399	400	400	401	402	402	402	401	398	398	397	396	397	398

B. At current prices:

(d) Depreciation	15·9	14·8	12·8	12·0	11·9	11·7	11·0	10·3	10·0	9·8	9·2	8·8	8·8	8·6	8·8	8·8	9·5	10·2	10·9
(f) Depreciated value*	578	475	377	347	350	343	326	314	294	288	276	259	242	231	226	225	228	235	235
(h) First cost value*	1219	1027	834	782	805	804	784	774	742	740	727	698	669	654	653	665	689	723	742

C. At 1930 prices:

(c) Gross fixed capital formation	5·8	5·9	4·7	4·5	3·6	3·4	3·4	2·9	3·0	3·1	3·0	3·0	2·7	2·1	3·6	4·4	5·1	6·3	5·1
(d) Depreciation	9·2	10·4	11·1	11·4	11·0	10·4	10·4	10·4	9·8	9·8	9·5	9·5	9·3	9·2	9·5	9·5	10·0	10·4	10·7
(f) Depreciated value*	344	339	333	326	319	311	304	296	282	276	269	262	255	249	244	239	235	235	230
(h) First cost value*	731	735	736	735	734	732	732	730	729	728	727	726	724	721	720	721	720	724	725

(4) Stocks on Farms

B. At current prices:

1. Livestock and poultry at 4 June	487	456	360	342	347	352	342	318	320	310	306	272	242	246	247	256	305	322
2. Crops at end of year	281	160	126	148	132	133	136	119	134	120	111	99	77	94	99	101	90	89

C. At 1930 prices:

1. Livestock and poultry at 4 June	305	313	313	315	318	320	323	326	319	313	321	331	337	334	333	334	333	338
2. Crops at end of year	146	108	132	122	132	118	126	111	117	109	111	106	95	96	95	93	90

(5) Other Information

1. Loose tools and other implements†

C. At 1930 prices:

(c) Replacements (= d)	1·4	1·3	1·3	1·3	1·3	1·3	1·3	1·2	1·2	1·2	1·2	1·2	1·2	1·2	1·1	1·1	1·1	1·1
(f) Depreciated value*	4·6	4·5	4·2	4·3	4·3	4·2	4·2	4·1	4·0	4·0	3·9	3·9	3·9	3·8	3·7	3·7	3·7	3·5
(h) First cost value*	13·9	13·5	12·7	12·8	12·8	12·7	12·6	12·5	12·4	11·9	11·8	11·7	11·6	11·4	11·1	11·0	11·0	10·6

2. Total farm tenants' capital.*

B. At current prices:	824	671	564	508	533	524	511	472	486	452	434	400	346	372	370	386	427	445
C. At 1930 prices:	491	462	486	476	488	474	483	470	468	452	457	467	461	456	459	459	458	460

3. Acreage of farm land under crops and permanent grass (million acres):

	33·7	33·3	33·2	33·1	33·1	32·9	32·8	32·7	32·6	32·5	32·4	32·3	32·2	32·1	32·0	31·9	31·8	31·8

4. Farm land and buildings as valued by the property market

B. At current prices	1182	953	953	1003	1012	1017	949	903	894	870	798	764	736	870	791	872	869	876

* At end of year. † Only the estimates at 1930 prices are given.

For Notes to Table see p. 72

NOTES TO TABLE 5.10

(1) Buildings

A. At historical prices:

(c) *Gross fixed capital formation*: A proportion of the value of all new work on buildings. See p. 73.

(d) *Depreciation*: Straight-line method, assuming a life of 100 years.

(f) *Depreciated value of buildings held at end of year*: For 1919 assumed to be one-half of A (h).

(g) *First-cost value of buildings scrapped*: Assumed to be negligible.

(h) *First-cost value of buildings held at end of year*: For 1919 by applying to the estimated maintenance expenditure on farmhouses and farm buildings the ratio for all premises of their first cost value to expenditure on their maintenance. See p. 73.

B. At current prices:

(i) *Land at end of year*: For 1913 by deducting A (f) for 1913 from the market value of farm land and buildings derived by capitalizing the gross annual value of land (including farmhouses and farm buildings) assessed to Schedule A. See p. 73. This value was extrapolated in proportion to the acreage under crops and permanent grass.

C. At constant (1930) prices:

(c) *Gross fixed capital formation*: A (c) deflated by index B.

(d) *Depreciation*: As for A (d).

(f) *Depreciated value of buildings held at end of year*: For 1919 derived from A (f) by the standard estimate that average historical costs of buildings (index B) were 50·8% of the costs at 1930 prices. (See chapter 2, p. 24).

(h) *First-cost value of buildings held at end of year*: For 1919 derived from A (h) by the same standard estimate as for C (f).

(i) *Land at end of year*: For 1930 by deducting C (f) for 1930 from the market value of farm land and buildings derived by multiplying the total acreage under crops and permanent grass by the estimated 1930 sale value of farm land and buildings. See p. 74 Extrapolation as for A (i).

(2) Machinery, Vehicles, etc.

1. Agricultural Machinery, Tractors, Vans and Lorries

This is the sum of three separate estimates. See p. 74. All estimates were made first in real terms and then multiplied by estimated average costs.

A. At historical prices:

(a) *Year's purchases*: For machinery and tractors by extrapolation of census year estimates of retained home production plus imports. See p. 74.

(b) *Proceeds of assets scrapped or sold*: 10% of A (g).

(c) *Gross fixed capital formation*: A (a) less A (b).

(d) *Depreciation*: Reducing balance method. For machinery at a rate of 18·75% and assuming a scrap value equal to 10% of the first cost. This corresponds approximately to a life of 13·7 years, which was the weighted average of the lives found for different types of agricultural machinery.[1] For the other components the life assumed was based on the standard depreciation rates allowed by the Inland Revenue.

(f) *Depreciated value of assets held at end of year*: For 1919 from (h) less the accumulated depreciation due (obtained by using the pre-1920 estimates of purchases derived under A (h)).

(g) *First-cost value of assets scrapped*: A three-year moving average of the purchases 15 years earlier.

(h) *First-cost value of assets held at end of year*: For machinery the starting point was the census of agricultural machinery taken in May 1942 (see p. 74), converted to an estimate in terms of tonnage. The valuation at historical prices rests on rough estimates of the pre-1920 purchases, taking special account of the heavy imports during the war years.[2] The end-1919 stock was assumed to have been accumulated over 15 years and the total stock in terms of tonnage at that date was spread over the 15 years in proportion to these estimates. The average values used to value this tonnage are described on p. 74.

For the other components the pre-1920 accumulation was negligible.

B. At current prices:

The series at 1930 prices multiplied by a special price index for each component. See pp. 74-5.

C. At constant (1930) prices:

The series in real terms valued at 1930 prices for each component. For agricultural machinery and for tractors the average 1930 prices were obtained from the 1930 [35] *Census of Production*, plus an addition of one-third for distribution costs, etc. For motor vehicles the average 1930 price used was that for commercial goods vehicles. (See 9.2, p. 165).

Further details as in the notes on the estimates at historical prices.

2. Horse-drawn Vehicles

A. At historical prices:

The depreciated and first-cost values were taken as 50% of the corresponding estimates at 1930 prices. Gross capital formation is equal to the series at current prices. Depreciation and scrapping then follow by the standard identities as in the estimates below at 1930 prices.

B. At current prices:

The series at 1930 prices multiplied by an index of the weekly wage rates of carpenters and joiners.[3]

C. At constant (1930) prices:

(c) *Gross fixed capital formation*: Replacements only, estimated as 1% p.a. of C (h).

(d) *Depreciation*: C (c) less annual change in C (f).

(f) *Depreciated value of vehicles at end of year*: For 1919 assumed to be one-third of C (h).

(g) *First cost value of vehicles scrapped*: C (c) less annual change in C (h).

(h) *First cost value of vehicles at end of year*: For each year the number of pairs of horses on farms[4] multiplied by the average 1930 cost of a horse-drawn vehicle. The average cost was based on data in the 1930 *Census of Production*, plus an allowance for distribution costs, etc.

(3) All Fixed Assets

The sum of items (1), (2) 1 and (2) 2.

(4) Stock on Farms

1. Livestock and Poultry on Farms at 4 June

Numbers enumerated on 4 June each year valued mainly[5] by means of weighted averages of market price quotations for store stock given in [2] *Agricultural Statistics*. See p. 75.

2. Stocks of Crops on Farms at end of year

Volume estimates made by the Crop Reporters in England and Wales, extended to the United Kingdom, and valued at the market prices given in [2] *Agricultural Statistics*. See p. 75.

(5) Other Information

1. Loose Tools and other Implements

This series is not included in all Fixed Assets, or in the national totals, but the depreciated value is included in the estimate below of tenants' capital.

A. At historical prices:
No estimate made.

B. At current prices:

The series at 1930 prices multiplied by an index of weekly wage rates in engineering.

C. At constant (1930) prices:

(c) *Gross fixed capital formation*: Replacements only, estimated as 10% p.a. of C (h).

(d) *Depreciation*: Equal to the replacements.

(f) *Depreciated value at end of year*: For 1919 assumed to be one-third of C (h).

(g) *First cost value of implements scrapped*: C (c) plus annual change in C (h).

(h) *First cost value at end of year*: For each year taken as 10 years' accumulation of an annual expenditure of £1 per person active in agriculture.

2. Farm Tenants' Capital

The sum of the depreciated values of items (2) 1, (2) 2, (4) 1, (4) 2 and (5) 1.

3. Acreage of Farm Land under Crops and Permanent Grass

4. Farm Land and Buildings as Valued by the Property Market

B. At current prices:

The total acreage under crops and permanent grass valued at the sale values of land and buildings compiled by [96] Britton, p. 128.

[1] [155] National Farmers Union, *An Interim Review of Agricultural Machinery Requirements* (London, 1945).

[2] These estimates of retained output plus imports were based on data in the 1907 Census of Production, and indications of the relationship between imports and home production. Cf. [49] Departmental Committee on Agricultural Machinery, *Report and Summaries of Evidence* (1919), Cmd. 506, p. 44.

[3] [1] *Abstract of Labour Statistics of the United Kingdom*.

[4] [2] Ministry of Agriculture and Fisheries, *Agricultural Statistics*, annual.

[5] The one exception is horses, where the price used was the lower of the average import or export value for geldings.

acreage was available. In 1925 rough grazings were valued at £21 m.,[1] which is about 2½% of the present estimate of the value of all agricultural holdings on acreage under crops or permanent grass.

The estimates of *motor vehicles* cover only those licensed at reduced rates because used for agriculture. All other motor goods vehicles used by farmers represent an omission from the sector and national totals though they are included in the supplementary estimate in chapter 9, p. 164 of vehicles engaged in road goods transport.

The estimates of *stocks* on farms cover only the specified livestock, poultry and harvested crops. Growing crops and other 'work in progress', purchased feeds, and miscellaneous stores are not included.

An estimate is also given of farm tenants' capital. This includes all assets used in agriculture as estimated in the present chapter, except for farm land and buildings.

METHODS OF ESTIMATION

Land and Buildings

(a) *Farm-houses and farm buildings.* The *gross capital formation at current (or historical) prices* was derived as a proportion of all new work on buildings (chapter 4, p. 60). For 1920–9 the proportion used for each year was the share of Farm-houses and Farm Buildings in the gross annual value of all buildings assessed to Income Tax, Schedule A, for the first time. This series was not collected after 1929 and the only alternative classification of buildings—that given in the data on plans approved collected by the Ministry of Labour from 146 local authorities—does not show farm buildings separately. The assumption made was, therefore, that expenditure on farm buildings moved together with that on residential dwellings and a fixed proportion was taken of the share of residential dwellings in total building as shown by the data on plans approved. The fixed proportion used was the average ratio for 1920–9 of the first assessments on Farm-houses and Farm Buildings to those on Dwelling-houses. For details of the first assessments to Schedule A, see chapter 10, p. 189 below.

The *first cost value at historical prices* at the end of 1919 was derived by multiplying an estimate of expenditure on maintenance of farm houses and buildings by the ratio of the first cost value of all houses and buildings to the expenditure on their maintenance.

The total allowance under Schedule A for repairs and maintenance to all farm lands and buildings in Great Britain in 1913/14 was £6·36 m. An addition of £216,000 was made to this for Northern Ireland.[2] In order to use this figure it was necessary to estimate the proportion of this total which was devoted to buildings. Unfortunately the best available statistics on this point were for Scotland only, and related to the war years 1940/1–1945/6.[3] The average share of all buildings in farm maintenance as shown by this investigation was 63%. This proportion was applied to the above figure of total maintenance, and an estimate of £4.14 m. for maintenance expenditure on United Kingdom farm houses and buildings was thus obtained.

For all houses and buildings in Great Britain in 1913/14 the allowance under Schedule A for repairs and maintenance was £35·58 m.,[4] and an allowance for Northern Ireland brings this to £35·7 m. The gross annual value of these premises in 1913/14 was £223·22 m.[5] and capitalizing this by means of the multiplier of 12·3 derived from the estimates for dwelling-houses (see chapter 10, p. 190), we obtain a first cost value in the United Kingdom at historical prices at the end of 1919 of £2746 m. The ratio of the first cost value to the repairs and maintenance allowance is thus 77:1. Multiplying the repairs and maintenance expenditure on farm buildings by this ratio we get a first cost value at end-1919 of £319 m.

The *depreciated value of buildings at historical prices* at the end of 1919 was then obtained by assuming that it was one-half of the corresponding first cost value. This estimate takes into account the fact that farm buildings were relatively older than most other buildings at this time.

Details of the other estimates, and of the series *at current and constant prices*, are given in the Notes to Table 5.10, p. 72.

(b) *Land (including improvements other than buildings).* The *market value of farm land* was estimated as the difference between the market value of total farm property (see below) and the depreciated value of buildings as estimated above. The term 'land' thus includes all improvements other than buildings.

For the series *at historical prices*, the market value of total farm property was estimated for 1913 by capitalizing the gross annual value of Lands (including Farm-houses, Farms, Buildings, etc.) assessed to Schedule A

---

[1] [**42**] Ministry of Agriculture and Fisheries, *The Agricultural Output of England and Wales, 1925*, Cmd. 2815 (1927), p. 115.

[2] [**25**] *58th Report*, p. 104. The adjustment for Northern Ireland was based on the proportion in 1923, when Northern Ireland was first shown separately.

[3] [**63**] Department of Agriculture for Scotland, *Scottish Farm Rents and Estate Expenditure* (1948), p. 15. (After these estimates were completed information relating to maintenance expenditure in England and Wales in 1956–9 was given by [**86**] J. R. Bellerby 'The Net Return to Farm Land', *The Farm Economist*, vol. IX (1960), p. 409. This indicates that 52% of owner-occupiers' maintenance expenditure in England and Wales was spent on buildings excluding dwellings.)

[4] [**25**] *58th Report*, p. 104.

[5] [**25**] *Ibid.*

in 1913/14.[1] The multiplier used to capitalize this annual value of £44·46m. was 19·52. This is the average for the ten years 1904/5 to 1913/14 of the number of years' purchase on the gross annual value of freehold agricultural land, as established for estate duty purposes.[2] The value obtained by this method is essentially the estimated pre-war current market price and this was taken to correspond for the inter-war years to the value at historical prices.

The depreciated value of farm buildings at historical prices at the end of 1913 (£169·5m.)[3] was deducted from the resulting value of £867·8m. to give the market value of the 'land' at historical prices at the end of 1913. This figure of £698·5m. was then extrapolated over the period 1920–38 in proportion to the acreage of farm land under crops and permanent grass.[4]

For the series at *constant prices* the value of 'land' at the end of 1930 was obtained by deducting the corresponding depreciated value of farm buildings from the 1930 market value of total farm land and buildings. This market value was derived by multiplying the acreage under crops and permanent grass by the 1930 sale value of farm land and buildings as estimated by D. K. Britton.[5] The value of 'land' obtained as the residual was extrapolated over the period 1920–38 in proportion to the acreage under crops and permanent grass.

The value *at current prices* was obtained by multiplying the above series at constant prices by an index of Britton's estimates of the sale value of farm land.

Agricultural Machinery, Tractors and Vehicles

This is an aggregate of three estimates, each made separately, working first in real terms. The agricultural machinery is by far the most important component: of the total gross fixed capital formation at 1930 prices in 1920–38 of £60·1m., machinery accounts for £47·0m. In 1938 the first cost value at 1930 prices of the machinery was £37·0m., for tractors it was £11·3m. and for motor vehicles £4·0m.

(a) *Agricultural machinery*. Estimates of the *gross fixed capital formation* in real terms (tonnage) were based on production data in the [**34, 35, 36**] *Census of Production* of 1924, 1930 and 1935, and the [**38**] *Import Duties Act Inquiries* of 1933, 1934 and 1937, together with the annual Trade Statistics of exports and retained imports. The years for which output data are available show a close relationship between imports and home production and estimates for the missing years between 1924 and 1938 were mainly based on this relationship. For 1920–3 production was assumed to have been at a constant level one-quarter above that in the census year 1924.[6]

The starting point for the estimate of the *first cost value* in real terms was the first census of machinery and implements in use, made in May 1942.[7] The numbers given for each type of machinery were converted to tons by means of coefficients derived from the [**37**] 1948 *Census of Production*. From this an estimate for the end of 1938 was derived by deducting the estimated purchases between the end of 1938 and the census of 1942; and an allowance for machinery scrapped in this period was made by increasing the residual by 20%.

For the series *at constant prices* these estimates in real terms were valued at the average cost of production per ton (ex works) of each sort of machinery as shown in the 1930 *Census of Production*, with an addition of one-third to the ex-works value for distribution costs, etc. This series was then converted to *current prices* by the weighted index of the average values of imports and exports. The index of the average values of exports was assumed to be representative of the changes in the prices of domestic products sold in the home market, and the weights were fixed on the basis of the relative contribution of domestic and imported machinery to total sales in the United Kingdom.

(b) *Tractors*. The estimates of *gross fixed capital formation* in real terms again rest on production data and on statistics of overseas trade. In addition the total number of tractors on British farms is known for June of 1925, 1931 and 1937 from the *Censuses of Agricultural Production*. Interpolation was based on the net increase between the censuses, and particularly in the 'twenties, on the assumption that retained imports were the main source of new tractors, as is suggested by information in the Censuses of Production for 1924 and 1930. Only in 1936–8 does the level of capital formation rise above £1m. per year.

The estimates of the *first cost value* were based on the statistics of the number of tractors on farms, and the census of agricultural tractors in use in May 1942. Valuation *at constant prices* was made in the same way as for agricultural machinery. This series at 1930 prices was then multiplied by an unweighted average of the

---

[1] [**25**] *Ibid.* £42·58m. for Great Britain plus an addition of £1·88m. for Northern Ireland, based on the proportions as shown in 1923.

[2] [**25**] *Ibid.*

[3] The value as estimated above for end-1919 is £159·4. Depreciation at 1% p.a. written off in the 6 years 1914 to 1919 was estimated at £9.8m. and added back, and it was assumed that there was no new building during these years.

[4] [**30**] *Statistical Abstract.*

[5] [**96**] Britton, p. 128.

[6] This assumption was based on evidence given to the Balfour Committee on Industry and Trade on behalf of the Agricultural Engineer's Association to the effect that employment in the industry was 25% higher in 1923 than in 1924. ([**61**] *Survey of Metal Industries*, H.M.S.O., 1928, p. 160.)

[7] [**4**] *Annual Abstract of Statistics*, No. 85, (1948), p. 159.

average values of imports and exports to get the estimate *at current prices*.

(*c*) *Motor vehicles*. Estimates of the *gross fixed capital formation* were first obtained in real terms from annual data on new registrations of exempt vehicles classed as 'agricultural vans and lorries'.[1] The estimate of the *first cost value* was similarly obtained from the classified statistics of licences current in each year. These series were valued by means of the price data used for commercial goods vehicles in chapter 9, p. 165.

Further details of the other estimates made to complete the standard estimates for agricultural machines, tractors and vehicles, and the estimates of horse-drawn vehicles and of loose tools and other implements, are given in the Notes to Table 5.10, p. 72.

Stocks on Farms

(*a*) *Livestock and Poultry*. The estimates are based on the enumeration by the Ministry of Agriculture and Fisheries[2] of livestock and poultry on farms on 4 June of each year. No adjustment was made to derive figures for the end of the calendar year. The prices used to value the livestock were taken from the annual averages of representative market prices collected by the Ministry.[3] Weighted averages of the quotations were taken for cattle, sheep and pigs to allow for differences in age and quality.

The total value of livestock in Table 5.10 shows only small changes, but this covers some significant changes in the composition of the total, as shown by the following details for three years:

Value of Livestock at 1930 Prices
(£m.)

		1920	1930	1938
Cattle:	(*a*) Dairy	81·7	90·1	102·1
	(*b*) Other	70·4	71·0	80·0
Sheep		56·7	69·2	75·1
Pigs		6·4	7·7	12·6
Horses		81·7	58·3	53·0
Poultry		7·7	14·0	15·5
Total		305	310	338

(*b*) *Stocks on Crops on Farms*. The estimates of the volume of the stocks on farms in England and Wales are based on the observations of the Crop Reporters,[4] and relate to stocks of the specified harvested crops remaining on farms at the end of each calendar year. No allowance is made for growing crops and work in progress. To obtain estimates for Scotland and Northern Ireland the ratios of stocks to crops in England and Wales each year were applied to the data on crops in Scotland and Northern Ireland. The stocks of turnips, swedes and mangolds were not given by the Crop

Reporters and estimates were made from data on the crops of these products by applying the ratio of stocks to crops for hay.

The average annual prices used to value the stocks were taken from the official data on representative market prices.[5] Wherever possible the prices selected for each crop were those on which the official index numbers of agricultural prices were based.

The composition of the total estimate in three years is shown below:

Value of Stocks of Crops on Farms at 1930 Prices
(£m.)

	1920	1930	1938
Wheat	5·3	4·6	6·8
Barley	5·1	2·9	3·0
Oats	8·5	7·9	6·6
Potatoes	7·3	6·2	7·7
Straw	18·0	11·6	12·4
Hay	37·8	35·1	21·9
Turnips, Swedes and Mangolds	64·5	42·9	31·3
Total	146·5	111·2	89·8

A COMPARISON WITH OTHER ESTIMATES

The present estimates of *farm tenants' capital* can be compared with the estimates obtained by the Ministry of Agriculture from the Crop Reporters, although the definition used is not exactly the same as in our estimates. Further, these cover only England and Wales and for purposes of comparison we have increased them to cover the United Kingdom in the proportion indicated by relative sales in the three years nearest to each census. On this basis the Ministry's estimate of tenants' capital in England and Wales at the end of 1925 was raised from £365 m.[6] to £460 m. This is £64 m. below the present estimate of £524 m. The Ministry's estimate of £280 m.[7] for 1930–1 was raised to £350 m., £84 m. below the present estimate of £434 m.

In 1925 the discrepancy is perhaps due mainly to the fact that the official estimate includes livestock

---

[1] [**30**] *Statistical Abstract*. The detailed classification of registrations is only available since 1927. For the earlier years rough estimates were made on the basis of the change in licences current.

[2] [**2**] *Agricultural Statistics*, annual.

[3] For example, [**2**] *Agricultural Statistics* (1938), vol. LXXIII, part I, Table 38, p. 81.

[4] From 1922 these were published each year by the Ministry of Agriculture and Fisheries in the weekly [**3**] *Agricultural Market Reports*. Estimates for 1920 and 1921 were based on unpublished information supplied by the Ministry.

[5] [**2**] *Agricultural Statistics*. For example 1938, vol. LXXIII, part I, Table 61, p. 104.

[6] [**42**] *The Agricultural Output of England and Wales, 1925*. Cmd. 2815 (1927), pp. 116–17.

[7] [**4**] *The Agricultural Output of England and Wales, 1930–1931*. Cmd. 4605 (1934), p. 6.

valued at farm prices, whereas the corresponding valuation in the present estimates was at market prices. In 1930–1 the discrepancy is too large to be explained by this factor alone and in part reflects the influence on the Crop Reporters' valuations of the depressed state of agriculture at that time.[1]

A number of estimates of tenants' capital have been prepared by the University of Oxford Agricultural Economics Research Institute.[2] These differ slightly in detail but are all derived from the same basic material. They are not, however, comparable with our estimates, either in total or in the details,[3] except for the one item of machinery and implements. This item is said to be valued 'on the basis of depreciated original cost' and to include an estimate of the capital value of cars, lorries and vans used in agriculture, and should therefore be broadly comparable with our estimates of the depreciated value of machinery, tractors and vehicles. There is, however, a very large discrepancy between their estimate of £85 m. for 1937/8 at current prices and our estimate of £20 m. Details of the Oxford methods were not published but it is likely that the difference is mainly in the allowance for depreciation, and our estimate of accumulated depreciation may be too high.

5.2 FORESTRY

ASSETS INCLUDED

The estimate in Table 5.20 covers all forestry whether public or private. The two main series relate to the annual increase in the value of standing timber, measured both gross and net of production (i.e. sales) of timber; and to the accumulated value of the stock of standing timber. These estimates include expenditure on new plantations.

Additional estimates are given of the value of bare land, and of buildings purchased by the Forestry Commissioners. These buildings are not carried into the national totals as they are assumed to be already included as parts of other estimates of buildings.

METHODS OF ESTIMATION

The *increase in the value of standing timber* was estimated as the sum of two series:

(a) Expenditure on new plantations.
(b) The value of the increments of standing timber.

(a) *Expenditure on New Plantations.* Expenditure on new plantations since 1919 is included in view of the fact that new plantations have practically no value as timber for several years after planting, although they do represent an addition to the accumulated capital in forestry. The net amount spent since 1919 was estimated to be £4·9 m. by 1930 and £14·3 m. by 1938.

The area of state forests planted annually is known[4] and estimates were made of the annual area of private and local authority forests planted.[5] The annual capital expenditure per acre on planting of new state forests[6] was then applied to this total acreage to obtain the *gross expenditure.*

For *net expenditure* the estimated expenditure on areas of clear felling was deducted from the gross expenditure.

(b) *The Value of the increments of standing timber.* Annual estimates were first made of the gross increments in cubic feet of standing timber. For this purpose it was necessary to reconcile official estimates of the net change in volume of standing timber from 1924 to 1938[7] and of the production of timber with estimates of the gross annual increments in 1924, 1938 and 1947–9.[8]

The next step was to value these estimates of the gross increments in cubic feet. The value at *constant (1930) prices* was taken as the average price per cubic foot of all standing timber in 1930 as estimated for the *1930 Census of Production of Home-grown Timber* (7.72d).

The value at *current prices* was obtained by multiplying the constant price series by a price index derived as an unweighted average of the wholesale price of good

[1] Cf. [98] H. Campion, *Public and Private Property in Great Britain* (London, 1939), p. 45.

[2] [88] A. J. Boreham, 'A Series of Estimates of Occupiers' Capital, 1867–1938', *The Farm Economist*, vol. VII, No. 6 (1953); [140] F. D. W. Taylor and J. R. Bellerby, 'Index of Farm Occupiers' Capital in the United Kingdom, 1937–8 to 1951–2', *The Farm Economist*, vol. VII, No. 7 (1954); [100] S. Cheveley and O. Price, *Capital in United Kingdom Agriculture Present and Future* (London, 1956); and [130] O. Price, 'Capital Needs of British Agriculture' in *Agriculture in the British Economy*, Ed. J. Scott Watson (London, 1957).

[3] The Oxford estimates for crops include harvested crops (not shown separately) and also crops in the ground, cultivations, cash reserves, debts, seeds, fertilizers in store, etc. The estimates for livestock relate to the estimated annual average numbers, not to the stock at 4 June, but this cannot account for more than a part of the amount by which our estimate for livestock exceeds theirs (the figures for 1937/8 are £313 m. and £186 m. respectively) and there must also be a substantial difference in the weighted store stock prices used to value the livestock. Finally, their total includes items omitted by us such as occupiers' fixtures (e.g. silos), purchased feeds and miscellaneous stores.

[4] [26] *Reports of the Forestry Commissioners*, annual.

[5] These estimates were derived from data published by the Forestry Commissioners on the acreage of new private plantations subsidized by the state, and estimates of the age structure of private forests given in the [39] *Census of Woodlands, 1924* (1928), and the [41] *Census of Woodlands, 1947–1949* (1951).

[6] [26] *Reports of the Forestry Commissioners*. The data used cover only the net cost of planting, excluding the cost of the land and overhead charges.

[7] [39] *Report of Census of Woodlands and Census of Production of Home-grown Timber, 1924*, p. 16; and [65] *Empire Forests and the War*: Statement presented by Great Britain to the Fifth Empire Forestry Conference (1947), pp. 3, 4, 11–15.

[8] [26] *Thirtieth Annual Report of the Forestry Commissioners*, p. 66; [40] *Report on the Census of Production of Home-grown Timber*, 1930; [64] *Interim Report of the Inter-Departmental Home-grown Timber Committee, 1933*; [41] *Census of Woodlands 1947–1949*, Summary Report; and [149] *Forest Record* (1951), no. 3.

TABLE 5.20 FORESTRY (£M.)

	1920	1921	1922	1923	1924	1925	1926	1927	1928	1929	1930	1931	1932	1933	1934	1935	1936	1937	1938
(4) Total Value of Standing Timber																			
A. At historical prices:																			
(a) Gross increase during the year	6·5	4·7	3·5	3·3	3·4	3·4	3·2	3·3	3·5	3·6	3·5	3·4	3·1	3·0	3·2	3·3	3·1	4·1	4·0
(b) Net increase during the year	2·4	1·8	1·5	1·3	1·4	1·5	1·5	1·6	1·7	1·7	1·8	1·7	1·6	1·6	1·7	1·8	1·8	2·3	2·4
(c) Total stocks*	86	88	89	90	92	93	95	96	98	100	101	103	105	106	108	110	111	114	116
B. At current prices:																			
(c) Total stocks*	140	143	84	86	84	80	78	80	83	86	84	80	76	74	76	80	73	100	94
C. At 1930 prices:																			
(a) Gross increase during the year	2·8	2·9	3·0	3·0	3·0	3·2	3·2	3·4	3·4	3·5	3·5	3·6	3·5	3·5	3·6	3·7	3·8	3·8	4·0
(b) Net increase during the year	1·1	1·1	1·3	1·2	1·3	1·4	1·5	1·6	1·6	1·7	1·8	1·8	1·8	1·8	1·9	1·9	2·0	2·1	2·2
(c) Total stocks*	70	71	72	73	74	76	77	79	80	82	84	86	88	89	91	93	95	97	99
D. In real terms (million cu. ft.):																			
(a) Gross increase during the year	77·3	78·3	79·3	80·2	81·2	82·2	83·1	84·1	85·1	86·0	87·1	88·4	90·4	91·9	93·6	95·8	98·2	101·3	104·3
(c) Total stocks*	2152	2178	2205	2233	2262	2292	2323	2355	2388	2422	2456	2493	2531	2569	2609	2652	2697	2744	2795
SUPPLEMENTARY ESTIMATE																			
(5) Land, Timber and Depreciated Value of Buildings*																			
A. At historical prices:	98	100	101	102	104	106	107	109	110	112	114	116	118	120	121	123	125	127	130
B. At current prices:	155	155	96	98	96	93	90	91	95	95	94	90	86	85	87	91	85	112	106
C. At 1930 prices:	79	80	81	82	84	85	87	88	90	92	94	96	97	99	101	103	105	107	109

* At end of year.

NOTES TO TABLE 5.20

1. *Value of Bare Land*

This item is not shown separately in Table 5.20. It was obtained as follows:

A. At historical prices:

The series at 1930 prices converted by the ratio found in 5.1 for agricultural land.

B. At current prices:

The series at 1930 prices multiplied by Britton's index of the sale value of farm property ([196] p. 128).

C. At constant (1930) prices:

The estimated area of woodlands in the United Kingdom[1] valued at the average cost of a plantable acre purchased by the Forestry Commission from 1920 to 1938. (This average was taken as the '1930 price' of forest land in order to eliminate the effect of short-period changes in the geographical distribution of the Commission's purchases).

2. *Buildings*

This item is not shown separately in Table 5.20 and is not included in the national totals. To complete the estimate for this sector, however, the estimated depreciated value is included in item (5) below. It was obtained by applying to the total acreage of woodlands the average cost of buildings per acre of plantable land purchased by the Forestry Commission.

(4) *Total value of Standing Timber*

This estimate combines net expenditure on new plantations with the value of the increments of standing timber. See p. 76.

A. At historical prices:

(a) *Gross increase during the year* and (b) *Net increase during the year*: Gross (net) increments at 1930 prices multiplied by a price index of home-produced and imported timber (see p. 76) plus the gross (net) expenditure on new plantations at current prices.

(c) *Total stocks*: For end-1919 total stocks of standing timber valued as explained on p. 79 (£85·2m.), plus net expenditure on new plantations from 1919 onwards (£0·3m.).

B. At current prices:

The series at 1930 prices multiplied by a price index of home-produced and imported timber (See p. 76), plus expenditure on new plantations.

C. At constant (1930) prices:

(a) *Gross increase during the year* and (b) *Net increase during the year*: Gross (net) increments in standing timber in real terms valued at 7·72d. per cu. ft. (See p. 76), plus the gross (net) expenditure on new plantations at 1930 prices.

(c) *Total stocks*: For end-1919 total stocks of standing timber valued at 7·72d. per cu. ft., plus net expenditure on new plantations from 1919 onwards.

D. In real terms (million cubic feet):

(a) *Gross increments of standing timber during the year*: See p. 76.

(c) *Total stocks of standing timber*: For 1919 derived from the 1924 [39] Census of Woodlands (see p. 79). For other years by adding net increments i.e. gross increments less sales of timber).

SUPPLEMENTARY ESTIMATE

(5) *Land, Timber and Depreciated Value of Buildings*

The sum of items (1) 1, (1) 2, and (4) (c).

[1] The annual area of State Forests in Great Britain is known for each year from the [26] Reports of the Forestry Commission. The area of private forests (2·75m. acres) is known for 1924 from the [39] Census of Woodlands and was assumed constant over the whole period. The total forest area in N. Ireland is known for each year from the [20] Annual Reports of the Ministry of Agriculture, Government of N. Ireland. The estimated total area was 2·88m. acres in 1920, rising to 3·2m. in 1930 and 3·5m. in 1938.

TABLE 5.30 FISHING (£M.)

(2) Fishing Vessels

	1920	1921	1922	1923	1924	1925	1926	1927	1928	1929	1930	1931	1932	1933	1934	1935	1936	1937	1938
A. At historical prices:																			
(c) Gross fixed capital formation	1·2	0·5	0·3	0·2	0·2	0·1	0·1	0·1	0·2	0·4	0·6	0·2	0·2	0·3	0·4	0·3	0·5	0·7	0·2
(d) Depreciation	0·4	0·4	0·4	0·4	0·4	0·3	0·3	0·3	0·3	0·3	0·4	0·4	0·4	0·4	0·4	0·3	0·4	0·3	0·3
(f) Depreciated value*	5	5	5	5	4	4	4	4	4	4	4	4	4	4	4	4	4	4	4
(h) First cost value*	10	10	10	10	10	10	10	10	10	10	11	11	12	12	12	12	13	12	12
B. At current prices:																			
(d) Depreciation	0·8	0·8	1·2	0·8	0·4	0·4	0·3	0·3	0·3	0·3	0·3	0·3	0·3	0·3	0·3	0·3	0·3	0·3	0·3
(f) Depreciated value*	10	9	13	8	5	4	4	3	3	4	4	4	4	4	3	4	4	5	4
(h) First cost value*	25	24	38	25	15	15	13	11	12	13	14	14	14	14	13	16	14	16	14
C. At 1930 prices:																			
(c) Gross fixed capital formation	1·3	0·2	0	0·2	0·2	0·1	0·1	0·1	0·2	0·4	0·6	0·2	0·2	0·2	0·4	0·3	0·7	0·4	0·1
(d) Depreciation	0·5	0·5	0·5	0·4	0·4	0·4	0·3	0·3	0·3	0·3	0·3	0·3	0·3	0·3	0·3	0·3	0·3	0·3	0·3
(f) Depreciated value*	6	5	5	4	4	4	4	4	4	4	4	4	4	4	4	4	4	4	4
(h) First cost value*	15	14	14	14	13	13	13	13	13	13	14	14	14	14	14	14	14	14	13

(5) Other Information

	1920	1921	1922	1923	1924	1925	1926	1927	1928	1929	1930	1931	1932	1933	1934	1935	1936	1937	1938
1. Fishing Gear (Depreciated value*)																			
B. At current prices	5·9	4·2	2·9	2·7	2·6	2·7	2·7	2·6	2·5	2·6	2·8	2·6	2·4	2·3	2·1	1·9	2·0	2·0	1·8
C. At 1930 prices	2·9	2·9	2·8	2·7	2·7	2·6	2·6	2·6	2·6	2·6	2·8	2·7	2·7	2·8	2·8	2·7	2·8	2·7	2·6
2. Tonnage of Steam and Motor Fishing Vessels registered (000 net tons):	271·5	271·1	267·0	259·0	251·3	247·0	243·7	242·2	241·7	247·0	260·5	257·5	259·5	260·4	264·0	259·5	262·0	253·0	241·7

NOTES TO TABLE 5.30

(2) Fishing Vessels

Note: All estimates were first made in terms of net registered tonnage and then valued at the average value per net registered ton of all ships exported.

A. At historical prices:

(a) *Year's purchases:* Tonnage registered for the first time valued at the average cost in the year of construction.

(c) *Gross fixed capital formation:* A (a) less proceeds of second-hand vessels sold abroad or scrapped, taken as equal to 10% of their first cost value.

(d) *Depreciation:* Straight line method assuming a life of 20 years.

(f) *Depreciated value at end of year:* A (h) less total depreciation due on each age-group of tonnage classified according to its year of registration.

(g) *First cost value of vessels sold or scrapped:* A (a) less annual change in A (h).

(h) *First cost value at end of year:* Tonnage classified according to its year of registration and each age-group valued at the average cost of the year of construction.

B. At current prices:

The series at 1930 prices multiplied by an index of the average costs of construction.

C. At 1930 prices:

As for the series at historical prices except that all tonnage was valued at the average cost of construction in 1930.

(5) Other Information

1. *Depreciated value of fishing gear:* The average value per net registered ton of fishing gear given in the [9] *Annual Reports of the Fishery Board for Scotland* applied to the total net registered tonnage of fishing vessels.

2. *Tonnage of Fishing Boats Registered:* Net tonnage of steam and motor vessels registered under part IV of the Merchant Shipping Act, 1894, [16] *Annual Statement of the Navigation and Shipping of the United Kingdom.*

building deal 4 in. × 11 in., and the average value of imported pitprops.[1]

The values at current and constant prices of the *net increments* of standing timber were obtained by applying the same price series to a series for the net increment in real terms. This was obtained by deducting annual sales of timber (to represent production of 'finished' timber) from the gross increments.

The value of the *stock of timber at historical prices* rests on the 1924 Census of Woodlands for estimates of the total stock and of its age-composition. In 1924 the acreage in the three age-groups—under 40 years, 40 to 80 years and over 80 years—was approximately equal. On this basis the simplifying assumption was made that the acreage in each comparable age-class at the end of 1919 could be treated as approximately equal. On this assumption estimates were made for each year back to 1850 of the annual increment in each year from each age-group old enough to enter into the calculation. These annual increments in each year were then valued at the prices of that year, represented by the import price of hewn timber.[2] The accumulated total of these increments thus represents the total value of the stock of timber at historical prices at the end of 1919.

For further details of the estimates see the Notes to Table 5.20, p. 77.

5.3 FISHING

ASSETS INCLUDED

The sector is defined by the tonnage of steam and motor boats registered as fishing vessels under the Merchant Shipping Act, 1894, i.e. registered under Part IV.[3] The major part of this tonnage consists of boats which are *also* registered under Part I of the Act and could thus be used for other purposes, but they are primarily engaged in fishing.

Three minor omissions must be noted: sailing boats, the depreciated value of which was never above £1 m.; fishing gear, which is shown at its depreciated value in Table 5.30, but is not included in the national totals; and stocks, the value of which was less than £0·5 m.

METHODS OF ESTIMATION

The estimates are based on the first registrations and age-composition of the tonnage of steam and motor boats registered as fishing vessels. The basic methods of estimation and the average costs per registered ton used to value the tonnage series are the same as those used in chapter 9 for the estimate of the merchant fleet but the calculations are made in terms of net (not gross) registered tonnage (see 9.3, p. 170).

For further details see the Notes to Table 5.30, p. 78, and chapter 9.

A COMPARISON WITH OTHER INFORMATION

Information is available in the [9] *Annual Reports of the Fishery Board for Scotland* on the average value per net ton of the vessels participating in the Scottish fishing season. If this average value is regarded as the depreciated value at current prices, and applied to the registered tonnage the result (except in the first few years) is about twice the corresponding value in the present estimates. In 1924, for example, the values are £9·5 m. and £4·8 m., in 1930 £9·8 m. and £3·9 m., and in 1938 £7·2 m. and £4·3 m.

[1] [30] *Statistical Abstract.*
[2] [113] W. E. Hiley, *The Economics of Forestry* (Oxford, 1930), pp. 69–72.
[3] [16] Board of Trade, *Annual Statement of the Navigation and Shipping of the United Kingdom.*

CHAPTER 6

MINING AND QUARRYING

This chapter covers the following trade groups:

6.1 Coal mining
6.2 Other mining and quarrying

6.1 COAL MINING

SOURCE OF INFORMATION

Two main sources of information were used. The first was a sample of company accounts covering approximately half the industry, which was grossed-up to yield estimates of the depreciated value of all fixed assets, of net capital formation and of stock-in-trade. The second was data obtained from the Board of Inland Revenue on wear and tear allowances in the Census of Assessments for 1938/9, and in samples of assessments examined in other years. These data were used to obtain the estimate of plant and machinery.[1]

ASSETS INCLUDED

The use of a sample of company accounts for the main estimates in Table 6.10 raises a number of important issues, firstly with regard to the scope of the estimates, secondly with regard to their accuracy.

(i) The method used to gross up the sample of accounts leads to an estimate of all assets *owned* by all business units classified by the Board of Inland Revenue as primarily engaged in coal mining.[2] On the one hand, this estimate understates the assets owned for the purpose of coal mining, because it excludes assets used by establishments engaged in coal mining, but owned by firms which were classified on the basis of their primary activity to some other industry. The main omission of this type is the coal mining assets owned by firms classified to the iron and steel industry. On the other hand, the present estimate overstates the assets owned for the purpose of coal mining by including the assets owned by firms whose primary activity was coal mining but which also engaged in other activities and owned assets for this purpose.

Four examples of these additional assets were apparent from the information given in the first accounts of the National Coal Board in 1947.[3] The most important are the houses owned by the collieries. The *First Report* of the National Coal Board discloses that the collieries owned 141,000 houses at the end of 1946. At historical prices the first cost value of these would be about £30 m. Second, there were the main-line railway wagons owned by the collieries and included in the present estimate of plant, vehicles, etc. The value at which these wagons were transferred to British Railways in 1947 was £12·3 m. Third, there was the farm land and buildings owned by the collieries (valued at approximately £2·7 m., see p. 81). Finally there were the brickworks owned by the collieries. An estimate made on the basis of data given in 1947 suggests that the depreciated value at the end of 1938 of those vested in the Coal Board was about £1·6 m. The value of brickworks not vested in the Coal Board is not known.

These assets, and any others owned by firms classified to this industry but used for other purposes (e.g. by subsidiary companies) not only introduce errors into the estimates of assets owned for the purpose of coal mining but also, in certain cases, lead to a duplication at the national level with estimates made for other sectors. This applies, in particular, to the dwellings included in this estimate and also in the comprehensive estimate of all dwellings made in chapter 12. It does not apply to the railway wagons or brickworks, which are not included in other estimates.[4]

These two types of error in the estimates for the coal mining industry will partially compensate for each other but it is not possible to determine their relative magnitude and thus their net effect on the estimates. Our impression is, however, that the assets excluded because owned by other trades probably exceeded those

---

[1] For a general discussion of the methods used to make the estimates from samples of accounts and Inland Revenue data on wear and tear allowances see chapter 2, appendix 2.1, p. 27.

[2] This corresponds to the [58] 1948 *Standard Industrial Classification* Minimum List Heading 10. See also chapter 13, pp. 221 and 227.

[3] [72] National Coal Board, *Annual Report and Statement of Accounts* for year ended 31 December 1947, pp. 77–84 and 128–143.

[4] An estimate of all privately-owned railway wagons is given in chapter 9, p. 156, but this is designed only as a supplement to the estimates for the railway sector and is not carried into the national totals.

included for the subsidiary activities of the colliery companies.[1]

(ii) The second problem is the reliability of the estimates made from samples of accounts, and especially of the estimate of gross capital formation.[2] This estimate is derived by adding an estimate of depreciation assumed to have been written off by the companies to the estimate of net capital formation given by the annual change in the (grossed-up) depreciated value of the assets shown in the companies accounts. The undisclosed amount of depreciation actually written off by the companies is thus implicit in this estimate and if the amount assumed to have been written off differs from this, then the estimate of gross capital formation will be in error to the extent of this difference. The possible errors may be material in the case of mine works, buildings, etc., where there were no official income tax rates to provide an underlying standard of depreciation from company to company and from year to year; and in an industry where, from 1926 onwards, the assumed depreciation added back was very large relative to the net capital formation.

METHODS OF ESTIMATION

Land and Buildings

(a) *Mines, Buildings and Structures.* The basic estimates of this item were derived from a sample of accounts of companies engaged in coal mining. In 1937 the depreciated value of all fixed assets owned by companies in the sample accounted for £97m., out of £181 m. estimated here for the whole trade group. The grossing-up factor by means of which the estimates were derived from the sample was obtained from the ratio of the wear and tear allowed to the sample companies in 1937 to the total allowed to all firms classified by the Inland Revenue as primarily engaged in coal mining.

The first estimate derived from the sample of accounts by the methods which are described in chapter 2, appendix 2.1, p. 27), was the depreciated value at historical prices of all fixed assets (including land and freehold coal) at the end of each year. The corresponding *depreciated value* of mines, buildings, and structures was then obtained by deducting from these totals the depreciated value of land, freehold coal and plant, machinery, etc. (The methods used to estimate these items separately are described below.) The residual obtained in this way is a composite item of building and civil engineering work including, for example, pit sinking, but it was not possible to make a further breakdown of this item, and the full amount is classified here and in the national totals as civil engineering work.[3]

The *gross fixed capital formation at current (or historical) prices* was then derived by adding the amount of depreciation assumed to have been written off each year to the first difference in the depreciated value.

The mixture of assets noted above made it difficult to find a fully satisfactory rate of *depreciation*. The rate finally adopted implied a length of life of 60 years. This was derived as a rough average of the approximate useful life of the houses, offices and other buildings not subject to heavy wear and tear from the working of machinery (100 years), and that of the more short-lived buildings and structures (40 years).

In order to estimate the *first cost value* at *historical prices* at the end of 1919, it was necessary to obtain some information on the age-structure of the stock of assets. For this purpose it seemed sufficient to use the long term growth of output as an indication of the growth of capacity. This suggested that the additions to the stock of assets in the 60 years before 1919 were fairly regular. Under such conditions the age-structure of a stock of assets (assumed to have been depreciated by the straight line method) would be such that the depreciated value was roughly one half of the first cost value.[4] The first cost value at the end of 1919 was derived from the corresponding depreciated value on this assumption.

The total *first cost value of buildings, etc., scrapped* during the period 1920–38 was assumed to be equal to the purchases 60 years earlier, i.e. in 1860–78. These purchases were estimated by assuming that they were the same proportion of the stock of buildings, etc., at the end of 1919 as the increase in output of coal between 1860 and 1878 (53m. tons) was of the output in 1913 (287m. tons), i.e. 18·5%. This total was spread in equal annual amounts.

For details of the series at *current and constant prices* see the Notes to Table 6.10, p. 83.

(b) *Land.* The estimate of the value of *land* included in the estimate of all fixed assets derived from the sample of accounts was obtained as the sum of two components.

The first was a constant amount of £2·7m. per annum to allow for farm land owned by the collieries. This estimate was obtained by applying a value of £12 per acre[5] to the 225,000 acres of farm land taken over by the National Coal Board in 1945.[6] This estimate is probably on the low side as the Board exercised their

---

[1] This impression is largely based on the distinction between assets not vested in the National Coal Board in 1947 but left to companies classified in the interwar years to coal mining, and those vested in the Board from companies classified to other industries.

[2] The problem is more fully discussed in chapter 2, appendix 2.1, p. 29.

[3] See chapter 13, p. 228.

[4] See chapter 2, p. 17.

[5] Derived from 5.1, p. 73.

[6] [72] *Annual Report and Statement of Accounts for 1947*, p. 82.

6

TABLE 6.10 COAL MINING (£M.)

	1920	1921	1922	1923	1924	1925	1926	1927	1928	1929	1930	1931	1932	1933	1934	1935	1936	1937	1938
(1) Mine Works, Buildings and Structures																			
A. At historical prices:																			
(c) Gross fixed capital formation	13·2	5·2	9·0	8·8	6·3	11·3	3·2	2·8	0	2·1	6·5	1·7	1·6	4·6	2·7	2·0	4·0	2·9	2·6
(d) Depreciation	2·7	2·8	2·9	3·0	3·1	3·3	3·3	3·3	3·3	3·3	3·4	3·4	3·4	3·5	3·5	3·5	3·5	3·6	3·6
(f) Depreciated value*	87	89	95	101	104	113	113	112	109	108	111	109	107	108	108	106	107	106	105
(h) First cost value*	164	167	175	182	187	197	199	200	198	199	204	204	205	208	209	210	212	213	215
(i) Land*	14	14	15	16	16	16	17	17	17	17	17	17	17	17	17	17	18	18	18
(j) Freehold coal*	8	8	8	8	8	8	8	8	8	8	8	8	8	8	8	8	8	8	8
B. At current prices:																			
(d) Depreciation	8·5	7·0	5·8	5·5	5·8	5·9	5·8	5·6	5·4	5·4	5·3	5·1	4·9	4·8	4·8	4·9	5·1	5·4	5·5
(f) Depreciated value*	257	208	172	165	171	177	169	164	152	149	147	138	128	126	124	124	127	131	131
(h) First cost value*	512	420	346	331	347	356	345	339	322	323	320	307	292	288	289	294	307	322	328
(i) Land*	40	33	27	26	27	28	27	27	25	25	25	24	23	23	23	23	24	25	26
(j) Freehold coal*	20	15	11	11	11	9	12	8	7	8	8	8	8	8	8	8	9	9	9
C. At 1930 prices:																			
(c) Gross fixed capital formation	7·7	3·7	8·0	8·2	5·7	10·2	3·0	2·7	0	2·0	6·5	1·8	1·8	5·1	2·9	2·2	4·2	2·9	2·6
(d) Depreciation	5·0	5·0	5·1	5·2	5·2	5·3	5·3	5·3	5·3	5·3	5·3	5·3	5·3	5·3	5·3	5·3	5·4	5·4	5·4
(f) Depreciated value*	149	148	151	154	155	160	157	154	149	146	147	144	140	140	137	134	133	131	128
(h) First cost value*	298	299	304	310	313	320	320	320	317	316	320	319	318	320	320	320	321	321	321
(i) Land*	24	24	24	25	25	25	25	25	25	25	25	25	25	25	25	25	25	25	25
(j) Freehold coal*	8	8	8	8	8	8	8	8	8	8	8	8	8	8	8	8	8	8	8
(2) Plant, Wagons, etc.																			
A. At historical prices:																			
(c) Gross fixed capital formation	4·6	5·3	6·4	7·9	7·2	2·1	3·3	4·6	3·9	7·0	2·4	5·2	2·9	2·3	4·3	3·3	3·9	5·3	6·1
(d) Depreciation	2·8	3·0	3·2	3·5	3·8	3·7	3·6	3·7	3·7	3·9	3·8	4·3	4·2	4·0	4·1	4·0	4·0	4·4	4·6
(f) Depreciated value*	38	40	43	48	51	49	49	50	50	53	52	53	51	50	50	49	49	50	51
(h) First cost value*	71	74	78	83	88	88	89	92	93	98	98	101	102	102	104	104	106	109	113
B. At current prices:																			
(d) Depreciation	6·3	4·2	3·3	3·7	4·0	3·7	3·7	3·7	3·6	3·9	3·6	3·8	3·8	3·7	3·8	3·9	4·1	5·1	5·1
(f) Depreciated value*	84	57	45	50	54	50	50	50	49	53	49	47	46	46	46	47	50	57	56
(h) First cost value*	164	110	85	91	97	93	93	94	93	100	94	91	92	93	96	99	106	124	123
C. At 1930 prices:																			
(c) Gross fixed capital formation	2·1	3·6	5·9	7·2	6·5	1·9	3·1	4·3	3·8	6·6	2·4	5·6	3·1	2·4	4·5	3·4	3·7	4·4	5·3
(d) Depreciation	2·8	2·9	3·1	3·4	3·6	3·5	3·4	3·5	3·5	3·7	3·6	4·1	4·0	3·9	4·0	3·9	3·9	4·3	4·4
(f) Depreciated value*	38	39	42	45	48	47	46	47	47	50	49	50	51	48	49	48	48	48	49
(h) First cost value*	74	75	78	83	87	86	87	89	90	94	94	97	98	98	100	101	102	104	107
(3) All Fixed Assets																			
A. At historical prices:																			
(c) Gross fixed capital formation	17·8	10·5	15·4	16·7	13·5	13·4	6·5	7·4	3·8	9·1	8·9	6·9	4·5	6·9	7·0	5·3	7·9	8·2	8·7
(d) Depreciation	5·5	5·8	6·1	6·5	6·9	7·0	6·9	7·0	7·0	7·2	7·2	7·7	7·6	7·5	7·6	7·5	7·5	8·0	8·2
(f) Depreciated value*	124	129	138	149	155	162	162	162	159	161	162	162	158	158	157	155	156	156	156
(h) First cost value*	234	241	253	266	275	285	288	292	292	297	302	305	306	309	312	314	318	323	328
(i) Land, freehold coal and depreciated value*	146	151	161	172	179	186	186	186	183	185	187	186	183	183	182	180	181	181	181

B. At current prices:																	
(d) Depreciation	14·8	11·2	9·1	9·2	9·8	9·6	9·5	9·3	9·0	8·9	8·7	8·5	8·6	8·8	9·2	10·5	10·6
(f) Depreciated value*	341	265	217	214	225	228	219	213	200	196	202	175	172	170	171	177	188	187
(h) First cost value*	676	530	431	422	443	449	438	432	415	414	423	384	382	384	393	413	446	451
(i) land, freehold coal and depreciated value*	402	314	255	252	263	265	258	248	233	229	235	202	202	201	202	209	223	222
C. At 1930 prices:																	
(c) Gross fixed capital formation	9·8	7·3	13·9	15·4	12·2	12·1	6·1	7·0	3·8	7·4	4·9	7·5	7·4	5·6	7·9	7·3	7·9
(d) Depreciation	7·8	7·9	8·2	8·6	8·8	8·8	8·7	8·8	8·8	9·4	9·3	9·2	9·3	9·2	9·7	9·8
(f) Depreciated value*	187	187	193	199	203	206	204	202	196	194	190	188	186	182	181	178	177
(h) First cost value*	372	374	382	393	399	406	407	409	411	416	416	418	420	420	423	425	428
(i) Land, freehold coal and depreciated value*	219	218	224	232	235	239	236	234	229	227	222	220	219	215	214	211	209

(4) Stock-in-Trade (Book value)*

B. At current prices	22	16	14	16	17	15	11	10	9	10	9	8	8	8	9	12	13
C. At 1930 prices	10	11	13	14	15	14	10	9	9	11	10	9	9	8	9	11	12

(5) Other Information

1. Supplies of coal at depths of 4000 ft. or less:																	
(a) Thousand million tons of coal (net)	133·6	133·4	133·2	132·9	132·6	132·4	132·3	132·0	131·8	131·3	131·1	130·8	130·6	130·4	130·2	130·0	129·7	129·5
(b) Capitalized Royalties (incl. freehold coal)	82·0	81·9	81·8	81·6	81·5	81·3	81·2	81·1	80·9	80·6	80·5	80·3	80·2	80·1	79·9	79·8	79·6	79·5

* At end of year.

NOTES TO TABLE 6.10

(1) Mine works, Buildings and Structures

A. At historical prices:

(c) *Gross fixed capital formation:* First difference in A (f), plus A (d).

(d) *Depreciation:* Straight line method assuming a life of 60 years. See p. 81.

(f) *Depreciated value of mines, etc. held at end of year:* For each year by deducting from the depreciated value of all fixed assets (see (3) below) the depreciated value of land (A (i)), of freehold coal (A (j)), and of plant, machinery, etc., (see (2) A (f)).

(g) *First cost value of mines, etc. scrapped:* The estimated amount due to be scrapped over the period (see p. 81) spread in equal annual amounts of £1·5m.

(h) *First cost value of mines, etc. held at end of year:* For 1919 derived from A (f) by imputing the age-structure estimated as described on p. 81. This makes A (f) equal one-half of A (h).

(i) *Land:* 7% of A (h), plus £2·7m. See p. 81.

(j) *Freehold Coal at end of year:* See p. 84.

B. At current prices

The series at 1930 prices multiplied by index B, except for freehold coal for which an index of the price of coal at the pits was used.

C. At constant (1930) prices:

(c) *Gross fixed capital formation:* A (c) deflated by Index B.

(d) *Depreciation:* As for A (d).

(f) *Depreciated values of mines etc. at end of year:* For 1919 derived from A (f) by the standard estimate that average historical costs of building over the period 1860–1913 (i.e. the period indicated by the age-structure estimated on p. 81) were 51·7% of the costs at 1930 prices. (See chapter 2, p. 24).

(g) *First cost value of mines, etc. scrapped:* As for A (g).

(h) *First cost value of mines, etc. held at end of year:* For 1919 derived from A (h) by the same standard estimate as for C (f).

(i) *Land at end of year:* Derived from C (h) by the ratio of A (i) to A (h).

(j) *Freehold coal at end of year:* Equal to A (j).

(2) Plant, Machinery, Wagons, etc.

A. At historical prices:

(c) *Gross fixed capital formation:* First difference in A (f), plus A (d).

(d) *Depreciation:* Reducing balance method; in 1936, 1937 and 1938 at the rates observed in samples of assessments collected by the Inland Revenue. For earlier years the rate for 1937, adjusted to take into account the additional allowances introduced in 1931 and 1937.

(f) *Depreciated value of plant, etc. held at end of year:* For 1937, the total wear and tear allowances in the Census of Assessments divided by the average rate of depreciation in the sample of assessments used in A (d). For extrapolation to other years see p. 84.

(g) *First cost value of plant etc. scrapped:* The total amount assumed due over the 19 years ($\frac{19}{30}$ of A (h) for 1919) derived from the average length of life given by A (d), and spread in equal annual amounts of £2·3m.

(h) *First cost value of plant, etc. held at end of year:* For 1919 derived from A (f) by imputing the age-structure estimated as described on p. 84. This makes A (f) equal 52·3% of A (h).

B. At current prices:

The series at 1930 prices multiplied by Index C.

C. At constant (1930) prices:

(c) *Gross fixed capital formation:* A (c) deflated by Index C.

(d) *Depreciation:* as for A (d).

(f) *Depreciated value at end of year:* For 1919 derived from A (f) by the standard estimate that average historical costs of plant, etc. (with an age-structure as estimated on p. 84) were 92·3% of the costs at 1930 prices. (See chapter 2, p. 24.)

(g) *First cost value of plant, etc. scrapped:* As for A (g).

(h) *First cost value of plant, etc. held at end of year:* For 1919 derived from A (h) by the same standard estimate as for C (f).

(3) All Fixed Assets

A. At historical prices:

i. *Depreciated value of all fixed assets (including land and freehold coal) held at end of year:* Derived from the chain of year-to-year changes in all fixed assets in a sample of company accounts grossed-up in 1937 as described on p. 81.

(4) Stock-in-Trade

A. At historical prices:

Derived from the chain of year-to-year changes in stocks in a sample of company accounts grossed-up in 1937 as described on p. 81.

B. At current prices:

C. At constant (1930) prices

The series at current prices deflated by a special index combining index C (weight 3) with the Board of Trade wholesale price index for coal (weight 1).

(5) Other Information

1. *Supplies of coal at a depth of 4000 feet or less:*

(a) Thousand million tons of coal (net). See p. 84.

(b) Capitalized royalties (including freehold coal). See p. 84.

option to take over farm land only in those cases where they considered it necessary for the economic running of the collieries. The second component was the standard estimate[1] of land as 7% of the first cost value of buildings, taken as 7% in this instance of the composite item of mines, buildings and structures. A possible over-estimation of this item is assumed to compensate in part for underestimation of the farm land.

(c) *Freehold Coal.* The estimated *depreciated value at historical prices*[2] of freehold coal was obtained as a proportion of the corresponding value of all coal deposits. This, in turn, was obtained by multiplying the volume of coal deposits at the end of each year by the average value per ton of the deposits.[3]

The volume estimate was taken from the investigations of the 1905 Royal Commission on Coal Supplies, according to which seams 1 ft. thick or more within 4,000 ft. of the surface contained 100,740 m. tons in proved coal fields, and 36,689 m. tons in unproved coal fields.[4] This figure was reduced by the subsequent tonnage of coal mined each year. The estimate of the average value per ton was based on the total value of royalties established by valuations under the Coal Act of 1938 and in its final form vested in the National Coal Board in 1947 at a value of £78·4 m.[5] This value was divided by the estimate derived above of coal deposits in that year.

The proportion of freehold coal contained in the total value of coal deposits was then obtained from data on the compensation paid after the war to the 687 collieries which owned freehold coal (£7·5 m.). The ratio of this compensation to the value of all coal deposits in 1938 was applied to the total value of deposits at the end of each year to obtain the value of the freehold coal.

Plant, Machinery, Wagons, etc.

The *depreciated value at historical prices* at the end of 1937 of plant, machinery, etc., was derived from the total wear and tear allowances in the Inland Revenue census of assessments for the year of assessment 1938/9. This total was divided by the average depreciation rates observed in a large sample of assessments for the same year collected by the Board of Inland Revenue. For 1923–38 the depreciated value at the end of 1937 was extrapolated by means of an index of the year-to-year changes in the wear and tear allowances in the annual samples of assessments collected by the Inland Revenue, taking into account the additional allowances which were introduced in 1931 and 1937. For the years 1920–22 this information was not available and the extrapolation was based on the changes in the horse-power of electric motors installed in the coal mines.

Depreciation was assumed to have been written off on the reducing balance method. In 1936, 1937 and 1938 the rates taken were those observed in the samples of assessments. In other years the 1937 rate was used with adjustments for the changes in allowances in 1931 and 1937.

The *gross fixed capital formation at current (or historical) prices* was then obtained from the annual changes in the depreciated value, plus the annual depreciation.

In order to relate the *first cost value* at the end of 1919 to the depreciated value it was necessary to determine the age-structure of the stock of plant and machinery. For this purpose the data on the horse-power of electric motors in the mines were used. This series indicated a particularly rapid rise in the years immediately before 1919.[6] To allow for this, the stock was assumed to contain two equal groups of assets: the first was assumed to have been accumulated by regular inflows during the 30 years before 1913; the second during the 12 years before 1919. With depreciation written off on the reducing balance method, the standard procedure described in chapter 2, p. 16 indicates a depreciated value under these conditions equal to 38% of the first cost value for the older assets, and 67% for the younger assets. This gives an average for the total stock of 52%.

For further details see the Notes to Table 6.10, p. 83.

A COMPARISON WITH OTHER INFORMATION

It may be of some interest to compare the present estimates of the depreciated value of fixed assets with the value at which the collieries were taken over by the National Coal Board at 1 January 1947. The fixed assets of the collieries were valued at a 'global sum' of £164·7 m.[7] to which must be added £12·3 m. for the private wagons transferred to British Railways. Our estimate for the depreciated value at historical prices of all fixed assets at the end of 1938 is £174 m. Numerical agreement between the two values is thus good, but the conceptual basis of the Coal Board valuation is *not* the

[1] See chapter 2, p. 15.

[2] The basis of valuation used leads essentially to a series at historical prices since the royalties capitalized in the value of coal deposits vested in the Coal Commission were in essence nominal charges determined by long-term contracts made in the past. As these charges were fixed for a long term or in perpetuity the series can, however, also be regarded as a valuation at constant prices.

[3] This estimated capitalized value of *all* deposits is given under section (v) of Table 6.10, p. 83.

[4] [46] Royal Commission on Coal Supplies. *Final Report*, Part I, *General Report*. Cd. 2355 (1905), p. 2 and *Final Report*, part IX, Cd. 2361 (1905), p. 4.

[5] [72] *Annual Report and Statement of Accounts* for 1947, p. 130.

[6] The horse-power of electric motors installed in coal mines was 56,000 H.P. in 1912, and this had risen to 1,013,000 H.P. at the end of 1919.

[7] [72] *Annual Report and Statement of Accounts* for 1947, p. 129.

TABLE 6.20 OTHER MINING AND QUARRYING (£M.)

	1920	1921	1922	1923	1924	1925	1926	1927	1928	1929	1930	1931	1932	1933	1934	1935	1936	1937	1938
(3) All Fixed Assets*																			
A. At historical prices:																			
(c) Gross fixed capital formation	0·7	0·7	0·6	0·9	1·0	1·0	0·9	0·7	0·8	2·8	1·4	1·1	0·9	0·8	1·6	0·8	1·6	2·1	2·0
(d) Depreciation	0·7	0·7	0·7	0·7	0·7	0·7	0·7	0·7	0·7	0·8	0·8	0·9	0·9	0·9	1·0	1·0	1·0	1·2	1·3
(f) Depreciated value†	17	17	16	17	17	17	17	17	17	20	20	20	20	20	20	20	20	21	22
(h) First cost value†	32	31	31	31	31	31	31	31	31	33	34	34	34	34	34	35	36	37	38
B. At current prices:																			
(d) Depreciation	2·2	1·5	1·1	1·1	1·1	1·1	1·1	1·0	1·0	1·1	1·1	1·2	1·0	1·1	1·1	1·1	1·2	1·5	1·7
(f) Depreciated value†	55	42	32	30	31	30	29	29	28	30	29	28	27	27	27	27	29	32	33
(h) First cost value†	106	78	58	56	56	54	53	52	51	52	50	48	47	47	47	48	50	56	57
C. At 1930 prices:																			
(c) Gross fixed capital formation	1·1	1·1	1·0	1·0	1·0	0·9	0·9	0·6	0·7	2·7	1·4	1·1	0·9	0·8	1·7	0·8	1·6	1·8	1·7
(d) Depreciation	1·1	1·1	1·0	1·0	1·0	1·0	0·9	1·0	1·0	1·1	1·1	1·2	1·2	1·2	1·2	1·2	1·2	1·3	1·4
(f) Depreciated value†	30	29	28	28	28	28	28	27	27	29	29	29	29	29	29	29	29	30	30
(h) First cost value†	54	53	52	51	51	51	50	50	49	50	50	50	50	50	50	49	50	50	51
(4) Stock-in-Trade (Book value)†																			
B. At current prices	4	4	3	3	3	3	3	2	2	2	2	2	2	2	2	2	3	4	4
C. At 1930 prices	2	3	3	3	3	3	3	2	2	2	2	2	2	2	2	2	3	4	4

* Only the total of all fixed assets is published for this trade group.   † At end of year.

NOTES TO TABLE 6.20

(1) Mines, Quarries, Buildings and Structures

A. At historical prices:

(c) *Gross fixed capital formation:* First difference in A (f), plus A (d).

(d) *Depreciation:* Straight line method, assuming a life of 50 years for the depreciating half of the stock of assets (see p. 86 for this assumed division into natural resources and man-made assets).

(f) *Depreciated value of assets held at end of year:* For each year by deducting from the depreciated value of all fixed assets (see (3) A (f) below) the depreciated value of plant, etc. (see (2) A (f)).

(g) *First cost value of assets scrapped:* For the man-made half of the assets, the total amount due over the 19 years taken as $\frac{9}{50}$ of half the first cost value at the end of 1919, and spread in equal annual amounts.

(h) *First cost value of assets held at end of year:* For 1919 derived from A (f) by imputing to the depreciating half of the assets the standard estimate of the age-structure of a stationary stock of assets, (see chapter 2, p. 16) making the depreciated value equal to about half the first cost value. The depreciated value of the other half of the assets was taken as equal to the first cost value.

B. At current prices:

The series at 1930 prices multiplied by index A.

C. At constant (1930) prices:

(c) *Gross fixed capital formation:* A (c) deflated by index A.

(d) *Depreciation:* As for A (d).

(f) *Depreciated Value of assets held at end of year:* For 1919 derived from A (f) by the standard estimate relating average historical costs of construction (index A) over the period 1860–1913 to costs at 1930 prices. (See chapter 2, p. 24).

(g) *First cost value of assets scrapped:* As for A (g).

(h) *First cost value of assets held at end of year:* For 1919 derived from A (h) by the same standard estimate as for C (f).

(2) Plant, etc.

A. At historical prices:

(c) *Gross fixed capital formation:* First difference in A (f), plus A (d).

(d) *Depreciation:* Reducing balance method, in 1936, 1937 and 1938 at the rates observed in samples of assessments collected by the Inland Revenue. For earlier years the rate for 1937 adjusted to take into account changes in the depreciation allowances in 1931 and 1937.

(f) *Depreciated value of plant, etc. held at end of year:* For 1937 the total wear and tear allowances in the Census of Assessments divided by the average rate of depreciation in the sample of assessments used in A (d). For 1923–36 and 1938 extrapolation was based on the chain of year-to-year changes in the wear-and-tear allowances in samples of assessments. Before 1923 all changes observed in the sample of accounts were assigned to plant, etc.

(g) *First cost value of plant, etc. scrapped:* The total amount assumed due over the 19 years ($\frac{19}{28}$ of A (h) for 1919) spread in equal annual amounts.

(h) *First cost value of plant, etc. held at end of year:* For 1919 derived from A (f) by imputing the standard estimate of the age-structure of a stationary stock of assets. (See Chapter 2, p. 16). Depreciation is assumed to have been written off by the reducing balance method with a life of 28 years.

B. At current prices:

The series at 1930 prices multiplied by index C.

C. At constant (1930) prices:

(c) *Gross fixed capital formation:* A (c) deflated by index C.

(d) *Depreciation:* As for A (d).

(f) *Depreciated value of plant, etc. held at end of year:* For 1919 derived from A (f) by the standard estimates relating average historical costs of machinery (index C) over the period 1884–1913 to costs at 1930 prices. (See Chapter 2, p. 24.)

(g) *First cost value of plant, etc. scrapped:* As for A (g).

(h) *First cost value of plant, etc. held at end of year:* For 1919 derived from A (h) by the same standard estimate as for C (f).

(3) All Fixed Assets

A. At historical prices:

(f) *Depreciated value at end of year:* Derived from the chain of year-to-year changes in a sample of company accounts grossed-up in 1937 by the ratio of the wear and tear allowed for the sample companies to the total allowed for all firms classified to the trade group in the Inland Revenue Census of Assessments for 1938/9.

(4) Stock-in-Trade

B. At current prices:

For each year derived from the depreciated value of all fixed assets by the ratios of stocks to fixed assets shown in the samples of accounts for each year.

C. At constant (1930) prices:

The series at current prices deflated by the index of the price of materials included in index A.

same as that of the present estimate, and it is also, of course, necessary to take into account two factors operative between 1938 and 1947: the depreciation of the assets and the rise in prices.

In the case of stocks a comparable alternative estimate can be made by multiplying the annual expenditure on stores shown in the interwar *Reports* of the Secretary for Mines[1] by the average ratio of stocks to expenditure on stores shown in the accounts of the National Coal Board for 1947 to 1953. The result is generally £2–3 m. above the present estimate of stocks at current prices. In 1924, for example, the present estimate is £16·6m. and the alternative estimate £18·0m.; in 1930 the figures are £10·1 m. and £12·9m.; and in 1938 £13·0m. and £17·8m.

6.2   OTHER MINING AND QUARRYING

SOURCE OF INFORMATION

The main sources of information were a sample of company accounts, from which estimates of the depreciated value of all fixed assets and of net capital formation were derived; and data on wear and tear allowances obtained from the Board of Inland Revenue. The sample of accounts covered 31·9% of the industry.

ASSETS INCLUDED

The estimates in Table 6.20 were designed to cover the mining and quarrying of iron ore, stone, slate, clay, sand, chalk, copper, lead, salt, etc. The minimum list headings of the 1948 *Standard Industrial Classification* are 11–14 and 19.[2]

The use of company accounts, and thus of the Inland Revenue classification, as the main basis for the estimate meant, however, that it was not possible to cover accurately the activities defined above, and the general remarks in 6.1, p. 80, about possible omissions and duplications are equally applicable to this trade group. It is, in fact, possible that a considerable part of the trade group is omitted from this estimate, but included in that for other trade groups. Cement companies, for example, might own their own clay pits, steel companies their own iron-stone quarries, and so on.

METHODS OF ESTIMATION

It was not possible to make a satisfactory division of the estimates into natural resources and man-made assets. For the estimates of depreciation the working assumption was made that one-half of the first cost value of assets classified as 'mine, quarries, buildings and structures' consisted of land and natural resources.[3]

This distinction was not made in the case of the gross fixed capital formation which therefore includes any expenditure on land and natural resources. The amounts involved are, however, very small.

A general discussion of the methods used to make estimates from sample of accounts and Inland Revenue data on wear and tear allowances is given in chapter 2, appendix 2.1, p. 27. Details for this trade group are given in the Notes to Table 6.20, p. 85.

A COMPARISON WITH OTHER INFORMATION

In the inter-war census years it was possible to make alternative estimates of stocks by multiplying figures for the value of production and of purchased materials by the ratios of stocks to flows in these items shown in post-war censuses. The estimates obtained in this way compare reasonably well with those made from the sample of accounts.

---

[1] **[14]** *Annual Report of the Secretary for Mines.*
[2] See also chapter 13, p. 221.
[3] The basis for this assumption was an impression gained from information in the **[45]** Royal Commission on Mining Royalties (1893), C.6980, *Final Report*, p. 12.

CHAPTER 7

ELECTRICITY, GAS AND WATER

The estimates presented in this sector cover:

7.1 Electricity supply undertakings.
7.2 Gas supply undertakings.
7.3 Water supply undertakings.

The complete set of standard estimates is given in Table 7.00 for the sector as a whole, and the estimates for the three component groups are given in Tables 7.10–7.30.

7.1 ELECTRICITY SUPPLY INDUSTRY

GENERAL PROCEDURE AND SOURCE OF INFORMATION

The main estimates are based directly on the annual *Electricity Supply: Return of Engineering and Financial Statistics*. This was published from 1921/2 by the Electricity Commissioners, together with their *Annual Reports*. It is an unusually comprehensive source of reliable information; showing, in particular, both the first cost value of the stock of each type of asset at historical prices at the end of each year, and also the capital expenditure during the year, net of any deductions for assets scrapped or sold. Gross fixed capital formation can thus be obtained from this expenditure plus the first cost value of any assets scrapped or sold.

A useful supplement to this is Garcke's *Manuals of Electricity Supply*, from which information about the industry's pre-1919 accumulation of assets was obtained.

ASSETS INCLUDED

The estimate in Table 7.10 covers all undertakings authorized by Parliament to engage in the business of supplying electricity to the public. The extent of the industry so defined is indicated by the following data extracted from the inter-war Censuses of Production:

Electricity supplied in Great Britain
(million kW-h)

	1924	1930	1935
By electricity supply industry	5,168	9,169	14,641
By other sources	4,173	7,593	9,417
TOTAL SUPPLY	9,341	16,762	24,058

No addition was made for Northern Ireland, where electricity sold by local authorities in 1924 was 44 m. kW-h and in 1935 141 m. kW-h. There is thus an understatement of the sectoral and national totals equal to just under 1% of the first cost value of the stock of assets.

METHODS OF ESTIMATION

Buildings

The first cost value at historical prices of buildings at the end of each year was taken directly from *Electricity Supply*.[1] This shows the cumulative total of expenditure at each date, less the first cost value of assets which have been scrapped, and thus provide exactly the figure that is required.[2]

The *gross fixed capital formation at current (or historical) prices* can be obtained from the annual change in this series plus the estimated first cost value at historical prices of the assets scrapped (or sold) each year. In the case of buildings no evidence of scrapping was found, and the assumption was made that there was no scrapping. The capital formation is thus simply the net increases in capital expenditure shown by the series of first cost values.

Depreciation was calculated on the straight-line method by assuming a length of life equal to the maximum period fixed by the Electricity Commissioners for the repayment of loans. For substantial buildings the period was 30 years.[3] It must be noted that this is an appreciably steeper rate of depreciation than that used in other sectors for similar buildings.[4]

The estimate of the *depreciated value at historical prices* at the end of 1919 was made by first reconstructing the

---

[1] [27] Electricity Commission, *Electricity Supply: Return of Engineering and Financial Statistics relating to Authorised Undertakings in Great Britain*, for the year ended 31 March for Public Authority Undertakings and 31 December for Company Undertakings, annual. The data in the returns for the year ended 31 March were adopted for the preceding calendar year without adjustment.

[2] Until 1931 buildings were shown separately in the *Returns*. For 1932–38 they were combined with land, and the first cost value of buildings was estimated by assuming that it remained the same proportion of land and buildings as in 1931.

[3] [10] *First Annual Report of the Electricity Commissioners* (1921), p. 27.

[4] Cf. chapter 2, p. 17.

TABLE 7.00 ELECTRICITY, GAS AND WATER (£M.)

	1920	1921	1922	1923	1924	1925	1926	1927	1928	1929	1930	1931	1932	1933	1934	1935	1936	1937	1938
(1) *Buildings and Works*																			
A. At historical prices:																			
(d) Depreciation	4	4	5	5	5	5	5	5	6	6	6	6	6	6	7	7	7	7	7
(f) Depreciated value*	183	191	196	200	207	214	222	230	236	243	250	257	261	265	269	276	286	293	303
(h) First cost value*	296	306	314	322	332	342	353	363	373	384	395	406	414	422	430	441	455	466	480
(i) Land*	13	13	13	14	14	15	16	17	18	19	19	20	20	21	21	22	23	24	25
B. At current prices:																			
(c) Gross fixed capital formation	8	12	10	9	12	12	13	13	12	13	13	13	10	10	11	14	17	14	17
(d) Depreciation	14	12	10	9	10	9	10	10	9	10	10	10	9	9	9	10	10	11	11
(e) Net fixed capital formation	−6	0	0	0	2	3	3	3	3	3	3	3	1	1	2	4	7	3	6
(f) Depreciated value*	593	508	401	374	385	386	382	382	376	377	372	369	352	347	348	359	378	404	427
(h) First cost value*	972	845	672	635	657	662	661	666	661	665	662	660	637	632	640	662	698	750	795
(i) Land*	40	33	27	26	27	27	28	28	28	29	29	28	27	27	27	29	31	34	35
C. At 1930 prices:																			
(c) Gross fixed capital formation	5	8	9	8	11	12	12	12	12	13	13	13	11	11	12	15	17	14	16
(d) Depreciation	8	8	8	9	9	9	9	9	9	10	10	9	10	10	10	11	10	10	10
(e) Net fixed capital formation	−3	0	1	−1	2	3	3	3	3	3	3	4	1	1	2	4	7	4	6
(f) Depreciated value*	352	352	353	352	354	357	360	363	366	369	372	376	377	378	380	384	391	395	401
(h) First cost value*	579	585	592	598	606	615	624	633	642	652	662	672	680	688	697	708	721	731	743
(i) Land*	23	24	24	24	24	25	26	26	28	28	29	29	29	30	30	31	32	33	34
(2) *Plant, Vehicles, etc.*																			
A. At historical prices																			
(d) Depreciation	7	8	9	10	12	13	14	16	17	19	21	23	22	24	25	26	28	30	31
(f) Depreciated value*	119	134	143	154	168	184	198	217	233	250	269	289	310	322	334	350	368	384	399
(h) First cost value*	242	262	277	294	316	341	361	391	419	450	484	522	559	590	621	658	697	738	779
B. At current prices:																			
(c) Gross fixed capital formation	16	23	18	21	26	29	28	35	33	36	40	43	43	36	37	42	46	46	46
(d) Depreciation	14	12	11	11	12	14	15	16	18	20	21	21	22	23	24	26	30	34	34
(e) Net fixed capital formation	2	11	7	10	14	15	13	19	15	16	19	22	21	13	13	16	16	12	12
(f) Depreciated value*	317	235	190	193	204	217	227	242	255	282	281	285	298	311	326	352	391	444	447
(h) First cost value*	613	464	381	380	396	416	431	454	478	528	526	531	552	585	619	675	758	877	902

C. At 1930 prices:

(c) Gross fixed capital formation	10	16	14	18	24	27	27	34	32	34	40	48	48	41	42	46	47	42	44
(d) Depreciation	8	8	9	10	11	13	14	16	17	19	21	24	24	26	27	28	30	31	33
(e) Net fixed capital formation	2	8	6	8	13	14	13	18	15	15	19	24	24	15	15	18	17	11	11
(f) Depreciated value*	152	160	166	174	187	201	214	232	247	262	281	305	329	344	359	377	394	405	416
(h) First cost value*	300	314	326	341	362	386	406	435	462	491	526	568	609	644	680	721	761	799	838

(3) All Fixed Assets

A. At historical prices:

(d) Depreciation	11	13	14	15	17	18	19	21	23	25	26	29	28	31	32	33	35	37	38
(f) Depreciated value*	302	324	339	354	375	398	420	447	469	493	519	546	571	587	603	626	654	677	703
(h) First cost value*	538	568	591	616	648	682	714	754	792	834	879	928	972	1012	1051	1099	1152	1204	1259

B. At current prices:

(c) Gross fixed capital formation	24	35	28	30	38	41	41	48	45	49	52	56	53	47	48	56	63	60	64
(d) Depreciation	28	24	20	21	22	23	24	26	27	30	30	30	31	32	33	36	40	45	46
(e) Net fixed capital formation	-4	11	8	9	16	18	17	22	18	19	22	26	22	15	15	20	23	15	18
(f) Depreciated value*	909	743	591	568	588	602	609	624	631	658	653	654	650	658	674	711	770	848	874
(h) First cost value*	1585	1309	1053	1015	1053	1078	1092	1120	1139	1193	1188	1191	1188	1217	1259	1337	1456	1627	1696

C. At 1930 prices:

(c) Gross fixed capital formation	14	24	23	26	35	38	39	46	44	46	52	61	58	52	54	61	65	57	60
(d) Depreciation	15	17	17	18	20	21	23	25	26	28	30	33	34	35	37	39	41	42	43
(e) Net fixed capital formation	-1	7	6	8	15	17	16	21	18	18	22	28	24	17	17	22	24	15	17
(f) Depreciated value*	505	512	518	526	541	558	574	595	613	631	653	681	705	722	739	761	785	800	817
(h) First cost value*	879	899	918	939	968	1000	1030	1068	1105	1144	1188	1240	1289	1332	1377	1429	1483	1531	1582

(4) Stock-in-Trade

*1. Book value**																			
B. At current prices	18	14	12	14	17	17	19	17	17	19	19	19	18	19	21	22	24	28	30
C. At 1930 prices	8	8	10	12	14	15	16	16	17	18	19	20	19	20	23	23	24	25	27
2. Investment in stocks†																			
B. At current prices	—	1	2	2	2	3	1	1	1	1	1	1	-1	1	2	0	1	1	2
C. At 1930 prices	—	1	1	2	3	2	1	1	1	1	1	1	-1	1	3	0	1	1	2

* At end of year. † See chapter 2, appendix 2.2, p. 33.

TABLE 7.10 ELECTRICITY SUPPLY UNDERTAKINGS (£M.)

(1) Buildings and Works

	1920	1921	1922	1923	1924	1925	1926	1927	1928	1929	1930	1931	1932	1933	1934	1935	1936	1937	1938
A. At historical prices:																			
(c) Gross fixed capital formation	1·7	1·7	1·6	1·0	1·9	2·1	3·8	4·0	3·9	4·0	2·9	2·9	1·9	2·1	1·6	3·8	3·9	2·8	4·1
(d) Depreciation	0·5	0·6	0·6	0·6	0·7	0·8	0·9	1·0	1·1	1·2	1·2	1·3	1·9	1·4	1·4	1·5	1·6	1·6	1·7
(f) Depreciated value*	10	12	13	13	14	16	19	22	24	27	29	31	31	32	32	35	37	38	40
(h) First cost value*	16	19	20	21	23	25	29	33	37	41	44	47	49	51	52	56	60	63	67
(i) Land*	2	3	3	3	3	4	4	5	6	6	7	7	7	7	8	8	9	9	10
B. At current prices:																			
(d) Depreciation	1·4	1·2	1·0	1·0	1·1	1·1	1·2	1·3	1·4	1·4	1·4	1·4	1·4	1·4	1·4	1·5	1·7	1·8	1·9
(f) Depreciated value*	26	22	19	18	19	19	22	24	26	28	30	30	30	30	30	35	38	41	44
(h) First cost value*	46	40	34	33	36	37	41	44	47	50	52	54	54	55	56	64	70	77	82
(i) Land*	7	6	5	5	5	5	6	6	7	8	8	8	8	8	8	9	10	11	12
C. At constant (1930) prices:																			
(c) Gross fixed capital formation	1·0	1·9	1·4	0·9	1·7	2·0	3·6	3·8	3·7	4·0	2·9	3·0	2·1	2·3	1·8	4·0	3·8	2·6	3·8
(d) Depreciation	0·8	0·9	0·9	0·9	1·0	1·0	1·1	1·3	1·4	1·4	1·4	1·4	1·5	1·5	1·5	1·6	1·6	1·6	1·7
(f) Depreciated value*	15	16	17	17	17	18	21	23	26	28	30	31	32	33	33	35	38	39	41
(h) First cost value*	27	28	30	31	33	35	38	42	46	50	52	56	58	60	62	66	70	72	76
(i) Land*	4	4	4	4	4	5	6	6	7	8	8	8	8	9	9	10	10	11	11

(2) Plant, Machinery, etc.†

	1920	1921	1922	1923	1924	1925	1926	1927	1928	1929	1930	1931	1932	1933	1934	1935	1936	1937	1938
A. At historical prices:																			
(c) Gross fixed capital formation	12·6	18·5	14·3	17·6	20·9	23·5	23·0	30·1	28·0	31·1	33·8	37·8	38·0	31·1	31·4	35·8	37·9	39·0	38·2
(d) Depreciation	4·1	5·5	6·3	7·6	8·7	10·1	11·2	12·9	14·3	15·8	17·2	19·9	18·8	20·7	21·6	22·8	24·4	26·0	26·9
(f) Depreciated value*	42	55	63	73	85	99	110	128	141	157	173	191	210	220	230	243	257	270	281
(h) First cost value*	105	122	135	149	168	188	205	231	255	283	313	347	380	408	434	467	501	536	572
B. At current prices:																			
(d) Depreciation	5·3	6·2	6·5	6·9	7·6	9·2	10·2	11·8	13·4	15·8	16·0	16·9	17·3	18·3	19·4	21·4	24·6	27·8	28·2
(f) Depreciated value*	59	65	66	68	77	92	103	119	135	157	162	172	184	195	208	229	258	291	296
(h) First cost value*	155	158	152	146	156	180	194	217	243	283	290	306	324	348	378	423	485	561	589
C. At 1930 prices:																			
(c) Gross fixed capital formation	8·1	12·5	10·6	15·1	19·7	21·8	21·8	29·2	27·1	28·6	33·8	40·8	42·6	35·6	35·8	39·4	39·3	36·8	36·7
(d) Depreciation	3·3	4·2	4·8	5·9	7·1	8·6	9·7	11·5	13·0	14·4	16·0	18·0	19·4	20·8	22·0	23·6	25·3	26·7	27·3
(f) Depreciated value*	36	45	50	60	72	86	98	116	130	144	162	184	208	222	236	252	266	277	287
(h) First cost value*	95	106	116	129	147	167	184	210	234	259	290	327	365	397	429	464	500	534	568

(3) All Fixed Assets

	1920	1921	1922	1923	1924	1925	1926	1927	1928	1929	1930	1931	1932	1933	1934	1935	1936	1937	1938
A. At historical prices:																			
(c) Gross fixed capital formation	14·3	21·1	15·9	18·6	22·7	25·6	26·7	34·1	31·8	35·1	36·7	40·8	40·0	33·2	33·0	39·6	41·8	39·0	42·3
(d) Depreciation	4·6	6·0	6·9	8·2	9·4	10·9	12·1	13·9	15·4	17·0	18·5	21·2	20·2	22·1	22·9	24·2	26·0	27·6	28·7
(f) Depreciated value*	52	67	76	86	100	115	129	150	166	184	202	222	241	252	263	278	294	308	322
(h) First cost value*	121	141	155	171	191	214	234	264	292	324	357	394	429	459	487	523	561	599	639
B. At current prices:																			
(d) Depreciation	6·7	7·5	7·4	7·9	8·6	10·3	11·4	13·1	14·8	17·1	17·4	18·2	18·6	19·6	20·7	22·9	26·2	29·6	30·1
(f) Depreciated value*	84	88	84	86	96	112	125	144	161	185	192	202	214	225	238	264	296	333	340
(h) First cost value*	200	199	186	180	192	217	234	261	290	332	342	360	379	403	434	486	555	638	670

C. At 1930 prices:

(c) Gross fixed capital formation

9·1	14·3	12·0	16·0	21·4	23·8	25·4	33·0	30·7	32·6	36·7	43·8	44·7	37·9	37·6	43·3	43·1	40·0	40·5

(d) Depreciation

4·0	5·0	5·7	6·9	8·1	9·6	10·8	12·7	14·4	15·8	17·4	19·4	20·9	22·3	23·5	25·2	27·0	28·3	29·0

(f) Depreciated value*

51	61	67	76	90	104	118	139	155	172	192	216	239	255	270	288	304	316	327

(h) First cost value*

121	135	146	160	179	201	222	252	279	309	342	382	423	457	490	530	569	606	644

(4) Stock-in-Trade (Book value)*

B. At current prices

4	4	4	4	4	5	5	6	7	7	8	8	8	9	10	11	13	13	16

C. At 1930 prices

2	2	3	3	3	4	4	5	6	7	8	8	8	9	11	13	13	16	15

* At end of year.   † Including transmission mains.

NOTES TO TABLE 7.10

Type of equipment	Method	Length of life
(i) Plant and machinery for generation	Reducing balance	20 years
(ii) Plant and machinery for distribution	Reducing balance	20 years
(iii) Main transmission	Reducing balance	40 years
(iv) Mains and services	Reducing balance	25 years
(v) Meters on consumers' premises	Reducing balance	10 years
(vi) Motors	Reducing balance	10 years
(vii) Miscellaneous[1]	Straight line	50 years

(1) Buildings and works

A. At historical prices:

(c) *Gross fixed capital formation*: Annual change in A (h). See p. 87.

(d) *Depreciation*: Straight-line method, assuming a life of 30 years.

(f) *Depreciated value of buildings held at end of year*: For 1919 by cumulating estimates of net fixed capital formation from 1900 to 1919, estimated as described on p. 92.

(g) *First cost value of buildings scrapped*: Assumed to be zero.

(h) *First cost value of buildings held at end of year*: For each year the accumulated total of capital expenditure on buildings recorded in *Electricity Supply*. (From 1932 the combined value of buildings and land is given and was split in the proportion shown in 1931.)

(i) *Land at end of year*: From 1921 to 1931 from *Electricity Supply*. From 1932 see A (h).

B. At current prices:

The series at 1930 prices multiplied by index B.

C. At constant (1930) prices:

(c) *Gross fixed capital formation*: A (c) deflated by index B.

(d) *Depreciation*: As for A (d).

(f) *Depreciated value of buildings held at end of year*: For 1919 by cumulating estimates of net fixed capital formation at 1930 prices from 1900 to 1919 (see p. 92). Deflation by index B.

(h) *First cost value of buildings held at end of year*: For 1919 by cumulating estimates of gross fixed capital formation at 1930 prices from 1900 to 1919 (see p. 92). Deflation by index B.

(i) *Land at end of year*: From C (h) by the ratio of A (i) to A (h).

(2) Plant, Machinery, etc.

This estimate was obtained as the sum of the separate estimates made of each of the types of plant listed under A (d).

A. At historical prices:

(a) *Year's purchases*: Annual change in A (h), plus A (g).

(b) *Proceeds of assets scrapped*: 10% of A (g).

(c) *Gross fixed capital formation*: A (a) minus A (b).

(d) *Depreciation*: The methods used, and the length of life, were:

(f) *Depreciated value of plant etc. held at end of year*: For 1919 by cumulated estimates of net fixed capital formation from 1900 to 1919, estimated as for (1) A (f).

(g) *First cost value of plant, etc. scrapped*: See p. 92.

(h) *First cost value of plant, etc., held at end of year*: For each year the accumulated total of capital expenditure on each type of plant recorded in *Electricity Supply*.

B. At current prices:

The series at 1930 prices multiplied by the following special indices for each type of equipment:[2]

(i) Plant and machinery for generation:
1920–38: Export price of generators.
1900–19: Average cost per unit of capacity. See p. 93.

(ii) Plant and machinery for distribution:
1920–38: Export price of convertors and transformers.
1900–19: Average weekly wage rates in Engineering.

(iii) Main transmission:
1900–38: An unweighted average of indices of: wholesale price of copper, buildings costs (index B), average weekly wage rates in Electrical Installation, and average weekly wage rates in Engineering.

(iv) Mains and services: as for high tension transmission mains.

(v) Meters:
1920–38: export price of electrical meters.
1900–19: average weekly wage rates in Engineering.

(vi) Motors and other apparatus on consumers' premises:
1920–38: export price of electrical motors.
1900–19: average weekly wage rates in Engineering,

(vii) Miscellaneous: 1900–38: unweighted average of indices of: wholesale prices, retail prices, average weekly wage rates of adult workers in all industries, and salaries in the professional services.[3]

C. At constant (1930) prices:

(c) *Gross fixed capital formation*: A (c) for each type of plant deflated by the special indices listed under (2) B.

(d) *Depreciation*: As for A (d).

(f) *Depreciated value of plant, etc. held at end of year*: For 1919 by cumulating estimates of net fixed capital formation at 1930 prices from 1900 to 1919 (see p. 92). Deflation by the special indices listed above under (2) B.

(g) *First cost value of plant, etc. scrapped*: As for A (g).

(h) *First cost value of plant etc. held at end of year*: For 1919 by cumulating estimates of gross fixed capital formation at 1930 prices from 1900 to 1919 (see p. 92). Deflation by the special indices listed above under (2) B.

(4) Stock-in-Trade

B. At current prices:

The depreciated value at current prices of all fixed assets at the end of each year multiplied by the ratios of stocks to all fixed assets in samples of accounts of large companies for each year.

C. At constant prices:

The series at current prices deflated by an unweighted average of indices of the wholesale index for coal, the price of building materials (see index B, p. 24), the wholesale price of copper, and the export prices of transformers, of electrical meters, and of electrical motors.

[1] No association with a specific type of asset could be traced for this item, and it was treated as though it comprised mainly preliminary expenses.

[2] Most of the price data were taken from the [30] *Statistical Abstracts*.

[3] [99] Chapman, p. 203.

first cost value for each year from 1899 to 1919 (see below). Estimates of the gross fixed capital formation and of depreciation, and thus of the net capital formation could then be obtained by the same method as in the inter-war years. The estimated annual net capital formation at historical prices was then cumulated to the end of 1919 to obtain the depreciated value of the stock of buildings.

The reconstruction of the pre-war series of first cost values was inferred from data given by Garcke.[1] A comparison of the composition of the average annual capital expenditure from 1899 to 1903, and of the stock of assets at the end of 1921/2 when the first analysis was made by the Electricity Commissioners, suggested that the structure of the fixed assets used by electricity supply undertakings remained fairly stable over the first two decades of the century.[2] It thus seemed reasonable to extrapolate back to 1900 the *composition* of the first cost value at the end of 1921/2, i.e. the same indicator was used for the extrapolation of each type of asset.

The indicator used was an index of changes in total capital raised by the industry, as recorded in Garcke's *Manual*. This covered both the loans authorized for electricity supply issued by local authorities, and the share and loan capital issued by electricity supply companies. At the beginning of the century, the accumulated capital expenditure obtained by this extrapolation was just over 10% of the level reached at the end of 1921.

The series of *current and constant prices* were obtained by the standard procedures. For details see the notes to Table 7.10, p. 91.

Plant, machinery, etc.

The estimate of plant, etc., shown in Table 7.10 is the sum of seven separately constructed estimates for different types of equipment. Each of these estimates was derived from *Electricity Supply* in the same way as those for buildings, except for the first cost value of plant scrapped or sold which could not be taken as zero. This affects also the annual estimate of the *gross fixed capital formation at current (or historical) prices*. This is equal to the net increase in capital expenditure shown by the series of first cost values, plus the first cost value of the scrapping or sales estimated to have been deducted from the accumulated capital expenditure each year, less the estimated proceeds of the plant scrapped or sold.

The *first cost value at historical prices of the scrapping* assumed to be due was estimated on the basis of the pre-1919 estimates of capital expenditure which, again, were derived in the same way as those for buildings. It

was assumed that the average life of all plant, machinery, mains, etc., was 25 years,[3] so that the total scrapping due over the period 1920–38 was equal to the estimated total capital expenditure on those assets from 1896 to 1913. (The assets acquired in these years, and thus assumed due for scrapping in the inter-war period, represented about 55% of the first cost value at the end of 1921, and about 12% of the first cost value at the end of 1938.)

Part of this total could be allocated to particular years on the basis of evidence of scrapping apparent in the technical information given in *Electricity Supply*. This showed that the capacity of the obsolete reciprocating steam plant declined from 374,000 kW in 1922 to 42,000 kW in 1937. The scrapping of this plant was used as an indicator of the scrapping of complete sets of generating equipment. This accounted for about a fifth of the total scrappings. The remainder was allocated more or less evenly over the years.

In connexion with this scrapping and replacement of plant the following comments made in 1949 by the British Electricity Authority are of interest.[4] They stated that they were satisfied from a scrutiny of the past records that the aggregate provision for depreciation made before vesting day was adequate. (By economic standards this means it was probably excessive.) They also found that: 'An important contribution to this satisfactory condition had arisen from the practice followed by many undertakers of meeting substantial amounts of capital expenditure out of revenue, thus making full provision for depreciation at the time of acquisition of the assets.'

The assumption was also made that the scrap value of the plant scrapped each year was equal to 10% of its first cost value. This amount is, therefore, deducted from the estimate of the year's purchases to obtain the estimate of gross fixed capital formation.

Depreciation was again estimated at rates corresponding to the maximum period fixed by the Electricity Commissioners for the repayment of loans. The rates used are listed in the notes to Table 7.10, p. 91.

Special price indices were constructed for the conversion of the estimates at historical prices to *current and*

[1] [**150**] *Manual of Electricity Supply*, annual.
[2] The percentage composition was:

	Average annual capital expenditure 1899–1903 (%)	First cost value of assets in 1921/2 (%)
Buildings and land	18	15
Plant and machinery	37	41
Mains	35	35
Meters, etc.	10	9

[3] Cf. above, p. 91.
[4] [**54**] British Electricity Authority, *First Report and Accounts* (1949), p. 108.

constant prices. Details are given on p. 91. The deflation of the annual expenditure on generating plant *before 1919* involved an important point of principle. As a result of technological progress and the use of bigger stations, the cost, even in money terms, of a unit of generating capacity was considerably lower in the inter-war period than before 1919. The extent of this unusual and perhaps unique development is shown below:

First cost value at historical prices of generating plant per kW of capacity installed

(£'s per kW)

1907	33·5	1916	25·4	1925	15·8
1910	29·1	1919	18·1	1930	13·8
1913	28·2	1921	17·1	1938	13·2

This sharp fall in costs in the period before 1919 completely outweighed the rise in prices, and in order to convert the pre-1919 inflows of generating plant to 1930 prices it was therefore decided to take as the price index the cost per unit of capacity. The series used was the average first cost value per unit of capacity of *all* generating plant installed up to the end of each year. The cost per unit of *new* plant installed each year could not be accurately measured because the data on capacity showed only the addition of completed units, while the capital expenditure covered also work in progress. In the inter-war years the effects of technological change were less marked relative to the rise in prices and a normal index of prices (the export price of generators) was used.

Stock-in-trade and work in progress

Electricity Supply gives no details of stocks, and a special estimate was made from a sample of accounts of electricity supply companies. For details see the notes to Table 7.10, p. 91.

7.2 GAS SUPPLY UNDERTAKINGS

GENERAL PROCEDURE AND SOURCE OF INFORMATION

The main estimates for the gas supply industry were derived from the *Return Relating to All Authorised Gas Undertakings in Great Britain*,[1] issued annually since 1882.

The estimate of the first cost value at historical prices of all assets (including stocks) was based on figures for the end of 1937 of the paid-up share and loan capital of companies, and of the total money borrowed by local authority undertakings.

The gross capital formation in all assets was estimated as the sum of (*a*) net additions, and (*b*) replacements of assets scrapped. The estimate of the former was derived from data on the increase in the paid-up capital of all companies and the expenditure out of loans by the local authority undertakings, adjusted in relation to the annual increase in the mileage of gas mains so as to allow for the discrepancies in timing between the capital raised and actual expenditure. The estimate of the expenditure on replacements was made separately for each type of asset by estimating the replacements due (and assumed to be made) at the end of the useful life of the assets as indicated by their approximate date of construction.

The first cost value and the net additions were allocated by type of asset, and the standard estimates then completed for each type of asset.

ASSETS INCLUDED

The estimates in Table 7.20 cover all assets owned by statutory gas supply undertakings in Great Britain. There are two minor omissions from the sector and national totals: non-statutory undertakings, which were responsible for 2·5% of total sales in 1947,[2] are not included; and no addition was made for Northern Ireland.

Coke ovens owned by collieries, steelworks and railways are not included in the gas industry but in the trade groups by which they are owned. There is a minor duplication of the estimates covering the ships owned by the gas industry, as they are included both in the present chapter and also in chapter 9 in the comprehensive estimate of all ships (see 9.3, p. 170). The value of ships (including barges, which are not covered by chapter 9) as shown in the 1949 Accounts of the Gas Council was £1·2 m.[3]

METHODS OF ESTIMATION

The primary point which must be considered is the use of financial data for the estimates of the first cost value and the annual capital expenditure.

(i) *Statutory companies*. The companies raised some two-thirds of their capital by the issue of shares, and the remainder by the issue of loans, usually with provision for redemption after a lengthy period. As the *First Report* of the Gas Council makes plain: 'Before vesting date there was no common practice in the accounting treatment of fixed assets in the accounts of gas companies. Most companies operated wholly or partially

---

[1] [28] Board of Trade, *Return Relating to All Authorised Gas Undertakings in Great Britain*: part II, Finance and Prices. Annual since 1920. Previously issued as a Return to the House of Commons.

[2] [75] The Gas Council, *First Report and Accounts, July 1948–March 1950* (London, 1951), p. 15.

[3] *Ibid.* pp. 142–3.

TABLE 7.20 GAS SUPPLY UNDERTAKINGS (£M.)

(1) *Buildings and Works*

	1920	1921	1922	1923	1924	1925	1926	1927	1928	1929	1930	1931	1932	1933	1934	1935	1936	1937	1938
1. *Buildings*																			
A. At historical prices:																			
(c) Gross fixed capital formation	0·5	0·7	0·5	0·5	0·6	0·8	0·8	0·8	0·8	0·9	0·9	0·9	0·8	1·0	1·1	1·1	1·5	1·1	1·2
(d) Depreciation	0·2	0·2	0·3	0·3	0·3	0·3	0·3	0·3	0·3	0·3	0·3	0·3	0·3	0·4	0·4	0·4	0·4	0·4	0·4
(f) Depreciated value*	9	10	10	10	10	11	11	12	12	13	14	14	15	15	16	17	18	18	19
(h) First cost value*	15	16	16	16	16	17	18	18	18	19	20	20	21	21	22	23	24	24	25
(i) Land*	3	3	3	3	3	3	4	4	4	4	4	4	4	4	4	4	5	5	5
B. At current prices:																			
(d) Depreciation	0·8	0·7	0·5	0·5	0·5	0·5	0·5	0·5	0·5	0·5	0·5	0·5	0·5	0·5	0·5	0·5	0·6	0·6	0·6
(f) Depreciated value*	30	24	19	18	19	19	19	19	19	19	19	19	18	18	19	20	21	23	24
(h) First cost value*	50	42	34	32	34	35	34	34	33	34	34	33	32	32	33	34	36	39	41
(i) Land*	10	8	7	6	7	7	7	7	6	7	7	7	6	6	6	7	7	8	8
C. At constant (1930) prices:																			
(c) Gross fixed capital formation	0·3	0·5	0·5	0·5	0·6	0·8	0·8	0·8	0·8	0·9	0·9	0·9	0·8	1·1	1·2	1·2	1·5	1·1	1·2
(d) Depreciation	0·5	0·5	0·5	0·5	0·5	0·5	0·5	0·5	0·5	0·5	0·5	0·5	0·6	0·6	0·6	0·6	0·6	0·6	0·6
(f) Depreciated value*	17	17	17	17	17	18	18	18	18	19	19	20	20	20	21	22	22	23	24
(h) First cost value*	29	30	30	30	31	31	32	32	33	33	34	34	35	36	36	37	38	39	40
(i) Land*	6	6	6	6	6	6	6	6	6	7	7	7	7	7	7	7	8	8	8
2. *Mains*																			
A. At historical prices:																			
(c) Gross fixed capital formation	1·7	2·2	1·7	1·4	2·0	2·5	2·7	2·7	2·6	2·6	3·1	2·8	2·3	2·9	3·5	3·7	4·8	3·3	4·1
(d) Depreciation	0·8	0·8	0·8	0·8	0·8	0·9	0·9	0·9	0·9	1·0	1·0	1·0	1·0	1·1	1·1	1·1	1·2	1·2	1·3
(f) Depreciated value*	27	28	29	30	31	33	35	36	38	40	42	44	45	47	49	52	55	57	60
(h) First cost value*	45	47	48	48	50	51	53	54	56	58	60	61	63	64	66	69	72	74	76
B. At current prices:																			
(d) Depreciation	2·5	2·2	1·7	1·6	1·7	1·7	1·7	1·7	1·7	1·7	1·7	1·7	1·7	1·7	1·7	1·8	1·9	2·0	2·2
(f) Depreciated value*	87	76	59	55	56	57	57	57	57	58	58	58	56	56	58	61	66	71	77
(h) First cost value*	149	132	104	98	100	101	101	103	103	103	103	104	100	100	102	105	112	121	130
C. At constant (1930) prices:																			
(c) Gross fixed capital formation	1·0	1·5	1·5	1·3	1·8	2·3	2·5	2·5	2·6	2·6	3·1	2·8	2·5	3·1	3·8	4·0	5·0	3·3	3·8
(d) Depreciation	1·5	1·5	1·5	1·5	1·6	1·6	1·6	1·6	1·7	1·7	1·7	1·7	1·8	1·8	1·8	1·9	1·9	2·0	2·0
(f) Depreciated value*	52	52	52	52	52	53	54	55	56	56	58	59	60	61	63	65	68	70	71
(h) First cost value*	90	91	92	92	93	95	96	98	99	101	103	105	106	108	110	113	116	118	120

(2) Plant, Vehicles, Ships, etc.

A. At historical prices:

Row	Values
(c) Gross fixed capital formation	2·3 3·0 2·4 2·1 3·0 3·6 3·7 3·8 3·7 3·9 4·6 4·1 3·4 4·2 4·8 5·2 6·8 4·8 6·0
(d) Depreciation	1·7 1·8 1·8 1·8 1·9 1·9 2·0 2·1 2·1 2·2 2·2 2·3 2·4 2·4 2·5 2·6 2·7 2·8 2·9
(f) Depreciated value*	36 37 38 38 39 41 42 44 46 48 50 52 53 54 57 59 64 66 69
(h) First cost value*	73 75 76 78 80 82 85 87 90 92 95 98 100 103 107 110 115 118 122

B. At current prices:

Row	Values
(c) Gross fixed capital formation	5·8 3·8 2·9 3·0 2·7 3·0 3·0 3·1 3·0 3·2 3·1 3·0 3·0 3·1 3·3 3·3 3·7 4·3 4·3
(d) Depreciation	
(f) Depreciated value*	122 80 59 58 59 58 58 58 56 60 58 55 56 58 63 60 70 80 80
(h) First cost value*	244 163 125 129 128 127 128 129 130 135 128 125 127 133 144 136 157 182 182

C. At constant (1930) prices:

Row	Values
(c) Gross fixed capital formation	1·0 2·1 2·2 1·9 2·7 3·3 3·4 3·6 3·7 3·7 4·6 4·4 3·7 4·4 5·0 5·3 6·5 4·1 5·2
(d) Depreciation	2·6 2·6 2·7 2·7 2·7 2·8 2·8 2·9 3·0 3·2 3·1 3·3 3·2 3·3 3·4 3·4 3·5 3·6 3·7
(f) Depreciated value*	55 54 54 53 54 54 55 56 58 60 58 59 60 61 62 64 67 68 69
(h) First cost value*	110 112 114 116 118 120 122 125 127 130 130 134 136 139 142 146 150 153 157

(3) All Fixed Assets

A. At historical prices:

Row	Values
(c) Gross fixed capital formation	4·5 5·9 4·6 4·0 5·6 6·9 7·2 7·3 7·1 7·4 8·6 7·8 6·5 8·1 9·4 10·1 13·1 9·2 11·3
(d) Depreciation	2·7 2·8 2·9 2·9 3·0 3·1 3·2 3·3 3·3 3·5 3·5 3·6 3·7 3·9 4·0 4·1 4·3 4·4 4·6
(f) Depreciated value*	72 75 77 78 81 84 88 92 96 100 105 110 112 116 122 128 137 141 148
(h) First cost value*	133 137 140 142 146 150 155 160 164 169 174 180 184 189 195 202 210 216 223

B. At current prices:

Row	Values
(c) Gross fixed capital formation	9·1 6·7 5·1 5·1 5·1 5·2 5·2 5·2 5·3 5·4 5·3 5·2 5·2 5·3 5·5 5·6 6·2 6·9 7·1
(d) Depreciation	
(f) Depreciated value*	239 180 137 132 134 134 134 133 135 136 133 132 130 133 137 144 157 175 181
(h) First cost value*	444 337 260 255 263 264 266 264 267 272 259 261 264 265 271 283 305 342 352

C. At constant (1930) prices:

Row	Values
(c) Gross fixed capital formation	2·3 4·1 4·2 3·7 5·1 6·4 6·7 6·9 7·0 7·2 8·6 8·1 7·0 8·6 9·4 10·5 13·0 8·5 10·2
(d) Depreciation	4·6 4·6 4·7 4·7 4·8 4·9 4·9 5·0 5·1 5·2 5·3 5·4 5·6 5·7 5·8 5·9 6·0 6·2 6·3
(f) Depreciated value*	124 124 123 122 124 124 126 128 130 132 135 135 138 139 142 146 151 158 164
(h) First cost value*	229 231 234 236 240 244 248 252 257 262 267 267 272 277 283 289 296 304 310 316

(4) Stock-in-Trade (Book value)*

Row	Values
B. At current prices	11 8 7 9 11 10 12 10 11 10 10 10 11 10 12 12 13 13 13
C. At 1930 prices	5 5 6 8 10 9 10 10 10 10 11 10 11 12 12 12 11 13 13

* At end of year.

For Notes to Table see p. 96

NOTES TO TABLE 7.20

The estimates of the annual net additions of fixed assets, and of the first cost value at historical prices of the stock of assets at the end of 1937, were first made for all assets and then allocated by type of asset. (See p. 97). The allocation (including a provisional allowance for stock-in-trade) was based on the composition of the assets vested in the Gas Council at 1 May 1949.[1] The allocation of the fixed assets is shown in column (1) below.

All the subsequent estimates for the fixed assets were made separately for each of the 5 types of asset. The same methods were used in each case except for (a) the assumed length of life of the asset, and (b) the index used for conversion from current to 1930 prices. These details are shown in columns (2) and (3) below:

Type of Asset	(1) Allocation of All Fixed Assets* %	(2) Assumed Length of Life Years	(3) Price Index Used
1. *Buildings (including land)*			
Offices	1·5	100	Index B
Other buildings	9·6	60	Index B
Land	2·2	—	—
2. *Civil Engineering Work*			
Mains and services	33·3	60	Index A
3. *Plant, vehicles, ships, etc.*			
Gas holders	8·9	60	Index C
Other plant, etc.	44·5	40	Index C

* For the estimates of gross fixed capital formation land was excluded and the other percentages adjusted proportionately.

(1), (2) and (3) The estimates for each type of fixed asset were made by the following methods:

A. At historical prices:

(c) *Gross fixed capital formation*: 1. *Net Additions*: Share of the adjusted increments in capital issued and money borrowed. See above p. 97.

2. *Replacements*: Assumed equal to A (g). See p. 98.

(d) *Depreciation*: Straight line method, assuming a length of life as listed above.

(f) *Depreciated value of assets held at end of year*: For 1919 derived from A (h) by imputing the age-structure derived from the length of gas mains constructed since 1882 and assuming for 1882 a depreciated value equal to one-half of the first cost value. (See chapter 2, p. 16). The accumulated depreciation deduced was estimated on the basis of the lengths of life assumed for each type of asset as listed above.

(g) *First cost value of assets scrapped*: C (g) multiplied by the appropriate price index as listed above.

(h) *First cost value of assets held at end-of-year*: For 1937 from the share of each type of fixed asset (see above) in the paid-up share and loan capital of companies plus the money borrowed by local authority undertakings, less the estimated stock-in-trade. See p. 98.

(i) *Land at end of year*: 2·2% of the total capital.

B. At current prices:

(c): A (c).

(g): A (g).

(d), (f) and (h): The series at 1930 prices multiplied by the appropriate index as listed above.

(i) From B (h) by the ratio of A (i) to A (h).

C. At constant (1930) prices:

(c) *Gross fixed capital formation*: A (c) deflated by the appropriate index as listed above.

(d) *Depreciation*: As for A (d).

(f) *Depreciated value of assets held at end of year*: For 1919 derived from A (f) by the standard estimate relating average historical costs to the costs at 1930 prices: i.e. for costs of building (index B) 50·8%; for costs of other construction (index A) 49·7%; and for costs of machinery (index C) 65·3%. (See chapter 2, p. 24).

(g) *First cost value of assets scrapped*: The total assumed due for scrapping over the 19 years taken as a proportion of C (h) for 1919. For the proportion, based on the imputed age-structure and varying with the assumed life of the asset, see p. 98. The total then spread in proportion to C (c) 1.

(h) *First cost value of assets held at end of year*: For 1919 derived from A (h) by the same standard estimates as for C (f).

(i) *Land at end of year*: From C (h) by the ratio of A (i) to A (h).

(4) *Stock-in-Trade*

B. At current prices:

The annual ratio of stocks to fixed assets in the accounts of a sample of statutory gas companies applied to the corresponding first cost value of all fixed assets.

C. At constant (1930) prices:

The series at current prices deflated by an unweighted average of index A, index C and the index of the wholesale price of coal.

[1] [75] *First Report and Accounts*, pp. 142-3.

on a renewals basis. . . . Some companies adopted depreciation accounting for assets with relatively short lives; others dealt with all assets on a renewals basis. It was rare for large companies to operate wholly on a depreciation basis.'[1]

Where the renewals system was used, some companies carried annual appropriations to the fund and charged actual renewals against this. Others were content to charge renewals expenditure to revenue in the year in which it was incurred. At times of heavy renewal programmes this latter practice was not always possible and the expenditure was often taken to a suspense account and spread over a period of years.[2] Accounting treatment was also influenced by the statutory limits imposed on prices and dividends.

In principle, therefore, the purchase of new assets (and major improvements) would be financed by the issue of share or loan capital, while replacements would be charged to revenue. The total share and loan capital issued would thus represent the stock of assets valued at the prices at which the first of the component items was acquired, i.e. at the 'original, historical' cost, not the historical cost of the assets actually in use at any particular date.

In practice the estimate we obtain from the total share and loan capital issued by the companies will only be an approximate representation of the stock as defined above. It will, for example, be too low to the extent that new assets and major improvements or, more commonly, replacements by improved types of asset (betterment), were charged to revenue; and also because the series for loan capital issued is net of any loans repaid. On the other hand, it will be too high if renewals were charged either wholly or in part to capital account, or if newly raised capital was used for the purchase of shares in other companies.

The most significant of these factors was probably the practice of charging to revenue as replacement what were, in effect, additional or improved assets. On balance, therefore, the paid-up capital is likely to underestimate the first cost value at historical prices of the stock of assets; and the increments in the paid-up capital will similarly underestimate the annual capital expenditure on net additions.

(ii) *Local authority undertakings*. Local authority undertakings raised almost all their capital by loans which were required to be repaid over periods intended to approximate to the estimated useful lives of the assets concerned. In fact, the periods prescribed were generally conservative.[3] In addition, capital expenditure of a minor nature was often met direct from revenue. The sinking funds required to repay the loans issued generally proved an effective means of providing

for depreciation and also obsolescence. Both new assets and replacements would thus be financed by borrowing, and, in principle, the use of the figure for the total money borrowed (including loans since repaid) to represent the first cost value at historical prices of the stock of assets, leads to considerable overstatement. This will be only partially offset by the capital expenditure charged direct to revenue.

The local authority undertakings accounted for only about one-third of the total supply of gas and thus of the total assets, but it is not possible to determine how far the probable overstatement in the estimate for these undertakings is offset by the probable understatement for the companies.

The estimated gross fixed capital formation by the local authority undertakings is based on the expenditure out of loans and will thus also include an element of expenditure on replacements.

With these reservations in mind, we can now describe more fully the actual methods used. The *gross fixed capital formation* in all assets *at current (or historical) prices* is the sum of two separate estimates: new construction for additions and extensions to the stock of assets: and replacement of assets scrapped.

The estimate of net additions was made separately for the two types of undertaking. The method used involved the re-allocation of the annual increase in the paid-up share and loan capital of the companies, or the expenditure out of loans of the local authority undertakings, in proportion to the length of gas mains added each year. This method was adopted in order to eliminate as far as possible the discrepancies in timing between the financial series of long-term capital raised and the actual capital expenditure. The first step was to allow for price changes by multiplying the annual increase in the length of gas mains from 1921 to 1937[4] by the index of the costs of civil engineering construction (index A, p. 24).

The average cost per adjusted mile of main was then obtained by dividing the overall increase in the paid-up capital from 1921 to 1937 by the total of the 17 adjusted increments in the length of mains. This average cost was then used to value each adjusted annual increase in the length of mains. The resulting annual total of all assets acquired for extensions was then allocated by type of asset. This allocation was essentially based on

---

[1] *Ibid.* pp. 59–60.
[2] For further discussion of the problems associated with the renewals system of accounting see chapter 1, appendix 1.1, p. 7.
[3] [75] *First Report*, p. 60.
[4] The data necessary for the full calculation were not available for 1920 and 1938.

7

the proportions shown for the stock of fixed assets vested in the Gas Council at 1 May 1949.[1]

The second component which has to be estimated is the acquisition of assets for replacements. This was derived separately for each type of asset on the assumption that all assets were scrapped at the end of their assumed lives and immediately replaced. This scrapping was first estimated in constant prices. The total first cost value of the assets due to be scrapped (and replaced) over the period 1920–38 was estimated by using the available data on the changes in the length of gas mains constructed as an indication of the age-structure of each type of asset. For example, for the plant, etc., with an assumed useful life of 40 years the proportion of the end-1919 stock due to be scrapped in 1920–38 is assumed equal to the plant purchased 40 years earlier, i.e. in 1880–98.[2] This in turn is assumed to be the same fraction of the end-1919 first cost value at 1930 prices as the increase in mileage of mains from 1880 to 1898 is of the total length of mains at the end of 1919. A similar method was used for assets with a life of 60 years.[3] It was assumed that for assets with a life of 100 years there was no scrapping in the period 1920–38.

The total scrapping (and replacements) estimated in this way were then spread over the period 1920–38 in proportion to the annual expenditure at constant prices on purchases for additions. Finally, the annual estimates at 1930 prices were converted to current prices by deflating by the appropriate price indices for each asset.

One implication of the use of the renewals system when prices are changing should be noted. So far as it was followed consistently so that all expenditure on replacements was charged to revenue, the accumulated total capital expenditure will always relate to the items first acquired even though the renewals done at later prices would, in time, physically constitute the greater part of the capital stock. Since the new items added to the present estimates of the capital stock (as the replacement component of the year's gross fixed capital formation) must be measured at current prices, it follows, logically, therefore, that for these series the items scrapped must be measured at the same price level if the capital stock is to remain unchanged. The first cost value of the scrapping *at historical prices* has thus to be taken as equal to the *current* cost of the replacements.[4]

The *first cost value at historical prices* of the stock of all assets at the end of 1937 was taken as equal to the paid-up share and loan capital at that date of the statutory companies, plus the gross amount borrowed by the local authority undertakings:[5]

	£m.
Company undertakings:	
Paid-up capital—Shares and stock	102·493
Loans (including Debenture stock) issued	46·694
Local authority undertakings:	
Money borrowed (including loans since repaid)	83·960
	233·147

The proportion of this total required for financing stock-in-trade was provisionally estimated at 5·2%,[6] and the balance of £221·0m. was then allocated between the fixed assets (including land) on the basis of the composition of the stock of assets vested in the Gas Council at 1 May 1949. The actual proportions are given on p. 96.

Details of all remaining estimates are given in the Notes to Table 7.20, p. 96.

7.3 WATER SUPPLY UNDERTAKINGS

GENERAL PROCEDURE AND SOURCE OF INFORMATION

The main sources of information were data on the local authority capital expenditure out of loans each year for water supply, and on the total of local authority loans outstanding issued for this service.[7] The expenditure figures were expanded to cover the statutory water supply companies and the total was taken as equal to the gross fixed capital formation. The total of loans outstanding in 1919 and 1938 was expanded to cover the companies and taken as corresponding to the depreciated value of the stock of all assets at historical prices.

These two estimates were then allocated by type of asset on the basis of the detailed information in the inter-war accounts of the Metropolitan Water Board.[8]

---

[1] [75] *First Report*, pp. 142–3. For further details see also p. 96.

[2] Cf. chapter 2, p. 16.

[3] The first date for which figures of the mileage of mains laid are available is 1882, and it was assumed that the mileage laid in 1860–78 was one-half of the length in 1882.

[4] The alternative would be to value the current cost of replacements at the historical prices of the asset first acquired, and this clearly seems less satisfactory.

[5] [28] Board of Trade, *Return Relating to All Authorised Gas Undertakings in Great Britain*.

[6] This proportion was based on the composition of the assets vested in the Gas Council at 1 May 1949. The resulting provisional estimate of £12.1m. differs slightly from the final estimate of £13.1m. obtained by applying the annual ratio of stocks to fixed assets in the accounts of a sample of statutory gas companies to the corresponding estimate of the first cost value of all fixed assets.

[7] [19] Ministry of Health, *Local Government Financial Statistics* (before 1934 [5, 6, 7] *Local Taxation Returns*), annual; and [30] *Statistical Abstracts*. Data for the financial year were taken for the preceding calendar year without adjustment.

[8] [68] Metropolitan Water Board, *Abstract of Accounts*, annual. The item in the accounts for 'reservoirs, wells, filters and filtration plant' was divided equally between the three main types of assets used in the present classification: buildings, mains and plant.

TABLE 7.30 WATER SUPPLY UNDERTAKINGS (£M.)

(3) All Fixed Assets*

	1920	1921	1922	1923	1924	1925	1926	1927	1928	1929	1930	1931	1932	1933	1934	1935	1936	1937	1938
A. At historical prices:																			
(c) Gross fixed capital formation	5·6	7·8	7·7	7·2	9·2	8·8	7·1	6·6	6·2	6·9	7·0	8·0	6·1	5·3	5·6	6·6	8·4	8·9	10·0
(d) Depreciation	3·5	3·7	3·8	3·8	4·0	4·0	4·1	4·2	4·3	4·3	4·3	4·4	4·5	4·6	4·7	4·7	4·8	4·9	4·9
(f) Depreciated value†	178	182	186	189	194	199	202	205	206	209	212	215	217	218	219	220	224	228	233
(h) First cost value†	283	290	297	303	311	318	325	330	336	342	347	354	359	364	368	374	381	389	397
(i) Land	7	7	7	8	8	8	8	8	8	9	9	9	9	9	9	9	9	10	10
B. At current prices:																			
(d) Depreciation	12·1	9·9	7·7	7·4	7·5	7·5	7·6	7·5	7·4	7·5	7·3	7·2	7·0	6·8	7·0	7·3	7·6	8·2	8·5
(f) Depreciated value†	586	475	369	350	359	357	350	346	337	336	327	319	306	301	299	303	316	341	352
(h) First cost value†	941	773	607	580	598	599	594	594	585	589	578	570	551	549	554	567	595	647	674
(i) Land	23	19	15	14	15	15	15	15	14	14	14	13	13	13	13	14	14	14	15
C. At 1930 prices:																			
(c) Gross fixed capital formation	3·1	5·4	6·8	6·8	8·4	8·2	6·7	6·2	6·1	6·7	7·0	8·2	6·5	5·7	6·0	7·0	8·6	8·5	9·2
(d) Depreciation	6·8	6·8	6·9	6·9	6·9	6·9	7·2	7·2	7·2	7·3	7·3	7·3	7·4	7·5	7·6	7·7	7·7	7·8	7·8
(f) Depreciated value†	329	328	327	327	329	330	330	329	328	327	327	328	327	325	323	323	324	324	326
(h) First cost value†	529	533	538	543	549	555	560	564	568	573	578	584	589	593	598	602	609	615	621
(i) Land	13	13	14	14	14	14	14	14	14	14	14	14	14	14	14	14	14	14	15

(4) Stock-in-Trade (Book value)†

	1920	1921	1922	1923	1924	1925	1926	1927	1928	1929	1930	1931	1932	1933	1934	1935	1936	1937	1938
B. At current prices	3	2	1	1	2	2	2	1	1	1	1	1	1	1	1	1	1	1	1
C. At 1930 prices	1	1	1	1	1	1	1	1	1	1	1	1	1	1	1	1	1	1	1

* Only the total is published for this sub-sector. It is the sum of the separate estimates for (1) Buildings and Mains and (2) Plant, vehicles, etc.
† At end of year.

NOTES TO TABLE 7.30

(1), (2) and (3) Separate estimates for each type of asset were obtained as follows:

A. At historical prices:

(c) *Gross fixed capital formation*: Expenditure out of loans for capital works by local authorities grossed up to cover statutory companies (see p. 100) and allocated by type of asset as follows: Buildings 16·7%, Mains 60·8% and Plant, etc. 22·5%.

(d) *Depreciation*: Straight line method, assuming a life of 100 years for buildings and 75 years for mains and plant.

(f) *Depreciated value of assets held at end of year*: For 1938 the loans outstanding of local authorities plus an estimate of the assets of statutory companies derived from a sample of accounts (see p. 100). Allocation by type of asset:

Land	4·0%
Buildings	21·9%
Mains	53·2%
Plant, etc.	20·2%
Stocks	0·7%

For 1919 the local authority loans outstanding expanded to cover statutory companies in the proportions estimated for 1938.

(g) *First cost value of assets scrapped*: For mains and plant purchases in 1845–63 taken as $\frac{19}{75}$ of the first cost value in 1878 (derived by means of the special indicator of age-structure, see p. 100), and spread in proportion to gross capital formation at 1930 prices. Scrapping of buildings assumed negligible.

(h) *First cost value of assets held at end of year*: For 1919 derived separately for each type of asset from the corresponding A (f) by imputing an appropriate age-structure. See p. 100.

(i) *Land at end of year*: 18·25% of the depreciated value of buildings as given for 1938 in (i) A (f).

B. At current prices:

The series at 1930 prices multiplied by index B for buildings, index A for mains and index C for plant.

C. At constant (1930) prices:

(c) *Gross fixed capital formation*: A (c) deflated by index B for buildings, index A for mains and index C for plant.

(d) *Depreciation*: As for A (c).

(f) *Depreciated value of assets held at end of year*: For 1919 derived from A (f) by the standard estimate relating average historical

costs to the costs at 1930 prices, i.e. for costs of building (index B) 50·8%, for costs of construction (index A) 49·7%, and for costs of machinery (index C) 65·3%. (See chapter 2, p. 24).

(g) *First cost value of assets scrapped*: As for A (g).

(h) *First cost value of assets held at end of year*: For 1919 derived from A (h) by the same standard estimates as for C (f).

(i) *Land at end of year*: 18·25% of C (f).

(4) Stock-in-Trade

B. At current prices:

$$\text{The ratio: } \frac{\text{Stocks of coal plus stores on hand}}{\text{total revenue}}$$

found in the accounts of the Metropolitan Water Board applied to the annual revenue of local authority water supply undertakings raised to a total for the United Kingdom proportionately to gross supply.

C. At 1930 prices:

The series at current prices deflated by an unweighted average of index A, index C and the wholesale index of coal prices.

The standard estimates were then completed for each type of asset.

ASSETS INCLUDED

The estimate covers the assets of all undertakings in the United Kingdom engaged in supplying water to the public. A stable four-fifths of the total supply was provided by local authorities (including water boards), the remainder by statutory companies.

METHODS OF ESTIMATION

The *gross capital formation* in all fixed assets *at current (or historical) prices* was estimated by taking the local authorities' expenditure out of loans for capital works for the supply of water, and expanding this (by approximately 26%) to cover the statutory companies. The weights were based on the relative quantities of water supplied.[1] This total was then allocated by type of asset in the proportions shown by the average composition of new assets purchased by the Metropolitan Water Board over the period 1920–38.

The *depreciated value at historical prices* of all assets (including stocks) at the end of 1938 was taken as the sum of the outstanding loan debt for water supply of local authorities at that date (including an allowance for Northern Ireland), plus the estimated depreciated value of the assets of statutory water companies. This latter was obtained by grossing-up a sample of company accounts for 1938 by the ratio of the gross production in 1935 of all water companies to the gross production of the companies in the sample.[2]

This total depreciated value was then allocated by type of asset in the proportions shown by the accumu-lated capital expenditure by the Metropolitan Water Board up to 1938.

The depreciated value at historical prices of all assets at the end of 1919 was obtained by assuming that the proportionate increase from 1919 to 1938 was the same as that for its main constituent: the outstanding loan debt of local authorities in Great Britain. Allocation by type of asset was again based on the corresponding data for the Metropolitan Water Board.

The end-1919 *first cost value at historical prices* for each asset, and the *depreciation* written off were then obtained by reconciling the above estimates in a consistent framework: thus, for each asset the depreciation over the period 1920–38 must equal gross fixed capital formation over the period less the increase in the depreciated value between end-1919 and end-1938.

The *first cost value of the mains and plant scrapped* was derived by using the series of Schedule D, Income Tax, gross assessments on the profits of waterworks in the United Kingdom[3] as an indication of the age-structure of the stock of assets. It was assumed that purchases in 1845–63 were $\frac{19}{75}$ of the 1878 first cost value; and this in turn was obtained on the assumption that it was the same proportion of the end-1919 value as the assessment in 1878/9 was of the assessment in 1913/14. (Cf. chapter 2, p. 16.)

For further details of the estimates see the Notes in Table 7.30, p. 99.

---

[1] [**34, 35, 36**] *Final Report* on the Census of Production, 1924, 1930 and 1935.

[2] An alternative estimate made by grossing up the local authority loans outstanding proportionately to gross production gives almost the same result for the depreciated value of company assets at the end of 1938: £50·6m., compared with the estimate of £52·6m. derived from the sample.

[3] [**25**] *Report of H.M. Commissioners of Inland Revenue*, annual.

CHAPTER 8

MANUFACTURING

8.12–8.54 TWENTY-ONE TRADE GROUPS

GENERAL PROCEDURE AND SOURCE OF INFORMATION

Capital formation in the manufacturing sector has been separately estimated for twenty-two trades or groups of trades. For all except one of these (cotton) the estimates are based on a sample of company accounts, and on Inland Revenue data on wear and tear allowances and rates of depreciation. The methods used to make estimates in this way are described at length in chapter 2, p. 27.

The individual details for each trade group are set out in tabular form in a Supplement to the Notes for Tables 8.12–8.54 (pp. 138–42). Cotton is dealt with separately below (see 8.11, p. 144). The tabular supplement shows for each trade group the proportion of the group covered by the accounts in the sample measured in terms of the depreciated value of all fixed assets. For manufacturing industry as a whole the samples of accounts covered 37·7% of the estimated total depreciated value in 1927, 43·3% in 1932 and 44·2% in 1937.

Two summary tables are given: Table 8.00 shows the complete set of standard estimates for the manufacturing sector as a whole, i.e., the aggregate for the 22 trade groups; and in Table 8.01 total gross fixed capital formation at 1930 prices is shown for each separate trade group.

Tables 8.10, 8.20, 8.30, 8.40 and 8.50 show the complete set of standard estimates for the five wider industrial groupings into which the twenty-two trade groups have been combined. Finally, the remaining twenty-two tables (8.11 to 8.54) show for each separate trade group the estimates for all fixed assets and for stock-in-trade and work in progress.

It may be desirable to stress again a point in connexion with estimates derived from company accounts.[1] The accounts yield direct estimates of net fixed capital formation, based implicitly on the undisclosed amount of depreciation actually written off by the company. Gross capital formation has then to be estimated by adding back the *assumed* depreciation, which may be very different. In trades where the depreciation added back is large relative to the net capital formation, the

possible errors in the estimates of gross capital formation on this account may be proportionately very large.[2]

ASSETS INCLUDED

Three important points should be noted with regard to the general coverage of the estimates.

(i) The use of company accounts leads to estimates of assets owned by all business units classified by the Inland Revenue to a particular trade group.[3] Units were classified to manufacturing if their primary activity was in this sector. As an estimate of assets owned for manufacturing, therefore, the present estimate is, on the one hand, overstated by the inclusion of assets owned by these units for the purpose of non-manufacturing activities; and, on the other hand, understated by the exclusion of the assets owned for the purpose of manufacturing activities by units which were classified by their primary activity to some other sector.

The most serious errors on this account arise in the case of those manufacturing trades such as clothing and footwear, where it is fairly common for firms to engage in both manufacturing and distribution. It is believed that in the inter-war period the usual practice was to classify such firms to retail distribution rather than to manufacturing, and to manufacturing rather than to wholesale distribution. On balance, therefore, the result is probably that manufacturing is understated and retail distribution overstated.[4]

(ii) The estimates will also understate the value of the assets owned for manufacturing by each trade group to the extent that assets (particularly buildings) were hired from other trade groups or from property companies; and will overstate the value to the extent that non-manufacturing assets were let to outside firms. Investigations made by the Statistical Division of the

---

[1] See also chapter 2, p. 29.
[2] The total effect of any such errors can, to a limited extent, be evaluated on the basis of the overall comparison of national totals measured from the supply and the ownership side. See chapter 13, pp. 230–7, especially p. 237.
[3] For details of the coverage of each Inland Revenue trade group in terms of the 1948 Standard Industrial Classification see chapter 13, Table 13.20, p. 224.
[4] For further discussion of this point see chapter 13, pp. 221 and 227–8.

TABLE 8.00 MANUFACTURING (£M.)

(1) Buildings and Works

	1920	1921	1922	1923	1924	1925	1926	1927	1928	1929	1930	1931	1932	1933	1934	1935	1936	1937	1938
A. At historical prices:																			
(d) Depreciation	11	11	12	12	12	13	13	14	14	14	15	15	15	15	15	15	16	17	17
(f) Depreciated value*	463	493	506	513	524	542	554	561	567	579	589	587	584	584	584	586	596	617	631
(h) First cost value*	664	703	725	741	761	789	812	829	846	868	890	899	906	916	926	939	961	997	1023
(i) Land*	46	49	51	52	53	55	57	58	59	61	62	63	64	64	65	66	67	70	72
B. At current prices:																			
(c) Gross fixed capital formation	70	41	25	19	23	31	25	21	20	26	25	13	12	15	15	17	26	38	31
(d) Depreciation	34	27	23	22	23	23	23	23	22	23	22	22	21	21	21	21	23	24	25
(e) Net fixed capital formation	36	14	2	−3	0	8	2	−2	−2	3	3	−9	−9	−6	−6	−4	3	14	6
(f) Depreciated value*	1394	1154	934	877	909	920	894	877	840	848	831	793	747	725	721	731	764	816	839
(h) First cost value*	2065	1721	1408	1337	1403	1428	1405	1392	1349	1374	1363	1317	1258	1238	1246	1278	1346	1443	1493
(i) Land*	144	121	98	94	98	100	98	97	95	96	96	92	88	87	87	89	94	101	105
C. At 1930 prices:																			
(c) Gross fixed capital formation	41	29	22	18	20	28	23	20	19	26	25	14	13	15	17	19	27	38	31
(d) Depreciation	20	20	20	20	21	21	21	22	22	22	22	23	23	23	23	23	24	24	24
(e) Net fixed capital formation	21	9	2	−2	−1	7	2	−3	−3	4	3	−7	−10	−8	−6	−4	3	14	7
(f) Depreciated value*	812	821	823	821	820	827	829	827	824	828	831	824	814	806	800	796	799	813	820
(h) First cost value*	1202	1223	1238	1251	1266	1287	1303	1315	1326	1345	1363	1368	1370	1375	1381	1389	1408	1437	1458
(i) Land*	85	86	87	88	89	90	92	93	93	94	96	96	95	96	97	97	99	101	102

(2) Plant, Vehicles, etc.

	1920	1921	1922	1923	1924	1925	1926	1927	1928	1929	1930	1931	1932	1933	1934	1935	1936	1937	1938
A. At historical prices:																			
(d) Depreciation	33	37	36	36	37	38	39	39	40	41	41	45	44	44	45	47	48	55	59
(f) Depreciated value*	408	447	452	454	456	470	478	487	502	511	513	507	501	495	510	523	543	576	595
(h) First cost value*	999	1043	1056	1065	1076	1098	1116	1134	1161	1181	1193	1202	1206	1211	1238	1264	1302	1358	1405
B. At current prices:																			
(c) Gross fixed capital formation	82	76	41	38	39	52	47	48	55	50	43	39	38	38	60	60	68	88	78
(d) Depreciation	95	64	47	47	47	46	46	46	46	47	44	45	45	45	46	49	53	67	68
(e) Net fixed capital formation	−13	12	−6	−9	−8	6	1	2	9	3	−1	−6	−7	−7	14	11	15	21	10
(f) Depreciated value*	1195	801	586	584	583	571	567	562	558	576	544	502	497	499	515	540	587	691	681
(h) First cost value*	3147	2083	1534	1541	1555	1511	1498	1479	1453	1496	1416	1316	1309	1324	1340	1387	1489	1734	1711

C. At 1930 prices:

(c) Gross fixed capital formation	38	52	38	35	35	48	44	46	53	47	43	42	41	40	63	60	64	74	67
(d) Depreciation	43	43	43	42	42	43	43	43	44	44	44	48	48	47	48	50	50	56	59
(e) Net fixed capital formation	−5	9	−5	−7	−7	5	1	3	9	3	−1	−6	−7	−7	15	10	14	18	8
(f) Depreciated value*	534	543	538	531	524	529	530	533	542	545	544	538	531	524	539	549	563	581	589
(h) First cost value*	1415	1418	1415	1407	1400	1404	1405	1407	1416	1418	1416	1412	1401	1391	1404	1413	1433	1459	1480

(3) All Fixed Assets

A. At historical prices:

(d) Depreciation	44	48	48	48	49	51	52	53	54	55	56	60	59	59	60	62	64	72	76
(f) Depreciated value*	871	940	958	967	980	1012	1032	1048	1069	1090	1102	1094	1085	1079	1094	1109	1139	1193	1226
(h) First cost value*	1663	1746	1781	1806	1837	1887	1928	1961	2007	2049	2084	2101	2112	2127	2164	2203	2263	2354	2428

B. At current prices:

(c) Gross fixed capital formation	152	117	66	57	62	83	72	69	75	76	68	52	50	53	75	77	94	126	109
(d) Depreciation	129	91	70	69	70	69	69	69	68	70	66	67	66	66	67	70	76	91	93
(e) Net fixed capital formation	23	26	−4	−12	−8	14	3	0	7	6	2	−15	−16	−13	8	7	18	35	16
(f) Depreciated value*	2589	1955	1520	1461	1492	1491	1461	1439	1398	1424	1375	1295	1244	1224	1236	1271	1351	1507	1520
(h) First cost value*	5212	3804	2942	2878	2958	2939	2903	2871	2802	2870	2779	2633	2567	2562	2586	2665	2835	3177	3204

C. At 1930 prices:

(c) Gross fixed capital formation	79	81	60	53	55	76	67	66	72	73	68	56	54	55	80	79	91	112	98
(d) Depreciation	63	63	63	62	63	64	64	65	66	66	66	71	71	70	71	73	74	80	83
(e) Net fixed capital formation	16	18	−3	−9	−8	12	3	1	6	7	2	−13	−17	−15	9	6	17	32	15
(f) Depreciated value*	1346	1364	1361	1352	1344	1356	1359	1360	1366	1373	1375	1362	1345	1330	1339	1345	1362	1394	1409
(h) First cost value*	2617	2643	2650	2658	2666	2691	2708	2722	2741	2763	2779	2780	2772	2766	2784	2801	2841	2896	2938

(4) Stock-in-Trade and Work in Progress

1. Book values*

B. At current prices	935	656	555	548	582	574	559	568	576	557	502	467	448	437	477	493	566	660	637
C. At 1930 prices	376	409	423	413	434	453	463	495	508	501	502	519	522	501	531	552	596	605	633

2. Investment in stocks†

B. At current prices	—	53	18	−13	28	24	12	37	15	−8	1	15	3	−7	6	19	42	10	28
C. At 1930 prices	—	33	14	−10	21	19	10	32	13	−7	1	17	3	−7	21	21	44	9	28

* At end of year. † See chapter 2, appendix 2.2, p. 33.

TABLE 8.01 MANUFACTURING (£M.)

GROSS FIXED CAPITAL FORMATION IN ALL FIXED ASSETS BY INDUSTRIES

At 1930 prices

Table No.	Industry	1920	1921	1922	1923	1924	1925	1926	1927	1928	1929	1930	1931	1932	1933	1934	1935	1936	1937	1938
8.11	Cotton	5·6	−1·8	3·2	1·1	1·5	4·5	2·4	1·2	0·3	−0·8	−0·9	−1·4	−2·3	−2·6	−2·5	−2·1	−0·8	−1·4	−1·2
8.12	Wool and worsted	1·9	3·9	2·4	2·3	3·7	3·4	1·9	3·3	1·2	1·6	2·5	1·7	3·5	1·6	3·3	4·6	4·2	4·9	2·6
8.13	Rayon and silk	0·8	0·6	0·5	1·0	1·6	3·8	4·0	4·6	3·6	5·1	3·5	1·6	1·4	1·6	3·2	3·1	3·7	3·1	2·5
8.14	Other textiles	3·6	1·5	2·4	1·3	1·5	1·3	2·1	2·1	2·4	1·4	1·4	2·4	2·2	1·8	2·1	1·8	2·7	1·7	2·6
8.15	Textile finishing	1·2	3·1	1·8	1·8	1·8	3·4	2·6	1·5	1·9	2·0	1·8	1·9	1·9	1·7	2·0	1·7	1·9	1·3	1·5
8.21	Iron and steel	7·1	9·4	9·1	7·9	6·5	7·4	6·5	6·5	7·8	7·0	6·5	7·4	8·6	8·1	12·4	10·4	15·5	20·5	19·0
8.22	Shipbuilding, railway and general engineering	7·4	7·5	5·6	6·8	6·0	6·6	7·1	6·3	7·5	7·8	7·1	6·7	5·3	5·4	8·5	7·7	8·7	13·5	11·8
8.23	Electrical engineering	7·8	5·4	3·5	3·1	2·2	4·7	3·0	2·2	3·2	2·6	3·3	2·6	2·3	2·0	2·6	3·9	3·7	3·9	4·8
8.24	Motor vehicles	3·8	3·8	1·2	0·8	1·2	1·3	1·7	2·4	3·4	1·6	3·6	5·2	5·8	3·1	4·7	6·2	6·4	9·0	7·5
8.25	Non-ferrous metals	2·2	1·1	1·1	0·9	1·3	1·5	1·4	0·9	2·0	1·8	1·3	2·1	1·4	1·8	2·5	2·9	3·1	4·0	3·0
8.31	Drink	2·3	2·9	1·4	2·1	2·1	3·5	1·8	2·5	2·3	2·4	2·7	1·5	1·0	1·6	2·0	2·8	2·7	3·0	2·9
8.32	Tobacco	0·7	1·5	0·9	0·6	1·0	0·9	0·5	0·9	0·9	0·7	0·7	0·8	0·5	0·7	0·7	0·9	0·7	0·9	1·2
8.33	Food	7·7	9·4	5·0	4·7	5·0	5·4	4·0	4·8	5·8	7·5	6·1	4·9	4·2	4·8	7·0	5·3	8·6	6·0	7·1
8.41	Chemicals	7·7	6·2	5·3	3·2	5·2	5·9	6·1	7·0	11·3	14·6	6·8	5·0	4·3	4·2	8·2	8·6	9·7	10·8	8·3
8.42	Leather and rubber	1·8	3·8	1·6	1·3	0·6	1·7	1·6	2·2	2·1	1·4	1·5	1·1	3·1	1·3	1·6	1·0	0·8	1·3	1·5
8.43	Clothing	3·3	3·3	5·1	3·5	3·9	4·6	4·1	1·4	1·9	3·0	3·2	2·5	2·1	1·8	1·5	1·9	1·6	4·2	3·6
8.44	Paper and hardboard	2·6	2·5	2·4	2·5	3·1	2·7	2·3	2·2	3·9	4·8	4·0	1·9	2·3	5·2	3·1	3·4	3·1	5·3	3·8
8.45	Newspapers, printing and stationery	2·2	6·7	2·8	3·8	2·9	5·0	5·9	4·5	3·9	3·4	2·7	2·8	2·4	2·6	4·1	5·3	6·0	6·6	5·1
8.51	Wood and cork; building and contracting	4·1	4·6	2·7	1·2	1·8	3·5	4·4	2·1	3·1	1·9	6·9	2·7	0·4	3·8	7·3	5·5	2·8	5·5	5·0
8.52	Cement, bricks and other clay	2·2	2·4	0·8	1·7	0·4	2·2	1·4	2·4	2·1	1·9	1·8	0·7	1·2	1·2	2·9	2·6	2·0	3·0	2·1
8.53	Glass and potteries	1·2	0·1	0·5	0·2	0·3	1·0	0·9	2·0	0·7	0·8	0·8	0·5	0·5	0·6	0·9	0·5	1·1	1·1	0·9
8.54	Toys, musical instruments and miscellaneous manufacturing	0·8	2·4	0·5	0·8	0·7	1·3	1·8	3·2	0·9	1·2	1·7	1·6	1·3	2·2	1·6	1·8	2·5	3·5	1·9
	Total Manufacturing	79	81	60	53	55	76	67	66	72	73	68	56	54	55	80	79	91	112	98

TABLE 8.10 TEXTILE INDUSTRIES (£M.)

(1) *Buildings and Works*

	1920	1921	1922	1923	1924	1925	1926	1927	1928	1929	1930	1931	1932	1933	1934	1935	1936	1937	1938
A. At historical prices:																			
(c) Gross fixed capital formation	8·2	0·0	4·2	1·3	2·3	4·3	3·2	1·8	1·3	1·4	1·2	−0·2	−0·6	−1·0	−1·3	−0·7	1·6	2·1	0·4
(d) Depreciation	2·2	2·2	2·2	2·3	2·3	2·4	2·5	2·5	2·5	2·5	2·7	2·6	2·6	2·5	2·5	2·4	2·5	2·5	2·4
(f) Depreciated value*	89	87	89	88	88	91	92	91	90	88	87	84	81	77	73	70	69	69	67
(h) First cost value	130	132	136	137	139	144	147	148	150	150	152	151	150	148	145	143	144	145	145
(i) Land*	9	9	10	10	10	10	10	10	10	10	11	11	11	10	10	10	10	10	10
B. At current prices:																			
(d) Depreciation	6·9	5·8	4·7	4·2	4·6	4·7	4·7	4·4	4·2	4·2	4·1	4·0	3·9	3·7	3·6	3·7	3·6	3·9	3·8
(f) Depreciated value*	282	225	182	168	172	173	166	161	152	149	143	134	123	115	110	108	110	114	113
(h) First cost value*	420	340	279	262	274	278	272	267	256	257	251	239	225	216	211	211	218	228	230
(i) Land*	30	24	20	18	19	20	19	19	18	18	18	17	16	15	15	15	15	16	16
C. At 1930 prices:																			
(c) Gross fixed capital formation	4·9	0·0	3·7	1·2	2·0	3·7	3·0	1·8	1·3	1·2	1·2	−0·1	−0·7	−1·1	−1·3	−0·8	1·6	2·0	0·4
(d) Depreciation	4·1	4·1	4·1	4·1	4·1	4·2	4·2	4·2	4·2	4·2	4·1	4·1	4·0	4·0	3·9	3·8	3·7	3·9	3·8
(f) Depreciated value*	164	160	157	155	156	154	154	152	149	146	143	139	134	128	122	118	116	114	111
(h) First cost value*	244	242	245	245	247	250	252	252	252	252	251	249	245	240	234	229	228	227	225
(i) Land	17	17	17	17	17	18	18	18	18	18	18	17	17	17	16	16	16	16	16

(2) *Plant, Machinery, Vehicles, etc.*

	1920	1921	1922	1923	1924	1925	1926	1927	1928	1929	1930	1931	1932	1933	1934	1935	1936	1937	1938
A. At historical prices:																			
(c) Gross fixed capital formation	17·9	10·9	7·2	7·1	8·9	13·8	10·6	11·5	8·4	8·6	7·1	5·8	7·0	5·1	9·0	9·7	10·6	9·0	9·0
(d) Depreciation	9·1	9·2	9·0	8·9	9·0	9·5	9·6	9·9	10·1	9·7	9·6	10·0	9·7	9·4	9·2	9·4	9·4	10·0	10·0
(f) Depreciated value*	120	122	120	118	118	122	123	124	123	121	119	115	112	107	107	107	109	108	106
(h) First cost value*	303	304	305	305	309	315	319	324	325	325	324	321	318	312	309	306	309	308	308
B. At current prices:																			
(d) Depreciation	27·9	17·7	12·7	12·5	12·3	12·5	12·3	12·2	12·1	11·8	10·7	10·7	10·4	10·2	10·0	10·3	10·7	13·0	12·3
(f) Depreciated value*	370	237	170	167	165	161	158	155	147	148	136	122	119	116	116	119	126	140	132
(h) First cost value*	983	637	469	469	476	463	458	452	438	445	419	382	374	370	362	363	383	427	409
C. At 1930 prices:																			
(c) Gross fixed capital formation	8·2	7·3	6·6	6·3	8·1	12·7	10·0	10·9	8·1	8·1	7·1	6·3	7·4	5·2	9·4	9·9	10·1	7·6	7·6
(d) Depreciation	12·6	12·0	11·6	11·4	11·1	11·5	11·6	11·7	11·7	11·1	10·7	11·4	11·0	10·7	10·2	10·4	10·3	10·9	10·6
(f) Depreciated value*	166	161	156	151	148	149	148	147	143	140	136	131	128	122	121	120	120	117	114
(h) First cost value*	444	436	432	431	431	432	432	429	429	424	419	412	403	391	382	372	370	362	356

TABLE 8.10 (cont.)

(3) All Fixed Assets

	1920	1921	1922	1923	1924	1925	1926	1927	1928	1929	1930	1931	1932	1933	1934	1935	1936	1937	1938
A. At historical prices:																			
(c) Gross fixed capital formation	26·1	10·9	11·4	8·4	11·2	18·1	13·8	13·3	9·7	10·0	8·3	5·6	6·4	4·1	7·7	9·0	12·2	11·1	9·4
(d) Depreciation	11·3	11·4	11·2	11·2	11·3	11·9	12·1	12·4	12·6	12·2	12·3	12·6	12·3	11·9	11·7	11·8	11·9	12·5	12·4
(f) Depreciated value*	209	209	208	206	206	212	214	215	212	210	206	199	193	185	181	178	178	176	173
(h) First cost value*	433	436	441	442	447	459	466	472	475	474	476	472	468	459	454	450	453	453	453
B. At current prices:																			
(d) Depreciation	34·8	22·5	17·4	16·7	16·9	17·2	17·0	16·6	16·3	16·1	14·8	14·6	14·4	13·9	13·6	13·9	14·4	16·9	16·1
(f) Depreciated value*	652	462	351	334	337	334	324	316	299	297	279	256	242	232	226	227	236	254	246
(h) First cost value*	1403	978	747	732	750	741	730	719	694	702	670	621	599	586	574	574	601	655	639
C. At 1930 prices:																			
(c) Gross fixed capital formation	13·1	7·3	10·3	7·5	10·1	16·4	13·0	12·7	9·4	9·3	8·3	6·2	6·7	4·1	8·1	9·1	11·7	9·6	8·0
(d) Depreciation	16·7	16·1	15·7	15·5	15·2	15·7	15·8	15·9	15·9	15·3	14·8	15·5	15·1	14·8	14·1	14·2	14·0	14·8	14·4
(f) Depreciated value*	330	321	316	308	303	305	302	299	292	286	279	270	261	250	243	238	236	231	225
(h) First cost value*	689	678	677	676	678	682	684	684	681	676	670	660	648	631	616	601	599	589	580
(4) Stock-in-Trade and Work in Progress (Book value)*																			
B. At current prices	207	134	135	136	143	130	120	121	134	118	97	85	93	94	103	98	123	137	123
C. At 1930 prices	60	86	93	87	80	79	89	92	97	92	97	106	121	116	116	115	131	126	137

* At end of year.

TABLE 8.11 COTTON INDUSTRY (£M.)

(3) All Fixed Assets

	1920	1921	1922	1923	1924	1925	1926	1927	1928	1929	1930	1931	1932	1933	1934	1935	1936	1937	1938
A. At historical prices:																			
(c) Gross fixed capital formation	11·6	−2·5	3·5	1·2	1·6	4·9	2·5	1·2	0·3	−0·8	−0·9	−1·3	−2·1	−2·3	−2·2	−2·0	−0·8	−1·3	−1·1
(d) Depreciation	4·8	4·6	4·5	4·4	4·2	4·3	4·2	4·2	4·1	3·9	3·8	3·7	3·5	3·3	3·1	2·9	2·8	2·8	2·6
(f) Depreciated value*	97	90	88	85	83	83	82	78	75	70	65	60	55	49	44	39	35	31	28
(h) First cost value	199	194	197	197	199	202	204	203	203	199	195	191	184	175	166	157	153	147	142
B. At current prices:																			
(d) Depreciation	14·9	10·0	7·4	7·0	6·9	6·8	6·6	6·2	5·8	5·7	5·2	5·0	4·6	4·3	4·0	4·0	3·8	4·4	4·0
(f) Depreciated value*	305	212	160	150	149	145	138	131	121	116	106	94	85	78	72	68	67	67	62
(h) First cost value*	656	452	350	342	352	347	340	332	319	318	299	275	259	246	232	222	227	238	226
C. At 1930 prices:																			
(c) Gross fixed capital formation	5·6	−1·8	3·2	1·1	1·5	4·5	2·4	1·2	0·3	−0·8	−0·9	−1·4	−2·3	−2·6	−2·5	−2·1	−0·8	−1·4	−1·2
(d) Depreciation	7·2	6·9	6·7	6·5	6·3	6·2	6·1	5·9	5·7	5·5	5·2	5·3	4·9	4·6	4·3	4·1	3·8	3·9	3·6
(f) Depreciated value*	156	148	144	139	134	132	128	124	118	112	106	99	92	85	78	72	67	62	57
(h) First cost value*	323	313	316	315	316	318	318	315	312	306	299	291	279	264	248	231	225	213	204

(4) Stock-in-Trade and Work in Progress (Book value)*

	1920	1921	1922	1923	1924	1925	1926	1927	1928	1929	1930	1931	1932	1933	1934	1935	1936	1937	1938
B. At current prices	79	55	51	50	48	45	39	35	38	38	30	26	24	23	23	23	24	26	25
C. At 1930 prices	20	34	34	30	26	26	30	27	28	30	30	33	30	29	27	26	27	26	29

Supplementary Estimate of all Fixed Assets

	1920	1921	1922	1923	1924	1925	1926	1927	1928	1929	1930	1931	1932	1933	1934	1935	1936	1937	1938
A. At historical prices:																			
(c) Gross fixed capital formation	12·0	1·7	3·5	1·8	1·7	5·9	3·3	2·3	1·3	0·6	0·5	0·1	0·1	0·1	0·3	0·8	0·2	0·6	0·3
(f) Depreciated value*	94	91	90	87	85	86	86	84	81	78	74	71	67	64	61	59	56	53	51
(h) First cost value*	193	190	193	194	195	199	201	201	200	198	195	192	187	181	175	169	166	162	158
B. At current prices:																			
(f) Depreciated value*	294	207	157	147	146	144	138	132	123	120	110	100	93	88	84	83	83	86	81
(h) First cost value*	638	443	341	335	343	339	334	327	315	316	299	277	265	256	247	243	251	267	258
C. At 1930 prices:																			
(c) Gross fixed capital formation	5·8	1·2	3·2	1·7	1·6	5·5	3·1	2·2	1·3	0·6	0·5	0·1	0·1	0·1	0·3	0·9	0·2	0·5	0·2
(d) Depreciation	7·1	6·7	6·6	6·3	6·1	6·1	6·0	5·9	5·6	5·4	5·2	5·3	5·0	4·8	4·6	4·5	4·3	4·3	4·1
(f) Depreciated value*	150	144	141	136	132	131	128	124	120	115	110	105	100	96	91	88	84	80	76
(h) First cost value*	313	306	309	308	309	311	311	310	308	303	299	293	285	275	265	254	250	242	236

(5) Other Information

	1920	1921	1922	1923	1924	1925	1926	1927	1928	1929	1930	1931	1932	1933	1934	1935	1936	1937	1938
1. Weighted index of spindles and looms (1930 = 100)	106·6	103·1	104·3	104·1	104·6	105·2	105·3	104·9	104·0	102·0	100·0	97·4	93·2	88·3	83·0	77·5	75·4	71·5	68·7

* At end of year.
Notes to Table on p. 108.

NOTES TO TABLE 8.11

(1) Buildings

A. At historical prices:

(c) *Gross fixed capital formation*: C (c) multiplied by index B.

(d) *Depreciation*: As for C (d).

(f) *Depreciated value of buildings held at end of year*: For 1919 derived from C (f) by the standard estimate that the average historical costs of buildings (index B) can be taken as 50·8% of the costs at 1930 prices (See chapter 2, p. 16).

(g) *First cost value of buildings scrapped or sold*: 50·8% of C (g) i.e., the same standard estimate relating average historical costs to 1930 costs is used each year as for A (f) for 1919.

(h) *First cost value of buildings held at end of year*: For 1919 derived from C (h) by the same standard estimate as for A (h).

(i) *Land at end of year*: 7% of A (h).

B. At current prices:

The series at 1930 prices multiplied by index B.

C. At constant (1930) prices:

(a) *Year's purchases*: The total from 1920–6 derived from Ryan's figures on the age-structure and spread in proportion to purchases of plant. See p. 145. Purchases after 1926 assumed to be nil.

(b) *Proceeds of buildings scrapped or sold*: C (g) for each year multiplied by the ratio of the depreciated value (C (f)) at the end of the previous year to the corresponding first cost value (C (h)).

(c) *Gross fixed capital formation*: C (a) minus C (b).

(d) *Depreciation*: Straight line method, assuming a life of 60 years.

(f) *Depreciated value of buildings held at end of year*: For 1919 67·7% of C (h). This ratio obtained by imputing the age-structure derived from the series of annual values of business premises (Premises not used as dwellings) assessed for Inhabited House Duty. (See chapter 2, p. 16).

(g) *First cost value of buildings scrapped or sold*: Assumed to be proportional to the scrapping of plant ((1) C (g)). The proportion used (61·4%) was the ratio of the first cost value of the buildings to that of the plant at the beginning of the period of heavy scrapping.

(h) *First cost value of buildings held at end of year*: For 1930, 62·6% of the first cost value of the plant ((2) C (h)). This proportion was derived from an analysis of construction costs. See p. 145.

(i) *Land at end of year*: 7% of C (h).

(2) Plant and Equipment

A. At historical prices:

(c) *Gross fixed capital formation*: C (c) multiplied by index C.

(d) *Depreciation*: As for C (d).

(f) *Depreciated value of plant, etc., held at end of year*: For 1919 derived from C (f) by the standard estimate that the average historical costs of plant (index C) over the period 1860–1913 can be taken as 64·0% of the costs at 1930 prices. (See chapter 2, p. 24).

(g) *First cost value of plant scrapped or sold*: 61·6 % of C (g). This is the standard estimate relating average historical costs to 1930 costs under index C for plant accumulated over the 40 years 1861–1900. See chapter 2, p. 24.

(h) *First cost value of plant held at end of year*: For 1919 derived from C (h) by the same standard estimate as for A (f).

B. At current prices:

The series at 1930 prices multiplied by index C.

C. At constant (1930) prices:

(c) *Gross fixed capital formation*: Spindles acquired multiplied by the 1930 cost per spindle of all plant. See p. 145.

(d) *Depreciation*: Reducing balance method at the rate found in a sample of assessments for 1937 collected by the Inland Revenue, with adjustments for the additional allowances introduced in 1931 and 1937.

(f) *Depreciated value of plant held at end of year*: For 1919 derived from C (h) by imputing the standard estimate for the age-structure of what is assumed to be a stationary population of assets, with a length of life corresponding to the depreciation rates given in C (d). (See chapter 2, p. 16.)

(g) *First cost value of plant scrapped or sold*: C (c) minus first difference in C (h).

(h) *First cost value of plant held at end of year*: An estimate for 1930 extrapolated by a weighted index of the number of spindles and looms. See p. 145.

(4) Stock-in-Trade and Work in Progress

B. At current prices:

From a sample of company accounts. See p. 146.

C. At constant prices:

B. Deflated by the Board of Trade wholesale price index for cotton.

Supplementary Estimate of all Fixed Assets

This is the estimate made on the assumption that buildings released by the cotton industry were not sold, but were retained in the industry (see p. 144). The estimates for plant are not altered in this estimate. The revised series for buildings were obtained as follows:

C. At constant (1930) prices:

(b) *Depreciated value of buildings scrapped*: Assumed to be negligible, (i.e. C (a) = C (c)).

(g) *First cost value of buildings scrapped*: The total amount assumed due over the nineteen years taken as $\frac{19}{60}$ of the first cost value in 1878 (given by the age-structure used in C (f)) and spread in equal annual amounts.

All other series, including those at historical and current prices were then derived in the same way as for the standard estimates.

(5) Other Information

Weighted index of number of spindles and looms. See p. 145.

TABLE 8.12 WOOL AND WORSTED INDUSTRY (£M.)

	1920	1921	1922	1923	1924	1925	1926	1927	1928	1929	1930	1931	1932	1933	1934	1935	1936	1937	1938
								(3) *All Fixed Assets*											
A. At historical prices:																			
(c) Gross fixed capital formation	3·8	5·7	2·7	2·7	4·2	3·7	2·0	3·5	1·2	1·8	2·5	1·6	3·3	1·5	3·1	4·4	4·3	5·5	2·9
(d) Depreciation	2·3	2·4	2·4	2·4	2·6	2·6	2·6	2·6	2·5	2·5	2·5	2·6	2·6	2·5	2·6	2·7	2·8	3·0	3·0
(f) Depreciated value*	42	45	45	45	46	48	47	48	46	46	46	45	45	44	45	47	48	50	50
(h) First cost value*	89	93	93	94	96	97	97	98	97	97	97	97	98	97	98	100	102	106	106
(j) Land and depreciated value*	43	46	47	47	48	50	49	50	49	48	48	47	48	47	47	49	51	53	53
B. At current prices:																			
(d) Depreciation	7·1	4·8	3·6	3·5	3·6	3·6	3·5	3·4	3·2	3·2	3·0	3·0	3·0	3·0	2·9	2·9	3·3	3·9	3·9
(f) Depreciated value*	133	97	74	72	74	73	70	69	65	65	62	58	57	55	56	59	63	70	69
(h) First cost value*	295	208	157	154	158	154	150	148	141	142	135	126	124	123	123	127	135	151	148
(j) Land and depreciated value*	138	102	78	76	78	77	74	73	69	68	66	61	60	58	59	62	66	74	73
C. At 1930 prices:																			
(c) Gross fixed capital formation	1·9	3·9	2·4	2·3	3·7	3·4	1·9	3·3	1·2	1·6	2·5	1·7	3·5	1·6	3·3	4·6	4·2	4·9	2·6
(d) Depreciation	3·4	3·3	3·3	3·3	3·2	3·3	3·3	3·2	3·2	3·0	3·0	3·2	3·1	3·2	3·1	3·1	3·2	3·5	3·5
(f) Depreciated value*	66	67	67	66	66	67	65	66	64	63	62	61	61	60	60	62	63	65	64
(h) First cost value*	143	143	142	141	142	142	140	140	138	136	135	134	134	132	132	133	134	135	135
(j) Land and depreciated value*	70	71	70	69	70	70	69	67	67	66	66	64	65	63	64	65	67	69	68
							(4) *Stock-in-Trade and Work in Progress (Book value)**												
B. At current prices	48	26	36	40	47	39	35	39	44	40	31	29	36	40	47	41	61	68	57
C. At 1930 prices	15	20	28	27	26	24	26	28	29	29	31	35	49	47	49	46	58	53	57

* At end of year.

TABLE 8.13 RAYON AND SILK INDUSTRY (£M.)

(3) All Fixed Assets

	1920	1921	1922	1923	1924	1925	1926	1927	1928	1929	1930	1931	1932	1933	1934	1935	1936	1937	1938
A. At historical prices:																			
(c) Gross fixed capital formation	1·5	0·9	0·5	1·1	1·7	5·3	4·3	4·8	3·7	5·4	3·5	1·4	1·3	1·5	3·1	3·1	3·8	3·6	2·9
(d) Depreciation	0·5	0·5	0·5	0·6	0·7	1·2	1·4	1·8	2·1	1·9	2·1	2·1	2·0	1·9	1·9	2·1	2·1	2·3	2·3
(f) Depreciated value*	10	11	11	11	12	16	19	22	24	27	29	28	28	27	28	29	31	32	33
(h) First cost value*	16	17	17	18	19	24	28	33	36	41	45	46	47	48	51	54	57	61	63
(j) Land and depreciated value*	11	11	11	12	13	17	20	23	25	28	30	29	29	28	30	30	32	34	34
B. At current prices:																			
(d) Depreciation	1·4	1·0	0·7	0·8	0·9	1·5	1·7	2·1	2·4	2·2	2·1	2·0	2·0	1·9	1·9	2·2	2·2	2·9	2·7
(f) Depreciated value*	30	21	16	16	17	21	23	25	26	29	30	28	26	26	27	29	32	36	36
(h) First cost value*	40	29	23	23	24	29	32	36	38	44	46	44	44	46	49	52	59	68	70
(j) Land and depreciated value*	31	22	17	17	18	22	24	26	27	30	31	29	27	27	28	30	33	37	37
C. At 1930 prices:																			
(c) Gross fixed capital formation	0·8	0·6	0·5	1·0	1·6	3·8	4·0	4·6	3·6	5·1	3·5	1·6	1·4	1·6	3·2	3·1	3·7	3·1	2·5
(d) Depreciation	0·7	0·6	0·6	0·7	0·8	1·4	1·6	2·0	2·3	2·1	2·1	2·1	2·1	2·0	1·9	2·2	2·1	2·5	2·4
(f) Depreciated value*	15	15	15	15	16	19	21	24	25	28	30	29	28	28	29	30	32	32	32
(h) First cost value*	23	24	21	24	25	30	33	38	41	46	49	50	51	52	55	58	61	64	66
(j) Land and depreciated value*	16	16	15	16	16	20	22	25	26	29	31	30	30	29	30	31	33	34	34

(4) Stock-in-Trade and Work in Progress (Book value)*

	1920	1921	1922	1923	1924	1925	1926	1927	1928	1929	1930	1931	1932	1933	1934	1935	1936	1937	1938
B. At current prices	7	4	4	4	4	6	7	8	10	10	9	7	7	6	6	7	8	9	11
C. At 1930 prices	2	2	3	2	3	4	6	7	9	9	9	8	10	8	8	9	11	10	14

* At end of year.

TABLE 8.14 FLAX, JUTE AND OTHER TEXTILE INDUSTRIES (£M.)

(3) All Fixed Assets

	1920	1921	1922	1923	1924	1925	1926	1927	1928	1929	1930	1931	1932	1933	1934	1935	1936	1937	1938
A. At historical prices:																			
(c) Gross fixed capital formation	7·0	2·2	2·7	1·4	1·7	1·4	2·2	2·2	2·5	1·5	1·4	2·1	2·1	1·7	1·9	1·8	2·9	1·9	3·0
(d) Depreciation	1·9	1·9	1·9	1·8	1·8	1·7	1·7	1·7	1·8	1·8	1·8	2·0	2·0	2·0	1·9	1·9	2·1	2·2	2·3
(f) Depreciated value*	28	28	29	29	29	28	29	29	30	29	29	29	29	28	28	28	28	28	29
(h) First cost value*	56	56	58	58	58	58	58	59	60	60	59	60	60	60	60	60	61	62	63
(j) Land and depreciated value*	29	29	30	30	30	30	30	31	31	31	30	30	30	30	30	29	30	30	30
B. At current prices:																			
(d) Depreciation	5·2	3·5	2·6	2·4	2·5	2·3	2·2	2·1	2·2	2·2	2·0	2·1	2·1	2·1	2·2	2·2	2·4	2·7	2·7
(f) Depreciated value*	78	56	43	41	41	40	39	39	38	37	35	34	33	32	32	32	34	36	36
(h) First cost value*	169	118	90	88	89	86	84	83	81	81	76	72	71	70	70	71	75	82	82
(j) Land and depreciated value*	81	58	45	43	44	42	42	41	40	40	37	36	35	34	34	34	36	38	39
C. At 1930 prices:																			
(c) Gross fixed capital formation	3·6	1·5	2·4	1·3	1·5	1·3	2·1	2·1	2·4	1·4	1·4	2·4	2·2	1·8	2·1	1·8	2·7	1·7	2·6
(d) Depreciation	2·5	2·4	2·3	2·2	2·2	2·1	2·0	2·1	2·1	2·1	2·0	2·2	2·2	2·2	2·2	2·2	2·3	2·3	2·4
(f) Depreciated value*	39	39	39	38	37	36	36	36	37	36	35	35	35	34	34	34	34	33	33
(h) First cost value*	82	82	82	81	80	79	79	79	79	78	76	76	77	76	75	74	75	74	74
(j) Land and depreciated value*	41	41	41	40	39	38	39	39	39	38	37	38	38	37	36	36	36	35	36

(4) Stock-in-Trade and Work in Progress (Book value)*

	1920	1921	1922	1923	1924	1925	1926	1927	1928	1929	1930	1931	1932	1933	1934	1935	1936	1937	1938
B. At current prices	58	40	37	35	36	33	32	32	36	26	23	21	22	21	23	24	26	31	27
C. At 1930 prices	17	24	24	22	21	20	23	24	25	20	23	26	28	27	29	30	31	34	34

* At end of year.

TABLE 8.15 TEXTILE FINISHING TRADES (£M.)

(3) All Fixed Assets

	1920	1921	1922	1923	1924	1925	1926	1927	1928	1929	1930	1931	1932	1933	1934	1935	1936	1937	1938
A. At historical prices:																			
(c) Gross fixed capital formation	2·2	4·5	2·0	2·0	2·0	3·8	2·8	1·6	2·0	2·1	1·8	1·8	1·8	1·7	1·8	1·7	2·0	1·4	1·7
(d) Depreciation	1·8	2·0	1·9	2·0	2·0	2·1	2·2	2·1	2·1	2·1	2·1	2·2	2·2	2·2	2·2	2·2	2·1	2·2	2·2
(f) Depreciated value*	33	35	35	35	35	37	38	37	37	37	37	37	36	36	35	35	34	34	33
(h) First cost value*	73	76	76	76	76	78	79	79	79	79	79	79	79	79	79	79	79	78	78
(j) Land and depreciated value*	34	37	37	37	37	38	39	39	39	39	38	38	38	37	37	36	36	36	35
B. At current prices:																			
(c) Gross fixed capital formation	6·2	4·2	3·1	3·0	3·0	3·0	3·0	2·8	2·7	2·7	2·5	2·6	2·6	2·6	2·6	2·6	2·6	3·0	2·8
(f) Depreciated value*	106	76	58	55	55	55	54	52	49	49	46	43	42	40	40	41	41	44	42
(h) First cost value*	243	170	128	125	127	125	123	119	115	116	110	103	101	100	100	101	105	115	112
(j) Land and depreciated value*	110	80	60	58	58	58	57	54	52	52	49	46	44	43	42	42	44	46	45
C. At 1930 prices:																			
(c) Gross fixed capital formation	1·2	3·1	1·8	1·8	1·8	3·4	1·5	1·5	1·9	2·0	1·8	1·9	1·9	1·7	2·0	1·7	1·9	1·3	1·5
(d) Depreciation	2·9	2·9	2·8	2·8	2·7	2·7	2·8	2·7	2·6	2·6	2·5	2·7	2·7	2·7	2·6	2·6	2·6	2·6	2·5
(f) Depreciated value*	53	53	52	51	50	50	50	49	48	48	46	46	45	44	43	42	41	39	38
(h) First cost value*	117	117	116	115	114	115	114	113	112	111	110	109	108	107	106	105	104	102	101
(j) Land and depreciated value*	55	55	54	53	53	53	53	52	51	50	49	48	47	46	45	44	44	42	41

(4) Stock-in-Trade and Work in Progress (Book value)*

	1920	1921	1922	1923	1924	1925	1926	1927	1928	1929	1930	1931	1932	1933	1934	1935	1936	1937	1938
B. At current prices	15	9	6	7	7	7	7	6	6	6	4	3	3	3	3	4	3	3	3
C. At 1930 prices	6	6	4	5	5	5	5	5	5	5	4	3	4	4	4	4	3	3	3

* At end of year.

TABLE 8.20 METALS AND METAL-USING INDUSTRIES (£M.)

	1920	1921	1922	1923	1924	1925	1926	1927	1928	1929	1930	1931	1932	1933	1934	1935	1936	1937	1938
(1) Buildings and Works																			
A. At historical prices:																			
(c) Gross fixed capital formation	30·4	15·0	6·1	6·1	5·0	9·8	6·4	6·3	5·3	7·7	8·7	5·2	6·0	5·6	5·4	6·4	10·0	18·7	14·5
(d) Depreciation	3·5	3·8	3·9	4·0	4·0	4·2	4·3	4·4	4·4	4·5	4·6	4·6	4·7	4·8	4·9	4·9	5·2	5·4	5·6
(f) Depreciated value*	152	163	166	168	169	174	177	179	180	183	187	187	188	189	190	191	196	210	218
(h) First-cost value*	213	227	232	237	241	250	255	260	264	270	278	281	286	291	295	300	309	326	339
(i) Land*	15	16	16	17	17	18	18	18	18	19	19	20	20	20	21	21	22	23	24
B. At current prices:																			
(d) Depreciation	10·6	8·9	7·2	6·8	7·1	7·3	7·1	7·1	6·9	6·9	7·0	6·8	6·5	6·4	6·5	6·7	7·1	7·7	8·0
(f) Depreciated value*	436	364	293	274	282	285	276	270	259	260	256	246	234	228	228	231	243	267	279
(h) First-cost value*	635	534	434	412	430	438	430	426	412	419	417	404	390	386	390	401	425	463	483
(i) Land*	44	37	30	29	30	31	30	30	29	29	29	28	27	27	27	28	30	32	34
C. At 1930 prices:																			
(c) Gross fixed capital formation	17·7	10·5	5·4	5·7	4·5	8·9	5·9	5·9	5·2	7·6	8·7	5·2	6·5	6·2	5·8	6·9	10·4	18·7	14·3
(d) Depreciation	6·2	6·3	6·4	6·4	6·5	6·6	6·7	6·7	6·7	6·8	6·9	7·0	7·1	7·2	7·2	7·3	7·5	7·6	7·8
(f) Depreciated value*	254	258	258	257	255	257	256	256	254	255	256	254	254	253	252	251	254	265	272
(h) First-cost value*	371	379	382	386	389	395	399	402	405	410	417	419	424	428	431	436	444	460	471
(i) Land*	26	27	27	27	27	28	28	28	28	29	29	29	30	30	30	30	31	32	33
(2) Plant, Machinery, Vehicles, etc.																			
A. At historical prices:																			
(c) Gross fixed capital formation	23·3	24·6	16·6	15·3	14·2	13·7	14·9	12·9	19·1	14·1	13·1	17·6	15·8	13·6	23·9	23·8	28·2	38·3	36·9
(d) Depreciation	10·3	11·5	11·8	12·1	12·3	12·4	12·5	12·5	13·1	13·1	13·2	14·9	15·0	14·8	15·6	16·4	17·2	20·4	22·7
(f) Depreciated value*	126	139	143	146	149	150	152	152	158	159	159	162	163	162	170	177	188	206	220
(h) First-cost value*	313	327	333	338	341	344	349	348	360	364	367	374	379	383	396	410	427	455	482
B. At current prices:																			
(d) Depreciation	29·6	20·1	14·9	15·0	15·2	14·7	14·5	14·2	14·4	14·6	13·9	14·5	14·8	15·0	15·8	17·0	18·6	24·4	25·9
(f) Depreciated value*	365	245	183	185	186	180	178	174	175	180	169	161	162	164	172	184	205	248	252
(h) First-cost value*	975	646	477	480	484	466	460	451	444	454	427	402	405	412	422	443	482	571	575
C. At 1930 prices:																			
(c) Gross fixed capital formation	10·6	16·7	15·2	13·8	12·7	12·6	13·8	12·4	18·7	13·2	13·1	18·8	16·9	14·2	24·9	24·2	27·0	32·2	31·8
(d) Depreciation	13·4	13·5	13·7	13·7	13·6	13·6	13·7	13·5	13·8	13·8	13·9	15·6	15·8	15·7	16·5	17·1	17·7	20·5	22·4
(f) Depreciated value*	164	167	168	168	167	166	167	166	170	170	169	172	173	172	180	187	196	208	217
(h) First-cost value*	438	439	439	437	435	432	431	428	431	429	427	431	433	432	442	451	462	479	496

8

TABLE 8.20 (cont.)

(3) All Fixed Assets

	1920	1921	1922	1923	1924	1925	1926	1927	1928	1929	1930	1931	1932	1933	1934	1935	1936	1937	1934
A. At historical prices:																			
(c) Gross fixed capital formation	53·7	39·6	22·7	21·4	19·2	23·5	21·3	19·2	24·4	21·8	21·8	22·8	21·8	19·2	29·3	30·2	38·2	57·0	51·4
(d) Depreciation	13·8	15·3	15·7	16·1	16·3	16·6	16·8	16·9	17·5	17·6	17·8	19·5	19·7	19·6	20·5	21·3	22·4	25·8	28·3
(f) Depreciated value*	278	302	309	314	318	324	329	331	338	342	346	349	351	351	359	368	384	415	438
(h) First-cost value*	526	553	565	574	582	594	604	608	624	634	644	655	665	673	691	710	736	782	821
B. At current prices:																			
(d) Depreciation	40·2	29·0	22·1	21·8	22·3	22·0	21·6	21·3	21·3	21·5	20·9	21·3	21·3	21·4	22·3	23·7	25·7	32·1	33·9
(f) Depreciated value*	800	610	476	459	468	464	454	445	434	440	425	406	396	392	400	416	448	514	531
(h) First-cost value*	1610	1180	911	892	914	904	890	876	856	873	844	806	794	797	812	845	907	1034	1058
C. At 1930 prices:																			
(c) Gross fixed capital formation	28·3	27·2	20·5	19·5	17·2	21·5	19·7	18·3	23·9	20·8	21·8	24·0	23·4	20·4	30·7	31·1	37·4	50·9	46·1
(d) Depreciation	19·6	19·8	20·1	20·1	20·1	20·2	20·4	20·2	20·5	20·6	20·8	22·6	22·9	22·9	23·7	24·4	25·2	28·1	30·2
(f) Depreciated value*	418	425	426	425	422	424	423	421	424	424	425	427	427	425	432	438	451	473	489
(h) First-cost value*	808	818	821	823	823	827	830	830	836	840	844	850	856	859	873	886	906	940	967
(4) Stock-in-Trade and Work in Progress (Book value)*																			
B. At current prices	290	204	153	163	170	167	159	168	162	164	153	141	127	123	139	158	185	236	230
C. At 1930 prices	128	123	125	134	141	148	133	158	159	157	153	145	134	130	149	186	184	206	203

* At end of year.

TABLE 8.21 IRON AND STEEL INDUSTRY (£M.)

(3) All Fixed Assets

	1920	1921	1922	1923	1924	1925	1926	1927	1928	1929	1930	1931	1932	1933	1934	1935	1936	1937	1938
A. At historical prices:																			
(c) Gross fixed capital formation	14·1	13·7	10·1	8·6	7·3	8·1	7·0	6·8	8·1	7·3	6·5	7·0	8·0	7·5	11·9	10·1	16·1	23·1	21·5
(d) Depreciation	5·3	5·7	5·9	6·1	6·1	6·2	6·2	6·2	6·5	6·5	6·5	7·0	6·9	7·0	7·4	7·6	8·3	9·8	11·2
(f) Depreciated value*	107	115	119	121	123	125	125	126	128	128	128	128	130	130	135	137	145	158	168
(h) First cost value*	212	221	226	230	233	237	239	238	245	247	249	252	255	258	265	271	282	300	317
(j) Land and depreciated value*	112	120	125	128	129	131	132	133	134	135	136	136	137	138	142	145	153	166	177
B. At current prices:																			
(d) Depreciation	16·4	11·7	8·9	8·8	8·9	8·7	8·5	8·3	8·3	8·4	8·0	8·0	7·9	7·9	8·3	8·8	9·9	12·5	13·7
(f) Depreciated value*	330	246	193	187	190	187	182	177	171	173	165	156	152	151	155	160	174	201	208
(h) First cost value*	687	496	383	376	384	378	370	363	353	358	344	326	320	321	327	338	363	415	425
(j) Land and depreciated value*	348	261	205	198	202	200	194	189	183	184	176	167	163	162	166	171	185	214	221
C. At 1930 prices:																			
(c) Gross fixed capital formation	7·1	9·4	9·1	7·9	6·5	7·4	6·5	6·5	7·8	7·0	6·5	7·4	8·6	8·1	12·4	10·4	15·5	20·5	19·0
(d) Depreciation	7·9	8·0	8·1	8·1	8·0	8·0	7·9	7·9	8·0	8·0	8·0	8·5	8·4	8·5	8·9	9·1	9·7	10·9	12·2
(f) Depreciated value*	170	172	173	173	171	171	169	168	168	167	165	164	164	164	167	169	174	184	191
(h) First cost value*	341	344	345	346	345	346	345	344	344	344	344	344	345	346	351	354	362	376	388
(j) Land and depreciated value*	180	182	183	183	182	182	180	179	179	178	176	175	176	176	179	180	186	196	203

(4) Stock-in-Trade and Work in Progress (Book value)*

	1920	1921	1922	1923	1924	1925	1926	1927	1928	1929	1930	1931	1932	1933	1934	1935	1936	1937	1938
B. At current prices	70	51	38	42	49	42	35	33	37	33	33	30	27	25	28	30	35	49	49
C. At 1930 prices	28	27	30	34	40	38	29	31	37	32	33	30	29	27	30	31	34	40	38

* At end of year.

TABLE 8.22 SHIPBUILDING, RAILWAY AND GENERAL ENGINEERING INDUSTRIES (£M.)

	1920	1921	1922	1923	1924	1925	1926	1927	1928	1929	1930	1931	1932	1933	1934	1935	1936	1937	1938
(3) All Fixed Assets																			
A. At historical prices:																			
(c) Gross fixed capital formation	14·4	10·9	6·2	7·5	6·7	7·1	7·6	6·7	7·7	8·2	7·1	6·4	4·9	5·1	8·1	7·5	8·8	15·2	13·1
(d) Depreciation	5·1	5·4	5·4	5·5	5·6	5·8	5·8	5·9	6·1	6·2	6·2	6·7	6·6	6·5	6·7	6·8	6·8	7·9	8·1
(f) Depreciated value*																			
1. Shipbuilding	23	25	25	26	26	26	26	26	26	25	25	24	23	22	22	22	22	22	22
2. Railway engineering	9	10	10	10	10	10	10	11	11	11	11	11	11	11	11	11	11	11	11
3. General engineering	68	70	72	72	73	75	76	76	78	80	82	82	82	81	82	83	85	92	96
4. Total	100	105	106	108	109	110	112	113	115	117	117	117	115	114	115	116	118	125	130
(h) First cost value*	193	199	201	205	207	210	213	215	218	222	225	226	227	228	232	235	239	250	258
(j) Land and depreciated value*	105	111	112	114	115	116	118	119	121	123	124	124	122	121	122	123	125	133	138
B. At current prices:																			
(d) Depreciation	15·6	11·0	8·2	8·1	8·2	8·1	8·0	7·9	7·8	7·9	7·6	7·6	7·5	7·4	7·6	7·8	8·1	10·1	10·1
(f) Depreciated value*	303	228	175	169	171	168	164	161	156	158	152	144	137	134	135	138	145	163	166
(h) First cost value*	617	450	344	336	343	337	331	325	317	322	310	295	286	285	287	295	311	348	351
(j) Land and depreciated value*	320	243	187	180	183	180	176	172	167	169	163	154	147	144	145	148	156	174	178
C. At 1930 prices:																			
(c) Gross fixed capital formation	7·4	7·5	5·6	6·8	6·0	6·6	7·1	6·3	7·5	7·8	7·1	6·7	5·3	5·4	8·5	7·7	8·7	13·5	11·8
(d) Depreciation	7·6	7·5	7·5	7·5	7·5	7·5	7·5	7·4	7·5	7·6	7·6	8·1	8·0	7·9	8·0	8·0	8·1	8·9	9·0
(f) Depreciated value*	159	159	157	156	155	154	154	152	152	153	152	151	148	145	146	146	146	150	153
1. Shipbuilding	60	61	61	61	61	61	61	60	60	59	58	57	56	55	55	54	54	54	52
2. Railway engineering	26	26	26	26	26	27	27	28	28	28	28	28	28	28	28	28	28	29	29
3. General engineering	225	224	223	222	222	222	222	220	221	223	224	225	224	223	225	226	228	235	239
4. Total	311	311	310	310	309	310	310	308	309	310	310	310	308	307	308	309	311	318	321
(j) Land and depreciated value*	169	169	167	167	165	164	164	162	163	163	163	161	159	156	157	156	157	162	165
(4) Stock-in-Trade and Work in Progress (Book value)*																			
B. At current prices	115	79	56	57	57	59	58	69	62	65	57	55	47	48	54	61	71	88	86
C. At 1930 prices	52	48	46	47	48	54	49	65	61	62	57	56	49	50	55	62	69	76	74

* At end of year.

TABLE 8.23 ELECTRICAL ENGINEERING INDUSTRY (£M.)

	1920	1921	1922	1923	1924	1925	1926	1927	1928	1929	1930	1931	1932	1933	1934	1935	1936	1937	1938
(3) All Fixed Assets																			
A. At historical prices:																			
(c) Gross fixed capital formation	13·7	7·9	3·9	3·4	2·4	5·2	3·3	2·3	3·2	2·7	3·3	2·5	2·1	2·0	2·5	3·8	3·7	4·5	5·3
(d) Depreciation	1·3	1·7	1·8	2·0	2·0	2·0	2·2	2·2	2·2	2·2	2·3	2·5	2·5	2·5	2·5	2·6	2·7	2·9	3·0
(f) Depreciated value*	35	41	43	44	45	48	49	49	50	51	52	51	51	50	50	52	53	54	56
(h) First cost value*	56	63	66	68	70	74	76	78	80	82	84	85	87	88	89	92	95	98	102
(j) Land and depreciated value*	37	43	45	47	47	50	52	52	53	53	55	54	54	53	53	55	56	57	90
B. At current prices:																			
(d) Depreciation	3·2	2·6	2·2	2·2	2·4	2·4	2·4	2·4	2·4	2·4	2·4	2·5	2·4	2·5	2·5	2·7	2·9	3·5	3·4
(f) Depreciated value*	80	67	54	53	55	57	57	55	54	55	54	52	50	49	49	51	55	61	62
(h) First cost value*	142	112	90	89	93	95	95	95	93	96	95	91	90	90	92	97	104	116	120
(j) Land and depreciated value*	85	71	58	57	58	61	60	59	58	59	58	56	53	53	53	55	59	65	67
C. At 1930 prices:																			
(c) Gross fixed capital formation	7·8	5·4	3·5	3·1	2·2	4·7	3·0	2·2	3·2	2·6	3·3	2·6	2·3	2·0	2·6	3·9	3·7	3·9	4·8
(d) Depreciation	1·7	1·8	2·0	2·1	2·1	2·1	2·3	2·3	2·3	2·3	2·4	2·6	2·7	2·7	2·7	2·7	2·8	3·1	3·1
(f) Depreciated value*	43	47	48	49	49	52	53	52	53	54	54	54	54	53	53	54	55	56	58
(h) First cost value*	74	78	81	82	83	87	89	89	91	93	95	96	97	98	99	102	104	107	111
(j) Land and depreciated value*	46	50	52	53	53	55	56	56	57	57	58	58	58	57	66	58	59	60	62
(4) Stock-in-Trade and Work in Progress (Book value)*																			
B. At current prices	57	41	31	35	37	37	37	36	34	36	34	28	25	24	27	32	40	52	49
C. At 1930 prices	26	25	26	29	30	33	31	34	33	35	34	29	26	25	28	33	39	45	43

* At end of year.

TABLE 8.24 MOTOR VEHICLE INDUSTRY (£M.)

(3) All Fixed Assets

	1920	1921	1922	1923	1924	1925	1926	1927	1928	1929	1930	1931	1932	1933	1934	1935	1936	1937	1938
A. At historical prices:																			
(c) Gross fixed capital formation	7·5	5·5	1·3	0·9	1·4	1·4	1·8	2·5	3·4	1·7	3·6	4·9	5·4	3·0	4·5	6·0	6·5	10·0	8·2
(d) Depreciation for the year	1·2	1·6	1·6	1·5	1·5	1·5	1·5	1·5	1·6	1·6	1·7	2·0	2·4	2·3	2·6	2·8	3·0	3·4	4·2
(f) Depreciated value*	19	23	23	22	22	22	22	24	25	25	27	30	33	34	36	39	42	49	53
(h) First cost value*	32	37	37	37	38	38	39	41	44	45	47	51	56	58	62	67	73	82	89
(j) Land and depreciated value*	20	24	24	23	23	23	23	25	27	27	29	32	35	35	37	41	44	51	55
B. At current prices:																			
(d) Depreciation	2·3	1·9	1·5	1·4	1·5	1·4	1·4	1·4	1·5	1·5	1·6	1·9	2·2	2·2	2·5	2·8	3·0	3·9	4·5
(f) Depreciated value*	38	32	25	24	24	24	24	25	26	26	27	29	31	32	34	38	44	54	57
(h) First cost value*	67	52	40	39	41	40	40	41	43	44	45	47	50	53	56	63	72	88	95
(j) Land and depreciated value*	40	34	26	25	25	25	25	26	27	28	29	31	33	34	36	40	46	56	60
C. At 1930 prices:																			
(c) Gross fixed capital formation	3·8	3·8	1·2	0·8	1·2	1·3	1·7	2·4	3·4	1·6	3·6	5·2	5·8	3·1	4·7	6·2	6·4	9·0	7·5
(d) Depreciation	1·1	1·3	1·3	1·2	1·3	1·4	1·4	1·3	1·5	1·4	1·6	2·0	2·3	2·3	2·6	2·9	2·9	3·3	4·0
(f) Depreciated value*	20	23	22	22	22	22	22	23	25	25	27	31	34	35	37	40	44	49	53
(h) First cost value*	33	36	36	36	37	37	38	39	42	42	45	49	54	57	60	66	71	79	86
(j) Land and depreciated value*	21	24	23	23	23	23	23	24	26	27	29	32	36	37	39	42	46	52	55
(4) Stock-in-Trade and Work in Progress (Book value)*																			
B. At current prices	29	18	15	16	16	16	16	18	17	17	16	15	15	14	17	19	20	26	24
C. At 1930 prices	14	12	12	13	13	15	15	17	16	16	16	15	15	14	19	22	22	27	25

* At end of year.

TABLE 8.25 NON-FERROUS METALS INDUSTRY (£M.)

(3) All Fixed Assets

	1920	1921	1922	1923	1924	1925	1926	1927	1928	1929	1930	1931	1932	1933	1934	1935	1936	1937	1938
A. At historical prices:																			
(c) Gross fixed capital formation	4·0	1·6	1·2	1·0	1·4	1·7	1·6	0·9	2·0	1·9	1·3	2·0	1·4	1·6	2·3	2·8	3·1	4·2	3·3
(d) Depreciation	0·9	0·9	1·0	1·0	1·1	1·1	1·1	1·1	1·1	1·1	1·1	1·3	1·3	1·3	1·3	1·5	1·6	1·8	1·8
(f) Depreciated value*	17	18	18	18	19	19	20	20	21	21	22	22	22	23	24	25	26	29	30
(h) First cost value*	32	33	34	34	35	35	36	36	38	39	39	40	41	42	44	45	48	51	54
(j) Land and depreciated value*	18	19	20	20	20	21	21	21	22	23	23	24	24	24	25	26	28	31	32
B. At current prices:																			
(d) Depreciation	2·7	1·8	1·3	1·3	1·3	1·4	1·3	1·3	1·3	1·3	1·3	1·3	1·3	1·4	1·4	1·6	1·8	2·1	2·2
(f) Depreciated value*	49	36	28	27	28	28	28	27	26	27	26	26	25	25	26	28	31	36	37
(h) First cost value*	98	71	54	53	54	54	53	52	51	52	51	49	48	48	50	53	57	66	68
(j) Land and depreciated value*	52	39	30	29	30	30	29	28	28	29	28	28	27	27	28	30	33	38	39
C. At 1930 prices:																			
(c) Gross fixed capital formation	2·2	1·1	1·1	0·9	1·3	1·5	1·4	0·9	2·0	1·8	1·3	2·1	1·4	1·8	2·5	2·9	3·1	4·0	3·0
(d) Depreciation	1·3	1·2	1·2	1·2	1·2	1·2	1·3	1·3	1·2	1·3	1·2	1·4	1·5	1·5	1·5	1·7	1·7	1·9	1·9
(f) Depreciated value*	26	26	25	25	25	25	26	25	26	26	26	27	27	27	28	30	31	33	34
(h) First cost value*	49	49	49	49	49	49	49	49	50	50	51	51	52	52	54	55	57	60	62
(j) Land and depreciated value*	27	27	27	27	27	27	27	27	28	28	28	29	29	29	30	32	33	35	36

(4) Stock-in-Trade and Work in Progress (Book value)*

	1920	1921	1922	1923	1924	1925	1926	1927	1928	1929	1930	1931	1932	1933	1934	1935	1936	1937	1938
B. At current prices	19	15	13	13	12	12	12	12	13	13	12	12	12	13	14	16	19	21	21
C. At 1930 prices	7	11	11	11	9	9	9	11	11	11	12	15	14	14	17	18	20	18	23

* At end of year.

TABLE 8.30 FOOD, DRINK AND TOBACCO INDUSTRIES (£M.)

(1) Buildings and Works

	1920	1921	1922	1923	1924	1925	1926	1927	1928	1929	1930	1931	1932	1933	1934	1935	1936	1937	1938
A. At historical prices:																			
(c) Gross fixed capital formation	8·0	8·6	3·7	4·6	4·0	4·7	2·7	3·8	3·1	3·1	3·5	2·7	1·7	2·4	2·1	2·8	4·4	3·6	3·7
(d) Depreciation	1·8	1·9	1·9	2·0	2·1	2·1	2·1	2·2	2·2	2·3	2·3	2·4	2·3	2·4	2·4	2·4	2·5	2·7	2·7
(f) Depreciated value*	67	74	76	78	80	83	84	85	85	86	87	87	87	87	86	86	89	90	91
(h) First-cost value*	105	112	116	120	123	127	129	132	134	136	139	141	142	144	146	148	152	155	158
(i) Land*	7	8	8	8	9	9	9	9	9	10	10	10	10	10	10	10	11	11	11
B. At current prices:																			
(d) Depreciation	5·6	4·7	3·9	3·7	3·9	3·9	3·8	3·8	3·7	3·8	3·7	3·6	3·4	3·4	3·4	3·5	3·7	3·9	4·0
(f) Depreciated value*	208	174	141	133	138	139	134	132	125	125	122	117	110	107	106	107	112	117	119
(h) First-cost value*	334	280	229	219	230	234	228	226	218	221	219	212	203	200	202	208	219	232	240
(i) Land*	23	20	16	15	16	16	16	16	15	15	15	15	14	14	14	15	15	16	17
C. At 1930 prices:																			
(c) Gross fixed capital formation	4·7	6·1	3·2	4·3	3·7	4·3	2·6	3·5	2·0	3·1	3·5	2·9	2·0	2·6	2·4	3·0	4·6	3·6	3·7
(d) Depreciation	3·2	3·3	3·3	3·4	3·4	3·6	3·6	3·6	3·6	3·6	3·7	3·8	3·8	3·8	3·8	3·8	3·8	3·9	3·9
(f) Depreciated value*	121	124	124	125	125	125	124	124	123	122	122	121	120	118	117	116	117	117	117
(h) First-cost value*	194	200	202	205	207	210	212	214	215	217	219	220	221	223	224	226	229	232	234
(i) Land*	14	14	14	14	14	15	15	15	15	15	15	15	15	16	16	16	16	16	16

(2) Plant, Machinery, Vehicles, etc.

	1920	1921	1922	1923	1924	1925	1926	1927	1928	1929	1930	1931	1932	1933	1934	1935	1936	1937	1938
A. At historical prices:																			
(c) Gross fixed capital formation	13·2	11·3	4·5	3·4	4·8	5·8	4·2	4·5	7·4	7·8	6·1	3·8	3·7	4·0	6·9	5·9	7·8	7·5	8·8
(d) Depreciation	4·1	4·5	4·5	4·4	4·5	4·7	4·6	4·5	4·9	5·0	5·1	5·4	5·3	5·2	5·4	5·4	5·5	6·2	6·6
(f) Depreciated value*	50	57	57	56	57	57	57	57	59	62	63	62	60	59	60	61	63	64	66
(h) First cost value*	118	126	127	126	128	130	130	131	135	139	141	142	142	142	145	147	151	155	160
B. At current prices:																			
(d) Depreciation	11·1	7·7	5·6	5·5	5·5	5·4	5·3	5·2	5·3	5·5	5·3	5·3	5·2	5·1	5·4	5·6	6·0	7·4	7·4
(f) Depreciated value*	141	97	70	69	69	68	66	64	65	69	66	60	59	59	61	63	68	78	77
(h) First-cost value*	368	246	181	180	181	175	172	168	166	172	164	151	150	152	154	159	170	195	192
C. At 1930 prices:																			
(c) Gross fixed capital formation	6·0	7·7	4·1	3·1	4·4	5·5	3·7	4·7	7·0	7·5	6·0	4·3	3·7	4·5	7·3	6·0	7·4	6·3	7·5
(d) Depreciation	5·0	5·1	5·1	5·0	5·0	5·0	4·9	4·9	5·0	5·2	5·3	5·6	5·6	5·5	5·6	5·6	5·7	6·2	6·5
(f) Depreciated value*	63	66	65	63	62	63	62	61	63	66	66	65	63	62	64	64	66	66	67
(h) First-cost value*	165	167	166	164	163	162	161	160	161	163	164	162	161	159	161	163	163	164	166

(3) All Fixed Assets

A. At historical prices:

(c) Gross fixed capital formation	21·2	19·9	8·2	8·0	8·8	10·5	6·9	8·3	10·5	10·9	9·6	6·5	5·4	6·4	9·0	8·7	12·2	11·1	12·5
(d) Depreciation	5·9	6·4	6·4	6·4	6·6	6·8	6·7	6·7	7·1	7·3	7·4	7·8	7·6	7·6	7·8	7·8	8·0	8·9	9·3
(f) Depreciated value*	117	131	133	134	136	140	141	142	144	147	150	149	146	146	146	146	152	154	157
(h) First-cost value*	223	238	242	246	251	257	260	264	269	275	280	283	284	286	290	295	303	310	318

B. At current prices:

(d) Depreciation	16·7	12·4	9·5	9·2	9·4	9·3	9·1	9·0	9·0	9·3	9·0	8·9	8·6	8·5	8·8	9·1	9·7	11·3	11·4
(f) Depreciated value*	349	271	211	202	208	207	200	196	190	194	188	177	168	166	166	170	180	195	196
(h) First-cost value*	703	527	410	398	411	409	400	395	384	394	382	364	353	352	356	366	389	428	432

C. At 1930 prices:

(c) Gross fixed capital formation	10·7	13·8	7·3	7·4	8·1	9·8	6·3	8·2	9·0	10·6	9·5	7·2	5·7	7·1	9·7	9·0	12·0	9·9	11·2
(d) Depreciation	8·2	8·4	8·4	8·4	8·4	8·6	8·5	8·5	8·6	8·8	9·0	9·4	9·4	9·3	9·4	9·4	9·5	10·1	10·4
(f) Depreciated value*	184	190	188	187	187	188	186	186	186	188	188	186	182	180	180	180	182	182	183
(h) First-cost value*	360	367	368	368	370	373	373	373	376	380	382	383	382	382	385	387	392	395	400

(4) Stock-in-Trade and Work-in-Progress (Book value)*

B. At current prices	158	119	104	93	104	102	103	110	109	105	90	87	84	78	86	90	102	108	113
C. At 1930 prices	85	83	85	78	88	89	94	98	98	97	90	94	91	88	95	98	108	107	116

* At end of year.

TABLE 8.31 DRINK INDUSTRY (£M.)

	1920	1921	1922	1923	1924	1925	1926	1927	1928	1929	1930	1931	1932	1933	1934	1935	1936	1937	1938
(3) All Fixed Assets																			
A. At historical prices:																			
(c) Gross fixed capital formation	4·7	4·2	1·7	2·2	2·3	3·8	1·9	2·6	2·4	2·5	2·7	1·3	0·9	1·5	1·8	2·7	2·8	3·3	3·2
(d) Depreciation	1·8	1·9	1·8	1·8	1·8	1·9	1·9	1·9	1·9	2·0	2·1	2·1	2·1	2·0	2·0	2·0	2·0	2·3	2·4
(f) Depreciated value*	33	35	35	36	36	38	38	39	39	40	41	40	39	38	38	39	39	40	41
(h) First cost value*	67	70	71	72	73	76	77	78	79	81	82	83	83	83	84	85	87	89	91
(j) Land and depreciated value*	36	38	38	38	39	41	41	42	42	43	44	43	42	41	41	42	43	44	45
B. At current prices:																			
(d) Depreciation	5·2	3·8	2·9	2·7	2·8	2·7	2·7	2·7	2·7	2·7	2·7	2·5	2·4	2·3	2·3	2·5	2·7	3·0	3·1
(f) Depreciated value*	102	78	60	57	58	59	57	56	54	54	52	49	46	45	44	45	48	52	52
(h) First cost value*	217	163	127	123	127	127	125	123	120	122	119	113	109	108	108	112	118	129	131
(j) Land and depreciated value*	110	84	65	62	64	65	62	61	59	59	58	54	51	49	49	50	53	57	58
C. At 1930 prices:																			
(c) Gross fixed capital formation	2·3	2·9	1·4	2·1	2·1	3·5	1·8	2·5	2·3	2·4	2·7	1·5	1·0	1·6	2·0	2·8	2·7	3·0	2·9
(d) Depreciation	2·6	2·6	2·5	2·5	2·5	2·5	2·5	2·5	2·5	2·5	2·7	2·7	2·7	2·6	2·6	2·6	2·6	2·7	2·8
(f) Depreciated value*	54	55	53	53	53	54	53	53	53	52	52	51	50	49	48	48	48	49	49
(h) First cost value*	113	114	113	114	114	116	116	117	117	118	119	118	118	118	118	119	120	121	122
(j) Land and depreciated value*	59	59	58	58	58	59	58	58	58	58	58	57	55	54	53	54	54	54	55
(4) Stock-in-Trade and Work in Progress (Book value)																			
B. At current prices	35	32	27	23	23	24	23	24	24	22	21	20	18	18	19	19	20	21	21
C. At 1930 prices	19	21	22	19	19	19	19	21	21	20	21	21	19	20	21	21	22	22	22
(5) Other Information																			
Public house and other properties owned by breweries†	140	143	145	147	150	154	159	167	169	171	171	171	173	174	175	180	182	186	191

* At end of year.

† This is the estimated first cost value at historical prices of these properties and is not included in the above estimates for 8.31.

TABLE 8.32 TOBACCO INDUSTRY (£M.)

(3) All Fixed Assets

	1920	1921	1922	1923	1924	1925	1926	1927	1928	1929	1930	1931	1932	1933	1934	1935	1936	1937	1938
A. At historical prices:																			
(c) Gross fixed capital formation	1·2	2·1	1·0	0·6	0·9	0·9	0·7	0·7	1·1	0·6	0·8	0·6	0·7	0·4	0·7	0·9	0·8	1·0	1·4
(d) Depreciation	0·3	0·3	0·3	0·3	0·4	0·4	0·4	0·3	0·5	0·4	0·4	0·4	0·4	0·4	0·5	0·5	0·6	0·6	0·7
(f) Depreciated value*	4	6	6	7	7	8	8	8	9	9	9	10	10	10	10	10	10	11	12
(h) First cost value*	8	10	11	12	12	13	14	14	14	15	15	16	16	16	16	17	18	18	19
(j) Land and depreciated value*	4	6	7	7	8	8	9	9	10	10	10	10	10	10	10	11	11	12	12
B. At current prices:																			
(d) Depreciation	0·7	0·6	0·5	0·5	0·5	0·5	0·5	0·5	0·5	0·5	0·5	0·5	0·5	0·5	0·6	0·6	0·6	0·7	0·7
(f) Depreciated value*	11	9	8	8	8	9	9	9	9	9	9	9	9	9	9	9	10	11	12
(h) First cost value*	25	20	16	16	17	18	18	17	17	18	17	17	16	16	17	17	18	21	22
(j) Land and depreciated value*	12	10	8	8	9	10	10	10	10	10	10	10	10	10	10	10	11	12	13
C. At 1930 prices:																			
(c) Gross fixed capital formation	0·7	1·5	0·9	0·6	1·0	0·9	0·5	0·9	0·9	0·7	0·7	0·8	0·5	0·7	0·7	0·9	0·7	0·9	1·2
(d) Depreciation	0·3	0·3	0·4	0·4	0·4	0·5	0·5	0·5	0·5	0·5	0·5	0·5	0·6	0·6	0·6	0·6	0·6	0·6	0·7
(f) Depreciated value*	6	6	7	7	8	8	8	8	9	9	9	10	10	10	10	10	10	10	11
(h) First cost value*	13	14	15	15	16	16	16	16	17	17	17	18	18	18	18	18	19	19	20
(j) Land and depreciated value*	6	7	8	8	9	9	9	9	10	10	10	10	10	10	11	11	11	11	12

(4) Stock-in-Trade and Work in Progress (Book value)*

	1920	1921	1922	1923	1924	1925	1926	1927	1928	1929	1930	1931	1932	1933	1934	1935	1936	1937	1938
B. At current prices	38	38	37	34	38	37	39	37	34	36	35	33	31	30	35	36	39	42	48
C. At 1930 prices	34	36	37	34	39	39	41	37	34	35	35	34	30	29	34	34	37	40	46

* At end of year.

TABLE 8.33 FOOD INDUSTRY (£M.)

(3) All Fixed Assets

	1920	1921	1922	1923	1924	1925	1926	1927	1928	1929	1930	1931	1932	1933	1934	1935	1936	1937	1938
A. At historical prices:																			
(c) Gross fixed capital formation	15·3	13·6	5·5	5·2	5·6	5·8	4·3	5·0	7·0	7·8	6·1	4·6	3·9	4·5	6·5	5·1	8·6	6·8	7·9
(d) Depreciation	3·8	4·2	4·3	4·3	4·4	4·5	4·4	4·5	4·7	4·9	4·9	5·3	5·1	5·2	5·3	5·3	5·4	6·0	6·2
(f) Depreciated value*	80	90	91	92	93	94	94	95	96	99	100	100	98	98	99	99	102	103	105
(h) First cost value*	147	158	161	163	165	168	170	172	175	180	183	184	185	187	191	193	199	203	208
(j) Land and depreciated value*	85	95	96	97	98	100	100	101	102	105	106	106	104	104	105	105	109	109	111
B. At current prices:																			
(d) Depreciation	10·8	8·0	6·1	6·0	6·1	6·1	5·9	5·8	5·8	6·1	5·8	5·9	5·7	5·7	5·9	6·0	6·4	7·6	7·6
(f) Depreciated value*	236	184	143	137	141	139	134	132	127	131	126	119	114	112	113	115	123	133	133
(h) First cost value*	461	344	267	260	267	264	258	254	247	254	247	234	228	228	231	237	253	278	279
(j) Land and depreciated value*	251	196	153	147	151	149	144	141	137	140	136	128	123	121	122	124	132	142	143
C. At 1930 prices:																			
(c) Gross fixed capital formation	7·7	9·4	5·0	4·7	5·0	5·4	4·0	4·8	5·8	7·5	6·1	4·9	4·2	4·8	7·0	5·3	8·6	6·0	7·1
(d) Depreciation	5·3	5·5	5·5	5·5	5·5	5·6	5·5	5·5	5·6	5·8	5·8	6·2	6·1	6·1	6·2	6·2	6·3	6·8	6·9
(f) Depreciated value*	125	129	128	127	127	127	125	124	125	126	126	125	123	122	123	122	124	123	123
(h) First cost value*	234	239	240	240	240	241	241	241	242	245	246	247	247	247	249	250	254	255	258
(j) Land and depreciated value*	133	137	137	136	136	136	134	134	134	135	136	134	133	131	132	131	134	133	133

(4) Stock-in-Trade and Work in Progress (Book value)*

	1920	1921	1922	1923	1924	1925	1926	1927	1928	1929	1930	1931	1932	1933	1934	1935	1936	1937	1938
B. At current prices	85	49	39	36	43	41	42	49	51	47	33	34	35	31	32	34	43	45	43
C. At 1930 prices	32	26	27	25	30	31	33	39	42	41	33	39	41	38	39	42	49	45	48

* At end of year.

TABLE 8.40 CHEMICAL, LEATHER, CLOTHING AND PAPER INDUSTRIES (£M.)

(1) *Buildings and Works*

	1920	1921	1922	1923	1924	1925	1926	1927	1928	1929	1930	1931	1932	1933	1934	1935	1936	1937	1938
A. At historical prices:																			
(c) Gross fixed capital formation	14·5	10·5	8·6	6·3	9·2	9·6	8·2	6·3	7·3	11·6	7·7	4·5	3·9	5·0	4·5	5·9	7·6	8·8	9·0
(d) Depreciation	2·2	2·2	2·3	2·4	2·5	2·6	2·8	2·9	3·1	3·2	3·3	3·4	3·4	3·4	3·5	3·6	3·6	3·7	4·0
(f) Depreciated value*	103	111	118	121	128	135	141	144	148	157	161	162	163	164	165	167	171	176	181
(h) First cost value*	140	150	158	164	172	181	189	194	201	212	219	222	226	229	233	238	245	253	261
(i) Land*	10	10	11	11	12	13	13	14	14	15	15	16	16	16	16	17	17	18	18
B. At current prices:																			
(d) Depreciation	6·6	5·5	4·6	4·3	4·7	4·7	4·7	4·7	4·6	4·8	4·8	4·8	4·5	4·5	4·5	4·6	4·9	5·2	5·6
(f) Depreciated value*	314	262	216	205	218	223	220	218	212	220	218	209	199	195	195	200	211	225	233
(h) First cost value*	441	369	305	292	311	319	317	316	309	321	320	311	300	296	300	311	329	353	367
(i) Land*	31	26	21	20	22	22	22	22	22	22	22	22	21	21	21	21	23	25	26
C. At 1930 prices:																			
(c) Gross fixed capital formation	8·3	7·5	7·6	5·8	8·3	8·6	7·7	5·9	7·1	11·5	7·7	4·5	4·2	4·3	5·0	6·4	8·0	8·7	8·8
(d) Depreciation	3·8	4·0	4·0	4·1	4·2	4·3	4·3	4·4	4·5	4·8	4·8	4·8	4·8	4·9	5·0	5·1	5·1	5·2	5·3
(f) Depreciated value*	183	186	190	192	196	201	204	206	208	215	218	218	217	216	216	218	221	224	228
(h) First cost value*	257	263	268	273	280	287	294	298	304	314	320	323	326	329	333	338	344	352	359
(i) Land*	18	18	19	19	20	20	20	21	21	22	22	23	23	23	23	24	24	25	25

(2) *Plant, Machinery, Vehicles, etc.*

	1920	1921	1922	1923	1924	1925	1926	1927	1928	1929	1930	1931	1932	1933	1934	1935	1936	1937	1938
A. At historical prices:																			
(c) Gross fixed capital formation	20·4	22·1	10·5	9·5	8·3	12·4	13·2	12·0	16·3	16·5	10·5	8·1	9·3	10·2	12·8	13·6	14·5	23·2	15·5
(d) Depreciation	6·5	7·6	7·9	7·8	7·9	8·3	8·6	8·5	8·9	9·4	9·4	10·1	9·9	10·0	10·2	10·4	11·0	12·7	13·1
(f) Depreciated value*	78	92	95	97	97	101	105	109	116	124	125	123	122	122	125	128	132	142	144
(h) First cost value*	180	197	203	207	210	217	226	232	244	255	261	264	266	272	280	289	300	318	329
B. At current prices:																			
(d) Depreciation	17·7	12·5	9·3	9·4	9·5	9·5	9·6	9·7	10·0	10·8	10·2	10·3	10·2	10·3	10·5	11·1	12·2	15·8	15·4
(f) Depreciated value*	215	152	113	114	115	114	116	117	121	130	123	113	112	114	117	123	132	159	154
(h) First cost value*	552	375	279	284	287	283	285	285	287	304	290	272	273	281	288	304	330	392	388
C. At 1930 prices:																			
(c) Gross fixed capital formation	9·3	15·0	9·6	8·5	7·4	11·3	12·3	11·4	16·0	15·7	10·5	8·8	10·0	10·8	13·5	13·8	14·1	19·5	13·5
(d) Depreciation	8·0	8·4	8·6	8·6	8·7	8·6	9·2	9·1	9·7	10·1	10·2	10·9	11·0	10·8	11·1	11·3	11·6	13·1	13·4
(f) Depreciated value*	96	103	104	104	103	106	109	111	117	123	123	121	120	120	122	125	127	133	133
(h) First cost value*	248	255	257	258	258	262	267	271	279	287	290	292	291	295	301	308	316	329	336

TABLE 8.40 (cont.)

(3) All Fixed Assets

	1920	1921	1922	1923	1924	1925	1926	1927	1928	1929	1930	1931	1932	1933	1934	1935	1936	1937	1938
A. At historical prices:																			
(c) Gross fixed capital formation	34·9	32·6	19·1	15·8	17·5	22·0	21·4	18·3	23·6	28·1	18·2	12·6	13·2	15·2	17·3	19·5	22·1	32·0	24·5
(d) Depreciation	8·7	9·8	10·2	10·2	10·4	10·9	11·4	11·4	12·0	12·6	12·7	13·5	13·3	13·4	13·7	14·0	14·6	16·4	17·1
(f) Depreciated value*	181	204	213	218	225	236	246	253	265	280	286	285	285	286	289	295	302	318	326
(h) First cost value*	320	347	361	371	382	398	414	427	445	467	479	486	492	500	513	527	544	571	590
B. At current prices:																			
(d) Depreciation	24·3	18·0	13·9	13·7	14·2	14·2	14·3	14·4	14·6	15·6	15·0	15·1	14·7	14·8	15·0	15·7	17·1	21·0	21·0
(f) Depreciated value*	529	414	329	320	332	337	336	335	332	349	341	322	311	309	312	323	343	384	387
(h) First cost value*	992	744	585	576	598	602	602	601	596	624	610	583	572	578	589	615	659	745	756
C. At 1930 prices:																			
(c) Gross fixed capital formation	17·6	22·5	17·2	14·3	15·7	19·9	20·0	17·3	23·1	27·2	18·2	13·3	14·2	15·1	18·5	20·2	22·1	28·2	22·3
(d) Depreciation	11·8	12·4	12·6	12·7	12·9	12·9	13·5	13·5	14·2	14·9	15·0	15·7	15·8	15·7	16·1	16·4	16·7	18·3	18·7
(f) Depreciated value*	279	289	294	296	299	306	313	317	325	338	341	339	337	336	339	342	348	358	361
(h) First cost value*	504	518	525	532	538	549	560	569	583	601	610	615	618	624	634	646	661	680	695

(4) Stock-in-Trade and Work in Progress (Book value)*

	1920	1921	1922	1923	1924	1925	1926	1927	1928	1929	1930	1931	1932	1933	1934	1935	1936	1937	1938
B. At current prices	177	122	109	103	100	104	103	101	103	100	91	87	82	80	84	88	93	107	103
C. At 1930 prices	55	71	76	68	69	72	77	84	87	87	91	103	107	100	100	109	106	98	113

* At end of year.

TABLE 8.41 CHEMICAL INDUSTRY (£M.)

(3) All Fixed Assets

	1920	1921	1922	1923	1924	1925	1926	1927	1928	1929	1930	1931	1932	1933	1934	1935	1936	1937	1938
A. At historical prices:																			
(c) Gross fixed capital formation	15·2	9·0	5·9	3·5	5·9	6·5	6·6	7·4	11·5	15·2	6·8	4·8	4·0	4·0	7·7	8·2	9·7	12·2	8·9
(d) Depreciation	4·2	4·3	4·4	4·2	4·1	4·3	4·5	4·1	4·5	5·0	4·9	5·2	5·2	5·1	5·2	5·4	5·6	6·2	6·3
(f) Depreciated value*	82	87	88	88	89	92	94	97	104	114	116	116	114	113	116	119	123	129	131
(h) First cost value*	147	154	157	158	162	166	170	174	183	196	200	203	202	204	210	216	224	234	241
(j) Land and depreciated value*	86	91	93	92	94	97	99	102	109	120	122	122	121	120	122	125	129	136	139
B. At current prices:																			
(d) Depreciation	11·8	8·3	6·3	5·9	6·1	5·9	6·0	6·1	6·1	6·8	6·5	6·5	6·3	6·2	6·3	6·6	7·1	8·6	8·4
(f) Depreciated value*	240	180	140	133	136	136	133	132	133	143	139	130	124	122	123	128	136	152	152
(h) First cost value*	453	331	256	250	257	256	253	252	252	268	260	248	241	241	247	258	278	313	316
(j) Land and depreciated value*	252	190	149	141	145	145	142	141	142	152	148	139	133	130	132	136	146	162	162
C. At 1930 prices:																			
(c) Gross fixed capital formation	7·7	6·2	5·3	3·2	5·2	5·9	6·1	7·0	11·3	14·6	6·8	5·0	4·3	4·2	8·2	8·6	9·7	10·8	8·3
(d) Depreciation	5·7	5·7	5·7	5·5	5·5	5·4	5·6	5·6	6·0	6·5	6·5	6·8	6·7	6·6	6·7	6·9	7·0	7·6	7·5
(f) Depreciated value*	125	125	125	123	123	123	124	125	130	138	139	137	134	132	134	135	138	141	142
(h) First cost value*	227	230	231	230	232	234	236	239	246	257	260	262	260	260	265	271	278	285	291
(j) Land and depreciated value*	132	133	133	131	131	131	132	134	139	147	148	146	144	141	143	145	148	151	152

(4) Stock-in-Trade and Work in Progress (Book value)*

	1920	1921	1922	1923	1924	1925	1926	1927	1928	1929	1930	1931	1932	1933	1934	1935	1936	1937	1938
B. At current prices	60	45	42	40	38	38	36	37	38	38	36	34	33	31	31	33	36	41	40
C. At 1930 prices	25	25	29	30	29	31	30	33	34	35	36	37	35	34	34	35	38	40	40

* At end of year.

TABLE 8.42 LEATHER AND RUBBER INDUSTRIES (£M.)

(3) All Fixed Assets

	1920	1921	1922	1923	1924	1925	1926	1927	1928	1929	1930	1931	1932	1933	1934	1935	1936	1937	1938
A. At historical prices:																			
(c) Gross fixed capital formation	3·7	5·4	1·7	1·4	0·6	1·8	1·7	2·3	2·2	1·3	1·5	1·0	2·9	1·1	1·4	1·0	0·8	1·5	1·6
(d) Depreciation	0·7	1·0	1·0	1·0	1·0	1·1	1·1	1·3	1·3	1·4	1·4	1·5	1·6	1·5	1·5	1·4	1·3	1·5	1·5
(f) Depreciated value*	11	15	16	16	16	17	17	18	19	19	19	19	20	20	20	19	19	19	19
(h) First cost value*	21	25	27	28	28	29	30	32	34	34	35	36	38	39	40	40	40	41	42
(j) Land and depreciated value*	11	16	17	17	17	17	18	19	20	20	20	20	21	21	21	20	20	20	20
B. At current prices:																			
(d) Depreciation	1·8	1·5	1·1	1·2	1·2	1·2	1·2	1·3	1·3	1·4	1·4	1·3	1·5	1·5	1·4	1·4	1·4	1·7	1·8
(f) Depreciated value*	28	24	19	19	19	20	20	20	21	21	20	19	20	20	20	20	20	22	22
(h) First cost value*	59	46	36	36	36	37	37	38	38	39	38	36	38	39	39	41	43	48	48
(j) Land and depreciated value*	29	25	20	20	20	20	21	21	21	22	21	20	21	21	21	21	21	23	23
C. At 1930 prices:																			
(c) Gross fixed capital formation	1·8	3·8	1·6	1·3	0·6	0·6	1·6	2·2	2·1	1·4	1·5	1·1	3·1	1·3	1·6	1·0	0·8	1·3	1·5
(d) Depreciation	0·9	1·0	1·1	1·1	1·1	1·1	1·2	1·2	1·3	1·3	1·3	1·4	1·6	1·5	1·5	1·4	1·3	1·4	1·5
(f) Depreciated value*	14	17	18	18	17	18	18	19	20	20	20	20	22	21	21	21	20	20	20
(h) First cost value*	29	32	33	33	33	34	35	36	37	38	38	39	41	41	42	42	42	43	43
(j) Land and depreciated value*	15	18	18	19	18	19	19	20	21	21	21	21	22	22	22	22	21	21	21

(4) Stock-in-Trade and Work in Progress (Book value)*

	1920	1921	1922	1923	1924	1925	1926	1927	1928	1929	1930	1931	1932	1933	1934	1935	1936	1937	1938
B. At current prices	24	16	13	11	11	14	15	14	15	13	11	10	9	9	12	13	12	14	12
C. At 1930 prices	9	12	10	7	7	5	7	7	9	10	11	14	16	13	15	15	12	11	13

* At end of year.

TABLE 8.43 CLOTHING INDUSTRY (£M.)

(3) All Fixed Assets

	1920	1921	1922	1923	1924	1925	1926	1927	1928	1929	1930	1931	1932	1933	1934	1935	1936	1937	1938
A. At historical prices:																			
(c) Gross fixed capital formation	6·1	4·7	5·7	3·9	4·4	5·2	4·4	1·5	1·9	3·2	3·2	2·4	1·9	2·7	1·4	1·9	1·6	4·7	3·9
(d) Depreciation	0·8	0·8	1·0	1·1	1·2	1·2	1·3	1·4	1·4	1·4	1·5	1·6	1·5	1·6	1·6	1·7	1·8	1·9	2·1
(f) Depreciated value*	31	34	39	42	45	49	52	52	53	55	56	57	57	57	57	57	57	60	62
(h) First cost value*	46	50	55	59	63	67	71	73	74	77	79	81	83	84	85	87	88	92	96
(j) Land and depreciated value*	33	37	42	45	48	53	56	56	57	59	60	61	62	62	62	62	62	65	66
B. At current prices:																			
(d) Depreciation	2·0	1·6	1·4	1·4	1·6	1·6	1·6	1·6	1·7	1·7	1·7	1·8	1·6	1·7	1·7	1·8	2·0	2·4	2·4
(f) Depreciated value*	89	75	64	63	68	72	72	71	69	71	70	68	66	65	64	66	68	75	77
(h) First cost value*	140	115	97	95	102	106	107	106	103	106	106	103	100	100	101	105	110	122	126
(j) Land and depreciated value*	97	82	70	69	74	78	79	77	75	77	76	74	71	70	70	72	74	81	84
C. At 1930 prices:																			
(c) Gross fixed capital formation	3·3	3·3	5·1	3·5	3·9	4·6	4·1	1·4	1·9	3·0	3·2	2·5	2·1	1·8	1·5	1·9	1·6	4·2	3·6
(d) Depreciation	1·1	1·1	1·2	1·4	1·5	1·4	1·5	1·5	1·6	1·7	1·7	1·8	1·8	1·8	1·9	1·9	2·0	2·1	2·2
(f) Depreciated value*	51	53	57	59	61	65	67	67	67	69	70	71	71	71	71	71	70	73	74
(h) First cost value*	79	81	85	89	92	96	99	100	101	103	106	108	109	110	111	112	113	117	119
(j) Land and depreciated value*	56	58	62	64	67	70	73	73	73	75	76	77	77	77	77	77	77	79	80
(4) Stock-in-Trade and Work in Progress (Book value)*																			
B. At current prices	41	30	29	26	26	25	25	23	24	21	18	17	16	16	15	17	19	20	20
C. At 1930 prices	11	19	19	16	14	15	18	17	17	16	18	22	21	20	18	20	21	20	24

* At end of year.

9

TABLE 8.44 PAPER AND HARDBOARD INDUSTRY (£M.)

(3) All Fixed Assets

	1920	1921	1922	1923	1924	1925	1926	1927	1928	1929	1930	1931	1932	1933	1934	1935	1936	1937	1938
A. At historical prices:																			
(c) Gross fixed capital formation	5·3	3·8	2·8	2·8	3·4	3·0	2·4	2·4	4·1	4·9	4·0	1·8	2·1	4·9	2·9	3·3	3·0	5·9	4·3
(d) Depreciation	1·2	1·4	1·4	1·4	1·5	1·6	1·7	1·7	1·8	1·8	1·9	2·0	1·9	2·1	2·2	2·2	2·3	2·6	2·8
(f) Depreciated value*	20	23	24	26	27	29	30	30	33	36	38	38	38	41	41	42	43	47	48
(h) First cost value*	40	43	44	46	49	51	52	54	57	61	64	65	66	70	72	74	76	81	85
(j) Land and depreciated value*	21	24	25	27	28	30	31	32	34	37	39	39	40	43	43	44	45	49	50
B. At current prices:																			
(d) Depreciation	3·3	2·4	1·8	1·9	1·9	2·0	2·0	1·9	2·0	2·1	2·1	2·0	2·0	2·1	2·2	2·3	2·5	3·1	3·2
(f) Depreciated value*	58	43	34	34	36	37	37	37	37	41	41	39	38	41	42	44	47	54	55
(h) First cost value*	123	88	68	68	71	71	71	71	71	76	75	71	71	75	76	80	86	99	101
(j) Land and depreciated value*	60	45	36	36	38	39	38	38	39	43	43	41	40	43	44	46	49	57	58
C. At 1930 prices:																			
(c) Gross fixed capital formation	2·6	2·5	2·4	2·5	3·1	2·7	2·3	2·2	3·9	4·8	4·0	1·9	2·3	5·2	3·1	3·4	3·1	5·3	3·8
(d) Depreciation	1·5	1·6	1·6	1·6	1·7	1·8	1·9	1·8	1·9	2·0	2·1	2·1	2·1	2·2	2·3	2·4	2·4	2·7	2·8
(f) Depreciated value*	29	30	31	32	33	34	34	35	37	39	41	41	41	44	45	46	47	50	50
(h) First cost value*	59	60	61	62	64	65	66	67	69	72	75	76	76	80	82	84	85	89	91
(j) Land and depreciated value*	30	31	32	33	34	35	36	36	38	41	43	43	44	47	48	49	49	52	53

(4) Stock-in-Trade and Work in Progress (Book value)*

	1920	1921	1922	1923	1924	1925	1926	1927	1928	1929	1930	1931	1932	1933	1934	1935	1936	1937	1938
B. At current prices	18	12	9	8	9	8	9	9	9	10	10	10	9	9	10	10	10	13	14
C. At 1930 prices	3	5	6	5	6	7	7	8	9	9	10	11	13	12	13	15	14	11	16

* At end of year.

TABLE 8.45 NEWSPAPERS, PRINTING AND STATIONERY INDUSTRIES (£M.)

(3) All Fixed Assets

	1920	1921	1922	1923	1924	1925	1926	1927	1928	1929	1930	1931	1932	1933	1934	1935	1936	1937	1938
A. At historical prices:																			
(c) Gross fixed capital formation	4·6	9·7	3·0	4·2	3·2	5·5	6·3	4·7	3·9	3·5	2·7	2·6	2·3	2·5	3·9	5·1	7·0	7·7	5·8
(d) Depreciation	1·8	2·3	2·4	2·5	2·6	2·7	2·8	2·9	3·0	3·0	3·0	3·2	3·1	3·1	3·2	3·3	3·6	4·2	4·4
(f) Depreciated value*	37	44	45	47	47	50	53	55	56	57	57	56	55	55	55	57	60	64	65
(h) First cost value*	67	76	77	80	82	86	91	94	97	99	101	102	103	104	107	110	116	123	127
(j) Land and depreciated value*	39	47	47	49	50	52	56	58	59	60	60	59	58	57	58	60	63	67	68
B. At current prices:																			
(d) Depreciation	5·4	4·2	3·3	3·3	3·4	3·5	3·5	3·5	3·5	3·6	3·4	3·5	3·3	3·3	3·4	3·6	4·1	5·2	5·2
(f) Depreciated value*	115	92	72	70	72	73	74	74	73	74	70	66	63	62	63	66	72	81	81
(h) First cost value*	217	165	128	127	131	132	134	134	132	136	131	125	122	123	125	131	143	162	165
(j) Land and depreciated value*	122	98	76	75	77	78	79	79	77	78	75	70	67	66	67	70	76	86	86
C. At 1930 prices:																			
(c) Gross fixed capital formation	2·2	6·7	2·8	2·8	2·9	5·0	5·9	4·5	3·9	3·4	2·7	2·8	2·4	2·6	4·1	5·3	6·9	6·6	5·1
(d) Depreciation	2·6	3·0	3·0	3·1	3·1	3·2	3·3	3·4	3·4	3·4	3·4	3·6	3·6	3·6	3·7	3·8	4·0	4·5	4·7
(f) Depreciated value*	61	65	64	65	65	67	69	70	71	71	70	70	68	68	68	69	72	74	75
(h) First cost value*	110	115	116	117	118	121	125	127	129	130	131	132	132	133	135	138	143	147	150
(j) Land and depreciated value*	65	69	68	69	69	71	74	75	75	76	75	74	73	72	73	74	77	79	80

(4) Stock-in-Trade and Work in Progress (Book value)*

	1920	1921	1922	1923	1924	1925	1926	1927	1928	1929	1930	1931	1932	1933	1934	1935	1936	1937	1938
B. At current prices	34	18	16	18	17	18	18	18	18	17	16	16	14	15	15	15	15	18	17
C. At 1930 prices	7	8	11	11	13	15	15	17	18	16	16	19	20	20	19	24	21	15	20

* At end of year.

TABLE 8.50 WOOD, CLAY AND MISCELLANEOUS MANUFACTURING INDUSTRIES (£M.)

(1) Buildings and Works

	1920	1921	1922	1923	1924	1925	1926	1927	1928	1929	1930	1931	1932	1933	1934	1935	1936	1937	1938
A. At historical prices:																			
(c) Gross fixed capital formation	8·3	6·7	2·8	1·4	2·5	2·8	4·6	2·9	3·2	3·1	4·8	1·4	0·3	2·5	4·6	3·2	2·6	4·7	3·8
(d) Depreciation	1·3	1·4	1·5	1·6	1·6	1·6	1·6	1·7	1·7	1·8	1·8	1·9	1·8	1·8	1·8	1·8	2·0	2·0	2·0
(f) Depreciated value*	51	56	58	57	58	60	62	64	65	66	70	69	66	67	70	71	72	74	76
(h) First cost value*	76	82	84	84	86	88	92	94	97	99	103	104	103	104	108	111	113	117	120
(i) Land*	5	6	6	6	6	6	6	6	7	7	8	8	7	7	8	8	8	8	8
B. At current prices:																			
(d) Depreciation	4·3	3·6	2·9	2·8	2·9	2·9	2·9	2·8	2·7	2·8	2·8	2·7	2·4	2·4	2·5	2·5	2·7	3·0	3·0
(f) Depreciated value*	154	129	104	96	99	99	98	96	93	94	94	88	81	79	82	84	87	93	95
(h) First cost value*	236	198	161	151	158	160	158	157	153	155	155	150	141	139	143	148	155	166	172
(i) Land*	16	14	11	11	11	11	11	11	11	11	11	10	10	10	10	11	12	12	12
C. At 1930 prices:																			
(c) Gross fixed capital formation	4·8	4·6	2·3	1·1	1·2	2·5	4·3	2·7	3·2	2·9	4·8	1·5	0·5	2·7	5·1	3·5	2·8	4·7	3·6
(d) Depreciation	2·4	2·4	2·5	2·5	2·5	2·5	2·5	2·6	2·7	2·8	2·8	2·8	2·8	2·8	2·9	3·0	2·9	3·0	3·0
(f) Depreciated value*	89	92	91	90	92	89	91	91	91	91	94	92	88	88	90	91	91	92	93
(h) First cost value*	137	141	142	142	142	144	147	148	150	151	155	156	153	155	159	161	162	166	168
(i) Land*	10	10	10	10	10	11	10	10	10	11	11	11	11	11	11	11	12	12	12

(2) Plant, Machinery, Vehicles, etc.

	1920	1921	1922	1923	1924	1925	1926	1927	1928	1929	1930	1931	1932	1933	1934	1935	1936	1937	1938
A. At historic prices:																			
(c) Gross fixed capital formation	7·6	7·1	2·4	3·0	2·3	5·9	4·4	7·4	3·7	3·2	6·4	3·8	2·8	4·8	7·3	6·8	6·7	10·0	7·3
(d) Depreciation	3·1	3·4	3·2	3·2	3·2	3·4	3·4	3·7	3·8	3·7	3·9	4·4	4·3	4·1	4·6	4·8	4·9	5·8	6·1
(f) Depreciated value*	36	40	39	39	38	40	41	45	45	44	47	46	45	45	48	50	52	56	57
(h) First cost value*	85	89	89	89	88	91	92	97	97	98	101	102	101	103	107	111	115	122	126
B. At current prices:																			
(d) Depreciation	8·8	5·8	4·3	4·3	4·1	4·2	4·1	4·2	4·2	4·2	4·1	4·3	4·2	4·3	4·6	4·8	5·2	6·8	7·0
(f) Depreciated value*	104	70	50	49	48	49	48	51	49	50	49	46	44	46	48	51	56	67	66
(h) First cost value*	268	178	128	128	127	124	122	123	119	121	116	108	107	109	113	118	124	150	147
C. At 1930 prices:																			
(c) Gross fixed capital formation	3·6	4·9	2·2	2·8	2·0	5·5	4·2	7·0	3·6	2·9	6·4	4·0	2·9	5·1	7·6	6·9	6·4	8·4	6·3
(d) Depreciation	3·9	4·0	3·9	3·7	3·8	3·8	3·9	3·9	3·9	3·9	4·1	4·5	4·4	4·4	4·7	4·9	5·1	5·7	6·0
(f) Depreciated value*	47	48	46	45	43	45	45	48	48	47	49	49	47	48	51	53	54	57	57
(h) First cost value*	120	121	118	117	114	115	114	117	116	114	116	114	114	114	118	120	122	126	127

(3) All Fixed Assets

A. At historical prices:

(c) Gross fixed capital formation	15·9	13·8	5·2	4·4	4·8	8·7	9·0	10·3	6·9	6·3	11·2	5·2	3·1	7·3	11·9	10·0	9·3	14·7	11·1
(d) Depreciation	4·4	4·8	4·7	4·8	4·8	5·0	5·0	5·4	5·5	5·5	5·7	6·3	6·1	5·9	6·4	6·6	6·9	7·8	8·1
(f) Depreciated value*	87	96	96	96	96	100	104	108	110	111	116	115	111	112	118	121	123	130	133
(h) First-cost value*	161	171	172	173	174	179	184	191	194	197	204	206	204	207	216	222	227	238	245

B. At current prices:

(d) Depreciation	13·1	9·4	7·2	7·1	7·0	7·1	7·0	7·0	6·9	7·0	6·9	7·0	6·6	6·7	7·1	7·3	7·9	9·8	10·0
(f) Depreciated value*	258	198	154	146	147	148	146	147	142	143	143	134	125	125	130	136	143	160	161
(h) First-cost value*	504	375	290	279	285	284	281	280	272	276	272	258	248	248	256	266	279	316	319

C. At 1930 prices:

(c) Gross fixed capital formation	8·3	9·5	4·5	3·9	3·2	8·0	8·5	9·7	6·8	5·8	11·2	5·5	3·4	7·8	12·7	10·4	9·2	13·1	9·9
(d) Depreciation	6·3	6·4	6·4	6·2	6·3	6·3	6·4	6·5	6·6	6·7	6·9	7·3	7·2	7·2	7·6	7·9	8·0	8·7	9·0
(f) Depreciated value*	136	139	137	135	135	134	136	139	139	138	143	141	136	136	141	144	145	149	150
(h) First-cost value*	257	261	260	258	256	259	261	265	266	266	272	271	268	269	276	281	284	291	295

(4) Stock-in-Trade and Work in Progress (Book value)*

B. At current prices	102	76	54	53	64	72	74	68	70	69	66	63	61	65	60	61	65	72	69
C. At 1930 prices	47	46	44	45	55	63	69	63	68	69	71	70	67	71	64	67	68	68	65

* At end of year.

TABLE 8.51 WOOD AND CORK; AND BUILDING AND CONTRACTING INDUSTRIES (£M.)

(3) *All Fixed Assets*

	1920	1921	1922	1923	1924	1925	1926	1927	1928	1929	1930	1931	1932	1933	1934	1935	1936	1937	1938
A. At historical prices:																			
(c) Gross fixed capital formation	7·6	6·7	3·0	1·4	3·1	3·8	4·7	2·2	3·1	2·0	6·9	2·6	0·3	3·5	6·8	5·2	2·9	6·1	5·6
(d) Depreciation	1·4	1·7	1·7	1·8	1·8	1·9	1·9	2·0	2·0	2·0	2·2	2·5	2·4	2·4	2·6	2·7	2·9	3·3	3·5
(f) Depreciated value*	33	38	40	39	41	42	45	45	46	46	51	51	49	50	54	57	57	60	62
(h) First cost value*	56	62	64	64	66	69	72	73	75	76	82	83	83	85	90	95	96	101	106
(j) Land and depreciated value*	36	41	43	42	44	45	48	49	50	50	55	55	53	54	58	61	61	64	66
B. At current prices:																			
(d) Depreciation	4·2	3·2	2·5	2·4	2·5	2·5	2·5	2·5	2·5	2·5	2·6	2·7	2·5	2·6	2·9	3·0	3·3	4·0	4·2
(f) Depreciated value*	95	77	62	58	60	61	62	60	59	59	62	59	54	55	59	62	65	72	73
(h) First cost value*	169	132	105	100	105	106	106	105	102	104	106	102	97	98	104	110	113	130	133
(j) Land and depreciated value*	102	83	67	63	65	66	67	65	64	64	67	64	59	59	64	67	70	78	79
C. At 1930 prices:																			
(c) Gross fixed capital formation	4·1	4·6	2·7	1·2	1·8	3·5	4·4	2·1	3·1	1·9	6·9	2·7	0·4	3·8	7·3	5·5	2·8	5·5	5·0
(d) Depreciation	2·1	2·2	2·3	2·2	2·3	2·3	2·4	2·3	2·4	2·4	2·6	2·8	2·7	2·7	3·0	3·3	3·2	3·6	3·8
(f) Depreciated value*	52	54	55	54	56	55	57	57	58	57	62	61	59	60	64	66	66	68	69
(h) First cost value*	90	93	94	93	94	96	99	99	100	100	106	107	105	107	113	117	118	122	125
(j) Land and depreciated value*	56	59	59	58	61	60	62	62	63	62	67	67	64	65	70	72	72	74	75
(4) *Stock-in-Trade and Work in Progress (Book value)**																			
B. At current prices	65	48	34	32	38	42	46	33	31	36	41	40	37	30	33	28	29	35	33
C. At 1930 prices	31	28	26	27	32	36	43	31	29	35	41	44	42	34	38	32	33	35	33

* At end of year.

TABLE 8.52 CEMENT, BRICKS AND OTHER CLAY INDUSTRIES (£M.)

(3) All Fixed Assets

	1920	1921	1922	1923	1924	1925	1926	1927	1928	1929	1930	1931	1932	1933	1934	1935	1936	1937	1938
A. At historical prices:																			
(c) Gross fixed capital formation	4·3	3·5	1·0	1·8	0·5	2·4	1·4	2·6	2·1	2·0	1·8	0·7	1·2	1·1	2·7	2·6	2·9	3·4	2·3
(d) Depreciation	1·5	1·6	1·5	1·5	1·5	1·5	1·4	1·5	1·5	1·6	1·6	1·7	1·6	1·5	1·6	1·7	1·8	2·0	2·0
(f) Depreciated value*	24	26	25	26	25	26	26	27	27	28	28	27	26	25	26	27	28	29	30
(h) First cost value*	48	51	50	51	50	51	51	52	53	54	54	53	53	52	54	55	56	58	59
(j) Land and depreciated value*	25	27	27	27	26	27	27	28	29	29	29	28	27	27	28	28	30	31	31
B. At current prices:																			
(d) Depreciation	4·5	3·1	2·3	2·3	2·2	2·2	2·1	2·0	2·0	2·0	1·9	1·9	1·8	1·8	1·8	1·9	2·0	2·5	2·5
(f) Depreciated value*	72	53	40	38	37	37	36	36	35	35	34	31	29	28	29	30	32	36	36
(h) First cost value*	152	110	83	81	81	80	77	76	74	75	71	66	63	62	63	65	69	77	76
(j) Land and depreciated value*	76	56	42	41	40	40	38	38	37	38	36	33	31	30	31	32	34	39	38
C. At 1930 prices:																			
(c) Gross fixed capital formation	2·2	2·4	0·8	1·7	0·4	2·2	1·4	2·4	2·1	1·9	1·8	0·7	1·2	1·2	2·9	2·6	2·9	3·0	2·1
(d) Depreciation	2·1	2·1	2·1	2·0	2·0	2·0	1·9	1·9	1·9	1·9	1·9	2·0	2·0	1·9	2·0	2·0	2·1	2·2	2·2
(f) Depreciated value*	37	37	36	35	34	34	33	34	34	34	34	32	31	30	31	32	32	33	33
(h) First cost value*	76	76	75	74	73	73	72	72	72	72	71	70	68	67	68	68	69	70	70
(j) Land and depreciated value*	39	39	38	37	36	36	36	36	36	36	36	35	33	32	33	34	35	35	35
(4) Stock-in-Trade and Work in Progress (Book value)*																			
B. At current prices	6	5	5	4	4	5	4	5	5	4	5	5	4	4	4	4	4	5	5
C. At 1930 prices	3	3	4	3	3	4	3	4	5	4	5	5	4	4	4	4	4	4	4

* At end of year.

TABLE 8.53 GLASS AND POTTERY INDUSTRIES (£M.)

	1920	1921	1922	1923	1924	1925	1926	1927	1928	1929	1930	1931	1932	1933	1934	1935	1936	1937	1938
(3) All Fixed Assets																			
A. At historical prices:																			
(c) Gross fixed capital formation	2·4	0·1	0·6	0·3	0·3	1·1	1·0	2·1	0·8	0·9	0·8	0·5	0·5	0·6	0·8	0·5	1·1	1·2	1·1
(d) Depreciation	0·7	0·6	0·6	0·6	0·6	0·6	0·6	0·7	0·8	0·7	0·7	0·8	0·8	0·7	0·8	0·8	0·8	0·8	0·9
(f) Depreciated value*	13	13	13	13	12	13	13	15	15	15	15	15	14	14	14	14	14	15	15
(h) First cost value*	25	25	25	24	24	25	25	27	27	28	28	28	28	28	28	28	29	30	30
(j) Land and depreciated value*	14	14	14	13	13	14	14	16	16	16	16	16	15	15	15	15	15	16	16
B. At current prices:																			
(d) Depreciation	1·9	1·3	1·0	1·0	0·9	1·0	1·0	1·0	0·9	1·0	1·0	0·9	0·9	0·9	0·9	0·9	0·9	1·2	1·2
(f) Depreciated value*	40	29	22	21	21	21	20	21	20	20	19	18	17	17	17	16	17	19	19
(h) First cost value*	80	57	44	42	42	42	41	42	41	41	40	37	36	36	36	37	39	43	43
(j) Land and depreciated value*	43	31	24	22	22	22	22	23	22	22	21	19	18	18	18	18	19	20	20
C. At 1930 prices:																			
(c) Gross fixed capital formation	1·2	0·1	0·5	0·2	0·3	1·0	0·9	2·0	0·7	0·8	0·8	0·5	0·5	0·6	0·9	0·5	1·0	1·1	0·9
(d) Depreciation	0·9	0·9	0·8	0·8	0·8	0·8	0·8	0·9	0·9	1·0	1·0	1·0	1·0	1·0	1·0	1·0	1·0	1·0	1·1
(f) Depreciated value*	21	20	20	19	19	19	19	20	20	20	19	19	18	18	18	17	17	17	17
(h) First cost value*	40	40	39	39	38	38	38	40	40	40	40	39	39	39	39	39	39	39	39
(j) Land and depreciated value*	23	22	21	21	20	20	20	21	21	21	21	20	20	19	19	19	19	19	19
(4) Stock-in-Trade and Work in Progress (Book value)*																			
B. At current prices	3	3	4	4	5	5	4	4	5	5	5	5	5	5	6	6	6	6	7
C. At 1930 prices	1	2	4	4	4	4	4	4	5	5	5	5	5	5	6	6	6	6	7

* At end of year.

TABLE 8.54 TOYS, MUSICAL INSTRUMENTS AND MISCELLANEOUS MANUFACTURING INDUSTRIES (£M.)

	1920	1921	1922	1923	1924	1925	1926	1927	1928	1929	1930	1931	1932	1933	1934	1935	1936	1937	1938
(3) All Fixed Assets																			
A. At historical prices:																			
(c) Gross fixed capital formation	1·6	3·5	0·6	0·9	0·9	1·4	1·9	3·4	0·9	1·4	1·7	1·4	1·1	2·1	1·6	1·7	2·4	4·0	2·1
(d) Depreciation	0·8	0·9	0·9	0·9	0·9	1·0	1·1	1·2	1·2	1·2	1·2	1·3	1·3	1·3	1·4	1·4	1·4	1·7	1·7
(f) Depreciated value*	16	19	18	18	18	19	20	22	22	22	22	23	22	23	23	23	24	27	27
(h) First cost value*	31	34	34	34	34	35	36	39	39	39	41	41	41	42	43	44	46	49	50
(j) Land and depreciated value*	17	20	19	19	19	20	21	23	23	23	24	24	23	24	24	25	26	28	28
B. At current prices:																			
(d) Depreciation	2·5	1·8	1·4	1·4	1·4	1·4	1·4	1·5	1·5	1·5	1·4	1·5	1·4	1·4	1·5	1·5	1·7	2·1	2·1
(f) Depreciated value*	51	40	30	29	29	29	29	30	29	29	28	27	25	26	26	27	29	34	33
(h) First cost value*	103	76	58	56	57	57	56	57	56	57	55	53	51	52	52	54	58	67	67
(j) Land and depreciated value*	54	42	32	31	31	31	31	32	31	31	30	29	27	28	28	29	31	36	36
C. At 1930 prices:																			
(c) Gross fixed capital formation	0·8	2·4	0·5	0·8	0·7	1·3	1·8	3·2	0·9	1·2	1·7	1·6	1·3	2·2	1·6	1·8	2·5	3·5	1·9
(d) Depreciation	1·2	1·2	1·2	1·2	1·2	1·2	1·3	1·4	1·4	1·4	1·4	1·5	1·5	1·6	1·6	1·6	1·7	1·9	1·9
(f) Depreciated value*	27	28	27	27	26	26	27	29	28	28	28	28	28	28	28	28	29	31	31
(h) First cost value*	52	53	52	52	52	52	52	55	54	54	55	55	55	56	56	57	58	61	61
(j) Land and depreciated value*	28	30	29	28	28	28	29	30	30	30	30	30	29	30	30	30	31	33	33
(4) Stock-in-Trade and Work in Progress (Book value)*																			
B. At current prices	27	20	11	12	17	20	20	25	27	24	18	17	17	22	22	21	25	26	24
C. At 1930 prices	12	14	10	11	16	19	19	24	26	23	18	18	18	24	23	21	24	22	20

* At end of year.

NOTES TO TABLES 8.12 TO 8.54

For a general description of the method of estimation from samples of accounts see appendix 2.1 to chapter 2 (p. 27).

The general details of the methods used for each individual trade group except cotton are given below for each type of asset, although only the aggregate of all fixed assets is published for the twenty-one individual trade groups in Tables 8.12 to 8.54. Additional specific details for each trade group are given in the supplement on pp. 139-42.

The estimates of each type of asset are given in Tables 8.10 to 8.50 for the following wider industrial groupings:

Table 8.10 *Textile Industries* This is the total of the estimates from the following tables:

8.11 Cotton; 8.12 Wool and worsted; 8.13 Rayon and Silk; 8.14 Other textiles; 8.15 Textile finishing.

Table 8.20 *Metal and Metal-using Industries* This is the total of: 8.21 Iron and Steel; 8.22 Shipbuilding, railway and general engineering; 8.23 Electrical Engineering; 8.24 Motor Vehicles; 8.25 Non-ferrous metals.

Table 8.30 *Food, Drink and Tobacco Industries* This is the total of:

8.31 Drink; 8.32 Tobacco; 8.33 Food.

Table 8.40 *Chemical, Leather, Clothing and Paper Industries* This is the total of:

8.41 Chemicals; 8.42 Leather and rubber; 8.43 Clothing; 8.44 Paper and hardboard; 8.45 Newspapers, printing and stationery.

Table 8.50 *Wood, Building, Clay and Miscellaneous Manufacturing Industries* This is the total of:

8.51 Wood and cork; Building and contracting; 8.52 Cement, bricks and other clay; 8.53 Glass and pottery; 8.54 Toys, musical instruments and miscellaneous manufacturing.

(1) Buildings and Works

A. At historical prices:

(c) *Gross fixed capital formation*: First difference in A (f), plus A (d).

(d) *Depreciation*: Straight line method, assuming a life of 60 years.

(f) *Depreciated value of buildings etc. held at end of year*: For each year by deducting from the depreciated value of all fixed assets derived from samples of accounts (see (3) A (j)) the estimated depreciated value of plant, etc. (see (2) A (f)) and an allowance for land (see A (i)).

(g) *First cost value of buildings etc. scrapped*: For most trade groups the total amount assumed due over the 19 years taken as $\frac{1\cdot9}{60}$ of the first cost value in 1878 (given by the age-structure used in A (h)) and spread in equal annual amounts. (See chapter 2,

p. 22). In a few cases, particularly the newer industries such as rayon or motor vehicles, special estimates were made.

(h) *First cost value of buildings etc. held at end of year*: For 1919 derived from A (f) by imputing the age-structure derived from the series of annual values of business premises (Houses etc. used solely for Trade, etc.) assessed for Inhabited House Duty. (See chapter 2, p. 16). This gives a ratio for A (f) to A (h) of 67·7%.

(i) *Land at end of year*: 7% of A (h).

B. At current prices:

The series at 1930 prices multiplied by index B.

C. At constant (1930) prices:

(c) *Gross fixed capital formation*: A (c) deflated by index B.

(d) *Depreciation*: As for A (d).

(f) *Depreciated value of buildings etc. held at end of year*: For 1919 derived from A (f) by the standard estimate that the average historical costs of buildings (index B) can be taken as 50·8% of the costs at 1930 prices. See chapter 2, p. 24.

(g) *First cost value of buildings etc. scrapped*: As for A (g).

(h) *First cost value of plant etc. held at end of year*: For 1919 derived from A (h) by the same standard estimate as for C (f).

(2) Plant, Vehicles, Equipment, etc.

A. At historical prices:

(c) *Gross fixed capital formation*: First difference in A (f) plus A (d).

(d) *Depreciation*: Reducing balance method at the rate found in a sample of assessments for 1937 (income tax year 1838-9) with adjustments for the additional allowances introduced in 1931 and 1937.

(f) *Depreciated value of plant etc. held at end of year*: For each year derived from samples of company accounts. On the basis of information available for each trade group one of three methods was chosen in the following order of preference:

1. the chain of year-to-year changes in the value of plant, etc. given in samples of accounts, grossed-up as for all fixed assets, (see (3) A (j)).

2. the ratio of plant to all fixed assets given in samples of accounts applied to the estimate of all fixed assets, (see (3) A (j)).

3. the chain of year-to-year changes in wear and tear allowances in samples of assessments investigated by the Inland Revenue, divided by the average rate of depreciation.

(g) *First cost value of plant etc. scrapped*: the total amount assumed due over the nineteen years taken as a fraction (19/L where L = average length of life given by A (d)) of A (h) for 1919, and generally spread in equal annual amounts.

(h) *First cost value of plant etc. held at end of year*: For 1919 derived from A (f) by imputing the standard estimate for the age-structure of what is assumed to be a stationary population of assets. Depreciation is assumed to have been written off by the reducing balance method at the rates given by A (d). See chapter 2, p. 16.

B. At current prices:

The series at 1930 prices multiplied by index C.

C. At constant (1930) prices:

(c) *Gross fixed capital formation*: A (c) deflated by index C.

(d) *Depreciation*: As for A (d)

(f) *Depreciated value of plant etc. held at end of year*: For 1919 derived from A (f) by the standard estimate that the average historical costs of machinery (index C) can be taken as 65·3% of the costs at 1930 prices. (See chapter 2, p. 24.)

(g) *First cost value of plant etc. scrapped*: As for A (g).

(h) *First cost value of plant etc. held at end of year*: For 1919 derived from A (h) by the same standard estimate as for C (f).

(3) All Fixed Assets

A. At historical prices:

(j) *Depreciated value of all fixed assets (including land) held at end of year*:

For each year from a chain of year-to-year changes in all fixed assets in the samples of company accounts excluding revaluations and transfers of assets. These samples were grossed-up on the basis of the wear and tear allowances for these companies as a proportion of the total allowances for the trade group in one of the inter-war censuses of assessments.

(4) Stock-in-Trade and Work in Progress

B. At current prices:

For each year derived from the samples of accounts. On the basis of the information available for each trade group one of the two following methods was chosen:

1. the ratio of stocks to all fixed assets in the accounts applied to the estimate of all fixed assets, (see (3) A (j)).

2. the chain of year-to-year changes in stocks observed in the accounts, grossed-up as for all fixed assets.

C. At constant (1930) prices:

The series at current prices deflated by the price indices given in the supplement to the Notes on pp. 139-42.

SUPPLEMENT TO NOTES TO TABLES 8.12 TO 8.54

No. of table	Trade or Industry and S.I.C. headings*	Per cent of group covered in 1937 by sample of accounts†	Method used to estimate		Price index used to obtain stocks at 1930 prices‖	Per cent of property let in 1937¶	Special notes
			Depreciated value of plant, etc.‡	Stocks at current prices§			
8.12	Wool and worsted 112, 120	12	Ratio of plant to all fixed assets	Ratio of stocks to all fixed assets	Wholesale index for wool	8·6	Samples of accounts grossed-up in year of assessment 1933/4
8.13	Rayon and silk 113, 114	70	Ratio of plant to all fixed assets	Ratio of stocks to all fixed assets	Average of indices of import price of silk cloth and export price of rayon cloth and wholesale index for all non-food commodities	2·5	The sum of two separate estimates: the first from information for three large concerns. The second (50·9%) from a sample of other firms grossed-up to represent the rest of the industry
8.14	Other textile 115–119, 121–122, 129	18	Ratio of plant to all fixed assets	Ratio of stocks to all fixed assets	Wholesale index for all textile materials	12·9	The sum of two separate estimates: the first group of samples covers headings 115, 116, 117, 122 and 129. The second covers the rest of the headings
8.15	Textile finishing 123	59	Ratio of plant to all fixed assets	Ratio of stocks to all fixed assets	Wholesale index for all non-food commodities	11·6	The estimate includes only the assets of firms classified as primarily engaged in this trade. Finishing is also done by many firms classified to the other textile trades. The sample of accounts was grossed-up in the year of assessment 1933/4
8.21	Iron and steel 40–43, 92 (part)	64	Changes in plant shown in Accounts combined with changes in wear and tear allowances	Ratio of stocks to all fixed assets	Average of wholesale index for coal and for iron and steel and index of price of 'basic materials' in index A	7·1	It is specially important to note that the figures of assets at historical prices anticipate all revaluations made up to 1938. (See p. 30.)
8.22	Shipbuilding, railway and general engineering 44, 50–58, 69, 82, 85, 89, 90–94, 99	32	Changes in wear and tear allowances	Ratio of stocks to all fixed assets	Average of wholesale index for coal and index C	18·3	See note in 8.21 above.

SUPPLEMENT TO NOTES TO TABLES 8.12 TO 8.54 *(cont.)*

140

No. of table	Trade or Industry and S.I.C. headings*	Per cent of group covered in 1937 by sample of accounts†	Method used to estimate — Depreciated value of plant, etc.‡	Method used to estimate — Stocks at current prices§	Price index used to obtain stocks at 1930 prices‖	Per cent of property let in 1937¶	Special notes
8.23	Electrical Engineering 70–75, 79	40	Changes in plant shown in Accounts	Ratio of stocks to all fixed assets	Average of wholesale index for coal and index C and index of price of 'basic materials' in index A	n.a.	The prewar classification of assessments did not separate this group. The reconstruction of the group omits units included in the pre-war classification in Retail Distribution. The group is thus narrower by about one-third than it would be if fully comparable with the post-war classification.
8.24	Motor vehicles 80–81, 83	50	Changes in plant shown in Accounts	Ratio of stocks to all fixed assets	Index of costs of motor vehicles	8·7	The sum of two separate estimates: the first from information for one large concern with an exceptional rate of development. The second from a sample grossed-up to cover the rest of the industry.
8.25	Non-ferrous metals 49, 95, 101–102	36	Changes in plant shown in Accounts	Changes in stocks shown in Accounts	Wholesale index for all non-food commodities	8·0	
8.31	Drink 163–164, 168	63	(a) Changes in plant shown in Accounts (b) Changes in wear and tear allowances	Changes in stocks shown in Accounts	(a) Wholesale index for all food (b) Average of prices of British wine, imported wine, cider and table waters. (See [139] Stone, p. 189)	(a) 31·1 (b) 25·3	The sum of two estimates: (a) Brewing and distilleries (b) Other drink industry. Public houses owned by breweries are excluded from this estimate on the basis of information in accounts giving the necessary breakdown of buildings. They are included with Hotels, Inns, etc. in chapter 10 (p. 192)
8.32	Tobacco 169	93	Ratio of plant to all fixed assets	Ratio of stocks to all fixed assets	Index of price of tobacco (Virginia leaf)	5·8	The sum of two separate estimates: the first for large concerns covering about 90% of the industry. The second for small firms from a sample grossed-up to cover the rest of the industry.

8.33	Food (a) 155 (b) 150–152 (c) 156, 157 (d) 153, 154, 162	(a) 96 (b) 26 (c) 26 (d) 26	(a), (b) Ratio of plant to all fixed assets (c), (d) Changes in wear and tear allowances	(a), (b) Ratio of stocks to all fixed assets (c), (d) Changes in stocks shown in Accounts	(a) Weighted average of wholesale index for all non-food commodities (weight 3) and index of price of sugar (1) (b) Average of wholesale index for cereals, for all food and for all articles and index of price of sugar (c) Weighted average of series included in (b) (each with weight 1) and indices of price of imported condensed milk (1) and of raw cocoa (2) (d) Weighted average of wholesale index for meat and fish (weight 3) and for cereals (1) and indices of price of imported butter (New Zealand 1st) (1), imported condensed milk (1), oil (palm kernel) (1) and sugar (1)	(a) 2·0 (b) 6·6 (c) 10·2 (d) 9·5	The sum of four estimates: (a) Sugar and glucose, (b) Grain milling, bread and biscuits, (c) Cocoa, confectionery and fruit preserving, (d) Miscellaneous. The interwar classification of assessment to this industry is narrower than the postwar, part of the industry having been included in Distribution. In estimates (a) and (d) information for one large firm was supplemented by an estimate from a sample of the remaining firms grossed-up to represent the rest of the sub-group
8.41	Chemicals (a) 30–34, 36, 39 (b) 35	53	Changes in plant shown in Accounts	Changes in stocks shown in Accounts	(a) Weighted average of wholesale index for all non-food commodities (weight 1) and index of price of chemicals (2)—this is an unweighted average of the price of sulphuric acid pyrites, ammonium sulphate, sodium carbonate, pure aniline oil and quinine sulphate (b) Average of wholesale index for all non-food commodities and indices of the price of chemicals (see (a) above) and of oil (palm kernel)	12·0	The sum of two estimates: (a) Chemicals and dyes, pharmaceutical preparations, etc., explosives, paint and varnish, mineral oil refining, and other oils, etc. Coke Ovens and By-product Works (heading 30) are not fully represented as a large number of these units are included with coal mining in chapter 6. (b) Soap, candles, glycerine, polishes, ink and matches. In both estimates information for large concerns was supplemented by an estimate from a sample of other firms grossed-up to represent the rest of the industry.
8.42	Leather and rubber 130, 131, 190	46	Changes in plant shown in Accounts	Ratio of stocks to all fixed assets	Average of indices of price of leather (price of ox and heifer hides and of cowhides) and of rubber (price of ribbed smoked sheets)	7·4	

SUPPLEMENT TO NOTES TO TABLES 8.12 TO 8.54 (*cont.*)

No. of table	Trade or Industry and S.I.C. headings*	Per cent of group covered in 1937 by sample of accounts†	Method used to estimate — Depreciated value of plant, etc.‡	Method used to estimate — Stocks at current prices§	Price index used to obtain stocks at 1930 prices‖	Per cent of property let in 1937¶	Special notes
8.43	Clothing and shoe 132, 140–143, 147–149, 287	44	Changes in wear and tear allowances	Ratio of stocks to all fixed assets	Wholesale index for all textile materials	19·6	A substantial part of the industry was classified to Distribution as being primarily engaged in that sector (see p. 101), and is thus excluded from the present estimate.
8.44	Paper and hard-board 180–181	49	Ratio of plant to all fixed assets	Ratio of stocks to all fixed assets	Index of price of paper—this is an average of the price of chemical wood pulp and of mechanical wood pulp	6·0	
8.45	Newspapers, printing and manufacture of stationery (*a*) 186, 189 (*b*) 182–183, 194	(*a*) 38 (*b*) 7	Changes in wear and tear allowances	Ratio of stocks to all fixed assets	Index of price of paper (see 8.44)	(*a*) 18 (*b*) 9	Sum of two estimates: (*a*) newspapers and other publishing, (*b*) printing and stationery.
8.51	Wood and cork; and building and contracting Orders XIV and XVII, 89, 192	4	Changes in wear and tear allowances	Ratio of stocks to all fixed assets	Average of indices of price of wood and price of 'basic materials' in index A	36·9	The sample is very small and may not be representative.
8.52	Cement, bricks and other clay 20, 24, 29	80	Changes in plant shown in Accounts	Changes in stocks shown in Accounts	Average of wholesale index for coal and index of price of all materials in index A	7·1	The sum of two separate estimates: one from information for cement concerns covering almost the whole sub-group and the second from a sample of other firms grossed-up to represent the rest of the industry.
8.53	Glass and pottery 21–23	19	Changes in plant shown in Accounts	Ratio of stocks to all fixed assets	Average of indices of price of glass and price of 'basic materials' in index A	8·3	
8.54	Toys, musical instruments and miscellaneous manufacturing 100, 103, 191–193, 199	15	Ratio of plant to all fixed assets	Ratio of stocks to all fixed assets	Index C	5·4	

* Minimum list headings in the 1948 Edition of the Standard Industrial Classification. See also chapter 13, Table 13.20, p. 224.
† Net value of all fixed assets in the samples of accounts as a percentage of the estimated total depreciated value. Unless otherwise stated the sample of accounts was grossed-up in the

‡ See technical notes (2) A (f) on p. 138.
§ See technical notes (4) (B) on p. 138.
‖ Unless otherwise stated the indices are of wholesale prices and the source is either the available Board of Trade index numbers of wholesale prices, or indices constructed from the

commodities. (See [30] *Statistical Abstract*). Averages are unweighted unless otherwise specified. For indices A, B and C see chapter 2, p. 24.
¶ Estimated in a special investigation by the Board of Inland Revenue.

Estimates of Stock-in-trade and Work in Progress
(Current Prices. £m.)

| | 1924 | | 1930 | | 1935 | |
	Census of Production	Accounts	Census of Production	Accounts	Census of Production	Accounts
Textile industries	153	143	89	97	88	98
Metals and metal-using industries	170	170	163	153	188	158
Food and drink industries*	59	66	51	55	49	53
Chemicals, leather, clothing and paper industries	119	100	113	92	111	88
Wood, clay, building industries†	22	47	24	51	27	39
Total manufacturing*†	523	527	440	448	463	436

* Stocks in the tobacco industry have been excluded from the above comparison because excise duties were not separated from the costs of materials in the inter-war censuses so that it is not possible to estimate stocks from the Censuses of Production.

† Stocks in the miscellaneous manufacturing industries have been excluded because of difficulties with the trade classification.

Board of Inland Revenue for 1937 established that about 16% of properties owned by manufacturing firms were let.[1] (The proportions for the indivdual trade groups are shown in the Supplement to the Notes for Tables 8.12 to 8.54.) No information is available on the extent to which assets are hired by a particular trade, and it is not possible to estimate the extent to which the discrepancies between ownership and use will in aggregate compensate for each other.

(iii) Thirdly, there is the possibility of duplication in the case of any assets owned by manufacturing firms for which an independent overall estimate was made elsewhere on a more comprehensive ('type of asset') basis. This duplication applies:

(a) to shops estimated in chapter 10 (p. 186) on the basis of first assessments to Schedule A, statistics of Inhabited House Duty, etc.;

(b) to dwellings estimated in chapter 12 (p. 212) on the basis of estimates of the value of houses built; and

(c) to ships estimated in chapter 9 (p. 170) on the basis of statistics of registered tonnage.

Only the first case is likely to be of any significance.[2] It does not apply:

(a) In the case of motor vehicles, since the estimate made in chapter 9 (p. 166) for inclusion in the national total relates only to road hauliers' vehicles. (The supplementary estimate made on the basis of registrations and licences current for all motor vehicles used in road transport is not included in the national totals.)

(b) In the case of buildings classified as hotels, inns, etc., owned by brewery companies. (See Trade Group 8.31.) The value of these was estimated

separately on the basis of information given in the accounts, and was excluded from the series for the manufacturing sector. The aggregate, estimated on the basis of the first assessments to Schedule A and the Inhabited House Duty Statistics, is shown in chapter 10 (p. 192).

Finally, it should be noted that neither the Royal Dockyards and Ordnance Factories, nor the railway workshops are included in the manufacturing sector. The former are entirely excluded from the estimates; the latter are included in the railway sector[3] where they are shown separately and so can be added to the manufacturing totals if required.

COMPARISON WITH OTHER ESTIMATES

A comparison with the estimates for manufacturing made by other authors from different sources is given in chapter 14, p. 238, below. In particular, there is a comparison with Redfern's estimates of gross fixed capital formation in industrial buildings on p. 241.

A rough comparison of the estimates of stock-in-trade and work in progress made from the company accounts can be made with alternative estimates derived from Census of Production statistics. These alternative estimates were made for each trade group by applying to the value of purchases and of finished products shown in the inter-war censuses the ratios respectively of stocks to purchases and stocks to finished products shown in the combined statistics of the 1949, 1950 and 1951 censuses. The comparison is set out in the table above for the five wider industrial groups.

[1] This percentage includes the very high proportion of public houses owned for letting by brewery companies. These buildings are, however, excluded from the estimates for this sector.

[2] See also chapter 13, p. 227.

[3] See 9.1, pp. 147-56.

The closeness of the agreement in the totals is broadly reassuring, although it conceals some large discrepancies in the constituents. These can be partly explained by several factors other than statistical differences in the two estimates, including differences in coverage and in timing, and the effect of changes in price according to the method of valuing stocks adopted in the accounts.

8.11   THE COTTON INDUSTRY

GENERAL PROCEDURE AND SOURCE OF INFORMATION

The periodic large-scale reorganizations in the cotton industry during the inter-war years made it undesirable to use information from company accounts for the estimates of capital formation and assets in this sector. Instead, estimates were made by working initially in physical terms with series for the numbers of spindles and looms. The reliability of these estimates is not very great.

Gross fixed capital formation was estimated on the basis of data on the age-structure (in ten-year age-classes) of spindles installed in 1930,[1] spread annually in proportion to the average of the number of spindles in course of erection at four dates during each year.[2] To obtain the value at 1930 prices of all plant, this series was then multiplied by the estimated 1930 replacement cost of all types of cotton plant, expressed as a price per spindle.

The first cost value of the plant at 1930 prices was estimated from the same estimate of replacement cost in 1930, and data on the number of machines available at the end of each year.[3]

The estimates on the two other price bases were then derived from the 1930 price series with the aid of the index of the price of unspecified plant and machinery (index C).

For buildings, estimates were derived by means of data relating the stock of buildings to the stock of plant.

ASSETS INCLUDED

The method employed for this industry leads to estimates of what might, in principle, be regarded as either:

(a) all assets used by firms and establishments engaged in the activities such as cotton spinning and weaving which define the industry (S.I.C. minimum list headings 110 and 111), irrespective of whether these assets are owned by those so engaged, or hired from outside.

(b) all assets owned by the cotton industry, which would then be defined so as to include not only firms or establishments engaged in cotton manufacture but also establishments which own assets (especially buildings) for the purpose of letting them out to those engaged in cotton manufacture.

In practice, it is not possible to make the detailed classification by establishments implied by either of the above approaches, and there is in consequence some omission and duplication which must be noted. First, assets owned for the purpose of some subsidiary activity by firms engaged primarily in cotton manufacture will be correctly omitted from the estimate for this industry, but will also in many cases be omitted from the estimate for the other industry, if that was made from a sample of accounts. The national totals will thus be understated to that extent.

Second, there will be some overlap with the estimates made from samples of accounts of firms which were classified to a particular industry on the basis of their primary activity, but which also, as a subsidiary activity, own assets for the purpose of cotton manufacture. The most important example of such duplication arises in the case of the rayon, nylon and silk industry (Trade Group 8.13).

On the national level the duplication of assets is believed to outweigh the omissions.

One aspect of the above problems is of particular importance in view of the large-scale closing of cotton mills during the latter half of the period covered by the estimates. In so far as these buildings were not sold they were either let to other industries, used by the cotton industry for other purposes or simply left unused. The method used to estimate the buildings owned for the purpose of cotton manufacture gives no indication of the way in which buildings released by the industry were treated. In the standard estimates the assumption has been made that they were sold when released for a price equal to their estimated depreciated value. This seemed in the circumstances of the period the most plausible assumption to make. A supplementary estimate has, however, been made showing what the position would be on the assumption that all buildings no longer used for cotton manufacture were still retained in the industry.

METHODS OF ESTIMATION

Plant

All estimates were first made at constant (1930) prices.

Gross fixed capital formation was estimated by valuing a

---

[1] [**134**] J. Ryan, 'Machinery Replacements in the Cotton Trade', *Economic Journal*, vol. XL (1930).

[2] [**152**] International Federation of Master Cotton Spinners' and Manufacturers' Associations: *International Cotton Statistics*.

[3] [**152**] *International Cotton Statistics*. The estimated number of spinning spindles existing in Great Britain on 1 February of each year was taken without adjustment as the number at the end of the previous year.

volume series of spindles acquired at the price of £2·98 per spindle.[1] This is the estimated 1930 replacement cost of all the plant, expressed as a price per spindle. The volume series was derived with the aid of an analysis of the age-structure (in 10-year age-classes) of spindles installed, obtained by J. Ryan in 1930 from a sample investigation of 200 Lancashire companies covering about one-third of the spinning mills.[2] The percentage of spindles in Ryan's sample which had been constructed in the decade 1920–9 was applied to the estimate of the total number of spinning spindles existing in Great Britain at the end of 1929.[3] This gave the estimated total number of spindles acquired during the decade. In order to spread this total over the ten years, the annual figures for the average number of spindles in course of erection at four dates during each year of this decade[4] were adjusted by a constant factor so as to sum to this total. The annual figures for the number of spindles in course of erection after 1930 were corrected by the same factor.

The corrected series was taken as an index of gross capital formation in physical terms and multiplied by £2·98. This estimate of the 1930 cost per spindle of the plant required for spinning, weaving and power was derived in three stages. Its basis was the estimate given by a Director of the English Sewing Cotton Company that the 1930 replacement cost per spindle of a complete spinning section (i.e., a spindle plus its complementary machinery such as carding engines and speed frames) was £2.[5] An addition of 17·78% was then made for power plant. This proportion was taken from a contemporary estimate of representative construction costs in a new cotton factory.[6] Finally, the resulting figure of £2·35 was raised by a further 26·25% to allow for the weaving machinery. This proportion is the average ratio of the value of the production of weaving machinery to that of spinning machinery (both complete) found from the data available in all the inter-war Censuses of Production and Import Duties Act Inquiries.

The *first cost value* of the plant at the end of 1930 was obtained from the absolute number of spindles at the end of 1930[7] multiplied by the above 1930 price per spindle of £2·98. This end-1930 first cost value was then extrapolated by a weighted index of the estimated number of spindles and looms existing in Great Britain at the end of each year. For this separate indices were constructed for spindles (treating a ring spindle as the equivalent of 1·5 mule spindles) and for looms.[8] These two indices (with 1930 = 100) were then combined in the ratio of 1:0·2625, this being the proportion of spinning to weaving machinery derived above.

Depreciation was calculated on the reducing balance method at the rate observed in a sample of cotton

company assessments for 1937 collected by the Inland Revenue, adjusted in earlier years for the additional allowances introduced in 1931 and 1937. *The depreciated value* at the end of 1919 was obtained from the corresponding first cost value by the standard procedure described in chapter 2 (p. 16). The length of life assumed corresponds to the rate of depreciation calculated above.

Finally, the *first cost value of the plant scrapped or sold* is equal to the annual gross fixed capital formation less the change in the first cost value at the end of each year.

For details of the remaining series *at historical and current prices* see the Notes to Table 8.11, p. 108.

Buildings

The estimates for buildings in the cotton industry are very rough. All estimates were first made at constant (1930) prices.

The first cost value of buildings (and land) at the end of 1930 was estimated as 67% of the corresponding first cost value of the plant, using the ratio of the cost of land and buildings to the cost of plant given in Greenhalgh's estimate of construction costs.[9]

The *year's purchases* of buildings from 1920 to 1926 were estimated as follows: the aggregate of purchases over this period was derived from Ryan's information[10] on the age-structure of the buildings owned by his sample of cotton companies, applied to the estimate of the first cost value at 1930 prices of the end-1930 stock of buildings. This total was then spread over the seven years in proportion to the corresponding fixed capital formation in plant. After 1926 it was assumed that in view of the contraction of the industry there were no further additions to the stock of buildings.

The *gross fixed capital formation* equals the year's purchases less the proceeds from the sale or scrapping of the buildings.

The *first cost value of the buildings scrapped or sold* each year was assumed to be proportional to the corresponding figure for plant. The proportion used was the ratio of the first cost value of buildings to that of plant at

---

[1] Strictly speaking, this gives an estimate of the year's purchases not of gross capital formation, but the difference (i.e. the proceeds of the plant scrapped or sold) was assumed to be very small and was ignored. Cf. chapter 2, p. 23.

[2] **[134]** Ryan, p. 571.

[3] **[152]** *International Cotton Statistics* (1930).

[4] *Ibid.*

[5] **[147]** *Annual Report* to the English Sewing Cotton Company, 1931.

[6] **[112]** F. Greenhalgh, *A Trade Policy for Cotton Spinners* (an address given to the General Committee of the Federation of Master Cotton Spinners' Association) (Manchester, 1932), p. 7.

[7] **[152]** *International Cotton Statistics.*

[8] *Ibid.*

[9] **[112]** Greenhalgh, pp. 7–10. Land was assumed to be 7% of the first cost value of the buildings.

[10] **[134]** Ryan, p. 572.

10

the beginning of the period of heavy scrapping. The *proceeds of the buildings scrapped or sold* each year were derived as a proportion of the corresponding first cost value of the scrapping. The proportion taken was the ratio of the depreciated value of the total stock of buildings at the end of the previous year to the corresponding first cost value.

Depreciation was assumed to have been written off on the straight line method with a life of 60 years.

For details of the remaining series *at historical and current prices* see the Notes to Table 8.11, p. 108.

Stock-in-Trade

A sample of company accounts (covering 34·6% of the cotton industry in 1937) was used to obtain the estimate of stock-in-trade *at current prices*. An index of the chain of changes in the value of stocks shown in these accounts was obtained and it was then necessary to estimate a base year value for this index. For this purpose the average ratio of stocks to production in three post-war Censuses of Production (1949, 1950 and 1951) was applied to the average annual production in all inter-war Censuses of Production and Import Duties Act Inquiries. The average value of the stocks thus obtained for these years was then equated to the average of the indices for the corresponding years.

CHAPTER 9

TRANSPORT AND COMMUNICATIONS

Estimates are presented in this chapter for a sector embracing the following trade groups:

9.1 Railways
9.2 Road transport (including highways and bridges)
9.3 Sea and inland water transport
9.4 Civil aviation
9.5 Postal, telephone and telegraph communications.

The complete set of standard estimates for the sector as a whole is given in Table 9.00. Estimates for the trade groups and their constituents are given in Tables 9.10–9.50.

9.1 RAILWAYS

GENERAL PROCEDURE AND SOURCE OF INFORMATION

The basic source of information was the comprehensive annual return covering the expenditure of all railways in Great Britain,[1] first issued in 1868. This was supplemented from 1934 by the annual Accounts of the London Passenger Transport Board.[2] Additional information was obtained from the accounts of the fifteen largest railway companies.[3]

The estimate of the first cost value of the permanent way and works was based on the book value of the accumulated capital expenditure at end-1919 as shown in the *Railway Returns*. Gross fixed capital formation was taken as equal to the annual net increase in the accumulated capital expenditure plus the expenditure out of revenue on complete renewals of the permanent way. For rolling stock special estimates were constructed for locomotives, carriages and wagons from data in the *Returns* on the number of units in stock and the number acquired each year, and from estimates of the average cost per unit.

ASSETS INCLUDED

The estimates in Table 9.10 cover all railway assets owned by railway companies in Great Britain, including the underground lines operated from July 1933 by the London Passenger Transport Board. All non-railway assets owned by these companies such as buses, steamboats, docks, canals and hotels are excluded from these estimates. They are included in their appropriate trade groups on the basis of information derived either from the *Returns* or from some more comprehensive source for the particular type of asset. Railway hotels, for example, are included with all other hotels in chapter 10.

The assets used for the railway manufacturing and repair workshops, and for catering services on stations and trains, are regarded as railway assets and are included in this trade group. The workshops are, however, shown separately in Table 9.10, and can be transferred from there to the manufacturing sector (trade group 8.22, p. 116) if desired. Except for this inclusion of the railway workshops, the estimate corresponds closely to the 1948 *S.I.C.* Minimum List Heading 220.

Estimates were made for privately-owned railway wagons, but they are not included in the totals for railway transport as they are already included in the estimates for the trade groups by which the wagons are owned (principally coal mining), and carried from there into the national totals.

The expenditure on the permanent way and works, less the estimated expenditure on land and compensation, is classified in the national totals as civil engineering work, although it in fact includes a significant amount for stations and buildings, signalling equipment, and so on. No adjustment is made for this, but in the national totals this is roughly offset by civil engineering work in other sectors which is classified as building.[4]

METHODS OF ESTIMATION

The Permanent Way and Works

These estimates raise in a very clear form the problems which arise where assets: (a) do not have a

[1] [22] Ministry of Transport, *Returns of the Capital, Traffic, Receipts and Working Expenditure, etc., of the Railway Companies of Great Britain*, annual.
[2] [67] London Passenger Transport Board, *Annual Report and Accounts*.
[3] Copies of these accounts are preserved in the historical archives of the British Transport Commission.
[4] See chapter 13, p. 228.

TABLE 9.00 TRANSPORT AND COMMUNICATION (£M.)

(1) Buildings and Works

	1920	1921	1922	1923	1924	1925	1926	1927	1928	1929	1930	1931	1932	1933	1934	1935	1936	1937	1938
A. At historical prices:																			
(d) Depreciation	12	13	13	13	14	14	14	14	14	15	15	15	15	15	15	15	16	16	16
(f) Depreciated value*	590	603	616	633	647	665	679	698	712	726	745	769	779	780	782	787	796	812	830
(h) First cost value*	1073	1095	1117	1142	1163	1191	1215	1243	1266	1290	1319	1352	1372	1379	1391	1405	1425	1450	1476
B. At current prices:																			
(c) Gross fixed capital formation	22	26	26	30	28	32	28	33	28	29	34	39	25	16	17	20	25	32	34
(d) Depreciation	41	36	28	27	27	27	27	27	26	26	26	26	24	24	24	24	25	26	27
(e) Net fixed capital formation	−19	−10	−2	3	1	5	1	6	2	3	8	13	1	−8	−7	−4	0	6	7
(f) Depreciated value*	1932	1694	1309	1220	1232	1231	1217	1219	1197	1187	1173	1169	1113	1085	1073	1083	1113	1171	1231
(h) First cost value*	3556	3154	2460	2309	2343	2355	2345	2359	2333	2329	2310	2306	2210	2170	2171	2209	2288	2425	2558
C. At 1930 prices:																			
(c) Gross fixed capital formation	13	18	22	27	26	30	26	32	27	29	34	39	27	18	19	22	26	32	34
(d) Depreciation	24	25	25	25	25	25	25	25	25	26	26	26	26	26	26	26	26	26	26
(e) Net fixed capital formation	−11	−7	−3	2	1	5	1	7	2	3	8	13	1	−8	−7	−4	0	6	8
(f) Depreciated value*	1154	1147	1144	1146	1147	1152	1153	1160	1162	1165	1173	1186	1187	1179	1172	1168	1168	1174	1182
(h) First cost value*	2125	2135	2150	2169	2181	2203	2223	2246	2265	2284	2310	2338	2356	2357	2367	2379	2396	2416	2435

(2) Plant, Vehicles, Ships, etc.

	1920	1921	1922	1923	1924	1925	1926	1927	1928	1929	1930	1931	1932	1933	1934	1935	1936	1937	1938
A. At historical prices:																			
(d) Depreciation	36	39	43	42	49	49	49	53	55	57	59	58	58	57	54	51	50	49	52
(f) Depreciated value*	444	491	572	602	620	640	639	635	652	656	650	632	600	562	537	529	540	558	582
(h) First cost value*	848	910	1013	1069	1116	1167	1185	1192	1226	1249	1268	1261	1249	1224	1215	1215	1238	1260	1310
B. At current prices:																			
(c) Gross fixed capital formation	95	86	124	72	67	69	48	49	72	61	53	40	26	19	29	43	61	67	77
(d) Depreciation	69	64	84	62	50	49	47	43	49	52	53	52	49	46	42	47	46	51	53
(e) Net fixed capital formation	26	22	40	10	17	20	1	6	23	9	0	−12	−23	−27	−13	−4	15	16	23
(f) Depreciated value*	867	808	1065	754	579	583	552	494	554	573	579	568	530	487	465	500	506	555	580
(h) First cost value*	2025	1873	2394	1698	1321	1318	1258	1116	1228	1264	1294	1284	1234	1167	1133	1227	1216	1312	1356
C. At 1930 prices:																			
(c) Gross fixed capital formation	54	46	55	48	60	63	44	57	73	65	53	39	23	15	32	44	62	64	70
(d) Depreciation	40	40	41	43	45	46	46	47	51	53	53	51	49	48	45	47	47	48	50
(e) Net fixed capital formation	14	6	14	5	15	17	−2	10	22	12	0	−12	−26	−33	−13	−3	15	16	20
(f) Depreciated value*	480	486	500	505	520	537	535	545	567	579	579	567	541	508	495	492	507	523	543
(h) First cost value*	1131	1129	1150	1162	1189	1221	1231	1238	1265	1284	1294	1275	1252	1215	1200	1196	1214	1230	1261

(3) All Fixed Assets

A. At historical prices:

(d) Depreciation	48	52	56	55	63	63	63	67	69	72	74	73	73	72	69	66	66	65	68
(f) Depreciated value*	1034	1094	1188	1235	1267	1305	1318	1333	1364	1382	1395	1401	1379	1342	1319	1316	1336	1370	1412
(h) First cost value*	1921	2005	2130	2211	2279	2358	2400	2435	2492	2539	2587	2613	2621	2603	2606	2620	2663	2710	2786

B. At current prices:

(c) Gross fixed capital formation	117	112	150	102	95	101	76	82	100	90	87	79	51	35	46	63	86	99	111
(d) Depreciation	110	100	112	89	77	76	74	70	75	78	79	78	73	70	66	71	71	77	80
(e) Net fixed capital formation	7	12	38	13	18	25	2	12	25	12	8	1	−22	−35	−20	−8	15	22	30
(f) Depreciated value*	2799	2502	2374	1974	1811	1814	1769	1713	1751	1760	1752	1737	1643	1572	1538	1583	1619	1726	1811
(h) First cost value*	5581	5027	4854	4007	3664	3673	3603	3475	3561	3593	3604	3590	3444	3337	3304	3436	3504	3737	3914

C. At 1930 prices:

(c) Gross fixed capital formation	67	64	77	75	86	93	70	89	100	94	87	78	50	33	51	66	88	96	104
(d) Depreciation	64	65	66	68	70	71	71	72	76	79	79	77	75	74	71	73	73	74	76
(e) Net fixed capital formation	3	−1	11	7	16	22	−1	17	24	15	8	1	−25	−41	−20	−7	15	22	28
(f) Depreciated value*	1634	1633	1644	1651	1667	1689	1688	1705	1729	1744	1752	1753	1728	1687	1667	1660	1675	1697	1725
(h) First cost value*	3256	3264	3300	3331	3370	3424	3454	3484	3530	3568	3604	3613	3608	3572	3567	3575	3610	3646	3696

(4) Stock-in-Trade

1. Book value*

B. At current prices	56	46	37	33	36	36	35	34	34	32	33	30	27	25	29	29	32	36	38
C. At 1930 prices	26	29	30	28	31	32	32	32	32	30	33	32	30	27	32	31	33	33	36

2. Investment in stocks†

B. At current prices	..	4	2	−2	3	1	1	0	0	−2	4	−1	−2	−3	4	0	2	0	3
C. At 1930 prices	..	4	2	−2	2	1	1	0	0	−2	4	−1	−2	−3	4	0	2	0	2

* At end of year.   † See chapter 2, appendix 2.2, p. 33.

TABLE 9.10 RAILWAYS (£M.)

I PERMANENT WAY AND WORKS
(1) Civil Engineering Works (plus Buildings, etc.)

	1920	1921	1922	1923	1924	1925	1926	1927	1928	1929	1930	1931	1932	1933	1934	1935	1936	1937	1938
A. At historical prices:																			
(c) Gross fixed capital formation	6·2	8·0	7·3	8·9	8·3	8·0	6·3	9·2	6·8	4·5	7·6	11·2	10·2	4·8	5·2	5·7	7·5	9·1	12·3
(d) Depreciation	6·6	6·7	6·7	6·8	6·9	6·9	7·0	7·0	7·1	7·1	7·2	7·3	7·3	7·4	7·4	7·4	7·5	7·6	7·7
(f) Depreciated value*	363	365	365	367	369	370	369	369	369	366	367	371	374	371	369	367	367	369	373
(h) First cost value*	659	665	671	678	685	692	696	702	707	710	716	725	734	737	740	744	750	757	768
(i) Land*	201	203	205	207	209	211	213	214	216	217	218	221	224	225	226	227	229	231	234
B. At current prices:																			
(d) Depreciation	22·4	19·6	15·3	14·3	14·6	14·5	14·4	14·4	14·2	14·0	13·8	13·7	13·1	12·9	12·9	13·1	13·6	14·5	15·4
(f) Depreciated value*	1225	1062	819	759	763	752	733	725	706	689	668	659	624	605	597	596	610	642	675
(h) First cost value*	2236	1960	1531	1435	1460	1455	1436	1438	1417	1403	1378	1372	1313	1293	1294	1310	1358	1448	1536
(i) Land*	683	599	468	438	446	444	439	439	433	428	421	419	401	395	395	400	415	442	469
C. At 1930 prices:																			
(c) Gross fixed capital formation	3·7	5·5	6·4	8·4	7·7	7·5	6·0	8·8	6·6	4·4	7·6	11·3	10·8	5·2	5·6	6·1	7·8	8·9	11·4
(d) Depreciation	13·4	13·4	13·5	13·5	13·6	13·6	13·6	13·7	13·7	13·7	13·8	13·9	13·9	14·0	14·0	14·0	14·1	14·1	14·2
(f) Depreciated value*	735	728	720	715	710	703	696	691	684	674	668	666	663	654	645	638	631	626	623
(h) First cost value*	1342	1344	1347	1352	1357	1361	1364	1370	1373	1374	1378	1386	1394	1396	1398	1401	1406	1411	1418
(i) Land*	410	410	411	413	414	416	416	418	419	420	421	423	426	426	427	428	429	431	433

II ROLLING STOCK
(2) Vehicles

	1920	1921	1922	1923	1924	1925	1926	1927	1928	1929	1930	1931	1932	1933	1934	1935	1936	1937	1938
A. At historical prices:																			
(c) Gross fixed capital formation	13·4	13·7	5·8	4·9	8·5	10·6	9·1	8·9	8·3	8·1	7·3	4·8	3·6	3·1	5·9	8·5	9·9	11·0	9·8
(d) Depreciation	4·3	4·6	4·6	4·6	4·8	5·1	5·3	5·4	5·6	5·7	5·7	5·7	5·6	5·6	5·6	5·8	5·9	6·0	6·4
(f) Depreciated value*	77	86	87	87	91	96	100	104	106	109	110	110	108	105	105	108	112	117	120
(h) First cost value*	165	175	178	180	186	192	197	202	204	206	206	205	203	200	199	201	204	210	214
B. At current prices:																			
(d) Depreciation	12·6	12·1	11·1	7·7	7·7	7·4	7·1	6·5	6·4	6·4	6·7	6·4	6·2	5·9	6·3	6·6	6·6	6·6	6·4
(f) Depreciated value*	201	195	177	122	122	118	114	105	104	106	113	111	106	100	107	112	113	116	117
(h) First cost value*	525	510	474	331	327	310	295	269	258	259	271	266	256	241	255	260	256	255	248
C. At 1930 prices:																			
(c) Gross fixed capital formation	6·9	7·0	2·9	3·9	7·1	9·0	8·2	9·1	8·3	8·1	6·8	4·5	3·4	2·9	5·5	7·6	9·0	10·3	8·8
(d) Depreciation	7·0	6·9	6·7	6·5	6·5	6·6	6·7	6·8	6·8	6·8	6·7	6·5	6·3	6·2	6·1	6·2	6·3	6·4	6·3
(f) Depreciated value*	110	106	106	104	104	107	108	110	112	113	113	111	108	105	104	106	108	112	115
(h) First cost value*	288	287	283	281	283	282	282	283	279	276	271	266	260	253	249	247	245	247	248

III POWER PLANT
(2) Plant†

	1920	1921	1922	1923	1924	1925	1926	1927	1928	1929	1930	1931	1932	1933	1934	1935	1936	1937	1938
C. At 1930 prices:																			
(c) Gross fixed capital formation	0·1	0·2	0·2	0·5	0·4	0·1	0·3	0·3	0·4	0·3	0·6	0·3	0·9	0·3	0·2	0·2	0·1	0·5	0·5
(d) Depreciation	0·4	0·4	0·4	0·4	0·4	0·4	0·4	0·4	0·4	0·4	0·4	0·4	0·5	0·6	0·6	0·5	0·5	0·5	0·5
(f) Depreciated value*	4	4	4	3	3	3	3	3	3	3	3	3	3	4	4	4	3	3	3
(h) First cost value*	10	10	10	8	9	9	9	9	8	9	9	9	10	14	14	14	13	14	14

IV ENGINEERING WORKSHOPS

(3) All Fixed Assets†‡

C. At 1930 prices:

(c) Gross fixed capital formation	0·5	0·6	0·4	0·1	0·5	0·3	0·4	0·4	0·4	0·5	0·8	0·5	0·3	0·6	0·9	0·3
(d) Depreciation	0·7	0·7	0·7	0·7	0·7	0·7	0·7	0·7	0·7	0·7	0·7	0·7	0·7	0·7	0·7	0·7
(f) Depreciated value*	16	16	16	16	17	17	18	18	18	19	19	19	20	20	20	20
(h) First cost value*	33	33	33	33	34	34	34	34	34	34	34	33	33	33	33	32
(i) Land*	2	2	2	2	2	2	2	2	2	2	2	2	2	2	2	2

V TOTAL RAILWAYS

(3) All Fixed Assets

A. At historical prices:

(c) Gross fixed capital formation	23·1	20·6	18·4	14·2	12·0	8·6	14·8	15·9	15·8	13·7	15·6	17·3	16·2	19·9	17·6	14·2	14·1	23·1	20·4
(d) Depreciation	15·1	14·6	14·4	14·2	14·0	14·1	13·8	13·9	13·8	13·7	13·6	13·3	13·2	12·9	12·6	12·2	12·1	12·1	11·7
(f) Depreciated value*	511	503	497	493	493	495	496	495	493	491	491	489	485	482	475	470	468	466	455
(h) First cost value*	1016	1000	988	979	974	972	967	960	951	945	940	933	922	912	899	885	877	868	851

B. At current prices:

(c) Gross fixed capital formation	23·1	20·6	18·4	14·2	12·0	8·6	14·8	15·9	15·6	13·7	15·6	17·3	16·2	19·9	17·6	14·2	14·1	23·1	20·4
(d) Depreciation	23·1	22·4	21·4	20·9	20·4	20·0	20·4	21·2	21·6	21·5	21·6	22·0	22·7	23·1	23·5	23·2	27·7	33·3	37·1
(f) Depreciated value*	812	778	742	726	723	725	749	789	802	817	831	853	871	895	910	905	1023	1292	1470
(h) First cost value*	1834	1752	1659	1614	1592	1577	1610	1680	1692	1706	1719	1753	1777	1811	1833	1811	2055	2532	2839

C. At 1930 prices:

(c) Gross fixed capital formation	21·7	21·7	17·6	14·4	11·4	8·9	15·4	16·5	15·6	12·6	15·6	18·6	15·4	17·3	15·2	12·1	10·3	13·4	11·0
(d) Depreciation	21·7	21·7	21·6	21·4	21·4	21·5	21·4	21·5	21·6	21·6	21·6	21·6	21·4	21·3	21·2	21·1	21·3	21·4	21·5
(f) Depreciated value*	760	760	762	766	773	780	791	797	802	808	817	823	826	832	836	842	851	862	870
(h) First cost value*	1713	1706	1698	1695	1695	1698	1698	1695	1693	1692	1695	1696	1689	1685	1681	1674	1674	1674	1673

(4) Stock-in-Trade (Book value)*

B. At current prices	24	21	18	17	17	16	17	20	22	21	23	24	24	25	24	21	23	33	39
C. At 1930 prices	21	19	18	18	18	17	18	20	22	21	22	23	22	23	22	19	20	21	19

VI SUPPLEMENTARY ESTIMATES: PRIVATELY-OWNED WAGONS

C. At 1930 prices:

(c) Gross fixed capital formation	0·8	1·5	1·3	0·7	0·8	0·6	0·2	0·1	0·6	1·2	3·4	1·0	4·0	1·5	4·3	0·5	4·3	0·4	1·0
(d) Depreciation	1·3	1·3	1·4	1·4	1·4	1·4	1·5	1·5	1·6	1·6	1·6	1·6	1·6	1·6	1·5	1·5	1·5	1·5	1·5
(f) Depreciated value*	17	18	18	18	18	19	21	20	23	25	25	24	25	24	25	20	23	22	23
(h) First cost value*	84	85	85	85	85	85	85	85	85	85	85	85	85	85	85	84	84	84	84

* At end of year.
† Only the estimate at 1930 prices is shown for this item.
‡ This is the sum of estimates for (1) Buildings and (2) Plant. The component estimates are not shown separately.

NOTES TO TABLE 9.10

I PERMANENT WAY AND WORKS

(1) Civil Engineering Works (Plus Buildings, etc.)

A. At historical prices:

(c) *Gross fixed capital formation:*
1. *New construction and major improvements:* Annual change in A (h).
2. *Renewals:* Expenditure out of revenue on 'complete renewals'.

(d) *Depreciation:* Straight line method assuming a life of 100 years.

(f) *Depreciated value of assets held at end of year:* A (h) less accumulated depreciation estimated by cumulating capital expenditure since 1831. See p. 154.

(g) *First cost value of assets scrapped or sold:* Assumed to be the same proportion of A (h) as in the series at current prices.

(h) *First cost value of assets held at end of year:* For 1919 accumulated capital expenditure given in the *Railway Returns* adjusted for exclusion of land, etc. as shown on p. 153.

(i) *Land:* For 1919 estimated as £200m. (see p. 153). Other years assumed to be the same proportion of A (h) as in 1919.

B. At current prices:

The series at 1930 prices multiplied by index A except for B (g), taken as equal to A (c) 2. See p. 154.

C. At constant (1930) prices:

(c) *Gross fixed capital formation:* A (c) deflated by index A.

(d) *Depreciation:* As for A (d).

(f) *Depreciated value of assets held at end of year:* A (f) by the ratio used for C (h).

(g) *First cost value of assets scrapped or sold:* Assumed to be the same proportion of C (h) as in the series at current prices.

(h) *First cost value of assets held at end of year:* For 1919 the ratio of historical to 1930 prices of the accumulated capital expenditure of 15 companies applied to the expenditure of all companies. See p. 154.

(i) *Land:* Same ratio to C (h) as A (j) to A (h).

II ROLLING STOCK

(2) Vehicles

The sum of separate estimates for locomotives, carriages and wagons. For a more complete explanation of the estimates see pp. 154–6.

A. At historical prices:

(a) *Year's purchases:* Number of new units acquired multiplied by average cost per unit in year of acquisition.

(b) *Proceeds of rolling stock scrapped or sold:* Assumed equal to the depreciated value of these vehicles: A (a) less A (d) less annual change in A (f).

(c) *Gross fixed capital formation:* A (a) minus A (b); (or A (d) plus annual change in A (f)).

(d) *Depreciation:* Straight line method assuming a rate of 3%, and a scrap value equal to 10% of the first cost.

(f) *Depreciated value of rolling stock held at end of year:* For 1919 derived by cumulating the capital expenditure on units still in use (as for A (h)) and deducting the accumulated depreciation due on these units.

(g) *First cost value of assets scrapped:* The number of units replaced (derived from the new units acquired less the change in the total number of units owned), multiplied by the average costs per unit in the assumed year of acquisition, i.e. 30 years earlier.

(h) *First cost value at end of year:* For 1919 derived by cumulating the annual capital expenditure (units acquired multiplied by the average cost per unit in the year of acquisition) over a period sufficient to cover the number of units held at the end of the year.

B. At current prices:

The series in terms of numbers of units multiplied by the estimated average costs per unit in the current year in question.

C. At constant (1930) prices:

The series in terms of numbers of units multiplied by the estimated average costs per unit in 1930.

III POWER PLANT

(2) Plant, etc.

The source of the estimates is [22] *Railway Returns* and also, from 1933, [67] *Reports of the London Passenger Transport Board.* The fall in the first cost value in 1923 is due to a transfer to tramways, and the rise in 1933 to a transfer from tramways to the L.P.T.B. The transfer of £3·2m. of tramways in 1933 is not included in gross capital formation or in the depreciated value of the plant.

A. At historical prices:

(c) *Gross fixed capital formation:* Annual change in A (h) plus expenditure on renewals out of revenue account.

(d) *Depreciation:* Reducing balance method assuming a life of 25 years.

(f) *Depreciated value of plant held at end of year:* By cumulating the annual change in the first cost value, less depreciation due, since 1905. Before that date the amounts involved were of little significance for the capital stock in the inter-war period.

(g) *First cost value of plant scrapped or sold:* Expenditure on renewals out of revenue account.

(h) *First cost value of plant held at end of year:* As shown in the *Railway Returns* and *Reports of the L.P.T.B.*

B. At current prices:

The series at 1930 prices multiplied by the price index used for plant and machinery for electrical generation (see chapter 7.1, p. 91).

C. At constant (1930) prices:

The series at historical prices deflated by the price index used for electrical generating plant (see chapter 7.1, p. 91). For C (f) and C (h) it was the annual estimates from 1905 onwards which were deflated and cumulated.

IV ENGINEERING WORKSHOPS

(1) Land and Buildings

A. At historical prices:

(c) *Gross fixed capital formation:* Annual change in A (h).

(d) *Depreciation:* Straight line method assuming a life of 60 years.

(f) *Depreciated value of buildings held at end of year:* For 1919 from A (h) by imputing the age-structure found for all industrial buildings (see chapter 2, p. 16).

(g) *First cost value of buildings scrapped:* Nil except in a few years where the *Returns* show transfers to other accounts.

(h) *First cost value of buildings held at end of year:* As shown in the *Railway Returns* and *Reports of the L.P.T.B.*

(i) *Land at end of year:* 7% of A (h).

B. At constant prices:

The series at 1930 prices multiplied by index B.

C. At constant (1930) prices

(c) *Gross fixed capital formation:* A (c) deflated by index B.

(d) *Depreciation:* As for A (d).

(f) *Depreciated value at end of year:* For 1919 derived from A (f) by the standard estimate that the average historical cost of buildings acquired over the period 1860–1913 was 51·7% of the cost at 1930 prices. (See chapter 2, p. 24.)

(h) *First cost value at end of year:* For 1919 derived from A (h) by the same standard estimate as for C (f).

(i) *Land at end of year:* 7% of C (h).

(2) Plant

A. At historical prices:

(c) *Gross fixed capital formation:* Annual change in A (h) plus A (g).

(d) *Depreciation:* Straight line method assuming a life of 30 years.

(f) *Depreciated value of plant held at end of year:* For 1919 derived from A (h) by imputing an age-structure such that A (f) = one-half A (h).

(g) *First cost value of plant scrapped:* 3·33% of A (h) for 1919.

(h) *First cost value at end of year:* As shown in the *Railway Returns* and the *Reports of the L.P.T.B.*

B. At current prices:

The series at 1930 prices multiplied by index C.

C. At constant (1930) prices:

(c) *Gross fixed capital formation:* A (c) deflated by index C.

(d) *Depreciation:* As for A (d).

(f) *Depreciated value of plant held at end of year:* For 1919 derived from A (f) by the standard estimate that the average historical costs of plant acquired over the 30 years 1884–1913 were 65·3% of the costs at 1930 prices (see Chapter 2, p. 24).

(g) *First cost value at end of year:* As for A (g).

(h) *First cost value at end of year:* For 1919 derived from A (h) by the same standard estimate as for C (f).

V TOTAL RAILWAYS

(3) All Fixed Assets

Sum of I (1) and IV (1); and II (2), III (2) and IV (2).

(4) Stock-in-Trade

B. At current prices:

As shown in the *Railway Returns* and the *Reports of the L.P.T.B.*

C. At 1930 prices:

The series at current prices deflated by an unweighted average of index C and the index of the price of building materials contained in index A.

normal life-cycle but rather are subject to a long series of expenditures which have simultaneously some of the characteristics of maintenance, of partial renewal and of modernization and improvement; and (*b*) are owned by enterprises which adopted the renewals system of accounting with the result, first, that there was no regular annual charge for depreciation, and second, that the balance sheet reflected the value of the capital stock at the prices at which the first assets were acquired, even though these assets were subsequently scrapped and replaced by assets acquired at different prices.

The conceptual aspects of these problems were discussed in a special appendix to chapter 1 (pp. 7–10), and are not taken up again here. When we turn to the practical task of constructing the necessary series we have inevitably to adopt a number of fairly arbitrary methods.

Gross fixed capital formation at current (or historical) prices is obtained as the sum of two components: expenditure on new construction and major improvements as charged by the companies to capital account; and revenue expenditure on complete renewals. The first component is obtained from the net increase in the accumulated capital expenditure on way and works.[1] This will be slightly too low since it is only the *net* increase, i.e. it excludes any deduction for assets scrapped without replacement, but as a partial offset to this no deduction has been made for any expenditure on land.

The estimate of renewals is more difficult both because the conceptual distinction between that part of revenue expenditure which constitutes a clear-cut renewal which should be capitalized and that part which merely preserves the asset unchanged in its original condition is particularly blurred in this instance, and because of the paucity of data. The only information available in the inter-war classification of the railway companies revenue expenditure on maintenance of way and works is a breakdown for the permanent way itself between 'complete renewals' and 'repairs and partial renewals'. The former is effectively defined as complete relaying, including points and crossings, with new materials throughout.[2] No breakdown is given for expenditure on other parts of the way and works. The 'complete renewals' of the permanent way can clearly be treated as capital expenditure and were included in our estimates of gross fixed capital formation. Some small part of the revenue expenditure on 'maintenance' of stations, bridges and other works will also be renewals which might be included but in the absence of any reliable data no addition has been made. The omission is, however, unlikely to be very significant as in many cases the renewal, when undertaken, would probably have represented a major improvement which would have been charged to capital account.

The *first cost value of the way and works at historical prices* at the end of 1919 was derived from the accumulated original capital expenditure as shown by the *Railway Returns*. It is, however, essential to make certain reservations with regard to this estimate since the accumulated capital expenditure does not fully correspond with our concept of the first cost value. In the first place it will be an understatement of the first cost value since it takes no account of the (mainly minor) improvements gradually incorporated through renewals charged to revenue as maintenance; though this may be wholly or partially offset (*a*) if companies failed to write off old unidentified assets on those occasions when the (major) improvements which replaced them were capitalized; and (*b*) if maintenance expenditure was too low, so that parts of the track were, in effect, scrapped without replacement, even though this was not reflected in the accounts. In the second place, there is the price factor mentioned above, i.e. the fact that after replacements have been made the book value does not relate to the original price of the assets actually in the stock at the date of the balance sheet.

Despite these defects the companies accumulated original capital expenditure on the permanent way and works is an interesting and significant aggregate representing the recorded experience of all railway companies, and has been accepted as the basis for the present estimates of the first cost value. The *Railway Returns* for 1919 give the accumulated expenditure on way and works in Great Britain at 31 December 1919 as £853 m., and the following adjustments were made to this figure: (i) In anticipation of revisions made in 1927 (when the final classification of expenditure was adopted) some minor adjustments, involving a net reduction of £6 m., were made. (ii) An addition of 1 % was made for Northern Ireland. (iii) The one substantial adjustment required was the separation of expenditure on land and compensation. A rough estimate of £200 m. was taken for this item.[3] We thus obtain a figure of £655 m. for the first cost value of the way and works in the United Kingdom at historical prices at end-1919.

---

[1] [**22**] *Railway Returns* and [**67**] London Passenger Transport Board, *Annual Report and Accounts*. Data in the latter accounts are only available for the year ended 30 June and were roughly adjusted to a calendar year basis.

[2] [**71**] *Form of Accounts and Statistical Returns, Annotated to show the manner in which they are to be compiled under the provisions of Section 77 (1) of the Railway Act, 1921.* Approved by and on behalf of the Ministry of Transport (1930).

[3] This figure was based on information provided by [**125**] Dr. B. R. Mitchell from his unpublished study of 'Capital Formation in the Railways of the British Isles, 1831–1919'.

The value *at constant prices* was then derived from this book value by means of information taken from the original published accounts of the fifteen largest companies. Using index A, the accumulated expenditure of these companies at the end of 1912 was converted to 1930 prices as follows: the total at the end of 1867 was deflated by the average of index A for the period 1845–67, and the annual capital expenditures (i.e. the annual changes in the accumulated series) from 1868 to 1912 were deflated by index A, and added to this. The ratio for the fifteen companies of this estimate at 1930 prices to their corresponding figure at historical prices was then applied to the accumulated capital expenditure at historical prices at the end of 1919 for all the companies.[1]

To obtain the end-1919 *depreciated value at historical prices* use was made of estimates of annual total capital expenditure by all railway companies from 1831 to 1919.[2] Annual expenditure on way and works was assumed to be the same proportion of these figures each year as the above estimate of the first cost value of the way and works at end-1919 was of the accumulated total of this expenditure. The resulting annual figures were then cumulated from 1831, depreciation was taken as 1% of the annual cumulated expenditures (see below) and the accumulated depreciation from 1831 to 1919 was then deducted from the end-1919 first cost value. The reduction of the annual estimates of pre-1919 expenditure to cover way and works only is clearly very approximate but as the major form of error will be to inflate one pre-1919 year at the expense of another the effect on the final estimate of the depreciated value will not be significant.

For estimating *depreciation* a life of 100 years was taken, and the estimates were made on the straight line method. This is a somewhat arbitrary life but should be considered as an average covering the mixture of assets which comprises the permanent way and works. Some parts such as the embankment (or those parts of it which are not abandoned), will last for more than 100 years, while others, such as the signalling and electrical equipment, will have a life appreciably less than this. The rate chosen is also designed to allow for closing of branch lines and other forms of obsolescence.

It is more difficult to arrive at a satisfactory estimate of scrapping. The formidable conceptual problems discussed in chapter 1, appendix 1.1, are aggravated by an absence of any reliable statistical information. The method adopted, with full recognition of its imperfections, was to assume that the *first cost value at current prices of assets scrapped* was equal to the expenditure on complete renewals included in gross capital formation. This will overstate the actual first cost value of assets

scrapped and replaced if, as is likely, the renewal includes an element of improvement, but this will be partly offset, or more than offset, by the exclusion of any allowance for assets scrapped without replacement. For conversion to historical and to 1930 prices the scrapping was assumed to be the same proportion of the first cost value of the capital stock at the end of the preceding year as in the estimates at current prices.

Rolling Stock

The use of the renewals system for a rapidly depreciating and changing asset such as railway rolling stock meant that the accumulated capital expenditure recorded in the accounts considerably overstated the depreciated value of the assets and considerably understated their first cost value. In this case, therefore, it seemed preferable to construct estimates on the standard pattern—with a regular charge for depreciation—rather than to use the figures recorded by the companies.[3] A complete set of standard estimates was made for each of the three main types of rolling stock: locomotives, carriages and freight wagons.

In the inter-war years, sufficient data for this purpose on the actual number of units of each type of rolling stock in use, and the number of units of each type acquired each year, are available in the *Railway Returns*; and estimates were made of their average cost

---

[1] It is interesting to note that for the fifteen companies the capital expenditure at historical prices at the end of 1912 was 48·8% of the value at 1930 prices estimated as above. The ratio which would be obtained by simply taking the average of index A for the whole period 1845–1913 is 49·4 %. This is thus a useful confirmation of our assumption that the average historical value in 1919 of a stock of assets was not appreciably influenced by the year to year fluctuations in investment and prices before the First World War.

[2] [125] Mitchell.

[3] It is of interest to note, in this connexion, that the accumulated expenditure recorded by the companies lies roughly midway between the present estimates of the depreciated value and the first cost value at historical prices (Table 9.10, p. 150). The figures are as follows:

Value of the stock of assets:	1920	1925	1930	1935	1938 (£m.)
In *Railway Returns:*	142	151	158	154	165
In the present estimate:					
Depreciated value	77	97	111	108	120
First cost value	165	192	206	201	214

The total of the net additions plus the major renewals out of revenue as recorded in the [22] *Railway Returns* is £106·8m. in 1920–9 and £76·4m. in 1930–8. The estimated year's purchases in Table 9.10 total £95·7m. in 1920–9 and £70·2m. in 1930–8.

See also [55] British Transport Commission, *Report and Accounts for 1948*, p. 211: 'The re-assessment of the book values of rolling stock, ships and other such assets . . . resulted in a considerable upward revision of the old book figures (which in the case of the Main Line Railways, for example, were largely related to the cost of the original assets purchased, perhaps 50 or 100 years ago, rather than to the cost of assets actually in service at 31 December 1947). At the same time the accrued depreciation required in respect of these assets was also computed and this, too, largely exceeded the renewal funds and depreciation provisions which had been provided by the vested undertakings. In the result, the net book value of rolling stock and other similar assets has been brought into the Commission's books at a figure of £46m. in excess of the net amounts previously standing in the books of the vested undertakings'.

per unit. These estimates of average cost were based on the annual capital expenditure on new units (including 'complete renewals') purchased or produced in the railway workshops, divided by the corresponding number of new units acquired. In order to minimize the effect of discrepancies in timing between the financial series and the data on new (completed) units, a three-year moving average of the series was used for valuing the units.

Estimates of the number of units in use and the number acquired each year, and of their average cost, were also needed for pre-war years for certain of the estimates at historical prices. The *Railway Returns* show only the total number of units owned and it was, therefore, necessary to construct a special estimate of the number replaced. Total expenditure each year on maintenance was apportioned between expenditure on renewals and expenditure on current maintenance and repair by estimating (on the basis of the figures for the inter-war years) the current maintenance required for the total number of units. The residual—expenditure on renewals—was then divided by the average cost per unit (see below), thus obtaining the estimated number of replacements for each type of rolling stock.

The average cost per unit of each type in the pre-1914 period was derived from the accounts of the fifteen largest companies. For each of these companies, the net changes in the accumulated capital expenditure on rolling stock was divided by the net changes in the number of units owned. Ten per cent of the observations at each extreme were eliminated and an average of the remaining series was then taken. As before, the final step was to reduce the discrepancies in timing by taking a three-year moving average of the series.

Complete estimates were then made for each type of rolling stock, first in terms of numbers of units and then on each of the three price bases.

The *year's purchases at current (or historical) prices* was obtained by multiplying the number of new units acquired each year (whether for additions or renewals) by the estimated average cost per unit. For the estimates *at 1930 prices* the units acquired were multiplied by the average costs per unit in 1930.

The *first cost value* of each type of rolling stock *at current prices and at 1930 prices* was obtained by multiplying the total number of units owned at the end of each year by the average costs per unit in the current year in question, and in 1930, respectively.

The *first cost value* at the end of 1919 *at historical prices* was derived by cumulating the estimated annual purchases over a sufficient period to account for all units still in use at the end of 1919, and deducting the esti-

mated scrapping. The number of units scrapped in each year before 1914 was taken as equal to the estimate made above of the number replaced and their first cost value at historical prices was found by valuing them at the average cost per unit in their assumed year of purchase, i.e. 30 years earlier. This assumed life was based on the period of time in which the stock of assets was completely replaced. For example, the accumulated replacements of wagons from 1869 to 1902 equalled the number in use in 1869, i.e. after 33 years. Similar periods were found for the other types of rolling stock and also for the replacements in the inter-war years.

In the inter-war years the number of units scrapped was again taken as equal to the number replaced, known for this period from the number acquired less the change in the total number of units owned. The *first cost value of scrapping at historical prices* was again obtained by multiplying the units scrapped by the average costs per unit thirty years earlier.

On the basis of the estimated length of life, *depreciation* was estimated at a rate of 3%, using the straight line method.

The *depreciated value at historical prices* at the end of 1919 was estimated by cumulating the estimated year's purchases of all units still in use at the end of 1919, and deducting the depreciation due at the above rate on those units. Units remaining in use after the assumed working life were retained in the depreciated value at an assumed scrap value equal to 10% of their original cost. For the *depreciated value at 1930 prices* the corresponding calculation in terms of numbers of units was multiplied by the average cost per unit in 1930, and for the series at current prices by the average cost per unit in the current year in question.

Finally, the proceeds of rolling stock scrapped or sold were assumed to be equal to the depreciated value of those units. This can be obtained from the identity:

Depreciated value of units scrapped or sold during the year
    equals *purchases* during the year
less *depreciation* during the year
less *change in the depreciated value of the rolling stock* during the year

Gross fixed capital formation is thus equal either to the year's purchases less the proceeds of scrapping or sales, or to depreciation during the year plus the change in the depreciated value of the rolling stock.

Details of the two remaining sets of estimates: for power plant, and for the buildings and plant in the railway manufacturing and repairing workshops, are given in the Notes to Table 9.10, p. 152.

Supplementary Estimate of Privately-owned Wagons

An estimate was first made in real terms on the basis of the censuses of privately-owned wagons in use, taken by the Board of Trade in 1918, 1928, 1937 and 1939.[1] Interpolation between these points was based on the series of registered new private wagons given since 1911 in the *Railway Returns*, and estimated scrapping. This series of new wagons registered was also the basis for the estimate of the year's purchases.

These series in real terms were then multiplied by the estimate made above of the average cost per unit of a freight wagon, and the standard estimates were completed in the same way as the estimates above for railway-owned rolling stock.

The estimates are shown, at 1930 prices only, at the foot of Table 9.10.

9.2　ROAD TRANSPORT

This section is set out in three parts:

Part 1. *Highways and bridges.*

Part 2. *Supplementary estimates:* classification by type of vehicle:

A. Road motor transport:
　1. Commercial goods vehicles.
　2. Buses and taxis.
　3. Passenger cars in the business sector.
B. Horse-drawn vehicles.

Part 3. *Estimates forming part of the national totals:* classification by *ownership* of vehicles in the following trade groups:

A. Assets owned by road hauliers:
　1. Commercial goods vehicles.
　2. Horse-drawn vehicles.
B. Assets owned by the public road passenger transport sector:
　1. Buses and taxis
　2. Tramways and trolley vehicles.

Highways and bridges are shown in Table 9.21; the supplementary estimates for all road vehicles in Table 9.22; and the estimates for all fixed assets owned by road hauliers and by the public road passenger transport sector in Tables 9.23 and 9.24.

PART I.　HIGHWAYS AND BRIDGES
GENERAL PROCEDURE AND SOURCE OF INFORMATION

The basic source for information on the capital expenditure on roads in the inter-war years is the *Report on the Administration of the Road Fund*.[2] This was supplemented by data in the study by Bretherton, Burchardt and Rutherford[3] of local authority and other public investment, and in the annual *Statistical Abstracts*.

The estimates of gross capital formation were obtained directly from these sources; and the estimates of the end-1919 first cost value at historical and 1930 prices were obtained in cumulating rather more approximate estimates (for the earliest years, allowances) for capital formation since 1820.

ASSETS INCLUDED

The estimates in Table 9.21 cover all public roads and bridges in the United Kingdom. Expenditure on public street lighting is not included. Some slight expenditure on road machinery is probably contained in the data but no allowance was made for this in the classification by type of asset.

METHODS OF ESTIMATION

The estimate for roads, like that for the permanent way of the railways, relates to an asset which does not have a normal life cycle since regular expenditure on maintenance (simultaneously incorporating an element of partial renewal and of improvement) appears to give the asset a more or less permanent character. While the conceptual problems are basically similar to those encountered in the case of railways in 9.1 of this chapter,[4] the practical difficulties are greater.

The first difficulty is that there is no clearly defined date at which the construction of the inter-war stock of roads can be said to have started, and there is no 'book value' for the roads corresponding to the records of accumulated capital expenditure kept by the railway companies. The concept of the 'stock of roads' is clearly very sophisticated and any attempt at measurement must inevitably be both arbitrary and approximate. The solution adopted in principle for the present estimates was that for the end-1919 stock the annual capital expenditure on new construction of roads should be cumulated over the period of 100 years from 1820 to 1919. The starting point is thus taken back to the age of Telford and McAdam, and it is assumed that no roads constructed before 1820 were maintained as part of the capital stock.

The second difficulty is the absence of any classification of the expenditure on maintenance, repairs and

---

[1] For 1918 and 1928 [22] *Railway Returns*, annual. For 1937 and 1939 [59] Central Statistical Office, *Statistical Digest for the War* (London, 1951), p. 188.

[2] [23] Ministry of Transport, *Reports on the Administration of the Road Fund*. Annual since 1919/20. Data in the Reports for years ended 31 March were adopted for the preceding calendar years without adjustment.

[3] [95] R. F. Bretherton, *et al.*

[4] See above p. 153 and also the more complete discussion of these conceptual problems in chapter 1, appendix 1, pp. 7–10.

TABLE 9.21 ROAD TRANSPORT: HIGHWAYS AND BRIDGES (£M.)

(1) Civil Engineering Works

	1920	1921	1922	1923	1924	1925	1926	1927	1928	1929	1930	1931	1932	1933	1934	1935	1936	1937	1938
A. At historical prices:																			
(c) Gross fixed capital formation	8·2	11·4	13·9	14·6	16·8	17·7	16·8	16·4	15·0	19·2	20·0	22·4	11·2	8·9	8·8	10·7	13·0	17·2	16·9
(d) Depreciation	1·6	1·8	1·9	2·0	2·2	2·4	2·5	2·7	2·8	3·0	3·2	3·4	3·5	3·6	3·7	3·8	3·9	4·1	4·3
(f) Depreciated value*	99	108	120	133	147	163	177	191	203	219	236	255	263	268	273	280	289	302	315
(h) First cost value*	164	175	189	203	219	236	252	268	283	301	320	342	353	361	370	380	393	409	426
B. At current prices:																			
(d) Depreciation	5·2	4·9	3·8	3·7	3·8	3·9	4·1	4·2	4·2	4·4	4·5	4·6	4·5	4·4	4·5	4·6	4·8	5·0	5·3
(f) Depreciated value*	304	287	225	217	227	241	253	263	268	279	291	302	294	292	292	302	314	331	351
(h) First cost value*	524	495	384	365	376	393	407	419	422	435	448	458	446	445	446	462	480	504	533
C. At 1930 prices:																			
(c) Gross fixed capital formation	4·8	7·3	11·8	13·5	15·8	16·6	15·8	15·6	14·6	18·9	20·0	22·9	12·1	9·8	9·8	11·8	14·1	18·4	17·7
(d) Depreciation	3·1	3·2	3·3	3·4	3·5	3·7	3·8	4·0	4·1	4·3	4·5	4·7	4·8	4·9	5·0	5·1	5·2	5·4	5·6
(f) Depreciated value*	179	183	191	201	214	227	239	250	261	275	291	309	316	321	326	333	342	355	367
(h) First cost value*	308	315	326	339	354	369	384	398	412	429	448	469	481	490	499	510	523	540	556

* At end of year.

NOTES TO TABLE 9.21

(1) Civil Engineering Works

A. At historical prices:

(c) *Gross fixed capital formation:*

1. *New construction:* Capital expenditure on new construction and major improvements. See p. 163.
2. *Renewals:* For 1920–31 taken as 10% of Expenditure on maintenance, repairs and minor improvements, and for 1932–38 as 5%. See p. 163.

(d) *Depreciation:* Straight line method assuming a life of 100 years.

(f) *Depreciated value of roads at end of year:* For 1919 A (h) less accumulated depreciation due on the first cost value at the end of each year after 1820.

(g) *First cost value of roads scrapped:* Total of £9·5m. in 1920–38 spread in proportion to C (c). See p. 164.

(h) *First cost value of roads at end of year:* For 1919 by cumulating the new construction and major improvements since 1820. See p. 163.

B. At current prices:

The series at 1930 prices multiplied by the special price index for road construction (see p. 163).

C. At constant (1930) prices:

(c) *Gross fixed capital formation:* A (c) deflated by the special price index for road construction (p. 163).

(d) *Depreciation:* As for A (d).

(f) *Depreciated value of roads at end of year:* For 1919 C (h) less accumulated depreciation due on the first cost value at the end of each year after 1820.

(g) *First cost value of roads scrapped:* Total of £19m. in 1920–38 spread in proportion to C (c).

(h) *First cost value at end of year:* For 1919 by cumulating the new construction and major improvements since 1820 deflated by index A.

TABLE 9.22 ROAD TRANSPORT: SUPPLEMENTARY ESTIMATE: ROAD MOTOR TRANSPORT AND HORSE-DRAWN VEHICLES (£M.)

A ROAD MOTOR TRANSPORT

I ROAD GOODS VEHICLES
(2) Vehicles

	1920	1921	1922	1923	1924	1925	1926	1927	1928	1929	1930	1931	1932	1933	1934	1935	1936	1937	1938
A. At historical prices:																			
(a) Year's purchases	11·5	8·1	10·1	10·2	12·0	8·8	10·7	11·1	11·4	16·6	16·3	17·0	14·5	15·0	15·7	16·7	18·8	19·6	18·0
(c) Gross fixed capital formation	11·5	8·1	10·1	9·7	11·3	8·1	9·5	9·8	9·9	14·7	14·3	14·7	12·3	12·7	13·3	14·2	16·2	16·9	15·3
(d) Depreciation	4·4	5·2	6·3	7·1	8·2	8·1	8·5	8·8	9·0	10·5	11·5	12·4	12·4	12·2	12·8	13·2	14·1	14·8	14·9
(f) Depreciated value*	15	18	22	25	28	28	29	30	31	35	38	40	40	40	41	42	44	46	46
(h) First cost value*	41	58	72	81	90	96	102	106	110	114	116	118	119	123	125	126	129	130	132
B. At current prices:																			
(d) Depreciation	5·1	5·2	5·8	6·3	7·2	7·1	7·5	8·1	8·4	10·3	11·2	12·8	12·4	12·2	10·7	12·0	13·2	14·3	15·3
(f) Depreciated value*	18	19	21	22	25	24	25	27	28	34	36	41	40	39	34	38	41	44	47
(h) First cost value*	57	67	70	71	76	79	82	89	94	104	107	119	117	118	99	107	113	118	129
C. At 1930 prices:																			
(a) Year's purchases	6·2	4·9	7·1	8·0	10·2	8·0	10·3	10·8	11·4	16·2	16·3	15·9	14·1	15·2	20·3	21·0	23·7	24·6	21·3
(c) Gross fixed capital formation	6·2	4·9	7·1	7·7	9·7	7·5	9·7	10·0	10·4	14·7	14·3	13·9	12·2	13·3	18·1	18·5	21·0	21·5	18·4
(d) Depreciation	2·7	3·1	4·0	4·9	6·1	6·4	7·2	7·9	8·4	10·1	11·2	11·9	12·0	12·4	13·8	15·0	16·6	17·9	18·0
(f) Depreciated value*	9	12	15	17	21	22	24	27	29	33	36	38	38	39	44	47	52	55	56
(h) First cost value*	31	41	49	56	64	71	79	87	94	101	107	111	114	119	127	133	141	147	152

II BUSES AND TAXIS
(2) Vehicles

	1920	1921	1922	1923	1924	1925	1926	1927	1928	1929	1930	1931	1932	1933	1934	1935	1936	1937	1938
A. At historical prices:																			
(a) Year's purchases	13·8	9·6	12·1	11·6	10·7	5·9	10·4	10·3	10·4	10·4	11·1	10·9	6·9	3·8	5·4	7·4	9·0	10·3	11·8
(c) Gross fixed capital formation	13·8	9·6	11·6	11·4	10·1	5·3	8·3	7·3	8·0	8·5	9·7	7·6	5·3	2·8	4·2	6·2	7·9	8·9	10·7
(d) Depreciation	5·6	6·4	7·5	8·4	8·7	7·8	8·1	8·3	8·4	8·5	8·7	8·8	8·0	6·6	5·9	5·9	6·3	6·9	7·8
(f) Depreciated value*	22	25	29	32	34	31	32	31	30	30	31	30	27	23	22	22	23	25	28
(h) First cost value*	96	106	113	127	138	143	140	126	119	116	117	101	98	97	96	98	99	99	104
B. At current prices:																			
(d) Depreciation	6·7	6·5	6·9	7·4	7·7	6·8	7·1	7·5	7·9	7·8	9·2	9·9	8·3	6·0	5·7	5·7	6·6	7·4	8·3
(f) Depreciated value*	28	27	28	29	30	27	27	27	28	27	32	33	28	21	21	21	25	27	31
(h) First cost value*	143	127	114	115	119	118	113	105	101	98	116	112	103	88	94	93	104	108	116
C. At 1930 prices:																			
(a) Year's purchases	8·4	6·7	9·6	10·2	9·8	5·9	11·0	11·0	11·4	12·1	11·1	9·8	6·6	4·3	5·7	7·9	8·7	9·5	10·3
(c) Gross fixed capital formation	8·4	6·2	8·8	9·9	9·3	5·5	9·5	8·6	9·6	10·5	9·7	6·5	5·0	3·3	4·6	6·7	7·3	8·1	8·9
(d) Depreciation	4·1	4·5	5·4	6·5	7·1	6·7	7·5	8·0	8·6	9·1	9·2	8·9	7·9	6·7	6·0	6·1	6·3	6·8	7·2
(f) Depreciated value*	17	19	22	26	28	27	29	29	30	32	32	30	27	23	22	23	24	25	27
(h) First cost value*	87	88	90	100	110	116	118	112	110	113	116	101	98	98	98	99	99	99	101

III PASSENGER CARS OWNED FOR BUSINESS USE

(2) Vehicles

A. At historical prices:

(a) Year's purchases	9·9	7·2	9·2	11·4	14·6	17·3	17·6	17·2	15·5	14·9	13·8	10·6	9·5	11·7	14·4	17·3	18·4	20·2	17·4
(c) Gross fixed capital formation	9·9	8·3	9·5	11·0	13·8	16·3	16·2	15·5	13·8	12·8	11·7	8·2	7·3	9·5	12·3	15·3	16·4	18·0	15·4
(d) Depreciation	3·8	4·6	5·6	6·9	8·7	10·6	12·1	13·0	13·2	13·1	12·6	11·5	10·4	10·1	10·5	11·6	12·8	14·2	14·5
(f) Depreciated value*	12	15	19	23	28	34	38	40	41	41	39	36	33	32	34	37	41	45	46
(h) First cost value*	28	39	53	63	74	86	97	105	111	115	117	112	109	108	109	114	120	125	131

B. At current prices:

(d) Depreciation	4·4	4·7	5·3	6·1	7·7	9·8	11·2	11·4	11·4	11·2	10·9	9·5	8·3	8·7	9·9	11·1	12·4	13·8	14·4
(f) Depreciated value*	14	16	18	20	25	31	35	35	35	34	33	29	26	27	31	35	39	43	45
(h) First cost value*	38	46	53	56	62	75	85	85	87	88	90	82	76	79	88	96	105	114	125

C. At 1930 prices:

(a) Year's purchases	4·1	3·2	4·7	6·8	9·5	11·4	12·1	13·5	14·2	13·1	13·1	12·1	12·2	15·2	18·4	22·7	25·3	27·3	23·2
(c) Gross fixed capital formation	4·1	3·7	4·6	6·4	9·1	10·9	11·4	12·6	13·1	11·7	10·4	10·7	10·3	13·5	16·6	21·0	23·1	24·9	21·0
(d) Depreciation	1·8	2·1	2·7	3·6	5·0	6·5	7·7	9·0	9·8	10·6	10·7	10·6	11·2	12·5	14·5	16·6	18·6	19·1	
(f) Depreciated value*	6	7	9	12	16	20	24	28	30	33	33	35	39	46	52	58	60		
(h) First cost value*	16	21	27	33	40	49	58	67	75	84	90	92	96	103	112	126	140	154	166

B HORSE-DRAWN VEHICLES

(2) Vehicles and Horses

B. Current prices: (h) First cost value*	42·6	37·2	29·5	24·1	20·6	21·6	18·1	16·2	16·4	12·4	11·9	9·2	7·1	7·2	6·3	6·5	9·1	11·0
C. At 1930 prices: (h) First cost value*	36·6	33·2	29·6	27·2	21·4	19·1	17·2	15·1	14·5	12·4	11·4	9·2	9·2	8·6	7·8	7·7	7·5	7·3

* At end of year.

NOTES TO TABLE 9.22

A. Road Motor Transport

This covers three separate estimates for road goods vehicles, buses and taxis and passenger cars owned for business use. Each of the estimates was first made in terms of numbers of vehicles.

(2) Vehicles

A. At historical prices:

(a) *Year's purchases:* New registrations multiplied by the estimated average cost per vehicle in the year of registration. See pp. 164-6.

(b) *Proceeds of vehicles scrapped or sold:* Assumed equal to the depreciated value of these vehicles: A (a) less A (d) less annual change in A (f).

(c) *Gross fixed capital formation:* A (a) less A (b); or A (d) plus annual change in A (f).

(d) *Depreciation:* Reducing balance method assuming a life of 8 years and a scrap value equal 10% of the first cost. See p. 165.

(f) *Depreciated value of vehicles at end of year:* Each age-group of surviving vehicles (estimated on the basis of a life-table, see p. 165) valued at the average cost per vehicle in the year of purchase, less the accumulated depreciation due for all age-groups, plus 'unexpected' survivors valued at 10% of their first cost. See p. 165.

(g) *First cost value of vehicles scrapped:* A (a) less annual change in A (h).

(h) *First cost value of vehicles at end of year:* Each age-group of surviving vehicles valued at the average cost per vehicle in the year of purchase, plus 'unexpected' survivors included at the average historical value of the expected survivors.

B. At current prices:

Estimates in terms of numbers of vehicles multiplied by the average cost per vehicle in the current year in question.

C. At constant (1930) prices:

Estimates in terms of numbers of vehicles multiplied by the average cost per vehicle in 1930.

B. HORSE-DRAWN VEHICLES

(2) Vehicles and Horses

B. At current prices:

(h) *First cost value of vehicles and horses at end of year:* The series of vehicles and horses at 1930 prices multiplied by their respective price indices. See p. 166.

C. At constant (1930) prices:

(h) *First cost value at end of year:* The number of horses used for transport multiplied by the average cost per horse in 1930; plus the equivalent number of vehicles multiplied by the average cost per vehicle in 1930. See p. 166.

TABLE 9.23 ROAD GOODS TRANSPORT: ASSETS OWNED BY ROAD HAULIERS (£M.)

(3) All Fixed Assets*

	1920	1921	1922	1923	1924	1925	1926	1927	1928	1929	1930	1931	1932	1933	1934	1935	1936	1937	1938
A. At historical prices:																			
(c) Gross fixed capital formation	2·4	1·8	2·2	1·3	1·7	2·2	1·7	3·8	2·2	3·1	2·8	3·2	2·8	2·5	3·8	3·5	3·5	3·7	3·3
(d) Depreciation	3·4	3·5	2·2	2·3	1·6	1·1	0·6	2·8	2·1	2·2	3·4	2·6	3·4	3·8	2·8	3·4	3·0	1·8	2·9
(f) Depreciated value†	13	11	11	10	11	12	13	14	14	15	15	15	15	13	14	15	15	17	17
(h) First cost value†	18	18	19	18	19	21	23	27	29	30	29	30	30	30	32	33	34	35	36
B. At current prices:																			
(d) Depreciation	1·7	1·5	1·5	1·4	1·4	1·6	1·7	2·1	2·2	2·5	2·6	2·8	2·7	2·6	2·5	2·9	3·0	3·4	3·6
(f) Depreciated value†	18	15	14	12	12	13	14	15	16	17	16	17	16	14	14	15	15	18	18
(h) First cost value†	29	25	23	21	21	23	24	28	29	32	31	33	32	31	30	32	33	36	38
C. At constant (1930) prices:																			
(c) Gross fixed capital formation	1·6	1·3	1·8	1·3	1·7	2·1	1·7	3·7	2·8	3·1	2·7	3·3	2·8	2·8	4·7	4·5	4·5	4·4	3·7
(d) Depreciation	2·6	2·7	1·1	1·3	1·4	1·8	1·5	2·3	2·2	2·5	2·6	2·9	3·1	2·8	3·6	3·9	3·8	4·2	4·5
(f) Depreciated value†	13	12	12	12	13	13	13	15	15	16	16	16	16	16	17	18	18	19	18
(h) First cost value†	19	18	20	19	20	22	22	27	29	30	31	32	32	33	36	38	39	41	40

* Only the total of all fixed assets is published for this sub-sector. It is the sum of separate estimates for (1) buildings and (2) road goods vehicles, horse-drawn vehicles and horses.
† At end of year.

NOTES TO TABLE 9.23

(1) Buildings

The sum of separate estimates of the garage space required for horse-drawn and motor vehicles.

A. At historical prices:

(g) *First cost value of buildings scrapped or sold:* From C (g) multiplied by the average of index B from 1850 to 1913.
(h) *First cost value at end of year:* For 1919 from C (h) multiplied by the average of index B from 1850 to 1913. All other items as for the series at current prices.

B. At current prices:

The series at 1930 prices multiplied by index B.

C. At constant (1930) prices:

(c) *Gross fixed capital formation:* Annual increase in the total units of garage space required per motor vehicle multiplied by the standard cost per unit of £54·5. See pp. 167-8.
(d) *Depreciation:* Straight line method assuming a life of 50 years.
(f) *Depreciated value at end of year:* For 1919 assumed to be one-half of C (h).
(g) *First cost value of buildings scrapped or sold:* Annual decrease in the total units required per horse-drawn vehicle multiplied by the standard cost per unit.

(h) *First cost value at end of year:* Total units of garage space required per vehicle multiplied by the standard cost per unit of £54·5. See pp. 167-8.
(i) *Land at end of year:* 10% of C (h).

(2) Vehicles

1. *Horse-drawn vehicles and horses*

A. At historical prices:

(h) *First cost value at end of year:* The series in part 2 for the first cost value of all horse-drawn transport multiplied by the ratio each year of:

$$\frac{\text{Horses owned by road hauliers}}{\text{All horses used for road transport}}$$

See p. 167. The *depreciated value* was taken as equal to the first cost value and *gross capital formation* as 10% of the first cost value. *Depreciation* and *scrapping* then follow from the standard identities.

B. At current prices:

Gross capital formation, depreciated and first cost value equal the corresponding series at historical prices. Depreciation and scrapping equal 10% of the first cost value.

C. At constant (1930) prices:

From the series in part 2 for the first cost value at 1930 prices of all horse-drawn transport in the same way as for the estimates at historical prices.

2. *Road goods vehicles*

A. At historical prices:

(b) *Proceeds of vehicles scrapped or sold:*
(d) *Depreciation:*
(f) *Depreciated value of vehicles at end of year:*
(h) *First cost value of vehicles at end of year:*

The corresponding series for all commercial goods vehicles in part 2 multiplied by the ratio for each year of:

$$\frac{\text{Number of goods vehicles owned by road hauliers}}{\text{Total number of goods vehicles in use}}$$

See p. 167. The remaining series then follow from the standard identities:

A (c) = A (d) plus annual change in A (f).
A (a) = A (b) plus A (c).
A (g) = A (a) minus annual change in A (h).

B. At current prices
C. At constant (1930) prices } In the same way as for the series at historical prices.

(3) All Fixed Assets

Sum of (1), (2) 1 and (2) 2.

TABLE 9.24 PUBLIC ROAD PASSENGER TRANSPORT (£M.)

I BUSES AND TAXIS*

(3) All Fixed Assets*

	1920	1921	1922	1923	1924	1925	1926	1927	1928	1929	1930	1931	1932	1933	1934	1935	1936	1937	1938
A. At historical prices:																			
(c) Gross fixed capital formation	16·0	11·0	11·8	12·7	11·2	6·0	8·6	8·1	9·5	10·1	10·8	7·6	5·3	2·8	4·3	6·9	8·6	9·7	11·6
(d) Depreciation	5·7	6·6	7·6	8·6	8·9	8·0	8·3	8·5	8·7	8·8	9·0	9·1	8·3	6·9	6·2	6·2	6·6	7·3	8·2
(f) Depreciated value†	28	32	36	40	43	41	41	41	41	43	44	43	40	36	34	35	37	39	42
(h) First cost value†	102	114	122	135	147	154	150	138	132	130	132	116	113	112	112	112	115	117	123
B. At current prices:																			
(d) Depreciation	7·0	6·8	7·1	7·6	8·0	7·1	7·4	7·8	8·2	8·2	9·6	10·3	8·7	6·4	6·1	6·1	7·0	7·8	8·7
(f) Depreciated value†	44	41	39	41	43	40	40	41	42	43	48	48	42	34	34	35	39	43	47
(h) First cost value†	162	143	128	128	134	133	128	121	117	116	136	130	120	104	110	110	123	129	139
C. At 1930 prices:																			
(c) Gross fixed capital formation	9·7	7·2	9·0	11·1	10·4	6·3	9·7	9·2	11·1	12·1	11·1	6·5	5·0	3·2	4·8	7·5	8·1	9·0	9·8
(d) Depreciation	4·3	4·7	5·6	6·7	7·4	7·0	7·8	8·3	8·9	9·5	9·6	9·3	8·3	7·1	6·4	6·5	6·7	7·2	7·6
(f) Depreciated value†	26	29	32	37	40	39	41	42	44	47	48	45	42	38	36	38	39	41	43
(h) First cost value†	97	100	102	112	124	130	133	127	127	131	136	120	117	117	117	118	120	120	123

II TRAMWAYS AND TROLLEY BUSES

(3) All Fixed Assets‡

	1920	1921	1922	1923	1924	1925	1926	1927	1928	1929	1930	1931	1932	1933	1934	1935	1936	1937	1938
A. At historical prices																			
(c) Gross fixed capital formation	2·6	4·3	3·1	4·3	1·4	3·4	2·8	2·6	2·1	1·5	3·0	1·3	0·7	1·0	0·8	1·9	2·1	2·7	2·4
(d) Depreciation	2·1	2·4	2·5	2·6	2·6	2·9	3·0	2·7	2·7	2·7	2·7	2·5	2·2	2·0	1·6	1·7	1·7	1·7	1·9
(f) Depreciated value†	24	26	26	28	27	27	27	27	26	25	25	24	22	18	18	18	18	19	20
(h) First cost value†	62	65	67	69	66	68	70	71	72	71	72	72	70	58	56	55	54	53	50
B. At current prices																			
(d) Depreciation	5·3	5·0	3·9	3·7	3·5	3·8	3·7	3·1	3·1	3·0	2·8	2·5	2·1	1·8	1·5	1·5	1·6	1·7	1·8
(f) Depreciated value†	64	58	43	39	35	34	32	31	30	28	26	24	21	17	17	17	18	19	20
(h) First cost value†	182	172	133	125	116	118	118	118	119	117	115	107	101	83	85	83	82	83	77
C. At 1930 prices																			
(c) Gross fixed capital formation	1·7	2·6	2·5	3·9	−0·4	2·7	1·9	2·0	1·5	1·2	2·2	0·9	0·7	1·1	0·8	1·5	1·9	2·2	1·7
(d) Depreciation	3·3	3·4	3·5	3·6	3·4	3·5	3·5	3·1	3·0	2·9	2·8	2·7	2·2	2·0	1·6	1·6	1·5	1·5	1·7
(f) Depreciated value†	39	38	37	38	34	33	31	30	29	27	26	25	23	19	18	18	18	19	19
(h) First cost value†	117	118	120	122	115	116	116	117	117	115	115	112	110	92	89	86	83	80	73

* Only the total of all fixed assets is published for this sub-sector. It is the sum of separate estimates for (1) Buildings and (2) Vehicles. The separate estimate for vehicles is given in Table 9.22.

† At end of year.

‡ Only the total of all fixed assets is published for this sub-sector. It is the sum of separate estimates for (1) The permanent way and (2) Power plant, lines and vehicles.

Notes to Table on p. 162

NOTES TO TABLE 9.24

BUSES AND TAXIS

(1) Buildings

Sum of separate estimates of garage space required by taxis and of all buildings required for buses. See p. 168.

A. At historical prices:

(c) *Gross fixed capital formation*: Increase in number of vehicles multiplied by the estimated cost of buildings per vehicle. See p. 168.

(d) *Depreciation*: Straight line method assuming a life of 50 years.

(f) *Depreciated value at end of year*: By cumulating capital formation A (c) less depreciation A (d) since 1905.

(g) *First cost value of buildings scrapped*: Assumed negligible.

(h) *First cost value at end of year*: For 1937: buses from *Reports* (see p. 168); taxis by cumulating capital formation A (c) since 1905.

(i) *Land at end of year*: 10% of A (h).

B. At current prices:

The series at 1930 prices multiplied by index B.

C. At constant (1930) prices:

(c) *Gross fixed capital formation*: A (c) deflated by index B.

(d) *Depreciation*: As for A (d).

(f) *Depreciated value at end of year*: By cumulating capital formation C (c) less depreciation C (d) at 1930 prices since 1905.

(h) *First cost value at end of year*: By cumulating capital formation C (c) at 1930 prices since 1905.

(i) *Land at end of year*: 10% of C (h).

(2) Vehicles

Equal to the estimate in part 2 for all mechanically-propelled public road passenger vehicles. See p. 158.

(3) All Fixed Assets

Sum of (1) and (2).

II TRAMWAYS AND TROLLEY BUSES

The series are affected by an internal rearrangement of accounts in 1924 (between power stations and electrical equipment of lines; by the transfer of power plant to the London Passenger Transport Board in 1933 (see above p. 152); and by other smaller and untraceable transfers.

(1) Civil Engineering Work. See p. 169.

1. *The Permanent Way.* See p. 169.

A. At historical prices:

(a) *Year's purchases*: Annual change in A (h) plus estimated renewals.

(b) *Proceeds of assets scrapped or sold*: A (a) less A (d) less annual change in A (f).

(c) *Gross fixed capital formation*: A (a) less A (b); (or A (d) plus annual change in A (f)).

(d) *Depreciation*: Straight line method assuming a life of 30 years.

(f) *Depreciated value at end of year*: By cumulating purchases less depreciation and disposals since 1897.

(g) *First cost value of scrapping*: Estimated expenditure on renewals plus transfers in the accounts to 'other trades' or to 'accounts of superseded assets'.

(h) *First cost value at end of year*: Accumulated capital expenditure on Permanent Ways, Street and Road Improvements and Unallocated Capital Expenses (less scrapping and transfers) since 1897.

B. At current prices:

The series at 1930 prices multiplied by the special price index for road construction (see p. 163).

C. At constant (1930) prices:

(a) *Year's purchases*: A (a) deflated by the index for road construction.

(b) *Proceeds of assets scrapped or sold*: As for A (b).

(c) *Gross fixed capital formation*: As for A (c).

(d) *Depreciation*: As for A (d).

(f) *Depreciated value at end of year*: By cumulating purchases less depreciation at 1930 prices since 1897.

(g) *First cost value of scrapping*: Expenditure on renewals at current prices deflated by the index for road construction, plus transfers taken as the same proportion of the first cost value as in the series at historical prices.

(h) *First cost value at end of year*: By cumulating C (a) less C (g) since 1897.

2. *Land*

A. At historical prices:

Accumulated capital expenditure on Other Land and Buildings (see p. 169).

B. At current prices:

The series at 1930 prices deflated by index A.

C. At constant (1930) prices:

Assumed to be the same proportion of the first cost value of the permanent way as in the series at historical prices.

(2) Plant and Vehicles

This is the sum of three separate estimates for power plant and lines; tramcars; and trolley vehicles. The estimates for vehicles were first made in real terms. See p. 169.

1. *Power Plant and Lines*

All items were estimated from data in the *Returns* on Power Stations and Electrical Equipment. See p. 169. The methods used were the same as those shown above for the permanent way, except that:

(a) Depreciation was written off by the reducing balance method with a life of 25 years.

(b) The price index used was a weighted average of the indices used for the assets owned by Electricity Supply Undertakings. (See chapter 7.1, p. 91.)

2. *Tramcars and Trolley Vehicles*

A. At historical prices:

(a) *Year's purchases*: The net additions plus replacements multiplied by the average cost per vehicle in the year of purchase.

(b) *Proceeds of vehicles scrapped or sold*: A (a) less A (d) less annual change in A (f) (= 10% of the original cost of the vehicles scrapped).

(c) *Gross fixed capital formation*: A (a) less A (b); (or A (d) plus annual change in A (f)).

(d) *Depreciation*: Reducing balance method at a rate of 15%, and assuming a scrap value equal to 10% of the first cost.

(f) *Depreciated value of vehicles held at end of year*: By cumulating purchases less depreciation since 1897.

(g) *First cost value of vehicles scrapped*: Roughly estimated for 1920–38.

(h) *First cost value of vehicles held at end of year*: By cumulating purchases C (a) less scrapping C (g) since 1897.

B. At current prices:

C. At constant (1930) prices: } Estimates in terms of number of vehicles multiplied by the average cost per vehicle in the current year in question, or in 1930.

minor improvements which would provide the basis for a distinction between major renewals and other repairs. The concept of renewal of a road is not very clear-cut, and the absence of any distinction in the accounts of those responsible for the roads undoubtedly weakens the case for attempting to make the separation with a view to capitalization of the renewals element. We have, however, taken a rather arbitrary proportion of the total expenditure on maintenance, repairs and minor improvements, partly on the general grounds outlined in chapter 1, appendix 1.1, and partly to maintain consistency with the estimates for other trade groups.

The proportions taken are designed to cover revenue expenditure on such work as complete resurfacing of significant lengths of road, the construction of new foundations or the strengthening of existing foundations, in each case with improved materials. The rapid growth of motor traffic led to greatly increased expenditure on existing roads on work of this sort after 1914 and much of it was not charged to capital account.

Detailed estimates were made in the light of the above points, and the more general principles suggested in chapter 1, appendix 1.1, by the following methods:

Gross fixed capital formation at current (or historical) prices in 1920–38 was taken as the sum of new construction and major improvements plus renewals. For 1930–38 the former was based on the figures given in the Road Fund *Reports* for annual expenditure on 'new construction' and 'major improvements'. For 1920–9 the basic estimates used were the figures given by Bretherton *et al* for capital expenditure on roads by local authorities.[1] This includes expenditure out of loans and out of other capital receipts such as government grants. Both series relate only to Great Britain and an addition was made for expenditure out of loans in Northern Ireland.[2] An amount was also added for central government capital expenditure on trunk roads in 1937 and 1938 as this was not covered by the Road Fund *Reports*. Finally the series was reduced by 17% each year to exclude expenditure on purchases of land.[3]

The renewals component was taken as 5% of expenditure on maintenance, repairs and minor improvements in 1932–8 and as 10% of this expenditure in 1920–31.[4] The higher proportion for the earlier period is designed to allow for the fact that in these years local authorities were assisted by the central government to undertake a considerable amount of maintenance work, much of which consisted of putting up-to-date surfaces and crusts onto existing roads.[5] After the autumn of 1931 this expenditure was substantially reduced as part of the general programme of economy measures introduced at that time. The actual proportions chosen have

no firm statistical basis, though some information on the percentage composition of expenditure on 'maintenance and minor improvements' is available for post-war years.

A special price index was used to convert the final estimate of gross capital formation at current prices to 1930 prices. It was constructed by taking a weighted average of the weekly wage-rates at the end of each year of labourers employed in local authority non-trading services (weight 4); and the average values of igneous rocks mined in the United Kingdom (1); imported asphalt (1); and exported cement (1).[6]

The end-1919 *first cost value at historical prices* was obtained by cumulating the annual capital expenditure on new construction and major improvements since 1820. (It is assumed that any renewals were balanced by an equivalent amount of scrapping.) For 1919 this was based on Bretherton *et al*, and for 1882–1918 on the local authority expenditure out of loans as given in the *Statistical Abstracts*. From 1910 to 1918 a small addition was made for capital expenditure other than out of loans, based on the annual payments under grants made for road purposes (mainly improvement of road crusts) by the central government through the Road Board.[7] These series were then reduced by 17% in 1910–19 and 10% in 1882–1909 to exclude expenditure on purchase of land.

Before 1882 the estimates are very much more approximate. For 1870–81 the above (adjusted) series was extrapolated by reference to the total loan expenditure in the United Kingdom (an analysis by type of service is not available for these years) and an analysis of the loan debt outstanding in 1884. For 1820–69 the very rough guess made was that, on average, capital expenditure on roads was £1m. per year.[8]

---

[1] [95] Bretherton *et al*., pp. 123–5 and Table 30, p. 421.

[2] [30] *Statistical Abstracts*.

[3] This proportion is based on the results of a sample investigation of the composition of local authority capital expenditure on roads and other services in 1929–36 made by [95] Bretherton *et al*., pp. 126–7.

[4] From 1930 onwards this expenditure is separately classified in the [23] Road Fund *Reports*, and it was only necessary to make an allowance for maintenance of trunk roads and for expenditure in Northern Ireland. In 1930–8 the expenditure on maintenance, repairs and minor improvements represented, on average, 74% of the total revenue expenditure (excluding loan charges), the balance being costs of cleansing, administration, etc. The corresponding estimates for 1920–9 were therefore obtained by taking 74% of the annual local authority revenue expenditure (excluding loan charges). This in turn was obtained from the expenditure 'other than out of loans' as given in the Road Fund *Reports*, reduced to exclude the estimated amount of capital expenditure contained under this head. (Cf. [95] Bretherton, *et al*., pp. 123–5.)

[5] See, for example, the [13] *Fourth Annual Report of the Road Board*, 1913–14, p. 5: '. . . the most pressing and the most universal need is the strengthening and improvement of the crusts (which include foundations as well as surface coatings) of existing roads'.

[6] All these series are given in [30] *Statistical Abstract*.

[7] [13] *Report of the Road Board*.

[8] After these estimates were completed, Dr. B. R. Mitchell made a detailed study (as yet unpublished) of capital expenditure on roads and bridges in the period 1831–1919. This shows an appreciably lower average per year than the figure of £1m.

The estimates *at 1930 prices* were then obtained by deflating the annual expenditure from 1870 to 1919 by means of index A and assuming that the average annual expenditure in 1820–69 was £2 m. at 1930 prices.

Depreciation was estimated on the straight line method, assuming a life of 100 years. The end-1919 *depreciated value at historical prices* was then obtained by estimating the depreciation due at this rate on the capital expenditure cumulated to the end of each year from 1820 onwards, and deducting the accumulated depreciation at the end of 1919 from the corresponding first cost value. A similar procedure was used for the estimate *at 1930 prices*.

Finally, the *first cost value of scrapping* in 1920–38 was very roughly allowed for on the assumption that it averaged £1 m. per year *at 1930 prices*, but that it fluctuated in proportion to the gross fixed capital formation at 1930 prices.

PART 2. SUPPLEMENTARY ESTIMATES: CLASSIFICATION BY TYPE OF VEHICLE

A. ROAD MOTOR TRANSPORT

GENERAL PROCEDURE AND SOURCE OF INFORMATION

The basic source for the estimate of all motor vehicles in the three groups: cars, goods vehicles and public passenger vehicles (hackneys) was information on the registration of motor vehicles. Two main series are available.[1] The first gives the number of new vehicles registered for the first time, and estimates of the year's purchases of vehicles were based on this series. The second gives the number of licences current at various dates in the year and this was the basis for the estimates of the first cost value of the stock of vehicles. The first series was only published from 1926 and other estimates have to be made for earlier years; the second is available from 1904.

Registration of motor vehicles was required by statute, and the Licensing Regulations defined the following groups of vehicles: Cars, Commercial goods vehicles, Motor hackneys, Motor cycles, Agricultural tractors and other dutiable vehicles, and Government-owned and other exempt vehicles. It is only the first three groups which are covered by the present estimates.

The series obtained in terms of numbers of vehicles from the registration data were then valued by estimates of the average cost per vehicle based on series given by K. F. Glover.[2]

ASSETS INCLUDED

This section covers all vehicles in the United Kingdom of the following types: mechanically propelled cars, commercial goods vehicles and public passenger vehicles such as buses and taxis. Separate estimates were made for each of these three types of vehicle and are shown in Table 9.22. These are supplementary estimates, and are not directly included in the national totals since they cover all vehicles in these three groups, irrespective of their ownership, and so duplicate estimates for other sectors.

In part 3 of this chapter estimates based on a classification by ownership are derived from the above estimates for these vehicles and it is these which form part of the national total.

The commercial goods vehicles are divided between those owned by the Road Haulage industry and those owned by sectors other than transport, principally Manufacturing (chapter 8) and Distribution (chapter 9). The former group is included in part 3. All public passenger vehicles are assumed to be owned by the public road passenger transport sector and are included in part 3. Private cars are not included in part 3. To the extent that they are owned by businesses they are assumed to be covered by the estimates for other sectors such as Manufacturing and Distribution. No information on the exact division between consumers and businesses is available; as a very rough guess it was assumed that roughly 30% of private cars were purchased by businesses in the inter-war years,[3] and it is only this 30% which is shown in Table 9.22.

Government-owned and other exempt vehicles are the only other group of vehicles covered by the registration statistics which should, in principle, form part of capital formation in the road motor transport section. Their value is not, however, of any consequence and they have been excluded from the present estimate. On a rough estimate, their first cost value at historical prices was about £3 m. in 1920, rising to just under £14 m. at the end of 1938.

METHOD OF ESTIMATION

A complete set of estimates was first made for each of the three groups in terms of the number of vehicles in the group. These estimates were then valued by means of the estimated average cost per vehicle.

From 1926 onwards, the estimated number of vehicles *purchased* was taken directly from the official

---

[1] [23] Ministry of Transport, and [29] *Road Vehicles in Great Britain*, Quarterly Returns. See also [161] Society of Motor Manufacturers and Traders Limited, *The Motor Industry of Great Britain*. Annual from 1926.
[2] [111] K. F. Glover, 'Gross Investment in Inland Transport in Great Britain'. Unpublished M.Sc. Thesis (1949), London University Library.
[3] This is consistent with the estimates in [139] Stone, vol. 2, where the remaining 70% of the purchases are allocated to consumer's expenditure.

series of the number of new vehicles registered for the first time in each of the statutory groups. For earlier years special estimates had to be made. Before 1916[1] the number of new vehicles was simply taken as the annual change in the stock of vehicles, as shown for this period by the number of licences current at 31 March each year. (Scrapping is thus omitted, but very little occurred in these years and it can be safely assumed that the effects of this omission on the post-war estimates of the stock is slight.)

From 1916 until 1922 the most suitable information available on new vehicles is the estimate given in [161] *The Motor Industry of Great Britain* of the total number of new vehicles of all types available each year for the home market. It was, however, necessary to allocate this total between the various types of vehicle. Data are available for each of these years on the number of licences current for each class of vehicle, but in the immediate post-war years the re-registration of vehicles not used during the war greatly increased the annual increments in this series. By the end of 1922, however, it seems that this process of re-registration was almost finished, since the number of new vehicles in that year again exceeded the net increase in licences current. It thus seemed reasonable to assume that the number of vehicles available for the home market in each group would be proportionate to the overall net increase in licences current for each group from the end of 1915 to the end of 1922.

From 1923 to 1925 *The Motor Industry of Great Britain* gives both the total number of vehicles available for the home market and also the number of cars available. It was thus only necessary to allocate the vehicles other than cars between the remaining groups. This was assumed to be proportionate each year to the increase in licences current for each of these groups of vehicles.

The *first cost value*, in terms of numbers, of the stock of vehicles was taken as equal to the number of licences current at a certain date during the year. Until 1920 the series related to the 31 March of each year. From 1920 to 1925 the series used was for the 31 August, as this was the quarterly date at which the number of licences current was at its highest. From 1926 onwards the figure taken was that given by the annual census of vehicles registered at the end of September. This was the seasonal peak of the year when the number of vehicles in use was closest to the actual number available.

The series for the number of vehicles *scrapped* each year then followed from the number purchased less the change in the stock of vehicles. It should be noted that this series was negative in the first few years because of the re-registration of vehicles which had been out of use during the war.

Factors such as the frequency of accidents and the consequent early scrapping of vehicles, and the wide variations in the extent to which vehicles are used, mean that the depreciated value of the stock of vehicles cannot be estimated in the usual way by imputing an age-structure based on some assumed normal life. Fortunately, a table of the life expectancy at the end of 1936 of a large sample of private motor cars is available.[2] This table shows the percentage of cars purchased which would 'survive' for periods of one year from six months to $17\frac{1}{2}$ years. By applying this table to the purchases in the preceding $17\frac{1}{2}$ years, it was possible to obtain each year the number of survivors from the previous $17\frac{1}{2}$ years' purchases which could be expected in the year in question; and also the age of each survivor.

Depreciation was written off over 8 years using the reducing balance method. The *depreciated value* at the end of each year of the expected survivors could then be obtained by deducting the accumulated depreciation due on all previous years' purchases from the expected number of survivors. In most years the actual number of survivors (as shown by the number of licences current) exceeded the number expected on the basis of the life-table used; the depreciated value of this excess was taken as 10% of its first cost and added to the estimated depreciated value of the expected survivors to obtain the depreciated value of the total stock of cars.

The same table was similarly used to estimate the depreciated value of the two other groups of vehicles,[3] with depreciation measured at the same rate.

Finally, *gross capital formation* can be obtained by adding the change during the year in the depreciated value of the stock of vehicles and the depreciation during the year.[4]

The standard estimates were then obtained by multiplying all the above estimates in terms of number of vehicles by the estimated average cost of the vehicles. For commercial goods vehicles the average cost from 1928 to 1938 was taken from the estimate made by Glover[5] from a detailed analysis of the sales of these vehicles. For years before 1928 Glover's estimate for

---

[1] Estimates are required for these years for certain of the series at historical prices.

[2] [161] *The Motor Industry of Great Britain*, 1938, p. 102. The table was used to make estimates for each type of vehicle in each of the inter-war years, although the discrepancy between actual and expected survivors was naturally larger in the earlier years and for other vehicles. For goods vehicles, for example, the excess was 2% of the actual stock in 1938, 21% in 1930 and 43% in 1921.

[3] See also the previous footnote.

[4] The 'negative scrapping' in 1920–2 was not taken into account when calculating gross (and net) capital formation.

[5] [111] Glover, appendix 4.

that year was extrapolated by a means of a weighted index of the quotations of prices for new vehicles in three size groups: up to 1 ton, 1 to 2½ tons and 2½ tons and over.[1]

For public passenger vehicles an estimate by Glover was again used for 1928 to 1938, and the 1928 figure was extrapolated by an unweighted index of the quotations for prices of two groups of vehicles: those of 2½ tons or more (to represent buses), and those of 1 ton (to represent taxis).

The estimated average value of cars was taken from Glover for 1928 to 1938, and extended to earlier years by means of a weighted average of the quotations of prices for the most popular makes of new cars.[2]

For the estimates *at 1930 prices* the estimated number of vehicles in each series was multiplied by the average cost per vehicle in 1930, and for the estimates *at current prices* by the average cost per vehicle in the appropriate current year.[3]

The first cost value *at historical prices* was estimated by multiplying each age-group of the surviving vehicles by the average cost per vehicle in the year of purchase, and adding this to the *average* first cost value at historical prices of the excess of actual over expected survivors, taken as equal to the average historical value estimated for the expected survivors. The depreciated value at historical prices was then obtained by deducting the accumulated depreciation due.

COMPARISON WITH OTHER ESTIMATES

A comparison with other estimates which have been made for vehicles will be found in chapter 14, p. 242.

B. HORSE-DRAWN VEHICLES

This is a supplementary estimate of the value of all horse-drawn vehicles used for road transport in the United Kingdom. Horse-drawn vehicles used in mines and on farms are excluded.

It is only the proportion of this total owned by professional road hauliers (see part 3, p. 167) which forms part of the national totals.

METHODS OF ESTIMATION

Horses

The total number of horses in Great Britain was established by official censuses from 1924 and 1934.[4] The number of these used for road transport was obtained by deducting thoroughbreds, riding horses, and horses on farms and in mines from these totals, and adding an allowance for Northern Ireland.

The figures for these two years were then extrapolated by means of an index which combines two series:

the number of horse-drawn hackneys registered in Great Britain,[5] and the number of horses used for road transport by the railways.[6] The resulting series decreases from 545,000 horses in 1920 to 187,000 in 1930 and 110,000 in 1938.

The *first cost value at current prices* of the horses used for road transport was derived by multiplying the number of horses by the estimated average price per horse in each year. This was taken as the lower of the average price each year for imported or for exported horses. The value at 1930 prices was similarly obtained from the average price per horse in 1930. No other series were estimated.

Vehicles

The number of vehicles was estimated on the assumption that one horse was required for every registered horse-drawn hackney, and that there was one other vehicle for every two of the remaining horses. These ratios were based on the data available for horses and vehicles owned by the railways.

For the estimate of the *first cost value at constant prices* the number of vehicles was multiplied by the estimated average value of a horse-drawn carriage, as shown by the 1930 Census of Production, plus an allowance for costs of distribution, harnesses, etc. To obtain the *current price* series the average price in 1930 was extended to other years by means of an index of the weekly wage rates of joiners.

PART 3. ESTIMATES FORMING PART OF THE NATIONAL TOTALS: CLASSIFICATION BY OWNERSHIP OF VEHICLE

Estimates covering all vehicles of a particular type, irrespective of which business sector they were owned by, were made in part 2, p. 164. These estimates in part 3 are based on a classification by ownership and cover only those vehicles not included elsewhere in this study as owned by some other sector.

---

[1] The quotations were taken from [**158**] *The Commercial Motor Index*, annual, Fletcher and Sons, Norwich.

[2] [**160**] *The Motor-Car Index*, annual, Fletcher and Sons, Norwich. The calculations for 1920–7 were taken from [**139**] Stone, vol. 2, where they are used for the estimates of consumers' expenditure.

[3] A slight defect in this procedure should be noted: the average cost in 1930 for (say) all goods vehicles, is a weighted average of the goods vehicles in various categories (unladen weight groups) purchased in that year, and this average will not be appropriate to other years in which the composition of vehicles purchased was different from that of 1930 (or to other measures, such as the first cost value where the average values should be weighted according to the compositions of the total number of vehicles in use each year). It would therefore have been better if the annual estimates at current and 1930 prices had been made separately for each of the main categories of goods vehicle.

[4] [**44**] *Report on the Census of Horses in Great Britain—1934*, H.M.S.O., 1935, gives the figures for both years.

[5] [**23**] *Report on the Administration of the Road Fund.*

[6] [**22**] *Railway Returns.*

A. VEHICLES (AND OTHER ASSETS) OWNED
BY ROAD HAULIERS

ASSETS INCLUDED

The present estimate relates to the commercial motor goods vehicles and horse-drawn vehicles owned by road hauliers. The road haulage services of the railways are included in this trade group. Goods vehicles not owned by the transport sector are included elsewhere, for example as part of the assets owned by Manufacturing (chapter 8).

An estimate of the buildings required to garage these vehicles and horses is also given.

METHODS OF ESTIMATION

The estimates of all commercial goods vehicles and horse-drawn vehicles were described above (pp. 164–6). The object in this section is to estimate the proportion of these totals owned by road hauliers.

The only direct information available is the number of vehicles in Great Britain owned under 'A' licences in 1937 and 1938.[1] These vehicles are mainly but not exclusively operated by road hauliers—a small number of the 'A' licences were held by operators who also held 'B' or 'C' licences, i.e. their 'A' licences were held only to make possible the occasional transport of other persons' goods. As a partial offset to this, no adjustment was made for road hauliers in Northern Ireland.

The extent of the road haulage services in other years can best be measured in terms of the numbers of wage-earners employed each year.[2] It was, therefore, necessary to estimate (a) the number of wage-earners operating motor vehicles and horse-drawn vehicles respectively; and (b) the appropriate relationship for each type of vehicle between the numbers employed and vehicles operated.

The best estimate which could be made of the number of men required to operate motor vehicles was based on [55] British Transport Commission *Report and Accounts* for 1948. At the end of that year the ratio of men employed (as drivers, loaders, and so on) to vehicles owned was roughly 4:3; and this ratio was adopted for the inter-war period for all motor goods vehicles. It was assumed earlier (p. 166) that for goods transport horses were generally used in pairs. The number of operatives per horse would be lower than the above ratio for motor vehicles, and the ratio chosen was one wage-earner per horse, i.e. two per horse-drawn vehicle. These two ratios were tested by applying them to the number of vehicles and horses owned at the end of each year by the railways,[3] and comparing the result with the estimated number of wage-earners

employed in the road haulage departments of the railways. This indicated that the ratios were reasonably accurate.

The next step was to estimate the total number of persons employed to operate each type of vehicle in each of the inter-war years. The number of vehicles operated under 'A' licences was 91,000 in June 1937 and 93,000 in June 1938. Applying the assumption that every three vehicles require four wage-earners we obtain the number employed to operate motor vehicles. The remaining wage-earners (69,000 in 1937 and 60,000 in 1938) were then taken as operating horse-drawn vehicles, and the assumption of one horse per wage-earner gives the number of horses owned by road hauliers in these two years. These figures for horses owned in 1937 and 1938 were then extrapolated back to 1920 proportionately to the trend in the number of horses owned by the haulage service of the railways.[4]

It was then possible to estimate the number of motor vehicles owned by road hauliers: the estimated number of horses and the assumption of one wage-earner per horse gives the number required for the horse-drawn vehicles; deducting this from the total number employed leaves the number of wage-earners available for motor vehicles; and finally the ratio of 4 men for 3 vehicles gives the number of vehicles owned each year. The estimate obtained in the way rises steadily from 13,000 in 1920 to 55,000 in 1930 and 93,000 in 1938. The corresponding figures for all commercial goods vehicles are 101,000, 355,000 and 504,000.

It may be noted that the results obtained correspond fairly well with a statement by the National Road Transport Federation in 1929, that it represented about 3,000 contractors employing at least 150,000 people and operating 50,000 lorries and 80,000 horse-drawn vehicles.[5]

With the aid of these series the standard estimates were then derived as follows:

Buildings (including land)

An estimate was made of the garage space needed for all vehicles owned by road hauliers, on the assumption that the necessary space was automatically built as each motor vehicle was acquired, or deducted as each horse-drawn vehicle was scrapped. The basic cost of a

---

[1] [11] Ministry of Transport, *Annual Report of the Licensing Authorities, 1936–1937*. 'A' licences are for vehicles which may only be used for the 'carriage of goods for hire or reward'.

[2] [99] A. Chapman, *Wages and Salaries in the United Kingdom, 1920–1938*. The estimates are given under the heading 'other road transport' on p. 143.

[3] [22] *Railway Returns*.

[4] The resulting series falls steadily from 119,000 in 1920 to 94,000 in 1930 and 60,000 in 1938.

[5] [51] Royal Commission on Transport 1931, *Final Report*, Cmd. 3751, p. 85.

standard unit of space, at 1930 prices, was assumed to be £60 of which £54·5 was the cost of the buildings, and 10% of this (£5·5) the cost of the land. For further details see the Notes to Table 9.23, p. 160.

Vehicles

The *first cost value at current and* 1930 *prices* of the horse-drawn vehicles was obtained by multiplying the corresponding estimates in part 2 (p. 166) by the ratio:

$$\frac{\text{Horses owned by road hauliers}}{\text{All horses used for road transport.}}$$

The annual estimates for motor goods vehicles owned by road hauliers of the stock at depreciated and first cost value, and of depreciation, were obtained by multiplying the corresponding estimates in part 2 by the ratio for each year:

$$\frac{\text{Number of goods vehicles owned by road hauliers}}{\text{Total number of goods vehicles in use}}$$

The remaining series followed by application of the standard identities. For further details of both sets of estimates see the Notes to Table 9.23, p. 160.

B. PUBLIC ROAD PASSENGER TRANSPORT

This estimate is in two parts. The first covers all mechanically propelled road passenger vehicles such as buses and taxis. The second covers the tramways and trolley vehicles, i.e. the electrically propelled road passenger vehicles.

No estimate is included for horse-drawn carriages. Their first cost value at 1930 prices was only about £5 m. in 1920 and had dropped to roughly £0·3 m. by 1938.

I. BUSES AND TAXIS

METHODS OF ESTIMATION

Land and Buildings

A special estimate was made of the buildings owned for these vehicles. For this purpose the vehicles were divided into two groups, according to whether their seating capacity was less or more than fourteen persons.

The number of public road passenger motor vehicles in each size group is known from September 1926 onwards.[1] For earlier years it was assumed that each group changed in the same proportion as the change in the total number of hackneys, known from the data on licences current (see above, p. 165).

The smaller vehicles, mostly taxis, were assumed to require only the 'standard unit' of garage space, valued at £60 per vehicle (including land) at 1930 prices.

The larger vehicles, mostly buses and coaches, were assumed to require not only garage space but also administrative and other buildings. The estimated number of these vehicles corresponded very closely to the number of vehicles operated in Great Britain by public passenger undertakings with six or more vehicles. Published reports on these vehicles for 1936/7 and 1937/8[2] show the accumulated capital expenditure on garages, workshops, bus stations, etc. This figure, plus that for the corresponding department of the London Passenger Transport Board, was taken as the first cost value of the buildings at historical prices at the end of 1937.

This total was assumed to have been accumulated in fixed proportion to the annual increase in the number of these vehicles with a seating capacity of fourteen or more persons. Capital expenditure on these buildings at current (or historical) prices in each year was taken as equal to the increase in the number of vehicles, multiplied by an assumed (constant) real cost of buildings per vehicle and adjusted (by means of index B) for changes in the cost of building. The assumed constant real cost of buildings per vehicle is the one unknown in this calculation, and it was found by putting the sum of each year's capital expenditure (estimated by the above calculation) from 1905 until 1937 equal to the known first cost value at the end of 1937.

For further details see the Notes to Table 9.24, p. 162.

Vehicles

It is assumed that all buses and taxis are owned by establishments engaged in road passenger transport. The vehicles owned are thus equal to the estimate for all public road passenger vehicles described in part 2, p. 164, as part of the supplementary estimate of all road motor transport.

2. TRAMWAYS AND TROLLEY VEHICLES

SOURCES OF INFORMATION

The main source is [31] *Annual Return of Tramways and Light Railways (Street and Road) and Trolley Vehicle Undertakings* issued by the Ministry of Transport.[3] For 1933–8 this was supplemented by information in [67] *Annual Reports of the London Passenger Transport Board.*

ASSETS INCLUDED

The estimate covers all electrically propelled passenger transport operating on public roads in Great Britain,

---

[1] [23] *Reports on the Administration of the Road Fund*, annual; and [29] *Road Vehicles in Great Britain*, Quarterly Returns.

[2] [15] Ministry of Transport: *7th Annual Report of the Traffic Commission*, 1937/8, pp. 110–11.

[3] Information in the *Returns* on Local Authority undertakings relates to financial years and was taken without adjustment for the preceding calendar year.

including assets transferred to the London Passenger Transport Board in 1933 by local authorities and companies.

The classification of expenditure used in the *Returns* does not provide an adequate breakdown by type of asset. In particular land, buildings and civil engineering work may all be included together under any of four headings: Permanent way, Street and road improvements (including purchase of land), Other land and buildings, and Power stations. The assumption was made that the value of all land owned by the undertakings was approximately equal to the accumulated expenditure on 'Other land and buildings'. No estimates are shown for buildings, but it is roughly estimated that the first cost value at historical prices in 1920 of the buildings included under other headings was £3·75 m.

It should also be noted that expenditure on Electrical Equipment of Lines is classified in the national totals under the heading, Plant, Vehicles, etc. No allowance was made for Northern Ireland but the omission is negligible.

METHODS OF ESTIMATION

Permanent way

The *year's purchases at current (or historical) prices* was taken from the *Returns* as the sum of the annual net increase in accumulated capital expenditure on the Permanent Way and on Street and Road Improvements, plus the estimated expenditure on renewals. This second component was derived as a proportion of the total expenditure on renewals out of the Reserve, Renewals and Depreciation Funds. Renewals expenditure is not classified by type of asset in the *Returns*, but an analysis is given each year of the expenditure on maintenance out of revenue, and expenditure on renewals was assumed to follow the same pattern.

The *first cost value at historical prices* of the permanent way was taken as equal to the accumulated capital expenditure on the Permanent Way, Street and Road Improvements and Unallocated Capital Expenses since 1897 (taken as the starting point for the electrification of tramways), less assets scrapped or transferred to 'other trades' or to 'accounts of superseded assets'.

Depreciation was estimated at a rate of 3·3% based on the maximum period allowed for repayment of loans on substantial buildings in electricity supply undertakings (see trade group 7.1, p. 87) and was written off on the straight line method. The *depreciated value at historical prices* was then estimated by deducting the accumulated depreciation and disposals since 1897 from the first cost value. In order to estimate the accu-

mulated depreciations due, estimates of the year's purchases from 1897 to 1919 were required and these were obtained in the same way as those for 1920–38 except that expenditure on renewals before 1920 was ignored in view of the very young age of the stock accumulated by 1914.

Gross fixed capital formation can then be obtained from the change during the year in the depreciated value, plus depreciation.

Plant, vehicles, etc.

This heading covers three separate estimates: power stations and plant and the electrical equipment of lines; tramcars; and trolley vehicles.

(*a*) *Power stations and plant, and lines.* The *year's purchases at current (or historical) prices* was estimated from the *Returns* as the sum of the annual net increase in the accumulated expenditure on these two items, plus the expenditure on renewals estimated in the same way as for the permanent way (see above).

Depreciation was assumed to have been written off by the reducing balance method, with a life of 25 years.

The *first cost and depreciated values at historical prices* were obtained in the same way as for the permanent way and it was again assumed that replacements before 1919 were negligible and could be ignored.

Gross fixed capital formation follows from the change during the year in the depreciated value, plus depreciation.

(*b*) *Tramcars.* The *year's purchases* of tramcars were first estimated in terms of units of new cars. Information is available on the total stock of cars, and the estimated number of replacements had, therefore, to be added to the annual net increase in the total stock. Replacement in the pre-war years was again assumed to be negligible, and a very rough estimate was made of replacements after the war.

This series in real terms was then valued at the estimated price per car. In pre-war years this was obtained by dividing the annual increase in the accumulated capital expenditure on electrical tramcars by the increase in the stock of cars. In the inter-war years the purchase of new trams rapidly declined and the average value used was based on the estimated average cost per unit of trolley vehicles. Three-year moving averages were used for the price and value series in order to smooth out the time-lags between changes in the financial accounts and in the data on the stock of vehicles.

The *first cost value* of the stock of tramcars *at 1930 prices* was obtained by multiplying the total number of trams owned by the estimated average cost per tram in 1930. The *first cost value at historical prices* was obtained

by cumulating the capital expenditure less scrapping since 1897.

Depreciation was written off on the reducing balance method, using the rate allowed by the Board of Inland Revenue for trackless trolley buses. The *depreciated value at historical prices* was then obtained by cumulating the net inflows since 1897.

Gross fixed capital formation follows from the change during the year in the depreciated value, plus depreciation.

(c) *Trolley buses.* Trolley buses were a very new form of transport during the period 1920–38 and replacements were negligible throughout. Apart from this the estimates were made in the same way as those for tramcars.

year. Similarly, the first cost value at 1930 prices is the total tonnage remaining on the register at the end of each year, multiplied by the average value per ton of ships exported in 1930.

For harbours and canals the estimates were mainly derived from the accounts of dock and harbour authorities and companies and from the *Railway Returns*.

ASSETS INCLUDED

This trade group covers:
  (a) All merchant ships other than fishing vessels.[2] (Table 9.31)
  (b) Harbours, docks, etc., including the warehouses, and cranes and other plant. (Table 9.32)
  (c) Canals. (Table 9.33)

Tramways and Trolley Vehicles
(£m. at 1930 prices)

	First Cost Value			Year's Purchases (Annual Averages)	
	1920	1930	1938	1920–9	1930–8
Permanent Way	75·2	70·9	38·3	1·0	0·6
Power Stations, Plant and Lines	14·4	17·0	12·2	0·7	0·7
Tramcars	26·9	25·9	16·0	0·7	—
Trolley vehicles	0·2	1·0	6·5	0·1	0·6
Land	14·2	16·8	11·6	—	—
All Fixed Assets	130·9	131·6	84·6	2·5	1·9

For Notes to Table see p. 162.

For further details of all the estimates for plant and vehicles see the Notes to Table 9.24, p. 162.

The total of all fixed assets is given in Table 9.24. The above table provides certain additional details analysed by type of asset.

9.3 SEA AND INLAND WATER TRANSPORT

GENERAL PROCEDURE AND SOURCE OF INFORMATION

The main source used for the estimates for the merchant fleet was the *Annual Statement of Navigation and Shipping of the United Kingdom*.[1] This shows the total tonnage remaining on the register at the end of each year, classified according to the year in which the tonnage was registered.

The basic series can be derived from this register in terms of tonnage, and these tonnage series were then valued by means of the average value per ton of ships exported. For example, the year's purchases at current prices is the tonnage registered in the year, multiplied by the average value per ton of ships exported in that

All sea-going passenger or cargo ships are included in (a), together with tugs and ferries and other port and river transport. Yachts are also included. Barges are omitted because they are not covered by the tonnage data from which the estimates are derived. Merchant vessels owned by the Admiralty are included,[3] but warships are not.

The sector thus corresponds quite closely to the 1948 *S.I.C.* Minimum List Headings 224, 225 and 226.

Since the estimates of all ships are derived from the comprehensive data on tonnage registered, there is some duplication with vessels owned by other sectors and thus included also in their estimates. The full extent of this duplication has not been determined, but by making an analysis of Lloyd's Register for 1937/8 it was possible to list the major overlaps. These occur in the case of the ships owned by harbours, canals, and local authorities; by the gas, electricity, coal and metal industries; by 'food and other' industries; and by

[1] [16] Board of Trade, annual.
[2] For fishing vessels see chapter 5, p. 79.
[3] They are treated in the same way as the army's married quarters, i.e. as assets in civil use. Cf. [57] *Sources and Methods*, p. 250.

TABLE 9.31 SEA AND INLAND WATER TRANSPORT: MERCHANT SHIPS (£M.)

	1920	1921	1922	1923	1924	1925	1926	1927	1928	1929	1930	1931	1932	1933	1934	1935	1936	1937	1938
(2) Merchant Ships																			
A. At historical prices:																			
(a) Year's purchases	63·1	58·9	101·0	39·5	34·9	36·6	19·4	19·3	39·7	33·7	29·3	14·6	4·9	4·1	6·9	17·1	27·5	28·2	25·7
(c) Gross fixed capital formation	54·9	47·0	93·0	40·4	29·3	33·2	12·8	13·2	37·1	27·4	19·3	10·8	2·0	-0·7	4·0	10·7	22·6	19·8	25·4
(d) Depreciation*	18·6	20·0	24·2	20·7	27·8	28·5	28·3	28·4	30·1	31·2	31·0	30·2	30·5	29·3	28·9	25·8	23·6	22·8	22·8
(f) Depreciated value*	269	296	365	384	386	390	375	360	367	363	349	330	301	271	246	231	230	227	230
(g) First cost value of ships scrapped or sold	12·5	28·2	17·5	5·9	18·8	12·9	16·2	18·8	12·2	19·7	20·2	15·7	17·3	26·4	21·7	28·8	22·2	32·3	7·1
(h) First cost value*	458	489	573	606	622	647	650	651	678	692	701	700	687	664	648	637	642	638	658
B. At current prices:																			
(d) Depreciation*	38·1	34·8	57·1	38·2	25·7	25·3	22·7	18·4	23·4	25·2	24·2	23·0	21·5	21·2	17·1	20·8	18·1	19·6	20·2
(f) Depreciated value*	479	453	748	495	309	311	277	222	276	285	282	274	247	219	189	212	199	220	228
(g) First cost value of ships scrapped or sold	19·0	74·3	58·4	44·9	31·1	21·4	22·5	21·0	18·6	23·7	26·5	22·2	25·4	37·7	24·5	30·8	21·3	30·2	16·2
(h) First cost value*	1046	972	1585	1050	654	657	609	490	603	623	628	632	600	566	504	578	535	585	608
C. At 1930 prices:																			
(a) Year's purchases	34·3	34·6	37·4	21·8	31·1	33·3	18·9	23·6	40·5	33·9	29·3	14·4	4·9	4·1	7·5	15·7	27·7	26·0	23·2
(c) Gross fixed capital formation	30·1	21·6	31·8	19·5	25·9	29·8	9·2	20·8	37·5	29·1	19·3	10·1	-1·0	-6·6	4·6	9·8	23·5	18·9	21·7
(d) Depreciation*	21·1	20·3	21·1	21·1	23·1	23·1	22·1	22·3	24·1	25·2	24·2	22·5	21·5	21·2	18·4	19·2	18·2	17·9	18·3
(f) Depreciated value*	264	265	276	274	277	284	271	269	282	287	282	269	247	219	205	196	201	202	205
(g) First cost value of ships scrapped or sold	10·4	43·5	21·5	24·8	27·8	19·5	22·1	25·5	19·0	23·8	26·5	21·9	25·4	37·7	26·7	28·3	21·5	27·8	14·5
(h) First cost value*	576	567	584	581	585	599	596	594	616	626	628	621	600	566	546	533	539	538	547
(4) Stock-in-Trade (Book value)*																			
B. At current prices	13	8	10	9	8	8	8	7	7	7	8	7	6	5	9	8	8	8	8
C. At 1930 prices	5	5	8	6	6	6	7	6	7	6	8	8	7	6	10	9	10	8	8

* At end of year.

NOTES TO TABLE 9.31

(2) Merchant Ships

The series were obtained from separate estimates for steam and motor vessels and for sailing vessels, made first in terms of gross registered tonnage and then valued at the average export value per gross registered ton.

A. At historical prices:

(a) *Year's purchases:* Tonnage registered as completed each year multiplied by the average export value per ton in that year.

(b) *Proceeds of ships scrapped or sold:* As for B (b).

(c) *Gross fixed capital formation:* A (a) less A (b).

(d) *Depreciation:* Straight line method, assuming a rate of 5% for steamers and 3⅓% for sailing vessels; and a scrap value equal to 10% of the first cost value.

(f) *Depreciated value of ships at end of year:* Total depreciation due on each 'age-group' of registered tonnage (classified according to its year of registration) deducted from the first cost value. See p. 176 and A (h). Ships remaining on the register beyond their assumed 'normal' life included at a scrap value equal to 10% of their first cost.

(g) *First cost value of ships scrapped or sold:* A (a) less annual change in A (h).

(h) *First cost value of ships at end of year:* Each 'age-group' of tonnage remaining on the register at the end of each year multiplied by the average export value per ton in the year of registration.

B. At current prices:

As for the series at historical prices except that all tonnage series are valued at the average export values per ton in the current year in question. For (b) Proceeds of ships scrapped or sold, see below pp. 175–6.

C. At constant (1930) prices:

As for the series at historical prices except that all tonnage series are valued at the average export value per ton in 1930.

(4) Stock-in-Trade

B. At current prices:

The ratio, derived from a sample of the accounts of shipping companies, of the value of stocks per gross registered ton of vessels owned, applied to the total registered tonnage.

C. At constant (1930) prices:

The series at 1930 prices deflated by the index of wholesale prices.

TABLE 9.32 SEA AND INLAND WATER TRANSPORT: HARBOURS, DOCKS, ETC. (£M.)

(1) Civil Engineering Works (plus Buildings)

	1920	1921	1922	1923	1924	1925	1926	1927	1928	1929	1930	1931	1932	1933	1934	1935	1936	1937	1938
A. At historical prices:																			
(c) Gross fixed capital formation	3·4	2·5	1·7	1·8	2·6	2·5	2·6	3·6	2·5	1·9	2·3	2·5	2·1	1·6	1·2	1·1	1·1	1·9	1·6
(d) Depreciation	1·8	1·9	1·9	1·9	1·9	1·9	1·9	2·0	2·0	2·0	2·0	2·0	2·0	2·0	2·0	2·0	2·1	2·1	2·1
(f) Depreciated value*	67	68	68	67	68	69	69	71	72	71	72	72	72	72	71	70	69	69	69
(h) First cost value*	137	139	140	141	142	143	145	146	148	149	150	151	152	153	153	154	154	155	156
(i) Land*	6	6	6	6	6	6	6	6	6	6	6	6	6	6	6	6	6	6	6
B. At current prices:																			
(d) Depreciation	5·8	5·1	4·0	3·7	3·8	3·7	3·7	3·7	3·6	3·6	3·5	3·5	3·3	3·2	3·2	3·3	3·4	3·6	3·8
(f) Depreciated value*	211	182	140	129	129	127	124	124	120	118	114	112	105	102	100	99	100	104	108
(h) First cost value*	440	385	300	280	284	282	278	277	272	269	263	261	248	244	243	246	254	270	285
(i) Land*	18	16	12	11	11	11	11	11	11	11	11	10	10	10	10	10	10	11	11
C. At 1930 prices:																			
(c) Gross fixed capital formation	2·0	1·7	1·5	1·7	2·4	2·3	2·5	3·4	2·5	1·8	2·3	2·5	2·3	1·8	1·3	1·3	1·1	1·8	1·5
(d) Depreciation	3·5	3·5	3·5	3·5	3·5	3·5	3·5	3·5	3·5	3·5	3·5	3·5	3·5	3·5	3·5	3·5	3·5	3·5	3·5
(f) Depreciated value*	127	125	123	121	120	119	118	118	117	115	114	113	112	110	108	106	103	102	100
(h) First cost value*	264	264	264	264	264	264	264	264	264	264	263	263	263	263	263	263	263	263	263
(i) Land*	11	11	11	11	10	10	10	10	10	10	10	10	10	10	10	10	10	10	10

(3) All Fixed Assets†

	1920	1921	1922	1923	1924	1925	1926	1927	1928	1929	1930	1931	1932	1933	1934	1935	1936	1937	1938
A. At historical prices:																			
(c) Gross fixed capital formation	4·4	3·3	2·7	2·5	3·5	3·3	3·5	4·7	3·4	2·6	3·1	3·3	2·9	2·4	1·8	1·7	1·7	2·6	2·3
(d) Depreciation	2·6	2·7	2·7	2·7	2·8	2·8	2·8	2·9	2·9	2·9	3·0	3·0	3·0	3·0	3·0	3·0	3·1	3·1	3·1
(f) Depreciated value*	83	84	84	84	84	85	86	87	87	87	88	88	88	87	86	85	83	83	82
(h) First cost value*	164	166	168	169	171	172	174	177	179	180	182	183	185	186	186	187	188	189	190
B. At current prices:																			
(d) Depreciation	8·5	6·9	5·3	5·0	5·1	5·0	5·0	5·0	4·9	4·9	4·8	4·7	4·5	4·4	4·4	4·6	4·8	5·1	5·3
(f) Depreciated value*	264	216	164	153	153	150	146	145	141	138	133	129	122	119	116	115	116	122	124
(h) First cost value*	529	444	344	324	329	326	321	321	315	313	306	300	288	285	285	288	299	321	335
C. At 1930 prices:																			
(c) Gross fixed capital formation	2·5	2·3	2·4	2·3	3·2	3·1	3·3	4·4	3·3	2·5	3·1	3·4	3·1	2·6	1·9	1·9	1·6	2·4	2·1
(d) Depreciation	4·7	4·7	4·7	4·7	4·7	4·7	4·7	4·7	4·8	4·8	4·8	4·8	4·8	4·8	4·8	4·8	4·8	4·8	4·8
(f) Depreciated value*	150	148	146	143	142	140	139	138	137	135	133	132	130	128	125	122	119	116	114
(h) First cost value*	304	304	304	304	304	304	305	305	305	306	306	306	306	306	306	306	306	306	306

* At end of year.
† The estimate for (2) Cranes and other equipment is not shown separately. It can be obtained from the difference between (1) Civil Engineering Works and (3) All Fixed Assets.

NOTES TO TABLE 9.32

HARBOURS, DOCKS, ETC.

Note: The proportions of the accumulated total capital expenditure taken as civil engineering work (80%), land (4%) and plant (16%) were based on the proportions shown in the accounts of the Port of London Authority in 1938,[1] covering their accumulated new capital expenditure from 1909 to 1938.

(1) Civil Engineering Works (Plus Buildings)[2]

A. At historical prices:

(c) *Gross fixed capital formation:* Annual change in A (h).
(d) *Depreciation:* Straight line method assuming a life of 75 years.
(f) *Depreciated value of harbours held at end of year:* A (h) less accumulated depreciation taken as 50% of the accumulated expenditure in 1882 plus 1·3% of the accumulated expenditure at the end of each subsequent year, roughly estimated on the basis of the data available for A (h).
(h) *First cost value of harbours held at end of year:* 80% of loans outstanding for local authority dock and harbour services in 1860, plus the cumulated net changes in their loans outstanding from 1860–82, plus the cumulated expenditure out of loans for capital works by local authorities and public boards from 1882 onwards;[3] and the total accumulated capital expenditure shown in the accounts of railway-owned harbours[4] and of other large harbour companies.[5]
(g) *First cost value of harbours scrapped:* Assumed to average £1m. p.a., but spread over 19 years in proportion to C (c).
(i) *Land at end of year:* 4% of accumulated capital expenditure as under A (h).

B. At current prices:

The series at 1930 prices multiplied by index A.

C. At constant (1930) prices

(c) *Gross fixed capital formation:* A (c) deflated by index A.
(d) *Depreciation:* As for A (d).
(f) *Depreciated value of harbours held at end of year:* For 1919 from A (f) by the ratio of C (h) to A (h) in 1919.
(g) *First cost value of harbours scrapped:* Assumed to average £2m. p.a. but spread in proportion to C (c).
(h) *First cost value of harbours held at end of year:* 80% of: local authority loans outstanding in 1860 deflated by the average of index A for the year 1845–60, plus the cumulated annual expenditure out of loans (or changes in loans outstanding) for docks and harbours of public authorities from 1860 onwards, deflated by index A.; plus the accumulated capital expenditure of railway-owned harbours and of harbour companies at the end of 1919, deflated by the ratio of 1930 to historical prices at that date for the harbours of local authorities.
(i) *Land at end of year:* From C (f) by the ratio of A (i) to A (f).

(2) Cranes and Other Plant

A. At historical prices:

(c) *Gross fixed capital formation:* Annual change in A (h) plus A (g).
(d) *Depreciation:* Straight line method assuming a life of 30 years.
(f) *Depreciated value of cranes, etc. held at end of year:* For 1919 from A (h) by imputing an age-structure based on the estimated inflows, taken as proportional to the expenditure out of loans by local authorities, plus renewals over 30 years of the assets owned at the end of 1889.
(g) *First cost value of cranes, etc. scrapped:* The total assumed due over the 19 years (27% of A (h) for 1919) spread in equal annual amounts. The total scrapping was estimated by deriving the proportion of the 1919 stock of assets purchased 30 years earlier (1890–1908), and so due for renewal during 1920–38, from the growth in the loans outstanding of local authorities.
(h) *First cost value of cranes, etc. held at end of year:* 16% of accumulated total capital expenditure as under (i) A (f).

B. At current prices:

The series at 1930 multiplied by index C.

C. At constant (1930) prices:

(c) *Gross fixed capital formation:* A (c) deflated by index C.
(d) *Depreciation:* As for A (d).
(f) *Depreciated value of cranes, etc. held at end of year:* For 1919 derived from A (f) by the standard estimate that average historical costs of plant and machinery over the 30 years 1884–1913 were 65·3% of the costs at 1930 prices. (See chapter 2, p. 24.)
(g) *First cost value of cranes, etc. scrapped:* As for A (g).
(h) *First cost value of cranes, etc. held at end of year:* For 1919 derived from A (h) by the same standard estimate as for C (f).

(3) All Fixed Assets

The sum of (1) and (2).

---

[1] [73] Annual *Report and Accounts* of the Port of London Authority.
[2] The estimate is classified in the national totals as civil engineering work, but since warehouses, etc. are also included this involves a slight error. See chapter 13, p. 228.
[3] [5] *Local Taxation Returns.*
[4] [22] *Railway Returns.*
[5] As shown by a collection of the accounts of the main dock and harbour companies.

TABLE 9.33 SEA AND INLAND WATER TRANSPORT: CANALS (£M.)

	1920	1921	1922	1923	1924	1925	1926	1927	1928	1929	1930	1931	1932	1933	1934	1935	1936	1937	1938
A. At historical prices:																			
(1) Civil Engineering Works																			
(c) Gross fixed capital formation	0·3	0·3	0·2	—	0·6	0·2	0·5	0·4	0·3	—	0·1	0·2	0·1	—	—	—	—	—	—
(d) Depreciation	0·5	0·5	0·5	0·5	0·5	0·5	0·5	0·5	0·5	0·5	0·5	0·5	0·5	0·5	0·5	0·5	0·5	0·5	0·5
(f) Depreciated value*	19	19	18	18	18	18	18	18	17	17	16	16	16	15	15	14	14	13	13
(h) First cost value*	38	38	38	38	38	38	38	38	38	38	38	38	38	37	37	37	36	36	36
(i) Land*	3	3	3	3	3	3	3	3	3	3	3	3	3	3	3	3	3	3	3
B. At current prices:																			
(1) Civil Engineering Works																			
(d) Depreciation	1·7	1·5	1·2	1·1	1·1	1·1	1·1	1·1	1·0	1·0	1·0	1·0	0·9	0·9	0·9	0·9	0·9	1·0	1·0
(f) Depreciated value*	63	54	41	38	38	37	35	35	33	32	30	29	27	26	25	24	24	25	25
(h) First cost value*	128	112	87	86	82	80	79	79	77	76	74	72	68	67	66	66	68	71	75
(i) Land*	9	8	6	6	6	6	6	6	6	5	5	5	5	5	5	5	5	5	5
C. At 1930 prices:																			
(c) Gross fixed capital formation	0·3	0·3	0·1	—	0·6	0·2	0·4	0·5	0·2	—	0·1	0·2	0·1	—	—	—	—	—	—
(d) Depreciation	1·0	1·0	1·0	1·0	1·0	1·0	1·0	1·0	1·0	1·0	1·0	1·0	1·0	1·0	1·0	0·9	0·9	0·9	0·9
(f) Depreciated value*	38	37	36	35	35	34	34	33	32	31	30	30	29	28	27	26	25	24	23
(h) First cost value*	77	77	76	76	76	75	75	75	75	74	74	73	73	72	71	71	70	70	69
(i) Land*	6	6	6	5	5	5	5	5	5	5	5	5	5	5	5	5	5	5	5

* At end of year.

NOTES TO TABLE 9.33

CANALS

Note: The allocation of the accumulated total capital expenditure between civil engineering work and land was based on the proportions shown in the accounts of the Manchester Ship Canal.

A. At historical prices:

(1) Civil Engineering Works

(c) *Gross fixed capital formation:* Annual change in A (h).

(d) *Depreciation:* Straight line method assuming a life of 75 years.

(f) *Depreciated value of canals held at end of year:* For 1919 assumed to be 50% of A (h).

(g) *First cost value of canals scrapped:* Assumed to average £0·3m. p.a.

(h) *First cost value of canals held at end of year:* 92·83% of accumulated total capital expenditure on railway-owned canals[1] and canals owned by other companies (as shown by their Accounts), plus an allowance for other canals.[2]

(i) *Land at end of year:* 7·17% of the accumulated capital expenditure derived as for A (h).

B. At current prices:

The series at 1930 prices multiplied by index A.

C. At constant (1930) prices:

(c) *Gross fixed capital formation:* A (c) deflated by index A.

(d) *Depreciation:* As for A (d).

(f) *Depreciated value of canals held at end of year:* For 1919 derived from A (f) by the standard estimate that average historical costs of civil engineering work over the period 1845–1913 were 49·4% of the costs at 1930 prices. (Cf. chapter 2, p. 24.)

(g) *First cost value of canals scrapped:* Assumed to average £0·6m. p.a.

(h) *First cost value of canals held at end of year:* For 1919 derived from A (h) by the same standard estimate as for C (f).

(i) *Land at end of year:* From C (f) by the ratio of A (i) to A (f).

[1] [22] *Railway Returns,* annual.

[2] These additional canals for which an allowance was made were those for which the accounts were not obtained for the inter-war years but were available for earlier years; or canals the existence of which was known from the [47] *Report of the Canals and Inland Navigation of the United Kingdom,* 1907, Cd. 3716.

wholesale distribution. If the average costs per ton of these ships were the same as those of all others, the minimum extent of the duplication would be 4·4% of the value of all ships registered. In fact, the higher than average costs of some of these ships (for example, those with refrigeration equipment owned by the food industry) and the fact that the above list is not exhaustive, means that the duplication is slightly larger than this.

There is no duplication of the ships owned by railway companies as these were expressly excluded from the railway sector. There is also no duplication of either the merchant ships owned by the Admiralty[1] or the ships owned by oil companies,[2] as the assets of these owners are not included elsewhere in the present study.

No allowance is made for the change in work in progress on ships.

METHODS OF ESTIMATION

Sea-Going Merchant Ships, Tugs, Ferries, etc.

The estimates described below were first made in full on the basis of the tonnage statistics for all vessels egistered under part I of the Merchant Shipping Act, 1894. The resulting estimates were then reduced by some 2% each year to exclude those vessels which were not registered *only* under part I, i.e. fishing vessels registered also under part IV. It is the lower aggregate which is reproduced in Table 9.31. The reduction was based on the figures of total net registered tonnage on the respective registers at the end of each year.

The *year's purchases of ships at current (or historical) prices* were estimated by multiplying the tonnage newly registered each year by the average value per ton of ships exported in that year.[3] This method of valuation was judged superior to the use of a price series based on wage-rates and the price of materials, because it overcomes the serious problems of timing caused by the long lag between the signing of the contract (when the price is usually fixed) and the moment of completion. It was also considered superior to the use of *Fairplay's* estimates[4] of the average contract price of a standard steamer, partly for the same reasons of timing, and partly because these estimates inevitably failed to reflect progressive changes in quality. In contrast, exported ships are a sample (even if not a perfectly representative one) of ships completed in the year, and the export value is the actual price paid for them.

A test of the accuracy of this measure of value per ton was made by a comparison of the present estimate with data[5] collected in a survey made for the National Shipbuilding Security scheme. This gave figures for the 'total contract or sale price or calculated value of vessels of 300 feet or more in length', launched by members. The survey was said to have included 93% of the ships

300 ft. or more in length, and from an examination of Lloyds Register we estimated that vessels of this length accounted for roughly 83% of all tonnage on the Register in 1930.[6] The survey would thus have covered about 77% of all registered tonnage.

The total value of all new vessels covered by the survey in the seven years 1924 to 1930[7] was £205m. and an estimate of the total value of all ships constructed was thus obtained by raising this figure to £267m. This total is broadly in agreement with the figure of £276m. obtained by adding to the present estimate of £213m. from Table 9.31 (2) A (a), the estimate of fishing vessels from chapter 5 and the value of ships exported.[8]

The estimates of the *year's purchases at 1930 prices* were obtained by multiplying the tonnage added to the register in each year by the average export value in 1930. The adoption of the one average export value for this purpose means that all changes in the average type or quality of ships built are ignored.

Gross fixed capital formation is equal to the year's purchases less the proceeds of ships sold abroad or for scrap. The register shows the tonnage sold abroad or scrapped, but no data on the proceeds of these sales were available, and the assumption made was that the proceeds were equal to the estimated depreciated value of these ships. The estimate of *gross fixed capital formation at current (or historical) and 1930 prices* can thus be obtained by deducting the depreciated value (at historical or 1930 prices) of the ships scrapped or sold abroad (see below, p. 176) from the year's purchases; or from the alternative identity:[9]

---

[1] Other assets of the Admiralty are excluded as the study covers only civil assets.

[2] For the oil companies it was only possible to make a satisfactory breakdown into domestic assets and those owned abroad in the case of the assets owned by subsidiary companies. The major domestic asset owned by the parent companies was their fleet of tankers and this is included in the shipping sector (and thus in the national total) from the tonnage statistics. Most other domestic assets of the parent companies represent an omission from the national total. (See chapter 13, p. 230).

[3] In 1932 and 1933 average export values were distorted by the very low volume of exports, and for those years the series has been adjusted on the basis of an index of the cost of shipbuilding materials.

[4] [148] *Fairplay's Weekly Shipping Journal.*

[5] Published annually in [156] *Reports of National Shipbuilding Security Ltd.*

[6] It appeared from the register that vessels of 300 ft. or more generally weighed not less than 2,500 to 3,000 gross tons.

[7] The seven years were taken together so as to minimize the effect of differences in timing between the survey (vessels launched) and the present estimate (vessels registered as completed).

[8] In raising the survey figure no allowance was made for the fact that vessels of less than 300 ft. would have a higher average cost per ton. On the other hand, war ships are included in the survey but not in the present estimate.

[9] The depreciated value of sales or scrapping at current prices will differ from the depreciated value of sales or scrapping at historical prices. The proceeds of sales or scrapping must however be the same at both current and historical prices and in the present estimates is assumed equal to the estimate of the depreciated value of ships sold or scrapped at historical prices.

Gross capital formation during the year
equals *Change in depreciated value of the stock of ships*
        during the year
plus *Depreciation* during the year.

The estimates of the *first cost value* of the stock of ships were derived from the data on the total registered tonnage. For the series *at current and at* 1930 *prices*, the first cost value was simply the total tonnage remaining on the register at the end of each year multiplied by the average value per ton of ships exported in the current year in question, or in 1930.

For the series *at historical prices* use was made of the valuable classification of the tonnage by the year of registration. Each 'age-group' of tonnage making up the total remaining on the register at the end of each year was multiplied by the average value per ton of ships exported in the year in which it was first registered.[1]

Assets were assumed to have been written down to a scrap value equal to 10% of their first cost, with depreciation calculated on the straight line method, at rates of 5% of the first cost value for steamers and $3\frac{3}{4}\%$ for sailing ships. The *depreciated value of the stock of ships* at the end of each year was then derived from the same age-classification of the total registered tonnage. Working first in terms of tonnage, the accumulated depreciation due on each age-group still on the register was calculated at the above rates and deducted from the tonnage on the register. Tonnage remaining on the register after the working life implied by the assumed rates of depreciation was retained in the estimate at an assumed scrap value equal to 10% of its first cost value.

The total written down tonnage was then valued on each price basis, using the average export values per ton in the same way as for the valuation at first cost.

The tonnage wrecked or sold abroad or for scrap each year can be calculated from the changes in the age-groups of tonnage remaining on the register. The *first cost value on each price basis of ships sold or scrapped* was obtained by multiplying this tonnage by the appropriate average export value per ton. The *depreciated value of ships sold or scrapped at current and* 1930 *prices* was then obtained by deducting from the corresponding first cost value the accumulated depreciation due according to the age of the ships concerned. Alternatively the series at historical and 1930 prices can be obtained by means of the following identity:

Depreciated value of ships scrapped or sold during the year
equals *Purchases* during the year
less *Depreciation* during the year
less *Change in the depreciated value of the stock of ships*
        during the year.

Harbours, Docks, etc., and Canals

These two sets of estimates (Tables 9.32 and 9.33) both relate mainly to assets which do not have a normal life-cycle. The estimates were therefore made in accordance with the principles suggested for such assets in chapter 1, appendix 1.1, pp. 7–10[2]. Details are given in the Notes to Tables 9.32 and 9.33, pp. 173–4.

Three general aspects which should be noted are: (*a*) no expenditure on renewals was capitalized which had not been charged to capital account by the owner of the assets; (*b*) the depreciation was written off over a life of 75 years; and (*c*) the series for scrapping of the assets is no more than an arbitrary allowance.

A comparison with independent estimates for the merchant fleet is given in chapter 14, pp. 242–3 and p. 248. These suggest that the present estimates may be too high.

9.4 CIVIL AVIATION

By 1936 the *first cost value at current prices* of civil aircraft engaged in regular transport was only about £330,000. This estimate is based on the number of civil aircraft as given in the annual report by the Air Ministry,[3] multiplied by the average value of aircraft exported. The standard measurements have, therefore, been omitted for this sector, but data from the accounts of Imperial Airways Limited from 1924–37 are shown in Table 9.40 and have been included in the national totals on all three price bases to represent civil aviation. An estimate has been added for 1938. No allowance was made for airports, etc.

9.5 POSTAL, TELEPHONE AND TELEGRAPH COMMUNICATIONS
GENERAL PROCEDURE AND SOURCE OF INFORMATION

The basic figures are all taken directly from the accounts and balance sheets contained in the annual [21] *Post Office Commercial Accounts.*

---

[1] For years before 1910 the average export values were extrapolated by means of a specially constructed index of the costs of shipbuilding. See [124] K. Maywald 'The Construction Costs and the Value of the British Merchant Fleet, 1850–1938', *The Scottish Journal of Political Economy*, vol. III (1956), p. 50. In part v of this article (pp. 60–6) the present estimates of the stock of all ships (including fishing vessels) are discussed and compared with alternative estimates.

[2] This does not apply to the cranes and other equipment which form part of the estimate for harbours, docks, etc., and the estimates for these assets were made in the usual way.

[3] [53] Air Ministry, Department of the Director-General of Civil Aviation *Report on the Progress of Civil Aviation*, 1936. Of a total of 1,682 registered aircraft in 1936, 116 were engaged in regular commercial air transport.

TABLE 9.40 CIVIL AVIATION (£M.)

	1920	1921	1922	1923	1924	1925	1926	1927	1928	1929	1930	1931	1932	1933	1934	1935	1936	1937	1938
							(2) *Aircraft*												
A. (= B, = C) At historical prices:																			
(c) Gross fixed capital forma-tion		—	—	—	—	0·11	0·11	—	—	0·2	0·0	0·4	0·1	0·0	0·1	0·2	0·5	1·2	1·2
(d) Depreciation		—	—	—	—	—	—	—	—	0·1	0·1	0·1	0·2	0·2	0·2	0·2	0·2	0·2	0·2
(f) Depreciated value*		—	—	—	0·1	0·1	0·2	0·2	0·1	0·2	0·2	0·4	0·4	0·2	0·1	0·1	0·4	1·4	2·4
(h) First cost value*		—	—	—	0·1	0·2	0·3	0·2	0·3	0·4	0·4	0·5	0·6	0·5	0·6	0·3	0·7	1·7	2·7

* At end of year.

TABLE 9.50 POSTAL, TELEGRAPH AND TELEPHONE COMMUNICATIONS* (£M.)

(2) Telegraph, Telephone and Other Plant

	1920	1921	1922	1923	1924	1925	1926	1927	1928	1929	1930	1931	1932	1933	1934	1935	1936	1937	1938
A. At historical prices:																			
(c) Gross fixed capital formation	8·0	11·5	9·2	11·0	12·9	14·8	13·3	13·1	12·8	12·4	12·6	11·3	9·8	8·7	9·7	11·8	14·7	18·8	22·2
(d) Depreciation	2·6	2·8	3·1	3·3	3·7	4·2	4·7	5·3	5·7	6·4	7·0	7·5	8·0	8·3	8·5	7·6	8·2	8·5	9·1
(f) Depreciated value†	36	44	50	58	67	78	86	94	101	107	113	117	119	119	120	124	131	141	154
(h) First cost value†	53	61	67	75	84	96	105	115	124	133	142	150	157	161	167	176	187	201	219
B. At current prices:																			
(d) Depreciation	5·2	5·0	4·4	4·3	4·6	5·1	5·4	5·8	6·2	6·8	6·9	7·0	7·1	7·1	7·3	7·9	8·8	10·1	10·9
(f) Depreciated value†	67	66	59	58	67	76	82	88	95	102	103	103	103	102	103	110	121	138	149
(h) First cost value†	113	109	96	85	100	111	118	126	136	151	150	151	153	154	158	171	191	218	235
C. At 1930 prices:																			
(c) Gross fixed capital formation	4·8	7·6	7·4	10·4	12·1	13·9	12·8	12·8	12·5	11·9	12·6	11·9	10·5	9·5	10·8	12·7	15·2	18·3	21·6
(d) Depreciation	3·1	3·4	3·6	3·9	4·3	4·8	5·2	5·7	6·1	6·4	6·9	7·3	7·6	7·9	8·1	8·6	9·1	9·7	10·6
(f) Depreciated value†	40	44	48	54	62	71	79	86	92	98	103	108	111	112	115	119	126	134	145
(h) First cost value†	67	72	77	84	94	104	114	123	132	141	150	158	165	170	176	186	197	211	228

(3) All Fixed Assets*

	1920	1921	1922	1923	1924	1925	1926	1927	1928	1929	1930	1931	1932	1933	1934	1935	1936	1937	1938
A. At historical prices:																			
(c) Gross fixed capital formation	8·5	12·1	9·2	11·4	13·7	15·9	14·4	14·3	14·0	13·6	14·0	12·8	11·1	9·6	11·1	13·2	16·2	20·4	24·7
(d) Depreciation	2·7	2·9	3·2	3·4	3·8	4·3	4·8	5·4	5·8	6·6	7·2	7·7	8·2	8·5	8·7	7·8	8·4	8·7	9·4
(f) Depreciated value†	44	53	59	67	77	89	98	107	115	122	129	134	137	138	141	146	154	166	181
(h) First cost value†	63	72	78	86	96	109	120	130	141	151	162	171	178	184	191	201	214	230	250
B. At current prices:																			
(d) Depreciation	5·5	5·2	4·6	4·5	4·8	5·3	5·6	6·0	6·4	7·0	7·1	7·2	7·3	7·3	7·5	8·2	9·1	10·4	11·3
(f) Depreciated value†	93	88	77	74	84	93	100	107	114	122	124	124	125	124	126	136	149	169	182
(h) First cost value†	142	133	116	103	120	131	139	148	159	174	174	176	179	180	185	201	224	254	274
C. At 1930 prices:																			
(c) Gross fixed capital formation	5·1	8·0	7·4	10·8	12·9	14·9	13·8	13·9	13·7	13·1	14·0	13·4	11·8	10·5	12·4	14·1	16·7	19·8	23·9
(d) Depreciation	3·3	3·6	3·8	4·1	4·5	5·0	5·4	5·9	6·3	6·6	7·1	7·5	7·8	8·2	8·4	8·9	9·4	10·0	10·9
(f) Depreciated value†	55	59	63	69	78	88	96	104	111	118	124	130	134	137	141	146	153	163	176
(h) First cost value†	84	90	95	102	112	123	134	144	154	164	174	184	192	198	206	217	230	245	265

(4) Stock-in-Trade (Book value)†

	1920	1921	1922	1923	1924	1925	1926	1927	1928	1929	1930	1931	1932	1933	1934	1935	1936	1937	1938
B. At current prices	3	5	4	3	3	4	4	3	3	3	3	4	4	3	3	3	5	6	6
C. At 1930 prices	2	3	2	2	3	3	3	3	3	3	3	4	4	4	4	4	5	6	6

* The estimates for buildings are not shown separately. They can be obtained from the differences between (2) Telegraph, telephone and other plant and (3) All fixed assets.

† At end of year.

NOTES TO TABLE 9.50

(1) Buildings

A. At historical prices:

All series were derived from the *Post Office Commercial Accounts*[1] as explained on p. 180, except that from 1920–22, the first cost value (prime cost) of assets was not shown. This was obtained by successive deduction of the 'net additions' from the first cost value at the end of 1923.

B. At current prices

The series at 1930 prices multiplied by index B.

C. At constant (1930) prices:

(c) *Gross fixed capital formation*: A (c) deflated by index B.

(d) *Depreciation*: The average rate of depreciation from 1920–38 used under A (d).

(f) *Depreciated value of buildings held at end of year*: For 1913 from A (f) on the assumption that the average historical costs as indicated by index B were roughly the same as if the expenditure had been incurred in the five years 1908–12, i.e. 54·1% of the costs at 1930 prices.

(g) *First cost value of buildings scrapped or sold*: Major transfers from C (h) for the previous year by the corresponding ratio of A (g) to A (h); plus other scrapping or sales deflated by the same assumption as for C (f).

(h) *First cost value of buildings held at end of year*: For 1913 from A (h) on the same assumption as for C (f).

(i) *Land at end of year*: From C (h) by the ratio of A (i) to A (h).

(2) Telephone and Other Plant

This series is the sum of separate estimates for the telephone service, the telegraph service, and light, heat and power plant.

A. At historical prices:

See (1) A.

B. At current prices:

For the telephone and telegraph service: The series at 1930 prices multiplied by a weighted average of indices of: wholesale price of copper (weight 2), price of building materials in index B (2), import price of electric motors (2), export price of electric motors (2), export price of convertors and transformers (2), average weekly wage rates in Engineering (5) and in Electrical Installation (5).[2]

For the light, heat and power plant: The series at 1930 prices multiplied by index C.

C. At constant (1930) prices:

(c) *Gross fixed capital formation*: A (c) for each type of plant deflated by the indices listed under B.

(d) *Depreciation*: The average rate of depreciation from 1920–38 used under A (d).

(f) *Depreciated value at end of year*: For 1913 from A (f) on the assumption that the average historical costs as indicated by the price indices listed under B were approximately the same as if the expenditure had been incurred over the five years 1908–12, i.e. 70% of the costs at 1930 prices.

(g) *First cost value of plant scrapped or sold*: Major transfers from C (h) for the previous year by the corresponding ratio of A (g) to A (h); plus revenue expenditure on renewals deflated by the price indices listed under B; plus assets 'permanently displaced' deflated by the same assumption as for C (f).

(h) *First cost value at end of year*: For 1913 derived from A (h) by the same assumption as for C (f).

(3) All Fixed Assets

The sum of (1) and (2).

(4) Stock-in-Trade

B. At current prices:

From the Post Office *Commercial Accounts*.[3]

C. At 1930 prices:

B. Deflated by a special index based on the indices of the prices of materials included in the special index described in (2), B above (i.e. excluding the two indices of wage rates).

---

[1] The [21] *Accounts* relate to the financial year ended in March and were taken without adjustment for the preceding calendar year.

[2] [30] *Statistical Abstract for the United Kingdom.*

[3] The accounts cover engineering stores only, but this is by far the largest item. A maximum estimate of other stores (stationery, motor vehicles, clothing, etc.) in 1938 would be about £1·0m.

ASSETS INCLUDED

All assets owned by post office establishments are covered by this sector, with the exception of: (*a*) the international cables, which were regarded as an asset outside the United Kingdom; (*b*) the Post Office Savings Department. (The buildings *used* by this Department are included in chapter 10); (*c*) the Post Office (London) Railway, which is included in 9.1, p. 147; and (*d*) short-lived assets such as road vehicles, letter boxes and furniture. (Expenditure on these assets was small and was always charged to revenue account in the Post Office *Accounts*. These short-lived assets are, therefore, omitted both from this and from the national total.) Cable and wireless services owned by the Post Office are included, but not the assets of the B.B.C. The sector thus corresponds very closely to the 1948 *S.I.C.* Minimum List Heading, 228.

Two further points may be noted. First, it appears from data in the Accounts on rent paid and received that these estimates of the value of buildings *owned* by the Post Office slightly understate the value of the buildings *used*. Second, buildings 'owned and occupied' by the Post Office do not form part of the estimate in chapter 10 of all shops, offices, etc., and there is, therefore, no double-counting in this respect.

METHODS OF ESTIMATION

All the information required for the series in Table 9.50 at historical prices can be obtained from the *Commercial Accounts*. It may be useful, however, to note some aspects of the system of accounting adopted by the Post Office.

The accounts at first cost show the prime cost of each of the main types of asset at the beginning of the year, and net additions during the year, the major transfers out (e.g. assets sold in 1922 to the Irish Free State) and the end-year prime costs. An annual charge for depreciation was made (on the basis of engineers'

estimates of the lives of the assets) and credited to a Depreciation Account; and the annual revenue expenditure on renewals was debited to this account, together with the charge for 'assets permanently displaced'. The balance on this account at the end of each year was then deducted from the prime cost to obtain the depreciated value.

The figures for depreciation and for the prime cost and depreciated value could be adopted for our estimates without adjustment. To complete our standard estimates it was necessary to have; (*a*) gross fixed capital formation; and (*b*) the first cost value of the assets scrapped or sold.

Gross fixed capital formation equals the purchases of additional assets plus the replacements for existing assets due to be scrapped.[1] The value of the former was obtained by adding back the 'assets permanently displaced' to the figure for the *net* additions during the year. The value of the latter was found from the expenditure on renewals out of revenue.

The first cost value of the assets scrapped or sold was taken as the sum of the revenue expenditure on renewals, major transfers out, and assets permanently displaced. It is thus assumed, with regard to the renewals, that when the expenditure was undertaken, assets to an equivalent amount (in real terms) were scrapped.[2] Any improvement element in the renewals is thus disregarded.

Details of the methods of estimation for the series *at current and at* 1930 *prices* are given in the Notes to Table 9.50, p. 179.

---

[1] Strictly speaking this gives the year's purchases not the gross capital formation. Except for 1922, however, when there were sales to the Irish Free State, the difference between the two series (equal to the proceeds of the assets scrapped or sold) was negligible.

[2] See chapter 1, appendix 1, p. 7. It should also be observed that acceptance of the accounting conventions used by the Post Office (in particular for the annual figure for the prime cost of the stock of assets) logically requires that since the revenue expenditure on renewals is the same measured at current and at historical prices, this must hold also for the estimate of scrapping if the value of the stock of assets is to remain unaltered except for additions.

CHAPTER 10

DISTRIBUTION AND OTHER SERVICES

Estimates are presented in this chapter for a sector embracing the following trade groups:

10.1 Wholesale distribution
10.2 Retail distribution, including semi-industrial retailers
10.3 Services by hotels, inns and restaurants
10.4 Municipal markets
10.5 Finance and miscellaneous services
10.6 Entertainment and sport
10.7 Professional services.

The complete set of standard estimates for the sector as a whole is given in Table 10.00. Estimates for the component trade groups are given in Tables 10.10–10.70 though for the less important trade groups only the series at constant prices are shown. The estimates for each trade group are fully described below, but one general point may be made. Several of the estimates involve a classification by type of asset or by ownership and this introduces an additional source of error, a large part of which is, however, cancelled out within the sector as a whole (for example, buildings which should strictly be restaurants may be classified as shops) and to this extent the overall estimate is more reliable than those for the component groups.

A comparison with an independent estimate by Redfern for the total buildings covered by this sector is given in Chapter 14, pp. 241 and 253–6 below.

10.1 WHOLESALE DISTRIBUTION

GENERAL PROCEDURE AND SOURCE OF INFORMATION

The estimates for this trade group were mainly derived from data obtained by grossing-up a sample of company accounts, and from Inland Revenue data on wear and tear allowances and rates of depreciation. The general methods used are described in chapter 2, appendix 2.1, p. 27.

ASSETS INCLUDED

The estimates in Table 10.10 cover all assets owned by firms classified by the Board of Inland Revenue as primarily engaged in wholesale distribution. Since all assets owned by these firms are included there will be some duplication with estimates made by the 'type of asset' method: in particular, with the shops assigned to retail distribution (trade group 10.2) and with the ships assigned to the shipping sector (chapter 9, trade group 9.3). In principle, the establishments owning these assets should be excluded from this trade group but this was not possible.[1]

Factories owned by firms classified to this trade group will also be included (though ideally they should be in chapter 8) but there is no duplication in this case as these factories will not be included in the manufacturing sector. In general, it is believed that the Inland Revenue practice was to classify firms undertaking more than one activity to manufacturing rather than to wholesale distribution, unless the manufacturing element was relatively small. In consequence the estimate for Manufacturing is probably slightly overstated at the expense of Wholesale distribution.

METHODS OF ESTIMATION

The estimate is based on a very small sample of accounts covering only 5.5% of the corresponding Inland Revenue trade group. Because of the variety in the composition of the assets owned by firms in this group the sample has been divided into four commodity groups: Food, Textile and general materials, Building and other materials, and Warehousing.

Separate estimates of the depreciated value of all fixed assets were made from the samples in each of the four groups. These were then weighted,[2] and grossed-up by the proportion of their gross profits in 1937 to those of all companies in the Inland Revenue trade group.[3]

---

[1] For a more complete discussion of the coverage of this and related estimates see chapter 13, p. 221.

[2] The relative weight given to Warehousing was based on its share in total wages and salaries in wholesale distribution as shown by [32] 1950 *Census of Distribution*. The weights for the other three groups were based on their shares in total wholesale sales in 1950. The weights used are: Food 49.7%, Textile and general materials 28.3%, Building and other materials 19.2%, and Warehousing 2.8%.

[3] The normal practice of using a grossing-up factor based on wear and tear allowances was not adopted in the present case because of the preponderance of assets such as stock-in-trade and buildings not containing fixed machinery, which are not reflected in these allowances.

TABLE 10.00 DISTRIBUTION AND OTHER SERVICES (£M.)

(1) Buildings

	1920	1921	1922	1923	1924	1925	1926	1927	1928	1929	1930	1931	1932	1933	1934	1935	1936	1937	1938
A. At historical prices:																			
(d) Depreciation	11	11	11	12	12	12	12	12	13	13	13	13	14	14	14	14	14	15	15
(f) Depreciated value*	629	647	648	660	675	682	687	691	700	711	727	728	726	729	742	756	764	781	791
(h) First cost value*	914	942	952	973	999	1016	1033	1046	1066	1088	1115	1125	1133	1147	1171	1197	1213	1242	1262
(i) Land*	66	68	69	70	72	73	74	75	77	79	80	81	82	83	85	87	88	90	92
B. At current prices:																			
(c) Gross fixed capital formation	51	29	12	24	27	19	17	16	22	24	29	14	12	17	27	28	22	32	25
(d) Depreciation	36	29	24	23	24	24	24	23	23	23	22	22	21	21	21	21	22	24	24
(e) Net fixed capital formation	15	0	−12	1	3	−5	−7	−7	−1	1	7	−8	−9	−4	6	7	0	8	1
(f) Depreciated value*	2008	1642	1316	1239	1289	1286	1243	1213	1165	1171	1153	1101	1043	1018	1026	1053	1094	1157	1180
(h) First cost value*	2968	2453	1991	1893	1988	2006	1962	1938	1879	1907	1891	1825	1746	1725	1751	1809	1892	2013	2065
(i) Land*	212	175	143	136	142	144	140	139	135	137	136	131	125	124	126	130	136	144	148
C. At 1930 prices:																			
(c) Gross fixed capital formation	30	21	10	22	24	17	17	15	22	23	29	15	13	18	29	31	23	32	24
(d) Depreciation	21	21	21	21	21	22	22	22	22	22	22	23	22	23	23	23	23	24	24
(e) Net fixed capital formation	9	0	−11	1	3	−5	−5	−7	0	1	7	−8	−9	−5	6	8	0	8	0
(f) Depreciated value*	1169	1169	1158	1159	1162	1157	1152	1145	1145	1146	1153	1145	1136	1131	1137	1145	1145	1153	1153
(h) First cost value*	1728	1746	1753	1771	1792	1806	1820	1830	1847	1866	1891	1897	1902	1917	1941	1967	1979	2005	2018
(i) Land*	123	125	125	127	128	129	130	131	132	134	136	136	136	137	139	141	142	144	145

(2) Plant, Vehicles, Equipment, etc.

	1920	1921	1922	1923	1924	1925	1926	1927	1928	1929	1930	1931	1932	1933	1934	1935	1936	1937	1938
A. At historical prices:																			
(d) Depreciation	9	10	10	11	12	13	13	14	15	17	17	20	20	20	21	21	22	24	26
(f) Depreciated value*	109	125	131	141	153	160	166	175	191	204	216	233	238	238	239	245	253	255	272
(h) First cost value*	237	255	264	278	295	308	319	335	359	381	403	432	450	462	477	497	520	538	574
B. At current prices:																			
(c) Gross fixed capital formation	35	26	16	21	24	20	19	23	31	30	29	37	25	20	22	27	30	26	43
(d) Depreciation	24	17	13	14	15	15	15	15	16	17	18	19	20	20	20	21	23	28	29
(e) Net fixed capital formation	11	9	3	7	9	6	4	8	15	13	11	18	5	0	2	6	7	−2	14
(f) Depreciated value*	293	217	166	171	182	184	185	190	201	217	218	222	225	228	231	244	264	297	306
(h) First cost value*	715	512	388	392	407	405	405	410	421	447	443	441	451	467	481	509	556	644	662
C. At 1930 prices:																			
(c) Gross fixed capital formation	16	18	15	19	21	19	18	22	30	28	29	40	27	21	23	28	29	22	38
(d) Depreciation	11	12	12	12	13	14	14	14	16	16	18	21	21	21	21	22	23	24	25
(e) Net fixed capital formation	5	6	3	7	8	5	4	8	14	12	11	19	6	0	2	6	6	−2	13
(f) Depreciated value*	140	146	149	156	164	169	173	181	195	207	218	237	243	243	245	251	257	255	268
(h) First cost value*	340	346	349	356	366	374	380	391	409	426	443	471	486	496	507	524	541	552	577

(3) All Fixed Assets

A. At historical prices:																			
(d) Depreciation	20	21	21	23	24	25	25	26	28	30	30	33	34	34	35	35	36	39	41
(f) Depreciated value*	738	772	779	801	828	842	853	866	891	915	943	961	964	967	981	1001	1017	1036	1063
(h) First cost value*	1151	1197	1216	1251	1294	1324	1352	1381	1425	1469	1518	1557	1583	1609	1648	1694	1733	1781	1836
B. At current prices:																			
(c) Gross fixed capital formation	86	55	28	45	51	39	36	39	53	54	58	51	37	37	49	55	52	58	68
(d) Depreciation	60	46	37	37	39	39	39	38	39	40	40	41	41	41	41	42	45	52	53
(e) Net fixed capital formation	26	9	−9	8	12	0	−3	1	14	14	18	10	−4	−4	8	13	7	6	15
(f) Depreciated value*	2301	1859	1482	1410	1471	1470	1428	1403	1366	1388	1371	1323	1268	1246	1257	1297	1358	1454	1486
(h) First cost value*	3683	2965	2379	2285	2395	2411	2367	2348	2300	2354	2334	2266	2197	2192	2232	2318	2448	2657	2727
C. At 1930 prices:																			
(c) Gross fixed capital formation	46	39	25	41	45	36	35	37	52	51	58	55	40	39	52	59	52	54	62
(d) Depreciation	32	33	33	34	34	36	36	36	38	38	40	44	43	44	44	45	46	48	49
(e) Net fixed capital formation	14	6	−8	8	11	0	−1	1	14	13	18	11	−3	−5	8	14	6	6	13
(f) Depreciated value*	1309	1315	1307	1315	1326	1326	1325	1326	1340	1353	1371	1382	1379	1374	1382	1396	1402	1408	1421
(h) First cost value*	2068	2092	2102	2127	2158	2180	2200	2221	2257	2292	2334	2368	2388	2413	2448	2491	2520	2557	2595

(4) Stock-in-Trade

1. Book values*																			
B. At current prices	1065	716	644	640	621	622	591	612	599	491	519	488	462	465	455	466	477	498	483
C. At 1930 prices	368	447	462	453	403	421	459	490	469	488	519	578	563	568	530	541	522	481	519
2. Investment in stocks†																			
B. At current prices	..	126	21	−13	−77	27	49	39	−27	23	31	50	−12	4	−33	10	−17	−42	35
C. At 1930 prices	..	79	15	−9	−50	18	38	31	−21	19	31	59	−15	5	−38	11	−19	−41	38

* At end of year.
† See chapter 2, appendix 2.2, p. 33.

TABLE 10.10 WHOLESALE DISTRIBUTION (£M.)

(1) Buildings

	1920	1921	1922	1923	1924	1925	1926	1927	1928	1929	1930	1931	1932	1933	1934	1935	1936	1937	1938
A. At historical prices:																			
(c) Gross fixed capital formation	20·2	11·5	3·5	5·3	5·1	0·8	1·2	0·8	4·3	2·7	11·5	0·8	0·8	1·9	8·4	8·5	0·8	10·3	0·8
(d) Depreciation	4·4	4·5	4·6	4·7	4·7	4·7	4·7	4·7	4·8	4·8	5·0	4·9	4·9	4·9	5·0	5·2	5·1	5·3	5·3
(f) Depreciated value*	179	186	185	186	186	182	179	175	174	172	179	175	171	168	171	174	170	175	170
(h) First cost value*	261	272	275	279	284	283	284	283	286	288	299	296	293	295	302	310	308	317	315
B. At current prices:																			
(d) Depreciation	13·9	11·5	9·4	8·9	9·3	9·2	9·0	8·8	8·5	8·5	8·5	8·1	7·6	7·5	7·6	7·9	8·1	8·7	8·7
(f) Depreciated value*	559	457	364	339	347	339	322	308	292	287	284	266	247	236	238	243	245	259	256
(h) First cost value*	835	692	562	532	556	555	538	526	508	512	511	485	457	449	457	473	487	520	525
C. At 1930 prices:																			
(c) Gross fixed capital formation	11·8	8·2	3·1	4·9	4·6	0·7	1·1	0·7	4·2	2·7	11·5	0·8	0·8	2·1	9·3	9·2	0·8	10·2	0·8
(d) Depreciation	8·1	8·2	8·2	8·3	8·4	8·3	8·3	8·3	8·3	8·3	8·5	8·4	8·3	8·3	8·4	8·6	8·5	8·6	8·5
(f) Depreciated value*	325	325	320	317	313	306	298	291	287	281	284	276	269	263	264	264	256	258	250
(h) First cost value*	486	493	494	498	501	499	499	497	499	501	511	504	498	498	506	514	509	518	513

(2) Plant, Machinery, etc.

	1920	1921	1922	1923	1924	1925	1926	1927	1928	1929	1930	1931	1932	1933	1934	1935	1936	1937	1938
A. At historical prices:																			
(c) Gross fixed capital formation	20·6	13·8	7·1	8·9	9·1	10·0	4·7	8·9	14·2	11·7	10·3	16·1	7·7	6·8	5·5	5·2	10·4	9·0	12·4
(d) Depreciation	3·7	4·5	4·7	5·0	5·3	5·7	5·6	5·9	6·5	7·0	7·2	7·9	8·6	8·5	8·2	8·0	8·4	8·9	9·1
(f) Depreciated value*	42	52	54	58	62	66	65	68	76	81	84	92	91	89	87	84	86	86	89
(h) First cost value*	86	98	102	109	115	123	125	132	143	153	160	174	179	184	187	190	198	204	214
B. At current prices:																			
(d) Depreciation	8·5	6·3	4·8	5·2	5·6	5·8	5·6	5·8	6·4	6·9	6·9	7·8	7·8	7·9	7·7	7·7	8·5	10·2	10·1
(f) Depreciated value*	99	73	56	60	65	67	65	68	74	80	80	83	83	83	81	81	88	99	99
(h) First cost value*	244	170	128	134	141	143	142	145	152	164	162	164	168	175	177	184	202	235	236
C. At 1930 prices:																			
(c) Gross fixed capital formation	9·3	9·4	6·5	8·1	8·3	9·3	4·4	8·4	13·8	11·1	10·3	17·3	8·2	7·2	5·8	5·3	10·0	7·6	10·7
(d) Depreciation	3·8	4·3	4·5	4·7	5·0	5·4	5·3	5·5	6·2	6·6	6·9	8·4	8·4	8·3	8·1	7·8	8·2	8·6	8·7
(f) Depreciated value*	44	50	52	55	58	62	61	64	72	76	80	88	88	87	85	82	84	83	85
(h) First cost value*	110	115	118	122	127	132	133	138	148	155	162	175	180	183	185	187	193	197	204

(3) All Fixed Assets

	1920	1921	1922	1923	1924	1925	1926	1927	1928	1929	1930	1931	1932	1933	1934	1935	1936	1937	1938
A. At historical prices:																			
(c) Gross fixed capital formation	40·8	25·3	10·6	14·2	14·2	10·8	5·9	9·7	18·5	14·4	21·8	16·9	8·5	8·7	13·9	13·7	11·2	19·3	13·2
(d) Depreciation	8·1	9·0	9·3	9·7	10·0	10·4	10·3	10·6	11·3	11·8	12·2	12·8	13·5	13·4	13·2	13·2	13·5	14·2	14·4
(f) Depreciated value*	222	238	239	244	248	248	244	243	250	253	262	267	261	257	257	258	256	261	260
(h) First cost value*	347	370	377	388	399	406	409	415	430	441	460	470	473	478	489	500	505	521	529
(j) Land and depreciated value*	241	259	260	265	269	270	265	264	272	275	285	289	284	279	280	281	279	285	283
B. At current prices:																			
(d) Depreciation	22·4	17·8	14·2	14·1	14·9	15·0	14·6	14·6	14·9	15·4	15·4	15·9	15·4	15·4	15·3	15·6	16·6	18·9	18·8
(f) Depreciated value*	658	530	420	399	412	406	387	375	365	368	364	349	330	320	319	324	333	358	355
(h) First cost value*	1079	862	690	667	697	698	680	671	660	676	672	649	625	624	634	657	688	755	761
(j) Land and depreciated value*	721	582	462	439	454	448	427	415	403	406	402	385	364	353	353	360	370	397	394

C. At 1930 prices:

(c) Gross fixed capital formation	21·1	17·6	9·6	13·0	12·8	9·9	5·5	9·1	18·0	13·8	21·8	18·1	9·0	9·3	15·1	14·5	10·8	17·8	11·5
(d) Depreciation	11·9	12·5	12·7	13·0	13·4	13·7	13·6	13·8	14·5	14·9	15·4	16·8	16·7	16·6	16·5	16·4	16·7	17·2	17·2
(f) Depreciated value*	370	375	372	372	371	368	359	355	357	364	357	365	357	350	348	347	341	341	335
(h) First cost value*	596	608	612	620	628	632	635	647	656	672	678	680	682	692	701	715	702	715	717
(j) Land and depreciated value*	406	412	409	409	409	405	397	392	395	402	403	395	387	387	385	379	380	380	374

(4) Stock-in-Trade (Book value)*

B. At current prices:

(a) Food	169	130	119	117	114	116	116	120	118	106	92	85	88	89	90	91	90	89	87
(b) Textiles and other commodities	366	205	197	204	202	208	188	204	196	166	161	150	142	144	139	142	148	142	132
(c) Building and other materials	56	34	27	44	50	53	54	59	65	61	54	50	48	53	53	62	53	55	59
Total	591	368	342	365	366	377	357	382	379	333	307	284	278	286	281	294	281	286	278

C. At 1930 prices:

(a) Food	79	91	96	87	88	95	100	103	106	97	111	104	102	98	104	102	98	89	89
(b) Textiles and other commodities	132	133	128	112	123	138	154	151	166	138	188	169	173	156	169	173	156	142	157
(c) Building and other materials	20	20	31	35	40	43	50	56	61	59	53	53	55	53	59	53	55	55	57
Total	201	231	256	234	251	276	304	310	333	284	349	352	326	334	352	326	309	286	302

* At end of year.

NOTES TO TABLE 10.10

(2) Plant, Vehicles, Equipment, etc.

A. At historical prices:

(c) *Gross fixed capital formation:* First difference in A (h), plus A (d).

(d) *Depreciation:* Reducing balance method at the rates allowed for 1937 in the samples of assessments collected by the Inland Revenue. For other years the rate for 1937 adjusted to take into account the additional allowances introduced in 1931 and 1937.

(f) *Depreciated value of plant etc. held at end of year:* For 1937 derived from the total wear and tear allowances in a census of assessments (adjusted to cover units not assessed because they made losses) divided by the average rate of depreciation allowed in the sample of assessments used in A (d). Extrapolation for 1924–36 and 1938 made on the basis of changes in wear and tear allowances in annual samples of assessments collected by the Inland Revenue. For 1920–3 the change in the depreciated value was assumed to be same proportion of the change in all fixed assets (as shown by the extrapolation of the grossed-up sample of accounts, see p. 28) as it was, on average in 1924–9.

(g) *First cost value of plant etc. scrapped:* The total amount assumed due over the 19 years ($\frac{19}{28}$ of A (h) for 1919) derived from the average length of life given by A (d) and spread in equal annual amounts. (See chapter 2, p. 22.)

(h) *First cost value of plant etc. held at end of year:* For 1919 derived from A (f) by imputing the standard estimate for the age-structure of what is assumed to be a stationary population of assets. (See chapter 2, p. 16.) Depreciation is assumed to have been written off by the reducing balance method, with a life of 28 years.

B. At current prices:

The series at 1930 prices multiplied by index C.

C. At constant (1930) prices:

(c) *Gross fixed capital formation:* A (c) deflated by index C.

(d) *Depreciation:* As for A (d).

(f) *Depreciated value of plant etc. held at end of year:* For 1919 derived from A (f) by the standard estimate that the average historical costs of machinery (index C) can be taken as 65·3% of the costs at 1930 prices. (See chapter 2, p. 24.)

(g) *First cost value of plant etc. scrapped:* As for A (g).

(h) *First cost value of plant etc. held at end of year:* For 1919 derived from A (h) by the same standard estimate as for C (f).

(3) All Fixed Assets

A. At historical prices:

(f) and (i) *Value of all fixed assets (including land) held at end of year:* Derived from the chain of year-to-year changes in all fixed assets in samples of company accounts, grossed-up in 1937. (See p. 181 and chapter 2, p. 28).

(4) Stock-in-Trade

B. At current prices:

The annual ratios of stocks to fixed assets in samples of accounts for the three commodity groups applied to the respective estimates of all fixed assets. (See p. 181.) Stocks in the sample of accounts for the fourth group, Warehousing, were negligible and no calculation was made.

C. At constant (1930) prices:

The series at current prices deflated by the following price indices.[1]

(a) *Food:* Wholesale index for food.

(b) *Textile and other commodities:* Wholesale index for textile materials.

(c) *Building and other materials:* Wholesale index for non-food commodities.

[1] [30] *Statistical Abstracts.*

---

(1) Buildings

A. At historical prices:

(c) *Gross fixed capital formation:* First difference in A (h), plus A (g).

(d) *Depreciation:* Straight line method, assuming a life of 60 years.

(f) *Depreciated value of buildings held at end of year:* For 1919 derived from A (h) by imputing the age-structure derived from the series of annual values of business premises assessed for Inhabited House Duty. (See chapter 2, p. 16.)

(g) *First cost value of buildings scrapped:* The total assumed due for scrapping over the 19 years taken as $\frac{19}{60}$ of the first cost value in 1878 and spread equally between the years after making special appropriations for those years in which the change in plant exceeded the change in all fixed assets. See chapter 2, p. 22.

(h) *First cost value of buildings held at end of year:* For each year by deducting from the value of all fixed assets (see (3) A (f)) the depreciated value of plant, etc. (see (2) A (f)) and the value of land (see (1) A (i)).

(i) *Land at end of year:* 7% of A (h).

B. At current prices:

The series at 1930 prices multiplied by index B.

C. At constant (1930) prices:

(c) *Gross fixed capital formation:* A (c) deflated by index B.

(d) *Depreciation:* As for A (d).

(f) *Depreciated value of buildings held at end of year:* For 1919 derived from A (f) by the standard estimate that average historical building costs (index B) can be taken as 50·8% of the costs at 1930 prices. (See chapter 2, p. 24.)

(g) *First cost value of buildings scrapped:* As for A (g).

(h) *First cost value of buildings held at end of year:* For 1919 derived from A (h) by the same standard estimate as for C (f).

Allowance was made for those units which had made losses in this year and also for units other than companies. Self-employed units are common in wholesale distribution, and as this has a distorting effect on gross profits the allowance for these other units was based on their respective wear and tear allowances rather than on gross profits.

The grossed-up data provide standard estimates of all fixed assets and of stock-in-trade, by the procedures described in chapter 2, p. 27.

The standard estimates for plant, machinery, vehicles, ships, etc., were then derived from data on wear-and-tear allowances (i.e. by the last of the three possible methods discussed in chapter 2, appendix 2.1, p. 28). Buildings were then obtained as a residual.

For specific details of the estimates see the Notes to Table 10.10, p. 185.

A comparison with other estimates is made in chapter 14, pp. 241 and 253–6.

10.2 RETAIL DISTRIBUTION

GENERAL PROCEDURE AND SOURCE OF INFORMATION

The estimates of gross capital formation in buildings in this trade group—all shops—was derived for 1920–9 as a proportion of the value of all new work on buildings (chapter 4, p. 57), and for 1930–8 as a proportion of the new work on dwellings (chapter 12, p. 219). The proportions were based on data on the share of shops in the annual value of buildings assessed to Income Tax, Schedule A, for the first time.[1]

The first cost value of the shops at historical prices was estimated for 1919 by capitalizing the 1913/14 Inhabited House Duty assessments on their gross annual value.[2] This was done by reference to the corresponding annual value of dwellings, and the estimate made in chapter 12 of the first cost value of dwellings.

The estimates of capital formation and capital stock for plant, vehicles, equipment, etc., were derived from Inland Revenue data on wear and tear allowances and rates of depreciation.

For stock-in-trade the estimates were based on the ratios of stocks to all fixed assets shown in samples of company accounts. These ratios were applied to the estimates of all fixed assets.

ASSETS INCLUDED

Different sources are used for buildings and for other fixed assets and the resulting definitions of the trade group do not completely coincide.

For buildings, the estimates relate only to one type of building: shops (as defined by the underlying data, see below, p. 190), but cover all shops so defined irrespective of ownership. Retail distribution is therefore defined in part as the trade group owning shops. Any shops owned by, say, a firm primarily engaged in manufacturing, are regarded as belonging to a retail distribution establishment of the manufacturing firm, and thus come within the scope of this chapter.

This has two important consequences. On the one hand shops owned by firms classified to sectors such as Manufacturing or Electricity supply will be included in the estimates derived from accounts for these sectors and will thus be counted twice in the national totals. On the other hand any factories, offices or warehouses owned by firms classified by the Board of Inland Revenue to retail distribution will be omitted entirely, since no use is made of the accounts of these firms in estimating the buildings owned by this trade group. On balance, Inland Revenue practice was to classify firms to retail distribution rather than to manufacturing in trades like food or clothing where both activities were undertaken. It is probable, therefore, that the factories and offices which are excluded outweigh on the national level the shops which are duplicated.[3]

For plant, vehicles, equipment, etc., the definition of the trade group is slightly different. The estimate is based on the amount of the wear and tear allowances for the following Inland Revenue trade groups:

E.3 Purely distributive retailers, (for example, grocers).

E.4 Semi-industrial retailers, (for example, carpenters, bakers or launderers).

The Inland Revenue classification of these groups defines the second component of our trade group, and it will, therefore, cover the plant and equipment owned by all firms primarily engaged in these forms of retail distribution. It should be noted that this includes the catering establishments of multiple shops which both sell goods (e.g. bread, milk and confectionery) and also serve meals and refreshments.

METHODS OF ESTIMATION

Buildings: Shops

Gross capital formation at current (or historical) prices was obtained as a proportion of the estimated total new work on buildings.[4] For 1920–9 the annual proportion

---

[1] [**25**] *Reports of the Commissioners of H.M. Inland Revenue*, annual, 1921–1932. The figures are reproduced on p. 190 below.
[2] [**25**] *58th Report*, pp. 74–86.
[3] For further discussion of this point, see chapter 13, p. 221.
[4] Table 4.22, p. 60.

was derived from the gross annual value of buildings assessed to Income Tax, Schedule A, for the first time, using the ratio of the first assessments for Residential Shops and Lock-up Shops to those for all buildings covered by Schedule A. This information was not collected after 1929 and the only alternative classification of buildings—that given in the data on plans approved collected by the Ministry of Labour from 146 local authorities—does not show shops separately. The assumption made was, therefore, that shop and residential building moved together each year and the share of shops was taken as a fixed proportion of the share of residential dwellings in each year from 1930 to 1938. The fixed proportion used was the average ratio for the period 1920–9 of the first assessments to Schedule A for Residential and Lock-up Shops to those for Dwelling-houses.

The *first cost value at historical prices* of the shops at the end of 1919 was based on the gross annual value of Residential Shops and Lock-up Shops as assessed for Inhabited House Duty in 1913/14.[1] The returns for that year are shown below:

Gross Annual Value of All Premises in Great Britain Charged to, and Exempt from, Inhabited House Duty, 1913/14

	£m.
Premises charged to duty:*	
Private dwelling-houses	69·3
Residential shops	14·7
Hotels, public houses, coffee-houses, etc.	8·2
Farmhouses occupied by a tenant or farm servants	0·8
Lodging-houses	1·7
Total charged	94·7
Premises exempt from duty:	
'Separate dwellings'	1·1
Houses of an annual value under £20†	64·6
Hospitals, schools, royal and diplomatic residences, etc.	5·0
Premises not used as dwellings, i.e. houses used solely for trade, etc.	58·6
Total exempt	129·3
Total charged or exempt	224·0

* Dwelling houses in the categories listed with an annual value of £20 or more.

† Includes all private dwelling houses, residential shops, hotels, public houses, coffee houses and lodging houses with an annual value under £20. (Farm-houses under the value of £20 are not included in the Inhabited House Duty Statistics.)

Source

[25] *58th Report of the Commissioner of H.M. Inland Revenue* (1915), pp. 74–86.

The gross annual value of Residential Shops with an annual value of £20 or more is thus known, but it is necessary to make a small allowance for those of lower annual value included with other premises exempt from

duty. Stamp[2] has estimated the approximate number of such shops by a comparison between the 1910–11 Inhabited House Duty returns and the classification of buildings given in the 1911 *Census of Population*. If we take an average annual value for these shops of £15 this suggests an addition of approximately £2 m. for the residential shops with an annual value of less than £20.

The gross annual value of Lock-up shops was normally included with Premises not used as dwellings, and was not separately distinguished. However, for 1911/12 a 'rough analysis' of this class of premises is given in the *Reports*;[3] and the value of Lock-up Shops in this year was extrapolated to 1913/14 proportionately to the movement of the assessments on all premises not used as dwellings. This gives a figure of £20·7 m., and adding this to the adjusted total for residential shops we obtain an estimate of £37·4 m. for the gross annual value in 1913/14 of all shops.

This annual value was then capitalized on the assumption that the ratio:

First cost value at historical prices in U.K. at end-1919

Gross annual value in Great Britain in 1913/14

was the same for shops as it was for dwellings.[4] For dwellings, the numerator, as estimated in chapter 12, is £1,642 m., and the denominator, taken from the table given above is £133 m.[5] We thus have a multiplier of 12·3, and applying this to the annual value of the shops gives a first cost value at historical prices of £460 m.

The first cost value of the shops *scrapped* each year was assumed to be the same proportion of the stock at the beginning of the year as that obtained for dwellings. (See chapter 12, p. 220).

Depreciation was assumed to have been written off on the straight line method with a life of 100 years.

The *depreciated value at historical prices* at the end of 1919 was derived separately for Residential Shops and for Lock-up Shops from their corresponding first-cost values by means of an imputed age-structure (see

[1] The assessments are made only for Great Britain and are the same as those for Schedule A, but the coverage is very slightly different because of the inclusion in the Inhabited House Duty statistics of farmhouses with an annual value of £20 or more, and of certain refreshment rooms at railway stations, etc., not assessed under Schedule A. There is a description of the classification of the buildings used in these statistics in [136] Stamp, chapter III.

[2] [136] Stamp, p. 127.

[3] [25] *58th Report*, p. 91. See also [136] Stamp, p. 122.

[4] Land is excluded from the numerator, but since the gross annual value is assessed on both land and buildings this assumption implies that the ratio of sites to buildings was the same for shops as for houses. To the extent that it was in fact higher for shops in 1913/14 this method will lead to some slight overstatement of the first cost value of the shops.

[5] Private dwelling-houses, £69·3 m., Separate dwellings, £1·1 m., and Houses of an annual value under £20, £64·6 m., less £2 m. for the approximate value of Residential Shops included in the last category.

TABLE 10.20 RETAIL DISTRIBUTION (£M.)

(1) Buildings

	1920	1921	1922	1923	1924	1925	1926	1927	1928	1929	1930	1931	1932	1933	1934	1935	1936	1937	1938
A. At historical prices:																			
(c) Gross fixed capital formation	17·1	11·7	4·7	12·8	18·1	15·1	13·1	11·7	13·2	15·3	12·0	9·7	8·5	10·8	13·6	14·6	15·5	16·5	17·0
(d) Depreciation	4·8	4·9	4·9	5·1	5·2	5·4	5·5	5·6	5·7	5·9	6·0	6·1	6·2	6·3	6·4	6·6	6·7	6·8	7·0
(f) Depreciated value*	338	345	345	353	366	375	383	389	397	406	412	416	418	422	430	438	446	456	466
(h) First cost value*	477	489	493	505	523	538	551	562	575	589	601	610	619	629	642	655	669	684	699
(i) Land*	33	34	34	35	37	38	39	39	40	41	42	43	43	44	45	46	47	48	49
B. At current prices:																			
(d) Depreciation	15·8	12·9	10·6	10·0	10·5	10·8	10·6	10·5	10·2	10·3	10·2	9·9	9·5	9·5	9·7	9·9	10·4	11·1	11·5
(f) Depreciated value*	1104	902	723	683	716	722	703	692	668	676	663	638	607	597	602	619	648	686	704
(h) First cost value*	1573	1298	1053	1002	1057	1074	1055	1047	1017	1036	1024	995	957	948	962	993	1045	1110	1144
(i) Land*	110	91	74	70	74	75	74	73	71	72	72	70	67	66	67	70	73	78	80
C. At 1930 prices:																			
(c) Gross fixed capital formation	9·9	8·4	4·1	11·9	16·3	13·6	12·2	11·1	12·9	14·9	12·0	10·1	9·3	12·0	15·1	15·9	16·2	16·4	16·6
(d) Depreciation	9·2	9·2	9·3	9·4	9·5	9·7	9·8	9·9	10·0	10·1	10·2	10·3	10·4	10·5	10·7	10·8	10·9	11·1	11·2
(f) Depreciated value*	643	642	637	639	646	650	652	653	656	661	663	663	662	663	668	673	678	683	689
(h) First cost value*	915	924	927	938	953	967	978	988	1000	1013	1024	1034	1042	1053	1067	1080	1093	1106	1119
(i) Land*	64	65	65	66	67	68	68	69	70	71	72	72	73	74	75	76	76	77	78

(2) Plant, Machinery, etc.

	1920	1921	1922	1923	1924	1925	1926	1927	1928	1929	1930	1931	1932	1933	1934	1935	1936	1937	1938
A. At historical prices:																			
(c) Gross fixed capital formation	8·2	6·9	4·9	7·6	9·6	6·0	8·8	9·7	10·3	11·1	12·9	14·4	12·1	7·8	9·2	15·7	12·6	8·9	23·1
(d) Depreciation	3·1	3·3	3·5	3·8	4·2	4·3	4·7	5·1	5·4	5·9	6·4	7·5	7·8	7·8	7·9	8·6	9·0	9·8	11·1
(f) Depreciated value*	38	42	43	47	52	54	58	63	68	73	79	86	90	90	92	99	102	102	114
(h) First cost value*	93	97	99	103	110	113	119	126	133	141	151	163	172	177	183	196	206	212	232
B. At current prices:																			
(d) Depreciation	9·0	6·0	4·5	4·7	5·2	5·1	5·3	5·6	5·8	6·3	6·5	7·2	7·6	7·7	7·9	8·7	9·6	11·8	12·6
(f) Depreciated value*	111	74	55	59	64	63	66	69	72	79	81	83	87	89	91	100	109	122	129
(h) First cost value*	296	196	145	149	156	152	155	158	160	170	170	169	177	184	189	206	226	262	273
C. At 1930 prices:																			
(c) Gross fixed capital formation	3·7	4·7	4·5	6·9	8·6	5·6	8·3	9·2	10·0	10·5	12·9	15·4	12·9	8·2	9·6	16·0	12·1	7·5	20·0
(d) Depreciation	4·0	4·1	4·1	4·3	4·6	4·7	5·0	5·3	5·6	6·0	6·5	7·7	8·1	8·1	8·2	8·8	9·2	9·9	10·9
(f) Depreciated value*	50	51	51	54	58	58	62	66	70	74	81	89	93	93	95	102	105	102	112
(h) First cost value*	133	133	133	136	140	141	145	150	155	161	170	180	189	193	198	209	217	220	235

(3) All Fixed Assets

	1920	1921	1922	1923	1924	1925	1926	1927	1928	1929	1930	1931	1932	1933	1934	1935	1936	1937	1938
A. At historical prices:																			
(c) Gross fixed capital formation	25·3	18·6	9·6	20·4	27·7	21·1	21·9	21·4	23·5	26·4	24·9	24·1	20·6	18·6	22·8	30·3	28·1	25·4	40·1
(d) Depreciation	7·9	8·2	8·4	8·9	9·4	9·7	10·2	10·7	11·1	11·8	12·4	13·6	14·0	14·1	14·3	15·2	15·7	16·6	18·1
(f) Depreciated value*	376	387	388	399	418	429	441	452	464	479	491	502	508	513	521	536	549	558	580
(h) First cost value*	570	585	592	609	633	651	670	688	708	731	752	773	791	806	825	851	875	896	931

B. At current prices:

(d) Depreciation	24·8	18·9	15·1	14·7	15·7	15·9	15·9	16·1	16·0	16·6	16·7	17·1	17·1	17·2	17·6	18·6	20·0	22·9	24·1
(f) Depreciated value*	1215	976	779	742	780	785	769	761	740	754	744	720	695	686	693	719	758	808	834
(h) First cost value*	1869	1494	1198	1151	1213	1226	1209	1204	1176	1206	1194	1163	1134	1132	1151	1199	1271	1372	1417

C. At 1930 prices:

(c) Gross fixed capital formation	13·6	13·1	8·6	18·8	24·9	19·2	20·5	20·3	22·9	25·4	24·9	25·5	22·2	24·7	31·9	28·3	23·9	36·6	
(d) Depreciation	13·2	13·3	13·4	13·7	14·1	14·4	14·8	15·2	15·6	16·1	16·7	18·0	18·5	18·9	19·6	20·1	21·0	22·1	
(f) Depreciated value*	693	692	688	693	703	708	714	719	726	736	744	751	755	757	762	775	783	786	800
(h) First cost value*	1048	1057	1060	1073	1093	1108	1123	1138	1155	1174	1194	1214	1231	1246	1264	1289	1310	1326	1354

(4) Stock-in-Trade (Book value)*

B. At current prices:

(a) Food	116	99	82	75	70	66	67	67	61	50	49	50	51	50	48	50	54	55	53
(b) Clothing	201	137	118	101	90	85	81	84	74	62	60	55	56	59	59	67	70	70	69
(c) Other commodities	136	98	89	89	76	74	73	72	69	65	63	64	66	67	67	72	76	76	75
Total	453	334	290	265	236	224	221	222	204	177	172	169	172	173	173	188	196	197	197

C. At 1930 prices:

(a) Food	54	60	63	61	53	54	56	56	53	50	56	57	62	57	55	54	49	55	
(b) Clothing	56	88	80	64	54	53	61	60	57	62	74	65	71	65	70	76	70	82	
(c) Other commodities	48	59	66	64	56	55	62	62	60	65	72	75	75	75	74	75	68	72	
Total	158	207	209	189	163	162	179	177	170	177	202	197	208	197	200	205	187	209	

* At end of year.

NOTES TO TABLE 10.20

(1) Buildings: Shops

A. At historical prices:

(c) *Gross fixed capital formation*: A proportion of all new work on buildings based mainly on the classification of first assessments to Schedule A. See p. 187.

(d) *Depreciation*: Straight line method, assuming a life of 100 years.

(f) *Depreciated value of buildings held at end of year*: For 1919 derived from A (h) by imputing the separate age-structure for Residential Shops and for Lock-up Shops derived from series of annual values as assessed for Inhabited House Duty. See p. 16.

(g) *First cost value of buildings scrapped*: The same proportion each year of the first cost value as for dwellings. (See chapter 12, p. 220.)

(h) *First cost value of buildings held at end of year*: For 1919 by capitalizing the gross annual values of Residential and Lock-up Shops assessed for Inhabited House Duty. (See p. 187.)

(i) *Land at end of year*: 7% of A (h).

B. At current prices: } As for Wholesale Distribution.
C. At constant (1930) prices: } See the Notes to Table 10.10, (1), p. 185.

(2) Plant, Vehicles, Equipment, etc.

A. At historical prices:

(c) *Gross fixed capital formation*: First difference in A (f) plus A (d).

(d) *Depreciation*: Reduced balance method at the rate found in a sample of assessments for 1937 collected by the Inland Revenue, with adjustments for the additional allowances introduced in 1931 and 1937.

(f) *Depreciated value of plant, etc. held at end of year*: For 1937 derived from the total of wear and tear allowances in the census of assessments for 1937, (adjusted for units excluded because of losses) divided by the average rate of depreciation allowed in the sample of assessments used in A (d). Extrapolation to 1924-36 and 1938 by means of the changes in the wear and tear allowances in annual samples of assessments collected by the Inland Revenue. For 1920-3 the change in the depreciated value assumed to be the same proportion of A (c) for buildings as it was, on average, in 1924-9.

(g) *First cost value of plant, etc. scrapped*: The total amount assumed due over the 19 years ($\frac{18}{19}$ of A (h) for 1919) derived from the length of life given by A (d) and spread in equal annual amounts. (See chapter 2, p. 22.)

(h) *First cost value of plant etc. held at end of year*: For 1919 derived from A (f) by imputing the standard estimate for the age-structure of what is assumed to be a stationary population of assets. (See chapter 2, p. 16.) Depreciation is assumed to have been written off by the reducing balance method with a life of 30 years.

B. At current prices: } As for Wholesale Distribution.
C. At constant (1930) prices: } See the Notes to Table 10.10, (2), p. 185.

(4) Stock-in-Trade

B. At current prices:

The annual ratios of stocks to fixed assets in samples of accounts for three commodity groups applied to the value of fixed assets in these groups estimated as described on p. 191.

C. At constant (1930) prices:

The series at current prices deflated by the following price indices:[1]

(a) *Food*: Wholesale index for food.
(b) *Clothing*: Wholesale index for textile materials.
(c) *Other*: Wholesale index for all non-food commodities.

[1] [30] *Statistical Abstract*.

Annual Value of New Buildings Assessed to Income Tax, Schedule A, for the first time in the years ended 5th April,* 1920–31

	1920	1921	1922	1923	1924	1925	1926	1927	1928	1929	1930	1931†
Dwelling-houses, including Flats, 'Separate Dwellings' and Almshouses	111·3	498·7	1911·1	3373·3	2529·8	3305·6	4711·6	5908·8	7400·8	6498·8	6341·0	6450·6
Shops: Residential	5·7	14·1	30·7	50·0	109·6	188·9	182·6	300·0	259·2	308·0	348·2	
Shops: Lock-up	12·2	53·4	117·2	117·2	220·6	393·6	353·8	304·7	343·0	338·7	436·8	
Hotels, Inns, Coffee-houses and Lodging-houses	5·8	5·9	7·4	12·0	41·0	33·1	20·7	56·6	70·1	65·6	55·5	
Farmhouses and Farm Buildings	1·5	6·6	13·3	14·3	10·7	13·3	11·7	14·3	11·8	11·4	10·9	
Places of Entertainment (theatres, cinemas, halls, etc.)	6·2	46·7	68·4	94·1	94·5	84·1	80·1	93·4	78·4	136·4	182·5	
Schools and Hospitals (including school houses and residential parts unless separately noted)	13·3	19·0	15·1	30·7	35·6	32·8	38·4	62·6	86·9	100·1	110·4	
Factories, Warehouses, Mills, Offices and other premises or parts thereof not used as dwellings (except by a caretaker) not included above	278·1	689·3	924·0	1064·2	790·6	941·2	987·0	1366·0	1317·3	1229·2	1526·8	
Total All Premises	434·16	1333·72	3087·20	4755·82	3832·3	4992·59	6385·7	8106·5	9567·4	8688·33	9012·03	9248·85

* This relates, broadly speaking, to buildings completed in the year ended the previous Michaelmas.

† Full details for this year are not available.

Source: [25] Reports of the Commissioners of H.M. Inland Revenue, 1919/20 to 1930/1.

chapter 2, p. 16). For the Residential Shops the age-structure imputed was based on the annual assessments for Inhabited House Duty since 1868. For the Lock-up Shops the age-structure was based on the total assessments on Premises not used as dwellings, available from 1874. The age-structure of the stock of Residential Shops in 1868 and of Lock-up Shops in 1874 was assumed to be such that the depreciated value was 50% of the corresponding first cost value.

All remaining estimates were obtained by the standard procedures. For details see the Notes to Table 10.20, p. 189.

Plant, Machinery, Vehicles, Equipment, etc.

The *depreciated value at historical prices* at the end of 1937 was derived by dividing the total wear and tear allowances for retail distribution in a census of assessments for 1937 (year of assessment 1938/9), with an

The *first cost value* at the end of 1919 was derived from the depreciated value by the standard procedure described in chapter 2, p. 16. The length of life assumed (30 years) was based on the rates of depreciation calculated above. This length of life was also used to calculate the total first cost value of the plant, etc., assumed to have been *scrapped* over the 19-year period: i.e. the total assumed scrapped was taken as $\frac{19}{30}$ of the first cost value of the plant, etc., at the end of 1919. This total was then spread evenly over the years.

The remaining estimates *at current and constant prices* were obtained by the standard procedures. For details see the Notes to Table 10.20, p. 189.

Stock-in-Trade and Work in Progress

In view of the wide variety of commodities covered by this trade group it was thought advisable to make the estimates separately for three main commodity

Retail Distribution
Stock-in-Trade at Current Prices
(£m.)

	Food		Clothing		Other Commodities		Total	
	Final	Provisional	Final	Provisional	Final	Provisional	Final	Provisional
1920	116	120	201	208	136	140	453	468
1925	70	68	90	82	76	82	236	232
1930	50	59	62	74	65	76	177	209
1935	48	53	59	69	67	80	173	202
1938	53	56	69	73	75	79	197	208

allowance for business units which made losses, by the average rate of depreciation observed in a large sample of assessments for the same year.

For 1924–36 and 1938 the 1937 value was extrapolated by means of an index of the year-to-year changes in the wear and tear allowances in the annual samples of assessments collected by the Inland Revenue. Adjustments were made for the additional allowances which were introduced in 1931 and 1937.[1] For 1920–3 the extrapolation was based on the assumption that the ratio of the change in the depreciated value of plant to the gross fixed capital formation in buildings was the same as it was, on average, in 1924–9.

Depreciation was assumed to have been written off on the reducing balance method at the rates observed in the samples of assessments for 1938/9, with adjustments for the additional allowances in 1931 and 1937.

The *gross fixed capital formation* was then obtained from the annual change in the depreciated value, plus the annual depreciation.

groups: Food, Clothing, and Other commodities. The estimates were made by multiplying series for all fixed assets by the ratios of stocks to all fixed assets found in samples of company accounts for each of the commodity groups. For this purpose it was first necessary to allocate the estimates made above for the stock of fixed assets to the three commodity groups. This was done separately for the depreciated value at historical prices of plant, etc., the first cost value at historical prices of buildings, and the value of land.[2]

The allocation of the plant for each year was made by means of (i) the ratios of plant to stocks found in samples of accounts for each commodity group, and (ii) the value of the stocks held by each group as shown by a provisional estimate of stocks made by a different

---

[1] See chapter 2, p. 22.
[2] The written-down value was taken for plant, etc., and the gross value for buildings, to correspond as far as possible with the usual valuation found for fixed assets in the accounts from which the ratios of stocks to all fixed assets were obtained.

method.[1] The provisional estimate of stocks in each group was multiplied by the plant:stocks ratio for the group to obtain an estimate of plant 'in terms of stocks' in each group. The actual estimate of the depreciated value of plant, etc., at the end of each year, was then allocated to the commodity groups in the proportions shown by these estimates.

The allocation of the first cost value of buildings was made in the same way, using the ratios of buildings to stocks found in samples of accounts. Land was allocated in the same proportions as the buildings.

The provisional estimates of stocks are compared above with the final estimates obtained for each group by multiplying the total for all fixed assets in each group by the corresponding ratio of stocks to all fixed assets.

10.3 SERVICES BY HOTELS, INNS AND RESTAURANTS

GENERAL PROCEDURE AND SOURCE OF INFORMATION

Gross fixed capital formation in buildings (hotels, inns and restaurants) in this trade group was derived as a proportion of the value of all new work on buildings, (chapter 4, p. 57).

The first cost value at historical prices at the end of 1919 was obtained by capitalizing the 1913/14 Inhabited House Duty assessments on the gross annual value of these buildings.[2]

For furniture, equipment, etc., the estimates were obtained as a proportion of the corresponding series for buildings, using the proportion found in the accounts of one very large company owning a chain of hotels.

ASSETS INCLUDED

The estimate for buildings relates to all hotels, inns, restaurants, etc. (as defined by the underlying data, see below) and all buildings of this type are assigned to this trade group. The group thus consists of all establishments owning buildings of this type. This includes the public houses owned by brewery companies[3] and the hotels owned by railway companies. Railway catering facilities at stations or on trains are not, however, included here, but are in chapter 9 (9.1).

The estimate for furniture, equipment, etc., is proportional to that for buildings and so has the same coverage. It should, however, be noted that the furniture and equipment of multiple shops serving meals and refreshments is included in trade group 10.2 (see p. 186 above). To the extent that the buildings owned by these firms were classified as hotels, inns, restaurants, etc.— and not as shops—there will be a small amount of duplication of the estimates for furniture, etc.[4]

METHODS OF ESTIMATION

Buildings: Hotels, Inns, Restaurants, etc.

Gross fixed capital formation at current (or historical) prices and the *first cost value at historical prices* were estimated on the same principles as the estimates for shops described above in 10.2, p. 186. For the capital formation the proportion of all building was based on the first assessments to Schedule A on Hotels, Inns, Coffee-houses, etc. and on Lodging-houses (see p. 190). For the first cost value the annual value capitalized was the Inhabited House Duty assessment in 1913/14 on Hotels, Public-houses, Coffee-houses, etc.,[5] and on Lodging-houses. The same multiplier (12.3) was used as for shops.

Depreciation was assumed to have been written off on the straight line method with a life of 100 years.

The *depreciated value at historical prices* at the end of 1919 was derived from the first cost value by imputing the age-structure given by the annual Inhabited House Duty assessments on Hotels, Public-houses, etc., since 1868. (See chapter 2, p. 16.) The age-structure of the stock in 1868 was assumed to be such that the depreciated value was 50% of the first cost value.

Scrapping of buildings was assumed to be negligible.

The remaining series at *current and constant prices* were obtained by the standard procedures. For details see the Notes to Table 10.30, p. 193.

Furniture, Equipment, etc.

The estimates for the furniture, etc., owned by this trade group were made on the basis of the accounts of

---

[1] The provisional estimates were derived from estimates by J. B. Jefferys of sales in each of 5 years for fifteen commodity groups. [116] *Retail Trading in Great Britain, 1850–1950.* (London, 1954), p. 453. These estimates of sales were multiplied by a stock: sales ratio for each of the fifteen groups, obtained from the ratios shown by the [32] 1950 *Census of Distribution*, extrapolated to the inter-war years by means of an index of the changes in the stock: sales ratios for the Cooperative Retail Societies. Data for the Co-operatives were available in a continuous series for 1920–38 in the [145] *Co-operative Yearbooks*, and for 1950 in the *Census of Distribution*. The resulting estimates for the fifteen groups were then aggregated into the three main commodity groups, and these estimates for five years were extended to the intervening years by interpolation.

[2] [25] *58th Report of the Commissioners of H.M. Inland Revenue* (1915), pp. 74–86.

[3] These public-houses were excluded from chapter 8, trade group 8.31, so that there is no duplication on this score.

[4] For the gross fixed capital formation it is the classification of the first assessments to Schedule A which is relevant; for the stock of assets it is the classification for Inhabited House Duty. So far as can be ascertained, for the former, a café or tea-room would generally have been classified as such, not as a shop. For Inhabited House Duty purposes, however, a building of this type would be classified to Hotels, Public-houses, Coffee-houses, etc., only if it was also (a) a dwelling-house, and (b) its annual value was £20 or more. If not, it would be included in the exempt categories of Houses with an annual value under £20, or Premises not used as dwellings.

[5] As noted in the previous footnote not all restaurants, etc., are in fact included in this category, but the net effect of the omission is probably slight and as no information is available no adjustment has been made. The first cost value is, therefore, a little too low on this account.

TABLE 10.30 SERVICES BY HOTELS, INNS, AND RESTAURANTS (£M.)

(3) All Fixed Assets*

	1920	1921	1922	1923	1924	1925	1926	1927	1928	1929	1930	1931	1932	1933	1934	1935	1936	1937	1938
A. At historical prices:																			
(c) Gross fixed capital formation	5·1	3·8	3·0	4·3	3·4	2·9	3·6	3·9	3·8	3·4	3·3	2·9	2·6	2·9	3·1	3·3	3·5	3·8	3·9
(d) Depreciation	2·3	2·3	2·4	2·5	2·6	2·6	2·7	2·7	2·8	2·8	2·8	2·9	3·0	3·0	3·1	3·1	3·1	3·2	3·2
(f) Depreciated value†	95	96	97	99	99	100	101	102	103	103	104	104	103	103	103	104	104	105	105
(h) First cost value†	159	162	164	167	169	171	174	177	179	182	184	186	188	190	192	194	196	199	202
B. At current prices:																			
(d) Depreciation	7·4	6·4	5·1	4·8	4·9	4·9	4·7	4·7	4·6	4·6	4·6	4·4	4·1	4·1	4·2	4·2	4·4	4·8	5·0
(f) Depreciated value†	307	254	203	189	193	192	184	180	173	172	167	159	149	146	146	147	152	160	162
(h) First cost value†	522	440	355	334	344	345	336	331	322	324	319	308	292	288	219	298	311	331	340
C. At 1930 prices:																			
(c) Gross fixed capital formation	3·1	2·5	4·4	3·9	3·1	2·6	3·4	3·7	3·7	3·4	3·3	3·0	3·0	3·3	3·5	3·7	3·7	3·8	3·8
(d) Depreciation	4·4	4·4	4·4	4·4	4·4	4·4	4·5	4·6	4·6	4·6	4·6	4·6	4·6	4·6	4·6	4·7	4·7	4·8	4·8
(f) Depreciated value†	180	178	176	176	175	173	172	171	170	169	167	166	164	163	162	161	160	159	158
(h) First cost value†	307	308	308	310	311	312	313	315	317	318	319	320	321	323	324	326	327	329	331

(4) Stock-in-Trade (Book value)†

	1920	1921	1922	1923	1924	1925	1926	1927	1928	1929	1930	1931	1932	1933	1934	1935	1936	1937	1938
B. At current prices	19	13	10	9	8	9	9	8	9	8	8	8	8	7	6	6	7	7	7
C. At 1930 prices	9	8	8	8	6	7	7	7	7	7	8	9	9	8	7	7	8	7	8

* This is the sum of (1) Buildings, and (2) Furniture, equipment, etc. The component estimates are not shown separately.
† At end of year.

NOTES TO TABLE 10.30

(1) Buildings: Hotels, Inns, Restaurants, etc.

A. At historical prices:

(c) *Gross fixed capital formation:* A proportion of all new work on buildings based mainly on the classification of first assessments to Schedule A. See p. 192.

(d) *Depreciation:* Straight line method, assuming a life of 100 years.

(f) *Depreciated value of buildings held at end of year:* For 1919 derived from A (h) by imputing the age-structure derived from the series of annual values of Hotels, Public Houses, etc., assessed for Inhabited House Duty. (See chapter 2, p. 16.)

(g) *First cost value of buildings scrapped:* Assumed to be negligible.

(h) *First cost value of buildings held at end of year:* For 1919 by capitalizing the gross annual value of Hotels, Public Houses, etc., assessed for Inhabited House Duty in 1913/14. See p. 192.

(i) *Land at end of year:* 7% of A (h).

B. At current prices: } As for Wholesale Distribution.
C. At constant (1930) prices: } See the Notes to Table 10.10, (1), p. 185.

(2) Furniture, Equipment, etc.

A. At historical prices:

(c) *Gross fixed capital formation:* C (c) multiplied by special index of furniture prices. See p. 194.

(d) *Depreciation:* As for C (d).

(f) *Depreciated value of furniture, etc. held at end of year:* For 1919 derived from C (f) by estimating the average historical costs of furniture assumed to have been evenly accumulated over the 30 years 1884–1913. (Cf. chapter 2, p. 24.) Using the index of furniture prices this gives a ratio of 49·5% of the estimate at 1930 prices.

(g) *First cost value of furniture etc. scrapped:* As for C (g).

(h) *First cost value of furniture etc. held at end of year:* For 1919 derived from C (h) by the same estimate as for A (f).

B. At current prices:

The series at 1930 prices multiplied by the index of furniture prices.

C. At constant (1930) prices:

(c) *Gross fixed capital formation:* 27·6% of the gross fixed capital formation in buildings, plus replacements of furniture etc. scrapped under C (g). See p. 194.

(d) *Depreciation:* Straight line method, assuming a life of 33 years.

(f) *Depreciated value of furniture etc. held at end of year:* For 1919 derived from C (h) by assuming an age-structure in 1919 such that the depreciated value was one-half of the first cost value.

(g) *First cost value of furniture etc. scrapped:* The total amount assumed due over the 19 years ($\frac{19}{33}$ of C (h) for 1919) derived from the length of life as in C (d) and spread in equal annual amounts.

(h) *First cost value of furniture held at end of year:* For 1919 taken as 27·6% of the first cost value of the buildings. See p. 194.

(4) Stock-in-Trade

B. At current prices:

The annual ratios of stocks to buildings in the accounts of Trust Houses Ltd., applied to the first cost value at historical prices of Hotels, Inns, etc.

C. At constant (1930) prices:

The series at current prices deflated by the Wholesale index for food.

one large company (Trust Houses, Ltd.) which owned some 200 units throughout the period investigated.[1] The ratio of furniture, etc., to buildings in the accounts of this company was thought to be broadly representative.

The calculations were first made in *constant prices*. In the accounts of Trust Houses Ltd., the total capital expenditure during 1920–38 on furniture, etc., was 27·6% of the capital expenditure on buildings. The *first cost value* of furniture, etc., at the end of 1919 was therefore taken as 27·6% of the corresponding estimate of buildings.

Purchases of new furniture, etc., each year, taken as equal to *gross fixed capital formation*, was estimated as (*a*) replacements of furniture, etc., scrapped, and (*b*) additional purchases. The annual additional purchases were estimated as 27·6% of each year's purchases of buildings at constant prices. The total replacements equal the total *first cost value of the furniture, etc., scrapped* over the 19 year period, and were assumed equal to $\frac{19}{33}$ of the first cost value of all furniture, etc., in 1919. This total was spread evenly over the period. This estimate was derived from the assumed length of life of 33 years. (See chapter 2, p. 16).

Depreciation was assumed to have been written off on the straight line method with this length of life.

The *depreciated value* at the end of 1919 was obtained on the assumption of an age-structure which reduced it to 50% of the corresponding first cost value.

A special price index to represent the price of furniture was used for the conversion of these series to *historical and current prices*. It combines in an unweighted average the indices of the import price of wood and of weekly wage-rates in the wood-working industry.[2] For further details see the Notes to Table 10.30, p. 193.

Stock-in-Trade

The annual value of the stocks held was found by multiplying the first cost value at historical prices of the buildings by the ratio of stocks to buildings given by the sample of accounts.

10.4 MUNICIPAL MARKETS
SOURCE AND METHOD OF ESTIMATION

These estimates were derived from items in the accounts of local authorities under the heading of Markets in England and Wales, and Slaughter-houses in Scotland.[3] They were assumed to relate entirely to buildings though it is possible that some 10–15% of the capital stock and expenditure figures should in fact be allocated to plant, vehicles, etc.

Gross fixed capital formation at current (or historical) prices was taken as equal to the annual expenditure out of

loans on this service. Expenditure on Land would be included in this but is assumed to be sufficiently small to be ignored.

The *depreciated value at historical prices* at the end of 1919 was taken as equal to the outstanding loan debt in that year for this service.

For details of the remaining estimates see the Notes to Table 10.40, p. 195.

10.5 FINANCE AND MISCELLANEOUS SERVICES
ASSETS INCLUDED

No estimate was made of the buildings owned by this trade group. The main implication of this is that there is no separate property-owning group in the present study. Shops owned by property companies are included in chapter 10 under Retail distribution, dwellings owned by property-owners are included in chapter 12, and so on. Offices owned by financial institutions (including those used for their own offices) property-owning companies and individuals are, however, omitted both here and at the national level. There are, however, certain offsetting errors in coverage; these are discussed in chapter 13, pp. 221–8.

The coverage of the estimate for furniture, equipment, etc., depends on the Inland Revenue classification.[4] The trade groups included in the present estimate cover British and foreign banks, insurance companies, stockbrokers and jobbers, finance companies and brokers; and a small group of miscellaneous services not included elsewhere, such as storage and film production.

METHOD OF ESTIMATION

The *depreciated value at historical prices* at the end of 1937 was derived by dividing the total wear and tear allowances for the groups listed above shown in a census of assessments for the 1938/9 year of assessment (with an allowance for units omitted because they made a loss), by the average rate of depreciation observed in a large sample of assessments for the same year.

The 1937 figure was extrapolated to other years by means of an index of the year-to-year changes in the wear and tear allowances in the annual samples of assessments collected by the Inland Revenue. Adjustments were made for the additional wear and tear allowances which were introduced in 1931 and 1937.

---

[1] A larger sample of accounts was examined but the information given in other accounts was less detailed and there were a number of discontinuities in the annual figures.

[2] [**30**] *Statistical Abstract*.

[3] [**5**] Ministry of Health, *Annual Local Taxation Returns* for years prior to 1934–5, and [**19**] *Local Government Financial Statistics*, annual, for 1934–5 onwards.

[4] See chapter 13, Table 13.20, p. 225.

TABLE 10.40 MUNICIPAL MARKETS (£M.)

(1) Buildings*

	1920	1921	1922	1923	1924	1925	1926	1927	1928	1929	1930	1931	1932	1933	1934	1935	1936	1937	1938
C. At 1930 prices:																			
(c) Gross fixed capital formation	0·2	0·1	0·1	0·1	0·2	0·3	0·2	0·4	0·6	0·9	0·6	0·4	0·2	0·3	0·3	0·3	0·4	0·2	0·3
(d) Depreciation	0·4	0·4	0·4	0·4	0·4	0·4	0·4	0·4	0·4	0·5	0·5	0·5	0·5	0·5	0·5	0·5	0·5	0·5	0·5
(f) Depreciated value†	14	14	13	13	13	13	12	12	12	13	13	13	13	13	12	12	12	12	12
(h) First cost value†	26	26	26	26	26	26	26	26	27	27	27	28	28	28	28	28	28	28	28

* Only the series at 1930 prices are shown for this sub-sector. There is no estimate of plant, etc.

† At end of year.

NOTES TO TABLE 10.40

(1) Buildings

A. At historical prices:

(c) *Gross fixed capital formation*: Expenditure out of loans by Local Authorities.

(d) *Depreciation*: Straight line method, assuming a life of 60 years.

(f) *Depreciated value of buildings held at end of year*: For 1919 the outstanding loan debt of Local Authorities in 1919 in respect of this service.

(g) *First cost value of buildings scrapped*: The total for the 19 years derived from the first cost value in 1919 and the assumed length of life. Distributed between the years in proportion to A (c).

(h) *First cost value of buildings held at end of year*: For 1919 derived from A (f) by an imputed age-structure. (See chapter 11, p. 208.)

(i) *Land at end of year*: Included with the stock of buildings (but assumed to be unimportant for the capital formation series).

B. At current prices: As for Wholesale Distribution.

C. At constant (1930) prices: See the Notes to Table 10.10, (1), p. 185.

TABLE 10.50 FINANCE AND MISCELLANEOUS SERVICES (£M.)

(2) Furniture, Equipment, etc.*

	1920	1921	1922	1923	1924	1925	1926	1927	1928	1929	1930	1931	1932	1933	1934	1935	1936	1937	1938
C. At 1930 prices:																			
(c) Gross fixed capital formation	0·5	0·7	0·8	1·0	1·5	0·4	1·0	0·8	1·2	2·3	0·9	2·1	0·7	1·5	3·1	1·3	1·9	1·9	1·5
(d) Depreciation	0·9	0·9	0·9	0·9	1·0	0·9	0·9	0·9	0·9	1·0	1·0	1·2	1·2	1·2	1·4	1·4	1·6	1·6	1·6
(f) Depreciated value†	9	9	9	9	9	9	9	9	9	10	10	11	11	11	13	12	13	13	13
(h) First cost value†	25	24	24	24	24	24	24	23	24	25	25	26	25	26	28	28	29	30	30

* Only the series at 1930 prices are shown for this sub-sector. There is no estimate of buildings.
† At end of year.

NOTES TO TABLE 10.50

(2) Furniture, Equipment, etc.

A. At historical prices:

(c) *Gross fixed capital formation:* First difference in A (f), plus A (d).

(d) *Depreciation:* Reducing balance method at the rate found in a sample of assessments for 1937 collected by the Inland Revenue, with adjustments for the additional allowances introduced in 1931 and 1937.

(f) *Depreciated value of equipment etc. held at end of year:* For 1937 derived from the total wear and tear allowances in the census of assessments, (adjusted for units not assessed because of losses), divided by the average depreciation rate allowed in the sample of assessments used in A (d). Extrapolation for 1924–36 and 1938 made by means of the changes in the wear and tear allowances in annual samples of assessments examined by the Inland Revenue. For 1920–3 the change in the depreciated value was assumed to be the same proportion of the change in the depreciated value of the plant in Retail Distribution, as it was, on average, in 1924–9.

(g) *First cost value of equipment etc. scrapped:* The total amount assumed due over the 19 years ($\frac{19}{24}$ of A (h) for 1919) derived from the average length of life given by A (d), and spread in equal annual amounts. (See chapter 2, p. 16.)

(h) *First cost value of equipment etc. held at end of year:* For 1919 derived from A (f) by imputing the standard estimate for the age-structure of what is assumed to be a stationary population of assets. Depreciation is assumed to have been written off by the reducing balance method with a life of 24 years. (See chapter 2, p. 16.)

B. At current prices:

The series at 1930 prices multiplied by index C.

C. At constant (1930) prices:

(c) *Gross fixed capital formation:* A (c) deflated by index C.

(d) *Depreciation:* As for A (d).

(f) *Depreciated value of equipment etc. held at end of year:* For 1919 derived from A (f) by the standard estimate that the average historical costs (under index C) of machinery accumulated over 20 years can be taken as 68·5% of the costs at 1930 prices. (Cf. chapter 2, p. 24.)

(g) *First cost value of equipment etc. scrapped:* As for A (g).

(h) *First cost value of equipment etc. held at end of year:* For 1919 derived from A (h) by the same standard estimate as for C (f).

All remaining estimates were obtained by standard procedures. For details see the Notes to Table 10.50, p. 196.

10.6 ENTERTAINMENT AND SPORT

GENERAL PROCEDURE AND SOURCE OF INFORMATION

Gross fixed capital formation in cinemas, theatres, etc., was derived as a proportion of the value of all new work on buildings, (chapter 4, p. 57). The first cost value at the end of 1937 was obtained by grossing-up a sample of company accounts.

For equipment, seating, etc., the estimates were derived from Inland Revenue data on wear and tear allowances and rates of depreciation.

ASSETS INCLUDED

For buildings the estimate of gross capital formation relates to all cinemas, theatres, halls, etc.; and all buildings of this type (Places of Entertainment) are assigned to this trade group. For the stock of buildings, however, the source is a sample of company accounts and the estimate therefore covers all buildings of whatever type owned by firms classified by the Board of Inland Revenue as primarily engaged in 'public amusements'. The coverage of the estimates of equipment, etc., is similarly defined. Any discrepancy between the coverage of the estimates for the gross capital formation in buildings and of all the remaining estimates is unlikely to be substantial.

METHODS OF ESTIMATION

Buildings: Cinemas, Theatres, Halls, Sports Grounds, etc.

Gross fixed capital formation at current (or historical) prices was estimated in the same way as the corresponding estimate for shops, described in 10.2, p. 186. The proportion of all new work on building was based on the series of first assessments to Schedule A on Places of Entertainment (see p. 190).

The *first cost value at historical prices* of buildings owned by the trade group was estimated for the end of 1937 from a sample of company accounts. In terms of wear and tear allowances the sample covered 36% of the trade group as defined by the Inland Revenue classification. This fraction was used to gross-up the sample to give the estimated value in 1937 of all fixed assets. The first cost of the buildings was then obtained by deducting from this the depreciated value of equipment, etc., (estimated below) and the value of the site.

Depreciation was assumed to have been written off on the straight line method with a life of 100 years.

The *depreciated value at historical prices* at the end of 1919 was derived from the corresponding first cost value by imputing an age-structure equal to that found for hotels, inns, restaurants, etc., from the Inhabited House Duty assessments since 1868.

A more complicated procedure than usual was used in estimating the *first cost value at historical prices of the buildings scrapped*. An estimate was made on the basis of data for the main type of building—cinemas—and this was assumed to be also applicable to the other types of buildings. The estimate of the total first cost value of the buildings scrapped over the 19 years was made initially in terms of the number of seats scrapped in cinemas. The basis for this was the excess of the estimated number of new seats built over the increase in the estimated number of cinema seats available.[1] This total of seats was then converted to an equivalent total value of buildings scrapped. The annual value of buildings scrapped was then obtained by spreading this total in proportion to the annual figures for purchases of buildings.

The series at *current and constant prices* were derived by the standard procedures. For details see the Notes to Table 10.60, p. 198.

Furniture, equipment, etc.

The equipment, etc., owned by cinemas and other places of entertainment and sport was estimated primarily from Inland Revenue data on wear and tear allowances, although annual samples of assessments such as those used above for distribution and finance were not available.

The calculations were first made *at historical prices*. The *depreciated value* at the end of 1937 was derived from the total of the wear and tear allowances in the Inland Revenue trade group in assessments for the year of assessment 1938/9 divided by the rate of depreciation found in a sample of assessments for that year, covering about seven-eighths of the group. The depreciated value at the end of 1927 was similarly calculated after adjusting the 1937 rate of depreciation for the additional allowances which were introduced in 1931 and 1937.[2] The net increase between 1927 and 1937 was distributed over the years in proportion to the gross capital formation in buildings. For the years before 1927 the ratio of the depreciated value of equipment, etc., to that of buildings at the end of 1927 was applied to the depreciated value of buildings at the end of each year.

[1] [**133**] S. Rowson, 'A Statistical Survey of the Cinema Industry in Great Britain in 1934', *Journal of the Royal Statistical Society*, vol. XLIV (1936), p. 76; [**4**] *Annual Abstract of Statistics*, No. 90, 1953, p. 74; [**153**] *Kinematograph Yearbook* for 1919; [**128**] *The British Film Industry*, P.E.P. (London, 1952), p. 34; and [**144**] *Annual Report* of the Rank Organization for 1956.

[2] See chapter 2, p. 28.

TABLE 10.60 ENTERTAINMENT AND SPORT (£M.)

(3) All Fixed Assets*

	1920	1921	1922	1923	1924	1925	1926	1927	1928	1929	1930	1931	1932	1933	1934	1935	1936	1937	1938
A. At historical prices:																			
(c) Gross fixed capital formation	12·7	5·9	3·6	4·1	3·0	2·6	2·4	1·8	3·6	4·6	5·2	3·2	2·8	3·6	4·3	4·9	5·0	5·5	7·2
(d) Depreciation	0·6	0·6	0·7	0·7	0·7	0·7	0·8	0·8	0·9	0·9	1·1	1·2	1·2	1·2	1·3	1·4	1·5	1·6	1·8
(f) Depreciated value†	31	36	39	42	45	46	48	49	52	55	59	62	63	65	68	72	75	79	85
(h) First cost value†	41	47	50	53	56	58	60	62	65	68	73	75	78	80	84	88	92	97	103
(j) Land and depreciated value†	34	40	44	47	50	52	54	55	58	61	66	68	70	72	76	80	83	87	93
B. At current prices:																			
(d) Depreciation	1·4	1·2	0·9	0·9	1·0	1·0	1·1	1·1	1·1	1·1	1·2	1·2	1·2	1·3	1·4	1·4	1·6	1·9	2·0
(f) Depreciated value†	73	64	54	54	58	60	60	60	60	63	66	65	64	65	68	73	80	88	94
(h) First cost value†	110	92	77	75	80	82	82	82	81	85	87	85	84	85	88	94	101	112	119
(j) Land and depreciated value†	84	73	62	62	66	67	67	67	67	71	74	73	72	73	76	82	88	98	105
C. At 1930 prices:																			
(c) Gross fixed capital formation	7·3	4·3	3·2	3·8	2·6	2·3	2·2	1·7	3·4	4·4	5·2	3·3	3·1	3·8	4·7	5·2	5·1	5·2	6·9
(d) Depreciation	0·8	0·8	0·8	0·9	0·9	0·9	0·9	0·9	1·0	1·1	1·2	1·3	1·3	1·3	1·5	1·5	1·6	1·7	1·9
(f) Depreciated value†	42	46	48	51	53	54	55	56	59	62	66	68	70	72	75	79	83	86	91
(h) First cost value†	62	65	68	71	72	74	76	77	80	83	87	89	91	94	97	101	105	109	114
(j) Land and depreciated value†	48	52	54	57	59	61	62	63	66	69	74	76	78	81	84	88	92	96	101

(4) Stock-in-Trade (Book value)†

	1920	1921	1922	1923	1924	1925	1926	1927	1928	1929	1930	1931	1932	1933	1934	1935	1936	1937	1938
B. At current prices	1·5	1·6	1·5	0·9	0·6	0·7	0·6	0·4	0·4	0·3	0·3	0·3	0·3	0·3	0·3	0·3	0·3	0·3	0·3
C. At 1930 prices	0·6	1·0	1·1	0·7	0·4	0·5	0·5	0·3	0·3	0·3	0·3	0·3	0·4	0·4	0·3	0·3	0·3	0·3	0·3

* This is the sum of (1) Buildings, and (2) Furniture, equipment, etc. The component estimates are not shown separately.
† At end of year.

NOTES TO TABLE 10.60

(1) Buildings: Cinemas, Theatres, Halls, etc.

A. At historical prices:

(c) *Gross fixed capital formation:* A proportion of all new work on buildings based mainly on the classification of first assessments to Schedule A. See p. 197.

(d) *Depreciation:* Straight line method, assuming a life of 100 years.

(f) *Depreciated value of buildings held at end of year:* For 1919 derived from A (h) by imputing the age-structure found for Hotels, Inns, etc. See p. 16

(g) *First cost value of buildings scrapped or sold:* Estimated on the basis of the number of cinema seats scrapped. See p. 197.

(h) *First cost value of buildings held at end of year:* For each year by deducting from the value of all fixed assets (see (3) A (f)) the depreciated value of equipment etc. (see (2) A (f)) and the value of land (see (1) A (i)).

(i) *Land at end of year:* 10% of A (h).

B. At current prices: } As for Wholesale Distribution. See the notes to Table 10.10,
C. At 1930 prices: } (1), p. 185.

(2) Furniture, Equipment, etc.

A. At historical prices:

(c) *Gross fixed capital formation:* First difference in A (f), plus A (d).

(d) *Depreciation:* Reducing balance method at the rate found in a sample of assessments for 1937 collected by the Inland Revenue, with adjustments for the additional allowances in 1931 and 1937.

(f) *Depreciated value of equipment, etc. held at end of year:* For 1937 derived from the total wear and tear allowances in the census of assessments divided by the average depreciation rate allowed in the sample of assessments used in A (d). For extrapolation to other years see p. 197.

(g) *First cost value of equipment etc. scrapped:* For 1920 to 1928 the total amount assumed due in this period was taken as $\frac{9}{25}$ of A (h) for 1919 and this was spread in equal annual amounts. From 1929 a more rapid rate assumed such that by the end of 1938 the 1928 stock was completely replaced. See p. 200.

(h) *First cost value of equipment etc. held at end of year:* For 1919 derived from A (f) by assuming that the depreciated value was two-thirds of the first cost value.

B. At current prices: } As for Finance and Miscellaneous Services. See the notes
C. At constant (1930) prices: } to Table 10.50, p. 196.

(3) All Fixed Assets

A. At historical prices:

(f) and (j) *Value of all fixed assets (including land) held at end of year:* Derived from the chain of year-to-year changes in all fixed assets in a sample of company accounts, grossed-up in 1937. See chapter 2, p. 28.

B. At current prices:

The annual ratios of stocks to fixed assets in the sample of accounts for this trade group applied to an estimate of fixed assets in the group.

C. At constant (1930) prices:

The series at current prices deflated by the Wholesale price index for all articles.

(4) Stock-in-Trade

TABLE 10.70 PROFESSIONAL SERVICES (£M.)

	1920	1921	1922	1923	1924	1925	1926	1927	1928	1929	1930	1931	1932	1933	1934	1935	1936	1937	1938
C. At 1930 prices:																			
(2) Equipment, etc.*																			
(c) Gross fixed capital formation	0·1	0·2	0·3	0·4	0·4	1·3	1·2	1·0	1·7	1·3	1·4	1·6	1·7	1·0	1·2	1·8	1·7	1·5	1·6
(d) Depreciation	0·1	0·1	0·2	0·2	0·2	0·3	0·4	0·4	0·5	0·6	0·7	0·8	0·8	0·9	0·9	1·0	1·0	1·1	1·1
(f) Depreciated value†	1	2	2	2	2	3	4	4	5	6	7	8	9	9	9	10	11	11	12
(h) First cost value†	3	3	3	3	4	5	6	7	8	9	11	12	14	14	16	17	19	20	22

* Only the series at 1930 prices are shown for this sub-sector. There is no estimate of buildings.

† At end of year.

NOTES TO TABLE 10.70

(2) *Equipment, Furniture, Vehicles, etc.*

A. At historical prices:

(c) *Gross fixed capital formation:* First difference in A (f) plus A (d).

(d) *Depreciation:* The depreciated allowances found in the censuses of assessments for 1927 and 1937, with extrapolation to other years on the basis of annual samples of assessments collected by the Inland Revenue.

(f) *Depreciated value of equipment etc. held at end of year:* For each year from A (d) by assuming depreciation to have been written off by the reducing balance method with a life of 25 years.

(g) *First cost value of equipment etc. scrapped:* The total amount assumed due over the 19 years ($\frac{19}{29}$ of A (h) for 1919) spread in equal annual amounts.

(h) *First cost value of equipment etc. held at end of year:* For 1919 derived from A (f) by assuming an age-structure in 1919 such that the depreciated value was one-half of the first cost value.

B. At current prices:

The series at 1930 prices multiplied by index C.

C. At constant (1930) prices:

(c) *Gross fixed capital formation:* A (c) deflated by index C.

(d) *Depreciation:* At the rates given by A (d) and A (h).

(f) *Depreciated value of equipment etc. held at end of year:* For 1919 derived from A (f) by the standard estimate that the average historical costs (under index C) of assets accumulated over the 25 years 1889–1913 can be taken as 68% of the costs at 1930 prices. (Cf. chapter 2, p. 24.)

(g) *First cost value of equipment etc. scrapped:* As for A (g).

(h) *First cost value of equipment etc. held at end of year:* For 1919 derived from A (h) by the same standard estimate as for C (f).

Depreciation was assumed to have been written off on the reducing balance method at the rates suggested by the 1937 sample of assessments, with adjustments for the allowances introduced in 1931 and 1937. The 1937 rates implied a life of about 25 years.

The *gross fixed capital formation* was then obtained from the annual change in the depreciated value, plus the annual depreciation.

The *first cost value* at the end of 1919 was estimated on the assumption that the corresponding depreciated value was equal to two-thirds of the first cost value. This implies that in 1919 the age of these assets was about 5 or 6 years.

The total *first cost value* of the equipment *scrapped* from 1920 to 1928 was assumed to have been $\frac{9}{25}$ of the first cost value at the end of 1919, spread in equal annual amounts. From 1929 a more rapid rate of scrapping became necessary as a result of the modernization of the cinema projection apparatus, and the scrapping was assumed to have been raised to a rate sufficient to permit the complete replacement of the end-1928 stock by the end of 1938.

For details of the remaining series *at current and constant prices* see the Notes to Table 10.60, p. 198.

Stock-in-trade

The value of stocks held at the end of each year was found by multiplying the above estimates for all fixed assets[1] by the ratios of stocks to all fixed assets found in samples of company accounts.

10.7 PROFESSIONAL SERVICES

ASSETS INCLUDED

The scope of this trade group is limited to the vehicles, instruments, furniture, etc., owned by members of the professions liable for income tax.[2]

METHOD OF ESTIMATION

Only very limited data are available for this trade group. The method used was based on the total of the depreciation allowances for the professions established by the Inland Revenue censuses of assessments for the years 1927 and 1937, and a chain of year-to-year changes in allowances compiled from samples of assessments prepared annually by the Board of Inland Revenue.

The calculations from these figures were first made *at historical prices*. The total *depreciation* was known for 1927 and 1937 and was estimated for other years by extrapolation on the basis of the chain of allowances shown by the annual samples. The *depreciated value* at the end of each year was then derived from this by assuming that the depreciation had been written off on the reducing balance method with an average life of 25 years.

The *gross fixed capital formation* was then obtained from the annual change in the depreciated value, plus the annual depreciation.

The *first cost value* at the end of 1919 was estimated by imputing an age-structure such that it was twice the depreciated value.

The total *first cost value* of equipment *scrapped* over the 19 years was assumed to have been $\frac{19}{20}$ of the first cost value at the end of 1919 and this amount was spread in equal annual amounts.

For details of the series *at current and constant prices* see the Notes to Table 10.70, p. 199.

---

[1] First cost value of buildings, plus land, plus the written-down value of equipment, etc., all at historical prices.

[2] The scope is further indicated by the following table of wear and tear allowances.

(£ thousands)

Profession:	1927	1932	1937
Law	11·7	15·1	31·2
Medicine and Dentistry	297·1	430·4	665·6
Literature and Art	4·7	8·7	16·2
Music and Drama	6·6	6·4	15·8
Accountancy	8·7	27·5	43·3
Architecture, Engineering and Surveying	34·5	46·5	96·0
Other	81·4	123·1	229·9
Total	444·7	657·6	1,098·0

Roughly speaking, capital expenditure on new instruments, etc., will be proportionately of the same order of magnitude as the wear and tear allowances.

CHAPTER 11

SOCIAL AND PUBLIC SERVICES

This chapter contains estimates covering the following groups:

11.1 Schools and Libraries

11.2 Hospitals

11.3 Local Authorities—Specified non-trading Services

11.4 Central Government—Specified Civil and Revenue Departments.

The complete set of standard estimates for the sector as a whole is given in Table 11.00. Estimates for the component sections are given in Tables 11.10–11.40. For the first three sections and for the sector as a whole the estimate for all fixed assets is very much more reliable than the breakdown by type of asset.

It should be noted that in sections 11.1 to 11.3 we have followed the classification of services made in the local authority accounts. This may, however, introduce some slight errors, either because information classified under one service should, for our purpose, more appropriately be included under another;[1] or because legislative changes led to changes in classification which do not reflect any change in the actual nature of the expenditure.[2] In both cases any error which results will cancel out in the estimate for the sector as a whole.

11.1 SCHOOLS AND LIBRARIES

SOURCE OF INFORMATION AND ASSETS INCLUDED

The estimates for this group relate only to schools and libraries owned by local authorities. They are derived from items in the published accounts of local authorities,[3] under the following headings for England and Wales:

Elementary Education
Higher Education
Public Libraries and Museums

and the corresponding headings for Scotland and Northern Ireland.

The major omissions are, therefore, the capital formation and assets owned by private schools and by universities. The only year for which any firm information is available is 1935 when the *Census of Production* shows £1·5 m. for new construction of private 'schools and college buildings.'[4] Some further indication of the extent of the private schools is given by data from the Census of Population: in 1921 the number of teachers in private schools was 16·1% of the number in local authority schools. In 1931 the proportion was 17·7%. For the universities a very rough guess would put the annual average gross capital expenditure on educational buildings and equipment in the 'thirties at about £·75 m.[5]

The accounts give no division of expenditure by type of asset and to obtain an approximate breakdown it was assumed that 70% of the purchases were buildings, 20% equipment and 10% sites.[6] Only the buildings and equipment are included in the present estimates of gross fixed capital formation.

METHODS OF ESTIMATION

The *gross fixed capital formation at current (or historical) prices* of buildings plus equipment was taken as equal to 90% of the local authorities annual expenditure out of loans for capital works on the specified services.[7]

---

[1] For example, capital expenditure on poor law institutions which provided medical services will be classified by the local authorities as Relief of the Poor and so will be included in 11.3, rather than with Hospitals, etc., in 11.2. (The extent of this particular item was estimated as £750,000 in 1938/9. See [**79**] B. Abel-Smith and R. M. Titmuss, *The Cost of the National Health Service in England and Wales* (Cambridge, 1956), p. 138.)

[2] For example, the abolition of the Boards of Guardians and other poor law authorities from 31 March 1930 (under the Local Government Act, 1929) may have caused some capital expenditure previously classified as Relief of the Poor to be transferred to Hospitals, etc. (These changes are, however, likely to have affected revenue expenditure on existing institutions rather than capital expenditure on new institutions.)

[3] [**5**] Ministry of Health, *Annual Local Taxation Returns*, or, from 1934–5, [**19**] *Local Government Financial Statistics*, and [**30**] *Statistical Abstracts*. Data for the financial year ended 31 March were taken for the preceding calendar year without adjustment.

[4] [**36**] *Fifth Census of Production, 1935*, part IV: section 1, *Final Report*, p. 5.

[5] Cf. [**76**] *Report of the University Grants Committee for the period 1929/30 to 1934/35* (1936).

[6] These proportions were based on data given in [**52**] *Memorandum on the Board of Education Estimates*, Cmd. 4824 (1935), p. 20, relating to proposals for expenditure in 1933 of £2,720,000.

[7] After 1928 the data for England and Wales include all capital expenditure. There may be some slight understatement of the estimates before 1928 because of the exclusion of capital expenditure other than out of loans.

TABLE 11.00 SOCIAL AND PUBLIC SERVICES (£M.)

(1) Buildings and Works

	1920	1921	1922	1923	1924	1925	1926	1927	1928	1929	1930	1931	1932	1933	1934	1935	1936	1937	1938
1. Buildings																			
A. At historical prices:																			
(d) Depreciation	3	4	4	4	4	4	4	4	4	5	5	5	5	5	6	6	6	6	7
(f) Depreciated value*	126	130	131	133	135	140	146	153	161	170	183	197	207	214	222	233	249	270	295
(h) First cost value*	215	223	227	232	238	246	256	266	277	290	307	325	339	351	364	379	399	424	455
(i) Land*	17	18	18	18	19	20	21	22	23	24	26	28	29	30	31	33	35	38	40
B. At current prices:																			
(c) Gross fixed capital formation	8	8	5	6	6	9	10	11	12	14	18	19	15	12	14	17	22	27	32
(d) Depreciation	11	9	8	7	8	8	8	8	7	8	8	8	7	8	8	8	8	9	10
(e) Net fixed capital formation	-3	-1	-3	-1	-2	1	2	3	5	6	10	11	8	4	6	9	14	18	22
(f) Depreciated value*	406	330	264	247	255	256	251	251	245	252	257	259	255	255	262	275	300	332	361
(h) First cost value*	709	586	478	454	476	484	479	480	471	486	492	490	481	483	496	520	560	611	650
(i) Land*	55	46	38	36	38	38	38	38	40	40	40	41	40	41	42	44	48	53	57
C. At 1930 prices:																			
(c) Gross fixed capital formation	5	6	5	5	6	8	9	11	11	13	18	20	17	14	15	18	23	27	32
(d) Depreciation	7	7	7	7	7	7	7	7	7	7	8	8	8	9	8	9	9	9	10
(e) Net fixed capital formation	-2	-1	-2	-2	-1	1	2	4	4	6	10	12	9	5	7	9	14	18	22
(f) Depreciated value*	236	235	233	231	230	231	233	237	241	247	257	269	278	283	290	299	313	331	353
(h) First cost value*	412	417	420	424	429	436	444	454	464	475	492	510	524	536	549	565	585	608	636
(i) Land*	32	33	33	34	34	34	35	36	38	39	40	43	44	45	47	48	50	53	56
2. Civil Engineering Works																			
A. At historical prices:																			
(d) Depreciation	3	3	4	4	4	4	4	5	5	5	5	6	6	6	7	7	7	8	8
(f) Depreciated value*	66	69	72	75	79	84	87	89	91	95	102	110	116	120	124	128	134	141	149
(h) First cost value*	114	119	125	132	139	148	154	160	167	175	186	199	210	219	229	238	250	264	279
B. At current prices:																			
(c) Gross fixed capital formation	5	6	7	7	8	9	7	7	7	9	12	14	12	10	11	11	13	15	16
(d) Depreciation	11	10	8	7	8	8	8	8	8	8	8	8	8	8	9	9	10	11	12
(e) Net fixed capital formation	-6	-4	-1	0	0	1	-1	-1	-1	1	4	6	4	2	2	2	3	4	4
(f) Depreciated value*	211	182	141	134	134	134	132	131	128	127	128	133	130	130	131	134	142	156	169
(h) First cost value*	370	328	262	250	260	265	267	272	273	278	282	290	286	290	298	311	331	364	398
C. At 1930 prices:																			
(c) Gross fixed capital formation	3	4	6	7	7	7	7	6	7	9	12	14	13	11	11	12	13	15	15
(d) Depreciation	6	6	7	7	7	7	7	8	8	8	8	8	9	9	9	10	10	10	11
(e) Net fixed capital formation	-3	-2	-1	0	0	2	0	-2	-1	1	4	6	4	2	2	2	3	5	4
(f) Depreciated value*	127	125	124	124	124	126	126	124	123	124	128	134	138	140	142	144	147	152	156
(h) First cost value*	222	225	230	236	241	248	254	259	265	272	282	293	304	313	322	332	343	355	367

(2) Plant, Vehicles, etc.

A. At historical prices:

Line																		
(d) Depreciation	1	1	1	1	1	1	1	1	1	1	2	2	1	2	2	2	2	2
(f) Depreciated value*	14	14	14	14	14	15	16	17	18	20	23	24	24	25	26	28	31	35
(h) First cost value*	28	28	28	28	29	30	31	32	34	36	39	41	42	43	45	48	51	56

B. At current prices:

Line																		
(c) Gross fixed capital formation	1	1	1	0	1	1	1	2	2	2	3	3	3	3	3	4	5	6
(d) Depreciation	3	2	2	2	2	2	2	2	2	2	2	1	2	2	2	2	2	3
(e) Net fixed capital formation	−2	−1	−1	−1	0	0	0	1	1	1	1	2	1	1	1	3	3	3
(f) Depreciated value*	44	28	19	19	19	19	19	20	21	22	22	23	24	25	27	30	37	39
(h) First cost value*	88	58	41	41	41	41	41	42	43	43	43	44	45	46	49	54	65	66

C. At 1930 prices:

Line																		
(c) Gross fixed capital formation	0	1	1	1	2	2	2	2	2	3	4	3	2	3	3	3	4	5
(d) Depreciation	1	1	1	1	1	1	1	1	1	2	2	2	2	2	2	2	2	2
(e) Net fixed capital formation	−1	0	0	0	1	1	1	1	1	2	2	1	0	1	1	1	2	3
(f) Depreciated value*	19	19	18	17	18	19	19	20	21	22	24	25	26	27	27	29	31	34
(h) First cost value*	40	39	38	38	38	39	40	41	43	45	46	47	48	48	50	52	54	57

(3) All Fixed Assets

A. At historical prices:

Line																			
(d) Depreciation	8	8	8	8	9	9	10	10	11	12	12	13	13	14	14	14	15	16	17
(f) Depreciated value*	206	213	217	222	229	239	249	259	270	284	306	331	348	359	371	387	410	441	479
(h) First cost value*	357	370	380	391	405	422	439	457	476	498	529	563	590	612	635	663	697	740	790

B. At current prices:

Line																		
(c) Gross fixed capital formation	14	15	12	13	16	13	16	18	19	20	20	21	24	26	30	38	47	55
(d) Depreciation	25	21	17	16	17	16	17	16	17	17	17	17	18	18	19	20	22	24
(e) Net fixed capital formation	−11	−6	−5	−3	−1	−3	−1	2	3	3	4	4	6	8	11	18	25	31
(f) Depreciated value*	661	540	425	398	409	402	400	392	400	407	414	408	409	418	436	472	524	569
(h) First cost value*	1167	972	781	778	791	787	793	785	806	816	823	811	818	841	880	945	1040	1115

C. At 1930 prices:

Line																		
(c) Gross fixed capital formation	8	10	12	13	14	18	18	19	20	20	25	27	29	33	34	32	40	52
(d) Depreciation	14	15	15	15	16	16	16	16	17	17	18	19	18	19	20	20	21	22
(e) Net fixed capital formation	−6	−5	−3	−2	−1	2	2	3	4	4	8	8	14	16	20	12	19	30
(f) Depreciated value*	378	373	372	374	376	379	383	391	400	407	407	414	427	441	449	458	470	489
(h) First cost value*	681	689	698	708	722	736	751	768	788	806	816	816	848	875	897	921	947	980

* At end of year.

TABLE 11.10 SCHOOLS AND LIBRARIES (OF LOCAL AUTHORITIES) (£M.)

(1) Buildings

	1920	1921	1922	1923	1924	1925	1926	1927	1928	1929	1930	1931	1932	1933	1934	1935	1936	1937	1938
A. At historical prices:																			
(c) Gross fixed capital formation	1·7	1·5	0·8	0·9	1·4	2·8	3·5	4·5	4·9	5·4	7·3	8·4	5·0	3·6	4·1	5·3	7·1	9·6	12·3
(d) Depreciation	0·5	0·6	0·6	0·6	0·6	0·6	0·7	0·7	0·7	0·8	0·9	1·0	1·0	1·0	1·1	1·1	1·2	1·3	1·4
(f) Depreciated value*	40	41	41	42	43	45	48	52	56	60	67	74	78	81	84	88	94	102	113
(h) First cost value*	54	55	56	57	58	61	65	69	74	80	87	95	100	104	108	113	120	130	142
(i) Land*	8	8	8	8	8	9	9	10	11	11	12	14	14	15	15	16	17	19	20
B. At current prices:																			
(d) Depreciation	1·8	1·5	1·2	1·1	1·2	1·2	1·2	1·2	1·2	1·3	1·4	1·4	1·4	1·4	1·4	1·5	1·6	1·8	2·0
(f) Depreciated value*	132	108	87	81	85	86	86	88	88	93	97	100	99	99	102	108	118	131	144
(h) First cost value*	178	147	119	113	119	122	122	124	124	130	135	138	137	138	142	150	163	181	196
(i) Land*	25	21	17	16	17	17	17	18	18	19	19	20	20	20	20	21	23	26	28
C. At 1930 prices:																			
(c) Gross fixed capital formation	1·0	1·1	0·7	0·8	1·3	2·5	3·3	4·3	4·8	5·3	7·3	8·7	5·5	4·0	4·5	5·7	7·4	9·6	12·0
(d) Depreciation	1·0	1·0	1·1	1·1	1·1	1·1	1·1	1·2	1·2	1·3	1·4	1·4	1·5	1·5	1·6	1·6	1·7	1·8	1·9
(f) Depreciated value*	77	77	76	76	76	78	80	83	87	91	97	104	108	110	113	117	123	131	141
(h) First cost value*	103	104	105	106	107	110	113	117	122	127	135	143	149	153	157	163	171	180	192
(i) Land*	15	15	15	15	15	16	16	17	17	18	19	20	21	22	22	23	24	26	27

(3) All Fixed Assets†

	1920	1921	1922	1923	1924	1925	1926	1927	1928	1929	1930	1931	1932	1933	1934	1935	1936	1937	1938
A. At historical prices:																			
(c) Gross fixed capital formation	2·2	1·9	1·0	1·2	1·8	3·6	4·5	5·8	6·3	7·0	9·4	10·8	6·4	4·6	5·3	6·8	9·1	12·4	15·8
(d) Depreciation	0·9	1·0	1·0	1·0	1·0	1·0	1·2	1·2	1·2	1·4	1·5	1·7	1·7	1·7	1·8	1·9	2·0	2·2	2·4
(f) Depreciated value*	48	48	49	49	50	52	56	60	65	71	79	88	93	96	99	104	111	121	135
(h) First cost value*	69	70	71	71	73	76	80	85	91	98	107	117	123	127	132	138	147	159	175
B. At current prices:																			
(d) Depreciation	3·2	2·4	1·9	1·8	1·9	1·8	1·8	1·9	1·9	2·0	2·1	2·1	2·1	2·2	2·2	2·3	2·5	2·9	3·2
(f) Depreciated value*	155	123	97	92	95	96	96	99	99	105	110	114	114	114	118	125	136	155	169
(h) First cost value*	225	177	142	135	141	143	143	146	146	154	158	162	161	163	168	178	194	218	235
C. At 1930 prices:																			
(c) Gross fixed capital formation	1·2	1·4	0·9	1·0	1·7	3·2	4·2	5·5	6·2	6·8	9·4	11·3	7·0	5·1	5·7	7·2	9·4	11·9	15·0
(d) Depreciation	1·6	1·6	1·7	1·7	1·7	1·7	1·7	1·8	1·8	2·0	2·1	2·1	2·3	2·3	2·4	2·4	2·6	2·7	2·9
(f) Depreciated value*	87	87	86	86	86	87	90	93	98	102	110	119	124	126	130	134	141	150	163
(h) First cost value*	124	125	126	126	127	130	133	138	143	150	158	169	175	180	185	191	200	211	226

* At end of year.

† The estimates for equipment etc. are not shown separately. They can be obtained from the difference between (1) Buildings and (3) All Fixed Assets.

NOTES TO TABLE 11.10

(1) Buildings

A. At historical prices:

(c) *Gross fixed capital formation*: 70% of expenditure out of loans by Local Authorities.

(d) *Depreciation*: Straight-line method, assuming a life of 100 years.

(f) *Depreciated value of buildings held at end of year*: For 1919 the total for all fixed assets was derived from the outstanding loan debt of Local Authorities in 1919. For the allocation of the total by type of asset see p. 206.

(g) *First cost value of buildings scrapped*: Assumed to be negligible.

(h) *First cost value of buildings held at end of year*: From the depreciated value of all fixed assets in 1919 and assumptions about its age-structure and asset composition. See p. 206.

(i) *Land*: 14·29% of A (h).

B. At current prices:

The series at 1930 prices multiplied by index B.

C. At constant (1930) prices:

(c) *Gross fixed capital formation*: A (c) deflated by index B.

(d) *Depreciation*: As for A (d).

(f) *Depreciated value of buildings held at end of year*: For 1919 derived from A (f) by the standard estimate for buildings that the average historical costs (index B) can be taken as 50·8% of the costs at 1930 prices. (See chapter 2, p. 24.)

(h) *First cost value of buildings held at end of year*: For 1919 derived from A (h) by the same standard estimate as for C (f).

(2) Equipment

A. At historical prices:

(c) *Gross fixed capital formation*: 20% of expenditure out of loans by local authorities.

(d) *Depreciation*: Straight-line method, assuming a life of 30 years.

(f) *Depreciated value of equipment held at end of year*: As for Buildings. See (1) A (f) and p. 206.

(g) *First cost value of equipment scrapped*: The total amount assumed due over the 19 years ($\frac{19}{30}$ of A (h) for 1919) derived from

the length of life in A (d), and spread in equal annual amounts.

(h) *First cost value of equipment held at end of year*: As for Buildings. See (1) A (h) and p. 206.

B. At current prices:

The series at 1930 prices multiplied by index C.

C. At constant (1930) prices:

(c) *Gross fixed capital formation*: A (c) deflated by index C.

(d) *Depreciation*: As for A (d).

(f) *Depreciated value of equipment held at end of year*: For 1919 derived from A (f) by the standard estimate that average historical costs of equipment (index C) can be taken as 68·5% of the costs at 1930 prices. (See chapter 2, p. 24.)

(g) *First cost value of equipment scrapped*: As for A (g).

(h) *First cost value of equipment held at end of year*: For 1919 derived from A (h) by the same standard estimate as for C (f).

(3) All Fixed Assets

The sum of (1) and (2).

The *depreciated value* of all fixed assets (including land) *at historical prices* at the end of 1919 was assumed to be equal to the outstanding loan debt in respect of the services listed above in 1919.

Depreciation was assumed to have been written off in all periods by the straight line method with a life of 100 years for buildings and 30 years for equipment.

The *first cost value* of all fixed assets (including land) *at historical prices* at the end of 1919 was then derived from the corresponding depreciated value by the following procedure:

(i) The age-structure of the assets in 1919 was assumed to be such that the ratio of the depreciated value to the first cost value was 75% for buildings (see below) and 50% for equipment.

(ii) The composition of the total first cost value was assumed to be 70% buildings, 20% equipment and 10% sites.

(iii) The depreciated value at historical prices at the end of 1919 as estimated above was £53·9m. Let the corresponding first cost value $= F$. We then have:

	First cost value	Depreciated value
Buildings	0·7F	0·75 × 0·7F
Equipment	0·2F	0·5 × 0·2F
Land	0·1F	1·0 × 0·1F

$$\text{Since } 0·525F + 0·1F + 0·1F = £53·9\text{m.}$$
$$F = £74·3\text{m.}$$

The age-structure of the buildings assumed in (i) above, and used also in 11.2 and 11.4 of this chapter, was obtained by the method described in chapter 2, p. 16, using the Inhabited House Duty assessments on Hospitals, Schools, Royal and Diplomatic Residences, etc., available since 1874/5.

The annual first cost value of equipment *scrapped* was estimated as $\frac{19}{30}$ of the first cost value of equipment at the end of 1919, and this total was spread in equal annual amounts. It was assumed that there was no scrapping of school buildings.

For details of the estimates at *current and constant prices* see the Notes to Table 11.10, p. 205.

11.2　HOSPITALS

SOURCE OF INFORMATION AND ASSETS INCLUDED

The estimates for this sector cover both local authority hospitals and voluntary hospitals. The estimates for the former were derived from items in the published accounts[1] of local authorities, under the following headings[2] for England and Wales:

Hospitals, Sanitoria, Dispensaries, etc.
Maternity and Child Welfare
Lunacy and Mental Deficiency

and the corresponding headings for Scotland and Northern Ireland.

The estimates for the voluntary hospitals were derived from *The Hospitals Yearbook*[3] and information given by the British Red Cross Society and the London County Council.[4] A small number of voluntary hospitals are omitted from these sources[5] and from our estimates.

No estimates were made of the stocks in this sector, but a rough estimate gave a value of about £3m. for stocks in 1930.

METHODS OF ESTIMATION

The *gross fixed capital formation at current (or historical) prices* was taken as equal to the annual expenditure out of loans for capital works by the local authorities, plus the annual capital expenditure by the voluntary hospitals recorded in the sources mentioned above.

On the basis of a sample of specifications for new buildings and extensions recorded in *The Hospitals Yearbook* in the 'thirties, the composition of total purchases was taken as buildings 83%, equipment 10% and sites 7%. Only the buildings and equipment are included in the present estimates of gross capital formation.

The *depreciated value at historical prices* at the end of 1919 of all fixed assets (including land) in local authority hospitals was assumed to be equal to the outstanding loan debt at that date in respect of the services listed above. It was assumed that the ratio of the depreciated values of the two groups of hospitals in 1919 was roughly the same as the ratio of their respective current expenditures. This was 41% in 1920–4 and an addition of this proportion was therefore made to the outstanding loan debt in 1919 to cover the depreciated value of all fixed assets in the voluntary hospitals.

Depreciation was assumed to have been written off by the straight line method, with a life of 100 years for buildings and 30 years for equipment.

[1] [5] Ministry of Health, *Annual Local Taxation Returns*, or from 1934–5 [19] *Local Government Financial Statistics*, and [30] *Statistical Abstracts*. Data for the financial year ended 31 March were taken for the preceding calendar year without adjustment.

[2] See footnotes 1 and 2, p. 201.

[3] [151] Central Bureau of Hospital Information, *The Hospitals Yearbook*, annual from 1931.

[4] [157] British Red Cross Society, *Report on the Financial Position of the Voluntary Hospitals in Great Britain, Excluding London*, annual, 1921–29; and [66] London County Council, *London Statistics*, annual.

[5] Cf. [79] Abel-Smith and Titmuss, p. 137.

TABLE 11.20 HOSPITALS (£M.)

(1) Buildings

	1920	1921	1922	1923	1924	1925	1926	1927	1928	1929	1930	1931	1932	1933	1934	1935	1936	1937	1938
A. At historical prices:																			
(c) Gross fixed capital formation	1·9	2·0	1·4	1·6	2·1	2·5	2·7	2·5	2·9	4·0	5·5	5·2	4·7	5·1	4·8	5·7	7·3	8·4	10·0
(d) Depreciation	0·3	0·3	0·3	0·3	0·4	0·4	0·4	0·4	0·5	0·5	0·6	0·6	0·7	0·7	0·8	0·8	0·9	1·0	1·1
(f) Depreciated value*	22	24	25	26	28	30	32	34	36	40	45	50	54	58	62	67	73	81	90
(h) First cost value*	29	31	32	34	36	38	41	44	47	51	56	61	66	71	76	82	89	97	107
(i) Land*	2	3	3	3	3	3	4	4	4	4	5	5	6	6	6	7	8	8	9
B. At current prices:																			
(d) Depreciation	0·9	0·8	0·7	0·6	0·7	0·7	0·7	0·7	0·7	0·8	0·8	0·8	0·9	0·9	0·9	1·0	1·1	1·2	1·4
(f) Depreciated value*	69	58	48	46	49	51	51	52	52	56	59	62	63	66	70	76	85	96	107
(h) First cost value*	93	78	64	62	67	69	70	71	71	76	80	82	83	86	91	98	110	124	136
(i) Land*	8	7	5	5	6	6	6	6	6	6	7	7	7	7	8	8	9	10	12
C. At 1930 prices:																			
(c) Gross fixed capital formation	1·1	1·4	1·2	1·5	1·9	2·2	2·5	2·4	2·8	4·0	5·5	5·4	5·1	5·6	5·3	6·2	7·6	8·4	9·8
(d) Depreciation	0·5	0·6	0·6	0·6	0·6	0·6	0·7	0·7	0·7	0·7	0·8	0·9	0·9	1·0	1·1	1·2	1·2	1·2	1·3
(f) Depreciated value*	40	41	42	43	44	46	48	49	52	55	59	64	68	73	77	82	89	96	104
(h) First cost value*	54	56	57	58	60	62	65	67	70	74	80	85	90	96	101	107	115	123	133
(i) Land*	5	5	5	5	5	5	6	6	6	6	7	7	8	8	8	9	10	10	11

(3) All Fixed Assets†

	1920	1921	1922	1923	1924	1925	1926	1927	1928	1929	1930	1931	1932	1933	1934	1935	1936	1937	1938
A. At historical prices:																			
(c) Gross fixed capital formation	2·1	2·3	1·6	1·8	2·4	2·8	3·0	2·8	3·3	4·5	6·2	5·8	5·3	5·7	5·4	6·4	8·3	9·4	11·2
(d) Depreciation	0·5	0·5	0·5	0·5	0·6	0·6	0·6	0·6	0·7	0·7	0·8	0·8	1·0	1·0	1·1	1·2	1·3	1·4	1·6
(f) Depreciated value*	24	25	26	28	30	32	34	36	39	43	48	53	57	62	66	71	78	86	96
(h) First cost value*	32	34	36	37	39	42	45	48	51	55	61	67	72	78	83	89	97	106	117
B. At current prices:																			
(d) Depreciation	1·4	1·1	0·9	0·8	0·9	0·9	0·9	0·9	0·9	1·1	1·1	1·1	1·2	1·2	1·2	1·3	1·5	1·7	1·9
(f) Depreciated value*	74	61	50	48	51	53	54	55	55	57	62	65	66	69	74	80	90	103	114
(h) First cost value*	103	85	69	67	72	74	75	76	76	81	85	87	88	92	98	106	118	134	147
C. At 1930 prices:																			
(c) Gross fixed capital formation	1·2	1·6	1·4	1·7	2·1	2·5	2·8	2·7	3·1	4·5	6·2	6·1	5·7	6·2	5·9	6·9	8·4	9·3	10·8
(d) Depreciation	0·7	0·8	0·8	0·8	0·8	0·8	0·9	0·9	0·9	0·9	1·1	1·2	1·2	1·3	1·3	1·5	1·6	1·6	1·8
(f) Depreciated value*	42	43	44	45	46	48	50	52	54	57	62	67	72	77	82	87	94	101	110
(h) First cost value*	59	60	61	63	65	67	70	72	75	79	85	91	96	102	108	115	123	132	142

* At end of year.

† The estimates for equipment, etc. are not shown separately. They can be obtained from the difference between (1) Buildings and (3) All Fixed Assets.

NOTES TO TABLE 11.20

A. At historical prices:

(1) Buildings

(c) *Gross fixed capital formation:* 83% of expenditure out of loans by Local Authorities plus 83% of capital expenditure by voluntary hospitals.

(d) *Depreciation:* Straight line method, assuming a life of 100 years.

(f) *Depreciated value of buildings held at end of year:* For 1919 the total for all fixed assets was derived from the outstanding loan debt of Local Authorities in 1919, raised by 4½% to allow for voluntary hospitals and Northern Ireland. For the allocation of the total by type of asset, see p. 206.

(g) *First cost value of buildings scrapped:* Assumed to be negligible.

(h) *First cost value of buildings held at end of year:* From the depreciated value of all fixed assets in 1919 and assumptions about its age-structure and asset composition. See p. 208.

(i) *Land:* 8·43% of A (h).

B. At current prices: As for the buildings of Schools and Libraries. See the Notes to Table 11.10, (1), p. 205.

C. At constant (1930) prices:

(2) Equipment

A. At historical prices:

(c) *Gross fixed capital formation:* 10% of expenditure out of loans by Local Authorities plus 10% of capital expenditure by voluntary hospitals.

(d) *Depreciation:* Straight line method, assuming a life of 30 years.

(f) *Depreciated value of equipment held at end of year:* As for buildings. See (1) A (f) and p. 206.

(g) *First cost value of equipment scrapped:* The total amount assumed due over the 19 years (19/30 of A (h) for 1919) derived from the length of life in A (d) and spread in equal annual amounts.

(h) *First cost value of equipment held at end of year:* As for buildings. See (1) A (h) and p. 208.

B. At current prices: As for the equipment of Schools and Libraries. See the Notes to Table 11.10, (2), p. 205.

C. At constant (1930) prices:

(3) All Fixed Assets

The sum of (1) and (2).

The *first cost value at historical prices* at the end of 1919 of all fixed assets in local authority and voluntary hospitals was then derived from the corresponding depreciated value by the method used for schools and libraries (above, p. 206). The asset composition of the total first cost value was assumed to be the same as that taken above for gross capital formation.

The annual *first cost value of plant scrapped* was estimated as $\frac{19}{30}$ of the first cost value of equipment at the end of 1919, and this total was spread in equal annual amounts. It was assumed that there was no scrapping of hospital buildings.

For details of the estimates at *current and constant prices* see the Notes to Table 11.20, p. 207.

11.3 LOCAL AUTHORITIES— SPECIFIED NON-TRADING SERVICES

SOURCE OF INFORMATION AND ASSETS INCLUDED

All the estimates for this group are based on information in the annual accounts of local authorities on the annual expenditure out of loans for capital works and the outstanding loan debt.[1]

Education, hospitals, housing and roads, and all trading services, are excluded, but all other local authority services are included. The relevant headings in the accounts are listed in the Notes on p. 209. 'Sewers and sewage disposal' is by far the largest single object of capital expenditure in the group.

The accounts do not give any basis on which a classification by type of asset can be made, and the estimates are given in Table 11.30 simply for 'All Fixed Assets'. In aggregating to the sector and national totals, however, it has been assumed that each of the individual services could be allocated in total to one of the three types of fixed assets. The allocations made are indicated in the Notes on p. 209.

Some expenditure on land is included in the annual loan expenditure but in view of the fact that most of the work was done on public places or sites already owned by local authorities it was assumed that the amount of the expenditure on purchase of land was small and no deduction has been made for this.

METHODS OF ESTIMATION

The *gross fixed capital formation at current (or historical) prices* was taken as equal to the annual expenditure out of loans for capital works.[2]

The *depreciated value at historical prices* at the end of 1919 and 1938 was assumed to be equal to the outstanding loan debt at those dates in respect of the services included.

Depreciation at historical prices for the 19 years was taken as the difference between the total estimated purchases of assets and the increase in the outstanding loan debt over the period 1920 to 1938. The repayments out of revenue of moneys borrowed for capital assets, usually made in accordance with a statutory scheme, were thus treated as the measure of depreciation. Depreciation was estimated on a straight line basis, with lives for the assets used in the various services as shown in the Notes on p. 209. These lives were chosen so as to give the right total amount of depreciation for each service over the 19 years, on the assumption of a reasonable age-structure for the assets in 1919.

This imputed age-structure determines the *first cost value at historical prices* at the end of 1919, and thus also the total *first cost value* of the assets *scrapped* in the 19 years. These scrappings were distributed between the years in proportion to purchases.

Estimates *at constant and current prices* were then derived by the standard procedures. For further details see the Notes to Table 11.30, p. 209.

11.4 CENTRAL GOVERNMENT— SPECIFIED CIVIL AND REVENUE DEPARTMENTS

SOURCE OF INFORMATION

The estimates are derived from information in the *Appropriation Accounts*[3] on expenditure on new works and on repairs and maintenance.

ASSETS INCLUDED

The estimates cover only the buildings in the United Kingdom owned by the Civil and Revenue Departments (other than the Post Office) of the Central Government. Buildings owned by the Defence Departments are not included.

Furniture and office equipment owned by the Central Government is not included. Annual purchases for the Civil and Revenue Departments may be roughly estimated at 30% of their capital expenditure on new works, i.e., an annual average of about £0·3 m. is

---

[1] [5] Ministry of Health, *Annual Local Taxation Returns*, or from 1934–5 [19] *Local Government Financial Statistics*; [6] Scottish Office, *Local Taxation Returns*, annual; [7] Ministry of Home Affairs (Northern Ireland), *Local Taxation Returns*, annual; and [30] *Statistical Abstracts*. Data for the financial year ended 31 March were taken for the preceding calendar year without adjustment.

[2] After 1928 the data for England and Wales include *all* capital expenditure. Capital expenditure other than out of loans was generally negligible for the services in this section before 1928.

[3] [17] Parliamentary Papers: Treasury, *Appropriation Accounts*, annual. Votes of expenditure by Civil and Revenue Departments (minus Post Office and buildings overseas) on new works, and on repairs and maintenance.

TABLE 11.30 LOCAL AUTHORITIES—SPECIFIED NON-TRADING SERVICES (£M.)

(3) All Fixed Assets*

	1920	1921	1922	1923	1924	1925	1926	1927	1928	1929	1930	1931	1932	1933	1934	1935	1936	1937	1938
A. At historical prices:																			
(c) Gross fixed capital formation	7·0	8·8	9·6	9·8	10·6	12·4	11·2	10·6	10·7	13·4	17·3	19·5	17·9	13·8	15·3	16·5	20·1	23·9	26·6
(d) Depreciation	5·8	6·0	6·3	6·5	6·8	7·1	7·4	7·6	7·9	8·2	8·7	9·2	9·6	10·0	10·3	10·7	11·2	11·8	12·5
(f) Depreciated value†	96	99	102	105	109	114	118	121	124	129	138	148	156	160	165	171	180	192	206
(h) First cost value†	204	211	220	228	237	248	257	266	275	287	302	318	334	346	359	373	390	410	433
B. At current prices:																			
(d) Depreciation	19·0	16·1	12·9	12·3	12·8	13·0	13·0	13·0	12·9	13·2	13·3	13·4	13·2	13·3	13·6	14·1	15·1	16·5	17·7
(f) Depreciated value†	306	253	195	180	182	180	175	172	165	165	165	168	166	163	165	170	181	199	218
(h) First cost value†	670	570	456	436	452	460	458	462	457	465	467	471	463	466	477	496	529	577	619
C. At 1930 prices:																			
(c) Gross fixed capital formation	4·1	6·0	8·5	9·8	11·5	11·5	10·5	10·1	10·3	13·1	17·3	19·9	19·2	15·1	16·6	17·6	20·8	23·4	25·0
(d) Depreciation	11·1	11·2	11·4	11·5	11·7	12·0	12·2	12·4	12·6	12·9	13·3	13·7	14·1	14·4	14·8	15·2	15·6	16·1	16·6
(f) Depreciated value†	180	175	172	170	168	167	165	163	161	161	165	171	176	177	179	181	186	194	202
(h) First cost value†	393	396	402	409	415	424	431	438	445	455	467	482	496	508	520	533	548	564	581

* Only the total of all fixed assets is published for this sector. See p. 208.
† At end of year.

NOTES TO TABLE 11.30

A. At historical prices:

(c) *Gross fixed capital formation*: Expenditure out of loans for capital works on the services in this sector listed in A (d).

(d) *Depreciation*: Straight line method with imputed length of life (estimated as explained on p. 208) as listed below:

Note. The series are grouped according to the type of asset to which they are allocated in the sector and national totals (see p. 208). It is assumed that errors in the individual allocations will, in total, be broadly compensated for.

1. *Civil engineering works*: Sewers and sewage disposal: 33 years; Parks, pleasure grounds and open spaces: 33; Land drainage, etc.: 33; Public lighting: 33; and Other works and Purposes: 33.

2. *Buildings*: Police and police stations: 40 years; Administration of justice: 40; Relief of the poor: 40; Baths, wash-houses, etc.: 33; Other public health services: 33; and Expenditure not allocated to specific services: 33.

3. *Plant, vehicles, etc.*: Fire brigades (engines, etc.): 25 years; and Collection and disposal of house and trade refuse: 20.

(f) *Depreciated value of assets held at end of year*: For 1919 the outstanding loan debt of Local Authorities in 1919 in respect of the services listed in A (d).

(g) *First cost value of assets scrapped*: The total for the years 1920–38 derived from the first cost value of the assets at the end of 1919 and their imputed length of life, and distributed between the years in proportion to A (c).

(h) *First cost value of assets held at end of year*: For 1919 derived from A (f) by means of an imputed age-structure. See p. 208.

(i) *Land at end of year*: Included with other assets but assumed to be unimportant in capital formation. See p. 208.

B. At current prices:

The series at 1930 prices multiplied by index A, B or C.

C. At constant (1930) prices:

(c) *Gross fixed capital formation*: A (c) deflated by index A, B or C.

(d) *Depreciation*: As for A (d).

(f) *Depreciated value of assets held at end of year*: For 1919 derived from A (f) by the standard estimate that the average historical costs can be taken as 49·7% of the costs at 1930 prices for civil engineering works (index A); 50·8% for buildings (index B); and 65·3% for machinery (index C). (See chapter 2, p. 24.)

(g) *First cost value of assets scrapped*: As for A (g).

(h) *First cost value of assets held at end of year*: For 1919 derived from A (h) by the same standard estimate as for C (f).

TABLE 11.40 CENTRAL GOVERNMENT—SPECIFIED CIVIL AND REVENUE DEPARTMENTS (£M.)

(1) Buildings*

	1920	1921	1922	1923	1924	1925	1926	1927	1928	1929	1930	1931	1932	1933	1934	1935	1936	1937	1938
A. At historical prices:																			
(c) Gross fixed capital formation	2·7	1·8	0·6	0·7	0·6	0·7	0·9	0·8	0·9	0·5	0·7	0·7	0·5	0·5	0·5	0·6	0·9	1·0	1·4
(d) Depreciation	0·5	0·5	0·5	0·5	0·6	0·6	0·6	0·6	0·6	0·6	0·6	0·6	0·6	0·6	0·6	0·6	0·6	0·6	0·7
(f) Depreciated value†	39	40	40	40	40	41	41	41	42	41	41	42	42	41	41	41	41	42	42
(h) First cost value†	52	54	54	55	56	56	57	58	59	59	60	61	61	62	62	63	64	65	66
(i) Land†	6	6	6	6	6	6	6	6	6	7	7	7	7	7	7	7	7	7	7
B. At current prices:																			
(d) Depreciation	1·7	1·4	1·1	1·1	1·1	1·1	1·1	1·1	1·1	1·1	1·1	1·0	1·0	1·0	1·0	1·0	1·0	1·1	1·1
(f) Depreciated value†	126	103	83	78	80	80	77	75	72	72	70	67	64	62	61	62	65	68	69
(h) First cost value†	169	140	114	108	112	113	111	110	106	107	105	102	98	96	97	100	104	111	114
(i) Land†	19	16	13	12	12	13	12	12	12	12	12	11	11	11	11	11	12	12	13
C. At 1930 prices:																			
(c) Gross fixed capital formation	1·6	1·3	0·5	0·6	0·5	0·7	0·8	0·8	0·8	0·4	0·7	0·7	0·6	0·4	0·6	0·7	1·0	1·0	1·3
(d) Depreciation	1·0	1·0	1·0	1·0	1·0	1·0	1·0	1·0	1·0	1·0	1·1	1·1	1·1	1·1	1·1	1·1	1·1	1·1	1·1
(f) Depreciated value†	73	73	73	72	72	72	71	71	71	70	70	70	69	69	68	68	68	67	68
(h) First cost value†	98	100	100	101	101	102	103	103	104	105	105	106	107	107	108	108	109	110	112
(i) Land†	11	11	11	11	11	11	11	12	12	12	12	12	12	12	12	12	12	12	12

* There is no estimate for plant, etc. for this sub-sector.
† At end of year.

NOTES TO TABLE 11.40

(1) Buildings

A. At historical prices:

(c) *Gross fixed capital formation:* 90% of the capital expenditure on new works by the Civil and Revenue Departments, excluding the Post Office and buildings overseas.

(d) *Depreciation:* Straight line method, with a life of 100 years.

(f) *Depreciated value of buildings held at end of year:* For 1919 assumed to be 75% of the first cost value. See p. 211.

(g) *First cost value of buildings scrapped:* Assumed to be negligible.

(h) *First cost value of buildings held at end of year:* For 1930 by applying to the expenditure on repairs and maintenance the average ratio of first cost value to expenditure on repairs and maintenance for buildings owned by the Post Office. See p. 211.

(i) *Land at end of year:* 11·1% of A (h).

B. At current prices:

C. At constant (1930) prices:

As for buildings owned by Schools and Libraries. See the Notes to Table 11.10, (1), p. 205.

omitted. Motor vehicles and other transport equipment used by the Civil and Revenue Departments are also omitted from the present estimates.[1]

METHODS OF ESTIMATION

The *gross fixed capital formation* in buildings *at current (or historical) prices* was taken as equal to 90% of the capital expenditure on new works by the Civil and Revenue Departments. The remaining 10% was assumed to be for land, which is not included in our estimates of capital formation.

The *first cost value* of the buildings *at historical prices* at the end of 1930 was assumed to bear the same ratio to the maintenance and repairs expenditure in 1930 of the Civil and Revenue Departments, as was found for the corresponding data for the Post Office[2] averaged over the 11 years 1926–36.

Depreciation was assumed to have been calculated on the straight line method with a life of 100 years. *Scrapping* of buildings was assumed to be negligible.

The *depreciated value at historical prices* at the end of 1919 was obtained from the first cost value by means of the ratio of depreciated to first cost value (75%) estimated in 11.1 above(p. 206) for buildings exempt from the Inhabited House Duty.

For details of the estimates at *current and constant prices* see the Notes to Table 11.40, p. 210.

---

[1] All these omitted short-lived assets were charged to revenue in the Government accounts.

[2] [21] Post Office *Commercial Accounts*, annual.

CHAPTER 12

RESIDENTIAL DWELLINGS

12.1 OWNERSHIP OF RESIDENTIAL DWELLINGS

GENERAL PROCEDURE AND SOURCE OF INFORMATION

The estimates of gross capital formation in residential dwellings for 1920–38 were obtained by multiplying the equivalent in units of completed houses of work done each year by annual estimates of the average cost per house. The estimate of work done was based on the official statistics of the number of houses completed each year; and the estimates of average cost were mainly derived from Ministry of Labour data showing the number and total cost of dwelling-houses for which building plans were approved by a sample of 146 local authorities.[1]

The first cost value at 1930 prices was obtained by cumulating estimates of the number of houses completed each year for a sufficient number of years to account for the total number of houses at the end of 1938, and valuing each year's building at its approximate average value at 1930 prices. The stock of houses in 1938 was calculated by extrapolating the figures given in the 1931 Census of Population.

ASSETS INCLUDED

The present estimates relate to all residential dwellings, irrespective of whether they are owned by, say, local authorities, property companies or individual owner-occupiers. The estimates should thus be regarded as constituting an 'ownership of residential dwellings' sector. Any landlord who owns more than one type of property is thus split into 'establishments', and the establishment owning dwellings is covered by this sector.

The term 'residential dwelling' includes self-contained houses and flats, and tenements in a block of dwellings, but not residential shops, hotels, inns, schools and so on. The estimate covers work on completed buildings plus the change in work in progress. It excludes all work on extensions, alterations and repairs to dwellings. An (implicit) allowance for architects' fees, legal fees, stamp duties, etc., is included.

METHODS OF ESTIMATION

Gross capital formation

For 1920 to 1938 the estimate of gross capital formation at current (or historical) prices was obtained by converting data on the number of dwellings completed into estimates of the equivalent in units of completed dwellings of the amount of work done, and multiplying this by the estimated average cost per dwelling.

Reliable official statistics of the number of houses completed in England and Wales are available for the period 1 January 1919 to 31 March 1920 and thereafter for every six months until 30 September 1939.[2] For houses constructed with state assistance figures are also available showing the number under construction at 31 March each year and, for 1935–8, at 30 September also. On the basis of this information it was possible to make reasonable estimates of the equivalent in completed houses of the work done in each calendar year. The difference between all work done and work done on completed houses (i.e. the equivalent in completed houses of the change in work in progress between the beginning and end of the year) is generally small, but is significant in years such as 1920 and 1933 when the level of work done was rising rapidly (and was reflected in an increased number of completed houses in the following year), or 1927 when there was a rush to complete houses by 30 September in order to qualify for a government subsidy.

The number of houses completed in Scotland[3] and in Northern Ireland[4] each year was generally too small to

---

[1] [1] 22nd *Abstract of Labour Statistics of the United Kingdom* (1937), and [70] *Ministry of Labour Gazette*. The series is available quarterly from 1924–38.

[2] Annual data for years ended 31 March are given in [30] *Statistical Abstracts*. There is a convenient summary of the half-yearly data to 31 March, 1935 in [105] L. R. Connor, 'Urban Housing in England and Wales', *Journal of the Royal Statistical Society*, Vol. 99 (1936) p. 8. After that date see [18] Ministry of Health, *Housing*, half-yearly.

The figures exclude a few houses with very high rateable values (over £105 in the Metropolitan Police District and £78 elsewhere). Each self-contained flat or tenement in a multiple building is treated as a separate house.

[3] The number of houses completed each (calendar) year is given in [8] *Annual Reports* of the Department of Health for Scotland.

[4] The total number of houses completed in each of the four years ended 31 March 1935 to 31 March 1938 is given in [4] *Annual Abstract of Statistics*, No. 84 (1948), Table 76. For earlier years annual figures are given in the [30] *Statistical Abstracts* but omit houses built without state

warrant correction for the change in work in progress, and was added without adjustment to the estimates for England and Wales. The total is shown on page 216.

It is much more difficult to obtain reliable estimates of the average cost of the houses built each year. Only one continuous and reasonably comprehensive series is available: for 1923 to 1938 the Ministry of Labour collected monthly data from 146 local authorities in Great Britain showing the number and estimated total cost of dwelling-houses for which building plans had been approved.

The estimates of average cost per dwelling-house which can be derived from this data raise three major problems which must be considered before the estimates can be used for our purpose. Firstly, the local authorities included are not a representative sample. Outer London is included but the area covered by the London County Council is not. More seriously, only urban areas are covered, and it seems likely that the cost (excluding land) of urban houses would in general exceed that of rural houses.

Secondly, the exact basis on which the estimates of the costs were made is not known: 'The cost of plans was not submitted to the Local Authorities and estimates based on the plans were, therefore, made by borough surveyors. The questionnaire requested that the cost of land be excluded, and this was probably done in most cases, but it is not clear whether the Local Authorities interpreted other costs consistently throughout'.[1]

Thirdly, there is the difficulty of timing. It is not clear whether the estimates made by the borough surveyors were based on the costs ruling at the time the plans were approved or those expected during the period of construction; and it is not known what time-lag there would, on average, have been between approval and completion.

On the other hand, the series does cover a very large sample of urban houses[2] on a continuous and, it may be presumed, at least for each authority, a consistent, basis from year to year; it does allow for changes in the size and type of house built as well as for changes in building costs; it relates to structurally separate dwellings defined in the same way as in the data on the number of houses completed;[3] and there is no other series available which might be more satisfactory.

Two alternative sources were examined in an attempt to check the accuracy of the average costs in the plans approved and to assess their scope. The first was the 1935 Census of Production report on the Building and Contracting Trade. This is the only one of the inter-war censuses in which sufficient detail is given to derive a separate estimate for one particular type of building.

The Final Report[4] gives a figure of £190 m. for total new construction of buildings. This includes work done by local authorities and by trades other than building and contracting, and includes an allowance for work done by firms employing not more than ten persons which were not required to make returns in 1935. The new work on dwellings would lie between £105 m. and £110 m., depending on the proportion of new building work by small firms given to housing.

Our estimate of work done in 1935 (page 216) is the equivalent of 348,000 houses and the plans approved series gives £499 as the average cost of dwellings approved in 1935. This gives an estimate for the value of work done of £174 m., or at least £64 m. more than the census estimate. An essentially similar comparison was made by Bowen and Ellis[5] in 1945: taking a three-year moving average of the number of houses completed annually from 1934 to 1936 (360,000) as an approximation to the amount of house construction in 1935, and valuing this at £499 per house they obtained an estimate of total work done of £181 m. On the basis of this calculation they considered that the value of the output of houses could not be lower than £166 m., and that there was, therefore, a serious understatement in the 1935 Census estimate of total new building done. Both authors were employed in the Ministry of Works during the war, Professor Bowen as Chief Statistical Officer, and their conclusions were widely accepted.[6]

They suggested two explanations for the understatement in the estimates given in the *Final Report* for 1935. The first is that where houses constructed by speculative builders were incomplete or unsold at the end of the year, builders were required to return the best possible estimate of the value of work done during the year, and this would frequently omit any allowance

---

assistance. The average number of unassisted houses completed in the period 1925–34 is given in the *Annual Abstract of Statistics*, No. 85, (1948), Table 76, and appropriate annual estimates were made on the basis of this average. The whole series was then converted to a calendar year basis.

[1] [90] I. Bowen and A. W. T. Ellis 'The Building and Contracting Industry' *Oxford Economic Papers*, No. 7. (March 1945) p. 123.

[2] The figures were designed to include all towns and boroughs outside the City and County of London with populations of 40,000 to 50,000 or more (*Ministry of Labour Gazette*, March 1925, p. 78). At the 1931 Census the population in the areas covered by the series was 15·6 million in England and Wales and 2·2 million in Scotland.

[3] 'It should be observed . . . that the term "dwelling-house" may apply either to a self-contained house, or to a flat, or to a tenement in a large block of dwellings . . .' *Ministry of Labour Gazette*, March 1937, p. 97.

[4] [36] *Fifth Census of Production, 1935*, part IV: section 1, *Final Report on the Building and Contracting Trade*, p. 9.

[5] [90] *Oxford Economic Papers*, No. 7, (March 1945).

[6] See, for example, [60] Central Statistical Office, *Studies in Official Statistics*, *No. 1*, *The Interim Index of Industrial Production* (London, 1949) p. 44, which made use of 'Figures from the 1935 Census of Production as amended by I. Bowen and A. W. T. Ellis'. I owe this reference to Mr. W. B. Reddaway.

for profits and overheads. The second is that inadequate allowance was made in the *Report* for work done by firms employing not more than 10 persons, which were not required to make returns in 1930 and 1935. (This second point has subsequently received confirmation from a careful comparison of the numbers employed in building and contracting as shown by each inter-war Census of Production, the 1931 Census of Population and the Ministry of Labour unemployment insurance records.)[1]

However, if we attempt to quantify the omissions due to these two factors the maximum it is possible to account for appears to be some £35m.[2] and this still leaves us at least £29m. short of the figure of £174m. obtained by using the plans approved series. How do we account for the remaining discrepancy? There are two further possible causes, in addition to the possibility of error in the plans approved series. The first is that the census would exclude professional fees for architects, surveyors and solicitors, and also stamp duties on the transfer of property, while it is possible that an allowance for these charges was included in the costs in the plans approved series. Consideration of the estimates of these fees made in chapter 4 above, and of the scale for professional fees, indicates a figure of perhaps £30 per house or £10m. in total.

The second possibility is that the costs in the plans approved series include not only the cost of building but also of site development, such as roads, paths, drains and gas, water and electricity services, both within and outside the curtilage of the house; whereas in the census return it is possible that part or all of this work was classified as work on, say, highways, sewers or gas mains and not as work on buildings. This is particularly likely to have happened on large estates where the work of site development was done by specialized contractors. If this is so, the cost in the plans approved series is too high for our purpose, since the work on site development is already covered by the separate estimates for highways, gas, electricity and water and sewerage.

The maximum estimate which can be derived by amending the census is thus £155m., giving an average cost per house for the 348,000 houses of £445, compared with the figure of £499 per house given by the plans approved series. Furthermore, it appears that the estimate from the plans approved series is too high to the extent that it includes the costs of site development and because it is based on a sample which excludes all rural houses. On the basis of the evidence so far considered it would seem to be necessary to reduce the average cost series derived from the plans approved data by up to 10%.

The second attempt to make an alternative estimate of the average cost of houses was based on estimates or actual costs culled from a number of sources, including the unpublished records of builders, building societies and estate agents, as well as newspaper advertisements and various published records.[3] However, a limited enquiry indicated that very little reliable data now exists. What little there is is not consistently defined (for example, some estimates include and others exclude the cost of land or of site development); the information available from building societies frequently covers the cost of both new and existing houses; the estimates are often very limited in geographical coverage—and if the cost of land is included the variation is, of course, very large; and estimates are seldom available on a consistent basis from year to year. It is therefore necessary to make numerous and arbitrary adjustments to the available information and the result is inevitably subject to a very

---

[1] [99] A. L. Chapman, *Wages and Salaries in the United Kingdom, 1920–1938*, pp. 109–10.

[2] A rough approximation to the profit and overheads omitted on work in progress can be obtained on the following assumptions: (*a*) if houses took 10 months to build the number under construction by private enterprise at 31 December 1935 would be roughly 210,000 and if they were, on average, half finished at that date the equivalent in completed houses of the work in progress would be 105,000 houses; (*b*) if the final cost of these houses was £550, the value of the work in progress would be some £58m.; (*c*) if the builders' overhead charges and profits were 20% of total cost the amount omitted would be £12m. (The 1948 Girdwood Report on *The Cost of House-building* suggests that on local authority housing before the war overheads and profits represented 7% of the total costs ([69] *First Report*, p. 21), so that an estimate of 20% for speculative building is likely to be on the high side.) Even if we add £3m. for houses completed but unsold the amount omitted is unlikely to have exceeded £15m. and might well be nearer £10m.

For the work done by small firms but omitted from the Census estimates the calculation is as follows: the correct number of wage and salary earners employed in private building and contracting in 1935 is estimated by [99] Chapman, pp. 111–12 to be 856,000, but this includes some 24,000 classified to building and contracting in the 1930 Census of Population but to other trades in the Census of Production (p. 109). We thus have a 'true' figure of some 832,000. The number employed by large firms which made returns was 502,000. We then have to add back 'working proprietors' in small firms as these were excluded by Chapman. On her assumption of one working proprietor in each small firm we have 87,000, making a total number of persons working in small firms of 417,000. The number allowed for in the Census estimates ([36] *Final Report*, p. 9) is 255,000 plus an adjustment of 'between 6 and 7%', say 272,000, i.e. about 145,000 too low. The census estimate of the value of all work done by these workers (free of duplication) was £86m., of which £35m. was new building construction. If we assume that gross output per head was the same for the 145,000 workers omitted, the under-statement in the value of all work done would be some £46m. If we assume further that the ratio of new building work to building repairs and other work was also the same, the under-estimate of new building work would be £18m. Not all of this would be new work on dwellings, so that the amount to be added to the census estimate of new construction of dwellings for small firms omitted is unlikely to have exceeded £20m. and might well be nearer £15m.

[3] I am particularly indebted to the National Federation of Building Trades Employers, to a number of their member firms, and to the Halifax, Abbey National, Co-operative Permanent and Woolwich Equitable building societies. Among the published sources consulted were [87] Sir Harold Bellman, *The Thrifty Three Millions* (London, 1935); [143] A. Whittick, *The Small House* (London, 1947, 1st edition); [138] Stolper; [126] Nevin; [12] Ministry of Health, *Annual Reports*; [24] *Annual Reports of the Chief Registrar of Friendly Societies*, part 5; and [159] *The Economist* 23 April, 1938.

large margin of error. The best estimate which could be made on the basis of the limited data at present available was an average relating broadly to the whole of the 1930's, and was obtained as a weighted average of separate estimates for four categories of dwelling.

approved for 1930–8 is £530. For what it is worth this very approximate estimate thus supports the previous evidence (page 214) suggesting that the costs in the plans approved are on the high side for our purpose, possibly because they included costs of site development.

Houses built by	Rateable value* (£)	Number of houses†		Estimated Final Selling Price‡ (£)
		(Thousands)	(Percentage)	
Local authorities	up to 13 (20)	527	23	350 ± 25
Private enterprise	up to 13 (20)	688	29	375 ± 25
Private enterprise	14–26 (21–35)	877	38	530 ± 50
Private enterprise	27–78 (36–105)	237	10	950 ± 50

* Figures in brackets are rateable values in the Metropolitan Police Area.

† Number built in England and Wales from 1 April 1931 to 31 March 1939, as classified by [92] Bowley, pp. 271–2.

‡ The estimate for local authority houses is derived from their estimated capital expenditure (see p. 217 below) and the number built; the remaining very approximate estimates were derived from various sources, including those listed on p. 214, note 3.

The estimates for each of the four categories are intended to indicate the final selling price inclusive of all fees, charges and profits other than the cost of land and site development. The average, weighted according to the numbers built in each category, is £485 ± 35. The average of the costs per dwelling in the plans

In the light of these considerations it seems that the average costs per dwelling as shown by the data on building plans approved should be reduced by anything up to 10%, although there is considerable uncertainty as to the exact size of the reduction necessary. For our final estimates (shown in the table on

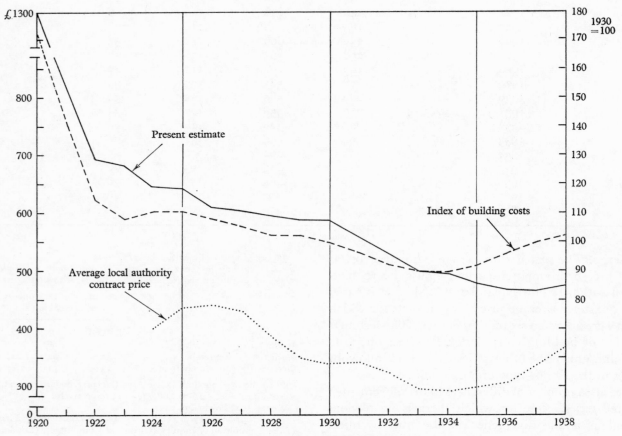

FIG. 5 Indices of average value or cost of houses built, 1920–38.

p. 216) we have reduced the series by 5%. The resulting series is intended to include all professional fees, legal charges, stamp duties, etc., but to exclude costs of site development.

With regard to the third problem referred to on p. 213, the timing of the plans approved series, it was assumed that the average cost per dwelling in the plans approved in any quarter represented the cost at which work was done in the three following quarters. Work done in the four quarters of, say, 1930 is thus valued at the average of the costs for each of the six quarters from the second quarter of 1929 to the third quarter of 1930, weighted 1, 2, 3, 3, 2 and 1 respectively.

The resulting estimate of average costs is shown in the table below and in Figure 5 it is compared with two

costs in 1924, and in the local authority tender prices in 1925 and 1926 but this is not reflected in the average cost of plans approved. The fact that the plans approved series falls more steeply after 1930 may be largely explained by the decline in the average size of the houses built by private enterprise;[2] and this decline, together with the probable economies derived from the increased scale of building, may well have been sufficient to offset the increase in building costs after 1934 suggested by index B. The contrasting rise in tender prices may also be partly due to a small increase in the average size of the houses built by local authorities.[3]

For 1920–2 the plans approved data on average costs were not compiled and for 1923 the method of weighting described above cannot be used without the data for

	Equivalent in completed houses of work done		Estimated average cost per dwelling (£)	Value of work done (2) × (3) (£m.)	Estimated capital expenditure by local authorities (£m.)
	England and Wales (Thousands)	United Kingdom (Thousands)			
	(1)	(2)	(3)	(4)	(5)
1920	46	48	1,300	62	33
1921	115	121	860	104	69
1922	97	109	690	75	42
1923	86	94	680	64	14
1924	139	146	646	94	20
1925	173	185	642	119	36
1926	219	237	606	144	53
1927	233	258	605	156	59
1928	172	197	592	117	42
1929	203	228	585	133	36
1930	180	208	585	122	33
1931	203	219	556	122	34
1932	205	223	528	118	28
1933	280	304	498	151	26
1934	319	345	492	170	25
1935	320	348	475	165	29
1936	338	366	465	170	36
1937	341	364	463	168	46
1938	332	359	472	169	53

Source: See text.

other series. The first is the average estimated cost at which three-bedroom non-parlour houses were built for local authorities in England and Wales. It is based on the quarterly average prices of contracts for which tenders were accepted six months earlier.[1] The second is the index of building costs (index B) given on p. 24 above, and unlike the other series, it does not allow for changes in the size or type of house built.

There are a number of differences in the movement of the three series. One for which there is no obvious explanation is the divergence in the mid-'twenties; there appears to have been a slight rise in the building

[1] [12] Ministry of Health, *Annual Reports.*

[2] The decline in the average size of houses built in England and Wales by private enterprise is indicated by the following figures:

	Percentage of new houses built with rateable values*		
	Up to £13	£14–26	£27–78
January 1919 to March 1931	1	66	33
April 1931 to September 1934	41	44	15
October 1934 to March 1939	37	51	12

* In the Metropolitan Police Area the corresponding rateable values were: up to £20, £21–35 and £36–105 respectively.

Source: [92] Bowley, p. 272.

[3] See [69] Ministry of Health, *The Cost of Housebuilding*, First Report of the Committee of Inquiry (Girdwood Committee), (London, 1948), p. 61.

1922. Alternative estimates were made as follows: separate estimates were made of the work done by local authorities and by private enterprise, and the former was valued on the basis of the capital expenditure on housebuilding by local authorities in Great Britain (see p. 217 below). The estimates for the latter were then based on the average costs per dwelling implicit in the local authority series.

For some purposes it may be useful to have separate series for capital expenditure on housing by local authorities and private enterprise. A separate estimate can be made for local authorities but from 1924 to 1938 the estimate for private enterprise can only be obtained as a residual and is, therefore, rather approximate.

The estimate of capital expenditure on housing by local authorities is given in the table on p. 216. The starting point is the series for Great Britain given by Bretherton, Burchardt and Rutherford.[1] This is taken from [19] *Local Government Financial Statistics*;[2] excludes capital expenditure on Small Dwellings, the greater part of which was advanced on loan by the local authorities to private individuals for the acquisition of houses; and includes capital expenditure other than out of loans before 1928/9.[3] Three adjustments are required. The first is the exclusion of expenditure on the purchase of land, legal costs, etc.; a sample investigation for 1929 to 1936 yielded a figure of 6·2% for this type of expenditure,[4] and this proportion was used for each year from 1919/20 to 1938·9. The second is the exclusion of sums 'repaid to lenders or transferred to sinking funds out of unexpended balances of loans or other capital receipts' which were included under the heading of capital expenditure. The relevant amount so included is known in total, but the extent to which it is included under the heading of housing is known only for one class of authority (county borough councils). A reduction equivalent to about 2% of capital expenditure on housing was made to exclude these sums. Finally, the figures for 1920–3 obtained by this procedure give an implied average cost per house which seems improbably high and a reduction was made to exclude what are assumed to be sums charged to the Housing Account by the local authorities for capital expenditure other than on construction of houses.[5]

The series given by Bretherton *et al.* ends in 1936/7 for England and Wales and 1933/4 for Scotland, and was continued to 1938/9 from the *Local Government Financial Statistics* and the *Annual Abstract of Statistics*.

First Cost Value

The estimate of the *first cost value at 1930 prices* was made by a type of perpetual inventory method. In place of the usual procedure involving some assumption about the length of life of the asset, however, the number of houses in Great Britain at the end of 1938 was taken as the starting point. Estimates of the number of houses completed each year were then carried back for as many years as was necessary to account for this stock, and valued at the appropriate average value per dwelling at 1930 prices.

The stock of houses in Great Britain at 26 April 1931 was counted at the 1931 *Census of Population*. This total was adjusted for houses built and scrapped since 1 January to obtain a benchmark for 31 December 1930 of 10,540,000 dwellings, (counting flats as separate dwellings). This figure was then extrapolated to 31 December 1938 by means of the data on the number of houses built in Great Britain and Stone's[6] estimates of the number of houses demolished. This gives a figure of 12,700,000.

B. Weber has estimated the number of houses built in Great Britain for each year from 1856–1916[7] and we know the number built from 1919–38. Making a small allowance for the missing war years we have a total for the period 1856–1938 of 9,562,000 dwellings.

A very rough guess can be made for the number of houses built from 1801 to 1855. The only comprehensive data on building available for this period are the decennial net increases in the stock of dwellings in England and Wales as shown by the Census of Population. Corresponding figures are not available for Scotland (before 1881) because of changes made in the definition of a house. Rough estimates of the number of houses in Scotland at each date were therefore derived on the assumption that in each decade between 1801 and 1881 the number of persons per house decreased at the same rate in Scotland as in England and Wales. The 'inter-censal' net increases in Great Britain thus obtained were then grossed-up by 10% in 1801–20 and by 20% in 1821–55 to allow for dwellings demolished and abandoned. (For the annual series required below

---

[1] [95] R. F. Bretherton, *et al.* Table 30, p. 421.

[2] Before 1933/4 [5] *Annual Local Taxation Returns*.

[3] Until the financial year 1928/9 the summary figures available in, for example, the [30] *Statistical Abstracts* included capital expenditure out of loans but not expenditure on capital account financed from capital grants from the central government, from the sale of assets, or by transfer from revenue or reserve funds. The [5] *Local Taxation Returns* do, however, contain detailed statements of annual capital expenditure however financed, and estimates were compiled from this source by [95] Bretherton *et al.*

[4] [95] Bretherton, *et al.*, pp. 126–7.

[5] This could, for example, include some of the initial costs incurred in the launching of the post-war housing programmes, and larger outlays on the purchase of land than are allowed for by our deduction of 6%.

[6] [139] R. Stone, vol. I, p. 221. The estimates were adjusted to calendar years.

[7] [141] B. Weber, 'A New Index of Residential Construction, 1838–1950', *Scottish Journal of Political Economy*, vol. II (1955), pp. 131–2.

for estimates of the depreciated value these figures were spread evenly over the decades.) We thus obtain a total of some 2,890,000 houses built in 1801–55. This leaves some 248,000 houses built before 1801 still unaccounted for, but no attempt was made to apportion these to particular years.

The cost of construction at 1930 prices of these houses (excluding sites) was then established as follows:

(i) *1920–38:* The estimates described above and shown in Table 12.00 gives a total of £2,376 m. for the cost at 1930 prices of houses built in this period. About 1% of this is for houses in Northern Ireland, giving some £2,350 m. for Great Britain.

(ii) *1856–1919:* The average cost per dwelling in 1907 appears to have been some £235–£250 at current prices,[1] say £450 at 1930 prices. This price was then extrapolated by an index designed to allow for the

If we now assume that the houses demolished were always the oldest in existence, so that we need go back only the minimum number of years to account for the houses standing in 1938, we can estimate the first cost value at 1930 prices of the end-1938 stock by summing the above estimates. The result, summarized below, is a figure of £5,370 m. Adding back the £26 m. for houses built in Northern Ireland in 1930–8 and adding 2·5%[3] to the figure for Great Britain for pre-1920 houses brings the total for the United Kingdom to £5,473 m.

The estimates made above indicate that more than 138 years building were necessary to accumulate the end-1938 stock of dwellings. It appears more reasonable, however, to estimate *depreciation* on the assumption that the probable life of the majority of houses included in the stock in the inter-war years would not exceed 100 years.

First Cost Value at 1930 Prices of the End-1938 Stock of Dwellings in Great Britain

(1) Period	(2) Number of years	(3) Number of houses completed (Thousands)	(4) Average 1930 cost per house (£)	(5) Value at 1930 prices (£m.)
1920–1938	19	4,227	555	2,350
1890–1919	30	2,736	445	1,215
1875–1889	15	1,365	405	555
1856–1874	19	1,234	375	465
1801–1855	55	2,890	250	725
pre-1801	—	248	250	60
		12,700		5,370

Source: see text.

Note: For 1856–1938 the average cost is obtained from cols. (3) and (5) and rounded to the nearest £5.

improvements during this period in the size of houses, the standard of building, the provision of sanitation, and so on. The index rises by ½ per cent per annum in each year from 1856 except in 1890 when there is a step of 5% to take account of the effects on the standard of building of the 1890 Housing of the Working Classes Act. The number of houses built in Great Britain each year as estimated by Weber was then multiplied by the resulting estimated price per dwelling, and a sum of £2,235 m. was obtained for the total cost at 1930 prices of houses built in Great Britain in this period.

(iii) *pre-1856:* The published information on the cost of the houses and cottages built in this period is very limited, but from the little that is available it would seem reasonable to take a figure of £250 as a very rough estimate of their average 1930 cost.[2] This gives a total value for the 3,138,000 houses built before 1856 of £785 m.

To obtain the end-1938 *depreciated value at 1930 prices* the first step was to cumulate the annual gross capital formation at 1930 prices from 1839 to 1938, and by taking 1% of the first cost value at the end of each year, to obtain the accumulated depreciation due on all houses built in this period. The second step was to obtain the accumulated depreciation on the pre-1839

[1] Professor A. K. Cairncross suggests a figure of £250 for the average cost (excluding land) of a new house built in 1907; [**97**] *Home and Foreign Investment, 1870–1914* (Cambridge, 1953) p. 108. This is based partly on an estimate of the total value of new houses built, derived by him from the [**33**] 1907 *Census of Production*, partly on the Inhabited House Duty statistics, and partly on references to a figure of £250 used by contemporary writers. [**69**] The Girdwood Report on The Cost of Housebuilding (p. 1) states that: '... houses built for local authorities immediately before the war were costing about £235 each ...'

[2] See, for example, [**135**] E. Smith, *The Peasant's Home, 1790–1875* (London, 1876), pp. 35–74; [**81**] T. S. Ashton, pp. 49–51; and [**74**] *Report of the Select Committee on Buildings Regulations and Improvement of Boroughs* (Parliamentary Reports from Committees, 1842, vol. x).

[3] Based on the number of dwellings in Northern Ireland and Great Britain in 1920 as given by [**139**] Stone, p. 221.

TABLE 12.00 RESIDENTIAL DWELLINGS (£M.)

	1920	1921	1922	1923	1924	1925	1926	1927	1928	1929	1930	1931	1932	1933	1934	1935	1936	1937	1938
A. At historical prices:																			
(d) Depreciation	17	18	19	19	20	21	23	24	26	27	28	29	30	32	34	35	37	38	40
(f) Depreciated value*	989	1075	1131	1176	1250	1348	1469	1601	1692	1798	1892	1985	2073	2192	2328	2458	2591	2721	2850
(h) First cost value*	1704	1807	1879	1940	2032	2150	2292	2445	2557	2686	2805	2925	3041	3189	3355	3514	3677	3837	3997
(i) Land*	119	126	131	267	142	150	160	171	179	188	196	205	213	223	235	246	257	268	280
B. At current prices:																			
(c) Gross fixed capital formation	62	104	75	64	94	119	144	156	117	133	122	122	118	151	170	165	170	168	169
(d) Depreciation	57	46	39	37	39	40	41	41	41	42	43	42	41	42	43	46	50	53	56
(e) Net fixed capital formation	5	58	36	27	55	79	103	115	76	91	79	80	77	109	127	119	120	115	113
(f) Depreciated value*	3197	2672	2197	2094	2228	2311	2345	2419	2399	2502	2527	2511	2472	2533	2664	2836	3068	3336	3512
(h) First cost value*	5614	4694	3865	3694	3924	4047	4067	4144	4086	4231	4255	4212	4133	4198	4370	4611	4947	5346	5599
(i) Land*	393	329	270	259	275	283	285	290	286	296	298	294	289	294	306	323	346	374	392
C. At 1930 prices:																			
(c) Gross fixed capital formation	36	74	66	60	85	107	134	147	115	130	122	127	128	168	188	179	178	167	165
(d) Depreciation	33	33	34	35	35	36	38	39	40	41	43	44	45	47	48	50	52	53	55
(e) Net fixed capital formation	3	41	32	25	50	71	96	108	75	89	79	83	83	121	140	129	126	114	110
(f) Depreciated value*	1861	1902	1934	1959	2009	2080	2176	2284	2359	2448	2527	2610	2693	2814	2954	3083	3209	3323	3433
(g) First cost value of assets scrapped or sold	—	1	5	6	3	2	4	7	10	8	7	4	5	8	12	15	15	17	17
(h) First cost value*	3268	3341	3402	3456	3538	3643	3773	3913	4018	4140	4255	4378	4502	4665	4845	5012	5175	5325	5473
(i) Land*	229	234	238	242	248	255	264	274	281	290	298	306	315	327	339	351	362	373	383

* At end of year.

NOTES TO TABLE 12.00

A. At historical prices:

(c) *Gross fixed capital formation:* Work done in units of completed dwellings multiplied by the estimated average value per dwelling. See pp. 212–17.

(d) *Depreciation:* As for C (d).

(f) *Depreciated value of dwellings held at end of year:* For 1919 derived from C (f) by the standard estimate that average historical costs of building (index B) can be taken as 50·8% of costs at 1930 prices. (See chapter 2, p. 24.)

(g) *First cost value of dwellings demolished:* Same proportion of A (h) for 1919 as for series at constant prices.

(h) *First cost value of dwellings held at end of year:* For 1919 derived from C (h) by the same standard estimate as for A (f).

(i) *Land at end of year:* 7% of A (h).

B. At current prices:

The series at 1930 prices multiplied by index B.

C. At constant (1930) prices:

(c) *Gross fixed capital formation:* A (c) deflated by index B.

(d) *Depreciation:* Straight line method, assuming a life of 100 years.

(f) *Depreciated value of dwellings held at end of year:* C (h) for 1938 less accumulated depreciation estimated at 1% of the first cost value at the end of each year of houses built from 1839 to 1938 plus 90% of houses built before 1839 and still in existence at end-1938.

(g) *First cost value of dwellings demolished:* The number demolished each year as given by Stone [139] p. 221 valued at an average 1930 cost per dwelling of £250.

(h) *First cost value of dwellings held at end of year:* For 1938 by cumulating annual gross capital formation at 1930 prices, going back for a sufficient number of years to account for the total number of houses at end-1938.

dwellings surviving to the end of 1938, i.e. those of more than 100 years. The end-1938 first cost value of these is equal to the difference between the figure of £5,473 m. obtained above and the figure of £4,923 m. obtained by cumulation of the gross capital formation from 1839 to 1938, and the accumulated depreciation on these was taken as 90% of their first cost value. We thus have a total accumulated depreciation of £2,040 m. and deducting this from the first cost value we obtain a depreciated value at 1930 prices at the end of 1938 of £3,433 m.

The number of dwellings *scrapped* each year was obtained from estimates by Stone,[1] and all houses scrapped were valued at a first cost value at 1930 prices of £250.

Site values were taken as 7% of the first cost value of the buildings.[2] It should be noted that this is a very rough estimate and as it assumes a constant relationship between building costs and site values it does not reflect adequately the increase in urban land values.

For details of the remaining estimates at current and historical prices see the Notes to Table 12.00, p. 219.

COMPARISON WITH OTHER ESTIMATES

A comparison with an alternative estimate can be made for the end-1919 depreciated value at historical prices. The market value of houses can be estimated by capitalizing their gross annual value (as assessed for Inhabited House Duty) by the number of years' purchase established for Estate Duty purposes. This represents the price which the property would fetch in the open market at the time of death if sold in such a manner and subject to such conditions as to obtain for the vendor the best price. As such, the resulting estimate of market value is conceptually distinct from the present estimates of actual '*ex post*' costs, but a comparison of the two estimates may be of interest.

The gross annual value of all dwellings in Great Britain was approximately £133 m. in 1913/14.[3] The average number of years' purchase on the gross annual value of Freehold House Property and Business Premises in the three years 1912/13 to 1914/15 was 14·24 years.[4] Multiplying by this factor gives a market value of dwellings (inclusive of sites) in 1913/14 of £1,894 m., and an allowance of 2·5% for Northern Ireland brings this to £1,940 m. This is essentially the value at 1912–14 prices, but in view of the long-term stability of pre-1914 building costs this will not differ very greatly from an estimate at historical prices.

Some slight deduction should be made for depreciation between 1913 and 1919 and this might reduce the market value at end-1919 to, say, £1,800 m. This is greatly in excess of our estimate of £1,059 m. for the end-1919 depreciated value at historical prices of dwellings plus land, and approximate more closely to our estimate of £1,757 m. for the first cost value plus land. The comparison thus indicates the extent to which market values will exceed the notional written-down value of property where it is maintained (and perhaps improved) by adequate current expenditure on repairs. It may also point to some understatement in our estimate of site values.

---

[1] [**139**], p. 221.
[2] See chapter 2, p. 15.
[3] See chapter 10, p. 187.
[4] [**25**] *58th Report of the Commissioners of H.M. Inland Revenue* (1915), p. 35.

CHAPTER 13

THE NATIONAL TOTALS

13.1 INTRODUCTION

In this chapter we bring together the estimates from chapters 5 to 12 of capital formation and of the stock of assets. The totals of these estimates are shown in Table 13.00, with the full set of standard estimates for the two groups of assets: (1) buildings and civil engineering work and (2) plant, machinery, vehicles, ships, and other equipment, and (3) for all fixed assets. The overall total of the estimates for stock-in-trade and work in progress is also given in Table 13.00.

A brief survey of the main features revealed by the present estimates was given with the summary of findings in chapter 3. The purpose of the present chapter is to examine certain aspects of the overall scope and accuracy of the national totals. In the opening sections we deal with the trade classification of the estimates; the known omissions and duplications in the classification and coverage; the known errors in the classification by type of asset; and the other known errors in the estimates. Then in 13.6 a detailed comparison is made for each of the main types of asset with the estimate of gross fixed capital formation derived from the Census of Production in chapter 4. This leads finally to an attempted evaluation of the reliability of the national totals estimated from the ownership side.

13.2 THE TRADE CLASSIFICATION OF THE ESTIMATES

The estimates of assets owned are classified into eight major sectors (chapter 5 to 12), and these sectors are in turn sub-divided into numerous sub-sectors or trade groups. The 1948 edition of the Standard Industrial Classification[1] (S.I.C.) was used as the framework for the estimates but the basic source material was too varied and *ad hoc* to permit a detailed grouping of the estimates in precisely the form prescribed by the S.I.C.

An attempt has nevertheless been made to indicate the approximate coverage of each trade group in relation to the minimum list headings and orders of the S.I.C., and the position is broadly as set out in Table 13.20. The table is in two parts. Part I covers Mining, Manufacturing and Distribution and other services where one of the basic sources[2] was data compiled by the Board of Inland Revenue. These data were classified into trade groups by the Board, and the coverage of our estimates is effectively determined by the classification used by the Board in the inter-war years. The minimum list headings of the S.I.C. which correspond to the Inland Revenue classification are shown in the Table, but the correspondence is inevitably rather approximate. Part II sets out the approximate relationship of the S.I.C. headings to the remaining trade groups. These estimates are largely independent of any formal classification, but on the whole correspond well with particular orders or headings of the S.I.C.

13.3 KNOWN ERRORS IN THE TRADE CLASSIFICATION AND COVERAGE OF THE ESTIMATES

The primary aim of the present study was to estimate the flows and stocks of capital, classified in principle according to the sector by which the assets were owned. In some cases, however, it was not possible to make the detailed analysis by establishments which would be required in order to fulfil this aim completely. In this section we shall consider the major errors which are known to be present in the trade classification and coverage of the estimates; other types of error such as arise from the deficiencies of the accounting data or the grossing up of the samples are not covered here.

(1) ERRORS AT THE LEVEL OF TRADE GROUPS

At the lowest level there are the errors which arise in the estimates for individual trade groups but which cancel out within the sector. This applies particularly to the estimates for the twenty-two trade groups in Manufacturing industry; and, to a lesser extent, to the estimates for Wholesale and Retail distribution.

The primary source of this type of error is that in these sectors the classification depends on the Board of Inland Revenue. The crucial feature of their classification was that all assessments on companies and most

---

[1] [**58**] Central Statistical Office, *Standard Industrial Classification*, 1948.
[2] The exceptions are the estimates for the cotton industry in chapter 8, and for shops, hotels, and cinemas in chapter 9.

TABLE 13.00 TOTAL UNITED KINGDOM DOMESTIC CAPITAL FORMATION AND CAPITAL STOCK, 1920–1938 (£M.)

(1) Building and Civil Engineering Works

	1920	1921	1922	1923	1924	1925	1926	1927	1928	1929	1930	1931	1932	1933	1934	1935	1936	1937	1938
A. At historical prices:																			
(d) Depreciation	68	71	73	76	76	80	83	86	88	91	94	96	98	101	104	106	110	114	117
(f) Depreciated value*	3301	3462	3558	3650	3779	3942	4109	4282	4413	4573	4739	4879	4988	5123	5286	5454	5642	5858	6070
(g) First cost value of assets scrapped or sold†	13	17	16	18	21	17	15	21	21	21	20	24	24	28	24	28	30	29	37
(h) First cost value*	5477	5696	5849	5999	6186	6413	6649	6888	7087	7318	7579	7772	7957	8168	8413	8662	8931	9234	9527
B. At current prices:																			
(c) Gross fixed capital formation	242	232	169	168	205	243	250	259	219	251	260	236	207	236	267	274	298	330	329
(d) Depreciation	223	186	152	144	150	152	152	151	148	151	151	148	143	143	144	149	160	170	178
(e) Net fixed capital formation	19	46	17	24	55	91	98	108	71	100	109	88	64	93	123	125	138	160	151
(f) Depreciated value*	10560	10844	7093	6680	6939	7031	6948	6957	6785	6893	6856	6725	6476	6443	6569	6813	7206	7729	8073
(g) First cost value of assets scrapped or sold†	37	43	35	35	42	34	33	40	40	40	37	43	42	44	40	48	55	59	70
(h) First cost value*	17890	15124	12226	11603	12123	12332	12237	12285	12043	12264	12232	12041	11646	11616	11853	12299	12997	13935	14561
C. At 1930 prices:																			
(c) Gross fixed capital formation	141	163	149	156	185	221	232	245	214	246	260	244	224	260	295	297	311	329	321
(d) Depreciation	131	131	134	135	137	138	141	143	146	148	151	152	154	158	159	164	166	169	171
(e) Net fixed capital formation	10	32	15	21	48	83	91	102	68	98	109	92	70	102	136	133	145	160	150
(f) Depreciated value*	6189	6221	6236	6257	6305	6388	6479	6581	6649	6747	6856	6948	7018	7120	7256	7389	7534	7694	7844
(g) First cost value of assets scrapped or sold†	24	30	30	32	37	31	30	37	39	40	37	45	45	50	46	51	56	60	68
(h) First cost value*	10490	10626	10745	10870	11022	11213	11416	11625	11801	12008	12232	12433	12614	12828	13081	13330	13586	13857	14111

(2) Plant, Ships, Vehicles, etc.

	1920	1921	1922	1923	1924	1925	1926	1927	1928	1929	1930	1931	1932	1933	1934	1935	1936	1937	1938
A. At historical prices:																			
(d) Depreciation	93	105	108	111	121	122	127	133	137	142	147	155	155	154	155	154	158	169	179
(f) Depreciated value*	1169	1290	1394	1449	1497	1552	1576	1610	1674	1723	1751	1768	1753	1720	1725	1753	1814	1889	1972
(g) First cost value of assets scrapped or sold†	29	84	78	63	72	73	90	103	92	97	99	108	98	110	101	110	101	111	82
(h) First cost value*	2515	2670	2817	2920	3023	3134	3205	3279	3395	3500	3592	3666	3715	3737	3804	3888	4016	4161	4345
B. At current prices:																			
(c) Gross fixed capital formation	240	226	212	166	169	177	151	167	201	191	175	172	140	121	160	182	219	244	263
(d) Depreciation	219	171	166	148	137	135	135	132	140	146	145	147	145	144	143	154	162	192	197
(e) Net fixed capital formation	21	55	46	18	32	42	16	35	61	45	30	25	−5	−23	17	28	57	52	66
(f) Depreciated value*	2880	2218	2136	1825	1670	1669	1644	1599	1677	1763	1734	1685	1657	1632	1646	1748	1869	2127	2158
(g) First cost value of assets scrapped or sold†	123	204	159	135	118	116	123	128	122	127	129	138	129	139	126	136	127	150	131
(h) First cost value*	6978	5306	5008	4306	3966	3929	3869	3736	3848	4013	3950	3832	3807	3804	3836	4069	4304	4889	4958

C. At 1930 prices:

(c) Gross fixed capital formation	126	143	133	133	152	164	141	170	197	187	183	175	183	148	124	172	189	219	219	235
(d) Depreciation	109	114	115	117	122	128	127	131	136	141	154	145	154	154	150	152	155	162	172	179
(e) Net fixed capital formation	17	29	18	16	30	36	14	39	61	46	29	30	29	−6	−26	20	34	57	47	56
(f) Depreciated value*	1415	1444	1462	1478	1508	1544	1558	1597	1658	1704	1763	1734	1757	1731	1751	1751	1785	1842	1889	1945
(g) First cost value of assets scrapped or sold†	56	133	108	107	105	105	118	122	126	126	141	129	147	136	131	131	137	123	133	119
(h) First cost value*	3443	3468	3503	3532	3585	3650	3686	3734	3816	3888	4002	3950	4018	4024	4067	4067	4129	4232	4329	4450

(3) All Fixed Assets

A. At historical prices:

(d) Depreciation	161	176	181	187	197	202	210	219	225	233	241	251	253	255	259	260	268	283	296
(f) Depreciated value*	4470	4752	4952	5099	5276	5494	5685	5892	6087	6296	6490	6647	6741	6843	7011	7207	7456	7747	8042
(g) First cost value of assets scrapped or sold†	42	101	94	81	93	90	105	113	118	124	132	132	122	138	125	131	138	140	119
(h) First cost value*	7992	8366	8666	8919	9209	9547	9854	10167	10482	10818	11171	11438	11672	11905	12217	12550	12947	13395	13872

B. At current prices:

(c) Gross fixed capital formation	482	458	381	374	334	420	401	426	442	420	435	408	347	357	427	456	517	574	592
(d) Depreciation	442	357	318	292	287	287	287	283	297	288	296	295	288	287	287	303	322	362	375
(e) Net fixed capital formation	40	101	63	42	87	133	114	143	145	132	139	113	70	59	140	153	195	212	217
(f) Depreciated value*	13440	11062	9229	8505	8609	8700	8592	8556	8656	8462	8590	8410	8075	8133	8215	8561	9075	9856	10231
(g) First cost value of assets scrapped or sold†	160	247	194	170	160	150	156	168	167	162	166	181	183	171	166	184	182	209	201
(h) First cost value*	24868	20430	17234	15909	16089	16261	16106	16021	16277	15891	16182	15873	15420	15453	15689	16368	17301	18824	19519

C. At 1930 prices:

(c) Gross fixed capital formation	267	306	289	289	337	385	373	415	433	427	435	427	372	384	467	486	530	548	556
(d) Depreciation	240	245	252	259	266	268	274	282	289	296	306	306	308	308	311	319	328	341	350
(e) Net fixed capital formation	27	61	37	37	78	119	105	141	129	121	129	121	64	76	156	167	202	206	
(f) Depreciated value*	7604	7665	7698	7735	7813	7932	8037	8178	8307	8451	8590	8711	8775	8851	9007	9174	9376	9583	9789
(g) First cost value of assets scrapped or sold†	80	163	138	140	144	136	148	166	161	166	166	186	181	177	188	179	193	187	
(h) First cost value*	13933	14094	14248	14402	14607	14863	15102	15359	15617	15896	16182	16435	16638	16846	17148	17459	17818	18186	18561

(4) Stock-in-Trade and Work in Progress

Value of physical increase‡

B. At current prices	97	−91	−65	−6	133	17	44	40	91	−3	−58	29	5	−6	60	83
C. At 1930 prices	53	−66	−49	1	86	17	34	33	91	1	−70	34	6	−7	56	82

Value of stocks held at end 1938§

B. At current prices	1743	..
C. At 1930 prices	1780	..

* At end of year.

† For most of the component sectors these estimates are not based on actual records of scrapping but simply reflect our assumption that assets are scrapped at the end of their estimated lives. The annual figures for this series are therefore of little value,

‡ See Table 3.60, p. 54 for source of this estimate and for estimates of book values at end of each year.

though the total over the period as a whole may be broadly correct.

§ This is the value at average current or 1930 prices not the book value. It is the sum of estimates from Table 2.80, 5.10 and 5.20.

.. Not available.

TABLE 13.20 COVERAGE OF THE ESTIMATES IN TERMS OF THE 1948 STANDARD INDUSTRIAL CLASSIFICATION

Part I. *Sectors in which the Coverage is determined by the pre-war Trade Classification of the Board of Inland Revenue*

Sector	Inland Revenue Classification	Approximate corresponding S.I.C. Order and Minimum List Headings				
		V Metal manufacture	VI[3] Engineering, shipbuilding, etc.	VII[4] Vehicles	VIII Metal goods n.e.s.	IX[5] Precision instruments
Chapter 6		**II. Mining and quarrying**				
6.1 Coal mining[1]	A 1	10				
6.2 Other mining and quarrying	A 2–A 4	11–14, 19				
Chapter 8, Textiles		**X Textiles**				
8.11 Cotton	—[2]	110–111				
8.12 Wool and worsted	B 2	112, 120				
8.13 Rayon and silk	B 3	113, 114				
8.14 Other textiles	B 4–B 6, B 8	115–119, 121–122, 129				
8.15 Textile finishing	B 7	123				
Metals and Metal-using						
8.21 Iron and steel	C 1–C2, C 5	40–42				
	C 14	43				
8.22 Shipbuilding	C 4		50–51		92 (part)	
Railway engineering[4]	C 3 (part), C 6			85, 86·2		
General engineering	C 3 (part)		52–56, 58, 69	82	91–92 (part)	
	C 8		57		90, 99	
	C 9	44			93, 94	
	C 10					
8.23 Electrical engineering[6]	C 3 (part)		70–75, 79			
8.24 Motor vehicles	C 7			80–81, 83		
8.25 Non-ferrous metals, etc.[7]	C 11–C 13, C 15	49			95	101–102
Food, Drink and Tobacco		**XIII Food, drink and tobacco**				
8.31 Drink[8]	D 1	163–164, 168				
8.32 Tobacco	D 3	169				
8.33 Food	D 2, D 4–D 7	150–157, 162				

Chemicals, Leather, Clothing and Paper

		IV Chemicals, etc.	XI Leather, etc.	XII Clothing	XV Paper and printing	XVI Other manufacturing	XXIV Miscellaneous services
8.41 Chemicals	D 8–D 11	30–36, 39					
8.42 Leather and rubber	D 12		130–131				
8.43 Clothing	D 13–D 14		132	140–143, 147–149		190	
8.44 Paper and board	D 15				180–181		
8.45 Newspapers, printing and stationery	D 16–D 18				182–183, 186–189	194	287

Wood, Building, Clay and Miscellaneous

		III Bricks, etc.	VII[9] Vehicles	IX[10] Precision instruments	XIV Manufacturing of wood and cork	XVI[11] Other manufacturing	XVII Building and contracting
8.51 Wood and cork Building and contracting	D 19 D 20				170–173, 179		200, 202
8.52 Cements, bricks, etc.	D 21	20, 24, 29					
8.53 Glass and pottery	D 22–D 23	21–23					
8.54 Toys and miscellaneous manufacturing	D 24–D 25		89	100, 103		192 191, 193, 199	

Chapter 10

		XVI[16] Other manufacturing	XIX Transport etc.	XX Distributive trades	XXI Insurance, Banking and Finance	XXIII Professional services	XXIV[17] Miscellaneous services
10.1 Wholesale distribution	E 1			240 (part), 241–242, 244			
10.2 Retail distribution[12]	E 3–E 4[13]		238 (part)	240 (part), 243 (part), 245–246			286
10.3 Services by inns, hotels, etc.	—[14]						285 (part)
10.4 Municipal markets	—[14]			243 (part)			285 (part)
10.5 Finance and miscellaneous services	J 1–J 5, K 4	195	238 (part) 239		250		
10.6 Entertainment and sport[15]	K 1						280–281
10.7 Professional services	H 1–H 7					270, 272 273 (part), 279	

Part II. *Other Sectors*

Sector	Approximate corresponding *S.I.C.* Order and Minimum List Headings
Chapter 4	I Agriculture, Forestry and Fishing[18]
5.1 Agriculture	1
5.2 Forestry	2
5.3 Fishing	3
Chapter 7	XVIII Gas, Electricity and Water
7.1 Electricity	211
7.2 Gas	210
7.3 Water	212
Chapter 9	XIX Transport and Communications,[19] plus VII Vehicles (part)[20]
9.1 Railways[21]	220, plus 84, 86
9.2 Road transport:	
Highways and bridges	—
Road goods transport	223
Public passenger transport	221–222
9.3 Sea and Inland water transport	224–226
9.4 Civil aviation	227
9.5 Postal, telephone and telegraph communications[22]	228
Chapter 11	XXII Public Administration and Defence (part), plus XXIII Professional Services[23]
11.1 Schools and libraries[24]	271
11.2 Hospitals[25]	273 (part)
11.3 Specified Local Authority non-trading services[26]	265
11.4 Central government civil and revenue departments	260 (part)

NOTES TO TABLE 13.20

1 Open-cast coal mining (part of 202) is here, not in 8.51.
2 Inland Revenue data were not used for this trade group.
3 Naval dockyards (50.1) and government ordnance factories (50.2) are excluded.
4 Manufacture and repair of locomotives, etc. (84, 86.1) by the railways is in 9.1. Manufacture and repair of carts, etc. (89) is in 8.51.
5 See also 8.54.
6 See also 9.5.
7 The Inland Revenue group C.15 is a residual called 'Miscellaneous metal industries' and has no corresponding S.I.C. minimum list heading.

8 Pubs owned by breweries are not here but in 10.3.
9 See also 8.22, 8.24 and 9.1.
10 See also 8.25.
11 See also 8.42, 8.45 and 10.5.
12 Inland revenue data used only for plant etc., not for buildings.
13 Note that E.4 covers semi-industrial retail distribution e.g. carpenters, bakers and tailors.
14 Inland Revenue data not used for these sectors.
15 Inland Revenue data not used for the estimate of gross capital formation for buildings.
16 See also 8.42, 8.45, 8.51 and 8.54.

17 See also 8.43.
18 Nurseries, market gardens etc. are omitted.
19 For 'other transport' (238) and storage (239) see 10.2 and 10.5.
20 See also 8.22, 8.24 and 8.51.
21 Ancillary services operated by the railways are excluded.
22 Manufacture of telegraph and telephone apparatus by the Post Office (72.1) is here, not in 8.23.
23 See also 10.7.
24 Covers only local authority schools and libraries.
25 For doctors' private equipment, vehicles, etc. see 10.7.
26 For details of the services see 11.3 p. 209.

assessments on individuals and firms related to the unit as a whole and not to its separate establishments.[1] Where a unit carried on two or more trades, it was assigned to the class from which the main profit was normally derived. Each trade group therefore includes all assets owned by a unit classified to the group on the basis of its primary activity. For example, the estimate for the wool and worsted industry (8.12) will include assets owned for, say, textile finishing (8.15) by a unit which is mainly engaged in weaving of woollens, but which also undertakes finishing of woollen fabrics.

The extent of this crossing of trade boundaries must be quite considerable, but no information is available on this point. However, since it will frequently work in both directions, the net effect on each trade group may not be very great.

(II) ERRORS ON THE LEVEL OF SECTORS

Units not only undertake more than one type of manufacturing activity, they may also engage in both manufacture and distribution. The same inability to classify by establishments thus means that the estimates for, say, companies engaged primarily in retail distribution,[2] will also include the plant owned by their manufacturing establishments; and conversely the estimates for those engaged primarily in manufacture will include all assets owned by their distributive establishments. This sort of boundary crossing was particularly common for firms in the clothing, footwear and food trades.

It is thought that, on balance, the effect of this is that the estimates for plant, vehicles, etc., owned by Retail distribution are overstated while those for all assets owned by Manufacturing and Wholesale distribution are understated.

As between Mining and Manufacturing, where the same problem occurs (for example, with coal mines owned by iron and steel companies) it seems that, on balance, it is the buildings and plant owned by Mining which are understated and those owned by Manufacturing which are overstated.

All the errors of this type will, however, cancel out on the national level, except for the complication with regard to buildings owned by Retail distribution, to be discussed below.

(III) ERRORS ON THE NATIONAL LEVEL

Finally there are the errors which arise within a sector or trade group which are not compensated for on the national level. Essentially the errors of this type occur because our methods of estimation fall into two broad categories. First, there are those derived from accounts (or from Inland Revenue data on wear and tear allowances classified in the same way as the accounts), leading to estimates of all assets owned by the trade group to which the accounts relate. This applies for example to the estimates discussed above for manufacturing, and to the estimates for the public utilities derived from aggregate accounts. We shall refer to this as the 'accounts method'.

Second there are estimates derived from data on all assets of a particular type, for example, ships or residential dwellings. This method of estimation, which we shall call the 'assets method', leads to an estimate covering all assets of the given type, and these are assigned to a sector which is defined as the sector owning all assets of that particular type. All ships, for example, were assigned to the shipping sector described in chapter 9. In principle, therefore, any ships included in the accounts of some other trade group in, say, manufacturing, should be regarded as owned by an establishment which would form part of the shipping sector, and should therefore be excluded from the manufacturing sector. In practice, this was not always possible with the result that there is an overestimate of the sector estimated by the 'accounts method', and double counting on the national level.

In some cases both methods are used. The estimate for Retail distribution, for example, combines one estimate by the 'accounts method' for plant, etc. with another by the 'assets method' for all shops.

The extent of this double counting or of any omissions can best be considered by taking each of the main types of asset separately.

Buildings

(a) *Dwellings*. The estimate in chapter 12 covers all residential dwellings (as defined by the underlying source of information) irrespective of ownership. These are all assigned to an 'ownership of dwellings' sector. The most substantial duplication arises in the case of the houses owned by colliery companies as these will also be included in the estimate derived from accounts in chapter 6. The first cost value at historical prices of these dwellings is estimated at about £30m. in 1946. Duplication in the inter-war estimate for gross capital formation will be very small.

Any dwellings owned by firms in Manufacturing or Wholesale distribution will also be duplicated; the value of these is not known but is unlikely to be significant.

---

[1] Fortunately, however, the unit classified in the care of groups of companies was generally the individual (subsidiary or holding) company, not the consolidated group.

[2] The estimates for buildings owned by Retail distribution are not classified in the same way as those for plant, vehicles, etc., and present a different problem. This is discussed below, p. 228.

(b) *Shops.* A similar estimate was made (10.2) covering all shops (as defined by the underlying source of information) irrespective of ownership. These are all assigned to Retail distribution, which is defined to cover all establishments owning shops together with retailers in the ordinary sense who rent their shops.

Some shops will, however, be included in the estimates derived from accounts for Manufacturing, Wholesale distribution and the public utilities. The extent of this duplication is not known but may be sizeable. It is believed, however, to be less than that of the corresponding omission of factories, offices and warehouses discussed below.

(c) *Hotels, inns and restaurants.* An estimate for these buildings was made by the 'assets method' and assigned to the sector covering Services by hotels, inns, etc. No duplication arises in the case of the hotels or pubs owned by the breweries and railways as the assets of this type have been excluded from the estimates for these two trade groups made by the 'accounts method'. (See 8.31 and 9.1.) Any remaining duplication is unlikely to be significant.

(d) *Factories, offices and warehouses.* No estimate of buildings of this type was made separately by the 'assets method': in general, they are owned by units within the sectors where the 'accounts method' was used and so included in the estimates. The major omissions are the offices and factories owned by units which were classified by the Board of Inland Revenue to retail distribution and those owned by private investors or—more important—by finance and property companies (including the banks' offices and other premises owned by such companies for their own use). An important example in the first group would be the clothing factories owned by firms regarded by the Inland Revenue as primarily engaged in the retail distribution of clothing; as previously noted (p. 186) a substantial number of units were classified to this sector and it is believed that they exceed the distributive establishments classified to manufacturing.

Plant, Vehicles, Ships, etc.

(a) *Plant, equipment, etc.* With only two exceptions all estimates for plant, etc., were derived from accounts, or from Inland Revenue data on wear and tear allowances classified in the same way as the accounts, and there is therefore no serious problem of duplication or omission. The exceptions are the estimates for agriculture (chapter 5) and for the cotton industry (8.11) and in neither case is there likely to be a significant duplication of other estimates.

(b) *Vehicles.* For goods vehicles and private cars owned by the business sector the main estimates included in the national totals were derived from accounts.[1] (Supplementary estimates covering all goods vehicles and cars were made by the 'assets method' in chapter 9, but these are not included in the national totals.) For buses and taxis an estimate was made by the 'assets method' and assigned in full to the road passenger transport sector for inclusion in the national totals. There is therefore no problem of duplication on the national level.

(c) *Ships.* The estimate of all ships (other than fishing vessels) made by the 'assets method' in 9.3 was assigned to the shipping sector. There is some slight duplication with ships owned by other sectors such as the gas industry, and included in estimates derived from their accounts. It is estimated that the extent of this duplication was a little over $4\frac{1}{2}\%$ of the value of all ships registered in 1937/8 (See chapter 9, p. 175). Ships owned by the railways are not duplicated as they were excluded from the railway sector.

Our overall conclusion is, therefore, that the two major sources of error in the trade classification and coverage are:

(a) *Plant, vehicles, etc.* Retail distribution is overstated at the expense of Manufacturing, but this cancels out in the national totals.

(b) *Buildings.* On the one hand factories and offices owned by Manufacturing are understated on the level of sectors; and on the national level offices, factories and warehouses owned by financial institutions, and property-owning companies and individuals or by firms classified by the Board of Inland Revenue to Retail distribution are omitted. On the other hand shops owned by firms classified to Manufacturing and Wholesale distribution, and those owned by the public utilities, are duplicated as they are also included in Retail distribution; and there is some duplication in the estimate for dwellings. On balance the net effect on this account is that there may be an underestimate in the national totals.

13.4 KNOWN ERRORS IN THE CLASSIFICATION BY TYPE OF ASSET

The estimates of capital formation and the capital stock are classified in the national totals (Table 13.00) into two main groups of assets:

(1) Buildings and civil engineering works
(2) Plant and machinery, vehicles, ships and other equipment

---

[1] One exception to this is the estimate for goods vehicles owned by road hauliers. This was obtained by allocating to the road haulage sector a proportion of the estimate for all goods vehicles.

There are no serious problems in this broad division but it is dependent on the classification made in the component trade groups and any errors at the lower level will be reproduced in Table 13.00 except insofar as they chance to cancel out. An example of the known but unidentifiable errors of this sort occurs in the estimates for Manufacturing (chapter 8) where the general procedure was to make one estimate for all fixed units and another for plant, vehicles, etc., and so to derive the series for buildings and works as a residual. A more special point is that for the local authority non-trading services included in 11.3, no allocation by type of asset was made for the individual services. In aggregating to the sector and national totals, however, the estimates for each service were allocated in full to whichever seemed

balance the effect is likely to be that buildings are understated on this account and civil engineering works overstated.

The second group of assets was also split into three main groups: (a) ships, (b) vehicles and (c) plant and machinery, etc. Sub-group (b) is further divided into five categories: roads goods vehicles, buses and coaches, passenger cars owned for business use, tractors and other road vehicles, and railway rolling stock. For ships the main estimates were made separately, (in 5.3 and 9.3) and so are readily available. Similarly the estimate for vehicles can be assembled from a number of separate estimates including the supplementary estimate for road motor vehicles in Table 9.22. The estimate for plant and machinery, etc. can then be obtained by

Sector	Components of estimate covering buildings and works allocated in full to	
	Buildings	Works
6.0 Mining and quarrying		Mines, works and buildings
7.1 Electricity supply	Buildings and works*	
8.0 Manufacturing	Buildings and works†	
9.1 Railways		Permanent way and works and buildings
9.2 Tramways		Permanent way and works and buildings
9.3 Harbours		Harbours and warehouses
10.1 Wholesale distribution	Buildings and works†	

* This does not include transmission lines etc. which are classified as plant.
† e.g. Site development and private sidings or ports.

the most appropriate type of fixed asset. (See 11.3, p. 209 for details). It was assumed that on balance the errors involved in this allocation would broadly cancel out.

For some purposes a more detailed classification by type of asset may be useful; an attempt has been made to provide this in chapter 3 (Tables 3.31, 3.41 and 3.51) but this classification is subject to very much larger errors than the more limited division given in the main tables and should be used with caution. The total for buildings and works is split into three: (a) Dwellings, (b) Other building, and (c) Civil engineering works. The separate estimate for dwellings is available from chapter 12 but there are certain difficulties about the division between other buildings and works. In certain sectors or sub-sectors it was not possible to separate buildings from works and an estimate covering both was assigned in full to whichever was the predominant component. This procedure was adopted in the sectors listed in the above table.

In aggregating to the national level the errors resulting from this procedure will partly cancel out but on

deducting the sum of these estimates for ships and vehicles from the national totals in Table 13.00 for all plant, ships and vehicles, etc. The weakness of this procedure is that the separate estimates for certain types of vehicle[1] were obtained from one source and the (unidentified) estimates included in the national total from a totally different source (the accounts of the owners—in which, in most cases, vehicles cannot be separated from other equipment). There will inevitably be differences between these two sets of estimates for vehicles[2] and these differences will be reflected in the residual estimate for plant and machinery, etc. The extent and sign of the resultant errors in the figures for plant and machinery, etc. are not known, but the errors may well be substantial.

---

[1] Goods vehicles other than those owned by road hauliers, passenger cars owned for business use and privately-owned rolling stock.

[2] One important example of the differences is that the supplementary estimate for passenger cars is based on the very rough assumption that a constant 30% of all cars were owned for business use. The actual amount of business expenditure on passenger cars included in the accounts each year is unknown but is most unlikely to have been the same as this estimate.

13.5 OTHER KNOWN ERRORS IN THE COVERAGE OF THE ESTIMATES

There are a few small additional known omissions in the estimates. First, the estimates are intended to cover the whole of the United Kingdom but there are two sub-sectors where no addition was made for Northern Ireland: electricity and gas supply (7.1 and 7.2). The addition required to make good this omission would represent less than 0·1 % of the national totals.

Second, the United Kingdom assets of oil companies, mining companies and other concerns which have their principal fixed assets abroad (Group L in the pre-war Inland Revenue classification) are not included except insofar as they are covered by one of the estimates made by the 'assets method'. For example, tankers owned by the oil companies (and registered in the United Kingdom) are picked up in the estimate for ships in 9.3, but the goods vehicles owned by these companies are omitted.

Finally there are a few minor known omissions for which no allowance was made: farm works, drainage, etc. (5.1); the assets of non-statutory gas companies (7.2); civil aerodromes (9.4); certain short-lived equipment and vehicles of the Post Office (9.5) and of other Government civil departments (11.4); and the buildings and equipment of universities and private schools (11.1). Estimates of the order of magnitude of most of these omissions are given in their respective chapters. In total they might represent very roughly about one per cent of the national totals.

13.6 COMPARISON OF OUR ESTIMATES OF GROSS FIXED CAPITAL FORMATION FROM THE SUPPLY SIDE AND THE OWNERSHIP SIDE

In this investigation we have made estimates of total gross fixed capital formation by two methods which may loosely be described as approaching the problem from the 'supply side' and from the 'ownership side' respectively. The former was described in full in chapter 4, the latter in chapters 5 to 12.

The basic principle behind the *supply* approach is that one starts from the Census of Production and other sources indicating the *output* of new goods and work done, and picks out those items which seem to be part of the flow of fixed assets, i.e. capital goods and new construction. Adjustments are needed for international trade, transport and distribution charges, legal and professional fees, assets scrapped or sold, etc., but in principle this approach should give figures for gross fixed capital formation analysed by the type of asset

which is supplied, but not (in the inter-war years) by the character of the purchaser.

On the *ownership* side the basic principle is to start from the purchaser's end, whether this be a company, government department, public utility or private individual, and to measure the *amount spent* on fixed assets each year by various categories of future owners. In the simplest case the owner's financial accounts provide just that information, but more commonly it has to be deduced indirectly from other data in the accounts, or from other sources. The end-product is a figure for gross fixed capital formation analysed by type of purchaser but not usually by type of asset or at most with a very broad division between buildings and works, and plant, vehicles, etc.

If it had been possible to cover the entire field independently on each approach a comparison of the two totals would constitute a most valuable internal check (though one which could only emerge when all the estimates on both sides had been completed). Unfortunately, however, the two estimates are not entirely independent; on both approaches it was necessary to import information from outside in order to close a gap or to remove part of an item which was not wanted. In some cases this meant that the *same* basic figure was used on both sides, and even where it was not used in the same way the independence of the two series was impaired.[1]

The two estimates of gross fixed capital formation are set out in rows 8 (a) and 8 (b) of Table 13.60. Taken at its face value the agreement between the totals is remarkably good, but if a proper appraisal of the comparison is to be made it is of course essential to take into account the inter-relationships already noted. This can best be done by considering separately the three main types of asset.

---

[1] The following cases illustrates the inter-dependence of the estimates:

(a) The simplest type of case is where the most reliable estimate can be obtained from a source which is neither the Census of Production nor the owner's accounts, and this estimate is then included in the total on both sides. Investment in ships, for example, or in buses and taxis, can most reliably be estimated from data on new registrations. (Goods vehicles and passenger cars for business use were also estimated from new registrations but these estimates were included on the supply side only; on the ownership side these vehicles were covered in the national totals by estimates from accounts.)

(b) A second straightforward case arises where no independent estimate was made on the supply side and the supply total was completed by including an estimate derived from the owners' accounts. This applied, for example, to the estimate for electricity supply mains and plant derived on the ownership side from the official return [27] *Electricity Supply*.

(c) A third and more complex case arises with certain types of building, including shops, hotels and cinemas, where the estimate on the 'ownership' side was in fact obtained by calculating the proportion of the total new building work done—as estimated from the supply side—which consisted of these specific categories of building.

(I) CIVIL ENGINEERING WORKS

On the ownership side estimates of new construction of civil engineering work can be obtained (in the main from published accounts) with only minor complications. These arise principally in the analysis by type of asset into civil engineering work and buildings.[1]

On the supply side we begin with estimates for the three census years but we can only derive from the censuses an estimate of *all* contracting work done, including repair and maintenance work. The census reports aggregate all contracting work under some such broad heading as 'construction, alteration, repair or maintenance', and even in census years it is not possible from the census alone to distinguish accurately between new work and repairs. Even in census years, therefore, there is no possibility of independent comparison with ownership estimates of new contracting work. It should also be observed that for several of the main sectors responsible for this work, for example, the railways and the Post Office, the census return of work done by the contracting departments in fact comes from the same organization as the return of expenditure on which the ownership estimates are based. As these contracting departments do most of the work covered by the expenditure figures the independence of the estimates would be more apparent than real.

In order to arrive at the estimate of building work done *in non-census years* it was necessary to extrapolate the overall census estimate of building and contracting work done, and then to deduct from this the estimated annual total for contracting work done. This total of contracting work done in non-census years was built up from separate estimates for each of its components (see Table 4.22, p. 60); and for most of the components this estimate could best be made by separate estimates for new work and for repairs, with the estimates of new work simply taken from the ownership side data.

(II) BUILDINGS

In the case of buildings the main problems of interdependence arise on the ownership, not the supply side. The supply side estimates of gross capital formation in buildings were derived from the Census of Production in chapter 4. On the ownership side the greater part of the estimates were derived from the owners' accounts or other sources, and are entirely independent of Census of Production data. However, the estimates for four specific types of building: shops, hotels, theatres, halls and cinemas and farm buildings were derived as a proportion of the supply side estimate of all new building work done. The information on the percentage of new building work composed of these specific types of building is independent of the Census of Production but the two overall estimates clearly cannot be regarded as independent. The two series are set out in Table 13.60 and are graphed in Fig. 6(a), p. 235 with the hybrid estimate for shops, etc. removed.

Little attention should be paid to the exceptionally large discrepancy in 1920. Some of this is due to the abnormal increase in work in progress to be expected with the upsurge in activity immediately after the war, but even if some allowance is made for this (as in chapter 12) it is clear that the supply side estimate for this year is too large. This may be partly due to a possible overstatement in the estimate for 1924 derived from the Census of Production[2] but the more important cause is the extrapolation of the 1924 estimate to 1920 without allowance for the fact that productivity in 1920 would have been lower than in 1924 as a result of postwar disorganization, scarcities of material, etc. Both these points probably apply also, though for the latter with rapidly diminishing effect, to the estimates for 1921–3, so that the supply estimates for these years may be too large.

From 1924 onwards the significant point is that the estimate from the ownership side consistently exceeds that from the supply side in every year except 1925 and 1928. Over the fifteen years 1924 to 1938 the discrepancy (ignoring sign) averages some £19 m. or 10% of the (independent) estimate from the ownership side. Is this primarily because the ownership side estimate is too high or because the supply side estimate is too low? This question can best be answered by considering first the overall estimates (including shops, etc.) for 1935, the year for which we have the Census of Production benchmark for the supply side.

We have already seen in chapter 12 (pp. 213–14) that the Census is generally believed to have understated the value of work done in 1935 on two counts: (*a*) because of inadequate allowance in the Census Report for work done by the firms employing not more than ten persons, which were not required to make returns in 1935 (or in 1930); and (*b*) because of the probable omission in many returns from speculative builders of the profits (including office overheads) on houses that were incomplete or unsold at the end of the year. A rough attempt to quantify the understatement due to these two factors suggested a figure of not more than £35 m.

The overall supply side estimate for 1935 given in Table 13.60 should therefore be raised by some £35 m. The estimate given in row 1 (a) of the Table is

---

[1] See p. 229 above.
[2] See chapter 4, p. 58 above.

TABLE 13.60 COMPARISON OF ESTIMATES OF GROSS CAPITAL FORMATION FROM THE SUPPLY SIDE AND THE OWNERSHIP SIDE AT CURRENT PRICES (£M.)

	1920	1921	1922	1923	1924	1925	1926	1927	1928	1929	1930	1931	1932	1933	1934	1935	1936	1937	1938
(1) 1. Buildings																			
1. *Total*																			
(a) Estimate from the supply side	362	258	174	160	169	192	191	202	193	190	186	150	125	155	191	217	239	267	264
(b) Estimate from the owner-ship side	200	190	122	119	157	185	205	213	180	207	203	175	163	199	231	236	249	274	268
2. *Buildings for which the estimates are not wholly independent*																			
(a) Estimates based on proportion of supply side total	32	19	9	18	22	18	17	15	18	20	17	13	11	14	18	20	21	22	24
3. *Other buildings*																			
(a) Estimate from the supply side (1(a)−2 (a))	330	239	165	142	147	174	174	187	175	170	169	137	114	141	173	197	218	245	240
(b) Estimate from the owner-ship side (1 (b)−2 (a))	168	171	113	101	135	167	188	198	162	187	186	162	152	185	213	216	228	252	244
(c) Discrepancy ((a)−(b))	162	68	52	41	12	7	−14	−11	13	−17	−17	−25	−38	−44	−40	−19	−10	−7	−4
(d) (c) as percentage of (b)	96	40	46	41	9	4	−7	−6	−9	−9	−9	−15	−25	−24	−19	−9	−4	−3	−2
(1) 2. Civil Engineering Works																			
4. *Total*																			
(a) Estimate from the owner-ship side	42	42	47	49	48	58	45	46	39	44	57	61	44	37	36	38	49	56	61
(2) Plant, Ships, Vehicles, etc.																			
5. *Total*																			
(a) Estimate from the supply side	441	218	219	184	179	183	168	177	197	199	182	156	129	125	157	191	239	255	273
(b) Estimate from the owner-ship side	240	226	212	166	169	177	151	167	201	191	175	172	140	121	160	182	219	244	263
6. *Plant etc., for which the estimates are not independent*																			
(a) Estimates used on both supply and ownership sides	101	93	128	77	72	77	57	58	83	76	69	59	43	34	44	57	79	85	93
7. *Other plant, etc.*																			
(a) Estimate from the supply side (5 (a)−6 (a))	340	125	91	107	107	106	111	119	114	123	113	97	86	91	113	134	160	170	180
(b) Estimate from the owner-ship side (5 (b)−6 (a))	139	133	84	89	97	100	94	109	118	115	106	113	97	87	116	125	140	159	170
(c) Discrepancy ((a)−(b))	201	−8	7	18	10	6	17	10	−4	8	7	−16	−11	4	−3	9	20	11	10
(d) (c) as percentage of (b)	145	−6	8	20	10	6	18	9	−3	7	7	−14	−11	5	−3	7	14	7	6

TABLE 13.60 (cont.)

	1920	1921	1922	1923	1924	1925	1926	1927	1928	1929	1930	1931	1932	1933	1934	1935	1936	1937	1938
(3) All Fixed Assets																			
8. Total																			
(a) Estimate from the supply side (1 (a) + 4 (a) + 5 (a))	845	518	440	393	396	433	404	425	429	433	425	367	298	317	384	446	527	578	598
(b) Estimate from the ownership side (1 (b) + 4 (a) + 5 (b))	482	458	381	334	374	420	401	426	420	442	435	408	347	357	427	456	517	574	592
9. Assets for which the estimates are not independent																			
(a) Estimates (2 (a) + 4 (a) + 6 (a))	175	154	184	144	142	153	119	119	140	140	143	133	98	85	98	115	149	163	178
10. Other assets																			
(a) Estimate from the supply side (8 (a)−9 (a))	670	364	256	249	254	280	285	306	289	293	282	234	200	232	286	331	378	415	420
(b) Estimate from the ownership side (8 (b)−9 (a))	307	304	197	190	232	267	282	307	280	302	292	275	249	272	329	341	368	411	414
(c) Discrepancy ((a)−(b))	363	60	59	59	22	13	3	−1	9	−9	−10	−41	−49	−40	−43	−10	10	4	6
(d) (c) as percentage of (b)	118	20	30	31	9	5	1	0	3	−3	−3	−15	−20	−15	−13	−3	3	1	1

NOTES TO TABLE 13.60

(1) Buildings

1 (a) See Table 4.22, row E 3.

1 (b) The total for Buildings and Works in Table 13.00, row (1) B (c) less Row 4 (a) of this table.

2 (a) This is the sum of the estimates for farm buildings (Table 5.10), shops (10.20), inns, hotels, etc. (10.30), and cinemas, halls, etc. (10.60).

2. Civil Engineering Works

4 (a) See Table 4.22, row D 4.

5 (a) See Table 4.30, row C 4.

5 (b) See Table 13.00, row (2), B (c).

(2) Plant, Ships, Vehicles, etc.

6 (a) This is the sum of the estimates of gross fixed capital formation for all the items for which the year's purchases is given in part B, rows 1–8 of Table 4.30, other than road goods vehicles not owned by road hauliers, passenger cars owned for business use and privately-owned railway wagons.

£217 m., and so would be raised to £252 m. made up as follows:

	£m.
New building work	198
Legal and professional fees, stamp duties, etc.	19
Adjustment for understatement	35
Total	252

In fact, however, the figure of £198 m. is too high and should be only £190 m. As explained in chapter 4 (p. 61) the benchmark taken in that chapter for

The discrepancy in the estimates for residential premises was considered at length in chapter 12 and our main interest here is in the remaining components. Excluding dwellings the adjusted supply side estimate exceeds the present ownership side estimate by £15 m. This appears to be largely accounted for by three factors: firstly, the known omission of ownership estimates for offices, churches and private schools; secondly, the reflection in the derived estimates for shops, etc. of the understatement in the total estimate from the supply side;[1] and thirdly, the classification of certain

NEW BUILDING WORK IN 1935
(£M.)

	Estimate based on Census returns	Adjusted supply side	Ownership side
	(1)	(2)	(3)
Residential premises	110	155	162
Shops, offices, hotels, warehouses, etc.	25	28	24
Factories and workshops (incl. electric power stations, gasworks, etc.)	24	26	25
Public buildings (except dwellings, factories and schools)	9·5	10	11
Public school and college buildings	4·5	5	5
Theatres, cinemas, etc.	3·5	4	4
Places of public worship and buildings connected therewith	1·5	2	4
Private school and college buildings*	1·5	2	—
Stations and railway buildings	3	3	—
Private hospitals*	1·5	2	2
Other buildings	6	7	3
Total	190	244	236

* So far as recorded separately.

Source

(1) [**36**] *Final Report on the Fifth Census of Production, 1935*, part IV, section 1, pp. 4–9.

(2) The adjustment consists of the addition of £35 m. to dwellings for the estimated understatement in the Census returns and the rough allocation of £19 m. for professional and legal fees, etc.

(3) This is based on the estimates in chapters 5–12.

contracting work done in 1935 was underestimated by £8 m., and as the benchmark for building was derived by deducting contracting work from the Census figure for new building and contracting work done it is correspondingly overstated. The best estimate from the supply side for new building work done in 1935 is thus £244 m. This exceeds by £8 m. the comparable estimate from the ownership side of £236 m.

There is insufficient information in the Census returns for a precise analysis by type of building of the new work done in 1935 but it is possible to make a broadly reliable estimate and this is done in the above table for comparison with the detailed estimates from the ownership side.

buildings (particularly stations and other railway buildings) as works, only partly offset by the classification of some works as buildings.[2]

The overall conclusions are, therefore:

(*a*) The supply side total for 1920–4 is too high and for 1925–38 too low.

(*b*) The fact that the ownership side estimates for the years from 1925 generally exceed the supply estimates is not an indication that they are too high and the detailed evidence for 1935 suggests that they are in fact

---

[1] This may be partly offset by a small overstatement in the *proportion* of the total allocated to these types of building.

[2] See above, p. 229.

too low. The estimate for dwellings is, if anything, slightly high and in the overall estimate this provides some compensation for the likely underestimate in the estimates for other buildings.

(III) PLANT, MACHINERY, VEHICLES, ETC.

For certain of these fixed assets the same estimates were used on both sides and for purposes of comparison must be excluded (see row 6 (a) of Table 13.60). This eliminates ships, buses and coaches, railway-owned rolling stock, telegraph and telephone plant, and electricity supply mains and services; together these items account for just over a third of the estimates.

In 1920 there is again a very great discrepancy between the independent estimates for the remaining assets (covering mainly plant and machinery, and vehicles other than buses). This may be due partly to the extrapolation from 1924 without allowance for the lower productivity in that year (cf. p. 231 above); and partly to the possibility that a part of the work done in 1920 represented an increase in work in progress and distributors' stocks which would not be reflected in the estimates from the ownership side of expenditure on finished goods.

For 1921–38, however, as Figure 6 (b) shows, agreement between the two independent estimates is good (see also Table 13.60, rows 7 (a)–(d).) The sign of the discrepancy is not consistent, but the ownership side

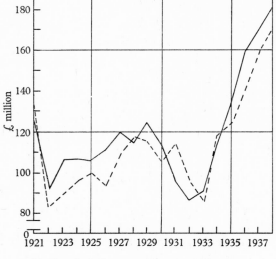

(b) Specified plant, machinery, vehicles, etc.

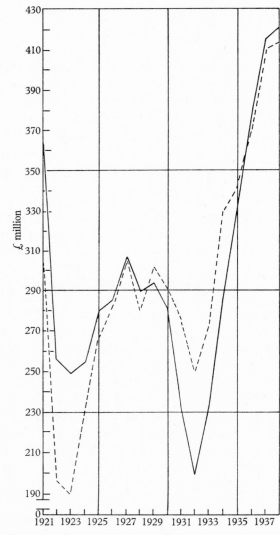

(c) Total independent estimates.

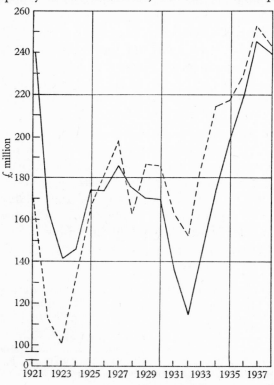

(a) Buildings excluding shops etc.

FIG. 6 Estimates of gross fixed capital formation from the supply side and the ownership side, 1921–38.

——————— Supply side   - - - - - - - - Ownership side

estimate is slightly lower[1] in 13 of the 18 years, with an average difference of less than 5%. Disregarding sign, the average discrepancy is just under £10m., or 9% of the estimate from the ownership side, and there are only two years (1923 and 1926) in which the discrepancy exceeds 15%. Both series show the same trend but the ownership side reaches a peak in 1928, one year earlier than the supply side, and a trough in 1933, one year later. The ownership side also has a rather dubious rise in 1931.

This broad measure of agreement is especially re-assuring in view of the sketchy nature of many of the data which were available on the ownership side for these assets. In particular, Inland Revenue data on wear and tear allowances and rates of depreciation were widely used to obtain estimates of the depreciated value of plant, vehicles, etc. The annual change in this series gives the estimated net fixed capital formation and in order to obtain the gross flow it was then necessary to add back our estimates of the amount of depreciation assumed to have been written off. This was the only source available from which estimates could be made for individual industry groups in Manufacturing, Mining and Distribution; and it seems in total to have yielded reasonably accurate results, although the component estimates are naturally likely to have a greater margin of error.

13.7 RELIABILITY OF THE ESTIMATES

There is no objective means of assessing the margin of error in the estimates presented in this study. It may, however, be of value to readers to give some indication of the subjective impression which we have formed on the basis of (i) knowledge of the primary sources used and the extent to which data originally assembled for some particular purpose are an appropriate basis for the estimates of capital formation made from them in this study; (ii) the various internal checks which can be made: for example, the comparison discussed in the preceding section; and (iii) the comparison in the following chapter with the results obtained by other estimators using different sources and methods.

For an excellent discussion of the types of error which can arise in social accounting estimates, and the diffi-culty of assessing the extent of such errors, reference should be made to R. Goldsmith's study of saving in the United States.[2] In Table 13.70, we set out an attempt to quantify our subjective impressions of the reliability of the present estimates of gross fixed capital formation at current prices, but it must be strongly

emphasized that this is necessarily a highly speculative process.

We have grouped the estimates into five categories according to the basic source from which they were derived, and have then classified all the main estimates in four reliability categories according to their probable margin of error:

		Probable Margin of error
A.	Good estimates	± less than 7%
B.	Fair estimates	± 7% to 15%
C.	Poor estimates	± 15% to 25%
D.	Rough estimates	± more than 25%

Our concept of 'probable margin of error' does not carry any precise definition but broadly speaking the categories are intended to indicate the distance from the 'true estimates' within which we expect the majority of the nineteen observations for each series for the period 1920–38 to lie. As a rule, estimates are likely to be more reliable in later than earlier years, since there was a general tendency for the quality of the basic information to improve. This applies particularly to the series in groups (i) and (ii) which were derived from accounts. The reliability categories take account of known omissions (for example of private schools in 11.1), but it is assumed that there is no error due to the principles adopted in the definition of our estimates— for example the inclusion of expenditure on renewals of roads and bridges in 9.2. Where the estimates for different types of asset were derived from different sources they are classified separately, but otherwise the grading relates to the estimate for all fixed assets in each sector or trade group. In general the estimates for all fixed assets in groups (i) and (ii) are more reliable than the component estimates for each type of asset.

Any attempt to indicate the probable error in the estimate of total gross fixed capital formation must be even more speculative than these given above for the components, since it is also necessary to take into account the nature and extent of the relationship between the errors in the components. At a guess the estimates for most years might lie within a range of error of between 7 and 15% from the 'true' estimate.

---

[1] Since the estimates for buildings owned by firms classified to manufacturing were obtained as a residual after deduction of these estimates of plant, etc. from estimates of all fixed assets owned by these firms there is possibly some correlation with the fact that the estimate for buildings was found to be probably too high (see chapter 14, p. 243). The position is uncertain, however, because the above estimates of plant, etc. cover firms in other sectors as well as those classified to manufacturing.

[2] [110] R. W. Goldsmith. *A Study of Saving in the United States* (Princeton, 1955), vol. II, pp. 129–47.

TABLE 13.70   RELIABILITY OF ESTIMATES OF GROSS FIXED CAPITAL FORMATION

	Sector or Trade Group	Type of Fixed Asset	Reliability Category
	(i) Estimates derived from aggregate accounts		
7.1	Electricity Supply	All	A
7.2	Gas supply	All	B
9.1	Railways	Permanent way and works	A
9.2	Road Transport	Highways and bridges	A
9.5	Post Office	All	A
11.1	Education	All	C
11.2	Hospitals	All	B
11.3	Local authority non-trading services	All	A
	(ii) Estimates derived from samples of accounts and Inland Revenue data		
6.0	Mining and quarrying	All	C
7.3	Water supply	All	B
8.0	Manufacturing: total	All	B
8.11–			
8.54	Manufacturing: individual trade groups	All	C or D†
9.3	Sea and inland water transport	Docks, canals, etc.	C
10.0	Distribution and other services	All	C
10.1	Wholesale distribution	All	D
10.2	Retail distribution	Plant, vehicles, etc.	C
	(iii) Estimates derived from numbers and average values		
9.1	Railways	Rolling stock	A
9.2	Road transport	Buses and taxis	B
		Goods vehicles*	B
		Passenger cars*	D
9.3	Sea and inland water transport	Ships	C
12.0	Residential dwellings	Dwellings	B
	(iv) Estimates derived as a proportion of supply side estimate of all building work done		
5.1	Agriculture	Buildings	C
10.2	Retail distribution	Shops	B
10.3	Services by hotels, inns, etc.	Hotels, etc.	C
10.6	Entertainment and sport	Theatres, halls, etc.	C
	(v) Other estimates		
5.1	Agriculture	Plant, tractors, etc.	C
10.3	Services by hotels, inns, etc.	Furniture, etc.	D

* Supplementary estimate.
† The reliability will depend in part on the size of the sample, for which see p. 139–42.

CHAPTER 14

COMPARISON WITH OTHER ESTIMATES

14.1 INTRODUCTION

In this chapter we shall compare our results with those obtained by other estimators. The first five sections deal with alternative estimates of gross and net capital formation, and 14.7–14.10 with four alternative estimates of the stock of capital. In 14.11 we consider certain alternative price indices. Wherever possible the coverage of the present estimates has been adjusted for purposes of comparison with these alternative estimates.

The most authoritative of the alternative estimates are those in 14.3 for gross and net fixed capital formation and depreciation in 1938 made by the Central Statistical Office. In this section we have therefore attempted to make a 'best estimate' for 1938 for each of these items, taking into account not only the results of the comparisons made in this chapter, but also all other indications of the reliability and completeness of the present estimates obtained in previous chapters. This 'best estimate' is intended to give what on the information now available seem to be the most reliable estimates which can be made for 1938 on the definitions used in the present study.

14.2 REDFERN'S ESTIMATES OF GROSS FIXED CAPITAL FORMATION, 1924–38

Estimates of gross fixed capital formation at 1948 prices for 1924 to 1938 were published in 1955 by Mr. P. Redfern.[1] They form part of a longer run of estimates which according to the author were: 'not in any sense a definitive set of figures, as they were obtained primarily as a step towards calculating depreciation.'[2] Nevertheless the estimates for the inter-war years were carefully compiled in considerable detail, and insofar as the sources of information and the methods of estimation used are independent of those in the present study the series provides a most useful check on our estimates 'from the ownership side'.

Redfern's estimates at 1948 prices for each type of asset have been converted to current prices[3] and the total is shown in Table 14.20. In order to compare this series with the present estimates at current prices it is

necessary to make several adjustments to the latter. First, the Redfern series for these years is incomplete. Among the assets omitted are private educational buildings and equipment, which are also omitted from our estimates; and farm buildings, fishing vessels, coal mining buildings and works, tramcars and tramways, hospitals (public and private), certain central government office buildings, and legal fees and stamp duties.[4] These latter assets are covered by the present estimates, but for purposes of comparison in Table 14.20 have been deducted. Secondly, the Redfern estimates exclude and the present estimates include a small amount of expenditure out of revenue on renewals of the railway way and works and an equivalent expenditure on renewal of roads,[5] and those items have also been deducted from our estimate. Finally, to arrive at the estimates of gross capital formation we have deducted the proceeds of ships, vehicles and other assets scrapped, sold abroad or sold to consumers, and there is no comparable deduction in the Redfern estimates for the inter-war years. The amount deducted in the present estimates has therefore been added back for purposes of comparison.

Our adjusted series at current prices is compared with Redfern's in Table 14.20, and the two totals are shown in Figure 7. The main components of the two

---

[1] [132] Redfern. See especially appendices A and B, pp. 169–81 for details of the methods and sources referred to in the subsequent pages.

[2] [132] Redfern, p. 150.

[3] [132] Redfern, Table 4, p. 155. The estimates for each type of asset except ships were converted to current prices by means of the price indices given by Redfern at p. 171. For ships see footnote 1 on p. 243 below.

[4] It was suggested in chapter 12 (pp. 213–15) that the average values used in estimating dwellings include an allowance for legal fees and stamp duties and since Redfern's estimates for dwellings were derived from the same source these charges will equally be allowed for in his estimates. For other assets these charges are assumed to be included in the present estimates where they were derived from accounts but are not covered by Redfern's estimates. The amount we have included cannot be separately identified and to the extent that they include legal fees and stamp duties the component estimates shown in Figures 8 and 9 and discussed in the following pages are larger than the corresponding estimates by Redfern. It is, however, possible to make a rough estimate of the *total* amount included and it is this total which is deducted in Table 14.20. The estimate is based on the data given in Table 4.40, p. 67. It averages some £14m. per annum.

[5] Our reasons for including this expenditure were given in chapter 1, appendix 1.1, p. 9 above. Other expenditure on renewals, for example by the Post Office, is included by Redfern.

TABLE 14.20   COMPARISON WITH REDFERN'S ESTIMATES OF GROSS FIXED
CAPITAL FORMATION, 1924–1938
(Current prices. £m.)

	Present estimates					
	Gross fixed capital formation	Proceeds of sales or scrapping	Items not covered by Redfern	Adjusted to Redfern definition and coverage (1) + (2) − (3)	Redfern	Percentage (5) to (4)
	(1)	(2)	(3)	(4)	(5)	(6)
1924	374	9	31	352	364	103
1925	420	8	38	390	391	100
1926	401	12	29	384	413	108
1927	426	10	30	406	444	109
1928	420	8	27	401	396	99
1929	442	12	30	424	450	106
1930	435	17	37	415	420	101
1931	408	11	28	391	407	104
1932	347	9	24	332	337	102
1933	357	15	30	342	354	104
1934	427	10	29	408	423	104
1935	456	15	31	440	467	106
1936	517	11	36	492	534	108
1937	574	14	36	552	586	106
1938	592	5	36	561	599	107

Source

(1) Table 13.00, p. 223, row (3) B (c).

(2) The estimates, mainly in chapter 9, of the proceeds of ships, vehicles and other assets scrapped or sold.

(3) The estimates in Chapters 5–11 above of: farm buildings, fishing vessels, coal mining buildings and works, tramway and tramcars, hospital buildings and equipment and central government buildings, plus the renewals expenditure on railway way and works and roads, plus part of the estimate from chapter 4 above of legal fees and stamp duties.

(5) [**132**] Redfern, Table 4, p. 155, converted to current prices by the indexes given at page 171.

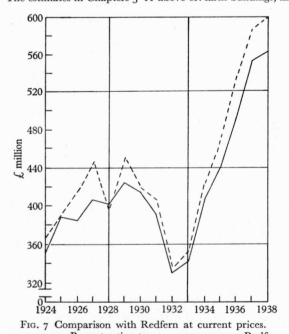

FIG. 7 Comparison with Redfern at current prices.
————— Present estimates   --------- Redfern

and the conversion to current prices in the inter-war years introduces a potentially large additional discrepancy into the comparison. For all other assets, the original calculations were made at current prices and the price indices used to convert back from 1948 to current prices are those originally used by Redfern to obtain the series at 1948 prices.

The outcome of the comparison between Redfern's series and the present estimates adjusted to a comparable coverage are most encouraging (Table 14.20). Except for one year, 1928, Redfern is consistently higher, though only by an average of some £20 m. or 4·5% of the present estimates. In no year do the series diverge by more than 9%. As Figure 7 shows, the two estimates also agree quite well on the trend of gross fixed investment over the period: slow ascent to a peak in 1929, a trough in 1932 and then a strong recovery to a much higher level in 1938.

If we look at the main components[1] of these two series, classified by type of asset (Figures 8 and 9), we totals are compared in Figures 8 and 9 below. It should be noted that for ships and road vehicles Redfern's original estimates were made at 1948 prices,

[1] The one small item omitted from Figures 8 and 9 is railway rolling stock for which the two estimates are derived from the same source, and though obtained by different methods are in very good agreement.

see that the present estimates are always, or almost always, lower for road goods vehicles and buses and taxis, for commercial buildings, and for dwellings. They are consistently higher for industrial buildings, ships and

the estimate for dwellings. Redfern's series is, on average, 4·5% higher than ours. Both series were obtained from the same basic data and by the same method but in the present estimates an attempt was

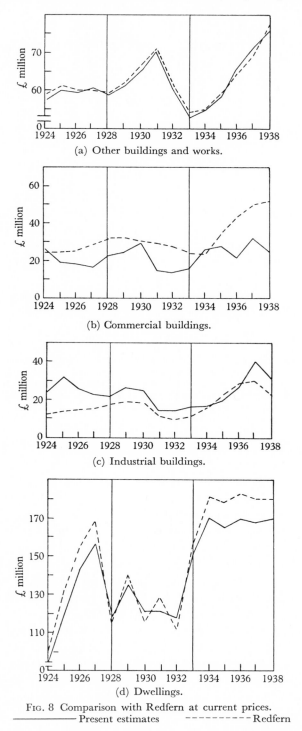

Fig. 8 Comparison with Redfern at current prices.
———————— Present estimates   - - - - - - - - Redfern

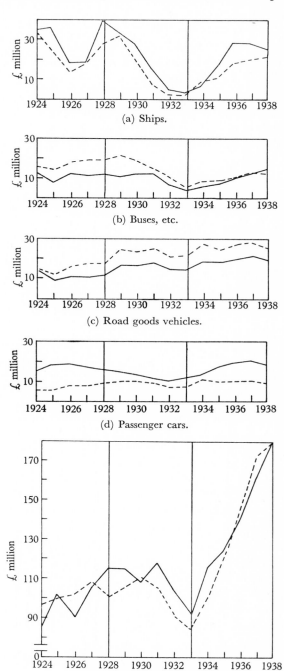

Fig. 9 Comparison with Redfern at current prices.
———————— Present estimates   - - - - - - - - Redfern

passenger cars, and on average for plant and machinery etc. For 'other buildings and works' the two estimates agree very closely. We shall now discuss each of these components in turn.

We begin with buildings. The largest component is

made to improve the result in three ways: an adjustment was made to the data on completed dwellings to allow for the change in work in progress, the series for the average value per dwelling was reduced by 5% because it was thought to be too high, and an adjust-

ment was made to the timing of the average value series. It is these adjustments and particularly the second, which account for the difference between the estimates; the case for making the adjustments is argued in chapter 12, p. 213 above.

Redfern's estimates for industrial and commercial buildings refer to specific buildings in these categories as defined in the Census of Production data taken as the starting points for his estimates. The present estimate shown in Figure 8 (c) as industrial buildings is the series from chapter 8 for buildings owned by firms classified to Manufacturing; and the estimate shown as commercial buildings is the series from chapter 10 consisting partly of buildings owned by firms classified to Wholesale distribution and partly of the specific estimates for shops, hotels, theatres, etc. There will be some differences in the coverage of the two pairs of estimates,[1] but there do not appear to be any significant *compensating* differences which would account for the fact that the present estimates for industrial buildings are consistently higher than Redfern's, while those for commercial buildings are lower in all but two years.

For industrial buildings Redfern's series starts from estimates derived from the Census of Production returns for the building industry for 1935 and 1930. These estimates were interpolated and extrapolated by reference to the series showing the value of plans approved in 146 towns for 'Factories and workshops', assuming a six months lag between plans passed and work done. In 1935, when the census classification of building work is most reliable, the present estimate agrees closely with the Redfern estimate; but in 1930 our figure is £9m. higher. For 1924 only an approximate estimate of industrial building can be derived from the census returns, but a figure of roughly £14m. is indicated. Redfern's estimate is £12m., and the present estimate is £23m. For non-censal years the indicator used by Redfern is not very reliable[2] but the present estimate could undoubtedly be substantially in error, and on this evidence is probably too high in most years. The present estimate is the sum of estimates for twenty-two separate industries but Redfern's method can only be applied at the level of all industrial building and so provides no guide to the accuracy of our series for individual industries.

For commercial buildings the same basic method was used by Redfern though the base-year figure was taken only from the 1935 Census of Production. The extrapolation was made by reference to the value of plans approved for 'Shops, offices, warehouses and other business premises'. In 1935 our estimate is some £6m. lower than Redfern's census estimate and this is not unreasonable in view of the probable underestimate for

shops and the omission of office building from our series. In most other years, however, the discrepancy is much larger, and it is particularly wide in 1936-8.

It is difficult to establish conclusively which is the more reliable series. The present series is composed partly of estimates for shops, hotels and restaurants, and theatres, cinemas, etc., and partly of estimates for buildings owned by firms classified to Wholesale distribution. The former were derived as a proportion of the value of all new work on buildings (as estimated in chapter 4); the earlier years are probably fairly reliable, since the omission of offices might be roughly balanced by a possible overstatement in the estimate of all work done, in the 'thirties, however, the present estimate is probably too low because of the understatement in the estimate for all new work. The estimates for the second component, buildings owned by wholesale distribution firms, are very weak. They are based on an extremely small sample of accounts and show large (and *prima facie* implausible) fluctuations in 1930 and 1934-8 (see Table 10.10, p. 184).

On the other hand we have already seen that the indicator used by Redfern is very unreliable.[3] Probably

---

[1] On the one hand our estimate for industrial building will be overstated to the extent that it includes shops or warehouses owned by firms classified to manufacturing, and on the other hand it will be understated to the extent that it excludes factories owned by firms classified to other sectors. It is thought that the net effect of *these* errors is that it is understated. (See chapter 8, p. 101). Our estimate for commercial building is understated because of the exclusion of office building and the absence of any compensating errors when taken alone. (See chapter 10, p. 186.)

[2] For a discussion of the defects in this indicator see [**142**] B. Weber and J. Parry Lewis, 'New Industrial Building in Great Britain, 1923-38', *Scottish Journal of Political Economy*, vol. VIII (1961). Their final verdict is that the series is: 'a somewhat hazardous estimate of costs of intended new building in a non-representative sample of towns' (p. 63). See also the following footnote.

[3] Cf. p. 213 above. As an instructive illustration of the magnitude of the errors which can arise in using the plans approved as indicators it is perhaps worth recording that we were not initially aware that Redfern had assumed a lag of six months between plans passed and work done, and we tried to reproduce his extrapolation for 1936-8 assuming first, no lag, and second, a lag of one year. The results obtained, starting in each case from £34m. in 1935, are (£m.):

	No lag	Lagged six months	Lagged one year
1936	37	43	53
1937	44	50	59
1938	40	52	69

When one considers that the actual lag will have varied from year to year, (as demonstrated for residential building by [**89**] I. Bowen, *Oxford Economic Papers*, No. 3 (1940), pp. 112-15); and that only a varying proportion of the plans approved would actually be carried out; and adds further that the classification by type of building was never precisely defined; that the values placed by the borough surveyors on buildings for which plans were approved were estimates and were not based on actual costs—the reservations expressed about the estimates made for dwellings would apply *a fortiori* to non-residential buildings; and finally, that the sample of plans was unrepresentative (since it excluded the London County Council area) and covered only about a fifth of all commercial building done (for industrial building the proportion was about one-third), it is clear why one cannot have much confidence in the use of this series for the purpose of extrapolating figures of work done.

the best conclusion, therefore, is that our estimates may be too low in most years but that the extent of the deficiency cannot be gauged from Redfern's series.

The last component, shown in Figure 8 (a), is 'other buildings and works' where the agreement between the two estimates is very good. However, the main components of this series are expenditure by local authorities and other public or semi-public enterprises such as the railways and electricity undertakings, and as both our estimates and Redfern's for these items are to a very large extent extracted from the same published accounts the agreement is to be expected.

We turn next to plant, ships and vehicles, etc., and consider first the three categories of vehicles shown in Figure 9. For road goods vehicles Redfern's estimates are consistently some 40% higher than ours. From 1927 the same series of new registrations was used in both estimates and any differences are due to the different average values by which the registrations have been multiplied.

Redfern's estimates were originally made at 1948 prices using 1948 replacement costs for three categories of vehicles. It is likely that part of the discrepancy arises simply in the conversion to current prices in the inter-war years. The crucial step in Redfern's price index is the link between 1948 and 1935 and this was assumed to be the same as that derived for buses and trolley buses from Census of Production average ex-factory values. Apart from this source of error, however, a comparison of Redfern's 1948 replacement costs[1] with the average ex-factory values shown by the 1948 Census of Production suggests that the former may be too high. The comparison is not exact because the categories used by Redfern do not correspond with those given in the Census, but the following figures give some indication of the divergence in 1948:

Average values in £s.

Unladen weight	Redfern (Retail)	Census of Production (ex-factory)
Not over 1½ tons	410	
Over 1½ but not over 4 tons	875	
Not over 3 tons		318

Even if an addition of 25% to cover the distributive margin is made to the Census figure for all goods vehicles not over 3 tons unladen weight it would still be lower than Redfern's figure for vehicles not over 1½ tons. The average values used in the present study are based on Glover's[2] estimates. These were obtained by a detailed examination of retail selling prices in each year, weighed according to the number of new registrations each year

in five categories (unladen weight groups) of goods vehicles, and within these categories a weighted mean of the prices collected was obtained on the basis of the estimated share of the market in each category enjoyed by each manufacturer. They are thus based on far more direct and more comprehensive evidence and are almost certainly more reliable.

For buses etc. Redfern is higher than the present estimates but by a variable amount. The discrepancy is large in 1927–30 but thereafter declines rapidly and is negligible after 1932. A minor cause of discrepancy is that taxis are included in the present estimates but not in Redfern's. For buses and trolley buses the same series of new registrations is used from 1927 in both estimates and the primary cause of the discrepancy in the earlier years is thus the different average values used. Redfern's estimates were originally made at 1948 prices, a link was established between 1948, 1937 and 1935, on the basis of Census of Production average ex-factory values in these years, and his inter-war average value index was then obtained by extrapolating the 1935 and 1937 figures by reference to an index of retail prices for all commercial vehicles. The present estimates are valued at the retail selling prices collected by Glover for commercial passenger vehicles and, for the reasons given above for goods vehicles, are almost certainly more reliable.

For passenger cars Redfern assumed that gross investment in cars at constant prices was equal to half the gross investment in road goods vehicles, and this implies that it was $\frac{1}{5}$ or less of the value of all cars newly registered. The present estimate was obtained by valuing all cars newly registered and assuming that business users acquired a constant 30% of this. Both assumptions are only guesses, and there is no means of choosing between them. Redfern's estimates are consistently below ours and the discrepancy is very slightly greater than Figure 9 shows since his series is intended to include taxis, whereas in the present estimate taxis are included with buses in road passenger transport.

The next comparison is between the two estimates for ships. The trends in the two series are in fairly close agreement, but this is largely explained by the fact that both estimates were made by multiplying data on tonnage built by estimated average costs per ton, and although the tonnage series are taken from different sources and differ in their timing[3] they are based on

---

[1] [**132**] Redfern, p. 168.

[2] [**111**] Glover, appendix IV.

[3] Redfern's estimates are based on Lloyds Register's figures of the tonnage of merchant vessels *launched* for home registration; the present estimates are based on the new tonnage registered (i.e. *completed*) shown in [**16**] Board of Trade, *Annual Statement of Navigation and Shipping of the United Kingdom*.

substantially similar and very reliable material. The level of capital formation is, however, generally higher in the present estimates, by amounts which are small in absolute terms but large relative to the level of the series. The present estimates of average export values per ton are some 30% above the values obtained by conversion of Redfern's average 1948 replacement costs to current inter-war prices. The conversion is very uncertain and could itself be a major source of the discrepancy.[1] The present comparison does, however, tend to confirm some evidence from the Census of Production that the average values used in the present estimates may be too high.[2]

The final comparison to be made is of the series for plant and machinery, etc. Redfern's estimates were obtained partly by extrapolation of a figure obtained from the 1948 Census of Production returns covering plant and equipment for agriculture, mining, and manufacturing, distribution and other services; and partly from published accounts for the public utilities. The former component accounts for slightly more than half the total. The present estimates were derived partly from samples of accounts and Inland Revenue data on wear and tear allowance and partly from the same published accounts for the public utilities. It is important to recall that it is a residual series, since the estimates derived from samples of accounts and Inland Revenue data included an unidentified amount of expenditure on vehicles, and the separate estimates (shown in Figure 9 (c) and (d)) for vehicles, which have to be deducted to obtain the residual, were derived from other sources and must be expected to differ from the unknown expenditure actually included. This danger applies particularly to our estimate of passenger cars for business use.

The independent element in both estimates, and perhaps particularly in ours, is somewhat uncertain and in view of this the measure of agreement revealed by Figure 9 (e) is not unsatisfactory. Disregarding sign, the difference between the two series averages £8m., or 7% of the present estimate, and in no year is the discrepancy more than 13%. The sign of the discrepancy fluctuates a good deal but on average the present estimate is very slightly higher.

We can sum up this detailed comparison with Redfern's estimates as follows:

(i) The estimates for railway rolling stock and 'other buildings and works' agree well, but this is largely because they are derived from the same or similar sources.

(ii) For road goods vehicles and road passenger vehicles the estimates are largely based on the same series of new registrations but are valued at different prices. The present estimates are lower and are likely to be more reliable. For passenger cars owned for business use both estimates are uncertain.

(iii) The estimates for ships are based on similar tonnage data and differ because of differences in the average values by which the tonnage was multiplied. The present estimates are higher by some 30%, and are probably too high.

(iv) The present estimate for dwellings is on average some 4·5% lower than Redfern's and is likely to be more accurate. It is, if anything, still slightly on the high side.

(v) There are significant differences in the estimates for industrial and commercial buildings. There is some indication that our estimates are in general too high for the former and too low for the latter, with the understatement probably slightly greater than the overstatement so that taken together they are on balance probably a little too low in most years. There are, however, considerable defects in the indicators used by Redfern to extrapolate his census benchmarks, so that his series cannot be used to gauge the extent of the errors in our series.

(vi) Finally for plant and machinery, etc., where the estimates are only partly derived from independent sources, there is broad agreement as to the trend of investment but significant differences in individual years and there is perhaps a slight presumption in favour of Redfern's series.

14.3 THE *BLUE BOOK* ESTIMATES OF GROSS AND NET FIXED CAPITAL FORMATION IN 1938

The estimates by Redfern which we have just considered omitted certain classes of assets, but for 1938 Redfern also made 'very rough estimates' of the omitted assets and of legal fees, stamp duties, etc. For this year, therefore, a more complete estimate of gross fixed capital formation was available, and this was taken over by the Central Statistical Office with slight adjustments in classification; and published in the *Blue Book*

---

[1] Redfern's price index for ships covers only 1938 and 1947–53. The extrapolation from 1938 back to 1924 necessary for purposes of comparison was based on the index used in the present estimates. The crucial step, however, is the link between 1938 and 1948, which Redfern based principally on Fairplay's index for the cost of a 9,500 d.w.t. motor cargo ship ([**132**] Redfern, p. 171). This index of the cost of a standard ship will not make allowance for changes between 1938 and 1948 in the type and quality of the ships built.

[2] See p. 248 below.

TABLE 14.30. COMPARISON WITH THE BLUE BOOK ESTIMATES OF GROSS FIXED CAPITAL FORMATION IN 1938

(Current Prices. £m.)

	Blue Book estimates (1)		Present estimates (2)	
Agriculture, forestry and fishing	15		5	
Mining and quarrying (a)	8		10	
Electricity, gas and water:				
Electricity	40		43	
Gas	8		11	
Water	10	58	10	64
Manufacturing and Distribution and other services:				
Industrial building (b)	23		31	
Commercial building (c)	52		25	
Plant and Machinery etc. (d)	104		96	
Vehicles (e)	30	209	28	180
Transport and communication:				
Railways—way and works	11		12	
Rolling stock, plant, etc. (a)	16		12	
Road passenger transport	15		15	
Shipping	20		25	
Harbours, docks and canals	2		2	
Air transport	1		1	
Postal and telephone communication	27	92	25	92
Dwellings		180		169
Social services:				
Education	24		16	
Health	12	36	11	27
Public Services:				
Roads	15		17	
Sewerage, etc.	29	44	28	45
Legal fees, etc. (f)		14		—
Total		656		592

Source

(1) The main classification and estimates are taken from [56] *National Income and Expenditure*, 1956, Table 48. Additional details are from Table 46, and from [132] Redfern, Tables 1, 2 and 9.

(2) The classification of the estimates in Chapters 5–12 below has been adjusted as indicated in the following notes in order to conform as far as possible with the *Blue Book* estimates:

  (a) Private wagons (£1m.) transferred from Mining and quarrying to Railways.

  (b) The estimate in Table 8.00 of buildings owned by firms classified to Manufacturing. (The *Blue Book* figure is for specific industrial buildings only.)

  (c) The estimate in Table 10.00 of shops, hotels and theatres, etc., plus buildings owned by firms classified to Wholesale Distribution. (The *Blue Book* figure is for specific commercial buildings only.)

  (d) The estimates in Tables 8.00 and 10.00 for plant, machinery, vehicles, etc. owned by firms classified to Manufacturing and to Distribution and other services, less the estimate for vehicles (other than those owned by road hauliers) described in note (e).

  (e) Vehicles owned by road hauliers (£3m.) plus 90% of the estimates in Table 9.22 of the remaining road goods vehicles and of the passenger cars owned for business use.

  (f) In the present estimate Legal fees, etc. are included in the estimates for each sector.

on *National Income and Expenditure*.[1] This is the only inter-war year for which there is an official estimate. Redfern also made estimates of depreciation and of net fixed capital formation for 1938 and these too were adopted, with minor modifications, as the *Blue Book* estimates.

We shall first compare our estimate of gross fixed capital formation at current prices in 1938 with the corresponding *Blue Book* estimate, and then consider the estimates of depreciation and net capital formation. The two gross estimates are set out in some detail in Table 14.30, classified by sector but with some additional detail by type of asset. The classification follows that adopted in the *Blue Book* (Table 48) and the present estimates from the ownership side have been rearranged to correspond as closely as possible with this. Some slight differences remain but do not affect the broad comparison and will be noted as we consider the individual items. The one significant difference is in the treatment of legal fees and stamp duties. These are shown as a separate item in the *Blue Book*,[2] whereas in the present estimates they are assumed to be included in the estimates for individual items and cannot generally be identified. (Architects' and other professional fees are, however, allocated by sector in the *Blue Book* estimates,[3] as they are in the present estimates.)

The *Blue Book* total of £656m. is £64m., or just under 11%, higher than our estimate.[4] This discrepancy arises largely on items accounting in 1938 for less than one-fifth of the total. There is also a difference of £11m. (6.5%) in the estimates for dwellings. For the remaining items, totalling some £346m. the two estimates are in very close agreement.[5] It should,

---

[1] The last published detailed estimates for 1938 were given in [56] *National Income and Expenditure, 1956* (1957). All references in this section to the 'Blue Book estimates' are to the figures in this edition, and to the underlying estimates by Redfern, which are available in more detail. I am greatly indebted to the Central Statistical Office for details of the adjustments made by them to the published Redfern estimates, and for other information about the Redfern and *Blue Book* estimates referred to in this chapter.

[2] For dwellings, however, the point made in footnote (4), p. 238 is equally applicable to the *Blue Book* estimates.

[3] See [132] Redfern, p. 179.

[4] The present estimate is reduced by a deduction for the proceeds of assets scrapped or sold abroad, amounting to £6m. On the other hand it includes £6m. for expenditure on renewals of railway way and works and of roads. Our treatment differs from that in the *Blue Book* on both these points, but on balance there is no adjustment required in the totals for purpose of comparison.

[5] For Mining and quarrying; Electricity, gas and water; machinery and vehicles for Manufacturing and distribution; Transport and communication; Health; and Public services the Blue Book estimate totals £348m. and the present total is £346m. For only one of the components (as classified in Table 14.30) making up these totals does the difference between the estimates exceed £5m.: this is the discrepancy of £8m. (less than 10%) in the estimates for plant and machinery in Manufacturing and distribution. But as the estimates for these assets were derived from completely different sources and as the scope for error in this sector is considerable, this divergence is not considered unsatisfactory.

however, be noted that the agreement claimed for vehicles in Manufacturing and distribution rests in part on the compensating differences in the constituent estimates for road goods vehicles and passenger cars owned by business users. (Cf. Figure 9, p. 240 above).

If we now turn to the items (other than dwellings) on which there are substantial discrepancies in the table we find four items on which the *Blue Book* estimate is higher than ours, to a total of £59m., partly offset by one item where the present estimate is higher by £8m. We consider first the items where the *Blue Book* is higher.

First, there is £14m. shown for legal fees, stamp duties, etc., in the *Blue Book*, whereas there is nothing shown separately for this item in the present estimates. However, as already noted, an allowance for this charge is assumed to be included in the present estimates for dwellings and in the estimates for other assets derived from data on expenditure. There is, therefore, no adjustment required. On the other hand there may be some duplication in the *Blue Book* estimate if, as is suggested, legal fees and stamp duties are implicitly included in the estimate for dwellings.

The second, and by far the largest, discrepancy is in the estimates for commercial buildings, where the *Blue Book* figure of £52m. is more than double our £25m. We have seen above (p. 241) that our estimates for commercial buildings are probably too low but that there is considerable uncertainty about the extrapolation of Redfern's census benchmark for 1935 (when the difference between the two series was only £6m.). Taking everything into account, therefore, an addition of £15m. to our estimate for 1938 might be reasonable.[1]

The third discrepancy is in the estimates for Agriculture, forestry and fishing, where the *Blue Book* shows £15m., against the present estimate of £5m.[2] Our estimate excludes expenditure on farm works and improvements but the amount allowed for this in the *Blue Book* is small, and their estimate for farm buildings seems too high. The *Blue Book* estimate for farm vehicles includes an allowance for passenger cars used by farmers, whereas we have not allocated any part of the estimated expenditure on cars for business use to this sector; but the *Blue Book* estimate seems to be high. On balance, we would not feel disposed to add more than about £3m. to our present estimate for this sector.

Finally, there is the discrepancy in the estimates for Education where the *Blue Book* estimate of £24m. exceeds the present estimate by £8m. This is more than accounted for by the £9m. included for capital expenditure on private education. This was omitted from the present estimates (for lack of reliable annual data), but

the evidence considered in chapter 11 (p. 201 above) suggests that the value of this expenditure in 1938 is unlikely to have exceeded £4m.

The one item where the present estimate is significantly the larger in 1938, as it is in most other years from 1924, is industrial building. Our estimate of £31m. exceeds Redfern's by £8m.[3] The discussion on p. 241 above emphasized the unreliability of the indicator used by Redfern to extrapolate his census year benchmarks, but noted that the present estimates are also poor; and a reduction of some £5m. might perhaps be made.

The net outcome, therefore, is that our figure of £592m. should perhaps be raised by roughly £17m. to obtain the best estimate for 1938, say £610m. A margin of error of at least ±£25m. should be attached to this estimate.

We next consider depreciation (capital consumption). The *Blue Book* estimates, supplemented by some additional details from Redfern, are set out in Table 14.31 for comparison with our estimates. The classification is by type of asset. Our total is larger by £16m. or less than 5%, and agreement for the component items is also on the whole good.

The treatment of legal fees, stamp duties, etc., in the *Blue Book* estimates again differs from ours. In the former, the whole of the amount included in gross capital formation each year is written off in the same year. In the present estimates it is capitalized together with other capital expenditure and written off over the life of the assets with which it is included; the amount included in our estimates of depreciation for 1938 cannot be shown separately.

For the industrial and commercial buildings our higher charge for depreciation is a reflection of the higher estimates obtained for the gross stock of capital in 1938 (see Table 14.70, p. 254 below), only partly offset by the fact that we have assumed a longer length of life for the purpose of estimating depreciation: 60

---

[1] The present estimate for Wholesale distribution is particularly low in 1938. The adjustment to commercial buildings would not need to be as large as £15m. in other years.

[2] The approximate asset composition of the estimates is:

	Blue Book (£m.)	Present Estimate (£m.)
Agricultural plant, machinery and tractors	6	3·9
Farm Buildings and works	5	0·4*
Farm vehicles	3	0·3
Fishing vessels	1	0·2
	15	4·8

* Farm buildings only.

[3] The excess would be £10m. if the proceeds of buildings sold (by the cotton industry) were added back.

years for industrial building compared with the life of 50 years assumed by Redfern, and 85 years[1] for commercial buildings compared with 75 years. For plant and machinery the present estimate is again slightly higher. The implicit weighted average length of life assumed is roughly the same in each case (about 30 years) and our higher charge for depreciation again reflects our higher estimate for the gross stock of plant and machinery. As we shall see below (p. 255) there is some reason to believe that Redfern's estimates of the capital stock are too low, so that we have some support for our higher estimates of depreciation for these items.

£16m., the difference in the estimates of net fixed capital formation (columns (3) and (4) of Table 14.31) is £80m., or 37% of our lower estimate of £217m.

Of this £34m. is the difference in the estimates for industrial and commercial buildings where from the considerations noted above it seems that the present net estimate is on the whole nearer the mark, even though it is probably some £10m. too low. On road vehicles there is a difference of £7m., and this is more than accounted for by the fact that the *Blue Book* gross estimate is £10m. higher and, as suggested on p. 242 above, is probably overstated. The present estimate for

TABLE 14.31   COMPARISON WITH BLUE BOOK ESTIMATES OF DEPRECIATION AND NET FIXED CAPITAL FORMATION IN 1938

(Current prices. £m.)

	Depreciation		Net Fixed Capital Formation	
	Blue Book estimates	Present estimates	*Blue Book* estimates	Present estimates
	(1)	(2)	(3)	(4)
Vehicles	43	40	7	4
Rolling stock, ships and aircraft	26	28	11	9
Plant and machinery	119	129	62	53
Dwellings	54	56	126	113
Industrial and commercial buildings	34	49	41	7
Other buildings and works	69	73	50	31
Legal fees, stamp duties, etc.	14	—	—	—
Total	359	375	297	217

Source
(1) and (3) [**56**] *National Income and Expenditure*, 1956, Tables 54 and 46; and [**132**] Redfern, Tables 2 and 9.

For the four remaining items: vehicles, rolling stock, ships and aircraft; dwellings; and 'other buildings and works' the estimates agree very well, though the agreement on the latter item (covering some twenty components) is due in part to the fact that there are a few small components where the present estimate is slightly lower balanced by one large component where it is higher. This large component is the estimate for local authority non-trading assets, which is based on the statutory loan repayments, implying a life of 33 years for most services,[2] against the 75 years assumed by the *Blue Book*. The longer life is more consistent with the estimates in other sectors, and the present estimate for depreciation might perhaps be reduced by some £10m., giving a best estimate of say £365m., with a margin of error of perhaps ±£20m.

As the present gross estimate was lower by £64m., and the present estimate of depreciation higher by

plant and machinery, etc., is lower by £9m. and this is due to the fact that our estimates of depreciation are higher, but they are probably more reliable. Finally, there is a difference of £19m. on other buildings and works, where the two main reasons for the difference are the extra £8m. for private educational building in the *Blue Book* gross estimate; and the higher present estimate for depreciation of local authority non-trading services.

Taking everything into account, therefore, the best estimate of net fixed capital formation in 1938 might be obtained by raising the present estimate by some £27m., making say £245m. The margin of error for this best estimate is perhaps ±£25m.

---

[1] This is the weighted average of the life of 60 years assumed for buildings owned by Wholesale distribution and of 100 years assumed for shops, hotels and theatres, etc.

[2] See chapter 11, p. 209.

TABLE 14.40 COMPARISON WITH ESTIMATES BY COLIN CLARK AND PHELPS BROWN AND WEBER OF GROSS FIXED CAPITAL FORMATION ESTIMATED FROM THE SUPPLY SIDE, 1924, 1930 AND 1935 (£M.)

		1924			1930			1935	
		Colin Clark	Phelps Brown	Present Estimate	Colin Clark	Phelps Brown	Present Estimate	Phelps Brown	Present Estimate
		(1)	(2)	(3)	(4)	(5)	(6)	(7)	(8)
A.	*Building and contracting, including repairs and maintenance*								
1	Total work done	346	339	355	402	395	399	428	426
2	*less* Electrical contracting and railway way and works	58	55	52	62	59	61	53	55
3	(1–2)	288	284	303	340	336	338	375	371
4	*less* Repairs and maintenance	124	110	117	153	120	127	135	144
B.	*New construction*								
5	Building and contracting (3–4)	164	174	186	187	216	211	240	227
6	Mechanical engineering	62	64	57	57	78	62	96	74
7	Electrical engineering and contracting	43	38	36	55	50	51	53	51
8	Shipbuilding	31	31	35	22	23	30	12	17
9	Commercial vehicles	6	6	24	10	10	29	10	27
10	Railway rolling stock and way and works	27	25	18	17	17	13	16	13
11	Total new construction	333	338	356	348	394	396	427	409

Source

Columns: (1) and (4) **[103]** Colin Clark, *National Income and Outlay*, pp. 170–8.

(2), (5) and (7) **[129]** Phelps Brown and Weber, p. 283.

(3), (6) and (8). Based on Tables 4.22 and 4.30. The following items are omitted from the Clark and Phelps Brown estimates, but included in our estimates from the supply side:

	£m.		
	1924	1930	1935
Total as above	356	396	409
Passenger cars owned for business use	15	14	17
Hotel furniture and fittings	2	2	2
Mine works and buildings	6	7	2
Proceeds of (used) ships and vehicles sold or scrapped	−9	−20	−14
Legal and professional fees, etc.	20	19	25
Renewals for roads and railway way and works	6	7	5
Total as in Table 13.60	396	425	446

14.4 PHELPS BROWN AND WEBER AND COLIN CLARK: ESTIMATES EXTRACTED FROM THE CENSUS OF PRODUCTION, 1924, 1930 AND 1935

Estimates of gross fixed capital formation derived from the Censuses of Production were published in 1937 by Colin Clark[1] for the census years 1924 and 1930; and in 1953 by Professor E. H. Phelps Brown and B. Weber[2] for the two earlier years and for 1935. These estimates are shown in Table 14.40 together with the comparable estimates made from the 'supply side' in Tables 4.22 and 4.30, pp. 60 and 64 above.

One substantial difference which must be noted is that the Clark and Phelps Brown estimates were con-

fined to data extracted from the Census returns. The present estimates include additional items (shown separately in Table 14.40) to a net total of approximately £40m. in 1924 and 1935 and £30m. in 1930. This consists of adjustments for items not covered by, or not separately identified in, the census returns, and includes additions for passenger cars acquired for business use, for legal and professional fees, stamp duties, etc., and for renewals expenditure on railway

---

[1] **[103]** Clark, (London, 1937), chapter VIII. His estimates for 1924 are more fully described in **[101]** *Investment in Fixed Capital in Great Britain*, London and Cambridge Economic Service, Special Memorandum No. 38, September 1934.

[2] **[129]** E. H. Phelps Brown and B. Weber. 'Accumulation, Productivity and Distribution in the British Economy, 1870–1938', *Economic Journal*, vol. LXIII (1953).

way and works and roads; partly offset by a deduction for the proceeds of ships and vehicles scrapped or sold. With the possible exception of the renewals expenditure it seems clear that the adjustments for these items are, in principle, correct.

For new construction of building and contracting work the estimates are in reasonably good agreement, though our figure for 1924 is somewhat higher than the others, and for 1935 is slightly lower. In the former case the present figure is probably too high;[1] in 1935 the difference is due largely to a discrepancy in the figure shown for repairs and maintenance where there is considerable scope for divergence in the estimate for contracting repair work. For electrical engineering and contracting agreement between the estimates is good in each year,[2] but for mechanical engineering the Phelps Brown estimates are higher than ours by £7m. in 1924, £16m. in 1930 and £22m. in 1935. There does not appear to be any specific reason for the discrepancy but all the estimates contain a good deal of rough estimation and judgment (for example, in the decision on which items should be classified as capital goods, or the allowances necessary to avoid duplication), and there is ample scope for divergence.

For shipbuilding, commercial vehicles and railway rolling stock the present estimates in Table 14.40 were not obtained from the censuses but from other sources which were regarded as more reliable and comprehensive,[3] and the table discloses some significant differences between our estimates for these assets and those derived from the censuses by Clark and Phelps Brown.

The present estimates for shipbuilding are consistently higher than those derived from the census. An initial cause of discrepancy is that the present estimates relate to the value of ships completed whereas the two other estimates are of work done. In 1935 the change in work in progress was positive: it is given in the Census of Production returns as £4m. and adjustment for this would increase the discrepancy. Work in progress was probably also positive in 1924, but is likely to have been negative in 1930 when the tonnage completed fell by more than half between 1930 and 1931. A more substantial factor is the discrepancy between the average values of completed tonnage given in the Census returns and the average export values used in the present estimates.

It is possible that some small part of the discrepancy may be due to the fact that some of the completed ships shown in the Census returns may not include machinery. Even if allowance is made for this, however, it does seem that the average values based on the ships exported are too high.

	Exports		Census of Production*	
	Tonnage exported ('000 gross tons)	Average value (£ per ton)	Tonnage completed ('000 gross tons)	Average value (£ per ton)
1924	151	34·6	288	20·3
1930	642	31·0	449	26·1
1935	62	33·6	512	25·8

* Based on the following data for steam and motor vessels: 1924 and 1930: Vessels wholly constructed in the year of return. 1935: Vessels wholly constructed in 1935 plus those completed but not wholly constructed in 1935.

For commercial vehicles (lorries, buses and taxis, etc.) the discrepancies are extremely large, the present estimates being two or three times higher in each year than those derived from the census returns by Phelps Brown and Weber and by Colin Clark. There appear to be two major reasons for this. First, the output recorded in the census is valued at ex-factory prices and the other estimates do not seem to include any allowance for distributive margins, which in the case of vehicles would be substantial.[4] The present estimates are valued (correctly, in principle) at retail selling prices.

The second and more important reason is that both Clark and Phelps Brown appear to have based their estimates on the census data for complete *vehicles* only, assuming that all complete *chassis* (and motor bodies) produced are duplicated in this data. In fact, however, a substantial number of chassis are not duplicated. It was, and still is, the practice for motor bodies to be fitted to chassis which were supplied by manufacturers; the chassis remained the property of the manufacturer or of the bus company or other customer to whose order the vehicle was being fitted, while the body-builder in effect worked on commission. This is the main but not the only source of error involved in the assumption that *all* chassis returned are duplicated in the census statistics for complete vehicles. The extent of the error can be roughly gauged from the large discrepancy between the number of complete commercial vehicles available for the home market as shown by the census returns (adjusted for exports) and the number of new registrations. (Compare rows A and B.3 of the table on p. 249).[5]

---

[1] See chapter 4, p. 58.

[2] Note that the present estimates for telegraph and telephone plant and electricity supply mains included under this heading were not derived from the census returns but from other sources. See chapter 4, p. 63.

[3] See chapter 4, p. 63.

[4] For passenger cars, the margin has been estimated at 20% of the ex-factory price in 1938. See [**115**] J. B. Jefferys, *The Distribution of Consumer Goods* (Cambridge, 1950), p. 352. For commercial vehicles it would perhaps be a little less than this.

[5] There are differences in the classification and timing of the two series but these can account for only a small part of the discrepancy.

It is clear from the table that a large *number* of complete chassis have to be taken into account in order to reconcile the census data and the new registrations; and since the chassis not duplicated were mainly for goods and passenger vehicles in the heavier categories, the proportionate omission is appreciably greater in terms of *value*. There is no doubt, therefore, that the estimates

14.5 JEFFERYS AND WALTERS' ESTIMATES OF GROSS AND NET FIXED CAPITAL FORMATION, 1924–1938

Estimates of gross fixed capital formation and of depreciation were published by J. B. Jefferys and D. Walters[2] in 1955, covering the years 1924–38 as part of

	Commercial vehicles* (Number of units in thousands)			
	1930	1934	1935	1937
A. New registrations	61·4	73·3	73·9	84·7
B. Available supply				
Complete vehicles:				
1. Output for sale	40·3	46·8	50·4	59·2
2. *less* exports	3·5	2·4	2·3	3·8
3. Supply to home market (1–2)	36·8	44·4	48·1	55·4
Complete chassis:				
4. Output for sale	28·5	39·7	41·5	55·1
5. *less* purchases by the vehicle trade	—†	—†	17·7	20·4
6. exports	3·1	11·4	11·4	16·6
7. Supply to home market (4–5–6)	25·4	28·3	12·4	18·1
8. Total domestic supply to home market (3+7)	62·2	72·7	60·5	73·5
9. *Add* Retained imports	1·5	1·6	1·8	4·6
10. Total available supply (8+9)	63·7	74·3	62·3	78·1

* Excluding taxis and tractors.   † Not stated separately.

Source A

   [161] *The Motor Industry of Great Britain*, 1954.

Source B

   [37] *Final Report on the Census of Production, 1948*, vol. II, Trade I, Table 8; [36] *Final Report on the Fifth Census of Production and Import Duties Act Inquiry, 1935*, part II; and [35] *Final Report on the Fourth Census of Production, 1930*, part II.

by Clark and by Phelps Brown and Weber are very much too low.

To sum up this comparison of the supply side estimates it may be said that taken in total there is a fairly good measure of agreement. With the exception of Clark's very low figure for 1930 no estimate is more than 5% greater or smaller than the mean estimate for that year. This agreement must be qualified in three respects. First, it is in part the outcome of compensating and uncorrelated differences in the components. Second, the comparison is necessarily confined to those items which are covered by all the estimates, and we have noted that the other estimates are incomplete. Third, any errors in the census returns[1] would be equally reflected in all three estimates.

a longer series. For 1938 they adopted the then latest estimates of the Central Statistical Office.[3] For 1924–37 their estimates were based, with one adjustment, on the series published by Phelps Brown and Weber. From their census year estimates of new construction Phelps Brown and Weber had deducted non-revenue-yielding construction and then interpolated annual values in each of six categories of 'new revenue-yielding construction'.[4] They also made annual estimates of depreciation, described below. The adjustment made by Jefferys and Walters was to replace the non-revenue-yielding construction by including an annual

---

[1] Cf. chapter 13, p. 231 above.

[2] [117] J. B. Jefferys and D. Walters (London, 1955), pp. 34–7.

[3] [4] *Annual Abstract of Statistics*, No. 89, 1952, Table 283.

[4] [129] Phelps Brown and Weber, pp. 283–4.

estimate of gross fixed capital formation by Central and Local Government non-trading services, based on unpublished estimates by J. E. G. Utting.[1] A corresponding addition from the same source was made to the Phelps Brown estimates of depreciation.

The (adjusted) estimates of gross fixed capital formation and depreciation are set out, together with the present estimates from the ownership side, in Table 14.50. The comparison is, in a sense, a further comparison of estimates from the 'supply side' and the 'ownership side', with the advantage that the two

only 4% of the present estimate, and it exceeds 5% in only three years: 1924, 1925 and 1934.

When we turn to compare the two estimates of depreciation given in Table 14.50 we find a startling discrepancy in both level and trend. The estimates by Jefferys and Walters are on average some £125 m. (over 40%) lower than our estimates each year, but they rise much more steeply over the period so that the discrepancy falls from £167 m. in 1924 to £110 m. in 1938.

TABLE 14.50   COMPARISON WITH JEFFERYS' AND WALTERS' ESTIMATES OF GROSS FIXED CAPITAL FORMATION AND DEPRECIATION, 1924–38
(Current Prices. £m.)

	Gross Fixed Capital Formation			Depreciation		
	Jefferys and Walters	Present estimate	Percentage (1) to (2)	Jefferys and Walters	Present estimate	Percentage (4) to (5)
	(1)	(2)	(3)	(4)	(5)	(6)
1924	347	374	93	120	287	42
1925	372	420	89	127	287	44
1926	388	401	97	133	287	46
1927	432	426	101	149	283	53
1928	414	420	99	156	288	54
1929	419	442	95	164	297	55
1930	414	435	95	166	296	56
1931	394	408	97	162	295	55
1932	343	347	99	156	288	54
1933	343	357	96	166	287	58
1934	384	427	90	186	287	65
1935	434	456	95	205	303	68
1936	515	517	100	235	322	73
1937	594	574	103	264	362	73
1938	600	592	101	265	375	71

Source

(1) and (4) [**117**] Jefferys and Walters, Table xv, p. 37.
(2) and (5) Table 13.00, p. 223.

series are independent to a greater extent than those considered in chapter 13, pp. 230–6. In the three census years the present estimates are higher by £27 m., £21 m. and £22 m., respectively, and this is largely explained by the differences between our estimates from the supply side and those of Phelps Brown and Weber already considered on pp. 247–9 above.[2]

In non-census years the sign and size of the discrepancy is irregular but the Jefferys and Walters' series rises relative to the present estimates in all except three years. The underlying interpolation made by Phelps Brown and Weber between the census estimates is probably less reliable than the similar exercise in chapter 4 above.[3] Despite this, there is still a very good measure of agreement between the two series. The average discrepancy (disregarding sign) is

In order to explain these differences in level and trend it is necessary to consider the four components which make up their total in each year: (i) the component based on the Schedule D allowances for wear and tear, to which we can add the constant £5 m. p.a.

---

[1] For the census years these estimates were slightly higher than the amounts excluded by Phelps Brown and Weber.

[2] The differences between the discrepancies in Table 14.40 and those given above are due to (*a*) the adjustment made to the Phelps Brown estimates by Jefferys and Walters: this reduces the discrepancy in each year; and (*b*) the difference between our estimates from the supply side in Table 14.40 and from the ownership side in Table 14.50: this reduces the discrepancy by £22 m. in 1924 but increases it by £10 m. in 1930 and in 1935.

[3] First the Phelps Brown interpolation and extrapolation did not make any use of the data for 1933, 1934 and 1937 in the Import Duties Act Inquiries; and second, when the present estimates were made, greatly improved information was available in [**99**] Agatha Chapman's series on numbers employed and wages and salaries paid.

included by Phelps Brown for equipment not covered by Schedule D; (ii) the annual estimate for revenue yielding buildings; (iii) the depreciation of Post Office telephones and telegraphs, based on the *Commercial Accounts*; and (iv) the amounts added by Jefferys and Walters for depreciation of public authority non-trading assets, based on loan repayments. The last two components agree well with the comparable series in the present estimates, though there are minor differences due mainly to the fact that both components are based on data representing historical costs, and only in the present estimates are these converted to current costs.

On components (i) and (ii), however, we find major differences, partly in estimation, and partly also in conceptual approach. We discuss first the estimate based on the Schedule D Allowances. The first point to make is that these allowances for wear and tear on plant and machinery, ships, vehicles and other equipment would not cover any of these assets owned by firms which were assessed on the renewals system, i.e. where the cost of any renewals in each year was allowed as a charge against profits *instead of* the wear and tear allowance. In the inter-war years this would apply to rolling stock and other plant owned by the railways, and to the plant and equipment of most gas and water undertakings and of a small number of other firms in trade and industry. The amount allowed for depreciation of these assets in the present estimates averages roughly £16m. p.a. When allowance is made for this and for the equipment owned by the Post Office and public authorities, the present estimates of depreciation at current prices for plant, ships, vehicles, etc., are *on average* only slightly above the amount estimated by Phelps Brown on the basis of the Schedule D allowances plus the constant £5m. p.a.

There are, however, substantial differences in trend which provide the major explanation for the much steeper increase shown by the Jefferys and Walters' estimates of depreciation. The difference arises primarily as a consequence of the Income Tax clause permitting firms making losses (or having an assessable profit lower than the allowance due) to carry forward their unclaimed wear and tear allowances to any later year; as any losses could themselves be carried forward first, the wear and tear allowance might not be claimed for several years after the year to which it actually related. The extent to which allowances were carried forward after the slump in the early 'thirties is not known, but it is likely to have been substantial and it seems probable, therefore, that it was mainly this factor which imparted the steep upward trend to the allowances and so to the Jefferys and Walters' estimates.

The second point is of very much more substance. It appears from the explanations given by Phelps Brown and Weber[1] that what they were attempting to estimate was not 'depreciation' as defined in the present study, but rather the 'replacement of scrapped equipment'. Thus they define Net (fixed) investment as equal to New construction less Replacement, and explain that they have 'modulated' the Schedule D allowances because they: 'show the amount of depreciation reckoned to be going on rather than the amount of actual replacement, which is likely to vary in sympathy with new construction'. In other words the estimates taken over by Jefferys and Walters were not intended as estimates of depreciation at all, but as estimates of what in the present study is described as the 'first cost value of assets scrapped or sold' measured at current prices.[2] Since, however, the basic assumption made by Phelps Brown and Weber for these assets was that depreciation and replacement would be about equal on average, this difference in intention does not, in principle, affect the validity of the Jefferys and Walters estimates of depreciation, though there would be inequalities (due to the imposed modulation) in the annual figures. When we turn to the other assets, however, this correspondence no longer holds[3] and the Phelps Brown figures become totally inadequate as measures of depreciation.

For their final component, revenue-yielding buildings, Phelps Brown and Weber described their series as 'annual estimates of depreciation of buildings (so far as not covered by repairs) taken very roughly at 0.25% of total value'.[4] As an estimate of the first cost value of

---

[1] [**129**] Phelps Brown and Weber, p. 284.

[2] The series for 'net fixed investment' obtained by deducting replacements from new construction thus corresponds neither with gross investment nor with net investment, as commonly defined. It is, however, precisely what is required to extrapolate an estimate of the gross stock of capital and it is just for this purpose that the estimate was made by Phelps Brown and Weber. It is not what was required by Jefferys and Walters for estimates of national product net of depreciation.

[3] Cf. chapter 3, pp. 50–1 above.

[4] [**129**] Phelps Brown and Weber, p. 284. The reasoning behind the phrase 'depreciation (so far as not covered by repairs)', and the explanation for why this definition was adopted for buildings but not for plant and equipment, seems to be the following: Phelps Brown and his colleagues were not interested in estimating depreciation as such but in obtaining a series for net investment as defined in the text above. They took as their benchmark the then current official estimates for 1938 (Cmd. 8203, April 1951) in which the gross series was defined so as to include all expenditure on the maintenance and repair of buildings and works, and with a correspondingly gross definition of depreciation. But as Phelps Brown and Weber's gross estimates consisted only of new construction, they assumed that all repairs to buildings and works should also be excluded from their estimate of depreciation: and thus, since they assumed depreciation and replacement to correspond on average, from their estimate of replacement. The assumption that the same absolute reduction should be made in the estimate of depreciation as in the estimate of gross investment was in fact erroneous, but it is admittedly easier to see this now than it was in 1951. (Cf. [**56**] Cmd. 8486, March 1952, where the narrower definition of gross investment was adopted for the first time.)

buildings replaced each year the resulting series is reasonably close to the present estimates of scrapping at current prices. As an estimate of depreciation as normally defined it implies a length of life for buildings of 400 years and is clearly unacceptable. This component accounts, on average, for some £77m. of the amount by which the Jefferys and Walters' estimates fall below ours.

Finally, it will be seen that the Jefferys and Walters' estimates contain no allowance for depreciation of civil engineering works other than those owned by public authorities. This accounts for a further £31m. of the average difference between the two estimates in Table 14.50.

To sum up, the Jefferys and Walters' estimate of 'depreciation' is a hybrid consisting of three components approximating to the required series (those based on the Schedule D allowances, public authority loan repayments and Post Office accounts) though calculated at historical and not current costs; and one component—for buildings—which is not in fact an estimate of depreciation but of scrapping, and falls short of our estimate of depreciation by an average of £77m. p.a. Furthermore, their estimate contains no allowance for depreciation of (a) plant and equipment owned by firms assessed on the renewals basis, which accounts for some £16m. p.a.; or (b) civil engineering works other than those owned by public authorities, a deficiency of some £31m. p.a. In total, therefore, it averages some £125m. less than the present estimates. The discrepancy has a downward trend mainly because the Schedule D allowances rise more steeply than actual wear and tear as a result of the carrying forward of the allowances in years during and after the slump when losses were incurred.

These discrepancies in the estimates of depreciation greatly outweigh the differences in the estimates of gross fixed capital formation. The Jefferys and Walters' estimates of net fixed capital formation are thus very substantially higher than the present estimates, the average excess over the period 1924–38 being £112m., or 82% of the present estimate.

14.6 BARNA'S ESTIMATES OF INVESTMENT IN STOCKS

Very approximate estimates of 'net investment in stocks' at current prices have been made for 1924–38 by Phelps Brown and Weber[1] on the assumption that it was equal to 40% of the first difference in national income. The same method was used by Jefferys and Walters[2] for 1924–37 to obtain a series at current prices described as the 'value of the physical increase in

stocks and work and progress'. In view of the method used no significance can be attached to these results.

A more direct attempt was published by T. Barna[3] in 1942, bringing together earlier work by Colin Clark[4] and A. Maisels.[5] We can first compare our estimate of the increase in value of stocks (excluding crops, livestock and growing timber) in 1924–38 with the comparable series given by Barna. These series are set out in columns (1) and (2) of Table 14.60. They have only a very limited significance for social accounting purposes but are the basic estimates obtained before adjustment for price changes and stock appreciation. As shown at the head of the table Barna's estimate of the end-1938 level of stocks (at book values) is appreciably higher than ours;[6] but it was derived on the same principles, i.e. by grossing-up the end-year book values in a sample of accounts.

The two series agree on the direction of the stock change in 11 out of the 15 years but differ widely in almost all years as to its magnitude. Barna's estimates of the change are generally very much greater and the discrepancy is particularly large in 1930 and 1931. Even if we exclude these years the average discrepancy disregarding its sign) is some £40m. which must be seen in relation to our estimate of an average change in stocks of about the same magnitude. The present estimates were based on a much larger sample of accounts, were built up in more detail for individual industries and were more carefully grossed-up, but the hazards of estimating the *change* in stocks are very great,[7] and neither set of estimates can be very reliable.

In columns (3) and (4) of Table 14.60 the two series are adjusted to the value of the physical increase in stocks at current prices,[8] the adjustment being equal to the estimates of stock appreciation shown in columns (5) and (6). These latter estimates are in general not too far apart. They agree as to the sign of the change in all but one year (1928) and the average size of the present adjustment (disregarding sign) differs from that estimated by Barna by roughly 20%. As Barna's adjustment for stock appreciation is generally larger, the agreement between the two estimates of the value

---

[1] [129] Phelps Brown and Weber, p. 284.

[2] [117] Jefferys and Walters, pp. 35–7. For 1938 they use the C.S.O. estimate discussed below, p. 253.

[3] [82] T. Barna, 'Valuation of Stocks and the National Income', *Economica*, New Series, vol. IX (1942), pp. 350–1.

[4] Colin Clark's estimates for 1924–31 were given in [102] *The National Income, 1924–1931* (London, 1932), pp. 141–3, and for 1932–34 in [103] *National Income and Outlay*, pp. 293–7.

[5] [121] Alfred Maisels, 'Consumption, Investment and National Expenditure in Wartime', *Economica*, New Series, vol. VIII (1941), p. 161.

[6] This is partly due to the apparent inclusion in Barna's series of stocks held by companies operating overseas. Cf. [102] Clark, p. 142.

[7] Cf. chapter 2, p. 32, note 5.

[8] See chapter 2, pp. 31–3 for an explanation of the adjustment made.

TABLE 14.60   COMPARISON WITH BARNA'S ESTIMATES OF INVESTMENT IN
STOCKS, 1924–38
(Current prices. £m.)

	Increase in Value of Stocks		Value of Physical Increase in Stocks		Stock Appreciation	
	Barna	Present estimate	Barna	Present estimate	(1)–(3) Barna	(2)–(4) Present estimate
	(1)	(2)	(3)	(4)	(5)	(6)
Book value of Stocks at end-1938	1743	1206				
1924	47	22	20	−18	27	40
1925	80	−9	258	130	−178	−139
1926	−37	−49	24	7	−61	−56
1927	−54	26	25	54	−79	−28
1928	25	−6	−13	12	38	−18
1929	−97	−28	30	52	−127	−80
1930	−325	−124	−98	89	−227	−213
1931	−186	−69	−97	−6	−89	−63
1932	−64	−50	−21	−16	−43	−34
1933	36	−11	−10	−56	46	45
1934	13	37	8	32	5	5
1935	35	27	−5	1	40	26
1936	142	91	46	−7	96	98
1937	200	127	70	61	130	66
1938	−51	−32	44	77	−95	−109

Source

(1) and (3): [82] Barna, p. 351.

(2) Annual change in row A 1, Table 3.60, p. 54.

(4) Table 3.60, row C 1.

Note. The above estimates exclude stocks on farms and standing timber.

of the physical increase is slightly better than that for the increase in value, but is still poor, particularly in 1925, 1930 and 1931. Excluding these years, the average size of the discrepancy (disregarding sign) is some £26 m. against an estimate of an average physical increase in stocks of £33 m.

Finally, we may note that for 1938 the Central Statistical Office[1] estimate of the increase in value of stocks at current prices is −£80 m., compared with our estimate of −£32 m.; and they estimate that there was no change in the value of the physical increase in stocks at current prices, against our estimate of £77 m.

14.7 REDFERN'S ESTIMATES OF GROSS AND NET FIXED CAPITAL IN 1938

The present estimates of the first cost and depreciated values of the stock of fixed assets at current prices in 1938 are set out in detail in Table 14.70, together with corresponding estimates by Redfern of gross and net fixed capital.[2] Except for shipping, described separately below, all Redfern's estimates were obtained by the perpetual inventory method, and therefore depend heavily on the length of life over which the estimates of

capital formation are cumulated, and on the estimates of gross capital formation, which have to be taken back as many as 100 years before 1938, with rapidly diminishing reliability.[3] As we shall see the results of this comparison are consistent with the view expressed by Barna (see below) that this method tends to produce estimates which are too low.

For the gross stock of fixed assets the present estimate exceeds Redfern's by some £3,700 m. or almost 20% of our figure. £1,350 m. of this is accounted for by our estimates for assets omitted by Redfern. For the common items, the present estimates are substantially higher for both industrial and commercial buildings, in each case by some £700 m.; for plant and machinery owned by Manufacturing and distribution by some £320 m.; for dwellings by £260 m.; for shipping by £220 m.; and for six other items by varying amounts to a total of £434 m. On the other side, there are only five items, totalling £270 m., where the present estimates are lower than Redfern's.

---

[1] [4] *Annual Abstract of Statistics*, No. 89, 1952, Table 283.

[2] [132] Redfern, Tables 7, 8 and 9, pp. 158–61. For conversion to 1938 prices see notes to Table 14.70, p. 254 below.

[3] *Ibid.*, pp. 145–47 and 140.

TABLE 14.70   COMPARISON WITH REDFERN'S ESTIMATES OF GROSS AND NET FIXED CAPITAL IN 1938

(Current prices. £m.)

	Gross Fixed Capital				Net Fixed Capital			
	Redfern (1)		Present estimates (2)		Redfern (3)		Present estimates (4)	
A. Items covered by both estimates:								
Agriculture (a)		40		49		22		16
Coal mining (b)		67		54		32		42
Electricity, gas and water:								
Electricity	724		670		449		340	
Gas	220		352		107		181	
Water	602	1,546	674	1,696	300	856	352	873
Manufacturing and Distribution and other services								
Industrial buildings (c)	802		1,519		437		858	
Commercial buildings (d)	1,351		2,045		860		1,171	
Plant and machinery, etc. (e)	1,863		2,179		957		921	
Vehicles (f)	282	4,298	237	5,980	140	2,394	91	3,041
Transport and communication:								
Railways: way and works,	1,410		1,536		574		675	
rolling stock, plant, etc. (g)	381		384		186		156	
Road passenger transport:								
buses, etc. (h)	107		124		45		35	
buildings and plant	42		35		30		22	
Shipping	387		608		189		228	
Harbours, docks and canals	411		410		177		149	
Air transport	4		3		3		2	
Postal and telephone communication	325	3,067	274	3,374	197	1,401	182	1,449
Public and social services								
Roads	455		533		285		351	
Other	993	1,448	882	1,415	618	903	398	749
Dwellings		5,339		5,599		3,550		3,512
Total		15,805		18,167		9,158		9,682
B. Items covered by present estimates but not by Redfern:								
Farm buildings		—	649			—	206	
Farm vehicles (i)		—	43			—	14	
Fishing vessels		—	14			—	4	
Coal mining buildings and works		—	328			—	131	
Tramcars and tramway		—	57			—	11	
Hospital buildings and equipment		—	147			—	114	
Central government buildings		—	114	1,352		—	69	549
Total		15,805		19,519		9,158		10,231

Source

(1) and (3): Redfern, Tables 7, 8 and 9. The estimates are given there at 1948 prices and were converted to 1938 prices by means of the indices given by Redfern at p. 171. This involved some assumptions as to the asset compositions of the estimates for certain industries (e.g. Electricity) but the net extent of any error in each case is negligible. The total is not affected by these assumptions as the breakdown of the total by type of asset is known.

(2) and (4): The classification and coverage of the estimates in chapters 5 to 12 above has been adjusted as indicated in the following notes to conform as far as possible with that in Redfern's estimates:

(a) Covers only agricultural plant, machinery and tractors.

(b) Covers only coal mining plant, machinery and vehicles other than privately-owned wagons (for which see note (g)).

(c) Buildings owned by firms classified to Manufacturing and to 'Other mining and quarrying'.

(d) Buildings owned by Distribution and other services, less Municipal markets, plus Road haulier's buildings.

(e) Plant and machinery, etc. owned by Manufacturing, by Distribution and other services, and by 'Other mining and quarrying'; less 90% of the goods vehicles not owned by Road Hauliers and of the passenger cars owned for business use (cf. note (f)); and less 20% of the privately-owned railway wagons (cf. note (g)).

(f) It was assumed that 90% of all goods vehicles not owned by Road Hauliers and of the passenger cars owned for business use are owned by Manufacturing and Distribution and other services, together with all the vehicles owned by Road hauliers. (Cf. [132] Redfern, p. 173). Redfern's estimates also include taxis.

(g) All privately-owned wagons are included.

(h) Taxis are included here in the present estimates but with vehicles owned by Manufacturing and Distribution in Redfern.

(i) Agricultural vans and lorries and horse-drawn vehicles.

We shall consider first the main items where the present estimate is higher. For industrial building and for plant and machinery owned by Manufacturing and distribution there is good reason to think that the present estimates are nearer the mark. This conclusion is based principally on the estimates which Barna has made for 1955 of fixed capital (excluding vehicles) in manufacturing.[1] His estimates were over 50% above Redfern's estimates for 1955, and after careful consideration of the two estimates Barna has concluded that the discrepancy is due to statistical (not conceptual) factors, which he gives in order of importance as follows:[2]

(i) The actual length of life of assets is longer than is implied in the income-tax depreciation rates on which the majority of Redfern's assumed lives were based.

(ii) Capital formation is under-reported in annual statistics of expenditure because, in general, a proportion of assets is charged to revenue.

(iii) Statistics of capital formation are subject to the usual statistical errors, which might have been important in the earlier years utilised by the perpetual inventory method.

It is likely that Barna's points about the underestimate in the assumed length of life and the possibility of error in the estimates for earlier years would apply with at least equal force to the estimate for commercial buildings, where our estimate is higher even though our annual estimates in the inter-war years (added on to the stock figure we obtained for 1919) were appreciably lower than Redfern's.

For dwellings, we found, when making our own estimate, that the life of 100 years assumed by Redfern was insufficient to account for the number of all houses in the known stock at the end of 1938,[3] and the fact that our estimate is higher by some £260m. is largely explained by the longer life implicit in the present estimates. The discrepancy on this account is, in fact, partly offset by the lower estimates we have made for capital formation in dwellings in the period 1924–38.

The two remaining items which call for comment are gas undertakings and shipping. On the former the discrepancy is (relatively) very large, and it is possible that our estimate is too high,[4] though it is difficult to say by how much, since all three of Barna's points would apply to Redfern's estimates of fixed capital in the gas undertakings.

For shipping the present estimate of £608m. is £221m. higher than Redfern's. Both estimates were made by multiplying a figure for the stock of tonnage by estimated average values, and the discrepancy results from four factors:

(i) The tonnage series on which Redfern's estimate was based excludes all vessels of less than 500 gross tons. These vessels, which should be included, have a total tonnage of roughly 0·9m. gross tons, and would be valued in the present estimate at approximately £30m.

(ii) Redfern specifically omitted from his estimate all passenger and dry cargo vessels of 25 years and over and all tankers of 20 years and over. This reduced his tonnage by some 1·8m. gross tons and in the present estimates this tonnage would be valued at some £62m. Redfern's reason for excluding these ships was that they had survived for longer than the life which he had assumed for the purpose of estimating depreciation. However, as the ships were still on the register they should, on the principles adopted in the present study, be included in estimates of the gross stock of capital.

(iii) The average export value used in the present estimates to value the tonnage on the register was £34·4 per ton. This is approximately 25% higher than Redfern's weighted 1948 average value converted to 1938 prices by means of his price index. This is quantitatively the most important factor and accounts for £102m. of the difference between the two estimates. The present estimate is probably too high,[5] though the likely error in the conversion of Redfern's estimate from 1948 to 1938 prices makes it difficult to gauge the extent of the overestimate.[6]

(iv) Finally Redfern's estimate for shipping excludes some £27m. for ships owned by other sectors. No deduction was made for this in the present estimate which thus relates to 'ships' rather than to 'shipping' and so duplicates ships owned by certain other sectors.[7]

We can thus summarize by saying that some £27m. of the discrepancy is a difference in classification; £92m. is due to the tonnage omitted by Redfern and here our estimate is clearly more correct; and £102m. is due to differences in average values where both estimates are uncertain, but the present estimate may well be too high.

We deal next with the few items for which the present estimates are significantly lower than Redfern's. The largest absolute difference is on 'Other public and social services', where the present estimate is £110m. or 11% lower. The main component (local authority non-trading services) was derived by making certain assumptions about the relationship between the gross

[1] These estimates are described on p. 256 below.
[2] [84] T. Barna, 'Alternative Methods of Measuring Capital', *Income and Wealth*, series VIII (London, 1959), p. 53.
[3] See chapter 12, p. 218 above, and [132] Redfern, p. 180.
[4] See chapter 7, pp. 93–7 above.
[5] Cf. p. 248 above.
[6] See p. 243 note 1, on the possibility of error in the link between 1948 and 1938.
[7] See chapter 9, p. 170-5 above.

and net stocks, taking the latter as equal to the amount of the loans outstanding for the specified services, and could be too low.

For Electricity and for Postal and telephone communication the present estimates are lower in each case by some £50 m. They were derived by converting to current prices data in aggregate published accounts on the gross stock at historical prices, and there is some possibility of error in the conversion. Redfern's estimates were based on annual expenditure figures from the same accounts cumulated over an assumed life and it may be that in these two cases, in both of which technical progress was rapid, the actual life of the assets was *less* than that assumed by Redfern, i.e. that the rate of scrapping in the inter-war years was higher than he assumed.

Finally, for vehicles owned by Manufacturing and Distribution we must first note that the divergence is in fact larger than appears from Table 14.70, since there is a compensating error in the component estimates for goods vehicles and passenger cars for business use. For the latter the present estimate is higher by some £37 m. and both estimates are very uncertain. For the former Redfern's estimate is higher by some £82 m. About half of this is due to the fact that his estimates were cumulated over a period of 10 years and for the period 1929–38 this gives a stock of goods vehicles over 20% higher than the number in use at September 1938 as shown by the number of licences current (on which the present estimates are based). The remainder of the excess is due to the higher average value used; this was discussed on p. 242 above.

The present estimate of net fixed capital is some £1,070 m. higher than Redfern's. This is reduced to some £520 m. when allowance is made for the items omitted by Redfern. (See cols. (3) and (4) of Table 14.70). On the comparable items the present estimate of accumulated depreciation in 1938 is higher by some £1,840 m. This figure is made up of higher estimates of accumulated depreciation on all but two items (Coal mining and Postal and telephone communications); and is generally explained by our higher figures for the gross stock of capital. For certain items, such as industrial and commercial building, this is partly offset by the fact that Redfern depreciated the stock more rapidly, i.e. he assumed a shorter life.[1] For Electricity, Redfern has a higher stock but a lower accumulated depreciation, and in this case the usual position was reversed and it was the lives assumed in the present estimates which were (slightly) shorter.

While this study was passing through the press Mr. G. A. Dean of the Central Statistical Office published new estimates of the end-1938 and post-war capital stock. His results were obtained by the perpetual inventory method and for manufacturing, distribution and other services represent a substantial upward revision of the Redfern estimates. The new series are based in part on the present estimates, and in the course of his work Dean was led to the conclusion that the present gross stock estimates for end-1938 are significantly too high for both industrial and commercial buildings.[2]

It has not yet been possible to examine his results in detail, but the suggestion that the present estimates for industrial building are too high is consistent with the point made on p. 29 above concerning the assumption that the book values derived from the samples of accounts can be regarded as the equivalent of the written-down value.

This point is not, however, applicable to the present estimate for commercial buildings since accounts were used only for the buildings owned by wholesale distribution and for these the book value was taken as the equivalent of the first cost value. For the remaining buildings the method used seems broadly reliable except perhaps for the point about site values raised in footnote 4 on p. 187, which would lead to some overstatement; but, on the other hand, there is the known omission from the present estimates of office buildings and this was expected to result in a figure which was, on balance, too low (see p. 228). It may be, therefore, that the gross fixed capital formation estimates used by Dean for these buildings are too low, and/or that the assumed life of 80 years leaves out of the capital stock a large number of the old shops and inns which are common in this sector. Where adequate expenditure on maintenance and repairs has maintained these pre-1859 buildings in good condition there is no reason why they should not be included, and they would be in the present estimates derived essentially from the gross annual value of the buildings as assessed for tax purposes.

14.8 BARNA'S ESTIMATES OF THE STOCK OF FIXED ASSETS IN MANUFACTURING IN 1955

In 1957 Barna[3] published estimates of the gross replacement cost of fixed assets (excluding vehicles) in manufacturing. They were based on fire insurance

---

[1] Cf. pp. 245–6 above.

[2] [**105ª**] G. A. Dean, 'The Stock of Fixed Capital in the United Kingdom in 1961', *Journal of the Royal Statistical Society*, Series A (General), vol. 127 (1964), pp. 330–1.

[3] [**83**] Barna, 'The Replacement Cost of Fixed Assets in British Manufacturing Industry in 1955', *Journal of the Royal Statistical Society*, Series A (General), vol. 120 (1957).

valuations for mid-1955 and do not involve any direct estimates for earlier dates which would come within the period covered by the present estimates. They are, however, conceptually comparable with the present estimates of the first cost value of fixed assets and it may be of some interest to extend our estimates to 1955 for comparison with Barna. We have done this in Table 14.80, using first the difference between Redfern's estimates for 1938 at 1938 prices and for 1952 at 1948 prices, and then following the same procedure as Barna

the view that it is, on balance, more likely to be an under-estimate rather than an over-estimate.[1]

14.9 CAMPION'S ESTIMATES OF THE MARKET VALUE OF REAL PROPERTY IN 1926–8 AND 1932–4

Mr. (now Sir Harry) Campion[2] has made estimates of the market value of public and private real property in Great Britain for the averages of two inter-war periods

TABLE 14.80 COMPARISON WITH BARNA'S ESTIMATES OF REPLACEMENT COST NEW OF FIXED ASSETS IN MANUFACTURING IN MID-1955

(£ thousand million)

	Plant and Machinery	Industrial Buildings	Total (excldg. Vehicles)
A. Our estimate adjusted:			
1. Our estimate: end-1938 at 1938 prices	2·2	1·5	3·7
2. Adjusted to end-1938 at 1948 prices	4·8	3·5	8·4
3. Mid-1955 at 1948 prices	6·8	4·1	10·9
4. Mid-1955 at 1955 prices	9·2	5·3	14·5
5. 80% of plant and 95% of buildings	7·4	5·0	12·4
6. War-time government expenditure	0·6	0·4	1·0
7. Adjusted total	8·0	5·4	13·4
B. Comparison with other estimates:			
8. Redfern	6·9	3·7	10·6
9. Barna	9·5	5·8	15·3
10. Percentage 7. to 9. (%)	84	93	88
11. Percentage 8. to 9. (%)	73	64	69

Notes

1. As in Table 14.70 for Manufacturing and distribution and other services.

2. Row 1 multiplied by the price indices given by [**132**] Redfern, p. 171.

3. Row 2 plus the sum of (a) the increase from 1938 to 1952 given by Redfern, p. 161 and (b) the increments used by Barna in bringing Redfern's estimates up to mid-1955. See [**83**] Barna, p. 21.

4. Row 3 multiplied by the implied price indices in [**56**] *National Income and Expenditure, 1956*, Tables 47 and 49.

5. Row 4 multiplied by the proportions given by [**83**] Barna (p. 21) to reduce the coverage of the estimates to manufacturing only.

6. The sum of (a) an estimate of £500m. given by [**83**] Barna (p. 21) to cover factories built by the government during the war and now leased to private firms plus assets for government research and develop-

ment; and (b) a very approximate allowance for war-time government financed capital formation in commercial factories still used after the war (cf. [**83**] Barna, p. 44) roughly taken as £500m. in the light of Barna's recent statement that this item, omitted from Redfern's estimates, accounts for 10% of the original difference of £5,000m. between his estimate and Redfern's. See [**85**] T. Barna 'On Measuring Capital' in *The Theory of Capital* Ed. F. A. Lutz and D. C. Hague (London, 1961), p. 93. The breakdown by type of asset is not known for either (a) or (b) and we have assumed that the total of £1,000m. should be divided in the same proportions as the main part of the capital stock in Row 5.

7. Rows 5+6.

8. Redfern brought to mid-1955 at 1955 prices as in [**83**] Barna, p. 21, plus £500m. as in note 6 (b).

9. [**83**] Barna, p. 21.

had used to bring Redfern's estimates for 1952 up to mid-1955 at 1955 prices. Essentially this means taking our estimate for 1938 as the starting point and cumulating on it the estimates for the years 1939–45 made by Redfern and those for the post-war years given in the *Blue Book*.

We find that our total, extended to mid-1955 and revalued at 1955 prices, falls short of Barna's total by just over 10%; Redfern's estimate, by contrast, falls short by over 40%. Barna's estimate is itself subject to errors of sampling and valuation, but he has expressed

of three years: 1926–8 and 1932–4. The estimates are based on the same principles as the earlier work by Lord Stamp,[3] and represent the most detailed and thorough attempt yet made to assess the market value of all real property in the inter-war period.

It is essential to emphasize that this concept of the market value of property is completely different from the concept underlying the present estimates of the

---

[1] [**83**], p. 22.
[2] [**98**] Campion.
[3] [**136**] Stamp, chapter XI; and [**137**], chapter I.

stock of capital, either at first cost or depreciated value. The estimates of the market or stock exchange value are made by capitalizing income flows (generally as assessed for purposes of taxation) by means of estimates of the number of years' purchase (or rate of interest) appropriate to each type of income. The result is a subjective estimate of the discounted value of the streams of income which the assets—or in the case of commercial assets, the enterprises owning the assets—are expected to yield in future. There are at least four major conceptual points on which it will differ from the present estimates.[1] First, it is a subjective valuation of *expected future incomes*, whereas the present estimates are based on *actual past outlays* (revalued at current replacement costs). Second, it includes an important element of goodwill attaching to the enterprise rather than the assets, whereas goodwill and any other intangible assets (such as patent rights) are omitted from the present estimates. Third, it will in principle vary according to the level of profits and the 'outlook' adopted by the market at the time the estimates are made, whereas estimates of the present type for any given date will, in principle, be the same whenever they are made. The difficulties experienced in this connection when attempting to estimate the market value were stressed by Stamp when he wrote in 1937 that there had been no point of time since the war when the outlook existing *at the period* over which any particular figures extended had not been 'completely falsified' by the time the figures of income became available.[2] Finally, assets on which no profit is made would be excluded from estimates of the market value whereas they would remain as part of the present estimates.

It is difficult to say *a priori* whether one would expect an estimate of the market value of the stock of capital to be closer numerically to an estimate of the present type of the original cost of the capital stock, or to the original cost less accumulated depreciation. The crucial issue is probably the extent to which the market reduces the value which it places on an asset to allow for obsolescence and for the fact that the asset is no longer new and has been subject to wear and tear. There are some assets, such as canals and railway tracks, which might be regarded as not depreciating so long as they are properly maintained. But for most types of buildings, plant and vehicles one might expect their market value to be related to the depreciated value, under conditions of stability, although the allowance made for age and wear and tear would almost certainly not fall linearly over time. In theory, therefore, one might expect the estimate of market value to be closer to our estimate of the depreciated value than to the estimated first cost value at current prices. In fact, however,

Table 14.90 shows that in both periods Campion's estimates lie between the depreciated and first cost values, but are very much closer to the latter.

TABLE 14.90   COMPARISON WITH CAMPION'S ESTIMATES OF THE MARKET VALUE OF REAL PROPERTY, 1926–28 AND 1932–34

(Current prices. £ thousand million)

	Campion	Present estimates	
		Depreciated value	First cost value
	(1)	(2)	(3)
1926–8	15·7	9·8	16·9
1932–4	15·6	9·0	16·1

Source

(1) [**98**] Campion: Private property, Table 6, p. 85 (Houses and buildings, Farmer's capital, Railways in Great Britain, Capital of industry, transport, commerce and finance); plus Public property, Table 8, p. 84 (Land and buildings—less an approximate 10% to exclude land, and Other property).

2. The estimates are at current prices. All fixed assets plus the book value of stock in trade from Tables 13.00 and 3.60, pp. 223 and 54; less roads from Table 9.21; less 2% for Northern Ireland.

14.10   PHELPS BROWN AND WEBER'S ESTIMATES OF THE CAPITAL STOCK IN 1924

The final estimates of the stock of capital which we shall consider are the widely used series constructed by Phelps Brown and Weber.[3] There is a certain ambiguity about the conceptual basis of their estimates which must first be classified. The starting point is derived from an estimate of *market value* in 1912 made by Stamp on exactly the same principles as those by Campion which we described above. This estimate was extrapolated to 1924; for buildings by reference to the increase in the total number of houses and the rise in building costs, and for all other capital by assuming that real equipment per occupied person was the same in 1924 as in 1912. For other years they cumulated on the 1924 figure the estimates of 'net investment' which we described on pp. 249–51 and 252 above. The result is intended to be a 'measure of physical stock valued at current replacement cost'. The concept of current replacement cost could refer to replacement with either new or second-hand assets, but Professor Phelps Brown has stated (in correspondence with the author) that it is the former which was intended.

---

[1] Cf. [**136**] Stamp, pp. 376–80.
[2] [**137**] Stamp, p. 4.
[3] [**129**] Phelps Brown and Weber, p. 283.

The position is, therefore, that the base-year figure for 1924 is intended to be comparable with our estimate of the first cost value (both estimates taken either at current or at constant prices) though it is in fact based on an estimate of the market value which is not conceptually comparable. As Table 14.100 shows, the two

TABLE 14.100 COMPARISON WITH PHELPS BROWN AND WEBER'S ESTIMATES OF THE GROSS STOCK OF REVENUE-YIELDING PROPERTY IN 1924

(Current prices. £ thousand million)

	Phelps Brown and Weber	Present estimates (First cost value)
	(1)	(2)
A. Revenue yielding buildings	7·5	7·5
B. Other capital	8·9	7·9
	16·4	15·4

Source

(1) [**129**] p. 287. The estimates are given at 1912/13 prices and have been converted to 1924 prices by means of the indices given at p. 287.

(2) The estimates at current prices in Tables 13.00 and 3.60, pp. 223 and 54 above, less farmers' capital and non-revenue-yielding buildings and works.

estimates for 1924 at current prices do agree fairly well, but this is solely because, as we have seen in the preceding section, the market value as estimated by Stamp and Campion in the inter-war years is much closer to the gross than to the written-down cost of the original outlays as estimated by us and revalued at current prices.

14.11 COLE'S INDEX OF MACHINERY PRICES, 1920–1938

The final comparison we shall make relates not to estimates of capital formation but to a price index. In the present study we have used three general indices. The indices of the cost of civil engineering and of building work (index A and index B, p. 24 above) were described in a published article,[1] and this also contained comparisons with the principal other indices of building costs. For plant and machinery the general index used in the present study (index C, p. 24 above) can be compared with an index constructed by H. J. D.

Cole.[2] Index C was based on indices of wage-rates and of iron and steel prices. Cole's index, by contrast, measures changes in average values per ton of specific classes of plant and machinery as shown in the export and import statistics. For the census years Cole also gives a comparable series based on the Censuses of Production and Import Duties Inquiries. (Cole's series was adopted by Redfern[3] for his price index of plant and machinery.)

Index C, Cole's annual index, and his index of average values for census years are shown in Figure 10.

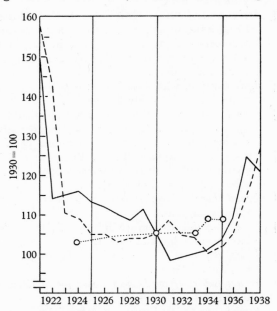

FIG. 10 Price indices for general plant and machinery, 1921–38.
——— Index C.   – – – – – – Cole's index.
······○······○······ Average values.

At several points the *movement* of the two annual indices shows considerable divergence: in 1930 and 1931, for example, index C falls sharply while Cole's index is rising; and in 1932–4 index C is rising while Cole's index is falling. For 1933–4 a rising trend is confirmed by the series of average values shown by the censuses. The general impression is that index C probably anticipates actual changes in machinery prices. Only in two years (1920 and 1922), however, do the *levels* of the annual indices diverge by more than 10%.

[1] [**122**] Maywald, vol. VII, 1954, pp. 202–3.
[2] [**104**] H. J. D. Cole, 'Machinery Prices between the Wars', *Bulletin of the Oxford University Institute of Statistics*, vol. 13 (1951).
[3] [**132**] Redfern, p. 171.

LIST OF WORKS CITED

I OFFICIAL PUBLICATIONS

1 GOVERNMENT RETURNS, STATISTICS, ETC.

[1] *Abstract of Labour Statistics of the United Kingdom*, Command Paper, issued at approximately three-year intervals up to 1937.

[2] *Agricultural Statistics* (Ministry of Agriculture and Fisheries), annual, part I: Reports on the acreage and production of crops, etc., in England and Wales, with summaries for Great Britain and the United Kingdom.

[3] *Agricultural Market Report* (Ministry of Agriculture and Fisheries) weekly from 1922.

[4] *Annual Abstract of Statistics* (Central Statistical Office), annual from no. 84, 1947, published in 1948. For earlier numbers in this series see item [30].

[5] *Annual Local Taxation Returns*, England and Wales (Ministry of Health), annual to 1933–4. For years after 1933–4 see item [19].

[6] *Annual Local Taxation Returns* (*Scotland*), (Scottish Office), annual.

[7] *Local Taxation Returns* (Ministry of Home Affairs, Northern Ireland), annual.

[8] *Annual Report of the Department of Health for Scotland*, Command Paper.

[9] *Annual Report of the Fishery Board for Scotland*, Command Paper.

[10] *Annual Report of the Electricity Commissioners* (Electricity Commission), annual from 1921.

[11] *Annual Report of the Licensing Authorities* (Ministry of Transport), annual from 1937.

[12] *Annual Report of the Ministry of Health*, Command Paper.

[13] *Annual Report of the Road Board*, H.C. paper, annual from 1911 to 1921.

[14] *Annual Report of the Secretary for Mines* (Mines Department of the Board of Trade).

[15] *Annual Report of the Traffic Commissioners* (Ministry of Transport), annual from 1930.

[16] *Annual Statement of the Navigation and Shipping of the United Kingdom* (Board of Trade).

[17] *Civil Services Appropriation Accounts and Revenue Departments Appropriation Accounts*, H.C. Papers, annual.

[18] *Housing* (Ministry of Health), half-yearly from September 1934.

[19] *Local Government Financial Statistics* (Ministry of Health), annual from 1934–5. For earlier years see item [5].

[20] Northern Ireland Government, *Annual Reports of the Ministry of Agriculture*.

[21] *Post Office Commercial Accounts*, H.C. Paper, annual.

[22] *Railway Returns: Returns of the Capital, Traffic, Receipts and Working Expenditure, etc. of the Railway Companies of Great Britain* (Ministry of Transport) annual.

[23] *Reports on the Administration of the Road Fund* (Ministry of Transport), annual.

[24] *Report of the Chief Registrar of Friendly Societies* Part 5, Building Societies, (Registry of Friendly Societies), annual.

[25] *Report of the Commissioners of H.M. Inland Revenue* (Board of Inland Revenue), annual.

[26] *Reports of the Forestry Commissioners*, H.C. Paper, annual.

[27] *Return of Engineering and Financial Statistics relating to Authorised Undertakings in Great Britain* (Electricity Commission) annual.

[28] *Returns relating to all Authorised Gas Undertakings in Great Britain* (Board of Trade), part II, Finance and Prices, annual.

[29] *Road Vehicles in Great Britain*. Mechanically-propelled Vehicles licensed pursuant to the Road Act, 1920. *Census of Vehicles*, quarterly from 1926.

[30] *Statistical Abstract for the United Kingdom*, Command Paper, annual up to the 83rd number, published 1940. For later numbers in the series see item [4].

[31] *Tramways and Light Railways (Street and Road) and Trolley Vehicle Undertakings, Returns of local authorities and companies* (Ministry of Transport), annual.

2 CENSUS REPORTS

[32] *Census of Distribution and other Services, 1950* (Board of Trade).

[33] *Census of Production of the United Kingdom, Final Report, 1907* (*First*), Cd. 6320, 1912.

[34] *Census of Production of the United Kingdom, Final Report, 1924* (*Third*), (Board of Trade).

[35] *Census of Production of the United Kingdom, Final Report, 1930* (*Fourth*), (Board of Trade).

[36] *Final Report on the Fifth Census of Production and the Import Duties Act Inquiry, 1935* (Board of Trade).

[37] *Final Reports on the Census of Production for 1948, 1949, 1950, 1951*, (Board of Trade).

[38] *Report on the Import Duties Act Inquiry* (1933) and (1934) (Board of Trade).

[39] *Report on the Census of Woodlands and Census of Production of Home-grown Timber, 1924*.

[40] *Report on the Census of Production of Home-grown Timber, 1930*.

[41] *Census of Woodlands, 1947–1949*.

[42] *The Agricultural Output of England and Wales, 1925*, Cmd. 2815, 1927.

[43] *The Agricultural Output of England and Wales, 1930–1931*, Cmd. 4605, 1934.

[44] *Report on the Census of Horses in Great Britain, 1934*.

3 COMMAND PAPERS
(*The order is chronological*)

[45] *Royal Commission on Mining Royalties, Final Report*, Cd. 6980, 1893.

[46] *Royal Commission on Coal Supplies, Final Report*, part I; *General Report*, Cd. 2355, 1905; *Final Report*, part IX, Cd. 2361, 1905.

[47] *Report on the Canals and Inland Navigation of the United Kingdom*, Cd. 3716, 1907.

[48] *Statement respecting allowances for Wear and Tear and Obsolescence of Plant and Machinery, etc.*, Cd. 9022, 1918.

[49] Departmental Committee on Agricultural Machinery, *Report and Summaries of Evidence*, Cmd. 506, 1919.

[50] *Report of the Royal Commission on Income Tax*, Cd. 615, 1920.

[51] *Royal Commission on Transport, Final Report*, Cd. 3751, 1931.

[52] *Memorandum on the Board of Education Estimates*, Cd. 4824, 1935.

4 OTHER OFFICIAL PUBLICATIONS

(a) *United Kingdom*

(*arranged in alphabetical order of issuing Department*)

[53] Air Ministry, Department of the Director-General of Civil Aviation, *Report on the Progress of Civil Aviation*, annual.

[54] British Electricity Authority, *First Report and Accounts*, 1949.

[55] British Transport Commission, *Report and Accounts for 1948*, 1949.

[56] Central Statistical Office, *National Income and Expenditure*, annual since 1952. Before that *National Income and Expenditure of the United Kingdom*, annual since 1946.

[57] Central Statistical Office, *National Income Statistics, Sources and Methods* (London, 1956).

[58] Central Statistical Office, *Standard Industrial Classification*, 1948.

[59] Central Statistical Office, *Statistical Digest of the War, History of the Second World War*, 1951.

[60] Central Statistical Office, *The Interim Index of Industrial Production*, Studies in Official Statistics, No. 1, 1949.

[61] Committee on Industry and Trade, (Balfour Committee), *Survey of Metal Industries*, being part IV of a survey of industries, 1928.

[62] Committee on National Debt and Taxation, (Colwyn Committee), *Minutes of Evidence*, 1927.

[63] Department of Agriculture for Scotland, *Scottish Farm Rents and Estate Expenditure*, 1948.

[64] Forestry Commission, *Interim Report of the Inter-Departmental Home-grown Timber Committee*, 1933.

[65] Forestry Commission, *Empire Forests and the War*, Statement presented by Great Britain to the Fifth Empire Forestry Conference, 1947.

[66] London County Council, *London Statistics*, annual.

[67] London Passenger Transport Board, *Annual Report and Accounts*.

[68] Metropolitan Water Board, *Abstract of Accounts*, annual.

[69] Ministry of Health, *The Cost of Housebuilding* (The Girdwood Report). First Report of the Committee of Inquiry appointed by the Minister of Health, 1948.

[70] Ministry of Labour, *Ministry of Labour Gazette*, weekly.

[71] Ministry of Transport, *Form of Accounts and Statistical Returns, Annotated to show the manner in which they are to be compiled under the provisions of Section 77 (1) of the Railway Act, 1921*, 1930.

[72] National Coal Board, *Annual Report and Statement of Accounts for 1947*.

[73] Port of London Authority, *Annual Report and Accounts*.

[74] Select Committee on *Buildings Regulations and Improvement of Boroughs*, Parliamentary Reports from Committees, 1842, vol. X.

[75] The Gas Council, *First Report and Accounts, July 1948– March 1950*, 1951.

[76] University Grants Committee, *Report of the University Grants Committee for the period 1929/30 to 1934/5*.

(b) *Publications of International Organizations*

[77] United Nations, *Studies in Methods*, Series F, No. 3. *Concepts and Definitions of Capital Formation*, (New York, 1953).

[78] United Nations, *Studies in Methods*, Series F, No. 8. *Methods of National Income Estimation*. New York, 1955.

II BOOKS AND ARTICLES

[79] Abel-Smith, B. and Titmuss, R. M. *The Cost of the National Health Service in England and Wales* (Cambridge, 1956).

[80] *A Critique of the United States Income and Product Accounts, Studies in Income and Wealth*, Volume twenty-two. National Bureau of Economic Research (Princeton, 1958).

[81] Ashton, T. S. 'The Treatment of Capitalism by Historians', *Capitalism and the Historians*, Ed. F. A. Hayek (London, 1954).

[82] Barna, T. 'Valuation of Stocks and the National Income', *Economica*, New Series, vol. IX (1942), p. 349.

[83] Barna, T. 'The Replacement Cost of Fixed Assets in British Manufacturing Industry in 1955', *Journal of the Royal Statistical Society*, Series A, (General) vol. 120 (1957), p. 1.

[84] Barna, T. 'Alternative Methods of Measuring Capital', *Income and Wealth*, Series VIII (London, 1959).

[85] Barna, T. 'On Measuring Capital', in *The Theory of Capital*, Ed. F. A. Lutz and D. C. Hague (London, 1961).

[86] Bellerby, J. R. 'The Net Return to Farm Land', *The Farm Economist*, vol. IX, No. 9 (1960), p. 393.

[87] Bellman, Sir Harold. *The Thrifty Three Millions* (London, 1935).

[88] Boreham, A. J. 'A Series of Estimates of Occupiers' Capital, 1867–1938', *The Farm Economist*, vol. VII, No. 6 (1953), p. 260.

[89] Bowen, I. 'Building Output and the Trade Cycle (U.K. 1924–38)', *Oxford Economic Papers*, No. 3 (1940), p. 110.

[90] Bowen, I. and Ellis, A. W. T. 'The Building and Contracting Industry', *Oxford Economic Papers*, No. 7 (March 1945), p. 111.

[91] Bowley, A. L. (Ed.). *Studies in the National Income, 1924–1938*, National Institute of Economic and Social Research (Cambridge, 1944).

[92] Bowley, M. *Housing and the State, 1919–1944* (London, 1945).

[93] Bowley, M. 'Housing Statistics', *Sources and Nature of the Statistics of the United Kingdom*, Ed. M. G. Kendall, vol. 1 (London, 1952).

[94] British Association. *Britain in Recovery*. Prepared by a Research Committee of the Economic Science and Statistics Section of the British Association (London, 1938).

[95] Bretherton, R. F., Burchardt, F. A. and Rutherford, R. S. G. *Public Investment and the Trade Cycle in Great Britain* (Oxford, 1941).

[96] Britton, D. K. 'The Sale Value of Farm Land between the Wars', *The Farm Economist*, vol. VI, No. 5 (1949), p. 125.

[97] Cairncross, A. K. *Home and Foreign Investment, 1870–1913* (Cambridge, 1953).

[98] Campion, H. *Public and Private Property in Great Britain* (London, 1939).

[99] Chapman, A. L. *Wages and Salaries in the United Kingdom, 1920–1938* (Cambridge, 1952).

[100] Cheveley, S. and Prince, O. *Capital in United Kingdom Agriculture Present and Future* (London, 1956).

[101] Clark, Colin. *Investment in Fixed Capital in Great Britain*, London and Cambridge Economic Service, Special Memorandum, No. 38 (September, 1934).

[102] Clark, Colin. *The National Income, 1924–1931* (London, 1932).

[103] Clark, Colin. *National Income and Outlay* (London, 1937).

[104] Cole, H. J. D. 'Machinery Prices between the Wars', *Bulletin of the Oxford University Institute of Statistics*, vol. 13 (1951), p. 78.

[105] Connor, L. R. 'Urban Housing in England and Wales', *Journal of the Royal Statistical Society*, Vol. 99 (1936), p. 1.

[105a] Dean, G. A. 'The Stock of Fixed Capital in the United Kingdom in 1961', *Journal of the Royal Statistical Society*, Series A (General), vol. 127 (1964), p. 327.

[106] Denison, E. F. 'Theoretical Aspects of Quality Change, Capital Consumption and Net Capital Formation', in *Problems of Capital Formation, Studies in Income and Wealth*, vol. *Nineteen*, National Bureau of Economic Research (Princeton, 1957).

[107] Domar, E. D. 'Depreciation, Replacement and Growth', *Economic Journal*, vol. LXIII (1953), p. 1.

[108] Feinstein, C. H. 'Income and Investment in the United Kingdom, 1856–1914', *Economic Journal*, vol. LXXI (1961), p. 367.

[109] Goldsmith, R. W. 'A Perpetual Inventory of National Wealth', *Conference on Research in Income and Wealth*, vol. Fourteen, National Bureau of Economic Research (New York, 1951).

[110] Goldsmith, R. W. *A Study of Saving in the United States* (Princeton, 1955).

[111] Glover, K. F. 'Gross Investment in Inland Transport in Great Britain'. Unpublished M.Sc. Thesis (1949), London University Library.

[112] Greenhalgh, F. *A Trade Policy for Cotton Spinners* (Manchester, 1932).

[113] Hiley, W. E. *The Economics of Forestry* (Oxford, 1930).

[114] Imlah, A. H. *Economic Elements in the Pax Britannia* (Cambridge, Mass., 1958).

[115] Jefferys, J. B. *The Distribution of Consumer Goods*, National Institute of Economic and Social Research (Cambridge, 1950).

[116] Jefferys, J. B. *Retail Trading in Great Britain, 1850–1950*, National Institute of Economic and Social Research (London, 1954).

[117] Jefferys, J. B. and Walters, D. 'National Income and Expenditure of the United Kingdom, 1870–1952'. *Income and Wealth*, series V (London, 1955).

[118] Kuznets, S. 'On the Measurement of National Wealth', *Studies in Income and Wealth*, vol. Two, National Bureau of Economic Research (New York, 1938).

[119] Lomax, K. S. 'Production and Productivity Movements in the United Kingdom since 1900', *Journal of the Royal Statistical Society*, Series A (General) vol. 122 (1959). p. 185.

[120] Mackintosh, R. M. 'A Note on Cheap Money and the Housing Boom', *Economic Journal*, vol. LXI (1951), p. 167.

[121] Maizels, Alfred. 'Consumption, Investment and National Expenditure in Wartime', *Economica*, New Series, vol. VIII (1941), p. 151.

[122] Maywald, K. 'An Index of Building Costs in the United Kingdom, 1845–1938', *Economic History Review*, vol. VIII (1954–5), p. 187.

[123] Maywald, K. 'Fire Insurance and the Capital Coefficient in Great Britain, 1866–1952', *Economic History Review*, vol. IX (1956–7), p. 89.

[124] Maywald, K. 'The Construction Costs and the Value of the British Merchant Fleet, 1850–1938', *Scottish Journal of Political Economy*, vol. III (1956), p. 44.

[125] Mitchell, B. R. *Capital Formation in the Railways of the British Isles, 1831–1919*. (Unpublished).

[126] Nevin, E. *The Mechanism of Cheap Money, A Study of British Monetary Policy, 1931–1939* (Cardiff, 1955).

[127] Peacock, A. T. and Wiseman, J. *The Growth of Public Expenditure in the United Kingdom*, National Bureau of Economic Research (Princeton, 1961).

[128] P.E.P. *The British Film Industry* (London, 1952).

[129] Phelps Brown, E. H. and Weber, B. 'Accumulation, Productivity and Distribution in the British Economy, 1870–1938', *Economic Journal*, vol. LXIII (1953), p. 263.

[130] Price, O. 'Capital Needs of British Agriculture', in *Agriculture in the British Economy*, Ed. J. Scott Watson (London, 1957).

[131] *Problems of Capital Formation, Studies in Income and Wealth*, vol. *Nineteen*, National Bureau of Economic Research (Princeton, 1957).

[132] Redfern, P. 'Net Investment in Fixed Assets in the United Kingdom 1938–1953', *Journal of the Royal*

Statistical Society, Series A, (General) vol. 118 (1955), p. 141.

[133] Rowson, S. 'A Statistical Survey of the Cinema Industry in Great Britain in 1934', *Journal of the Royal Statistical Society*, vol. 44 (1936), p. 67.

[134] Ryan, J. 'Machinery Replacements in the Cotton Trade', *Economic Journal*, vol. XL, 1930, p. 568.

[135] Smith, E. *The Peasant's Home, 1760–1875* (London, 1876).

[136] Stamp, J. C. *British Incomes and Property* (London, 1916).

[137] Stamp, J. C. *The National Capital* (London, 1937).

[138] Stolper, W. F. 'British Monetary Policy and the Housing Boom', *Quarterly Journal of Economics*, vol. LVI, No. 1 (part II) (November 1941), p. 1.

[139] Stone, R. *Measurement of Consumers' Expenditure and Behaviour in the United Kingdom 1920–1938*, vol. I (Cambridge, 1954); vol. II, in preparation.

[140] Taylor, F. D. W. and Bellerby, J. R. 'Index of Farm Occupiers' Capital in the United Kingdom, 1937–8 to 1951–2', *The Farm Economist*, vol. VII, No. 7 (1954), p. 305.

[141] Weber, B. 'A New Index of Residential Construction, 1838–1950', *Scottish Journal of Political Economy*, vol. II (1955), p. 104.

[142] Weber, B. and Parry Lewis, J. 'New Industrial Building in Great Britain, 1923–38', *Scottish Journal of Political Economy*, vol. VIII (1961), p. 57.

[143] Whittick, A. *The Small House* (London, 1947).

III PERIODICAL PUBLICATIONS, YEARBOOKS AND OTHER SOURCES

[144] *Annual Report of the Rank Organization for 1956.*

[145] *Co-operative Yearbooks* 1920–38.

[146] *Cotton Year Book.*

[147] *Director's Annual Report to the English Sewing Cotton Company*, 1931.

[148] *Fairplay's Weekly Shipping Journal.*

[149] *Forest Record*, No. 3, 1951.

[150] *Garcke's Manual of Electricity Supply*, annual.

[151] *Hospitals Yearbooks*, Central Bureau of Hospital Information, annual.

[152] *International Cotton Statistics*: International Federation of Master Cotton Spinners' and Manufacturers' Associations, annual.

[153] *Kinematograph Year book* for 1919.

[154] *London and Cambridge Economic Bulletin*, published in *The Times Review of Industry*, quarterly.

[155] National Farmers Union, *An Interim Review of Agricultural Machinery Requirements*, 1945.

[156] *Reports of National Shipbuilding Security Ltd.*

[157] *Report on the Financial Position of the Voluntary Hospitals in Great Britain, excluding London*, annual 1921–29, British Red Cross Society.

[158] *The Commercial Motor Index*, Fletcher and Sons, Norwich, annual.

[159] *The Economist*, 23 April 1938.

[160] *The Motor Car Index*, Fletcher and Sons, Norwich, annual.

[161] *The Motor Industry of Great Britain*, Society of Motor Manufacturers and Traders, annual from 1926.

INDEX

(f. = FIGURE; n. = FOOTNOTE TO TEXT OR TABLES; t. = TABLE)